GENESIS·

OR,

THE FIRST BOOK OF MOSES.

WITH A COMMENTARY.

BY

RT. REV. E. HAROLD BROWNE, LORD BISHOP OF ELY,

AUTHOR OF "EXPOSITION OF THE THIRTY-NINE ARTICLES," "SERMONS ON THE ATONEMENT," "THE PENTATEUCH, IN REPLY TO COLENSO," ETC.

(This forms a part of the volume of the "SPEAKERS' COMMENTARY" *on the Pentateuch.)*

New York:

SCRIBNER, ARMSTRONG & CO.,

654 BROADWAY.

1873.

PUBLISHERS' NOTICE.

THE general adoption by the Sunday Schools of the International Uniform Series of Lessons has created a demand for a concise and intelligible Commentary upon Genesis, which should present, in an authoritative and popular form, the results of the most recent research. This want is fully met in Dr. E. HAROLD BROWNE's exposition of this book, as given in the volume of the "Speaker's" Commentary, devoted to the Pentateuch. In order to bring it within the reach of every teacher and scholar, it is herewith presented in a separate form, and at a price ($1.50), which cannot fail to secure for it a very wide circulation.

Dr. E. HAROLD BROWNE, the Lord Bishop of Ely, is widely known to the American public from his *Exposition of the Thirty-Nine Articles*, while his very able work on the Pentateuch, in reply to Colenso, exhibits his special fitness for the undertaking, which he has so ably accomplished in this volume. His Commentary on Genesis, while bearing evidence of the ripest and most devout scholarship, is nowhere overburdened with a useless parade of learning. It is compact, but exhaustive, and throughout intelligible to every Bible student. For general use in connection with that portion of the Holy Scriptures now under study in our Sunday Schools it must prove very generally acceptable.

In this connection, tne attention of teachers is urgently invited to the volume of LANGE'S COMMENTARY on *Genesis*, translated and edited by Dr. Tayler Lewis and Dr. Gosman, under the general supervision of Dr. Schaff. The additions to this volume by Dr. Tayler Lewis, in particular, have attracted the widest notice in England as well as in this country, and have everywhere been justly regarded as among the most important of recent contributions to sacred literature. These two volumes give the student the best and ripest results of modern biblical scholarship. Lange's *Genesis* is a volume of nearly 700 pages, royal 8vo, and is sold at $5 in cloth.

PREFACE.

IT is about seven years since the Speaker of the House of Commons, the Right Hon. J. Evelyn Denison, conceived the idea of the present Commentary, and suggested its execution.

It appeared to him that in the midst of much controversy about the Bible, in which the laity could not help feeling a lively interest, even where they took no more active part, there was a want of some Commentary upon the Sacred Books, in which the latest information might be made accessible to men of ordinary culture. It seemed desirable that every educated man should have access to some work which might enable him to understand what the original Scriptures really say and mean, and in which he might find an explanation of any difficulties which his own mind might suggest, as well as of any new objections raised against a particular book or passage. Whilst the Word of God is one, and does not change, it must touch, at new points, the changing phases of physical, philological, and historical knowledge, and so the Comments that suit one generation are felt by another to be obsolete.

The Speaker, after mentioning this project to several prelates and theologians, consulted the Archbishop of York upon it. Although the difficulties of such an undertaking were very great, it seemed right to the Archbishop to make the attempt to meet a want which all confessed to exist; and accordingly he undertook to form a company of divines, who, by a judicious distribution of the labour amongst them, might expound, each the portion of Scripture for which his studies might best have fitted him.

The difficulties were indeed many. First came that of

treating a great and almost boundless subject upon a limited scale. Let any one examine the most complete Commentaries now in existence, and he will find that twenty or thirty ordinary volumes are not thought too many for the exhaustive treatment of the Scripture text. But every volume added makes a work less accessible to those for whom it is intended; and it was thought that eight or ten volumes ought to suffice for text and notes, if this Commentary was to be used by laymen as well as by professed divines. Omission and compression are at all times difficult; notes should be in proportion to the reader's needs, whereas they are more likely to represent the writer's predilections. The most important points should be most prominent; but the writer is tempted to lay most stress on what has cost him most labour.

Another difficulty lay in the necessity of treating subjects that require a good deal of research, historical and philological, but which could not be expected to interest those who have had no special preparation for such studies. In order to meet this, it was resolved that subjects involving deep learning and fuller illustration should be remitted to separate essays at the end of each Chapter, Book or division; where they can be found by those who desired them.

The general plan has been this. A Committee was formed to select the Editor and the Writers of the various sections. The Rev. F. C. Cook, Canon of Exeter, and Preacher of Lincoln's Inn, was chosen Editor. The work has been divided into Eight Sections, of which the present volume contains the Pentateuch. Each book has been assigned to some writer who has paid attention to the subject of it. The Editor thought it desirable to have a small Committee of reference, in cases of dispute; and the Archbishop of York with the Regius Professors of Divinity of Oxford and Cambridge agreed to act in this capacity. But in practice it has rarely been found necessary to resort to them.

The Committee were called upon, in the first place, to consider the important question, which has since received a much fuller discussion, whether any alterations should be made in the authorized English Version. It was decided to reprint that Version, without alteration, from the edition of 1611, with the marginal references and renderings; but to supply in the notes amended translations[1] of all passages proved to be incorrect. It was thought that in this way might be reconciled the claims of accuracy and truth with that devout reverence, which has made the present text of the English Bible so dear to all Christians that speak the English tongue. When the Prayer Book was revised, the earlier Psalter of Coverdale and Cranmer was left standing there, because those who had become accustomed to its use would not willingly attune their devotions to another, even though a more careful, Version: the older Psalter still holds its place, and none seem to desire its removal. Since then, knowledge of the Bible has been much diffused, and there seems little doubt that the same affection, which in the middle of the seventeenth century clung to the Psalter and preserved it, has extended itself by this time to the Authorized Version of 1611. Be that as it may, those who undertook the present work desired that the layman should be able to understand better the Bible which he uses in Church and at home; and for this purpose that Bible itself gives the best foundation, altered only where alteration is required to cure an error, or to make the text better understood.

This volume is sent forth in no spirit of confidence, but with a deep sense of its imperfections. Those who wish to condemn will readily extract matter on which to work. But those who receive it willing to find aid in it, and ready to admit that it is no easy matter to expound, completely, fully and popularly, that Book which has been the battle-field of all sects and parties, which has been interpreted by all the ages, each according to its measure of light, will do justice to the spirit that has guided the writers. Such will find in it something that may help them better to appreciate the Sacred Text.

[1] These emendations are printed throughout in a distinctive type, darker than the rest of the note.

PREFACE.

"As for the commendation," says Coverdale, "of God's holy Scripture, I would fain magnify it as it is worthy, but I am far insufficient thereto, and therefore I thought it better for me to hold my tongue than with few words to praise or commend it." Our English Bible has come down to us, won for us by much devoted labour, by persecution, by exile, even by blood of martyrdom. It has still much work to do, and when we consider the peoples to whom we have given our language, and the vast tracts over which English-speaking peoples rule, we feel how impossible it is for us to measure the extent of that work. We humbly desire to further it in some small measure, by removing a stumblingblock here, and by shedding light upon some dark places there. Such human efforts are needed, but the use of them passes, whilst the Word of God of which they treat will endure to the end. Yet it is permitted to offer them with an aspiration after the same result that attends the Word of God itself; and that result is, in the words of inspiration, "that ye might believe that Jesus is the Christ, the Son of God; and that believing ye might have life through His name." (John xx. 31.)

More than seven years have elapsed since this Commentary was first projected. It will, doubtless, be admitted that this period is not longer than might be reasonably demanded for the preparation of any considerable portion of such a work: but it is due to all concerned with this volume to state that but for unforeseen circumstances it would have been published much earlier. We have to deplore the premature death of no less than three contributors, two of whom had undertaken the commentary on Exodus and Numbers. All the writers in this volume had, in consequence of this and of other circumstances, a much larger amount of work imposed upon them than they were prepared for, long after the commencement of the undertaking. For one book they had to write the entire commentary; for another to re-write, with a special view to condensation, notes which had been prepared with great ability and learning by Mr Thrupp. This statement is made simply to account for the delay in the publication. The other parts of the work are now far advanced, and two volumes, including the historical and poetical books, will probably be printed within twelve months.

CONTENTS.

GENESIS.

INTRODUCTION. BY THE BISHOP OF ELY.

Document Hypothesis 21
Unity of plan and purpose throughout 22
Division of book into Toledoth . . . *ib.*
Of the names of God, as used in Genesis 24
" " and in Exodus vi. 2, 3 25
Proper names compounded with JAH . 26
Meaning and antiquity of the name JEHOVAH, with further reference to Exodus vi. 2, 3 . . . . *ib.*
Elohistic and Jehovistic passages . . 28
Alleged inconsistency with modern science 29

COMMENTARY AND CRITICAL NOTES. BY THE BISHOP OF ELY.

pp. 31—236.

PAGE

On the Days of Creation. Chap. i. 5 . 36
On the Creation and Primitive State of Man. Chap. ii. 7 43
On the Effect of the Fall. Chap. iii. 19 . 47
On the Historical Character of the Temptation and the Fall. Chap. iii. 22 . . 48
Cherubim. 49
§ 1. Traditional accounts. § 2. Tabernacle and Temple. § 3. Seen in Visions of Isaiah, Ezekiel, and St John. § 4. The Cherubim of Paradise. § 5. Etymology of name. Chap. iii. 24.
On the Early Civilization of Mankind. Chap. iv. 2 58
Difficulties in the Chronology of Chap. v. 61
§ 1. Difference of texts. § 2. Longevity of Patriarchs. § 3. Antiquity of Human Race, as deduced from (1) Geology, (2) History, (3) Language, (4) Ethnology.
The Deluge. Chap. viii.. 74
§ 1. Was it historical? § 2. Was it universal?
On Circumcision. Chap. xvii. 10 . . . 121
§ 1. Reasons for the rite. § 2. Origin of circumcision, whether pre-Abrahamic or not.
The Dead Sea, Site of Sodom and Zoar. Chap. xix. 25 131
§ 1. Characteristics of Dead Sea. Testimonies ancient and modern. § 2. Geological formation. § 3. Were Sodom, Zoar, &c. on the north or south of the Dead Sea?
On the Chronology of Jacob's life. Chap. xxxi. 41 177
§ 1. Difficulty of the question. Common reckoning. § 2. Suggestion of Dr Kennicott. § 3. Dates on this hypothesis. § 4. Greater facility for explaining the events thus obtained.
On Shiloh. Chap. xlix. 10 232
§ 1. Different renderings of the word, § 2. Choice of renderings, either 4 or 5. § 3. Messianic, by consent of Jewish and Christian antiquity. § 4. Answer to objections.

GENESIS.

INTRODUCTION.

	PAGE
Document Hypothesis	21
Unity of plan and purpose throughout .	22
Division of book into Toledoth . .	22
Of the names of God, as used in Genesis	24
— — — *Exod. vi. 2, 3*	25
Proper names compounded with JAH .	26
Meaning and antiquity of the name JEHOVAH, with further reference to Exod. vi. 2, 3	26
Elohistic and Jehovistic passages .	28
Alleged inconsistency with modern science	29

IF it be once admitted that the Pentateuch, as a whole, is due to Moses, there can be no difficulty in admitting that Genesis, the most ancient part of the Pentateuch, is due to him. If he wrote the history of the Exodus, he, either as author or compiler, must have written the introductory history of the times of the patriarchs. The unity of design is very manifest throughout. Moses was employed to mould and form a simple and previously enslaved people into an organized nation. He had to give them a code of laws, civil and ecclesiastical, for the guidance of their national life. The infant people was to be a theocracy, the germ and embryo of a theocracy greater than itself, guarded and isolated for fifteen centuries, till by a new revolution it should expand into the Church of Christ. It was obvious therefore, that he, who had to write the earliest chapters of its history, should begin by tracing down its descent from those who had from the first been the depositaries and witnesses of the truth.

If, however, adverse criticism has been busy in trying to dislocate all portions of the Pentateuch, to disprove its unity, and so to shake the evidence for its Mosaic origin; it has been signally busy in so dealing with Genesis. If Moses wrote the later books, he certainly wrote Genesis; and on the other hand, if he did not write Genesis, he wrote nothing. Hence to shake the foundation of Genesis is to destroy the fabric of the Pentateuch. The progress of the criticism has been sufficiently gradual. It was suggested long since by Vitringa, that Moses may have had before him "documents of various kinds coming down from the times of the patriarchs and preserved among the Israelites, which he collected, reduced to order, worked up, and where needful, filled in," *schedas et scrinia patrum, apud Israelitas conservata, Mosem collegisse, digessisse, ornasse, et ubi deficiebant, complesse* ('Obs. Sac.' I. c. 4). A conjecture of this kind was neither unnatural nor irreverent. It is very probable that, either in writing or by oral delivery, the Israelites possessed traditions handed down from their forefathers. It is consistent with the wisdom of Moses, and not inconsistent with his Divine inspiration, that he should have preserved and incorporated with his own work all such traditions, written or oral, as had upon them the stamp of truth.

The next step in the theory was, that taken by Astruc in 1753, who taught, that the names of God (Elohim and JEHOVAH), occurring in the book of Genesis may distinguish respectively the documents or memoirs from which Moses compiled his history. He believed that there were no fewer than twelve documents, the two chief being the Elohistic and the Jehovistic.

Later writers again have varied this theory with every possible variation; some believing that there was one Elohist, and one Jehovist document; others that there were more than one Elohist, and many Jehovists; and exercising a subtle ingenuity, most convincing at least to themselves, they have traced minutely the transitions from one document to another, sometimes even in the midst of a sentence, guided by some catchword or form of expression, which they have, as others think most arbitrarily, assigned to the first or second Elohist, to the first, second, third, or fourth Jehovist, according to the number of authors in which they respectively believe[1]. Another step has been to suggest, that the different documents, often, as it is alleged, giving different versions of the same story, have been carelessly and clumsily put together. And a further still has been to deny, that Moses could be either the Elohist, the Jehovist, or the compiler and redactor, it being evident that the whole was a later work, due perhaps to Samuel, perhaps to Hilkiah or Jeremiah, perhaps still later to Ezra or some survivor from the captivity, or possibly to a collection of the labours, the piously fraudulent labours, of them all.

The salient points in their arguments are these. There appear to be two versions of the history of the creation, the first from Gen i. 1 to Gen. ii. 3, in which only the name Elohim occurs, the other from Gen. ii. onwards, in which the name of JEHOVAH occurs in combination with Elohim. Again, there appear two accounts of the Flood, which though interlaced in the book of Genesis, may be disentangled. These also are characterized respectively by the same variety in the names of God. Similar phenomena are said to prevail throughout the book, and even throughout the Pentateuch, but these are the two most observable. Then comes the well-known passage in Ex. vi. 3, where the Most High says to Moses that He was known to the fathers by the name of El-Shaddai, but by the name JEHOVAH He was not known to them; whence the introduction of the name Jehovah in the history of Adam, Noah, Abraham, &c., is argued to be a proof of later authorship.

It may be well then to shew:

First, that the Book of Genesis is not an ill-digested collection of fragmentary documents, but a carefully arranged narrative with entire unity of purpose and plan.

Secondly, that the use of the names of God is neither arbitrary nor accidental, but consistent throughout with the Mosaic authorship, and the general scope of the history.

1. *Unity of plan and purpose throughout.*

First then, as to the organic structure of the book, though it may be somewhat obscured by the modern division into chapters and verses, as it was of old by the Jewish division of the Pentateuch into *perashim* or sections; careful examination will shew, that the arrangement is methodical and orderly from first to last.

The book begins with a general introduction, from ch. i. 1 to ch. ii. 3, wherein the creation of the universe is related in language of simple grandeur, very possibly in words handed down from the remotest antiquity, than which none could be more fitted here for the use of the sacred historian.

After this the book consists of a series of *Toledoth*, or genealogical histories, the first of which is called "the Toledoth of the heavens and the earth," ch. ii. 4; the others being the respective histories of the different families of man, especially of the ancestors of the people of Israel, from Adam to the death of Joseph[1]. The

[1] An abstract of the different theories from Astruc to the present day may be seen in Havernick ('Int. to Pent.' p. 45, Translation, Clark, Edinburgh), and 'Aids to Faith,' M'Caul's Essay on 'Mosaic Record of Creation,' p. 191.

[1] The word *Toledoth* has by some been rendered "origins," as "generations" cannot properly be used of the creation of heaven and earth; but it is not necessary to drop the figurative language in a translation. By an easy metaphor, the word, which described well the family history of a race of men, was applied to the history of the material creation. The word, moreover, as used in Genesis, does not mean a

great divisions of the book will be found to be:

1. The Introduction, from ch. i. 1 to ch. ii. 3.

2. "The generations of the heavens and the earth," beginning with ch. ii. 4, and extending on through the history of the fall to the birth of Seth, ch. iv.

3. "The book of the generations of Adam," from ch. v. to vi. 8.

4. "The generations of Noah," giving the history of Noah's family till his death, from vi. 9 to end of ix.

5. "The generations of the sons of Noah," giving an account of the over-spreading of the earth, from x. 1 to xi. 9.

6. "The generations of Shem," the line of the promised seed, down to Abram, Nahor, and Haran, the sons of Terah, xi. 10 to 26.

7. "The generations of Terah," the father of Abraham, from whom also in the female line the family was traced through Sarah and Rebekah, from xi. 27 to xxv. 11[1].

8. "The generations of Ishmael," from xxv. 12 to xxv. 18.

9. "The generations of Isaac," containing the history of him and his family from the death of his father to his own death, xxv. 19 to end of xxxv.

10. "The generations of Esau," xxxvi. 1—8.

11. "The generations of Esau in Mount Seir," xxxvi. 9 to xxxvii. 1.

12. "The generations of Jacob," giving the history of Jacob and his sons to his own death and the death of Joseph, xxxvii. 2 to the end of ch. l.

history of the mode in which persons or things came into existence, but rather the history of those who descended from them. Thus "the Toledoth of Adam" gives the history of Adam and his posterity. In like manner "the Toledoth of the heavens and the earth" is the history of the material universe and its productions. See Keil on the 'Pentateuch,' Vol. I. pp. 70 sqq. (Clark, Edinburgh).

[1] It seems strange that the "generations of Abraham" should not be given distinctly from those of his father, and Quarry thinks that the title may have existed, and have fallen out of the MS. just before the last clause of xii. 4. The reason, however, which he himself assigns, seems sufficient to account for the omission, viz. that the history contained in this section is that of Abraham, Lot, Sarah, and of Isaac and Rebekah (all descendants of Terah), down to the death of Abraham.

Some of these sections relate only to collateral branches and are brief. The larger sections will be found to have subdivisions within them, which are carefully marked and arranged. As a rule, in each of these successive *Toledoth*, the narrative is carried down to the close of the period embraced, and at the beginning of each succeeding portion a brief repetition of so much as is needed of the previous account is given, and with it, very often, a note of time. Thus the Introduction is ushered in with the words "In the Beginning." Then the second section, referring to what has just been recorded, announces "The generations of the heavens and of the earth when they were created, in the day that the Lord God made the earth and the heavens," ch. ii. 4. Then again ch. v. 1, having the same note of time ("In the day," &c.) refers back to the account of creation, "In the likeness of God made He him, male and female created He them," &c. The next section, vi. 9, "The Toledoth of Noah," recapitulates the character of Noah, the degeneracy of man, and God's purpose to destroy all flesh. In xi. 10, the age of Shem and the birth of his son two years after the flood, are named. The like plan is observable in the "Toledoth of Terah," xi. 27; "the Toledoth of Ishmael," xxv. 12; "of Isaac," xxv. 19, "who was forty years old when he took Rebekah to wife;" "of Esau," xxxvi. 1, where his marriages are recorded again: and lastly, in the case of Jacob (xxxvii. 2), we find, in the verse immediately preceding (viz. xxxvii. 1), a note telling us the position of Jacob at the time, and again in vv. 2 and 3 the age of Joseph ("Joseph was seventeen years old"), taking us back to a point of time twelve years before the death of Isaac, which had been before recorded, that so we might see the new starting-point of the history.

Space will not allow the tracing of similar recapitulations and notes of time in the smaller sub-sections of the history. It must suffice to observe that they are very characteristic of the whole book, and are had recourse to wherever perspicuity of narrative seems to require[1].

[1] They are traced at length by Quarry ('Genesis,' pp. 326 to 340).

This brief review of the divisions of Genesis shews that it was not a loosely compacted structure, carelessly or clumsily thrown together by some one, who found a variety of heterogeneous materials and determined to mass them all in one: but that it was drawn up carefully, elaborately, and with distinct unity of purpose; whether from pre-existing documents or not it matters comparatively little to enquire.

2. *Of the names of God as used in the Book of Genesis.*

The names by which the Supreme Being is called in the Old Testament, and especially in Genesis, are chiefly two, *Elohim* and JEHOVAH, the one generally rendered in the versions God, the other LORD. We meet also with *El* (which is but a shorter form of Elohim), with *Elion*, Most High, (in the Pentateuch occurring only in Gen. xiv. 18 in connection with *El; El-Elion*, God most High, though in the Psalms it is found with Elohim and Jehovah, and also stands alone), and *Shaddai*, Almighty (in the Pentateuch generally with *El, El-Shaddai;* elsewhere standing alone).

The name *Elohim* is derived either from the Arabic root *Alaha*, "to fear, reverence, worship," or, much more probably, from אָלָה (*alah*) = אול "to be strong, to be mighty[1]." It is the simple, generic name of God, "The Mighty." It does not occur in the singular in the earlier books of Scripture, except in the abbreviated form of El. The plural is probably a plural of excellence and majesty. As in Prov. ix. 1, "wisdom," occurs in the plural *Chochmoth*, to signify wisdom in the abstract, including in itself all the treasures of wisdom and knowledge; so *Elohim* in the plural is applied to God, as comprehending in Himself the fulness of all power and all the attributes which the heathen ascribe to their several divinities (see Smith's 'Dict. of Bible,' Art. JEHOVAH). Still the word is a title rather than a name. It is applied to false gods, as well as to the true. The heathen nations round about the Israelites would have recognized the existence and the divinity of El and of the Elohim.

[1] It is more probable that the verb to signify "fear and worship" is derived from the name of the Deity, than that the name of the Deity was derived from the verb signifying "to fear."

JEHOVAH, on the contrary, is as clearly a proper name as Jupiter or Vishnu. *Elohim* and *Jehovah* are therefore as distinguishable as *Deus* and *Jupiter;* the difference being only in this, that, whereas the worshippers of Jupiter admitted "gods many and lords many," a multitude of *Dii*, the worshippers of Jehovah, on the other hand, believe in no Elohim except JEHOVAH. We may see at once, then, that there may be good reasons for expecting the title Elohim to be chiefly employed in some passages, whilst the proper name JEHOVAH would be chiefly employed in others. For instance, in the general account of creation it is very natural that Elohim, the Mighty One, the God of creation and providence, should be the word in use. So, where foreigners, people of heathen nations, as Hagar, Eliezer of Damascus, the Egyptians, &c. are introduced, it is most natural that the word Elohim should be more frequent than JEHOVAH, unless where some distinct acknowledgment of JEHOVAH is intended. On the contrary, when the history of the chosen people or their ancestors is specially concerned, and the stream of the Theocracy traced down from its fountain head, then the special name of Him, who was not ashamed to be called their God, would probably be of more frequent use. This, if kept clearly in view, will explain many of the so-called Elohistic and Jehovistic phenomena in Genesis. Another thing to be noted is this. The Semitic tongues, especially the more ancient and simpler forms of them, deal much in repetition, and where our modern Aryan languages would put a pronoun, they very frequently repeat the noun. From this general habit of repetition, and especially the habit of repeating the noun rather than using the pronoun, when in any one chapter or section we find either the word Elohim or the name JEHOVAH, we are very likely to find the same frequently recurring. In consequence of this, the several passages will to an European eye look as if they were strongly marked either by the title Elohim, or by the name JEHOVAH. For instance, it is alleged that in the first account of creation, ch. I, ii. 1—3, Elohim occurs thirty-five times, and that there is here no other name of God: but it has been replied, that, if it occurred once, it was only natural, owing to the uniformity of the whole passage, that it should have occurred again at each account of a separate creation, and also that in modern language a pronoun would have been substituted in many cases for the repeated title or name. Hence the thirty-five are in effect reducible to one. The passage is scarcely more really marked as Elohistic by the name Elohim occurring thirty-five times, than if it had occurred but once; for its having occurred once would inevitably lead to its continued and frequent recurrence[1].

The most important passage in relation to this question is, of course, Exod. vi. 2, 3, where according to the Authorized Version, "God spake unto Moses, and said unto him, I am JEHOVAH; and I appeared unto Abraham, unto Isaac, and unto Jacob, by the name of God Almighty, but by my name JEHOVAH was I not known to them." The inference derived from this passage has been this. The person, who recorded these words of God to Moses, would never have written a history of still earlier times, in which the name JEHOVAH should be introduced not only in the narrative, but in the mouths of the various speakers, from Eve downwards. Hence, no doubt, in his earlier history the writer of this passage would surely have been an Elohist. The parts of Genesis then, which are characterized by the use of the title Elohim, may probably be attributed to him: but all the parts in which JEHOVAH predominates were evidently added afterwards, and must be due to some one who was not alive to the incongruity of introducing Jehovistic language into a history of events and speeches prior to the revelation of the name JEHOVAH. It follows, of course, that the very first who could possibly have written the original Elohistic narrative was Moses, the Jehovistic portions being necessarily much later than Moses. It is further argued, however, that names compounded with the sacred name of JAH or JEHOVAH do not occur till the time of Samuel, hence it is added that the name could not have been known, nor the sixth chapter of Exodus written, till the time of Samuel: and further, it is now alleged that the name JEHOVAH is unknown even to the writer of the earlier Psalms, and that therefore probably David learned it late in life from its inventor Samuel.

The romance of modern criticism is as remarkable as its perverse ingenuity: for when once a theory has been suggested, its author and his followers proceed forthwith to construct an elaborate history upon it, as much as if, instead of excogitating a theory, they had discovered a library of authentic records. The wider the theory is from all that has hitherto been believed from concurrent testimony and careful enquiry, the more it finds acceptance and is hailed as a discovery. If we look a little closely

[1] Quarry, 'on Genesis,' pp. 341, 400, 401. The following table of the alternation of the names in the first 11 chapters is given by the learned author, and will shew how different the *virtual* occurrence of the respective names is from the apparent, superficial occurrence on which so much has been built:

			E.	J.
Ch. i. ii. 1—3.	Elohim	35 times	=1	
iii. 1—5.	Elohim	3 ...	=1	
iv. 1.	Jehovah	1 ...		=1
2—16.	Jehovah	8 ...		=1
25.	Elohim	1 ...	=1	
26.	Jehovah	1 ...		=1
v. 1.	Elohim	2 ...	=1	
22—24.	Elohim	3 ...	=1	
29.	Jehovah	1 ...		=1
vi. 2—4.	Elohim	2 ...	=1	
3.	Jehovah	1 ...		=1
5—8.	Jehovah	4 ...		=1
9—22.	Elohim	5 ...	=1	
vii. 1—5.	Jehovah	2 ...		=1
9.	Elohim	1 ...	=1	
16.	Elohim	1 ...	=1	
	Jehovah	1 ...		=1
viii. 1.	Elohim	2 ...	=1	
15.	Elohim	1 ...	=1	
20—21.	Jehovah	3 ...		=1
ix. 1—6.	Elohim	2 ...	=1	
8—17.	Elohim	4 ...	=1	
26.	Jehovah	1 ...		=1
	Elohim	1 ...	=1	
27.	Elohim	1 ...	=1	
x. 9.	Jehovah	2 ...		=1
xi. 5—9.	Jehovah	5 ...		=1
			15	12

"Hence for the purposes of the present enquiry, and as evidence of any predilection of either name, the case is just as if in these eleven chapters, in the order of succession and at the distances here indicated, the name Elohim had recurred singly 15 times, and the name Jehovah 12 times."

into the foundations of the theory, it will appear as baseless as other dreams.

First, as regards the names compounded with JAH, we have at all events Jochebed, Joshua, Jonah, Jotham, Micah and Jonathan and mount Moriah, besides three named in Chronicles, Azariah (1 Chr. ii. 8), Abiah (1 Chr. ii. 24), Ahijah (1 Chr. ii. 25), all of which at least appear to have been so compounded, and which it is a gratuitous slander to say were the inventions of later days. Moreover, it by no means follows, that one age should have had the fashion of a special form for the composition of names, because we find that fashion prevailing some centuries later. Names compounded with *any* name of God are rare in the early ages, but became common in the later. Secondly, as regards the Psalms, there is no foundation whatever for saying that the earlier Psalms are Elohistic and the later only Jehovistic. Many of the manifestly and confessedly later Psalms (as the 78th, 82nd, 114th, &c.) are eminently Elohistic, whilst many of the earliest (as the 24th, 27th, 34th, &c.) are as eminently Jehovistic[1].

But again, the form and derivation of the name JEHOVAH points to a pre-Mosaic origin. Some of the German writers indeed have tried to trace the name to an attempt at expressing in Hebrew letters the name of the Phœnician god, *Iao*. Time will not allow of a lengthened consideration of this theory here. Suffice it to say that its chief support is an oracular response of the Clarian Apollo quoted by Macrobius ('Sat.' I. c. 18) about 400 A.D.; which has been clearly proved by Jablonsky to have originated in a Judaizing gnostic[2].

It is now generally admitted by competent Semitic scholars, that the word signifies "the existent" or something nearly akin to this. The true pronunciation, of course, is lost; but there can be no reasonable doubt, that, as the name of God declared to Moses in Ex. iii. 14, viz. אהיה, I AM, is the first person present of the substantive verb, so the name JEHOVAH is part of the same, but probably the third person present, or, as others think, the same tense of a causative (Hiphil) form[1]. But if so, there can be no question, as even Ewald fully admits, that the name must have been pre-Mosaic. In Hebrew the verb is always *hayah*, though in Syriac and Chaldee it is always *havah*. A name therefore derived from *havah* and existing in ancient Hebrew, must have come down from a time prior to the separation of the Hebrews from their kindred Aramæans, *i.e.* not later than the time of Abraham. In fact the name יהוה (IHVH) could not have been found among the Hebrews, at any period of history from the descent into Egypt to the captivity of Babylon: and as it undoubtedly exists in Hebrew writings prior to the captivity, so it must have originated before the time of Joseph.

We must conclude, then, that the name JEHOVAH was not unknown to the patriarchs, nor do the words of Exodus necessarily mean that it was. These words literally are, "I am JEHOVAH: and I appeared (or was manifested) to Abraham and to Isaac and to Jacob by El-Shaddai, but My name JEHOVAH was I not known to them:" that is to say, "I manifested myself to the patriarchs in the character of El-Shaddai, the Omnipotent God, able to fulfil that which I had promised; but as to my name (*i.e.* my character and attributes of) JEHOVAH I was not made manifest to them[2]." (So LXX. Vulg. οὐκ ἐδήλωσα, *non indicavi*). The words strictly and naturally imply this. The ancient versions seem to confirm this interpretation. It is no new one framed to meet modern objections, but was propounded by Aben Ezra and Rashi among the Jews, and by many of the most illustrious Christian commentators of past times.

The theory then of the late invention of this sacred name has really no foundation. That its use was very much more

[1] The Editor has shewn this more at length in his tract, called 'The Pentateuch and the Elohistic Psalms' (Longman).

[2] See the whole question discussed in Smith's 'Dict. of Bible,' I. p. 953, and Quarry, 'Genesis,' p. 300 sqq.

[1] Thus it corresponds in form with such names as Isaac, Jacob, Joseph, which are all the third persons singular present of verbs.

[2] "In El-Shaddai" is interpreted to mean "as El-Shaddai," "in the character of El-Shaddai," (Gesen. Lex. s.v. בְּ div. C.). "The name of Jehovah," as meaning the character of Jehovah, is very common. Cf. Ps. v. 11, viii. 1, ix. 10, Is. xxvi. 8, xxx. 27.

prevalent after the revelation to Moses in Exodus than it had been before, there can be no reasonable doubt. God made His special covenant with Abram, beginning with the emphatic words, "I am El-Shaddai," Gen. xvii. 1. So again on a like occasion He spake to Jacob, Gen. xxxv. 11. Hence both Isaac and Jacob seemed to lay especial stress upon that name in times of trouble and anxiety (see Gen. xxviii. 3, xliii. 14), as recalling to them the faithfulness and the power of their covenant God. But to Moses the words are frequently spoken, "I am JEHOVAH," and the covenant, which had been assured to the patriarchs by God as El-Shaddai, the Mighty God, is now assured to the people of Israel, by the same God, as JEHOVAH, the self-existent, the cause of all being, governing the past, the present, and the future. Let us then suppose, that Moses had access to, or knowledge of, oral or written traditions concerning the Creation, which must from the nature of the case have been originally matter of revelation, the Flood, the history of Abraham, Isaac and Jacob; it is most likely that he would have made these the ground-work of his history. If the name, JEHOVAH, was known to the patriarchs, but had, as seems most likely from the first chapters of Exodus, been latterly but little used, perhaps wholly disused, among the Israelites in Egypt; then it is pretty certain that these traditions or documents would have had El, Elohim, or Elion, for the name of God, perhaps even to the exclusion of the name JEHOVAH. In working up these materials into a continuous history, some of the documents would be preserved entire, others might be so arranged and so worded as to fit them to be connecting links one with the other, while we should probably find many portions of the history in the hand of the author or compiler himself. If Moses was that author, though he would often use the name Elohim, we might naturally expect to find that he had a fondness for that sacred name by which the Most High had declared Himself as the special Protector of His people; and hence we might look for that name in passages where another writer perhaps would not have introduced it. If, as we infer from Josh. xxiv. 14, the Israelites in Egypt had learned to serve strange gods, there would be the more reason why Moses should set before them the one true God, as their own God, and exhibit Him under His name, JEHOVAH, thereby the more clearly to mark Him off from the false Elohim of Egypt, and the false Elohim of Canaan.

Now the facts of Genesis remarkably coincide with all this probability. Some portions of the narrative do indeed present what is called an Elohistic aspect; and especially those portions, which, of their very nature, are most likely to have existed in the traditions current from old time among the Israelites, viz. the general account of the Creation, the Flood, the covenant of circumcision made with Abraham, and the genealogical tables. These then Moses appears to have adopted, much as he found them, perhaps perpetuating, word for word, in his writings what before had been floating in unwritten record. Yet these portions of the narrative are not loosely thrown in, but rather carefully and organically incorporated and imbedded in the whole.

For instance, in the history of creation, we have first, in Gen. i. ii. 1—3, that which was very probably the ancient primeval record of the formation of the world. It may even have been communicated to the first man in his innocence. At all events, it very probably was the great Semitic tradition, handed down from Noah to Shem, from Shem to Abraham, and from Abraham through Isaac, Jacob and Joseph, to the Israelites who dwelt in Egypt. Without interfering with the integrity of this, the sacred author proceeds in the same chapter to add a supplementary history, briefly recapitulating the history of creation, with some little addition (in vv. 4—7), and then proceeding to the history of Paradise, the Fall, the expulsion, and the first bitter fruits of disobedience. In the first part of this second or supplementary history we meet with a signal phenomenon, viz. that, from ch. ii. 4 to the end of chapter iii. the two names (or rather the generic and the personal names) of God, JEHOVAH and Elohim, are used continually together. There is no other instance in Scripture of this continued and repeated use of the united names. It is evident, that the author, who adopted the first ancient record and stamped it with authority, and who desired to bring his people to a worship of the great self-existent JEHOVAH, used this method of transition from the ancient Elohistic document to his own more immediate narrative, in order that he might more forcibly impress upon his readers, that the Elohim who created all things was also the JEHOVAH, who had revealed Himself to Moses, and who was now to be spoken of as the Protector and King of the great Theocratic race, whose history was to be traced down even from the very creation of Adam. The consistency and close connection of the two parts is admitted by some, who are far from admitting the Divine original or high inspiration of the Pentateuch. "The second account," says Kalisch (*in loc.*) "is no abrupt fragment; it is not unconnected with the first; it is not superfluous repetition; it has been composed with clear consciousness after, and with reference to, the first. The author of the Pentateuch added to an ancient document on creation the history of man's disobedience and its consequence. ...The first account was composed independently of the second; but the second is a distinct and deliberate continuation of the first....It does not merely recapitulate, but it introduces new facts and a new train of thought." The consistency of the two narratives, and a consideration of the alleged inconsistencies, will be seen in the commentary (on ch. ii. especially). One singular point of resemblance it may be well to point out here. In ch. i. 26, in the so called Elohistic document, we have the remarkable words, "Let us make man," the plural pronoun used by the Almighty Himself, and the appearance of deliberation. In ch. iii. 22 (in the so called Jehovistic portion) we have again, "Behold the man is become as one of us:" again the very observable plural, and again perhaps even more markedly anthropomorphic language, as though the Most High were taking counsel, before executing His judgments. This identity of thought and speech is very observable, The like occurs again in ch. xi. 6; where neither Elohim, nor JEHOVAH-Elohim, but JEHOVAH alone is the name of God made use of[1]. There is not space to go through the book of Genesis and shew how similar principles prevail throughout. If the basis of the history of the Flood were an ancient Elohistic document, Moses appears to have interwoven it with a further narrative of his own. The one portion may be marked by the prevalence of one name, the other by that of another name of God; but the consistency of the one with the other is complete throughout (see notes on the history, infra). The same will appear in other portions of Genesis, though the creation and the flood most clearly exhibit both the phenomena relied on by the theorists and the facts leading to a refutation of their theory.

It must not, however, be thought that the variety in the employment of the sacred names could have resulted only from the variety of the materials used by Moses and the additional matter introduced by himself. Careful observation will shew, that, whilst often it was a matter of indifference whether the one or the other name was introduced, yet there was no mere carelessness in the introduction. On the contrary, in most passages it is impossible to doubt that the choice of the name adopted is the happiest possible.

Thus in the first history of creation we have Elohim, the mighty one, God of Creation and Providence, then in order to mark the transition of subject and yet the unity of the Being spoken of, we have for two chapters JEHOVAH Elohim; but when we come to the ivth chapter and to Eve's exclamation, when she hoped that her firstborn should be the ancestor of the promised seed, the words ascribed to her connect her hope with JEHOVAH, Him whom the Israelites learned to look on as their covenant God, who was to make good all the promises to the fathers. Again, in ch. v. the genealogy from Adam to Noah has no Divine name except Elohim, till we come, in v. 29, to the birth of Noah, and his father's pious anticipation that he should be a comfort to his race, in

[1] See Quarry, p. 348.

reference to the earth, which had been cursed. The use of the name JEHOVAH in this verse points us at once to the fact that Noah became the second head of the Theocratic race, the new depositary of the promises of God. If we pass on to ch. xiv. we are introduced to Melchizedek, priest and king of a Canaanitish people. He is a worshipper of *El-Elion*, God most High, this being evidently the name by which the Almighty was known to him and to his countrymen. Once, however, the name JEHOVAH occurs in the chapter, but it is in the mouth of Abraham, and Abraham evidently uses it that he may shew that he acknowledges the El-Elion worshipped by Melchizedek to be one and the same with the JEHOVAH, who was the God of Hebrews. "I have lift up my hand to JEHOVAH, El-Elion, possessor of heaven and earth," xiv. 22. A similar propriety of usage prevails throughout Genesis, and will frequently be referred to in the notes.

Again, verbal peculiarities are said to distinguish the so called Jehovistic from the so called Elohistic portions of the Pentateuch, so that, besides the variety in the use of the names of God, it is possible for a keen eye to disentangle the different documents the one from the other by noting the phraseology peculiar to each. It will be plain that, if even this were proved and patent, it would still not interfere with the Mosaic origin of Genesis, so long as we admit that Moses may have used the so called Elohistic MSS. or traditions. The Elohistic phraseology would then be characteristic of the more ancient documents, the Jehovistic would belong to Moses himself. It is, however, very clear, that the peculiarities are greatly magnified, if they exist at all. Sometimes indeed the theorists discover that a passage must belong to the Elohist for instance, because it contains Elohistic expressions; but then, though the name JEHOVAH occurs in it, that name must be a later insertion because it does not correspond with the general wording of the chapter. Thus the name JEHOVAH in ch. xvii. 1 is argued to be evidently out of place, because Elohim occurs everywhere else (ten times) in the chapter. Surely this is constructing a theory in despite, not in consequence, of the facts on which it ought to stand[1].

Again anthropomorphisms are said to characterise the Jehovist passages. This is by no means unlikely, considering that JEHOVAH is the personal name of God, and that by which He was pleased to reveal Himself familiarly to His people; yet they are far from exclusively belonging to the Jehovistic portions. Lastly, all the indications of a more advanced civilization, such as the use of gold, jewels, earrings, musical instruments, camels, servants, &c. are assigned to the Jehovist, and are thought to mark a period later than that of Moses. But surely the Israelites, who had dwelt for centuries in the fairest province in Egypt, and Moses who had been bred up in the court of a powerful and luxurious Pharaoh, must have been familiar with a civilization considerably in advance of anything that we read of in Genesis. Indeed the graphic account which Genesis gives of the simple habits of Abraham and the other patriarchs is one proof of its antiquity and its truth. It is very doubtful whether an author even in the time of Samuel, more than doubtful whether one in the reign of Solomon, of Josiah, or one of those who returned with Ezra from captivity, could have written the history of the forefathers of his race with all the truthfulness, all the simplicity, and all the accuracy of detail to be found in the Book which is called the First Book of Moses. Moses could have written it, for he had every conceivable qualification for writing it. The writer of after times, who could have produced that book, must have been himself a wonder, unsurpassed by any of those wonders which he is supposed to have devised and recorded.

The supposed inconsistency of the statements in Genesis with the recent

[1] The distinction between the Elohistic and Jehovistic words and phrases is carefully and elaborately investigated by Mr Quarry ('Genesis,' pp. 578 sqq.). The conclusion at which he arrives is the very reverse of the conclusion arrived at by the believers in the fragment theory.

discoveries of science will be found treated of in the notes to the earlier chapters. It may be well here only to say, that in the present state of our knowledge, both critical and scientific, a patient suspension of judgment on many points seems our wisest attitude. It is plain that a miraculous revelation of scientific truths was never designed by God for man. The account of creation is given in popular language; yet it is believed that it will be found not inconsistent with, though not anticipatory of, modern discovery. And after all, modern discovery is yet in a most imperfect condition, the testimony of the rocks and of the stars but imperfectly read, whilst there is room for no small diversity of sentiment on the meaning of many of the expressions in Genesis. At present the greatest inconsistency alleged as between Genesis and science is to be found in the question of the antiquity of man. Whilst there is at least good reason for withholding confident assent from the conclusions of some eminent geologists as to the evidence of the drift; it is quite possible to believe that Genesis gives us no certain data for pronouncing on the time of man's existence on the earth. The only arguments are to be drawn from the genealogies. As those given by the Evangelists are confessedly incomplete, there cannot be sufficient reason for maintaining that those in Genesis must have been complete. It is true that we have only conjecture to lead us here: but if the genealogies, before and after the Flood, present us only with the names of leading and "representative" men; we can then allow no small latitude to those who would extend the duration of man upon the earth to more than the commonly received six thousand years. The appearance of completeness in the genealogies is an undoubted difficulty; yet perhaps not insuperable, when we consider all that may have happened (no where more probably than here) in the transmission of the text from Moses to Ezra and from Ezra to the destruction of Jerusalem.

Let us suppose that it had pleased God to reveal to Moses the fact that the earth revolves round the sun, a fact familiar now to children, but unknown to astronomers for more than three thousand years after the Exodus. The effect of such a revelation would probably have been to place the believer and the astronomer in a state of antagonism. The ancient believer would have believed the truth; yet the observer of the heavens would have triumphantly convicted him of ignorance and error. We can see plainly that the wise course for both would have been to suspend their judgments, believing the Bible and yet following out the teaching of nature. A Galileo would then have been, not feared as a heretic, but hailed as a harmonist. There appears now to some an inconsistency between the words of Moses and the records of creation. Both may be misinterpreted. Further research into science, language, literature and exegesis, may shew that there is substantial agreement, where there now appears partial inconsistency. It would evidently have served no good purpose, had a revelation been vouchsafed of the Copernican system, or of modern geological science. Yet there may be in Scripture truth popularly expressed concerning the origin of all things, truth not apparent to us, because we have not yet acquired the knowledge to see and appreciate it. Certainly as yet nothing has been proved which can disprove the records of Genesis, if both the proof and the records be interpreted largely and fairly.

THE FIRST BOOK OF MOSES,

CALLED

GENESIS.

CHAPTER I.

1 The creation of heaven and earth, 3 of the light, 6 of the firmament, 9 of the earth separated from the waters, 11 and made fruitful, 14 of the sun, moon, and stars, 20 of fish and fowl, 24 of beasts and cattle, 26 of man in the image of God. 29 Also the appointment of food.

[a] Psal. 33. 6. & 136. 5. Acts 14. 15. & 17. 24. Hebr. 11. 3.

IN [a]the beginning God created
the heaven and the earth.

2 And the earth was without form,
and void; and darkness *was* upon the
face of the deep. And the Spirit of God
moved upon the face of the waters.
3 And God said, [b]Let there be [b] 2 Cor. 4. 6
light: and there was light.
4 And God saw the light, that *it*
was good: and God divided [†]the
light from the darkness.

† Heb. *between the light and between the darkness.*

CHAP. I. 1. *In the beginning*] Not "first in order," but "in the beginning of all things." The same expression is used in Joh. i. 1, of the existence of the "Word of God," "In the beginning was the Word." The one passage illustrates the other, though it is partly by the contrast of thoughts. The Word *was*, when the world was *created*.

God created] In the first two chapters of Genesis we meet with four different verbs to express the creative work of God, viz. 1, to create; 2, to make; 3, to form; 4, to build. The first is used of the creation of the universe (v. 1); of the creation of the great sea-monsters, whose vastness appears to have excited special wonder (v. 21); and of the creation of man, the head of animated nature, in the image of God (v. 27). Everywhere else we read of God's *making*, as from an already created substance, the firmament, the sun, the stars, the brute creation (vv. 7, 16, 25, &c.); or of His *forming* the beasts of the field out of the ground (ch. ii. 19); or lastly, of His *building up* (ii. 22, margin) into a woman the rib which He had taken from man. In Isai. xliii. 7, three of these verbs occur together. "I have *created* him for my glory, I have *formed* him, yea, I have *made* him." Perhaps no other ancient language, however refined or philosophical, could have so clearly distinguished the different acts of the Maker of all things, and that because all heathen philosophy esteemed matter to have been eternal and uncreated. It cannot justly be objected that the verb *create*, in its first signification, may have been sensuous, meaning probably to *hew* stone or to *fell* timber. Almost all abstract or spiritual thoughts are expressed by words which were originally concrete or sensuous; and in nearly all the passages of Scripture in which the verb in question occurs, the idea of a true creation is that which is most naturally implied. Even where the translators have rendered it otherwise, the sense is still clearly the same, *e.g.* in Numb. xvi. 30, "If the LORD *make a new thing* (lit. *create a creation*), and the earth open her mouth;" or again, Ps. lxxxix. 47, "Wherefore hast Thou *made* (Heb. *created*) all things for nought?" The word is evidently the common word for a true and original creation, and there is no other word in Hebrew which can express that thought.

the heaven and the earth] The universe popularly described according to its appearance as earth and sky. In similar language, as Grotius notes, the new creation, to be hereafter looked for, is described 2 Pet. iii. 13, as "new heavens and a new earth." The Hebrew word for *heaven* is always plural, whether as expressive of greatness, or perhaps of multitude, like the old English plural, *welkin*.

2. *And the earth was without form, and void*] **Desolate and void.** These two words express devastation and desolation. They are used of the desert, Job xii. 24; xxvi. 7; of the devastated city, Isa. xxiv. 10; of "the line of wasting, and the plummet of destruction," Isa. xxxiv. 11. In Jer. iv. 23 they describe the utter wasting of a condemned and desolated land. Whether in the present verse they indicate entire absence of life and order, or merely that the world was not then, as now, teeming with life; whether they express primeval emptiness, or rather desolation and disorder succeeding to a former state of life and harmony, cannot immediately be determined. The purpose of the sacred writer is to give a history of man, his fall,

5 And God called the light Day, and the darkness he called Night. †And the evening and the morning were the first day.

† Heb. *And the evening was, and the morning was, &c.*

his promised recovery, then specially of the chosen seed, and of the rise of the Theocracy. He therefore contents himself with declaring in one verse generally the creation of all things, and then in the next verse passes to the earth, man's place of abode, and to its preparation for the habitation of man. Countless ages may have elapsed between what is recorded in v. 1, and what is stated in v. 2. Some indeed have insisted on the close connection of v. 2 with v. 1, because they are united by the word *And:* but this particle, though necessarily implying transition, does by no means necessarily imply close connection. The Book of Leviticus begins with "And the Lord called unto Moses." The Book of Exodus begins with the same word *And*, though centuries intervene between its history and that of the Book of Genesis; and so our translators have very reasonably rendered the Hebrew particle in that passage not *And*, but *Now*. The meaning of the verse before us evidently is, "In the beginning God created the universe;" but, at the time now to be spoken of, the earth, which is our chief concern, was shapeless and waste. The verb "was" as used in this verse implies, not succession, but condition at the time in question.

darkness was upon the face of the deep] No light penetrated to the desolate and disordered ruin. The *deep* may mean either the confused mass itself, or, as more frequently, the abyss of waters and the clouds and mists with which the earth was surrounded.

the Spirit of God moved upon the face of the waters] The Targum of Onkelos and many Jewish commentators render "a mighty wind was moving," &c., which is favoured, though not proved, by the absence of the article. The common rendering is the more natural, especially if the word "moved" signifies, as some think, not merely *fluttering* or *hovering*, as of a bird over its nest, but also *brooding*, as of a bird sitting on its eggs. (See Deut. xxxii. 11, where it is used of the eagle fluttering over her young.) The Spirit of God appears to be represented as the great quickening principle, hovering or brooding over the earth and the ocean, and breathing forth upon them light and life.

3. *God said*] In the cognate languages the word here rendered *said* has the force of *commanded.*

Let there be light: and there was light] Was light created before the creation of the sun and other luminous bodies? That this is possible has been shewn by Dr McCaul, 'Aids to Faith,' p. 210, &c.; but very probably the creation of the sun is related in v. 1, where under the word heaven (or heavens) may be comprehended the whole visible universe of sun, moon, and stars. Now, the history is going on to the adaptation of the earth for man's abode. In v. 2 a thick darkness had enveloped it. In this 3rd verse the darkness is dispelled by the word of God, the light is separated from the darkness, and the regular succession of day and night is established. Still probably there remains a clouded atmosphere, or other obstacle to the full vision of sun and sky. It is not till the fourth day that these impediments are removed and the sun appears to the earth as the great luminary of the day, the moon and the stars as reigning in the night. Light may, perhaps, have been created before the sun. Yet the statement, that on the first day, not only was there light, but the succession of day and night, seems to prove that the creation of the sun was "in the beginning," though its visible manifestation in the firmament was not till the fourth day.

4. *God saw the light, that it was good*] The earlier the records, the more we find in them of anthropopathic language, as the better fitted to simple understandings. The design of words like these is to express emphatically, that all the works, as they came direct from the hand of God, were good, and that the evil did not result from any defect in the workmanship, but from the will of the creature not according with the will of the Creator.

divided the light from the darkness] In the chaotic condition described in v. 2, all things were confused and commixed; but, when God called the light out of darkness, He set bounds to both of them, and caused a succession of day and night, calling the light day and the darkness night.

5. *And the evening and the morning were the first day*] Literally, "And it was (or became) evening, and it was (or became) morning, day one."

Some think the evening is put before the morning, because the Jews reckoned their days from evening to evening. Others think, that, as the darkness was first and the light called out of darkness, so the evening (in Heb. *ereb*, the time when all things are mixed and confounded) is placed before the morning; and thus the whole period of chaotic darkness may have been the first night, and the first day that period of light which immediately succeeded the darkness.

See Note A at end of the Chapter.

c Psal. 136. 5. Jer. 10. 12. & 51. 15. † Heb. *expansion.*

6 ¶ And God said, c Let there be
a † firmament in the midst of the
waters, and let it divide the waters
from the waters.
7 And God made the firmament,
and divided the waters which *were*
under the firmament from the waters
which *were* above the firmament:
and it was so.

d Jer. 51. 15.

8 And God called the d firmament Heaven. And the evening and
the morning were the second day.

e Psal. 33. 7. & 136. 5. Job 38. 8.

9 ¶ And God said, e Let the
waters under the heaven be gathered
together unto one place, and let the
dry *land* appear: and it was so.
10 And God called the dry *land*
Earth; and the gathering together of
the waters called he Seas: and God
saw that *it was* good.

† Heb. *tender grass.*

11 And God said, Let the earth
bring forth † grass, the herb yielding
seed, *and* the fruit tree yielding fruit
after his kind, whose seed *is* in itself,
upon the earth: and it was so.
12 And the earth brought forth
grass, *and* herb yielding seed after his
kind, and the tree yielding fruit,
whose seed *was* in itself, after his
kind: and God saw that *it was* good.
13 And the evening and the morning were the third day.

f Deut. 4. 19. Psal. 136. 7.

14 ¶ And God said, Let there
be f lights in the firmament of the

---

6. *Let there be a firmament*] The earth is spoken of as covered with waters, partly, that is, the waters of the sea, partly the heavy clouds and vapours, which hung round it in its state of desolation and darkness. The dispersion of some of these vapours lets in the light. Then, in the present verse, the clouds and mists are described as raised up above the firmament, the firmament itself dividing between the waters of the ocean and the clouds of heaven. It is plain from this that the word rendered *firmament* embraces the atmosphere immediately surrounding the surface of the earth, which bears up the clouds floating in it, in or on the face of which also the birds are described as flying (see v. 20). In v. 14 the word is extended further to embrace the whole region of the sky in which sun and moon and stars appear. In this respect, as Le Clerc notices, it corresponds with the classical word *cœlum*, which meant at times the air just round us, at other times the place of the stars and planets; and so likewise of our own English word *heaven*, we may say the birds of heaven, the clouds of heaven, or the stars of heaven. The original sense of the word has been much debated, but is of little consequence; for the sacred writer would use the common language of his people, and not go out of his way to devise one which would be philosophically accurate. The verb, from which the substantive is derived, signifies (1) to beat or stamp upon, Ezek. vi. 11, xxv. 6; (2) to spread abroad by stamping, 2 S. xxii. 43; (3) to beat out metal into thin plates, or gold into gold leaf, Ex. xxxix. 3, Num. xvi. 38, Isai. xl. 19; (4) to spread forth, extend, stretch out, Job xxxvii. 18, Ps. cxxxvi. 6, Is. xlii. 5, xliv. 24. The most probable meaning of the substantive therefore is *the expanse* or *the expansion*. The LXX. rendered it *firmament* (see here Quarry 'on Genesis,' p. 79); and hence it has been argued that Moses taught the sky to be a hard, metallic vault, in which the sun and stars were fixed; but the most learned modern commentators, including Gesenius, Kalisch, &c., believe the true etymology of the word to shew that *expanse*, not *firmament*, is the right translation. The teaching however of the present passage does not depend on the etymology of the word. If a writer in the present day uses the English word *heaven*, it does not follow, that he supposes the sky to be a vault *heaved* up from the earth. Neither would it follow that the inspired writer had taught, that the portion of atmosphere, intervening between the sea and the clouds, was a solid mass, even if the word used for it had etymologically signified *solidity*.

11. *Let the earth bring forth grass*] We have here the first calling forth of life upon the earth, vegetable life first, soon to be succeeded by animal life. The earth was made fruitful, and three kinds of vegetation were assigned to it; the tender grass, the common covering of the soil, fit chiefly for the use of the lower animals; herb bearing seed, which should be adapted to the service of man; and trees, with their conspicuous fruits; all three so ordained, that their seed should be in themselves, that they should contain, not a principle of life only, but a power also of fecundity, whereby the race should be perpetuated from generation to generation.

14. *Let there be lights*] Lit. **luminaries**, *light-bearers*, spoken of lamps and candlesticks, Ex. xxv. 6, Num. iv. 9, 16. The narrative only tells what sun, moon, and stars are in relation to the earth. When the clouds and mists are dispelled from its surface, the

† Heb. *between the day and between the night.*
heaven to divide †the day from the
night; and let them be for signs,
and for seasons, and for days, and
years:
15 And let them be for lights in
the firmament of the heaven to give
light upon the earth: and it was so.
16 And God made two great
lights; the greater light †to rule the
day, and the lesser light to rule the
night: *he made* the stars also.
† Heb. *for the rule of the day, &c.*
17 And God set them in the
firmament of the heaven to give light
upon the earth,
18 And to [g]rule over the day
and over the night, and to divide the
light from the darkness: and God
saw that *it was* good.
[g] Jer. 31. 35.
19 And the evening and the morning were the fourth day.
20 And God said, [h]Let the waters
[h] 4 Esdr. 6. 47.
bring forth abundantly the ‖moving
creature that hath †life, and fowl
that may fly above the earth in the
†open firmament of heaven.
‖ Or, *creeping.* † Heb. *soul.* † Heb. *face of the firmament of heaven.*
21 And God created great whales,
and every living creature that moveth,
which the waters brought forth abundantly, after their kind, and every
winged fowl after his kind: and God
saw that *it was* good.
22 And God blessed them, saying,
[i]Be fruitful, and multiply, and fill
the waters in the seas, and let fowl
multiply in the earth.
[i] chap. 8. 17. & 9. 1.
23 And the evening and the morning were the fifth day.
24 ¶ And God said, Let the earth
bring forth the living creature after
his kind, cattle, and creeping thing,
and beast of the earth after his kind:
and it was so.

---

seas confined within their boundaries, and the first vegetation springs up; then the sky is cleared up, the sun, moon, and stars appear and assume their natural functions, marking days and nights, seasons and years; and God makes or appoints them, the sun to rule the day, and the moon to rule the night.

16. *he made the stars also*] The purpose of the sacred narrative being to describe the adaptation of the earth to the use of man, no account is taken of the nature of the stars, as suns or planets, but merely as signs in the heavens. The words in the text may be a kind of parenthesis, not assigning the special time of the creation of the stars. Moreover, the word used is "made," not "created," see on v. 1. When the Sun and Moon became great lights to rule the day and to rule the night, then also the stars shone forth; the heavens were lit up by the sun in the day-time, by the moon and stars in the night-season, all of them declaring the glory of God and shewing His handy-work.

20. *the moving creature*] The versions render *reptiles*. The word is of wide significance, most frequently used of reptiles and fishes; the verb from which it comes, and which is here translated "bring forth abundantly," means *to swarm, to creep, to propagate itself rapidly*. We may probably therefore understand here the insect creation, the fishes of the sea, and the reptiles and saurians of sea and land.

that hath life] Literally perhaps, "Let the waters swarm with swarms of the breath of life." Let the waters teem with innumerable creatures, in which is the breath of life. The word *nephesh*, which we have rendered *breath*, corresponds nearly with the classical *psyche*, the vital principle. It is used of the breath, of the living principle, of the soul or seat of feelings and affections, and of living beings themselves.

and fowl, &c.] **and let fowl fly.**

21. *great whales*] **Great sea monsters.** The word is used of serpents, Ex. vii. 9, Deut. xxxii. 33, Ps. xci. 13, Jer. li. 34, and of the crocodile, Ezek. xxix. 3, xxxii. 2. It is not likely that the Israelites should have had much knowledge of the larger species of whales which do not frequent the shores of the Mediterranean. Their early acquaintance with Egypt had impressed them with a horror of the crocodile, and in the desert they had become familiar with large serpents. In Is. xxvii. 1, and perhaps in Job vii. 12, this name apparently belongs to sea monsters; but we may remember that the Hebrews applied the term *sea* to great rivers also, like the Nile and the Euphrates. (See Is. xix. 5, Jer. li. 36, Ezek. xxxii. 2, Nahum iii. 8.) It seems, on the whole, most probable, that the creatures here said to have been created were serpents, crocodiles, and other huge saurians, though possibly any large monsters of sea or river may be included. The use of the word *created* in this place has already been remarked on v. 1. Another reason for its use may be, that, as he Egyptians paid idolatrous worship to crocodiles, the sacred historian would teach that they also were creatures of God.

24. The fifth day was chiefly occupied in peopling the waters with fishes and reptiles,

25 And God made the beast of the
earth after his kind, and cattle after
their kind, and every thing that creepeth upon the earth after his kind: and
God saw that *it was* good.

26 ¶ And God said, [k]Let us make k chap. 5. 1.
man in our image, after our likeness: & 9. 6.
and let them have dominion over the 1 Cor. 11. 7.
fish of the sea, and over the fowl of Ephes. 4. 14.
the air, and over the cattle, and over Col 3. 10.

---

and the air with birds. The work of the sixth day gives inhabitants to the land, "cattle" (*i.e.* the well-known animals, which afterwards became domesticated, though the name was not exclusively attached to them), "and creeping things," such as serpents, lizards, crawling insects and the like, "and beast of the earth," *i. e.* either the wilder and fiercer beasts, as distinguished from cattle, or perhaps more generally animals of all kinds.

26. *And God said, Let us make man*] It has been observed by commentators, both Jewish and Christian (*e. g.* Abarbanel, *in loc.* Chrysost. *in loc.*), that the deliberation of the Creator is introduced, not to express doubt, but to enhance the dignity of the last work, the creation of man. So even Von Bohlen, "A gradual ascent is observed up to man, the chief work of creation, and in order to exalt his dignity, the act of his creation is accompanied by the deliberations of the Creator." The creative fiat concerning all other creatures runs, "Let the waters bring forth abundantly," "Let the earth bring forth," &c. Man is that great "piece of work," concerning which God is described as taking forethought and counsel, as making him in His own image, and (ch. ii. 7) as breathing into him the breath of life. Three times in *v.* 27 the verb *created* is used concerning the production of man; for, though his bodily organization may, like that of the beasts, have been produced from already created elements ("the dust of the ground," ch. ii. 7); yet the complex being, man, "of a reasonable soul and human flesh subsisting," was now for the first time called into being, and so was, unlike the beasts, wholly a new creation.

Let us make] The Jews vary much in their explanation of these words. Philo speaks of "the Father of all things addressing his own powers" ('De Profugis,' p. 359). The Talmud says, "The Holy One, Blessed be He, does nothing without consulting the family which is above" (*Sanhed.* c. iv.). Moses Gerundinus says, that God addressed the earth, for, as the earth was to give man the body, whilst God was to infuse the spirit, so "in our likeness" was to be referred both to God and to the earth. Abenezra writes, "When, according to God's commandment, the earth and the sea had brought forth plants and living beings, then God said to the angels, 'Let us make man, we will be occupied in his creation, not the seas and the earth.'" So he considers man to have been made after the likeness of the angels. To a similar effect Maimonides, 'More Nevochim,' p. ii. ch. 6. See Munster *in loc.*, Cleric. *in loc.*, Heidegger, p. 32.

Some interpreters, both Jewish and Christian, have understood a plural of dignity, after the manner of kings. This is the opinion of Gesenius and most of the Germans. But the royal style of speech was probably a custom of much later date than the time of Moses. Thus we read Gen. xli. 41–44, "I have set thee over the land of Egypt . . . . I am Pharaoh." Indeed this royal style is unknown in Scripture. Some of the modern rationalists believe (or affect to believe) that the plural name of God, *Elohim*, was a mere relic of ancient polytheism, and that though Moses habitually attaches a singular verb to the plural nominative, yet here "the plural unconsciously escaped from the narrator's pen" (Von Bohl.). The ancient Christians with one mind see in these words of God that plurality in the Divine unity, which was more fully revealed, when God sent His only begotten Son into the world, and when the only begotten Son, who was in the bosom of the Father, declared Him to mankind. So *e. g.* Barnabas (ch. iv.), Justin M., Irenæus, Theophil., Epiphan. ('Hæres.' xxxiii. 4–2), Theodoret ('Quæst. in Gen.').

in our image, after our likeness] Many Christian writers think that nothing is meant except that man was created holy and innocent, and that this image of God was lost when Adam fell. That holiness, indeed, formed part of the likeness may be inferred from Col. iii. 10, "the new man, which is renewed after the image of Him that created him;" but that the image of God was not wholly obliterated by the fall seems clear from Gen. ix. 6, Jas. iii. 9. And, if so, then that image did not simply consist in perfect holiness. Some, both Jewish and Christian, have supposed that it referred to that dominion, which is here assigned to man. As God rules over all, so man was constituted the governor of the animal world. St Basil M. in 'Hexaemeron' (qu. by Clericus) considers that the likeness consisted in freedom of will. This probably is a most important point in the resemblance. The brute creatures are gifted with life and will and self-consciousness, and even with some powers of reason; but they have no self-determining will, no choice between good and evil, no power of self-education, no proper moral character,

all the earth, and over every creeping
thing that creepeth upon the earth.
27 So God created man in his *own*
image, in the image of God created he
[l] Matt. 19. 4. him; [l] male and female created he them.
Wisd. 2. 23. 28 And God blessed them, and God
[m] chap. 9. 1. said unto them, [m] Be fruitful, and multiply, and replenish the earth, and sub-
due it: and have dominion over the
fish of the sea, and over the fowl of
the air, and over every living thing
† Heb. *creepeth.* that † moveth upon the earth.
† Heb. *seeding seed.* 29 ¶ And God said, Behold, I have
given you every herb † bearing seed,
which *is* upon the face of all the earth,
and every tree, in the which *is* the fruit
of a tree yielding seed; [n] to you it [n] chap. 9. 3.
shall be for meat.
30 And to every beast of the earth,
and to every fowl of the air, and to
everything that creepeth upon the
earth, wherein *there is* † life, *I have given* † Heb. *a living soul.*
every green herb for meat: and it
was so.
31 And [o] God saw every thing that [o] Ecclus. 39. 16.
he had made, and, behold, *it was* very
good. And the evening and the morning were the sixth day.

---

and so no true personality. God is the essentially personal Being, and in giving to man an immortal soul, He gave him also a true personality, self-consciousness, power of free choice, and so distinct moral responsibility. All this was accompanied at first with perfect purity and innocence; and thus man was like his Maker, intelligent, immortal, personal, with powers of forethought and free choice, and at the same time pure, holy and undefiled.

NOTE A on CHAP. I. v. 5. ON THE DAYS OF CREATION.

THE vexed question of the duration of the days of creation cannot readily be solved from consideration of the wording of this verse. The English Version would seem to confine it to natural days, but the original will allow much greater latitude. Time passed in regular succession of day and night. It was an ingenious conjecture of Kurtz, adopted by Hugh Miller, that the knowledge of pre-Adamite history, like the knowledge of future ages, may have been communicated to Moses, or perhaps to the first man, in prophetic vision, that so perhaps vast geological periods were exhibited to the eye of the inspired writer, each appearing to pass before him as so many successive days. It has been said moreover that the phenomena under the earth's surface correspond with the succession as described in this chapter, a period of comparative gloom, with more vapour and more carbonic acid in the atmosphere, then of greater light, of vegetation, of marine animals and huge reptiles, of birds, of beasts, and lastly of man. (See Kurtz, Vol. I. p. xxvii. sq., Hugh Miller, 'Test. of Rocks,' passim, &c.) In the present condition of geological science, and with the great obscurity of the record of creation in this chapter, it may be wise not to attempt an accurate comparison of the one with the other. Some few points, however, seem clearly to come out. In Genesis, first of all, creation is spoken of as "in the beginning," a period of indefinite, possibly of most remote distance in the past; secondly, the progress of the preparation of the earth's surface is described as gradually advancing from the rocks to the vegetable world, and the less perfectly organised animal creation, then gradually mounting up through birds and mammals, till it culminates in man. This is the course of creation as popularly described in Genesis, and the rocks give their testimony, at least in the general, to the same order and progress. The chief difference, if any, of the two witnesses would seem to be, that the Rocks speak of (1) marine plants, (2) marine animals, (3) land plants, (4) land animals in their successive developements; whereas Moses speaks of (1) plants, (2) marine animals, (3) land animals; a difference not amounting to divergence. As physiology must have been nearly and geology wholly unknown to the Semitic nations of antiquity, such a general correspondence of sacred history with modern science is surely more striking and important than any apparent difference in details. Efforts have been made to compare the Indian cosmogony with the Biblical, which utterly fail. The cosmogony of the Hindoos is thoroughly adapted to their Pantheistic Theology, the Hebrew corresponding with the pure personal Monotheism of the Old Testament. The only important resemblance of any ancient cosmogony with the Scriptural account is to be found in the Persian or Zoroastrian; which is most naturally accounted for, first by the fact, which will be noticed hereafter, that the Persians, of all people, except the Hebrews, were the most likely to have retained the memory of primitive traditions, and secondly, that Zoroaster was probably brought into contact with the Hebrews, and perhaps with the prophet Daniel in the court of Darius, and may have learned much from such association.

CHAPTER II.

1 The first sabbath. 4 The manner of the creation. 8 The planting of the garden of Eden, 10 and the river thereof. 17 The tree of knowledge only forbidden. 19, 20 The naming of the creatures. 21 The making of woman, and institution of marriage.

THUS the heavens and the earth
were finished, and all the host
of them.

2 [a]And on the seventh day God [a] Exod.
ended his work which he had made; 20. 11. & 31. 17.
and he rested on the seventh day from Deut. 5. 14.
all his work which he had made. Heb. 4. 4

3 And God blessed the seventh day,
and sanctified it: because that in it
he had rested from all his work which
God †created and made. † Heb.
4 ¶ These *are* the generations of *created to make.*

CHAP. II. 3. *And God blessed the seventh day*] The natural interpretation of these words is that the blessing of the Sabbath was immediately consequent on the first creation of man, for whom the Sabbath was made (Mar. ii. 27). It has been argued from the silence concerning its observance by the patriarchs, that no Sabbatic ordinance was really given until the promulgation of the Law, and that this passage in Genesis is not *historical* but *anticipatory*. There are several objections, which seem fatal to this theory. It is first to be observed, that this verse forms an integral part of that history of the creation, which, if there be any truth in the distinction, is the oldest portion of the Pentateuch, the work of the Elohist, very possibly handed down from the earliest ages of the world, and taken by Moses as the very groundwork of his inspired narrative. Secondly, the history of the patriarchs extending over at least 2500 years is all contained in the book of Genesis, and many things must have been omitted, much more memorable than the fact of their resting on the Sabbath, which in their simple pastoral life would seldom have called for special notice. Thirdly, there are indications even in Genesis of a division of days into weeks or hebdomades. Thus Noah is said twice to have waited seven days, when sending the dove out of the ark, Gen. viii. 10, 12. And the division of time into weeks is clearly recognized in the history of Jacob, Gen. xxix. 27, 28. The same hebdomadal division was known to other nations, who are not likely to have borrowed it from the Israelites after the time of the Exodus. Moreover, it appears that, before the giving of the commandments from Mount Sinai, the Israelites were acquainted with the law of the Sabbath. In Ex. xvi. 5 a double portion of manna is promised on the sixth day, that none need be gathered on the Sabbath. This has all the appearance of belonging to an acknowledged, though perhaps neglected, ordinance of Divine Service, not as if then for the first time the Sabbath were ordained and consecrated. The simple meaning of the text is therefore by far the most probable, viz. that God, having divided His own great work into six portions, assigned a special sacredness to the seventh on which that work became complete; and that, having called man into being, He ordained him for labour, but yet in love and mercy appointed that one-seventh of his time should be given to rest and to the religious service of his Maker. This truth is repeated in the IVth Commandment, Ex. xx. 11; though there was a second and special reason why the Jews should observe the Sabbath day, Deut. v. 15: and very probably the special day of the seven, which became the Jewish Sabbath, was the very day on which the Lord brought them from the land of bondage, and gave them rest from the slavery of Egypt. If this reasoning be true, all mankind are interested in the sanctification of the Sabbath, though Jews only are required to keep that Sabbath on the Saturday; and not only has it been felt by Divines that the religious rest of the seventh day is needful for the preservation of the worship of God, but it has been acknowleged even by statesmen and physiologists that the ordinance is invaluable for the physical and moral benefit of mankind. The truly merciful character of the ordinance is fully developed in the Law, where it is extended not only to the manservant and maidservant, but to the ox and the ass and the cattle, that they also should rest with their masters, Ex. xx. 10, Deut. v. 14.

which God created and made] Lit. "**which God created to make.**" So the Targum of Onkelos and the Syriac version render it. The Vulgate has "which God created that He might make it." On the difference between the verbs *create* and *make* see on ch. i. 1. The natural meaning of the words here is, that God first created the material universe, "the heavens and the earth," and then made, moulded and fashioned the new created matter into its various forms and organisms. This is the explanation of the R. Nachmanides, "all His work which He had created out of nothing, in order that He might make out of it all the works which are recorded in the six days." (Quoted by Fagius, 'Crit. Sacri.')

4. *These are the generations*, &c.] The Jews tell us, that, when these words occur without the copulative *and*, they separate the words following from those preceding, but

the heavens and of the earth when they were created, in the day that the LORD God made the earth and the heavens,

5 And every plant of the field before it was in the earth, and every herb of the field before it grew: for the LORD God had not caused it to

that when they have the *and*, then they unite with the preceding. It is apparent, that the narrative proceeds in direct order from Gen. i. 1 to this verse, ii. 4, and that from this verse there is a return to the first formation of plants and vegetables and to the creation of man, a kind of recapitulation, yet with some appearance of diversity. This has been noticed long ago. In the 17th century (1655) Is. Peyreyrius wrote a book to prove, that the account of the creation of man in ch. i. related to a pre-Adamite race, from which sprang a great majority of the Gentiles, whereas the account in ch. ii. was of the creation of Adam, the direct ancestor of the Israelites and of the nations in some degree related to them. The book was condemned and suppressed. Some modern writers have more or less embraced its views, but it seems that the whole Bible, both Old and New Testament, refers to Adam as the head of the whole human race, so that, if pre-Adamite man existed at all, the race must probably have been extinguished before Adam was created. Moreover, ch. ii. 4 sqq. is evidently a continuation of ch. i., although there is a return or recapitulation in vv. 4, 5, 6, 7, in order to prepare the way for an account of Paradise and the fall. See note at end of the chapter.

The word "generations," *toledoth*, which occurs for the first time in this verse, meets us again continually at the head of every principal section of the Book of Genesis. Thus ch. v. 1, we have "the book (or account) of the generations of Adam," in which the descendants of Adam are traced to Noah. From ch. vi. 9 we have the generations of Noah, where the history of Noah and his sons is given. In ch. x. 1 we come upon the generations of the sons of Noah, where the genealogical table and the history of the descendants of Shem, Ham, and Japhet are recorded. Ch. xi. (10—26) gives us the generations (or genealogical table) of Shem. Ch. xi. 27 begins the generations of Terah, the father of Abram. Ch. xxv. 12 gives us the generations of Ishmael. Ch. xxv. 19 the generations of Isaac. Ch. xxxvi. 1, the generations of Esau; xxxvii. 2, the generations of Jacob, which are continued to the end of the book.

The word itself naturally signifies the generation or posterity of any one. It is used in general to usher in a history of the race or descendant of the heads of the great patriarchal families. The application of the word here is very appropriate. The primary creation of all things had just been recorded; the sacred writer is about to describe more in detail the results of creation. The world had been made; next comes a history of its natural productions, its plants and trees, and chief inhabitants. And as the history of a man's family is called the "book of his generations," so the history of the world's productions is called "the generations of the heavens and the earth."

when they were created] By these words the inspired writer reveals the truth set forth in the former chapter, that heaven and earth were creatures of God, "the generations" referring to what is to come after, not to what preceded, as though the universe had sprung from generation or natural production.

the LORD *God*] It has long ago been observed that the sacred name JEHOVAH occurs for the first time here in verse 4. The Jews give as a reason, that the works being now perfected, the perfect name of God, "the LORD God," is for the first time adopted. It seems most probable, that the sacred writer, having in the first chapter recorded the creation as the act of God, giving to Him then His generic name as the Supreme Being, now passes to the more personal history of man and his immediate relation to his Maker, and therefore introduces the more personal name of God, the name by which He became afterwards known to the patriarchs, as *their* God. The union of the two names JEHOVAH Elohim throughout chapters ii. iii. is singularly appropriate, as indicating that the Elohim of the first chapter is the same as the JEHOVAH who appears afterwards in the fourth chapter, and from time to time throughout the history. On the names of God and the documents in Genesis, see Introduction to Genesis.

5. *And every plant of the field*] So the LXX. and the Vulg. But the Targums, the Syr., Rashi, and the most distinguished modern Hebraists, such as Rosenmüller, Gesenius, &c., translate, "**Now no plant of the field was yet in the earth, and no herb of the field had yet sprouted forth; for the LORD God had not caused it to rain upon the earth, and there was not a man to till the ground.**"

It was objected long ago, and the objection is repeated with all its force by the German critics of the day, that this is opposed to ch. i. 11, where we read, "God said, Let the earth bring forth grass," &c. Hence it is

rain upon the earth, and *there was* not
a man to till the ground.
6 But ‖there went up a mist from
the earth, and watered the whole face
of the ground.
7 And the LORD God formed man
†*of* the [b]dust of the ground, and breathed into his nostrils the breath of life;
and [c]man became a living soul.
8 ¶ And the LORD God planted a
garden eastward in Eden; and there
he put the man whom he had formed.

‖ Or, *a mist which went up from*, &c.

† Heb. *dust of the ground.*

[b] 1 Cor. 15. 47.

[c] 1 Cor. 15. 45.

---

inferred that the first and second chapters constituted two independent and contradictory traditions, clumsily put together by the compiler of Genesis. The difficulty had been anticipated by R. Nachman, who observes, that this passage does not refer to the produce of the earth created on the third day, but to those herbs and plants, which are raised by the cultivation of man. L. de Dieu also ('Critica Sacr.' in loc.) notices, that the words rendered *plant*, *field* and *grew*, never occur in the first chapter, they are terms expressive of the produce of labour and cultivation; so that the historian evidently means, that no cultivated land and no vegetables fit for the use of man were yet in existence on the earth.

the LORD *God had not caused it to rain upon the earth, and there was not a man to till the ground.* (6). *But there went up a mist*, &c.] It is objected here also, that the first chapter speaks of the earth as enveloped in waters and vapours, and that there could therefore have been no lack of rain and moisture. The inconsistency is again more apparent than real. In the first place, the mist, or vapour, or cloud, here mentioned as watering the ground, may perhaps tally well with that watery condition of the atmosphere, of which we read in ch. i. But next, the purpose of ch. ii. is to give an account, not of the creation or adaptation of the whole earth, but of the preparation of a special chosen spot for the early abode of man. That spot may have been in a region where little or no rain fell, and which derived all its moisture from vapours or dews. It may not have been wholly without vegetation, but it was not a cultivated field; no herbs, or shrubs, or fruit-trees fitted for man's use grew there; no rain was wont to fall there (as some render it, "not even a mist went up to water the ground," or more probably), "yet there went up a mist and watered the whole face of the ground." When the Creator made Adam, that he might not wander about a helpless savage, but that he might have a habitation suited to civilized life, a garden or cultivated field was planted for him, provided with such vegetable produce as was best adapted to his comforts and wants.

7. *And the* LORD *God formed man of the dust of the ground*, &c.] Here again, as in i. 26, 27, the formation of man is ascribed to the direct workmanship of God. In ch. i. God is said to have *created* man in His own image, because the production of a rational, personal, responsible being clothed with a material body was a new creation. Spiritual beings existed before; animal natures had been called forth from earth and sea; man had an animal nature like the beasts, but his spiritual nature was in the likeness of his Maker. So in this chapter again the Creator is described as forming man from the earth, and then breathing into him a living principle. It is probably not intended that the language should be philosophically accurate, but it clearly expresses that man's bodily substance was composed of earthly elements, whilst the life breathed by God into his nostrils plainly distinguishes that life from the life of all inferior animals. All animals have the body, all the living soul, ch. i. 20, 21, but the breath of life, breathed into the nostrils by God Himself, is said of man alone. Cp. "the body, soul and spirit" of ancient philosophy and of the Apostle Paul.

See note A at the end of this chapter.

8. *a garden*] The versions render *a Paradise*, which is a Persian word, signifying rather a park than a garden, pleasure grounds laid out with shrubs and trees.

in Eden] The word *Eden* signifies delight, and the Vulgate renders *a garden of delight*, *a pleasure garden*; but the word is a proper name, and points to a region, the extent of which is unknown. Two countries are mentioned in Scripture with the same name, viz., one in Mesopotamia near the Tigris, 2 K. xix. 12, Is. xxxvii. 12, Ez. xxvii. 23; the other in the neighbourhood of Damascus, Amos i. 5; but neither of these can be identified with the region in which Paradise was placed. Much has been written on the site of Paradise, but with no very definite result. The difficulty consists in discovering the four rivers mentioned in vv. 11, 12, 13, 14. It is generally agreed that one, Phrath (v. 14) is the Euphrates, and that another, Hiddekel, is the Tigris, and so it is rendered by all the ancient VSS. The name of the Tigris in Chaldee is Diglath, in Syriac Diklath, in Arabic Dijlat, all closely corresponding with Hiddekel, and from one of them the word Tigris itself is probably a corruption. The following are the principal opinions as to the names of the other rivers, and consequently as to the site of Paradise.

9 And out of the ground made the LORD God to grow every tree that is pleasant to the sight, and good for food; the tree of life also in the midst of the garden, and the tree of knowledge of good and evil.

---

1. Josephus identified the Gihon with the Nile.

2. Calvin, Huet, Bochart, and others believed the river of Paradise to have been the united streams of the Tigris and Euphrates called the Shat-el-Arab, which flows by Bassora. Its four heads, on their shewing, would have been, on the north, the two separate streams of the Tigris and Euphrates, on the south, Gihon, the eastern, and Pison, the western channels, into which the united stream again branches out below Bassora, before it falls into the sea. Havilah would then be the north-eastern part of Arabia, and Cush the region of Kissia, Susiana or Chuzestan. A general exposition of this view may be found in Wells, 'Geog. of the O. T.,' ch. i.

3. J. D. Michaelis, Rosenmüller, and Karl Von Raumer, who appear to be followed by Kurtz, identify Eden with the Armenian highlands, making Pison to be the Phasis or Araxes, and Gihon to be the Oxus, Havilah is with them the country of the Chwalissi, which is said even now to be called by the Russians Chwaliskoje More.

4. Heidegger believed that Eden was a portion of the Holy Land.

5. Others again find the site in India or Circassia.

Of these opinions No. 1 is utterly untenable. The identification of Gihon with the Nile probably originated with the Alexandrian Jews, who for the honour of their country would have had the Nile to be one of the rivers of Paradise. This was confirmed by the mistranslation of *Cush* into *Ethiopia*. It is impossible, however, setting aside all questions of inspiration, that one so familiar with Egypt as the writer of Genesis should have conceived of the Nile as connected with the Tigris and Euphrates. See Kurtz, 'Hist. of Old Covenant' (Clark's Library), Vol. I. p. 73.

No. 2 has the advantage of pointing to a single river, which might in primitive times have been described as branching out into four divisions or heads. Moreover, Arabia, in which certainly was a region called Havilah, is near to the western channel, whilst Chuzestan, which may have corresponded with the land of Cush, borders on the eastern channel.

The chief difficulty in No. 3 is that at present there is no junction between the heads of the four rivers, Tigris, Euphrates, Oxus, and Araxes, though all may take their rise in the same mountain system, and may possibly in more ancient times have been more nearly related. The question is one which has been much discussed, and is not likely soon to be set at rest: but the weight of argument and of authority seems in favour of No. 2, or something nearly corresponding with it; and it is the solution (more or less) adopted by the best modern interpreters.

9. *made the* LORD *God to grow*] We must understand this of the trees of Paradise only.

the tree of life also in the midst of the garden] Jewish and many Christian commentators consider that there was a virtue in this tree, which was calculated to preserve from diseases and to perpetuate animal life. Kennicott ('Two Dissertat.' Diss. i.) argued that the word "tree" is a noun of number, whether in the Hebrew or the Greek (comp. Rev. xxii. 2), and that all the trees of Paradise, except the tree of knowledge, "the true test of good and evil," were trees of life, in the eating of which, if man had not sinned, his life would have been perpetuated continually. The fathers inclined to the belief that the life to be supported by this tree was a spiritual life. So St Augustine ('De Gen. ad lit.' VIII. 4) says, "In other trees there was nourishment for Adam; but in this a sacrament," *i.e.* The tree was a sacrament or mystic image of, and perhaps also supporting, life eternal. Its reference, not to temporal, but to eternal life, seems to be implied in Gen. iii. 22. In Prov. iii. 18, Wisdom is compared to the tree of life: and in Prov. xiii. 12, we read, "When the desire cometh, it is a tree of life," which connects it with the hope of the future. And so perhaps we may say pretty confidently, that whatever was the physical effect of the fruit of this tree, there was a lesson contained in it, that life is to be sought by man, not from within, from himself, in his own powers or faculties, but from that which is without him, even from Him who only hath life in Himself. God only hath life in Himself; and the Son of God, who by eternal generation from the Father hath it given to Him to have life in Himself, was typified to Adam under this figure as "the Author of eternal salvation." Joh. i. 4, xiv. 6, Rev. ii. 7, xxii. 2 (see Fagius in loc. and Heidegger, 'Hist. Patriarch.' Exerc. IV.).

the tree of knowledge of good and evil] Onkelos paraphrases, "of the fruit of which they who eat learn to distinguish between good and evil." The tree appears to have been the test, whether man would be good or bad; by it the trial was made whether in keeping God's commandments he would attain to good, *i.e.* to eternal life, or by breaking them he should have evil, *i.e.* eter-

10 And a river went out of Eden to
water the garden; and from thence
it was parted, and became into four
heads.
11 The name of the first *is* [a] Pison: [a] Ecclus. 24. 29.
that *is* it which compasseth the whole
land of Havilah, where *there is* gold;
12 And the gold of that land *is*
good: there *is* bdellium and the onyx
stone.
13 And the name of the second
river *is* Gihon: the same *is* it that
compasseth the whole land of † Ethiopia. † Heb. *Cush.*

14 And the name of the third river
is Hiddekel: that *is* it which goeth
‖ toward the east of Assyria. And the ‖ Or, *eastward to Assyria.*
fourth river *is* Euphrates.
15 And the LORD God took ‖ the ‖ Or, *Adam.*
man, and put him into the garden of
Eden to dress it and to keep it.
16 And the LORD God commanded the man, saying, Of every tree
of the garden † thou mayest freely † Heb. *eating thou shalt eat.*
eat:
17 But of the tree of the knowledge
of good and evil, thou shalt not eat of

---

nal death. The lesson seems to be, that man should not seek to learn what is good and evil from himself but from God only; that he should not set up an independent search for more knowledge than is fitting, throwing off the yoke of obedience and constituting himself the judge of good and ill. Some have thought that the tree had not this name from the first, but that it was given it after the temptation and the fall, either because the tempter had pretended that it would give wisdom, or because Adam and Eve, after they had eaten of it, knew by bitter experience the difference between good and evil.

12. *bdellium*] a transparent gum obtained from a tree (*Borassus flabelliformis*) which grows in Arabia, India, and Media (Plin. 'H. N.' XII. 9. § 19). This is the translation of Aqu., Symm., Theod., Vulg.: Josephus and many moderns, as Celsius ('Hierob.' I. 324), Cleric. in loc. adopt it. The LXX. renders "the carbuncle;" the Arabic, "sardius;" Kimchi, Grotius, Bochart, Gesenius, and others, with great probability take it to mean "pearls," of which great abundance was found in India and the Persian Gulf, and this falls in well with Bochart's belief, that Havilah bordered on the Persian Gulf. It appears far more probable that it should mean either pearls or some precious stone than a gum like bdellium, which is of no great value.

the onyx] Most of the versions give "onyx" or "sardonyx;" Onkelos has "beryl."

13. *Ethiopia*] **Cush.** This is a word of wide extent. It generally belongs either to Arabia or to Ethiopia. From Gen. x. 7 sqq. it will appear how widely the sons of Cush spread forth: their first settlement appears to have been in Arabia. Nimrod founded the kingdom of Babylon. Afterwards they settled largely in Ethiopia. In the more ancient books of Scripture, the Asiatic Cush is more frequently, perhaps exclusively, intended. Later the name applies more commonly to African Cush, *i.e.* Ethiopia.

14. *toward the east of Assyria*] The name Asshur included Babylonia, and even Persia: see Ezra vi. 22, where Darius is called King of Assyria: but in the time of Moses probably Assyria proper would be understood, a region of low land on the left bank of the Tigris, perhaps only including the country afterwards called Adiabene. It is hardly correct to say, that the Tigris runs "to the East of Assyria." Perhaps the renderings in some of the versions "towards" or "before Assyria" may be correct.

17. *thou shalt not eat of it*] It has been questioned why such a test as this should have been given; whether it be consistent with God's goodness to create a sin by making an arbitrary enactment; and how "the act of eating a little fruit from a tree could be visited with so severe a penalty." But we may notice that if there was to be any trial of man's obedience in Paradise, some special test was almost necessary. His condition of simple innocence and happiness, with no disorder in the constitution of his body or in the affections of his soul, offered no natural temptations to sin. Adam and Eve had none but each other and their Creator near them; and they could have had no natural inclination to sin against God or against their neighbour. If we take the ten Commandments as the type of the moral law, we shall find none that in their state of healthy innocence they could naturally desire to break (see Joseph Mede, Bk. I. Disc. 40). Their position was one of freedom indeed, but of dependence. Their only danger was that they should prefer independence upon God, and so seek for themselves freedom in the direction of evil as well as in the direction of good; and the renouncing dependence upon God is the very essence of evil in the creature. Now the command concerning the fruit of the tree, simple and childish as it may appear, was one exactly suited to their sim-

it: for in the day that thou eatest
thereof †thou shalt surely die. († Heb. *dying thou shalt die.*)
18 ¶ And the LORD God said, *It*
is not good that the man should be
alone; I will make e him an help † meet (e Ecclus. 17. 5.)
for him. († Heb. *as before him.*)
19 And out of the ground the LORD
God formed every beast of the field,
and every fowl of the air; and brought
them unto ‖Adam to see what he would (‖ Or, *the man.*)
call them: and whatsoever Adam call-
ed every living creature, that *was* the
name thereof.
20 And Adam †gave names to all († Heb. *called.*)
cattle, and to the fowl of the air, and
to every beast of the field; but for
Adam there was not found an help
meet for him.
21 And the LORD God caused a
deep sleep to fall upon Adam, and he
slept: and he took one of his ribs,
and closed up the flesh instead thereof;
22 And the rib, which the LORD
God had taken from man, †made he († Heb. *builded.*)
a woman, and brought her unto the
man.
23 And Adam said, This *is* now
bone of my bones, and flesh of my
flesh: she shall be called Woman,
because she was f taken out of man. (f 1 Cor. 11. 8.)

---

ple and childlike state. Moreover it is not inconsistent with God's general dealings with mankind, that he should at times see fit to test faith and obedience by special and unusual trials. Compare Gen. xxii. 1, Matt. xix. 21.

thou shalt surely die] St Jerome ('Qu. in Gen.') proposes to adopt the translation of Symmachus, "Thou shalt become mortal or liable to death." It is needless so to translate, but the meaning of the threat probably was that the effect of eating of the fruit of that tree should be to poison the whole man, soul and body, with a deadly poison, making the body mortal, and the soul "dead in trespasses and sins." With the day of transgression a life commences, which is a living death. St Paul uses the expression, "Death worketh in us." There was, however, doubtless some remission of the sentence, so that they did not die instantly, as was the case with the Ninevites (Jonah iii. 10); and then a remedy was provided which might ultimately turn the curse into a blessing. Still the sentence was never wholly reversed, but the penalty took effect at once.

19. *the* LORD *God formed*] The account of the formation of the brute animals here does not, as some have supposed, necessarily imply that they were created after Adam; but it is introductory to the bringing them one by one to Adam that he may name them, and it is intended to lead up to the statement that they were none of them suited to be Adam's chief companions. They were formed by God of earthly materials; but the breath of Divine life had not been breathed into them.

brought them unto Adam to see what he would call them] The power of speech was one of those gifts which from the first distinguished man from all other animals; but, as tending to that civilized condition in which it was God's will to place Adam, in order to mature his mental powers, and to teach him the use of language, the animals are brought to him that he might name them. Nouns are the first and simplest elements of language; and animals, by their appearance, movements and cries, more than any other objects suggest names for themselves.

20. *there was not found an help meet for him*] There is some obscurity in the original of the words "an help meet for him;" they probably mean "a helper suited to," or rather "matching him."

22. *the rib...made He a woman*] lit. **The side He built up into a woman.** The word which primarily means "rib" more frequently signifies "side:" whence many of the rabbins adopted the Platonic myth (see Euseb. 'Præp. Evang.' XII. 12), that man and woman were originally united in one body, till the Creator separated them. The formation of woman from the side of man is without question most mysterious: but it teaches very forcibly and beautifully the duty of one sex towards the other, and the close relationship between them, so that neither should despise or treat with unkindness the other. That respect for the weaker sex, which we esteem a mark of the highest refinement, is taught by the very act of creation as recorded in the earliest existing record. The New Testament tells us that marriage is a type of the union of Christ and His Church; and the fathers held that the formation of Eve from the side of Adam typified the formation of the Church from the side of the Saviour. The water and blood which flowed from that side were held the one to signify baptism, the other to belong to the other great Sacrament, both water and blood cleansing from sin and making the Church acceptable to God.

23. *Woman, because she was taken out of*

Matt. 19. 24 [g]Therefore shall a man leave
Mark 10. 7. his father and his mother, and shall
Cor. 6. 16. cleave unto his wife: and they shall be
Eph. 5. 31. one flesh.

25 And they were both naked, the man and his wife, and were not ashamed.

---

man] Hebrew "Ishsha because she was taken out of Ish." Hence many have argued that Hebrew must have been the primitive language. The same, of course, is inferred from other names, as Eve, Cain, Abel, &c., all having appropriate significance in Hebrew. The argument is inconclusive, because it is quite possible to translate names from one language into another, and to retain the meaning which those names had in their original tongue.

24. *Therefore*, &c.] These may have been the words of Adam, or of the inspired historian. Matt. xix. 5 seems to refer them to the latter, which also is the more natural interpretation. Then too they have more obviously that Divine authority which our Lord so emphatically ascribes to them. Such incidental remarks are not uncommon in Scripture; see for instance ch. xxxii. 32.

NOTE A on CHAP. II. v. 7. ON THE IMMEDIATE CREATION AND PRIMITIVE STATE OF MAN.

ON the question of man's direct creation in distinction to the hypothesis of development, and on his original position as a civilized being, not as a wild barbarian, we may remark, 1st, It is admitted even by the theorists themselves, that in the present state of the evidence the records beneath the earth's surface give no support to the hypothesis that every species grew out of some species less perfect before it. There is not an unbroken chain of continuity. At times, new and strange forms suddenly appear upon the stage of life, with no previous intimation of their coming. 2ndly, In those creatures, in which instinct seems most fully developed, it is impossible that it should have grown by cultivation and successive inheritance. In no animal is it more observable than in the bee: but the working bee only has the remarkable instinct of building and honey-making so peculiar to its race; it does not inherit that instinct from its parents, for neither the drone nor the queen-bee builds or works; it does not hand it down to its posterity, for itself is sterile and childless. Mr Darwin has not succeeded in replying to this argument. 3rdly, Civilization, as far as all experience goes, has always been learned from without. No extremely barbarous nation has ever yet been found capable of initiating civilization. Retrogression is rapid, but progress unknown, till the first steps have been taught. (See Abp. Whately, 'Origin of Civilization,' the argument of which has not been refuted by Sir John Lubbock, 'Prehistoric Man.' Both have been ably reviewed by the Duke of Argyll, 'Primeval Man'). Moreover, almost all barbarous races, if not wholly without tradition, believe themselves to have been once in a more civilized state, to have come from a more favoured land, to have descended from ancestors more enlightened and powerful than themselves. 4thly, Though it has been asserted without any proof that man, when greatly degenerate, reverts to the type of the monkey, just as domesticated animals revert to the wild type; yet the analogy is imperfect and untrue. Man undoubtedly, apart from ennobling influences, degenerates, and, losing more and more of the image of his Maker, becomes more closely assimilated to the brute creation, the earthly nature overpowering the spiritual. But that this is not natural to him is shewn by the fact, that, under such conditions of degeneracy, the race gradually becomes enfeebled, and at length dies out; whereas the domesticated animal, which reverts to the type of the wild animal, instead of fading away, becomes only the more powerful and the more prolific. The wild state is natural to the brutes, but the civilized is natural to man.

Even if the other parts of the Darwinian hypothesis were demonstrable, there is not a vestige of evidence that there ever existed any beast intermediate between apes and men. Apes too are by no means the nearest to us in intelligence or moral sense or in their food and other habits. It also deserves to be borne in mind, that even if it could be made probable that man is only an improved ape, no physiological reason can touch the question, whether God did not when the improvement reached its right point, breathe into him "a living soul," a spirit "which goeth upward," when bodily life ceases. This at least would have constituted Adam a new creature, and the fountain head of a new race.

On the derivation of mankind from a single pair, see Prichard's 'Physical Hist. of Mankind,' Bunsen, 'Philosophy of Universal History,' Smyth, 'Unity of the Human Race,' Quatrefages, 'L'unité de l'espèce Humaine,' &c.

CHAPTER III.

1 *The serpent deceiveth Eve.* 6 *Man's shameful fall.* 9 *God arraigneth them.* 14 *The serpent is cursed.* 15 *The promised seed.* 16 *The punishment of mankind.* 21 *Their first clothing.* 22 *Their casting out of paradise.*

NOW the serpent was more sub-
til than any beast of the field
which the LORD God had made. And
he said unto the woman, †Yea, hath († Heb. *Yea, because, &c.*)
God said, Ye shall not eat of every
tree of the garden?
2 And the woman said unto the
serpent, We may eat of the fruit of
the trees of the garden:
3 But of the fruit of the tree which
is in the midst of the garden, God hath
said, Ye shall not eat of it, neither
shall ye touch it, lest ye die.
4 [a]And the serpent said unto the (a 2 Cor. 11. 3. 1 Tim. 2. 14.)
woman, Ye shall not surely die:
5 For God doth know that in the
day ye eat thereof, then your eyes
shall be opened, and ye shall be as
gods, knowing good and evil.
6 And when the woman saw that
the tree *was* good for food, and that
it *was* †pleasant to the eyes, and a († Heb. *a desire.*)
tree to be desired to make *one* wise,
she took of the fruit thereof, [b]and (b Ecclus. 25. 26. 1 Tim. 2. 14.)
did eat, and gave also unto her hus-
band with her; and he did eat.
7 And the eyes of them both
were opened, and they knew that
they *were* naked; and they sewed fig
leaves together, and made themselves (‖ Or, *things to gird about.*)
‖aprons.

CHAP. III. 1. *Now the serpent*] "Almost throughout the East the serpent was used as an emblem of the evil principle," Kalisch, ad h. l.: but Kalisch himself, Tuch and others deny that the evil spirit is to be understood in this narrative of Genesis. Yet not only did the East in general look on the serpent as an emblem of the spirit of evil, but the earliest traces of Jewish or Christian interpretations all point to this. The evil one is constantly called by the Jews "the old serpent," *Hannachash hakkadmoni* (so also in Rev. xii. 9, "that old serpent the devil"). In Wisd. ii. 24, we read, "By the envy of the devil death entered into the world." Our Lord Himself says, "the Devil was the murderer of man from the beginning" (Joh. viii. 44). Von Bohlen observes that "the pervading Jewish view is the most obvious, according to which the serpent is considered as Satan; and the greatest confirmation of such an interpretation is the very general agreement of the Asiatic myths" (ad h. l.). Some have thought that no serpent appeared, but only that evil one, who is called the serpent; but then he could not have been said to be "more subtle than all the beasts of the field." The reason why Satan took the form of a beast remarkable for its subtlety may have been, that so Eve might be the less upon her guard. New as she was to all creation, she may not have been surprised at speech in an animal which apparently possessed almost human sagacity.

Fit vessel, fittest imp of fraud...
...For in the wily snake
Whatever sleights none would suspicious mark,
As from his wit and nature subtlety
Proceeding, which in other beasts observed
Doubt might beget of diabolic power,
Active within beyond the sense of brute.
'Paradise Lost,' IX. 91.

5. *God doth know*] The tempter represents God as envious of His creatures' happiness, the ordinary suggestion of false religion and unbelief. Then he suggests to Eve the desire of self-dependence, that which is in fact the origin of all sin, the giving up of dependence on God, and the seeking for power, wisdom, happiness in self.

as gods] Or more probably, "as God." The plural word *Elohim* stands at times for false gods, at times for angels, but most commonly for the one true God.

knowing good and evil] Having a clear understanding of all great moral questions; not like children, but like those of full age, who "by reason of use have their senses exercised to discern both good and evil" (Heb. v. 14). This was the serpent's promise, though he knew that the result would be really a knowledge of evil through the perversion of their own will and their own ill choice.

6. *to make one wise*] Gesenius and others, after the LXX. and Vulgate, render *to look upon.*

7. *the eyes of them both were opened, &c.*] "Their eyes were truly opened as the serpent had promised them, but only to see that in the moment when they departed from God they became slaves of the flesh, that the freewill and independence of God, and knowing the good and the evil, delivers them up to the power of evil. Man, who had his glorious destiny before him of becoming by means of the knowledge and love of God, and by obedience, the free lord of the world, ceases, by disobedience, to be master of himself." (O. Von Gerlach, 'Comment.' ad h. l.).

fig leaves] Celsius, Tuch, and Gesenius, have doubted whether this was the Ficus

8 And they heard the voice of the LORD God walking in the garden in the †cool of the day: and Adam and his wife hid themselves from the presence of the LORD God amongst the trees of the garden.

9 And the LORD God called unto Adam, and said unto him, Where *art* thou?

10 And he said, I heard thy voice in the garden, and I was afraid, because I *was* naked; and I hid myself.

11 And he said, Who told thee that thou *wast* naked? Hast thou eaten of the tree, whereof I commanded thee that thou shouldest not eat?

12 And the man said, The woman whom thou gavest *to be* with me, she gave me of the tree, and I did eat.

13 And the LORD God said unto the woman, What *is* this *that* thou hast done? And the woman said, The serpent beguiled me, and I did eat.

14 And the LORD God said unto the serpent, Because thou hast done this, thou *art* cursed above all cattle, and above every beast of the field; upon thy belly shalt thou go, and dust shalt thou eat all the days of thy life:

15 And I will put enmity between thee and the woman, and between thy seed and her seed; and it shall

---

Carica of Linnæus, supposing it to have been the *Musa Paradisiaca;* but the word is that used throughout Scripture for the well known fig tree (see Rœdiger in Ges. 'Lex.' p. 1490).

8. *the voice of the* LORD *God*] The whole of this history of the creation and the fall is full of these anthropomorphic representations. The Creator is spoken of as if consulting about the formation of man (i. 26), as reflecting on the result of His creation, and declaring it all very good (i. 31), as resting from His work (ii. 2), as planting a garden for Adam (ii. 8), bringing the animals to him to name them (ii. 19), then building up the rib of Adam into a woman, and bringing her to Adam to be his bride (ii. 22). Here again Adam hears His voice as of one walking in the garden in the cool of the day. All this corresponds well with the simple and childlike character of the early portions of Genesis. The Great Father, through His inspired word, is as it were teaching His children, in the infancy of their race, by means of simple language, and in simple lessons. Onkelos has here "The Voice of the Word of the LORD." It is by this name, "the Word of the LORD," that the Targums generally paraphrase the name of the Most High, more especially in those passages where is recorded anything like a visible or sensible representation of His Majesty. The Christian fathers almost universally believed that every appearance of God to the patriarchs and prophets was a manifestation of the eternal Son, judging especially from Joh. i. 18.

cool of the day] Lit. "wind of the day," which is generally understood of the cool breezes of evening. Paradise had been to man the place of God's presence, which brought heretofore happiness, and security. Now that sin had come upon him, the sense of that presence was accompanied with shame and fear.

14. *cursed above all cattle*] We can hardly doubt that these words were in part directed against the animal, which was made the instrument of man's ruin, as in the law the ox which gored a man was to be put to death like a malefactor. Thus the serpent was ever to bear about the remembrance of that evil, which he had been made the means of producing, was to be the enemy of man, causing him suffering, but in the end suffering from him utter destruction; yet, as the serpent was but the outward form of the spirit of evil, so the language of the Almighty, which outwardly refers to the serpent, in its spiritual significance is a curse upon the evil one. And as the curse is for the sake of man; so in it is contained a promise that the human race shall finally triumph over that which first caused its fall. The most natural interpretation of the curse might indicate, that the serpent underwent some change of form. It would, however, be quite consistent with the narrative, even in its most literal acceptance, to understand that it merely implied continued and perpetual degradation coupled with a truceless war against mankind.

15. *seed*] Allix, as quoted by Bishop Patrick, observes that in this promise God did a kindness to Adam, who otherwise by the temptation might have been estranged from his wife; but here the promise of redemption is through the seed of the *woman*. "Marriage, which had been the vehicle of the fall, is now also to become that of salvation; the seed of the woman is to bruise the head of the Serpent." (Kurtz, I. 78.) The promise is, no doubt, general, that, though the seed of the serpent (mystically Satan and all his servants) shall continually wage war against the descendants of Eve, yet ultimately by God's appointment mankind (the whole seed of the woman) shall triumph over their spi-

bruise thy head, and thou shalt bruise
his heel.
16 Unto the woman he said, I will
greatly multiply thy sorrow and thy
conception; in sorrow thou shalt bring
forth children; and thy desire *shall be*
‖to thy husband, and he shall [c]rule
over thee.
17 And unto Adam he said, Because thou hast hearkened unto the
voice of thy wife, and hast eaten of the
tree, of which I commanded thee, saying, Thou shalt not eat of it: cursed
is the ground for thy sake; in sorrow
shalt thou eat *of* it all the days of thy life;
18 Thorns also and thistles shall
it †bring forth to thee; and thou shalt
eat the herb of the field;
19 In the sweat of thy face shalt
thou eat bread, till thou return unto

‖ Or, *subject to thy husband.*
c 1 Cor. 14. 34.
† Heb. *cause to bud.*

---

ritual enemy. If there were no more than this in the language used, even so there would be, an obscure indeed, but still a significant promise of some future deliverance. But the last words of the verse seem not merely general but personal. In the first clause it is said, that there should be "enmity between thy *seed* and her *seed*;" but in the second clause it is said, "It (or he) shall bruise *thy* head." It was the head of the particular serpent (not of the seed of the serpent only), which the seed of the woman was to bruise. And though we must not lay stress on the masculine pronoun "*he*," because the word for *seed* is masculine in Hebrew, yet there is the appearance here of a personal contest, and a personal victory. This inference is strengthened by the promise being made to the seed of the *woman*. There has been but one descendant of Eve, who had no earthly father; and He was "manifested that He might destroy the works of the devil." Though the Jewish writers do not directly interpret the promise of the Messiah; yet the Targums of Jerusalem and of the Pseudo-Jonathan both say that this victory over the serpent shall be "in the days of the Messiah."

It is well known that Roman Catholic divines have attributed the victory to the Virgin Mary, misled by the rendering of some MSS. of the Latin, *Ipsa*, she. The original Hebrew is perfectly unequivocal; for, though the pronoun might be so pointed as to signify either *he* or *she*, yet the verb is (according to the Hebrew idiom) masculine. Moreover the LXX. has *seed* in the neuter, but the pronoun referring to it, "*he*," in the masculine, which would naturally refer it to some individual son of the woman. The Syriac Version also has a masculine pronoun.

shall bruise] The LXX. followed by the Vulgate and Onkelos has "shall watch," probably meaning to watch and track as a hunter does his prey; but the word in Chaldee signifies "to bruise or crush." In this, or nearly this sense it is used in the only other passages in which it occurs in Scripture, viz. Job ix. 17, Ps. cxxxix. 11, and so it is rendered by most ancient Versions and Comm. as Syr. Sam. Saad. St Paul refers to it in the words "The God of peace shall bruise Satan under your feet shortly." Rom. xvi. 20.

16. *Unto the woman He said*] It is noticed by Tertullian, that though God punished Adam and Eve, He did not curse them, as He did the Serpent, they being candidates for restoration ('adv. Marcion.' ii. 25).

I will greatly multiply thy sorrow and thy conception] Some suppose this to be a *hendiaduoin* for "the sorrow of thy conception." The words rather mean that woman's sorrow and her conception should both be multiplied. The mother has not only the pains of childbirth, but from all the cares of maternity greater sorrow connected with her common offspring than the father has. The threat of multiplying conception indicates, not that Eve had already borne children, but that childbirth would not have been unknown had the first pair remained in Paradise.

Thy desire shall be] Desire here expresses that reverential longing with which the weaker looks up to the stronger. The Vulgate therefore renders, "Thou shalt be under the power of thy husband." This is also the interpretation of Abenezra and of many moderns. The comparison with ch. iv. 7 shews that there is somewhat of dependence and subjection implied in the phrases.

17. *And unto Adam He said*] Here for the first time *Adam* occurs without an article, as a proper name.

cursed is the ground for thy sake] The whole earth partakes of the punishment, which the sin of man, its head and destined ruler, has called down. The creature itself is subjected to vanity, Rom. viii. 20. Death reigns. Instead of the blessed soil of Paradise, Adam and his offspring have to till the ground now condemned to bear thorns and thistles, and this is not to end, until the man returns to the earth from which he was taken. Yet even here there is some mark of mercy: for, whereas the serpent is cursed directly, and that with a reference to the earth he was

the ground; for out of it wast thou taken: for dust thou *art*, and unto dust shalt thou return.

20 And Adam called his wife's name †Eve; because she was the mother of all living.

† Heb. *Chavah.*

21 Unto Adam also and to his wife did the LORD God make coats of skins, and clothed them.

22 ¶ And the LORD God said, Behold, the man is become as one of us, to know good and evil: and now, lest he put forth his hand, and take also of the tree of life, and eat, and live for ever:

23 Therefore the LORD God sent him forth from the garden of Eden, to till the ground from whence he was taken.

24 So he drove out the man; and he placed at the east of the garden of Eden Cherubims, and a flaming sword which turned every way, to keep the way of the tree of life.

---

to travel over; here on the contrary the earth, rather than the man, is cursed, though for the man's sake and with reference to him. (Tuch.)

19. See note A at end of Chapter.

20. *Eve*] *Chavvah, Life.* Not only because she gave birth to all living, but perhaps with a further prophetic meaning, in reference to the promise just given, because the race of man, now subject to death, should be made alive by the Offspring of the woman.

22. *the man is become as one of us*] Man was not a mere animal, following the impulse of sense, without distinction of right and wrong. He had also a spiritual personality, with moral will and freedom of forechoice. His lower nature, though in subjection to the higher, as that was in subjection to God, yet acted as a veil, screening from him what might have been visible to pure spiritual intelligence: hence, though he knew good from knowing God and living in dependence on Him, yet he knew not evil, having had no experience of it hitherto. His fall therefore, although sinful, was not like the sin of angels, who had no animal nature to obscure vision or to tempt by sense. *Their* fall must have been more deliberate, more wilful, less pardonable. But, when man by fatal mischoice learned that there was evil in the universe as well as good, then he had acquired a condition like to that of spiritual beings, who had no veil to their understanding, and could see both on the right hand and on the left. The meaning then of this mysterious saying of the Most High may be, that now by sin man had attained a knowledge like the knowledge of pure spiritual existences, a knowledge which God has of necessity, a knowledge which the angels have, who might have fallen but who stood upright, a knowledge, which evil angels have from their own deliberate choosing of evil instead of good. The difficulty of this interpretation is, that it supposes God to speak of Himself as One among other spiritual beings, whereas He cannot be likened to any one, but is infinitely above and beyond all created natures. Some therefore would understand here and elsewhere, the plural as a mere plural of majesty. Still there is a manifest plurality of person. It is not merely "like Us," but "like one of Us." Hence it was the universal belief of the early Christians, that here as in Gen. i. 20, God was speaking to, and of, His coeternal Son and Spirit.

See note B at end of Chapter.

lest he put forth his hand] Vatablus, who looks on the tree of life as no more than a mystical emblem, understands that it was as though God had said, "Lest he should have a vain expectation excited in him by laying hold of this symbol of My promise; that shall be taken from him which might give him such a hope of immortality," ad h. l. But Augustine, who spoke of the tree of life as a sacrament, probably meant by a sacrament something more than a mere emblem; and many of the fathers looked on this judgment of God, whereby man was excluded from the reach of that, which might have made him immortal, as rather a mercy than a judgment. If his life had now been perpetuated, it would have been an immortality of sin. So Gregory Nazianzen says the exclusion from the tree of life was "that evil might not be immortal, and that the punishment might be an act of benevolence." (Greg. Naz. 'Orat.' XXXVII. n. 1. See Patrick).

24. *Cherubims*] See note C at end of Chapter.

NOTE A on CHAP. III. v. 19. ON THE EFFECT OF THE FALL.

NOTHING can really be plainer than that the narrative describes a most deplorable change in the condition of the first parents of mankind, a change from a state of holiness resulting from the presence of God and a life in dependence on His support, to a state of sin and shame following on disobedience to His will and a desire to become independent of Him. It is the distinctest possible account of a sin and of its punishment. Moreover in all subsequent teaching of Scripture the whole human race is represented as sharing in the exile of Adam from his Maker, and hence in his sinfulness; for holiness and happiness are inseparable from the presence and the Spirit of God. It may be impossible fully to explain all the justice or the mercy of this dispensation. Yet we may reflect that man was created a reasonable, free-willing, responsible being. All this implies power to will as God wills, and power to will as God does not will. It implies too something like a condition of trial, a state of probation. If each man had been put on his trial separately, as Adam was; judging from experience as well as from the history of Adam, we may see the probability that a large number of Adam's descendants would have sinned as he sinned. The confusion so introduced into the world would have been at least as great as that which the single fall and the expulsion once for all of our first parents from Paradise have actually brought in. And the remedy would have been apparently less simple and more complicated. As the Scripture history represents it to us, and as the New Testament interprets that history, the Judge of all the earth punished the sin of Adam by depriving him of His presence and His Spirit (that "original righteousness" of the fathers and the schoolmen, see Bp. Bull, Vol. II. Dis. v. and Aquinas, 'Summa,' ii. 1. qu. 82. art. 4), and thus subjecting him to death. But though He thus "concluded all under sin," it was indeed "that He might have mercy on all," Rom. xi. 32. The whole race of man condemned in Adam, receives in Adam also the promise of recovery for all. And in the Second Adam, that special *Seed of the woman*, the recovery of the whole race is effected, insomuch that as in Adam all died, even so in Christ all shall be made alive. And thus in truth the mystery of sin can only be cleared up by the mystery of redemption; whilst both exhibit the justice of God brought out into its fullest relief only under the light of His love.

NOTE B on CHAP. III. V. 22. ON THE HISTORICAL CHARACTER OF THE TEMPTATION AND THE FALL.

THE traditions of all, especially Eastern nations, have more or less of resemblance to the record of the first three chapters of Genesis. This is, according to some, to be explained by mere similarity in all early mythology. According to others it results from the Hebrew histories borrowing the myths of neighbouring countries and propounding them as historical truths. There can be no reasonable doubt, that the writer of Genesis puts forth his history as history. Hence some of the early rationalists admitted an historical foundation, though they thought it coloured by subsequent fancy. Eichhorn for instance ('Urgeschichte,' Th. 2. B. 2) supposed that Adam dreamed of the formation of Eve out of his side. Eve (as Abarbanel had also imagined) saw the serpent eating poisonous fruit, then ate of it herself and gave it to her husband; and thus awakened in them both sensual thoughts and the first feelings of shame. A thunderstorm seemed to them the voice of God; they fled in terror from Paradise, and in the unkindliness of a sterile land, the toils of agriculture and the pangs of childbirth found a punishment for their fault. But such forced explanations soon gave way to mythical interpretation. Paradise is but the golden age of the Hebrews; the tree of life is the Ambrosia or Amrita of Greece or India; the tempter finds a parallel in the contests of Krishna with the serpent, or in the Persian myth of Ahriman deceiving the first human beings under a serpent's form. The Indian cosmogony and the history of Krishna certainly bear some resemblance to the Jewish history, though widely distinguished from it by the gross Pantheism of the Hindoo Theology: but that the Hebrews can owe nothing to these is evident from the fact that they are not contained in the Vedas and the most ancient Sanscrit literature, from which alone it is possible that even the later Jewish writers could have borrowed. Indeed the history of Krishna first appears in the 'Bhagavat Gita,' a work assigned to the 3rd century after Christ, and which is supposed to have drawn largely from Christian or Pseudo-Christian sources. The nearest resemblance, however, is traceable between the Biblical record and the teaching of the Zendavesta. As there is a likeness in the history of Creation and in the description of Paradise, so there is a special similarity in the account of the fall. According to the doctrine of Zoroaster, the first human beings, created by Ormuzd, the good principle, lived in a state of innocence in a happy garden with a tree which gave them life and immortality; but Ahriman, the evil principle, assuming the form of a serpent, offered them the fruit of a tree, which he had himself created; they ate and became subject to evil and to a continual contest between light and darkness, between the good motions of Ormuzd, and the evil suggestions of Ahriman. As the Hindoo traditions are disfigured by Pantheism, so are the Persian by dualism; and both are markedly contrasted with the pure monotheism of the Bible History. But Hartmann, Von Bohlen, and other mythical interpreters, have imagined that the Mosaic account was really borrowed from the Zoroastrian; a theory which could only be established by proving that the early chapters of Genesis were not written till after the Babylonish captivity; for it was then that the Jews first came into close contact with the Persians, and might have borrowed some of their superstitions.

Against so late a date the language of the first chapter of Genesis is conclusive. There are indeed a few Aramaisms in Genesis; but it has been ruled most justly, that "Aramaisms in a book of the Bible are proof either of a very early or of a very late origin." The Patriarchs, who came from Ur of the Chaldees, may have naturally spoken a Hebrew not unmixed with Chaldaisms, and some names, as that of Eve (Chava) and that of the *LORD* (JEHOVAH), both of which have a Chaldee or Aramaic form, could not possibly have been invented later than the age of Moses, unless they were invented after the Babylonian Captivity, when the Jews again came into contact with the Chaldeans in Babylonia. That the Aramaisms of Genesis really mark antiquity, not novelty, should almost be self apparent to one familiar with the original. The Hebrew of the first three chapters of the Bible is most emphatically archaic. It cannot therefore be a modern Chaldaized Hebrew, but is a Hebrew so ancient as still to retain strong traces of its original union with its sister dialect Chaldee. Its peculiar conciseness is the exact opposite of the diffuse and verbose style of the Chaldee in Daniel or Ezra. The 3rd verse of Genesis owes much of its proverbial grandeur to this very conciseness. So many thoughts are perhaps nowhere else in the world uttered in so few syllables. The very reverse of this is true of the language when it had become infected by the Chaldee of the Captivity. But, if the legends of the Zendavesta were not borrowed by the Jews in their captivity, then the real contact point between them and the Jewish history must be found in pre-Mosaic times, in the days of the early patriarchs; and then the fact, that the traditions of Persia were of all others the nearest to the Jewish traditions may easily be explained. Let us suppose the account in Genesis to be the great Semitic tradition, perhaps delivered direct from Shem to Abraham, from Abraham to Jacob, from Jacob to Joseph, and incorporated under Divine guidance by Moses in his history. Is it unlikely that Japhet may have given the very same account of his own posterity? and where would it have been so well preserved, as in Iran, that spot, or at least near to that spot, where the Aryan races seem longest to have dwelt together, and where the tradition was most likely to have been undisturbed by constant migrations? The Persians prided themselves on their pure and ancient descent; and modern ethnologists have given to those tribes which peopled India and Europe the name of Aryan, after the inhabitants of Iran and the noblest race among them, the Arii. If the Hebrews retained the Semitic tradition pure and uncorrupted, through their adherence to the worship of the true God, whilst the Persians had the Japhetic tradition, though corrupted by dualism, the resemblance between their respective accounts would be in every way natural, and the real historical basis of them both would be the simplest solution of the difficulty.

It may only be necessary to add that this reasoning will not be affected, even if we should concur with those who argue, that the history of the fall is a true history though veiled under allegorical imagery, *i. e.* that Adam and Eve were created innocent and holy, that they were subjected to a trial and fell under it, thereby bringing in sin and death upon mankind, but that the description given of this in Genesis is not literal but emblematical and mystical (see for instance Quarry 'on Gen.' p. 112, and Warburton quoted by him).

NOTE C on CHAP. III. V. 24. CHERUBIM.

(1) Traditional accounts of the Cherubim. (2) Cherubim figured in Tabernacle and Temple. (3) Cherubim seen in visions of Isaiah, Ezekiel, St John. (4) Cherubim of Paradise. (5) Etymology of name.

IN this passage the Cherubim appear to be living beings, angels of God, fulfilling the will of God. Elsewhere (except in brief allusions as Ps. xviii. 10; 2 Sam. xxii. 11) we find them as sculptured or wrought figures in the Tabernacle and the Temple; or as images in the visions of prophets, which visions have always more or less of the other imagery of the Temple presented in them (Ez. i. x; Rev. iv. and perhaps Is. vi.).

Tradition gives no satisfactory account of the appearance of these cherubic figures. Josephus, ('Ant.' III. 6. § 5) says that they were "winged animals in form like nothing seen by man." It is possible that Josephus' Pharisaic prejudice in interpreting the second commandment may have led him to this profession of utter ignorance concerning the forms of the Cherubim, for he charges Solomon with a breach of the law on account of the oxen under the brazen sea ('Ant.' VIII. 7. § 3), and in the face of Exod. xxvi. 31 (compared with Ezek. x. 20), he denies that the veil of the tabernacle had any living creatures on it ('Ant.' III. 3. § 6). Still the Apostle (Heb. ix. 5), who speaks of "the Cherubim of glory shadowing the mercy seat," adds, "of which we cannot now speak particularly," as though, after the captivity and the destruction of the first Temple, not only had the sacred figures never been restored, but even the memory of their shapes had been lost.

1. *The Tabernacle and the Temple*] When Moses is commanded to make the ark, we learn that he was to make the *Capporeth*, the mercy seat or covering of the ark, of pure gold, and Cherubim looking towards the mercy seat, stretching forth their wings on high to cover the mercy seat. The Cherubim were to be of a piece with the mercy seat, or at least of the same material (Ex. xxv. 17—20). There is no appearance of more than one face to each Cherub, nor of more than two wings. The Cherubim on the mercy seat in the Tabernacle appear to have been exactly imitated by Solomon in the Temple, unless they were the very Cherubim of the Tabernacle removed to the Temple. Their height is said to have been ten cubits, and their wings touched the walls on either side (1 K. vi. 27). Besides the two Cherubim on the mercy seat, figures of Cherubim were wrought on the curtains of the Tabernacle (Ex. xxvi. 1, 31, xxxvi. 8, 35), and were afterwards engraven on the walls and doors of the Temple, along with palms and flowers, (1 K. vi. 29, 32, 35): also on the bases of the ten lavers, on the borders that were between the ledges were "lions, oxen and Cherubims." (1 K. vii. 29). Then again were four wheels a cubit and a half high, and again we find "Cherubims, lions and palm trees." (v. 36.)

The special offices of the Cherubic figures in the Tabernacle appear to have been, first, the watching and guarding of the ark and the sacred law deposited within the ark, towards which they are represented as looking and over which they spread their outstretched wings, and secondly, to attend and bear up that mystic presence of God, which appeared in the Cloud of glory over the mercy seat. That Cloud of glory had led Israel through the Red Sea and the wilderness, the guide and guardian of God's people, the symbol of His presence, especially in the giving of the law, having a twofold aspect, at times as darkness, at times as a pillar of light; now a glory settling on the Tabernacle or resting above the ark, at another time accompanied with fire and lightnings, so that the people durst not look on it. (Ex. xiii. 21, 22, xiv. 19, 24, xvi. 10, xix. 16, 18, 20, xx. 18, xxiv. 16, 17, xxxiii. 9, xxxiv. 5, xxxvii. 6—9, xl. 34—38; Num. ix. 15—23, xii. 5—10, xvi. 19—42). When the Tabernacle is set up, the Law is deposited in the Ark, the cloud is promised to rest upon the covering of the Ark, and, as the Cherubim guard the Law and the Testimony of God, so they may be supposed reverently to surround the throne of His glory.

If we went no farther, we should naturally conclude, that the Cherubim were winged human figures, sculptured in the Tabernacle and the Temple, representing either the personal angels of God, or at least those ministers and agents of His in creation which do His pleasure and wait upon His will. We should infer, that their offices were (1) to guard what is sacred and unapproachable, the gate of Paradise (Gen. iii. 24), the ark of the covenant of the LORD, in which were deposited the two tables of the Law (compare Ezek. xxviii. 14—16, where the Prince of Tyre is compared to a Cherub, who in Eden covers with his wings the precious stones): (2) to surround the mystic throne of God and to attend His presence (hence the Most High is constantly spoken of as dwelling between the Cherubim, *i.e.* by His Shechinah on the mercy seat, 1 S. iv. 4; 2 S. vi. 2; 2 K. xix. 15; Ps. lxxx. 2, xcix. 1; Is. xxxvii. 16): (3) perhaps to bear up the throne of God upon their wings, and to carry Him when He appeared in His glory. (Comp. 2 S. xxii. 11; Ps. xviii. 10, "He rode upon a Cherub, and did fly: yea, He did fly upon the wings of the wind.")

2. *The visions of Isaiah, Ezekiel and St John*] It is doubtful whether the Seraphim in the vision of Isaiah ch. vi. (the only place in which they are named in Scripture) be the same as the Cherubim or not. The scene is the same as in the Cherubic visions of Ezekiel and St John, viz. in the Temple (vv. 1. 6). The Seraphim occupy a place like that of the Cherubim, viz. just by the Throne of God; and their taking the live coal from the altar seems to connect them with the burning coals of Ezekiel's Cherubim (Ez. i. 13). As far as we can judge these Seraphim resemble the Cherubim of the Tabernacle and the Temple in having human forms and single faces, but they have six wings each: "With twain he covered his face, and with twain he covered his feet, and with twain he did fly."

We come now to the visions of Ezekiel and St John. These visions also have their seat in the Temple as the image of Heaven. (See Ezek. x. 2, 3, 5, 18, where we meet with the altar fire and the courts of the Temple: and Rev. *passim*, where all the imagery is drawn from the Temple, *e.g.* the candlestick ch. i. 12, the High Priest ch. i. 13, the altar ch. vi. 9, &c.) In both visions the throne corresponds with the place on which the Cloud of glory rested between the Cherubim. The Cherubim then are described as living creatures (Ezek. i. 5; Rev. iv. 6), in the form of a man (Ezek. i. 5) with four (Ezek. i. 8, ii. 23, x. 7, 8—21), or with six wings (Rev. iv. 8), having eyes all over (Ezek. i. 18, x. 12; Rev. iv. 8). In Ezekiel they have each four faces, viz. of a man, of a lion, of an ox, of an eagle (Ezek. i. 10, x. 16). In St John they have but one face each, these faces being respectively of a man, of a lion, of a calf and of an eagle (Rev. iv. 7). Their feet appear to Ezekiel as straight feet, like the feet of oxen (Ezek. i. 7). In Ezek. x. 14, we have the very singular phenomenon that the face of a Cherub seems identified or synonymous with the face of a calf or an ox. (Comp. Ezek. i. 10; Rev. iv. 7.) It is thought by many, that in these latter visions we have a fuller description of the Cherubim of the Tabernacle and the Temple than we could gather from the earlier accounts in Holy Scripture. It is supposed that they too, like the Cherubim in the visions, must have been composite creatures, if of human form, yet with heads of other animals, either as described by Ezekiel or by St John. Moreover, as such composite figures must plainly have been emblematical, it has been thought that the Cherubim by their faces of a man, a lion, a bull and an eagle, perhaps expressed the strength and wisdom of the Divine Majesty, or perhaps the strength and the swiftness, with which His ministers do His will. Again, as they surround the throne and guard the Law of the Most High, so perhaps we may understand, that the natural and the spiritual creation being knit up together in one great scheme, these symbolic creatures indicate that all things, all creation, wait upon God, all do His will, all work together for good to the godly and for judgment on the ungodly. They guard His law, and execute its judgments, and keep off the sinner from the blessing of its rewards.

The existence of composite winged emblematical figures amongst nations more or less connected with the Hebrews is now well known. The Sphinx and the Griffin have long been familiar to us: but it has been remarked as singular that Mr Layard should have discovered in Nineveh gigantic winged bulls with human heads, winged lions, and human figures with hawk or eagle heads, corresponding so nearly with the winged Cherubim of the visions of Ezekiel and St John. These gigantic figures too are generally placed as guards or sentinels at the entrances of temples and palaces, like the guarding Cherubim of Holy Writ. Moreover, they are evidently not objects of idolatrous worship, but appear rather as worshippers than as divinities. It is argued, that it is not improbable that Moses should have adopted similar emblems, opposing the true worship to the false, and placing in the temple of the true God emblems of protection, watchfulness, power, and glory, similar to those used in the temples of the gods of the nations. (See Lämmert, 'Die Cherubim' in 'Jahrbücher für Deutsche Theol.' Zwölfter Band, Viertes Heft, Gotha, 1867). It is, however, to be observed, that nothing connects Moses with Assyria or the Assyrian sculptures: and indeed those found by Mr Layard in the Temple of Kojundjik, which are most to the point, are not considered by him to be of great antiquity. Far more likely is it that some Egyptian type should have been followed: and we find in the Egyptian Sculptures, and in the 18th dynasty, which was probably the dynasty of the Exodus, examples of a shrine or ark wonderfully calculated to remind us of the ark of the Covenant made by Moses. It is carried by persons of the sacerdotal race, by staves, as the Levites carried the ark. In the centre is the symbol of the Deity, and two winged human figures spread out their wings around and over it. (Lepsius, 'Denkm.' III. Bl. 14.) These two figures, however, represent the goddess Ma, under the two-fold notion of "justice" and "truth." This is clear from the ostrich feathers on the heads of the figures. This goddess is often called "the double Ma," and it is very doubtful, whether, notwithstanding this apparent similarity, there is any relation between these figures and the Cherubim of the Tabernacle.

What then is to be said of the vision of Ezekiel and of St John who nearly repeats the imagery in Ezekiel? We may observe, that Ezekiel was a priest (Ezek. i. 3). He was therefore probably familiar with the sculptures in the Temple, especially the Cherubim carved on the bases of the ten lavers, along with bulls and lions, and with four wheels curiously connected with them. His vision, the scene of which was the Temple, naturally was mixed up with objects in the Temple. The connection of his Cherubic figures with wheels is explained by 1 Kings vii. 29, 30, 33. Even the lion and bull-heads of these figures may have come from the mingling of the Cherubim with the bulls and lions in the Temple. But, besides this, he saw these visions by the river Chebar in the land of the Chaldeans; and there he and his people would, no doubt, have become familiarized with the gigantic winged guardians of the temples and the palaces in Babylonia and Assyria, the bulls and lions and eagle-headed men, and human-headed bulls. It is highly probable that the difference between the Cherubim in Ezekiel's vision (repeated with certain variations in St John's), and the Cherubim in the Tabernacle and the Temple resulted in part from this. In God's dealings with man, He constantly uses for lessons things just before men's eyes. And so He may have done in this case with Ezekiel. It is almost certain that Ezekiel's visions did not represent accurately that to which he had been used in the Temple. Hence he appears not at first to have recognized them as being Cherubim; but at the end of his second vision he tells us, that now he knew they were Cherubim (Ezek. x. 20). To Moses, on the other hand, but still on the same principle, God had dictated the carving of figures like those which he had seen in Egypt, figures emblematical of guardianship, and of the reverence of those who wait constantly upon God, but which had never been objects of idolatrous worship. Thus He sanctioned, or at least tolerated, that which seems so dear to religious humanity, the use of symbolism, where dangers from its abuse were not great. We conclude, therefore, notwithstanding much authority to the contrary, that in all probability the Cherubim of glory shadowing the mercy seat were winged human figures, with human faces too.

The Cherubim of Paradise] It is noticed that Moses describes the placing of the Cherubim at the gates of Eden in words suggested by that which he had to carve in the Tabernacle. "He placed...Cherubim" is in the Hebrew יַשְׁכֵּן "He made to dwell," a term specially belonging to the dwelling of the glory of God in the Shechinah, the cloud of glory. And the Paradise Cherubim were to keep, lit. "to guard," (לִשְׁמֹר) the way to the tree of life, as the Cherubim in the Tabernacle guarded the Ark of the Covenant. Those, who believe the Cherubim in the Tabernacle to have been like those seen by Ezekiel, naturally believe also that they were but emblems of those powers of nature and creation by which the Creator so constantly works His will. The Cherubim and the flaming sword at the East Gate of Paradise to them mean only that the way back to Eden and to the tree of life was closed by such natural hindrances as the Author of nature saw fit to interpose. It is not impossible that even if the Cherubim of the Tabernacle were not composite creatures, but simply winged human figures, much the same may have been meant. There are doubtless hosts of spiritual beings that surround the throne of God and do His will; but all things serve Him. He maketh the winds His angels, and a flame of fire His ministers. The stern, mechanical, turning every way of the sword of flame perhaps points to this; and the sacred writer may possibly have signified under the symbols of angelic beings the great ministering powers of nature.

This at least is taught us by the Cherubim guarding the way to the Tree of life. Paradise had been lost by sin; but it was not gone for ever. The tree of life, and the garden where it grew, were still in full glory under the keeping of God and of His holy angels. The forfeited life is not irrecoverable: but it can only be recovered through fighting and conquest, suffering and death. There were between it and man the ministers of righteous vengeance and the flaming sword.

The Etymology of the word *Cherub* is very obscure. Some derive it from כָּרַב (Cherab) "to plough," it being inferred from Ezek. i. 10 compared with x. 14, that the true Cherub form was that of an ox. Others compare קָרוֹב (Kerob) "near," *i.e.* admitted to the special presence of God. The Talmudists assert that the name signifies "a child," and that the faces of the Cherubim were the faces of children. Eichhorn and others compare the Greek γρύψ, γρύπος, from the Persian *greifen* "to hold," and consider the name to be nearly equal in significance, as well as in derivation, with the fabulous Griffin or Gryphon of the East. Gesenius suggests the root כרב (Charab) = חרם (Charam) "to shut out," "to consecrate" (hence *haram*, a sacred shrine). According to this derivation, the Cherubim would be the guardians and defenders of that which is consecrated, of the Shrine or the Paradise. Canon Cook (see Appendix to this volume) has traced the word to an Egyptian root, which probably means "carve," or at any rate "shape." In Matt. xviii. 2, χερεβ is the Coptic for μορφή.

CHAPTER IV.

1 The birth, trade, and religion of Cain and Abel. 8 The murder of Abel. 11 The curse of Cain. 17 Enoch the first city. 19 Lamech and his two wives. 25 The birth of Seth, 26 and Enos.

AND Adam knew Eve his wife; and she conceived, and bare Cain, and said, I have gotten a man from the LORD.

2 And she again bare his brother †Abel. And Abel was †a keeper of sheep, but Cain was a tiller of the ground.

3 And †in process of time it came

† Heb. *Hebel.*
† Heb. *a feeder.*
† Heb. *at the end of days.*

CHAP. IV. 1. The last Chapter was a history of the first birth of sin; this gives us an account of its developement, as also of the first out-spreading of the human race. Cain and Abel are respectively types of the two opposing principles discernible throughout the sacred history; Cain of the unchecked dominion of evil, Abel of the victory of faith.

I have gotten a man from the LORD] LXX. "by means of the Lord;" Onk. "from the Lord;" Syriac "for the Lord;" Pseudo-Jonathan "a man, the angel of the LORD." Following the latter paraphrast, Luther, Munster, Fagius, Schmidt, Pfeiffer, Baumgart. and others, have rendered "I have gotten a man, even JEHOVAH," as though Eve understood that the *seed*, who was to bruise the serpent, should be incarnate Deity, and supposed that Cain was that seed. We can, however, scarcely see ground enough to believe that Eve's knowledge was so advanced, or her faith in the Messiah so lively as to

to pass, that Cain brought of the fruit of the ground an offering unto the LORD.

4 And Abel, he also brought of the firstlings of his †flock and of the fat thereof. And the LORD had [a]respect unto Abel and to his offering:

† Heb. *sheep*, or *goats*.
[a] Heb. 11. 4.

---

have called forth such an exclamation. It is more probable that the particle rendered in our Version *from* is a preposition (it is in the next chapter (v. 24) rendered *with*), and that it signifies, as the LXX. has it, *by means of*, or, as Gesenius, *by the help of*. There is, however, little doubt that her words had some pregnant meaning, and that she looked on Cain as at all events one of that race which was destined to triumph over the seed of the Serpent.

"The use of the name (JEHOVAH) is significant, though we cannot think that Eve already knew this name of God, which was first revealed to man at a later period of his history, and which is of Hebrew origin, whereas that language probably did not exist until the time of the dispersion at Babel. Yet, doubtless, the historian expresses the true meaning of Eve's speech which she spoke, inspired by that help which had been graciously given her of God" (Keil, 'Bibl. Comment.').

2. *Abel.*] She called her first-born Cain (*possession*), but this second Hebel (*breath*, *vapour*, *vanity*, *nothingness*), because all human possession is but vanity. Yet it is not said, that Abel was so named by Eve herself, as Cain had been. Hence it is possible, that the name Abel was that by which he became known, after his life had passed away like a breath or a vapour.

Abel was a keeper of sheep, but Cain was a tiller of the ground] The word rendered *sheep* includes sheep and goats. It is observed that the wildest nations live by hunting, those, who have thrown off the first barbarism, are nomadic, feeding sheep and cattle, those more civilized are agriculturists (see Rosen.). Hence the rationalist view coincides with the heathen, that a state of nature was pure barbarism, and that man gradually emerged from it into nomadic, then into agricultural, and finally into civilized life. In contradistinction to this, the account of Genesis represents man as placed by his Maker in a state of very simple civilization. Adam in Paradise was "to dress and to keep" the garden (Gen. ii. 15). His sons must have learned from him the knowledge which he had thus acquired. It is not likely to have been extensive knowledge, probably the very simplest possible, but still sufficient to rescue them from a state of pure barbarism, and from the necessity of living by the chase.

See note A at the end of this Chapter.

3. *in process of time*] Lit. "at the end of days." Abenezra understands "at the end of the year." So Fagius, Bochart, Clericus, Dathe, Rosenmüller, and many others. Clericus quotes from Aristot. 'Ethics,' VIII. 2. "It appears that ancient sacrifices were offered after the gathering of the fruits of the earth, they being a kind of first fruits. Moreover, at that time, men were most at leisure."

an offering] The word here used always signifies an unbloody oblation. It is frequently translated "a meat offering." Its nature is defined, Lev. xi. 1 seq.

4. *of the firstlings of his flock and of the fat thereof*] There has been in all times a difference of opinion as to the Divine or human origin of sacrifice. Sacrifices were so thoroughly sanctioned by the Divine law in after times, so generally accepted by God, and made so conspicuously types of the Lamb of God, that it is difficult to conceive how they should have arisen but from a Divine command. Yet, there is a deep silence as to any such command, whilst the institution of the Sabbath and of other positive ordinances is distinctly recorded. Hence, many have thought that sacrifice was dictated by an instinct of natural religion, and then, by a condescension to man's infirmity, sanctioned for a temporary purpose, and constituted an image of redemption. It is impossible to say what the view of the Apostolic fathers was; but from the time of Justin Martyr ('Apol.' II. 5; 'Dial.' pp. 237, 292), the fathers generally adopted the belief that sacrifice was a human, not a Divine ordinance. A remarkable exception to this appears in a passage of the most learned of the 4th century divines (Euseb. 'Dem. Evang.' I. 10), in which he distinctly ascribes the origin of sacrifice to a Divine inspiration, though even this does not necessarily imply a Divine command. It may be fairly said, that no certain conclusion on this question can possibly be arrived at, in the silence of Scripture. The principal arguments on the side of the Divine origin may be seen in Bp. Jer. Taylor, 'Duct. Dub.' Bk. II. R. XIII. §§ 27, 30; Witsii 'Ægypt.' III. 14; Kennicott, 'Two Dissertations,' II. p. 184 sq.; Magee 'On Atonement,' Disc. II. and notes; Faber, 'Three Dispensations,' Vol. I. The arguments on the opposite side may be found in Spencer, 'De Legibus Heb.' Lib. III. Diss. ii.; Warburton, 'Div. Legat.' Bks. VI. IX.; Davison's 'Remains,' art. *on origin of Sacrifice*. The work of Outram, 'De Sacrificiis,' should by all means be consulted, which takes an impartial survey of the whole question.

had respect unto] Comp. Num. xvi. 15;

5 But unto Cain and to his offering
he had not respect. And Cain was
very wroth, and his countenance
fell.
6 And the LORD said unto Cain,
Why art thou wroth? and why is thy
countenance fallen?
7 If thou doest well, shalt thou not
‖be accepted? and if thou doest not
well, sin lieth at the door. And ‖unto
thee *shall be* his desire, and thou shalt
rule over him.
8 And Cain talked with Abel his
brother: and it came to pass, [b]when

‖ Or, *have the excellency?*
‖ Or, *subject unto thee.*
[b] Wisd. 10. 3. Matt. 23. 35. 1 John 3. 12. Jude 11.

Amos v. 22. How did the Almighty express His approval of Abel's offering? According to the ancient Greek translation of Theod., it was by sending down fire to consume the sacrifice, as in Lev. ix. 24; Jud. vi. 21; 1 K. xviii. 38; 1 Chr. xxi. 26; 2 Chr. vii. 1. This explanation has been adopted by St Jerome, Rashi, Abenezra, Kimchi, Luther, Grotius, Delitzsch, and many others. Nothing but conjecture can guide us in this matter. We must be content to suppose, that some sign, intelligible to both the brothers, was given from above. The reason, as well as the mode, of the acceptance of Abel's gift has been greatly debated. Ver. 7, and Heb. xi. 4, seem to prove that the difference of spirit in which the two offerings were made caused the diversity of acceptance. The Apostle says, "By faith Abel offered a more excellent sacrifice." Faith, therefore, was the motive power; yet the result may have been that the sacrifice so offered was a better, fuller, and more acceptable sacrifice. Some have maintained that Cain brought fruits only, that Abel brought both fruits and the firstlings of his flock (see Kennicott, as above, p. 194). The wording of the original does not seem to warrant this. But, whilst we may see in the different spirit and disposition of the offerers a reason why one should be accepted and the other rejected, still "the view so often expressed, that Abel's bloody sacrifice resulted from a more profound religious apprehension than that of Cain, which was 'without shedding of blood,' seems to agree with the general bearing of the text" (Kurtz, 'Hist. of O. C.' Vol. I. p. 89); even if it be not admitted that a Divine ordinance had already sanctioned animal sacrifices.

5. *countenance fell*] Cp. the original of Nehem. vi. 16.

7. *shall thou not be accepted*] **Is there not acceptance?** Lit. "lifting up" either of guilt (*i.e.* pardon), or of the countenance, as when a suppliant bending down his face is accepted, and so his face raised up and cheered. Or more probably as the A. V., Is there not acceptance? Shalt thou not be accepted by God?

if thou doest not well, sin lieth at the door] This is generally explained as meaning that sin crouches at the door of the soul, like a wild beast, ready to devour it. Others understand *sin* to mean *the punishment of sin*, in which sense the word is sometimes used, see Zech. xiv. 19 (so Onk., Vatablus, Cornel. a Lapide). Some again interpret "a sin offering" (another frequent sense of the Hebrew word) which in the form of an animal victim lies or crouches at your door (see Kennicott, as above, p. 216, and Lee, 'Lex.' s. v. חַטָּאת). The chief objection to this latter interpretation is that there is no instance of this use of the word before the giving of the Law; which Law appears to have brought out into clearer relief the knowledge of sin and the need of sin-offering. See Rom. iii. 20.

And unto thee shall be his desire, &c.] There are two principal interpretations of these words, which have divided commentators in all times, the one set referring *his desire* to *Abel*, the other to *sin*. The LXX. Version clearly refers it to Abel, which interpretation is adopted by Chrysost., Ambrose, Augustine, and most of the fathers, by Grotius, Vossius, Heidegger, by our own translators, and by a majority of English commentators. The sense will then be, that Cain, whose jealousy had been excited by God's acceptance of Abel, need not, if he behaved well, fear that Abel should be preferred before him; his pre-eminence of birth should still be preserved to him: the desire of the younger brother should be towards him (an idiomatic expression specially noting the longing of one who looks up to another as an object of reverence, and so noting dependence, as of a younger brother on an elder, cp. Gen. iii. 16). The other interpretation, which is apparently, though not certainly, favoured by the Vulgate, is given in the Targums of Jerusalem and Pseudo-Jonathan, and adopted by Rashi, and most Jewish writers, by Luther's translation, Munster, Pererius, Rosenmüller, Von Bohlen, Delitzsch, Knobel, Keil, and most of the Germans. The sense of the passage on this supposition would be, "Sin lieth crouching like a wild beast at the door of the soul; its desire is towards thee, yet thou art not given over into its power; but if thou wilt, thou shalt be able to keep it in subjection." The former of these interpretations, which is also the more ancient, seems both more natural and more according with the simple meaning of the original.

8. *Cain talked with Abel*] The original

they were in the field, that Cain rose
up against Abel his brother, and slew
him.
9 ¶ And the LORD said unto Cain,
Where *is* Abel thy brother? And he
said, I know not: *Am* I my brother's
keeper?
10 And he said, What hast thou
done? the voice of thy brother's †blood
crieth unto me from the ground.
11 And now *art* thou cursed from
the earth, which hath opened her
mouth to receive thy brother's blood
from thy hand;
12 When thou tillest the ground, it
shall not henceforth yield unto thee
her strength; a fugitive and a vagabond shalt thou be in the earth.
13 And Cain said unto the LORD,
‖My punishment *is* greater than I can
bear.
14 Behold, thou hast driven me
out this day from the face of the
earth; and from thy face shall I be
hid; and I shall be a fugitive and a
vagabond in the earth; and it shall
come to pass, *that* every one that
findeth me shall slay me.

‖ Or, *My iniquity is greater than that it may be forgiven.*

---

means more naturally "Cain *said* to Abel." Accordingly in some few of the Masoretic MSS. there is the mark of an omission here. The Samaritan Pentateuch, the LXX., Syr., Vulg., read "Cain said to Abel his brother, Let us go into the field." These latter words, however, do not occur in the Greek Versions of Aquila, Symmachus, Theodotion, or the most ancient Targum, that of Onkelos It is probable that the words were inserted in the Sam., LXX., &c. as a gloss, from the difficulty of explaining the passage without them; and that this is really an example of an ancient and obsolete usage of the verb *to say*, which here means either *to talk with*, as the A. V., or to *tell*, as Jerome, or to *command*, to *lay a command upon*, according to Arabic usage, as Prof. Lee.

10. *the voice of thy brother's blood crieth unto me*] The verb "crieth" here agrees with "blood," which is in the plural, in which form it is used specially of blood shed, drops of blood, above all of blood shed by violence and murder. Murder is a crime which cries to heaven for vengeance, and though the blood may be hidden, its voice cannot be silenced.

11. *now art thou cursed from the earth*] The words are variously rendered (1) "Cursed art thou from the ground," *i.e.* the curse shall come upon thee from the earth, which shall not yield thee her fruit (Abenezra, Kimchi, Knobel). (2) "Cursed art thou away from the land," *i.e.* Thou art cursed and banished from the land, in which thou hast dwelt, and in which thy father and brethren are dwelling (Rosenm., Vater, Tuch, Knobel). (3) "Cursed art thou even more than the earth" which had been cursed (ch. iii. 17). Of these (3) seems quite inadmissible; either of the others yields a pertinent sense. The second is the most probable.

12. *When thou tillest*, &c.] The curse was in effect, that Cain should be banished from the land inhabited and cultivated by Adam and his family, should wander about without a settled habitation or a fertile dwelling place, living hardly in a barren and inhospitable wilderness.

13. *My punishment*] There is great variety of interpretation here. The Hebrews constantly expressed *sin* and *punishment for sin* by the same words; moreover to *bear*, and *to take away* or *forgive*, were thoughts closely connected. Hence (1) "My sin is too great to be forgiven" (as in the Marg.) is the rendering of LXX., Onk., Syr., Vulg., Saad. Whilst (2) Abenezra, Kimchi, and the majority of modern commentators, render as the A. V., "My punishment is greater than I can bear." Both these renderings can be defended on good grounds by Hebrew usage. The latter seems more accordant with the temper of Cain's mind, and is probably correct.

14. *from thy face shall I be hid*] Though God no longer constantly manifested His presence as in Eden, yet there were at times some indications of that presence, (*e.g.* see v. 4). It may perhaps be inferred that some special place had already been set apart for Divine worship and sacred service. (On this subject see Blunt, 'Undesigned Coincidences,' I. p. 9, eighth Edition, 1863).

every one that findeth me shall slay me] Josephus, Kimchi, Michaelis, and others, have supposed that Cain feared death from the beasts of the field; but most commentators rightly understand that his fear was from the vengeance of his own kindred. It is observed by Kurtz that, according to hints gathered from Gen. iv. 25, the murder of Abel probably took place just before the birth of Seth, *i.e.* 130 years after the creation of man, Gen. v. 3. We need not suppose that Cain, Abel, and Seth, were the only sons of Adam. Indeed, from Gen. v. 4, we infer that there were others. Cain, Abel, and Seth, are mentioned for obvious reasons; Abel for his piety and his early death, Cain for his wickedness

15 And the LORD said unto him,
Therefore whosoever slayeth Cain,
vengeance shall be taken on him seven-
fold. And the LORD set a mark upon
Cain, lest any finding him should kill
him.
16 ¶ And Cain went out from the
presence of the LORD, and dwelt in
the land of Nod, on the east of Eden.
17 And Cain knew his wife; and
† Heb. *Chanoch.* she conceived, and bare †Enoch: and
he builded a city, and called the name
of the city, after the name of his son,
Enoch.
18 And unto Enoch was born Irad:
and Irad begat Mehujael: and Mehujael begat Methusael: and Methusael begat †Lamech. † Heb. *Lemech.*
19 ¶ And Lamech took unto him
two wives: the name of the one *was*
Adah, and the name of the other Zillah.

---

and the worldly wisdom of his posterity, Seth because he was the ancestor of the promised seed. There may then, in 130 years, have grown up a very considerable number of children and grandchildren to Adam and Eve. An Eastern tradition assigns to them no less than 33 sons and 27 daughters.

15. *Therefore*] The LXX., Symm., Theodot., Vulg., Syr., read *Not so.* So Dathe and others.

whosoever slayeth] Cain, though guilty of a terrible sin, may not have had the full and fixed purpose to commit murder, but in a moment of furious anger have seized a weapon and dealt a murderous blow, perhaps hardly aware of its deadly consequences. Hence, it may be, the Most High forbids him to be put to death, but sentences him to a perpetual banishment from his early home, and to a life of misery and sorrow. Kalisch well observes, "The early death of Abel can be no punishment; he seemed in fact to enjoy the peculiar favour of God; his offering was graciously accepted. We find, therefore, in this narrative the great and beautiful thought, that life is not the highest boon; that the pious find a better existence and a more blessed reward in another and a purer sphere; but that crime and guilt are the greatest evils; that they are punished by a long and wearisome life, full of fear and care and compunction of conscience."

set a mark upon Cain] **Gave a sign to Cain.** LXX. The interpretation that God provided Cain with some mark which would make him known is adopted by Pseudo-Jonathan, most of the Jewish Commentators, Luther, Calvin, Piscator, Wogal, &c. Most modern commentators agree that God gave some sign to Cain to assure him that he should not be slain, (Abenezra, Gabe, Dathe, Rosenm., Gesen., Maurer, Hitzig, V. Bohl., Tuch, Baumg., Kalisch, Delitzsch). Of what nature the sign may have been, we have now no means of learning.

16. *the presence of the Lord*] It is questioned whether this means merely from conversing with the Lord, or whether Eden, though not the *garden* of Eden, in which Adam had dwelt since the fall, was esteemed a sacred spot, a spot in which still a peculiar presence of God was looked for by man. See on v. 14.

Nod] *i.e.* "wandering." It is impossible to say where Nod was situated, except that it lay east of Eden.

17. *Enoch*] It has been contended that in these genealogies Adam = Enosh, Enoch or Chanoch = Enoch, Cain = Kenan, Irad = Jered, Mehujael = Mahalaleel, Methusael = Methuselah. In the first place, however, there is a manifest difference in the roots of the names so identified; next, the paucity of names at this early period may have naturally led to similar names being adopted in different families; 3rdly, the relationship of the families of Seth and Cain, and the probably occasional intercourse between them, would not unnaturally tend to the same result. Dettinger is quoted by Kurtz (Vol. I. p. 91), as having called attention to the fact, that the text furnishes more detailed particulars about Enoch and Lamech, whose names were so similar to Sethite names, in order to prevent the possibility of their being confounded, and to shew more clearly that the direction in which these two lines tended was markedly opposite. See Kurtz as above, Hävernick, 'Introd. to Pentateuch,' p. 109.

builded a city] Rather "began to build a city," lit. "was building a city." It is not necessary to suppose that the city was built immediately on the birth of Enoch. It may have been built when Cain had lived many years and was surrounded by children and grandchildren. The word *city* is, of course, not to be interpreted by modern ideas: a village of rude huts, which was distinguished from the booths or tents of the nomads, would satisfy all the conditions of the text.

19. *Lamech took unto him two wives*] Here we have the first example of polygamy; which, though afterwards tolerated, had its rise among the sons of Cain, and is evidently mentioned for reprobation.

20 And Adah bare Jabal: he was
the father of such as dwell in tents,
and *of such as have* cattle.
21 And his brother's name *was*
Jubal: he was the father of all such
as handle the harp and organ.
22 And Zillah, she also bare Tu-
bal-cain, an †instructer of every arti- † Heb. *whetter.*
ficer in brass and iron: and the sister
of Tubal-cain *was* Naamah.
23 And Lamech said unto his wives,
Adah and Zillah, Hear my voice; ye ‖ Or, *I would slay a man in my wound, &c.*
wives of Lamech, hearken unto my
speech: for ‖I have slain a man to
my wounding, and a young man ‖to ‖ Or, *in my hurt.*
my hurt.

---

20. *the father of such as dwell in tents, and...have cattle*] Jabal invented tents and introduced the custom of pasturing cattle round the tents, and perhaps even of stalling them in tents. Moreover, the word here used for cattle implies larger cattle, whereas that used of Abel v. 2 applied only to smaller cattle: Jabal therefore was the first who introduced the thorough nomadic life. (See Bochart, 'Hieroz.' P. I. Lib. II. c. 44.)

21. *the harp and the organ*] The *kinnur*, which descended to the Greeks and was by them called Kinura, is described by Josephus as having ten strings and as played on by a plectrum; but in 1 Sam. xvi. 23, xviii. 10, xix. 9, David is said to have played on it with his hand. It was probably, when invented by Jubal, the simplest form of stringed instrument. The word rendered *organ* was apparently a pipe, bagpipe, panpipe, or some very simple wind instrument: Onkelos renders it by pipe or flute. "It is not an accidental fact, that the lyre and the flute were introduced by the brothers of a nomadic herdsman. It is in the happy leisure of this occupation that music is generally first exercised and appreciated." Kalisch.

22. *an instructer of every artificer in brass and iron*] So Onkelos. Perhaps (with LXX. and Vulg.) *a sharpener of every instrument in bronze and iron.* The word rendered *brass* is certainly either *bronze*, or, more probably, a native metal, *copper* (see Smith's 'Dict. of the Bible,' art. *Brass*). Bronze is an alloy of copper and tin, very much harder than either of them and also than brass, with a little more tin it becomes bell-metal. Previously to this time all weapons for defence or instruments of husbandry may have been of flint, or wood, or bone. Uncivilized nations at the present time have weapons made of flint, wood, bone, shark's teeth, &c. Where nations have lost the usages of more civilized life, they seem to have fallen back on a flint age, then to have invented bronze weapons (in the case of South America weapons of gold), and lastly to have discovered the use of iron. Tubal Cain is here described as the first who made metal instruments and sharpened them. It is not to be objected, that this was too early for the invention of metals. If Tubal Cain was contemporary with Enoch (the descendant of Seth in the same degree) he must have been born at least 500 years after the creation of Adam, according to the Hebrew Chronology, or 1000 years according to the LXX. Chronology. Whether we must understand that he invented the use of both copper and iron, or only of copper or bronze, which led in course of time to the farther invention of iron, it may be difficult to decide from the concise and obscure wording of the text. That the most ancient inhabitants of Europe were ignorant of the use of metal, as indicated by the discovery of flint weapons in the gravel, can be no proof that they were unknown to the early descendants of Adam. If the colonists of Australia were for the next thousand years to be separated from all connection with the rest of the world, it is quite possible, notwithstanding their present high state of civilization, that they might utterly lose many of the arts of civilized life, and perhaps, if there were a deficiency of coal, or lime, or native metals, even the use of metallic instruments.

Nothing can be more natural or probable than the difference of character and development in the descendants of Cain and Seth respectively. In the former we see the children of this world wise in their generation, rapidly advancing in art and the acquirement of riches, but sensual, violent and godless. In the latter we find less of social and political advancement, but a life more regulated by the dictates of conscience and by faith in the Providence and Grace of God.

Resemblances to the names of Lamech's family have been traced in the names of those to whom the Latins attributed similar inventions. Thus Tubal Cain has been thought = Vulcan, Naamah, "the lovely, or beautiful," may then = Venus, Jubal, the inventor of the lyre = Apollo. It is observed also that the refinement and perhaps the luxury of the descendants of Cain appear in the names of their wives and daughters, Naamah, lovely, Adah, beauty or ornament, Zillah, shadow.

23, 24. *And Lamech said*, &c.]

And Lamech said unto his wives,
Adah and Zillah, hear my voice,
Ye wives of Lamech, give ear unto my speech,
For I slay a man if he woundeth me,
Even a young man, if he hurteth me,
Lo! Cain would be avenged seven-fold,
But Lamech seventy-and-seven fold.

24 If Cain shall be avenged seven-
fold, truly Lamech seventy and seven-
fold.
25 ¶ And Adam knew his wife
again; and she bare a son, and called
his name †Seth: For God, *said she*,
hath appointed me another seed instead of Abel, whom Cain slew.
26 And to Seth, to him also there
was born a son; and he called his
name †Enos: then began men ‖to
call upon the name of the LORD.

† Heb. *Sheth.*

† Heb. *Enosh.*

‖ Or, *to call* themselves *by the name of the LORD.*

The speech of Lamech has exercised the skill of translators and interpreters of all times. Its obscure and enigmatical character is admitted as a mark of its remote antiquity even by the most unfavourable critics. The apparent meaning of the words is this. Amid the violence of the times, especially among the descendants of Cain, Lamech comforts his wives with the assurance that with the aid of the bronze and iron instruments now in his hands, he could kill any one who injured him ("I slay or would slay a man for wounding me"); and that, if it had been promised to Cain, that he should be avenged seven fold, there was power in the hands of Lamech's family to avenge seventy-seven fold. The speech is one of confident boasting. Lamech trusts in his weapons of brass and steel to maintain his cause, even when referring to words used by God to his forefather Cain.

The chief difficulty lies in the use of the perfect tense in the verb *slay:* lit. "I have slain," (which is the rendering of the LXX. Vulg., Syr., &c.). That difficulty seems to have suggested the supposition that a *not* may have fallen out (which is the rendering of Onkelos, "I have not slain,") or that it should be rendered interrogatively ("Have I slain?"): but the more probable explanation is, that in this ancient distich the perfect tense is used to express the arrogant confidence of the boaster; even as at times the perfect is adopted in the most sure word of prophecy, the future being represented as having all the certainty of the past. The words rendered in the A. V. "to my wounding"—"to my hurt"—probably mean "for my wounding," &c. *i. e.* "for wounding me," or "in revenge for his wounding me."

25. *Seth*] *i.e.* "Foundation," from the word signifying *to place*, rendered here "appointed." Seth came into the place of Abel, as the ancestor of the Theocratic race and of the promised seed.

26. *then began men to call upon the name of the Lord*] **Then began he to call on the name of the LORD.** There is great diversity in the interpretation of these words. The Samaritan Pentateuch and the Vulgate refer them to Enos, "Then he, *i.e.* Enos, began to call on the name of the LORD." The LXX. has "Then he hoped," &c. it being possible to refer the verb to a root signifying "to hope," whence some have understood, that the birth of Enos inspired a new hope that the promise to Eve should be fulfilled. The Targum of the Pseudo-Jonathan has "In those days men began to make themselves idols, which they called after the name of the Word of the LORD." This interpretation is adopted by some celebrated Jewish commentators (Kimchi, Rashi, &c.), who derive the verb from a root signifying "to profane," and render "Then was there profanation in calling on the name of the LORD." Jerome ('Quæst.') mentions this as the opinion of many Jews in his days. The most natural sense of the Hebrew is, that when Enos was born, Seth his father in gratitude and hope then began to praise the LORD and to call on Him with reassured hope in His mercy and His promises. There is nothing to connect the verb with Enos as its nominative case rather than with Seth; nor again is there any good ground for the notion that emphasis is to be placed on the special name of God, JEHOVAH; as though then for the first time He was invoked under that name. The sacred narrative has all along used the name JEHOVAH; and whether we believe it to have been known from earlier times or to have been revealed first to Moses, there is nothing whatever to connect its revelation and acknowledgment with the birth of Enos.

NOTE A. ADDITIONAL NOTE ON CHAP. IV. V. 2. ON THE EARLY CIVILIZATION OF MANKIND.

HAVERNICK ('Introd. to the Pentateuch,' Translation, p. 104) has shewn that the traditions of ancient nations, the Phœnicians, Egyptians, Greeks, &c. refer the invention of agriculture to the earliest mythic ages; and that the investigators of history, Herder, Link, Schlosser, &c. have been led to the conclusion that "the discovery of the breeding of cattle, of agriculture, and of the preparation of metals, belong to prehistoric times, and that in the historic period these arts have made comparatively no great advances." The recent discoveries of human remains, and of the implements of human industry in the gravel and drift formations on the Earth's surface, may seem to contradict all this. Ethnologists distinguish a flint age, a bronze age, and an iron age, as having existed in ancient Europe; during the first of which only flint instruments, during the second bronze, during the third, iron instruments appear to have been in use. And, as for the most part in the earlier periods, the skulls seem to have been smaller and of a lower type than those of later date, the theory of early barbarism and of progressive civilization has been thought to derive confirmation from Geology. Sir Charles Lyell says also, that "had the original stock of mankind been really endowed with superior intellectual power and with inspired knowledge, and had possessed the same improvable nature as their posterity, the point of advancement, which they would have realized ere this, would have been immeasurably higher" ('Antiquity of Man,' p. 378). He goes on to say that, instead of rude pottery and flint weapons, we should in that case have found works like those of Phidias and Praxiteles. It may be answered, that Scripture does not represent the first man as "endowed with superior intellectual power and with inspired knowledge." All that we learn is, that Adam was placed in Eden to till it, that his power of speech was exercised by having to name the brute creation, that he had a simple command given him, and afterwards a special promise. Morally he may have been, in the first instance, in a state of innocence, without being intellectually in a condition of eminence. As for the advance of knowledge, many nations have been in a state of mental cultivation and of art knowledge incomparably beyond that of Adam and his children, and yet have remained for centuries upon centuries without any apparent progress; for instance, the people of China. All that we say is, that his primary state was not a state of savageness, but rather of rudimentary civilization. And this is really not opposed, but confirmed, by the records of Geology. "We must remember, that as yet we have no distinct geological evidence, that the appearance of what are called the inferior races of mankind has always preceded in chronological order that of the higher races" (Lyell, as above, p. 90). On the contrary, some of the most ancient remains of man and man's art give indications of considerable civilization. In the valley of the Ohio there are hundreds of mounds, which have served for temples, for places of defence and of sepulture, containing pottery, ornamental sculpture, articles in silver and copper, and stone weapons, with skulls of the Mexican type. Above these have grown a succession of forests, in which the Red Indians for centuries may have housed and hunted (Lyell, pp. 39, 40). They prove that in those very ancient days there must have been a civilization, of which all traces have vanished above the surface of the earth. As regards the fossil skulls found in Europe, that known as "the Neanderthal Skull" is of the lowest type, and is said to be the most apelike skull ever seen, though its capacity, 75 cubic inches, is greater than that of some individuals of existing races. It was discovered in a cavern with the thigh of a bear: but there is nothing to prove its great antiquity. It may be very ancient, but may be comparatively modern. But the skull found at Engis near Liege, which appears to have been contemporary with the Mammoth, and is assigned by Lyell to the post-pliocene age, although the forehead is somewhat narrow, may be matched by the skulls of individuals of European race (Lyell, p. 80): and the skull of the fossil man of Denise, though said to be contemporary with the Mammoth and coeval with the last eruption of the Puy Volcanoes, and therefore as old as, or older than, any other human skull yet discovered, is of the ordinary Caucasian or European type (Lyell, p. 200). No prudent Geologist will admit, concerning any of these crania, more than that they bear marks of rude as compared with civilized races, rather more mastication, more prominent marks of muscular attachment and the like, all things of every day occurrence. So, in fact, the argument from Geology is really coincident with the testimony of Scripture and of universal primitive tradition, viz. that man, in his original condition, was not a helpless savage, but had at least the rudiments of civilization and intelligence.

When we read that Cain was a tiller of the ground, we do not necessarily conclude, that he cultivated wheat and barley; he may have known only of fruits, vegetables, roots, &c. Yet it is observable, that cereals have been discovered with some of the very early remains of human industry.

CHAPTER V.

1 *The genealogy, age, and death of the patriarchs from Adam unto Noah.* 24 *The godliness and translation of Enoch.*

Chron. THIS *is* the [a]book of the generations of Adam. In the day that
God created man, in the likeness of
God made he him;
2 [b]Male and female created he [b] Wisd. 2.
them; and blessed them, and called 23.
their name Adam, in the day when
they were created.

CHAP. V. 1. *the book of the generations*] The record or recounting of the genealogical history of Adam and his descendants. See ch. ii. 4.

3 ¶ And Adam lived an hundred
and thirty years, and begat *a son* in
his own likeness, after his image; and
called his name Seth:
4 [c] And the days of Adam after he (c 1 Chron. 1, 1. &c.)
had begotten Seth were eight hundred
years: and he begat sons and daughters:
5 And all the days that Adam lived
were nine hundred and thirty years:
and he died.
6 And Seth lived an hundred and
five years, and begat †Enos: († Heb. *Enosh.*)
7 And Seth lived after he begat
Enos eight hundred and seven years,
and begat sons and daughters:
8 And all the days of Seth were
nine hundred and twelve years: and
he died.
9 ¶ And Enos lived ninety years,
and begat †Cainan: († Heb. *Kenan.*)
10 And Enos lived after he begat
Cainan eight hundred and fifteen
years, and begat sons and daughters:
11 And all the days of Enos were
nine hundred and five years: and he
died.

12 ¶ And Cainan lived seventy
years, and begat †Mahalaleel: († Gr. *Maleleel.*)
13 And Cainan lived after he be-
gat Mahalaleel eight hundred and
forty years, and begat sons and
daughters:
14 And all the days of Cainan were
nine hundred and ten years: and he
died.
15 ¶ And Mahalaleel lived sixty
and five years, and begat †Jared: († Heb. *Jered.*)
16 And Mahalaleel lived after he
begat Jared eight hundred and thirty
years, and begat sons and daughters:
17 And all the days of Mahalaleel
were eight hundred ninety and five
years: and he died.
18 ¶ And Jared lived an hundred
sixty and two years, and he begat
Enoch.
19 And Jared lived after he begat
Enoch eight hundred years, and begat
sons and daughters:
20 And all the days of Jared were
nine hundred sixty and two years:
and he died.

---

3. *Adam lived*, &c.] The genealogy given is that of the Sethites, probably as the line of the promised seed. The genealogy of the Cainites was given much more imperfectly in the last chapter, and with no dates or chronological marks, because, says Keil, being under the curse of God, they had no future. He quotes Baumgarten as saying, that this genealogy was "a memorial witnessing both the truth of God's promises and also the faith and patience of the fathers." The chronology of this chapter is very different in the Hebrew, the Samaritan and the Septuagint, as will be seen in the following table of the generations from Adam to the flood (see also note infra).

	Hebrew Text.			Samaritan Text.			Septuagint.		
	Years before birth of Son.	Rest of Life.	Whole Life.	Years before birth of Son.	Rest of Life.	Whole Life.	Years before birth of Son.	Rest of Life.	Whole Life.
Adam	130	800	930	130	800	930	230	700	930
Seth	105	807	912	105	807	912	205	707	912
Enosh	90	815	905	90	815	905	190	715	905
Cainan	70	840	910	70	840	910	170	740	910
Mahalaleel	65	830	895	65	830	895	65	730	895
Jared	162	800	962	62	785	847	62	800	962
Enoch	65	300	365	65	300	365	165	200	365
Methuselah	187	782	969	67	653	720	187	782	969
Lamech	182	595	777	53	600	653	188	565	753
Noah	500			500			500		
Shem at the Flood	100			100			100		
Date of Flood	1656			1307			2262		

6. *Enos*] *i.e.* man. Adam signifies *man*, *mankind*, generally. Enos, or Enosh, is rather *mortal*, *miserable man*. The now growing experience of human sorrow and fragility may have suggested this name.

9. *Cainan*] *i.e.* possession.

12. *Mahalaleel*] The Praise of God.

15. *Jared*] The root of this name signifies *to descend*, Descent.

18. *Enoch*] *i. e.* consecrated.

21 ¶ And Enoch lived sixty and
five years, and begat † Methuselah: († Gr. *Mathusala.*)
22 And Enoch walked with God
after he begat Methuselah three hundred years, and begat sons and daughters:
23 And all the days of Enoch were
three hundred sixty and five years:
24 And [d] Enoch walked with ([d] Ecclus. 44. 16. Heb. 11. 5.)
God: and he *was* not; for God took
him.
25 And Methuselah lived an hundred eighty and seven years, and begat
† Lamech: († Heb. *Lemech.*)
26 And Methuselah lived after he
begat Lamech seven hundred eighty
and two years, and begat sons and
daughters:
27 And all the days of Methuselah
were nine hundred sixty and nine
years: and he died.
28 ¶ And Lamech lived an hundred eighty and two years, and begat
a son:
29 And he called his name † Noah, († Gr. *Noe.*)
saying, This *same* shall comfort us
concerning our work and toil of our
hands, because of the ground which
the LORD hath cursed.
30 And Lamech lived after he begat Noah five hundred ninety and five
years, and begat sons and daughters:
31 And all the days of Lamech
were seven hundred seventy and seven
years: and he died.
32 And Noah was five hundred
years old: and Noah begat Shem,
Ham, and Japheth.

---

21. *Methuselah*] Perhaps "the missive of death." Bochart interprets "His death the sending forth," as indicating that his death was contemporary with the pouring forth of the waters, for Methuselah must have died in the very year of the flood. Gesenius gives the sense of the word as *vir teli*, "the man of the sword" or "of the dart." From its frequent occurrence in Phœnician inscriptions, &c., there can be little doubt that Methu = Betha = man.

24. *he was not; for God took him*] The LXX. rendering seems to interpret this of translation. So do all the Targums. In Ecclus. xliv. 16, we read "He pleased the Lord and was translated (into Paradise, according to the Vulgate), being a pattern of repentance." The words are, no doubt, obscure. Yet, when we remember how universally the promise of the Old Testament is of life and blessing in this world, not of an early and happy death, we could scarcely doubt that the ancient interpretation was the true one, even if it had not been that given in Heb. xi. 5. The history of Enoch is reasonably supposed to be the origin of the Phrygian tradition concerning a certain Annacus or Nannacus, who lived upwards of 300 years, concerning whom it was prophesied that after him all would be destroyed. This caused great grief among the Phrygians, whence "to weep as in the days of Annacus" became a proverb. At his death came the deluge of Deucalion, and all men were destroyed (Suidas, v. Νάννακος, Steph. Byz. v. Ἰκόνιον).

29. *he called his name Noah, saying, This same shall comfort us*, &c.] The name "Noah" signifies "Rest," and the connection between the thought of rest and that of comfort is obvious. Lamech appears as one oppressed with the toil and labour needful to subdue the earth, and with the feeling that God had cursed it and made it sterile. He expresses a hope, that Noah would be a comfort to his parents and the bringer of rest; whether the mere natural hope of a father that his son should be a support and comfort to him, or a hope looking to the promise made of old to Eve, or a hope inspired by prophetic vision that Noah should become the second founder of a race, the head of a regenerated world, it may be hard to say. There may have been an unconscious prophecy in the expression of a merely pious hope.

Which the LORD *hath cursed*] This occurs in a chapter which modern critics call Elohistic. Therefore they consider this an interpolation. The truer inference would be that the Elohistic theory is unfounded.

NOTE A. ON THE CHRONOLOGY IN CH. V.

Difficulties in the Chronology. 1 Difference of texts. 2 Longevity of Patriarchs. 3 Antiquity of human race, as deduced (1) from Geology, (2) from History, (3) from Language, (4) from Ethnology.

THE genealogies in this chapter and in chapter xi. are the only sources extant for the construction of a chronology of the patriarchal ages. The questions which arise are of the same kind in both genealogies, and may be considered together. The difficulties which suggest themselves may be arranged as follows:

1. The disagreement between the Hebrew, Samaritan and Septuagint texts.

2. The extreme longevity assigned to the patriarchs.

3. The insufficient time allowed for the existence of man upon the earth.

1. The first of these difficulties is such as to render it impossible to arrive at a certain conclusion as to the exact dates of the creation of man, the Deluge and the call of Abraham; but it in no degree affects the veracity of the Sacred Record. It is true, that there appears something like design in the alterations which must have taken place; thus the Hebrew gives the age of Adam as $130 + 800 = 930$, whilst the LXX. give $230 + 700 = 930$, and so on in the case of most of the Patriarchs, the results being frequently made to tally, whilst the constituents of these results disagree. Hence, whilst some have charged the Alexandrian translators with lengthening the periods, in order more nearly to satisfy the demands of Egyptian chronology, others have supposed that the rabbins shortened the time, to escape the force of the Christian's argument, that the world was six thousand years old, and that therefore the Messiah must have come. If either of these charges be true, it only brings us in face of what is already familiar to all critics, viz. that the errors of copyists were sometimes intentional, but that even these do not affect the general integrity of the text. It is well known that there have been some few designed corruptions in the text of the New Testament. It need not surprise us therefore, if we find reason to think that there were some attempts of a like kind in the text of the Old Testament. If anywhere the temptation to correct existed, it could never be stronger than in the genealogical tables of the ancestors of the Jewish race. Indeed, as numbers are of all things the most liable to become confused in ancient documents, very great errors in restoring them may be consistent with the most honest intention on the part of the restorers. And, though we believe in the Divine guidance and inspiration of the original writer, we have no right to expect that a miraculous power should have so watched over the transmission of the records, as to have preserved them from all possible errors of transcription, though a special Providence may have guarded them from such loss or mutilation, as would have weakened their testimony to Divine and spiritual truth.

2. As to the extreme longevity of the Patriarchs, it is observable that some eminent physiologists have thought this not impossible; and even Buffon, by no means inclined to credulity on the side of Scripture, admitted the truth of the record, and could see physical causes for such long life in early times. (See 'Aids to Faith,' p. 278.) It is undoubted, that the traditions of ancient nations, as Greeks, Babylonians, Egyptians, Hindoos, and others, point to the great longevity of the early inhabitants of the globe; and though sceptics argue that this only places the Scriptural account on a level with other mythic histories (see Von Bohlen, Vol. II. p. 100), yet we may reply that, if the Scripture account were true, the traditions of other nations would be almost sure to preserve some traces of the truth, and that this is a more probable explanation of the fact, than the supposition that all these nations, however unconnected with each other, should have stumbled upon the same fabulous histories.

It is well observed by Delitzsch; "We must consider that all the old-world population was descended from a nature originally immortal (in Adam and Eve), that the climate, weather, and other natural conditions were very different from those which succeeded, that the life was very simple and even in its course, and that the after-working of the Paradisiacal state was not at once lost in the track of antiquity." To this Keil adds, that this long life must have been very favourable to the multiplication of mankind, for the formation of marked characters, and the developement of the good and evil qualities of different races. Family affection, piety, good discipline and morality would strike their roots deeper in pious families; whilst evil propensities would be more and more developed in godless races. Supposing, however, that physiology should ultimately decide that the extreme longevity of the patriarchs was not possible, without a continued miracle, we should only be driven to the principle already conceded, that numbers and dates, especially in genealogical tables, are liable in the course of transcription to become obscured and exaggerated.

3. The third objection is derived from the opinion now very generally gaining strength, that man must have been in existence on the earth more than four or even six thousand years before the Christian era.

The arguments for the antiquity of man are:

(1) Geological.
(2) Historical.
(3) Linguistic.
(4) Ethnological.

(1) The very eminent British geologist, Sir C. Lyell, has attempted to prove, that man, having been contemporary with the mammoth and other extinct mammalia, must have been living at least 100,000 years on the earth. Although unfortunately in physical science a great name always carries with it a crowd of followers, far more than in politics, literature or religion, yet in the present instance Sir C. Lyell has failed to carry conviction to some of the most eminent of his contemporaries. Elie de Beaumont on the continent and several of the most distinguished geologists in England demur to his conclusions. The conclusions are based on two principal assumptions; first, that relics of

man, flint instruments or the like, are found in recent and post-pliocene formations, which have been deposited in juxtaposition with bones of the mammoth and other extinct mammalia; secondly, that the present rate of deposition must be reckoned as the normal rate, and that at that rate the beds, which overlie the extinct mammal and human remains, must have taken a vast time to form. Of course much depends on the argument from uniformity. There are many men of science, who, accepting Lyell's general principles, yet believe that in former ages there were causes at work, which would have produced much speedier deposition and greater rapidity in the formation of beds of all kinds, than we see going on at present. It may perhaps be true, that man was coeval with the mammoth; but a mammoth was found early in this century in Siberia preserved in the ice, with skin and hair fitting it to live in a cold climate, and with flesh upon it, of which it was possible to make soup. Now, even allowing for the great preserving power of ice, there is neither proof nor probability that this animal had been dead 100,000 years or even more than 6,000 years. But again, it seems probable that man was in existence at a time when animals now inhabiting tropical climates roamed at large in the forests of Gaul and Britain. How long it may have taken to reduce the climate of Great Britain from a tropical to its present temperate condition, is a question very difficult to solve. A change in the Gulf Stream, an alteration in the respective elevation of land and water, let alone all question of the gradual cooling down of the earth itself, would do much towards this. Besides, not *human bones*, but only flint instruments are found in the gravel and caverns with bones of extinct mammals. Moreover, the present opinions of geologists rather go to negative entirely the tropical character of the British climate in the mammoth and tiger periods. Sir Chas. Lyell admits that even now "the Bengal tiger ranges occasionally to latitude 52° North" (*i.e.* the latitude of England, and probably in a climate much colder than England), "and *abounds* in latitude 48°, to which the small tailless hare or pika, a polar resident, sometimes wanders southwards" ('Antiq. of Man,' p. 158). We may see therefore many contingencies which might have brought human remains into contact with the remains of tropical animals, at a period much more recent than that assigned to such proximity by this eminent writer.

Difficulties of various kinds attach to Sir Charles Lyell's very large numbers; for instance, at anything approaching to the present rate of increase the descendants of a single couple would have multiplied to nearly the number of the present population in about 6000 years. Again, according to Sir C. Lyell's own admission, "we must remember, that as yet we have no distinct geological evidence that the appearance of what are called the inferior races of mankind has always preceded in chronological order that of the higher races." p. 90. On the contrary, it was shewn above that the evidence which we have points to some degree of civilization in the earliest periods. Indeed had it not been so, it is hardly possible that man should not soon have become extinct in the presence of so many animals whose mere physical powers were so much greater than man's. But then is it credible, that for some 90,000 years the human race should have been stationary, having acquired almost from the first the art of making flint instruments, but all farther progress in the arts of civilization having apparently been reserved to the last 6,000 years? On the whole, it seems impossible not to conclude that the geological evidence as to the antiquity of man is as yet imperfect and imperfectly read.

(2) The historical arguments are chiefly derived from Egyptian sources; for, though the Indians, the Chinese, and the Babylonians profess to go back to hundreds of thousands of years of past history, it is generally admitted that their historic times do not at the very utmost extend farther back than to the 27th century B.C. The eminent Egyptologers, Bunsen and Lepsius, relying on the monuments of Egypt and the statements of Manetho, claim for Egypt a national history from nearly 10,000 years B.C. It is, however, quite certain that much of the evidence for this is of the vaguest possible character, and that very large deductions must be made for myth and for contemporary dynasties. In all probability the earliest Egyptian dynasty cannot be dated farther back than B.C. 2700. (See 'Aids to Faith,' Essay VI. 17, pp. 252 sq., also 'Biblical Dict.' Arts. *Chronology*, *Egypt*, and the Excursus at the end of this volume).

(3) The linguistic argument is of this nature. Languages are of slow growth. The divergence of several modern European languages from Latin has been comparatively inconsiderable in 1500 years. Can we then believe all languages to have been formed, and to have diverged so widely from each other, since the dispersion at Babel? One answer to this is, that only those languages which have a literature change slowly. As long as the Authorised Version of the Scriptures and the works of Shakspeare are read in English, the English language will never be much unlike what it is now, or what it was three centuries ago. But where there is no literature, a few years create a complete revolution; wild tribes in a single generation cease to understand each other. And, even keeping out of sight the miracle of the dispersion at Babel, emigration, which carried no literature with it, would soon have created an endless diversity of tongues. The chief difficulty, however, is in the slow growth of

languages to a high degree of grammatical perfection, such as of Greek to the language of Homer some 900 years B.C., and of Sanskrit to the language of the Vedas, nearly 1200 years B.C. But we must remember, that the Samaritan and LXX. chronology allow an interval of more than 3000 years from the Flood to the Christian era, and 1800 years (the difference between 3000 and 1200) will give considerable scope for grammatical developement.

(4) The ethnological argument is grounded principally on the apparently unchanging character of some of the races of mankind. Especially it is observed, that in very ancient Egyptian monuments the negro race is depicted with all its present features and peculiarities. It would therefore be impossible, it is argued, that all the varieties of man should have sprung up, if their ancestors were a single pair, brought into being not more than 6000 or 8000 years since. It is replied, that supposing, which is disputed, the alleged antiquity of the monuments in question, still a race, continuing under nearly the same circumstances, is not likely to change since first its peculiarities were produced by those very circumstances. Such has been the case with the negroes since the time of the Egyptian monuments. If we take the LXX. chronology as correct, the negroes may have been in Africa for nearly 1500 years before the reign of Sethos I., when we find them so clearly depicted on the monuments. Their change to that climate, their fixed habits of life, and isolation from other races, may have soon impressed a character upon them, which whilst continuing to live under the same condition ever since, they have never lost for a period extending now to more than 3000 years. But we witness rapid changes in race when circumstances rapidly change. The European inhabitants of the North American States are said even in two or three generations to be rapidly acquiring a similarity of feature and conformation to the original inhabitants of the soil, though not losing their European intelligence and civilization. Many similar facts are noticed; which prove that changes of race, though sometimes so slow as to be imperceptible, are at other times extremely rapid. The early condition of mankind, with its frequent migrations, wide separations and little intercommunion, must have been favourable to rapid change, whilst its later more stationary condition is favourable to continuance and perpetuity of type.

There is one other important objection made to the genealogies in this chapter and in Chapter xi. viz. that each gives a catalogue of but ten generations; which looks as if neither were historical. A probable solution of this difficulty would seem to be, that the genealogies neither were, nor were intended to be, complete. Like other genealogies or pedigrees, sacred and profane, they omitted certain links, and perhaps only recorded and handed down to posterity those ancestors of the race who, for some reason or other, were more than the rest deserving of remembrance. This solution would be entirely satisfactory, if it were not for the appearance of chronological completeness which both the genealogies exhibit in their present form; the age of the patriarch at the birth of his son and successor, and the number of years which he lived after that birth, being given in every case. If therefore the above explanation be adopted, it would almost be necessary to add that, in the course of transmission and transcription, a greater appearance of completeness had been given to the catalogues than had existed in the original record. Such hypotheses are never to be too lightly adopted; but they are far more probable than those of the modern critical school, which reject the historical truth of the earlier books of the Bible. The genealogies of our Lord given in the Gospels have undoubtedly some links omitted, and yet are reduced to a form of great completeness. This is a strong argument for believing that the genealogies in Genesis may have been treated in the same manner. We may observe that this supposition, viz. that some links are omitted, will allow a much greater antiquity to the race of man, than may at first appear on the face of the text of Scripture. In fact, if it be correct, the time which it would allow, is almost unlimited.

CHAPTER VI.

1 *The wickedness of the world, which provoked God's wrath, and caused the flood.* 8 *Noah findeth grace.* 14 *The order, form, and end of the ark.*

AND it came to pass, when men
began to multiply on the face of
the earth, and daughters were born
unto them,
2 That the sons of God saw the
daughters of men that they *were* fair;
and they took them wives of all which
they chose.
3 And the LORD said, My spirit

CHAP. VI. 1. *And it came to pass*] The inspired writer has now given us an account of the first rise of sin, of its terrible manifestation in the murder of Abel, of its further

shall not always strive with man, for that he also *is* flesh: yet his days shall be an hundred and twenty years.

developement in the race of the first murderer, and of the separation from the profane of the descendants of the pious Seth. He proceeds in this chapter to assign a reason for the still more universal spread of ungodliness throughout the world, such as to call down from heaven a great general judgment on mankind.

2. *the sons of God saw the daughters of men*] Who were the sons of God? and who the daughters of men?

1. Perhaps the most ancient opinion was that the sons of God were the young men of high rank (as in Ps. lxxxii. 6, "I have said, Ye are gods, and ye are all the sons of the most Highest"), whilst the daughters of men were the maidens of low birth and humble condition; the word for *men* in this passage being a word used at times to signify men of low estate (cp. Isai. ii. 9, v. 15). According to this interpretation the sin lay in the unbridled passions of the higher ranks of society, their corrupting the wives and daughters of their servants and dependants, and the consequent spread of universal licentiousness. This seems to have been the earliest interpretation among the Jews. It is adopted by the Targums of Onkelos and Jonathan, by Symmachus, Abenezra, Rashi, Kimchi, and by some moderns, Selden, Vorstius, and others. The chief objection to this is that there is scarcely proof enough that the name "sons of God" was ever given to men of high rank, or that the word for man (*Adam*) ever meant people of low rank, except when contrasted with another word for man (namely, *Ish*). Compare *vir* and *homo* in Latin.

2. A second interpretation, also of great antiquity, is that the sons of God were the angels, who, moved to envy by the connubial happiness of the human race, took to themselves human bodies, and married the fair daughters of men. This interpretation is supposed to have the support of some ancient MSS. of the LXX. (as mentioned by August. 'De Civ. Dei,' xv. 23). It is argued that St Jude (6, 7) evidently so understood it, as he likens the sin of the angels to the sin of the cities of the plain, "the going after strange flesh." The same is thought to be alluded to in 2 Pet. ii. 4. Philo ('De Gigant.' Vol. I. p. 262); Josephus ('Antiq.' Lib. I. c. 4, § 1): and the most ancient of the Christian fathers, as Justin Martyr, Tatian, Athenagoras, Clement of Alexandria, Tertullian, Cyprian, Lactantius, moved probably by their reading of the LXX. and being ignorant of Hebrew, adopted this interpretation. The Apocryphal Book of Enoch and some of the Jewish writers also expounded it so. The later fathers, Chrysostom, Cyril of Alexandria, and Theodoret, condemn this view as monstrous and profane. The rationalistic interpreters (Gesenius, Rosenmüller, Von Bohlen, Tuch, Knobel, Ewald, Hupfeld, Kalisch, Davidson, &c.) naturally prefer it, as favouring their belief, that the first chapters of Genesis exhibit merely the Hebrew mythology. But it is also adopted by several of the more orthodox German commentators, as Hofmann, Baumgarten, Delitzsch, Kurtz, who contend that some very portentous wickedness and excess of sin must have been the cause of the Deluge; a complete subverting of the whole order of God's creation, so that the essential condition of man's social life was imperilled and overthrown. The chief arguments in favour of this view are (1) that "sons of God" mostly mean angels, see Ps. xxix. 1, lxxxix. 7; Job i. 6, ii. 1, xxxviii. 7; Dan. iii. 25; (2) that the "daughters of men" can only be antithetic to something not human; (3) that the context assigns a monstrous progeny to this unnatural union; (4) that St Jude and St Peter appear to sanction it; (5) that any ordinary promiscuous marriages are not sufficient to account for the judgment of the flood.

3. The third interpretation is that "the sons of God" were the descendants of Seth, who adhered to the worship and service of the true God, and who, according to some interpretations of ch. iv. 26, were from the time of Enos called by the name of the Lord, and that "the daughters of men" were of the race of the ungodly Cain. This was the belief of the eminent Church fathers, Chrysostom, Cyril of Alexandria, Theodoret, Augustine, and Jerome. It was adopted by Luther, Calvin, and most of the reformers, and has been the opinion of a great majority of modern commentators.

4. It was suggested, by Ilgen, that the Cainites were called "sons of the gods" because of their ingenuity and inventions, and that their intermingling themselves with the other races of men caused the general corruption of mankind.

5. The author of 'the Genesis of the earth and of man' suggests that "the sons of the gods" (so he would render it) may mean the worshippers of false gods. These he looks on as a pre-Adamite race, and would render, not "daughters of men," but "daughters of Adam." The pre-Adamite worshippers of the false gods intermarried with the daughters of Adam.

Of these interpretations it appears most probable that the right is a modification of 3. We are not probably justified in saying that there were but two races descended from

4 There were giants in the earth in those days; and also after that, when the sons of God came in unto the daughters of men, and they bare *children* to them, the same *became* mighty men which *were* of old, men of renown.

5 ¶ And God saw that the wicked-

Adam, the race of Cain and the race of Seth. Adam may have had many sons; but the history of the Cainites is preserved because both of their impiety, and of their ingenuity; that of the Sethites, because at least in one line of that race piety and true religion flourished, and of them came the family of Noah which was preserved in the ark. There appears to have been a growing corruption of mankind, more rapid, no doubt, in the family of Cain than in any other race, but still spreading far and wide. The line of the Sethites, traced in ch. v., alone appears to have kept itself pure, the little Church of God, in the midst of gathering darkness of the world around. This little Church may well have been called "the children of God," a term by no means limited in Scripture to the holy angels. They alone were the salt of the earth; and if that salt should lose its savour, all would become worthless and vile. When therefore some of these "sons of God" went out from their own little home circle, to make mixed marriages with the general heathenized races round them, the elements of corruption were brought from the world into the Church, the Church itself became corrupted, and the single family of Noah appears to have been kept pure from that corruption, just as afterwards the family of Lot was the only family in Sodom free from the pollution and depravity of the cities of the plain. The salt had lost its savour. At all events too little was left to purify and to save the world. It could but save the souls of the few righteous that were therein.

Concerning the *giants*, see note on v. 4.

3. *My spirit shall not always strive*] Is rendered, (1) "shall not dwell" by LXX., Vulg., Syr., Onk., Saad., and others. (2) "Shall not judge," or which probably is the same thing, "shall not strive," by Symm., Targg. Joh. and Jerus., Rashi, Kimchi, Luther, Rosenmüller, &c. This is the rendering of the A. V. and is probably correct. (3) "Shall not rule," by De Wette, Rosenmüller, Maurer, Knobel, Delitzsch, &c. (4) "Shall not be humbled," Gesenius, Tuch, &c. No great difference in the general significance of the passage will be produced by adopting a different translation. Kimchi, and some of the German commentators, understand, not that the Holy Ghost shall no longer dwell or strive with man, but that the spiritual principle implanted by God in man shall no longer rule in him, or no longer contend against his animal nature.

for that he also is flesh] The modern interpreters, Gesenius, Vater, Schum, Tuch, render "Because of his error he is become wholly flesh," or, as Rosenmüller, "whilst their flesh causeth them to err." The objection to the reading of the Authorized Version, which is that of all ancient Versions and commentators, is that the particle rendered *that* never occurs in the Pentateuch, but only in the later Psalms and other clearly more modern books of the Old Testament. It is in fact an Aramæan particle. But it must never be forgotten, that Aramaisms are to be expected, either in the most modern, or *in the most ancient portions of Scripture.* There is therefore good reason to adhere to the Authorized Version.

yet his days shall be an hundred and twenty years] Josephus ('Ant.' I. 3, 2) and after him, Tuch, Ewald, Hävernick, Baumgarten, Knobel, Hupfeld, Davidson, &c., suppose that this alludes to the shortening of the term of human life. But all the Targums, Saad., Luther's Version, Rosenm., Hengst., Ranke, Hofmann, Kurtz, Delitzsch, understand "There shall yet be a respite or time for repentance of 120 years, before the threatened vengeance shall overtake them." The normal duration of human life did not, as Delitzsch truly observes, become from this time 120 years, and the whole context shews, that the judgment impending was that of the Flood, and that it was a respite from that, which is here promised, that time might be given for Noah's preaching, and man's repentance. The only argument, that can even appear to have weight against this interpretation is that of Tuch, repeated by Bp. Colenso, viz. that Noah was 500 years old (cp. ch. v. 32) when this saying, "His days shall be 120," is ascribed to the Almighty, and that he was 600 years old (c. vii. 6) when the Flood came. Hence there were but 100 years, not 120 given as a respite. But there is really no ground whatever for asserting that all which is related in ch. vi. took place after Noah was 500 years old. What is said in v. 32 is that Noah was 500 years old, when his three sons were born. The Deluge may have been threatened long before this.

4. *There were giants in the earth in those days, and also after that*, &c.] It is hence argued that by "Sons of God" must be meant angels or fallen angels; from the union of whom with the daughters of man sprang the race of giants. But there is no-

ness of man *was* great in the earth, and
that ‖every imagination of the thoughts
of his *a*heart *was* only evil †continu-
ally.
6 And it repented the LORD that
he had made man on the earth, and
it grieved him at his heart.
7 And the LORD said, I will destroy man whom I have created from
the face of the earth; †both man, and
beast, and the creeping thing, and the
fowls of the air; for it repenteth me
that I have made them.
8 But Noah found grace in the
eyes of the LORD.
9 ¶ These *are* the generations of
Noah: *b*Noah was a just man *and*
‖perfect in his generations, *and* Noah
walked with God.

)r, *the* *hole ima-* *nation.* he Hebrew word gnifieth t only *e imagi-* *ation,* t also *e pur-* *ses and* *sires.* chap. 8. . att. 15. . Heb. *ery day.* Heb. *om man* *to beast.*

Ecclus. . 17. Pet. 2. 5.)r, *right.*

10 And Noah begat three sons,
Shem, Ham, and Japheth.
11 The earth also was corrupt before God, and the earth was filled
with violence.
12 And God looked upon the earth,
and, behold, it was corrupt; for all
flesh had corrupted his way upon the
earth.
13 And God said unto Noah, The
end of all flesh is come before me;
for the earth is filled with violence
through them; and, behold, I will
destroy ‖them with the earth. ‖ Or, *from the earth.*
14 ¶ Make thee an ark of gopher
wood; †rooms shalt thou make in the † Heb. *nests.*
ark, and shalt pitch it within and
without with pitch.
15 And this *is the fashion* which

thing said of a race of giants springing from this union. "In those days were the (well-known) *Nephilim* in the earth" cannot have such a sense, especially when what follows is taken into account, "and also after that, when the sons of God went in unto the daughters of men, and they bore children to them, these became mighty men, men of renown." Evidently the passage shews, that *Nephilim* were on earth before this union, and afterwards also from these marriages sprang men of warlike spirit, who made themselves a name. The result was, as when the Israelites afterwards made marriages with the Midianites, a great and general corruption of manners. The warlike character and perhaps bodily strength of these *Nephilim* is specially noted, as explaining what is said in v. 13, that the earth was filled with *violence.*

Nephilim. The LXX., Vulg., Syr., and Targum render "Giants;" Aq. and Symm. "violent men." Most derive the word from a root signifying to *fall;* and understand "the fallen" (whether men or angels), or, more probably, "those who fall on others," *robbers* or *tyrants.* (Aquila, Rosenm., Gesenius, Kurtz.) Others (among whom Tuch and Knobel) derive from a root signifying *wonder*, and understand *monsters*, *prodigies.* We meet with the name again Num. xiii. 33, as that of one of the Canaanitish tribes, who appear to have been men of large stature, as were the Rephaim, the Anakim and others. This very likely was the reason, why the word came to be rendered "giants," which does not seem to have been its original meaning.

6. *it repented the* LORD] All the language of this portion of Scripture is suited to the infant condition of the world. Hence human sentiments are even more than in the later books of Scripture attributed to the Almighty. No sound criticism would see any appearance of myth in this.

9. *These are the generations of*] See note on ch. ii. 4.

14. *an ark of gopher wood*] The word for *ark* occurs only here and in Exod. ii. 3, 5 of the ark or boat of papyrus or bulrushes. This word might perhaps lead us to suppose that the ark was of the form of a vast chest or coffer, rather than of the form of a ship; fitted to carry a heavy burden, not to sail over the waters; yet the proportions given are those of a ship, though of rather greater width than usual, *see on* v. 15.

gopher wood] It is uncertain what this wood was. The Targumists followed by many Jewish and Christian commentators rendered *Cedar*, others *Juniper* or *Box.* Fuller, Bochart and Celsius suggested *Cypress*, in which they have been followed by most modern commentators. The affinity between the roots *gophar* and *cupar* is great, and cypress is a wood well fitted for ship-building and abounding in the parts of Syria next to Babylon, which many have supposed to be the country inhabited by Noah.

rooms] literally *nests*, different compartments fitted for the habitation of men and animals.

pitch] more probably asphaltos, **bitumen**, which is said to be particularly suited for closing up the interstices of the timbers and making a vessel watertight.

15. *this is the fashion*] The actual form of the ark is not described. The proportions only are given, which are not very

thou shalt make it *of:* The length of
the ark *shall be* three hundred cubits,
the breadth of it fifty cubits, and the
height of it thirty cubits.
16 A window shalt thou make to
the ark, and in a cubit shalt thou
finish it above; and the door of the
ark shalt thou set in the side thereof;
with lower, second, and third *stories*
shalt thou make it.
17 And, behold, I, even I, do bring
a flood of waters upon the earth, to
destroy all flesh, wherein *is* the breath
of life, from under heaven; *and* every
thing that *is* in the earth shall die.
18 But with thee will I establish
my covenant; and thou shalt come
into the ark, thou, and thy sons, and
thy wife, and thy sons' wives with
thee.
19 And of every living thing of all
flesh, two of every *sort* shalt thou

---

different from those of "The Great Eastern." Reckoning the cubit at 21 inches; the proportions would be length 525 ft., breadth 87 ft. 6 in., height 52 ft. 6 in.; those of "The Great Eastern" being length 680, breadth 83, depth 58. (See Smith's 'Dict. of Bible,' Art. *Noah.*) The length of the cubit is doubtful, as there appear to have been 2 or 3 different measures so called. In all probability it means the length from the elbow to the end of the hand, a variable measure, of course, but sufficiently accurate for the purposes of those simple times. It is mentioned by the German commentators that Peter Jansen in 1609 built a vessel of the same proportions as the ark, though smaller, viz. Length 120, width 20, depth 12 ft. It was found most convenient for stowage, containing one-third more freight than ordinary vessels of the same tonnage, though it was unsuited for making way quickly through the water.

John Temporarius quoted by Heidegger ('Historia Sacra,' I. p. 338) made a curious calculation, according to which the ark would have afforded abundant room for all the animals then known, and food for their voyage. Tiele also in his commentary calculates that there was room for 7000 distinct species. (See Kurtz, I. p. 101.)

16. *A window shalt thou make to the ark, and in a cubit shalt thou finish it above*] There is a great variety of interpretation here, some rendering *a window*, others *light*, or *daylight* or a *transparent substance*, others, after the LXX., *an inclined roof*, or *sloping deck*. Much too has been said against the historical truth of a narrative, which could assign but one window of a cubit long to so vast a ship. The interpretation of Gesenius seems evidently the true, viz. that the unusual word translated "window" (the word in ch. viii. 6, is quite another word) means really a set of windows, a window course, a system of lighting: and the use of the feminine gender in the pronoun suggests to the same high authority, that the right rendering would be, "A window system shalt thou make to the ark, and in a cubit shalt thou finish them from above." It is quite possible that it may have been a window course running for a cubit long under the top or deck of the ark, lighting the whole upper story very similar to the clerestory of churches (see Knobel here). The word is translated by Symmachus "*a transparency*." It seems not impossible that some transparent substance was used. This may easily have been known to the Antediluvians, who had made the progress in arts described ch. iv. 21, 22. Perhaps the invention was lost after the Deluge, an event which must have reduced mankind to almost original simplicity and rudeness. It is by no means clear, that these windows were all in the roof or deck. They may have been in the gunwales, *i.e.* on the higher part of the sides of the vessel, like the port-holes of a modern ship of war. And, if they were covered with a transparent substance, it is quite possible that they may not have been confined to the upper story of the ship, as the word "*above*" does not necessarily mean on the upper part of the vessel, but may mean the top of the window course.

the door of the ark] There was naturally but one opening beside the window course, through which all the inhabitants of the ark were to be let into it.

19. *two of every sort shalt thou bring into the ark*] Of course if we will admit nothing out of the ordinary course of nature, we shall be unable to receive the Mosaic history of the Deluge. Yet, even on natural principles, we may in some measure explain Noah's power over the beasts. When a terrible catastrophe is closely impending, there is often a presentiment of it in the brute creation. Under the pressure of great danger or great suffering, the wildest animals will at times become perfectly tame and tractable. Most likely too, Noah and his family would choose pairs of very young animals, just old enough to feed themselves, as being the most tractable and as requiring less room than those full grown.

bring into the ark, to keep *them* alive
with thee; they shall be male and
female.

20 Of fowls after their kind, and
of cattle after their kind, of every
creeping thing of the earth after his
kind, two of every *sort* shall come
unto thee, to keep *them* alive.

21 And take thou unto thee of all
food that is eaten, and thou shalt
gather *it* to thee; and it shall be for
food for thee, and for them.

Heb. 11. 22 [c]Thus did Noah; according to
all that God commanded him, so did he.

CHAPTER VII.

1 Noah, with his family, and the living creatures, enter into the ark. 17 The beginning, increase, and continuance of the flood.

AND the [a]LORD said unto Noah, [a] 2 Pet. 2. 5.
Come thou and all thy house
into the ark; for thee have I seen
righteous before me in this generation.

2 Of every clean beast thou shalt
take to thee by †sevens, the male and † Heb. seven seven
his female: and of beasts that *are* not
clean by two, the male and his female.

3 Of fowls also of the air by sevens,
the male and the female; to keep
seed alive upon the face of all the
earth.

4 For yet seven days, and I will
cause it to rain upon the earth forty
days and forty nights; and every living substance that I have made will I
†destroy from off the face of the earth. † Heb. blot out

If the ark was to hold, not only birds and quadrupeds, but insects and reptiles, possibly eggs or larvæ may have been preserved.

CHAP. VII. 1. *And the* LORD *said unto Noah*] The preceding chapter accounts for a period of 120 years. At the beginning of that period, God had declared His will to destroy mankind by a flood, unless they profited by the time still given them for repentance. Noah is ordered to prepare an ark, the building of which may have occupied the greater part of this season of respite He is told at the very first that he and his sons are to go into the ark, and that a pair of every kind of cattle and fowls and moving things should go in with him and be preserved alive. In the present chapter we reach the end of the 120 years. The ark has been built in the prescribed form with due preparation and capacity. Noah has done according to all that God had commanded him (ch. vi. 22), and now the Lord gives to Noah fuller directions concerning the animals which he was to take with him.

2. *Of every clean beast thou shalt take to thee by sevens, the male and his female*] It is questioned whether there were to be seven or seven pairs of every clean beast. Some think there were to be only seven, the odd number being accounted for by the fact that the clean beasts were preserved for sacrifice, that therefore more of them were needed than of unclean beasts, and the number seven was adopted as a sacred number. The addition of the words "the male and his female" (comp. v. 9), seems to favour the belief that seven pairs are intended. In any case there is no inconsistency between this verse and ch. vi. 20, "two of every sort." The command here is but an amplification of the former injunction, which had probably been given 120 years before. In the first instance it was said that Noah's family should be preserved together with a pair of every kind of beast. In the second, that, whilst the general rule should be the saving of a single pair, yet, in the case of the few clean beasts, there should be preserved, not one pair only but seven. The objection that this was an anticipation of the Levitical distinction of beasts into clean and unclean, is wholly groundless. The boundary line between clean and unclean animals is marked by nature. Every tribe of mankind would distinguish between the sheep and the hyæna, between the dove and the vulture. Whether animal food was eaten before the Deluge or not, it is certain that flocks and herds were fed for the sake of their milk and wool, and that of them victims were offered in sacrifice. This alone would separate between the clean and the unclean. It is not improbable, that the distinction even of the names "clean and unclean" had been fully established by custom, long before it was recognized and ratified by the Law.

3. *Of fowls also of the air by sevens*] In the Samaritan, the LXX. and Syr. this verse runs, "And of all the fowls of the air which are clean by sevens, the male and the female, and of all fowls which are not clean by two, the male and the female, to keep seed alive upon the face of all the earth." This must have been a very ancient reading; but it appears to have arisen from a gloss or commentary having crept into the text. It probably gives the true sense of the passage.

4. *yet seven days*] The 120 years ended and the ark prepared for the saving of his house, Noah is allowed yet seven days more

5 And Noah did according unto all that the LORD commanded him.

6 And Noah *was* six hundred years old when the flood of waters was upon the earth.

7 ¶ And Noah went in, and his sons, and his wife, and his sons' wives with him, into the ark, because of the waters of the flood.

8 Of clean beasts, and of beasts that *are* not clean, and of fowls, and of every thing that creepeth upon the earth,

9 There went in two and two unto Noah into the ark, the male and the female, as God had commanded Noah.

10 And it came to pass ‖ after seven days, that the waters of the flood were upon the earth.

‖ Or, *on the seventh day.*

11 ¶ In the six hundredth year of Noah's life, in the second month, the seventeenth day of the month, the same day were all the fountains of the great deep broken up, and the ‖ windows of heaven were opened.

‖ Or, *floodgates.*

12 And the rain was upon the earth forty days and forty nights.

13 In the selfsame day entered Noah, and Shem, and Ham, and Japheth, the sons of Noah, and Noah's wife, and the three wives of his sons with them, into the ark;

14 They, and every beast after his kind, and all the cattle after their kind, and every creeping thing that creepeth upon the earth after his kind, and every fowl after his kind, every bird of every † sort.

† Heb. *wing.*

15 And they went in unto Noah into the ark, two and two of all flesh, wherein *is* the breath of life.

---

for gathering all safely into the place of refuge before the flood sets in.

9. *two and two*] This again is no contradiction to v. 2. The rule was that all animals, clean or unclean, should go in two and two, that rule was not broken, but amplified, by the direction in verse 2, that of clean animals there should be more than a single pair, viz. seven or seven pairs.

11. *In the six hundredth year of Noah's life, in the second month, the seventeenth day of the month*] The questions concerning the Deluge year are complicated by the uncertainty, 1. whether the year was the old civil year beginning with the month Tisri in the autumn, or the sacred year which from the time of the Exodus was appointed to begin with the month Abib, the Passover month, in the spring: 2. whether the calculation be Lunar or Solar.

As regards the first question, we may notice that the year did not begin from Abib, until the time of the Exodus, and that even then the civil year was reckoned from Tisri. Hence we may naturally conclude, that the year of the Flood began with Tisri, or about the autumnal Equinox. If so, the 17th day of the second month would bring us to the middle of November, the beginning of the wintry and rainy season.

The second question seems at first sight resolved by comparing this verse (vii. 11) with vii. 24 and viii. 4, from which comparison it appears that the flood began on the 17th of the second month, lasted 150 days, i.e. five months of 30 days, and had subsided, so that the ark could rest on Ararat on the 17th of the seventh month. Thus the 17th of the seventh month appears to have been exactly five months of thirty days after the 17th of the second month. This would make the Noachic year a year of 360 days, corresponding with the old Egyptian year, unless any intercalation of five days was made use of. On the presumption that this reckoning is conclusive, it has been argued that the account of the Flood must have been of much later date than Moses, as the Israelites never learned to reckon by solar time till after the Babylonish captivity. It is certain however that the Egyptians used solar time long before the date of the Exodus, which is answer enough to this difficulty.

With regard to the forty days' rain, it seems pretty certain that those were not additional to, but part of, the 150 days of the prevalence of the flood. Supposing the above calculation to be correct, we have the very remarkable coincidences that on the 17th day of Abib the ark rested on Mount Ararat—on the 17th day of Abib the Israelites passed over the Red Sea—on the 17th day of Abib Christ our Lord rose again from the dead.

were all the fountains of the great deep broken up, and the windows of heaven were opened] It cannot be imagined, that this is a philosophical explanation of the flood. The use of Scripture is always to describe the phenomena of nature, not to trace their hidden causes. The words here written express only the effect produced upon man's senses. There was a flood of waters from above and

16 And they that went in, went
in male and female of all flesh, as God
had commanded him: and the LORD
shut him in.
17 And the flood was forty days
upon the earth; and the waters increased, and bare up the ark, and it
was lift up above the earth.
18 And the waters prevailed, and
were increased greatly upon the earth;
and the ark went upon the face of
the waters.
19 And the waters prevailed exceedingly upon the earth; and all the
high hills, that *were* under the whole
heaven, were covered.
20 Fifteen cubits upward did the
waters prevail; and the mountains
were covered.
21 [b]And all flesh died that moved
upon the earth, both of fowl, and of
cattle, and of beast, and of every creeping thing that creepeth upon the earth,
and every man:
22 All in whose nostrils *was* †the
breath of life, of all that *was* in the
dry *land*, died.
23 And every living substance was
destroyed which was upon the face of
the ground, both man, and cattle, and
the creeping things, and the fowl of
the heaven; and they were destroyed
from the earth: and [c]Noah only remained *alive*, and they that *were* with
him in the ark.
24 And the waters prevailed upon
the earth an hundred and fifty days.

[b] Wisd. 10. 4.

† Heb. *the breath of the spirit of life.*

[c] Wisd. 10. 4. 2 Pet. 2. 5.

CHAPTER VIII.

1 The waters asswage. 4 The ark resteth on Ararat. 7 The raven and the dove. 15 Noah, being commanded, 18 goeth forth of the ark. 20 He buildeth an altar, and offereth sacrifice, 21 which God accepteth, and promiseth to curse the earth no more.

AND God remembered Noah, and
every living thing, and all the
cattle that *was* with him in the ark:
and God made a wind to pass over
the earth, and the waters asswaged;
2 The fountains also of the deep
and the windows of heaven were
stopped, and the rain from heaven
was restrained;
3 And the waters returned from off
the earth †continually: and after the
end of the hundred and fifty days
the waters were abated.
4 And the ark rested in the seventh
month, on the seventeenth day of the
month, upon the mountains of Ararat.

† Heb. *in going and returning.*

---

from beneath. The clouds poured down rain, and the seas and rivers swelled and burst their boundaries; so that to one who witnessed it it seemed as though "the fountains of the great deep were broken up, and the windows of heaven were opened."

16. *and the* LORD *shut him in*] By some providential or supernatural agency the door of the ark, which could not have been secured with pitch or bitumen by Noah, was secured and made water-tight.

17, 18, 19. In these verses the frequent repetition of the same thought in almost the same words has been supposed by Astruc and others to evidence the work of different hands. Repetition, however, is universal in a simple state of society, wherever great strength of expression is aimed at. Even in late Hebrew such repetition is familiar, but in early Hebrew it meets us at every turn.

20. *Fifteen cubits upward*] *i. e.* from 25 to 28 feet: a depth apparently above the neighbouring mountains, perhaps depressed by convulsion, or otherwise. See note on the Deluge at the end of the eighth chapter.

CHAP. VIII. 1. *God remembered Noah*] As it is said, 1 Sam. xv. 11, "It repenteth Me that I have anointed Saul to be king," *i.e.* I have decreed to put another in his place, and above (Gen. vi. 7), "It repenteth Me that I have made man," *i.e.* I have determined to destroy man; so here "The Lord remembered Noah" does not point to a previous forgetfulness, but to God's great mercy towards him (Theodoret).

2. *The fountains*, &c.] The clouds were dispersed by a wind, the waters no longer increased, and the effect was, as though, after the forty days of rain and flood, the fountains of the deep and the windows of heaven were closed.

4. *Ararat*] The belief that this is the mountain-range now commonly called Mount Ararat, the highest peak of which rises nearly 17,000 feet above the level of the sea, rests on a very uncertain foundation. Far more probable is the opinion that Ararat was the ancient name of Armenia itself, or, rather, of the Southern portion of Armenia. The name occurs only here, and in 2 Kings xix. 37; Is. xxxvii. 38, where it is mentioned as the place

† Heb. *were in going and decreasing.*

5 And the waters †decreased continually until the tenth month: in the
tenth *month*, on the first *day* of the
month, were the tops of the mountains
seen.
6 ¶ And it came to pass at the end
of forty days, that Noah opened the
window of the ark which he had
made:
7 And he sent forth a raven, which
went forth †to and fro, until the waters
were dried up from off the earth.

† Heb. *in going forth and returning.*

8 Also he sent forth a dove
from him, to see if the waters were
abated from off the face of the
ground;
9 But the dove found no rest for
the sole of her foot, and she returned
unto him into the ark, for the waters
were on the face of the whole earth:
then he put forth his hand, and took
her, and †pulled her in unto him into
the ark.
10 And he stayed yet other seven

† Heb. *caused her to come.*

---

to which the sons of Sennacherib fled, after the murder of their father. Most of the ancient VSS. render the word by *Armenia* (Aq., Symm., Theod., Vulg., and in Kings and Isaiah the LXX., though in Gen. the LXX. leave it untranslated). The Targums render Kardu or Kardon, probably meaning Kurdistan, or the Gordyæan mountains, which run to the South of Armenia, dividing the valley of the Tigris from Iran, on, or near to which mountains, in the Chaldæan tradition of the Deluge preserved by Berosus, Xisuthrus is said to have landed. Jerome ('on Isai.' xxxvii.) tells us, that "Ararat is a champaign country of incredible fertility, situated in Armenia, at the base of Mount Taurus, through which flows the river Araxes." Moses, Archbishop of Chorene, A.D. 460, the famous historian of Armenia, also tells us that Ararat was a region, not a mountain. A Mohammedan tradition has no doubt placed the site of the ark's resting on the top of the highest ridge of the mountain, called anciently Macis, by the Persians Coh Noah; and this has been thought to correspond with what is related by Nicolaus of Damascus, that there was a mountain in Armenia called Baris, to which people escaped in the general Deluge, and on which a vessel struck, parts of which long remained (Joseph. 'Ant.' I. 4). All this, however, is somewhat vague. We can only say with certainty that, so long as the time when the LXX. VS. was made, Ararat was believed to correspond with, or to constitute a part of Armenia. Moreover, general belief has pointed to the neighbourhood of Armenia as the original dwelling-place of the first fathers of mankind.

Yet the claims, not only of the central mountain peak, but even of any portion of Armenia, to be the site of Noah's landing-place, have been disputed by many. In Gen. xi. 2 the migration of the sons of Noah towards Shinar is said to be "from the East." If so, it could not have been from Armenia. It is, however, most probable that the right rendering should be, as in Gen. ii. 8, xiii. 11, not "from the East" but "eastward," and such is the marginal rendering of the A.V. which though not supported by the VSS. is accordant with other Hebrew idioms (see Quarry, 'Gen.' p. 397). Another objection to Armenia is found in the statement of Strabo (lib. XI. p. 527), that the vine does not grow there (cp. Gen. ix. 20). Accordingly Hardouin contends that Ararat could not have been in Armenia, but is to be sought for in the North of Palestine, where it borders on Antilibanus and Syria ('De Situ Parad. terres.' in Franzii, Edit. Plin. 'Nat. Hist.' Tom. X. pp. 259, 260). Yet the 10,000 are said to have found old wine in Armenia (Xen. 'Anab.' 4. 4, 9); and vines are said at this day to grow in the highlands of Armenia, at a level of 4000 feet above the sea. (See Ritter, quoted by Knobel, on ch. IX. 20.) Von Bohlen, arguing from Gen. xi. 2 that Ararat lay eastward of Shinar, identifies it with Aryavarta, the sacred land to the North of India, to which the Hindoo tradition points. The Samaritan VS. places it in the Island of Ceylon. Though on such a question certainty is impossible, the arguments in favour of Armenia are very strong.

6. *the window*] or *opening*, from a verb meaning *to perforate* or *open*. This is quite a different word from that used vi. 16. The A.V. would suggest the idea, that Noah was commanded (vi. 16) to make a window, and that now he opened that window; whereas the original expresses the fact, that Noah was commanded to make a window-course, or light system, and that now he opens the window, or casement, in the ark, which he had made on purpose to open.

7. *went forth to and fro*] It has been supposed that there were carcases of men and beasts floating on the waters, that from them the raven found a place to light upon, and also food; and hence, though it returned from time to time and rested on the ark, it never again sought an entrance into it.

8. *a dove*] Noah, finding no sufficient indication from the raven, now sends forth the dove, a bird which rests only on dry places and feeds only on grain.

days; and again he sent forth the
dove out of the ark;

11 And the dove came in to him
in the evening; and, lo, in her mouth
was an olive leaf pluckt off: so Noah
knew that the waters were abated
from off the earth.

12 And he stayed yet other seven
days; and sent forth the dove; which
returned not again unto him any more.

13 ¶ And it came to pass in the
six hundredth and first year, in the
first *month*, the first *day* of the month,
the waters were dried up from off the
earth: and Noah removed the covering of the ark, and looked, and, behold, the face of the ground was dry.

14 And in the second month, on
the seven and twentieth day of the
month, was the earth dried.

15 ¶ And God spake unto Noah,
saying,

16 Go forth of the ark, thou, and
thy wife, and thy sons, and thy sons'
wives with thee.

17 Bring forth with thee every
living thing that *is* with thee, of all
flesh, *both* of fowl, and of cattle, and
of every creeping thing that creepeth
upon the earth; that they may breed
abundantly in the earth, and be
fruitful, and multiply upon the
earth.

18 And Noah went forth, and his
sons, and his wife, and his sons' wives
with him:

19 Every beast, every creeping
thing, and every fowl, *and* whatsoever creepeth upon the earth, after
their †kinds, went forth out of the † Heb. *families.*
ark.

20 ¶ And Noah builded an altar
unto the LORD; and took of every
clean beast, and of every clean fowl,

---

11. *an olive leaf*] Theophr. 'Hist. Plant.' L. IV. c. 8, and Pliny, 'Hist. Nat.' L. XIII. c. 25, are cited as saying that the olive grew under water in the Red Sea, and bore berries there. Whether this be so or not, it is probable that the olive may live more healthily under a flood than most other trees. It is eminently hardy, and will grow in a favourable soil without care or culture. The following passage illustrates the extraordinary powers of adaptation to circumstances possessed by some plants. "The formation of sprouts gives the plant the means of attaching itself to the most varied conditions, of persisting through periods of continued cold and heat, damp or drought, according as the climate may produce, and guarding against death in all cases of frustrated seed-development...... Thus *Littorella lacustris*, which never flowers under water, maintains and increases itself by lateral runners, year after year, at the bottom of the lakes of the Black Forest, and only comes into flower when the water retreats in the driest years, which scarcely occur oftener than once in ten" (A. Braun, 'Rejuvenescence in Nature,' p. 41, 42, Ray Society). The olive (Olea Europea) is generally a plant of the Mediterranean: other species occur at the Cape of Good Hope, the Himalaya mountains, and elsewhere.

pluckt off] rather, as Vulg., **fresh.**

20. *every clean beast*] Probably not every beast which was afterwards permitted to the Israelites for food, but those which were esteemed clean for sacrifice; viz. oxen, sheep and goats, doves and pigeons. Some of the German commentators see in the account of this sacrifice a late interpolation, derived from the Mosaic or Levitical customs of sacrifice. Delitzsch justly observes that in most of the traditions of the Deluge, external to the Israelites, as the Phœnician, Indian, Greek, &c., a sacrifice forms part of the legend. The pretence, therefore, that in the Biblical narrative this was an afterthought of a Jehovist interpolater must be gratuitous.

21. *a sweet savour*] Lit. "the savour of satisfaction or delectation," the word *Nichoach*, "satisfaction," having a reference to *Noach*, "rest." Cp. like expressions in Lev. ii. 12, xxvi. 31; Ezek. vi. 13, xx. 41. The gratitude of Noah, and his faith as manifested by the sacrifice, were acceptable to God.

for the imagination of man's heart is evil from his youth] In ch. vi. 5, it is written that God's anger was moved, "because every imagination of the thoughts of his heart was only evil continually." Here, on the contrary it is said, that "the Lord said in His heart, I will not curse the ground any more for man's sake, for the imagination of his heart is evil from his youth." The Germans discover an inconsistency between the words of the Elohist in vi. 5, and those of the Jehovist here. Some have endeavoured to reconcile these passages by translating "although" instead of "for." The true solution is, that in the first instance (ch. vi. 5) the actual sinfulness of man, the constant tendency of every imagination of his thoughts to evil, is represented as moving the anger of God, and tend-

and offered burnt offerings on the
altar.
21 And the LORD smelled †a sweet
savour; and the LORD said in his
heart, I will not again curse the
ground any more for man's sake;
for the [a] imagination of man's heart
is evil from his youth; neither will I
again smite any more every thing living,
as I have done.
22 †While the earth remaineth,
seedtime and harvest, and cold and
heat, and summer and winter, and
day and night shall not cease.

† Heb. *a savour of rest.*

[a] chap. 6. 5. Matt. 15. 19.

† Heb. *as yet all the days of the earth.*

---

ing to man's destruction; but in the present instance (ch. viii. 21) the Lord is described as considering the feebleness of his nature, and pitying that natural propensity to evil, which every man inherits at his birth.

The word in the original for *imagination*, is the word which the Rabbins used to express that desire of evil, which results from original sin (Buxt. 'Lex. Chald.' p. 973; Ges. 'Thes.' p. 619). Accordingly in ch. vi. we see God's righteous indignation against the hardened, impenitent, unbelieving sinner. Here, on the contrary, we read of the Lord's compassionate kindness to His feeble and erring creatures, and how He is moved not to curse, but to pity and to bless those who turn to Him with penitent hearts, and faith in that great Sacrifice, of which Noah's offering was a type and a prophecy.

22. *seedtime and harvest*] The Deluge had confounded earth and sea. There reigned as it were one long winter, almost one unbroken night, over the whole world. But thenceforth the Lord decreed, that seasons should follow in their course, the season of sowing and the season of reaping, the cold and the heat, the summer and the winter, the day and the night.

NOTE A on CHAP. VIII. THE DELUGE.

1. Was it historical? (*α*) Traditions among all races of men. (*β*) Explicable only on the supposition of historical foundation. 2. Was it universal? (*a*) How to judge of the narrative. (*β*) Universal probably to mankind. (*γ*) Geological difficulties. (*δ*) Rationale of Deluge.

Two great questions concerning the Flood of Noah naturally present themselves: 1. Is the account of it historical or mythical? 2. Was the Deluge partial or universal?

1. Many of the Germans, and according to Davidson "all good critics" have abandoned the historical character of the narrative. The physical difficulties are supposed to be insuperable. The whole therefore is said to be "mythical, embodying the old Hebrew belief in the retributive character of sin" (Davidson, 'Introd. to O. T.' Vol. I. p. 187). How then, it may be asked, does it happen, that so many nations retained a recollection of the same great event? The races of mankind have been divided by modern Ethnologists into Semitic, Aryan (Iranian or Indo-European) and Turanian. It will be found, that in all these races there are traditions of a flood, which destroyed all mankind except one family. The Semitic account is to be found in the Bible and in the Chaldæan tradition, which is the nearest to that of the Bible, and which comes down to us in the fragments of Berosus preserved by Josephus and Eusebius. According to that tradition, Sisuthrus or Xisuthrus being warned of a flood by the god Cronus, built a vessel and took into it his relatives and near friends, and all kinds of birds and quadrupeds. The vessel was five stadia in length and two in breadth. When the flood had abated, he sent out birds, which first of all returned to him, but, after the second trial, returned no more. Judging then that the flood was abated, he took out some of the planks of the vessel, and found that it had stranded on the side of a mountain. Whereupon he and all his left the ship, and offered sacrifice to the gods. The place of landing was in Armenia; where part of the vessel still remained, from which the people of the country scraped off the bitumen and made amulets (see Cory's 'Ancient Fragm.' pp. 22, 29, 1st Edition). Of the Aryan traditions, first, the Greek is to be found in the well known classical legend of the floods of Ogyges and Deucalion. Pindar ('Ol.' IX. 37), first mentions the flood of Deucalion. The account is given at length by Ovid; by whom the reason assigned is the general prevalence of violence and wickedness ('Metam.' I. 240, &c.). Apollodorus (Lib. I.) ascribes the deluge of Deucalion to the determination of Jupiter to destroy the men of the brazen age. And Lucian ('De Syra Dea') speaks of it as having destroyed the whole human race. The Persian tradition may be that embodied in the Koran, though there probably incorporated with the Scriptural narrative. The Hindoo tradition represents Manu as warned by a great fish to build a ship, that he might be preserved during an impending deluge. The ship was saved by being lashed on to the horn of the fish, and was ultimately landed on a northern mountain. (See the tradition at length, Hardwick, 'Christ and other Masters,'

p. ii. ch. III. § 3.) The Phrygian story of Annakos (supposed to be Enoch) who foretold the Deluge, is singularly confirmed by a medal struck at Apamea (called Apamea Kibotus, i.e. Apamea, the Ark) in the reign of Septimius Severus, on which is depicted an ark or chest floating on the waters. Two people are seen within it and two going out of it. On the top of the ark a bird perches, and another flies towards it with a branch between its feet, on the vessel; in some specimens of this coin, are the letters ΝΩ. It can hardly be doubted, however, that this coin, and the tradition connected with it, come somewhat directly from Hebrew sources. The third division of the Human Race, the Turanian, has also everywhere traditions of the Deluge. In China, Fa-he, the reputed founder of Chinese civilization, is represented as escaping from the waters of a deluge, and he reappears as the first man at the production of a renovated world, attended by his wife, three sons and three daughters (Hardwick, Part III. p. 16). The inhabitants of the Polynesian Islands, who are probably of Malay origin, especially the Figi islanders, have distinct accounts of a deluge, in which a family, eight in number, was saved in a canoe (Hardwick, III. 185). Similar traditions prevailed throughout the continent of America, the aboriginal inhabitants of which are now generally believed to be all of one stock, and by their physical and linguistic peculiarities are by the greatest ethnologists identified with the Turanian races of Asia. (See Bunsen, 'Philos. of Univ. Hist.' Vol. II. p. 112.) In Central America, the inhabitants of Mexico had paintings representing the Deluge, a man and his wife in a bark or on a raft, a mountain rising above the waters, and birds, the dove, the vulture, &c. taking part in the scene. In North America, the Cherokee Indians had a legend of all men destroyed by a deluge, except one family saved in a boat, to the building of which they had been incited by a mysterious dog, which recalls the Indian fable of the friendly fish (see Hardwick, Part III. pp. 161—164).

Thus among the more civilized countries of Europe, and in well nigh every portion of Asia and America, in every different race of mankind, we find traditionary accounts of this great catastrophe, and of the miraculous deliverance of a single family. The mythical interpreters insist, that every nation had its mythic age, its mythic traditions, and that as we discover the same myth of a deluge in all other nations, we naturally conclude that the Hebrew narrative is in like manner mythical. But how can it be explained, that in all parts of the world, people have stumbled on the same myth? What is there, apart from tradition, that so commends the fable of a Deluge and of the saving of one household to the imagination and invention of mankind? The existence of cosmogonies, more or less alike, may be easily conceived of. But, that in all parts of the world, among races the most remote and dissimilar, there should prevail a belief, that, after man was created on the earth, all men but one family, were destroyed by a Deluge, is intelligible only on the supposition, that some such event actually did occur; an event simply, graphically and accurately related in the Book of Genesis, but variously distorted and disguised in the legends of the heathen world. An universal belief, not springing directly from some instinctive principle in our nature, can with reason only be ascribed to tradition of an historical fact. The only other explanation suggested is utterly impossible, viz. that in many parts of the world among the more civilized and the most barbarous alike, remains of marine animals found beneath the Earth's surface had suggested the same belief, viz. that there must have been an universal Flood. Even supposing this possible, how does this account for the similarity of the tradition not generally only, but in minute particulars in the remotest parts of the inhabited world?

2. The second question, Was the Deluge Universal? has long divided those who believe that it was historically true, and that it is correctly related by Moses. The most literal interpretation of the language, especially of the words, Gen. vii. 19, "all the high hills that were under the whole heaven, were covered," would lead to the conviction that it must have been universal. Yet it is certain, that many, who accept implicitly the historical truth of the narrative, believe the inundation to have been partial. Of such we may distinguish two classes of writers, 1st those who think that all the then living race of man was destroyed; but that those regions of the earth not then inhabited by man were unaffected by the Flood: 2nd, those who believe that the Flood swept away only that portion of mankind with which the Sacred narrative is chiefly concerned; and which had become corrupted and vitiated by the promiscuous marriages mentioned in ch. vi. 1, 2.

In order to place ourselves in a fair position for judging of these questions, it may be well to consider the nature of the narrative, and the common use of language among the Hebrews. And if we do so carefully, we shall surely be led to conclude, that the Deluge is described as from the point of view of an eye-witness. It has been so much our wont to look on all the early portions of Genesis as a direct revelation from God to Moses, that we rather consider the picture to be drawn, if we may speak so, as from the point of view of the Omnipotent. Yet, even if we are right in esteeming all as a simply direct revelation, it may be, that the revelation was given in prophetic vision, and that Moses wrote, not merely what he had heard, but also, and rather, what he had seen. But we may remember too, that the custom of Scripture is to refer historical records to the evidence of eye-witnesses. This is very much the case in the New Testament. The Apostles and Evangelists constantly claim to have been present at the scenes which they relate (see especially Luke i. 1, 2; Joh. xix. 35, xxi. 24; Acts i. 3; 1 Cor. xv. 3—8; 2 Pet. i. 16; 1 Joh. i. 1); and they relate them as those scenes appeared to them. The baptism of Jesus, the transfiguration, the walking on the waters, the multiplying the loaves and fishes, the Crucifixion, the Resurrection, the Ascension, the tongues of fire at Pentecost, are all simply painted as they who were present saw and conceived of them. And this is equally true in the Old Testament. Take for instance the much debated miracle of the sun and the moon standing still at the command of Joshua. The phenomenon is related just as the contending armies witnessed it. It is not referred to its natural causes, whatever they may have been. That merely is related which actually appeared. At Joshua's command, and of course by Divine intervention, the Sun and the Moon, which would naturally have seemed to describe an arc in the heavens and to descend into the west, then, on the contrary, seemed to stand still in the midst of heaven. Now just so is the Deluge described in Genesis. It is pictured, as it would have presented itself to the eyes of Noah and his family. Moreover, on the principle just mentioned, it is in the highest degree probable, that the description is really that which was given by one of such eye-witnesses. It would have been very strange if no such description had been given and preserved. Shem would almost certainly have related it, over and over again, to his children and grand-children. They would have treasured it up in their memories and have handed it on. As has been so notoriously the case among later nations (see Max Müller's 'Sans. Lit.' p. 500) the very words of the original narrative would be carefully recorded from father to son, whether in writing or by oral tradition; and so, in all probability, we have in Genesis the very syllables in which the Patriarch Shem described to the ancestors of Abraham that which he himself had seen, and in which he had borne so great part. The Divine authority of the narrative would be no more affected by this, than the authority of the Gospel of St Mark is affected by the probable fact that St Mark relates that which St Peter communicated to him as the result of his own ocular and aural experience. Let us then view it thus. One of the eight human beings saved in the ark relates all that he saw. He mentions first God's warning to Noah and denunciation of judgment on mankind. He describes the building and the proportions of the ark. He narrates the 40 days of rain and the swelling of the rivers and of the ocean, in the words which most forcibly describe that great catastrophe (Gen. vii. 11). He then describes how the waters prevailed, till the ark was raised up and floated over them (v. 18). At length, not only did the ark float, but the highest hills disappeared (v. 19); nothing was visible under the whole vault of heaven, but sea and air. The very words are "All the high hills under the whole heaven were covered." Where the ark was at this time, or where Noah and his family had been dwelling before, we cannot tell. The country may have been mountainous, and so, in order to hide the hills from view, the waters must have been very deep, or it may have been a plain country, as many think the region round about Babylon, with few hills in sight and those not of great altitude; in which case but a moderate depth of water would have sufficed to cover all the highest hills under the whole canopy of heaven. The inhabitants of the ark probably tried the depth of the Deluge by a plumb line, an invention surely not unknown to those who had acquired the arts of working in brass and iron (ch. iv. 22), and they found a depth of 15 cubits. Then all flesh, all that was on the dry land, died. And, as the gathering of the waters is thus described, so in ch. viii. the subsidence is given in the same simple graphic style. At length, on a specified day, the ark rests. It is found that it had stranded near to some of the hills in a generally plain country, perhaps to the south of Armenia, perhaps in the north of Palestine, perhaps somewhere in Persia, or in India or elsewhere. The waters continually decrease, it may be the vapours also clear off; and at length the summits of the surrounding hills become visible, though the plain country still is flooded. Noah then sends out the Raven. It goes to and fro, but returns no more to the ark. No account is given of its wanderings; what appears to Noah and his family is all that we learn. So too of the Dove. It goes forth and, finding no rest, comes back again. Once more it is sent out. Whither it goes no one can tell, all that appears is, that it has found dry land. It brings back an olive leaf in its beak; and Noah judges that the waters were abated. From first to last the description is just that which Shem or Noah would have given of all that he had himself seen.

If this be the true explanation of the narrative, we may then more readily see how the question of the universality of the Deluge stands. The words used may certainly mean that the Deluge was universal, that it overwhelmed, not only all the inhabited parts of Asia, but also Europe, Africa, and America, Australia, New Zealand, and Oceanica; most, if not all, of which Islands and Continents were probably then without human inhabitants. Yet, if only the inhabited world was inundated, and all its inhabitants destroyed; the effect would have been the same to Noah, and would, most likely, have been described in the same words. The purpose of God was to sweep away the sinful race of Adam That purpose would have been effected by a Deluge, which covered the whole of that portion of the globe, which may be called the cradle of the human race. The words of the narrative are perhaps no stronger than would have been naturally used to describe such a catastrophe. The most striking is the passage, "All the high hills under the whole heaven," ch. vii. 19. But this is no more than such expressions as, "I begin to put the dread of thee upon the nations that are under the whole heaven," Deut. ii. 25: "all countries came into Egypt to Joseph to buy corn," Gen. xli. 57: "as the Lord thy God liveth, there is no nation or kingdom whither my lord hath not sent to seek thee, &c.," 1 Kings xviii. 10. When the ancients speak of the whole world, they mean at most the whole world as known to the ancients. When they speak of the whole heaven, they mean the whole visible canopy or expanse of the sky; and so, when they speak of the earth, the land, the dry ground, they mean at times very limited portions indeed of the earth's surface. The strictest interpretation of the record, according to the habit of speech among Semitic nations, will allow us to understand that a Deluge prevailed, extensive enough to destroy all the living race of man, and to cover with water the whole visible face of nature. It is another question, whether we may admit, that any portion of the human race, except the eight persons miraculously preserved, can have escaped. Some suppose the descendants of Cain to have peopled China, and not to have been involved in the Deluge, which, in their belief, was sent on purpose to destroy those apostate and degenerate Sethites, who had defiled the chosen race by intermarrying with unbelievers. Others think that the Nephilim of Numb. xiii. 33 were descendants of the Nephilim of Gen. vi. 4, who must therefore have survived the Deluge. Others again, as the authors of 'The Genesis of the Earth and Man,' and of 'Adam and the Adamites,' suppose that there was a pre-Adamite race of men, and that the history in Genesis relates only the fortunes of the Adamites, having no reference to the rest. Without pronouncing too hastily on any fair inference from the words of Scripture, we may reasonably say, that their most natural interpretation is, that the whole race of man had become grievously corrupted, since the faithful had intermingled with the ungodly; that the inhabited world was consequently filled with violence, and that God had decreed to destroy all mankind, except one single family; that therefore all that portion of the earth, perhaps as yet a very small portion, into which mankind had spread, was overwhelmed by water. The ark was ordained to save the one faithful family; and lest that family, on the subsidence of the waters, should find the whole country round them a desert, a pair of all the beasts of the land and of the fowls of the air were preserved along with them, and along with them went forth to replenish the now desolated continent. The words of Scripture (confirmed as they are by an universal tradition), appear, at least, to mean as much as this. They do not necessarily mean more.

The geological objections to the history of the Deluge are chiefly such as the discovery of loose scoriæ on the tops of the extinct volcanoes of Auvergne and Languedoc, the impossibility of the waters extending to the height of 15 cubits above the mountains, and the permanent distribution of the animal kingdom over the different parts of the world.

It is said the loose scoriæ on the mountains of Auvergne and Languedoc must have been swept away by an universal flood. It is, however, quite conceivable, even if the Deluge extended to those regions and to the tops of those hills, that the gradual rise and subsidence of the waters may have left there remains of volcanic action, which are not so light as has been asserted, almost untouched. The difficulty in conceiving of the waters rising 15 cubits above the highest mountains is a difficulty in the mind of the objector, not in the text of Scripture, which nowhere speaks of such a rise. (See the earlier part of this note.) The possibility of vegetation surviving has been considered in the note on ch. viii. 11. The most serious difficulty in conceiving of a Flood universal (not only to the world inhabited by man, but to the whole surface of the globe) is in the history of the distribution of the animal kingdom. For example, the animals now living in South America and in New Zealand are of the same type as the fossil animals which lived and died there before the creation of man. Is it conceivable that all should have been gathered together from their original habitats into the ark of Noah and have been afterwards redistributed to their respective homes? The difficulty, however, vanishes entirely, if the sacred narrative relates only a submersion of the human race and of its then dwelling-place, a sense of that narrative, which exact criticism shews to be possible, perhaps even the most probable, irrespective of all questions of natural science. The cavils against the single window, the proportions of the ark, &c. have been considered in their respective places. The peculiar unfairness of the objections urged is to be found, not so much in the objections themselves, as in the insisting at the same time on an interpretation of the Scripture narrative, on principles which would not be applied to any other history whatever. Not only are we required to expound ancient and Eastern phraseology with the cold exactness applicable only to the tongues of Northern Europe, but moreover to adhere to all the interpretations of past uncritical ages, to believe that there was but a single window in the ark, that the ark stranded on the top of a mountain, within sight of which it very probably never sailed, that the waters of the Flood rose three, or even five miles above the sea level, and other prodigies, which the sacred text, even in its most natural significance, nowhere either asserts or implies.

If it be inquired, why it pleased God to save man and beast in a huge vessel, instead of leaving them a refuge on high hills or in some other sanctuary, we perhaps inquire in vain. Yet surely we can see, that the great moral lesson and the great spiritual truths exhibited in the Deluge and the ark were well worth a signal departure from the common course of nature and Providence. The judgment was far more marked, the deliverance far more manifestly Divine, than they would have been, if hills or trees or caves had been the shelter provided for those to be saved. The great prophetic forepicturing of salvation from a flood of sin by Christ and in the Church of Christ would have lost all its beauty and symmetry, if mere earthly refuges had been sufficient for deliverance. As it is, the history of Noah, next after the history of Christ, is that which perhaps most forcibly arrests our thoughts, impresses our consciences and yet revives our hopes. It was a judgment signally executed at the time. It is a lesson deeply instructive for all time.

CHAPTER IX.

1 *God blesseth Noah.* 4 *Blood and murder are forbidden.* 8 *God's covenant,* 13 *signified by the rainbow.* 18 *Noah replenisheth the world,* 20 *planteth a vineyard,* 21 *is drunken, and mocked of his son,* 25 *curseth Canaan,* 26 *blesseth Shem,* 27 *prayeth for Japheth,* 29 *and dieth.*

AND God blessed Noah and his
sons, and said unto them, [a]Be [a] Chap. i. 28 & 2. 17.
fruitful, and multiply, and replenish
the earth.

2 And the fear of you and the
dread of you shall be upon every beast
of the earth, and upon every fowl of
the air, upon all that moveth *upon* the
earth, and upon all the fishes of the
sea; into your hand are they delivered.

3 Every moving thing that liveth
shall be meat for you; even as the
[b]green herb have I given you all [b] chap. i. 29.
things.

CHAP. IX. 1. *And God blessed Noah,* &c.] Noah, now become the second head of the human family, receives a blessing, the former part of which is but a repetition of the blessing first pronounced on Adam, ch. i. 28. The sin of man had frustrated the intent of the first blessing. The earth had been filled with licentiousness and violence, fatal to the increase of mankind, and at length bringing down a judgment, which swept all but one family away. Now all begins anew; and God repeats the promise of fecundity, which sin had made of none effect.

2. *the fear of you and the dread of you*] The small remnant of mankind just rescued from the Deluge might have perished from the attacks of wild beasts, which had probably been young and tame in the ark, but were now adult or adolescent and returning to their own wild natures. The assurance given in this verse was therefore a very needful comfort to Noah and his family.

3. *Every moving thing that liveth shall be meat for you*] In the primal blessing (ch. i. 28, 29, 30) there had been mention of man's supremacy and power over the inferior animals. It has been a question whether there had been a permission of animal food or not. The almost universal opinion of the ancients was that only vegetable food was then permitted; and if we remember that most probably the early race of men lived in a warm and genial climate, and that even now some of the Eastern nations are contented and healthy upon a vegetable diet, we shall be the more disposed to acquiesce in an interpretation which seems to do less violence to the text. It cannot, however, be said that there was from the first a *prohibition* of animal food. From very early times we find sheep and cattle kept at least for milk and wool, and slain for sacrifice, ch. iv. 2, 20. Whether then it had been conceded or not from the first; it is likely that those who fed and sacrificed sheep, like Abel, who kept cattle, like Jabal, or who handled instruments of bronze and iron, like Tubal Cain, would in the course of time have learned the use of animal food. If so, we may consider the words of this verse as a concession to the infirmities or the necessities of mankind, coupled with restrictions,

Lev. 17. 4 [c]But flesh with the life thereof,
4. *which is* the blood thereof, shall ye
not eat.
5 And surely your blood of your
lives will I require; at the hand of
every beast will I require it, and at
the hand of man; at the hand of
every man's brother will I require the
Matt. 26. life of man.
2. 6 [d]Whoso sheddeth man's blood,
Lev. 13. by man shall his blood be shed: [e]for
5. chap. 1. 7. in the image of God made he man.
7 And you, be ye fruitful, and
multiply; bring forth abundantly in
the earth, and multiply therein.
8 ¶ And God spake unto Noah,
and to his sons with him, saying,
9 And I, behold, I establish my
covenant with you, and with your
seed after you;
10 And with every living creature
that *is* with you, of the fowl, of
the cattle, and of every beast of the
earth with you; from all that go

---

which may have been called for by the savage practices of the Antediluvians.

4. *flesh with the life thereof*] Rashi and some other Jewish commentators understand a prohibition of the practice of eating flesh cut from the living animal, and so Luther translated, "the flesh which yet lives in its blood." The monstrous wickedness of the Antediluvians, by which the earth was filled with violence, may have taken this form among others; and these words without doubt condemn by implication all such fiendish cruelty. They prohibit also the revolting custom of eating raw flesh; for civilization is ever to be a handmaid to religion. But over and above all this, there is reference to that shedding of blood, or pouring out of life, which formed so great a part of typical sacrifice, and which had its full significance in that pouring out of the soul unto death, which won for man the resurrection to eternal life. We need not look for any scientific explanation of the connection between life and blood here, or in the subsequent legal enactments (*e.g.* Lev. iii. 17, vii. 26, xvii. 10; 1 Sam. xiv. 32; Ez. xxxiii. 25). The ancients no doubt generally believed the blood to be the seat of the life; but it is also literally true, that the shedding of blood is equivalent to the destruction of life; and so in these early injunctions the God of mercy taught the value not only of human, but of all animal being, and along with the forbidding of manslaughter forbade wanton cruelty and indifference to the sufferings of His brute creatures.

5. *And surely your blood of your lives will I require*, &c.] There have been many proposed translations of this verse. The A.V., which accords with the most important ancient versions, no doubt gives the true meaning. "The blood of your lives" probably signifies "your life blood." Under the law the ox that gored was to be killed (Ex. xxi. 28), which seems a comment on this passage. In Ps. ix. 12 God is said to be the requirer of blood, a phrase identical with that made use of here.

6. *Whoso sheddeth man's blood*] Here the manner in which God will require the blood of the murdered man is specified. There shall be a legal retribution, life for life.

for in the image of God made he man] The slaughter of brute animals was permitted, though wanton cruelty towards them was forbidden; but man was made in the image of God, and to destroy man's life has in it the sin of sacrilege. Moreover, the image of God implies the existence of a personal, moral, and therefore, in the creature, a responsible will. Though the holiness, which was part of the likeness, was lost in the fall, still the personality and the moral being remained. To destroy the life of such an one is therefore to cut short his time of probation, to abridge his day of grace, to step in between him and his moral Governor, to frustrate, as far as may be, God's purposes of love and mercy to his soul. Hence the sin of murder is the greatest wrong which man can do to his brother man; perhaps also the greatest insult which man can offer to Him who is the loving Father of all men. The Jews held that there were seven precepts given to Noah, which were binding on all mankind, to be observed by proselytes of the gate and by pious Gentiles, viz. abstinence from murder, from eating the flesh of living animals, from blasphemy, idolatry, incest, theft, and the submission to constituted authority; the first two and the last are expressly enjoined in the words recorded in this chapter, the other four result from the dictates of natural religion.

9. *I establish my covenant with you, and with your seed after you*] A new covenant is now made with all the human beings rescued from the flood, and through them even with the beasts of the field, that there should not again be a flood to destroy all flesh. This, perhaps, more than any other part of the history, seems to prove that the Deluge extended at least to the destruction of all the then living race of man.

10. *from all that go out of the ark, to every beast of the earth*] An idiomatic ex-

out of the ark, to every beast of the earth.

f Isai. 54. 9.

11 And f I will establish my covenant with you; neither shall all flesh be cut off any more by the waters of a flood; neither shall there any more be a flood to destroy the earth.

12 And God said, This *is* the token of the covenant which I make between me and you and every living creature that *is* with you, for perpetual generations:

13 I do set my bow in the cloud, and it shall be for a token of a covenant between me and the earth.

g Ecclus. 43. 11, 12.

14 g And it shall come to pass, when I bring a cloud over the earth, that the bow shall be seen in the cloud:

15 And I will remember my covenant, which *is* between me and you and every living creature of all flesh; and the waters shall no more become a flood to destroy all flesh.

16 And the bow shall be in the cloud; and I will look upon it, that I may remember the everlasting covenant between God and every living creature of all flesh that *is* upon the earth.

17 And God said unto Noah, This *is* the token of the covenant, which I have established between me and all flesh that *is* upon the earth.

18 ¶ And the sons of Noah, that went forth of the ark, were Shem, and Ham, and Japheth: and Ham *is* the father of † Canaan.

† Heb. *Chenaan.*

19 These *are* the three sons of Noah: and of them was the whole earth overspread.

20 And Noah began *to be* an husbandman, and he planted a vineyard:

21 And he drank of the wine, and was drunken; and he was uncovered within his tent.

---

pression, signifying that the covenant shall extend not only to those that go out of the ark, but also to every beast of the earth. Not only those preserved in the ark, but all other animals are to be interested in this promise. From which we can hardly fail to infer that the destruction of the lower animals was confined to a certain district, and not general throughout the earth.

13. *I do set my bow in the cloud*] Lit. I have set My bow. The covenant was an universal covenant; the sign of the covenant was therefore to be one visible to all nations, and intelligible to all minds. It appears at first sight as if the words of the sacred record implied that this was the first rainbow ever seen on earth. But it would be doing no violence to the text to believe, that the rainbow had been already a familiar sight, but that it was newly constituted the sign or token of a Covenant, just as afterwards the familiar rite of baptism and the customary use of bread and wine were by our Blessed Lord ordained to be the tokens and pledges of the New Covenant in Christ between His Heavenly Father and every Christian soul.

20. *Noah began to be an husbandman*] Husbandry had been much used before the flood; but now there was a new condition of the earth, and all was, as it were, begun again. As an incursion of barbarians has often swept away the civilization of a whole region or continent, so the flood had reduced mankind almost to the simplicity of the days of Adam. Still, without doubt, many of the inventions of the antediluvian race would have been preserved by the family of Noah; and probably among the rest the cultivation of the vine.

21. *he drank of the wine*] Many have supposed that Noah was the discoverer of the art of making wine, and even that he was the great planter of the vine. So they have palliated his fault by ascribing it to ignorance of the effects of wine. It is hardly probable that, with all the difficulties of his new position, Noah should have invented fermentation. More likely is it, that the ingenious and intemperate descendants of Cain had long before discovered it. Noah may have been but little used to strong drink, and hence may not have known that it would so soon overcome him; yet we may well follow the wisdom of Calvin, and say, "Leaving all this in uncertainty, let us learn from Noah's intemperance how foul and detestable a vice drunkenness is." The Holy Scriptures never conceal the sins even of God's greatest saints, and the sins of saints are sure to meet with chastisement. Noah's piety is plainly recorded. It is also plainly recorded that he fell into sin, whether partly of ignorance or wholly of infirmity; that sin brought with it shame, and, as is so often found, was the occasion of sin to others, and led on to consequences disastrous to the descendants of all those who

22 And Ham, the father of Canaan,
saw the nakedness of his father, and
told his two brethren without.
23 And Shem and Japheth took a
garment, and laid *it* upon both their
shoulders, and went backward, and
covered the nakedness of their father;
and their faces *were* backward, and
they saw not their father's nakedness.

24 And Noah awoke from his wine,
and knew what his younger son had
done unto him.
25 And he said, Cursed *be* Canaan;
a servant of servants shall he be unto
his brethren.
26 And he said, Blessed *be* the
LORD God of Shem; and Canaan
shall be ‖ his servant.
27 God shall ‖ enlarge Japheth, and

‖ Or, *servant to them.*
‖ Or, *persuade.*

in any degree shared in the guilt of it. Noah sinned, Ham sinned, perhaps, too, Canaan sinned. So there was a heritage of sorrow to the descendants of Noah in the line of Ham, to the descendants of Ham in the line of Canaan.

22. *Ham, the father of Canaan*] The great difficulty in this history is that Ham appears to have sinned, and Canaan is cursed. Some see in this simply the visiting of the sins of the fathers on their children. But then why only on one of those children? A propriety has been discovered in the curse on Canaan, as he was Ham's youngest son, just as Ham was the youngest son of Noah. Yet this is all gratuitous and without authority from the text of Scripture. It has been thought, once more, that Noah's prophecy extended to all the posterity of Ham, but that only that portion which affected Canaan was preserved by Moses, in order to animate the Israelites in their wars against the Canaanites; others again have conjectured, that in the prophecy of Noah, instead of "cursed be Canaan," we ought to read, "cursed be Ham the father of Canaan," but such conjectures, without authority of MSS. are quite inadmissible. The extreme brevity of the narrative renders it impossible to explain it fully. Nothing is said, save only that Ham saw his father naked, and then told his brethren. We are even left to infer that he told this scoffingly; but for the curse that follows, we might suppose that he had only consulted them as to how best to conceal their father's shame. Something therefore there plainly is, which requires to be supplied in order fully to clear up the obscurity. Yet this cannot now be discovered. Conjecture only is possible.

Origen mentions as a tradition among the Jews, that Canaan first saw the shame of his grandfather and told it to his father. In that case, it may have been that the chief sin lay with Canaan, and hence that he especially inherited the curse. Many commentators have adopted this opinion, and it would certainly solve most of the difficulty.

24. *His younger son*] Ham is always named second among the sons of Noah; but it has sometimes been thought, that Japheth was the eldest and Ham the youngest, the order being changed for the sake of putting first Shem, who was the progenitor of the chosen seed. Yet many writers of great authority, both Jewish and Christian, understand by the term here used, "his younger (lit. little) son," not his son Ham, but his grandson Canaan. (So Levi Ben Gerson, Abenezra, Theodoret, Procopius, Joseph Scaliger, &c.). This would correspond with the tradition mentioned by Origen (see last note), that the sin of Ham was shared by Canaan, or perhaps that Canaan was the guilty person, his father only not having condemned, but rather joined in his wickedness.

25. *Cursed be Canaan*, &c.] In the patriarchal ages, when there was no regular order of priests or prophets, the head of the family was the priest, and these blessings and curses spake they not of themselves, but being high priests they prophesied. Yet we can hardly fail to see also in these histories a lesson, that a parent's blessing is to be valued, a parent's curse to be dreaded.

26. *Blessed be the* LORD *God of Shem*] The prophecy here assumes the form of a thanksgiving to God, from whom all holy desires and good counsels come, and who had put into the heart of Shem to act piously. At the same time, it is clearly implied, that the Lord, JEHOVAH, should be very specially the God of Shem, which was fulfilled in the selection of the descendants of Abraham to be the peculiar people of God.

Canaan shall be his servant] Noah foretells the subjugation of the land of Canaan by the people of Israel, when the Canaanites should become servants of the descendants of Shem.

27. *God shall enlarge Japheth*] There is a paronomasia on the name Japheth, which probably signifies "enlarged." The Hebrew word "shall enlarge" is, neglecting the vowel points, letter for letter the same as the word Japheth. The prophecy looked forward to the wide territory which was assigned to the descendants of Japheth, reaching from India and Persia in the East to the remotest boun-

he shall dwell in the tents of Shem; and Canaan shall be his servant.

28 ¶ And Noah lived after the flood three hundred and fifty years.

29 And all the days of Noah were nine hundred and fifty years: and he died.

CHAPTER X.

1 The generations of Noah. 2 The sons of Japheth. 6 The sons of Ham. 8 Nimrod the first monarch. 21 The sons of Shem.

NOW these *are* the generations of the sons of Noah, Shem,

---

daries of Europe in the West, and now spreading over America and Australia.

and he shall dwell in the tents of Shem] (1) The Targum of Onkelos, Philo, Theodoret and some other interpreters, Jewish and Christian, understood He *i.e.* God, shall dwell among the descendants of Shem." (2) Many more, (*e.g.* Calvin, Bochart, Rosenm., Tuch, Del., Reinke, Keil), following the Targum of the Pseudo-Jonathan, consider Japheth to be the subject of the proposition. Jonathan's paraphrase is "The sons of Japheth shall be proselyted and dwell in the schools of Shem," and the majority of Christian interpreters understood the prophecy to be similar to that in Isai. lx. 3, 5, "Gentiles shall come to thy light, and kings to the brightness of thy rising ...the abundance of the sea shall be converted unto thee, the forces of the Gentiles shall come unto thee." Nearly all those nations whose history and language shew them to be Japhetic have been converted to a belief in the religion of the God of Shem, which has long been the religion of all Europe, and which is now making way even among the Aryan races of Asia. (3) It has been suggested by some, though with little ground of probability, that instead of "tents of Shem," we should render "tents of renown," the tabernacles of Japheth being spoken of as famous and illustrious. Of the three interpretations, (2) may be pronounced somewhat confidently to be the true. By that the continuity of the whole prophecy is preserved. The first part, v. 25, refers only to the descendants of Ham and Canaan. The second is the blessing on Shem, with a repetition of the condemnation of Canaan. The third is the blessing on Japheth, concluding also with the condemnation of Canaan.

The prophecy then embraces the following particulars: 1. That the world should be divided among the descendants of Noah, but that Japheth should have the largest portion for his inheritance. 2. That the descendants of Shem should preserve the knowledge of the true God, and be specially chosen to be His inheritance and His peculiar people. 3. That the descendants of Japheth should ultimately dwell in the tents of Shem, that is, according to Jewish interpretation, should learn from the descendants of Shem the knowledge of the true God. 4. That Canaan, and perhaps other Hamitic nations, should be depressed and reduced to a condition of servitude.

How fully all these predictions have been carried out in the history of Asia, Europe and Africa, hardly need be said.

28. *And Noah lived*, &c.] These two verses seem the natural conclusion of ch. v. but are disjoined from it in order to insert the history of the life of Noah.

CHAP. X. 1. *Now these are the generations*] From the history of Noah the sacred narrative proceeds to the genealogy of the sons of Noah. It is admitted on all hands that there exists no more interesting record, ethnological and geographical, independently of its Scriptural authority.

The genealogy traces the origin of all nations from a single pair. The human race descended from Adam had been destroyed by the flood, with the exception of Noah and his family. Though it is quite possible to interpret the language of the sacred narrative consistently with the belief that the Deluge was not universal, it at least appears most probable that the man-inhabited world was submerged. And again, although some have contended that the different races of man are so dissimilar, that they must have descended from different primitive stocks; yet the inquiries of naturalists and physiologists at present tend rather to diminish than to increase the number of distinct species, both in the animal and the vegetable world, and so to make it even the more certain that human beings constitute but one species deducible from a single pair. The same anatomical structure, especially of the skull and brain, the same intellectual capacities, though differently developed in different nations, the same general duration of life, the same liability to disease, the same average temperature of the body, the same normal frequency of the pulse, the fruitful intermarriage of all races, and that with no instinctive natural repugnances, are manifest indications of an unity of species (Del.). From the time of Blumenbach (whose book 'De naturæ generis humani unitate' is still a standard work on this subject) down to the present day, the most eminent physiologists agree in considering these and similar arguments well nigh conclusive in favour of the unity of the human race. (Consult especially Prichard, 'Phys. Hist. of Mankind;' Smyth, 'Unity of Human Race;' Quatrefages, 'L'unité de l'espèce humaine,' and his report on 'Anthropologie'). To these physiological considera-

Ham, and Japheth: and unto them
were sons born after the flood.
1 Chron. 5. 2 [a]The sons of Japheth; Gomer,
and Magog, and Madai, and Javan,
and Tubal, and Meshech, and Tiras.

---

tions we may now add the evidence to be derived from human language. "It was a profound saying of William Humboldt, that man is man only by means of speech, but that in order to invent speech, he must be man already" (Lyell, 'Antiquity of Man,' 468). This alone is an argument for the unity of that race which is distinguished from all other animals by the possession of articulate language. But, moreover, the greatest philologists of the present day seem to be approaching the conclusion that the evidence of comparative grammar, so far as it goes, is in favour of the original unity of human language. "One of the grandest results of modern comparative philology has been to shew that all languages belonging to one common stock—and we may say, enlarging this view, all languages of the earth—are but scattered indications of that primitive state of human intellect, and more particularly of the imitative faculty, under the higher excitement of poetical inspiration, in which the language originated, and with which every language remains connected, as well through the physiological unity of the human race, as through the historical unity of the family to which it more especially belongs" (Meyer ap. Bunsen, 'Christianity and Mankind,' Vol. III. p. 163). So writes Dr Meyer: and Prof. Max Müller says, "These two points Comparative Philology has gained. (1) Nothing necessitates the admission of different independent beginnings for the material elements of the Turanian, Semitic, and Aryan branches of speech: nay, it is possible even now to point out radicals, which, under various changes and disguises, have been current in these three branches ever since their first separation. (2) Nothing necessitates the admission of different beginnings for the formal elements of the Turanian, Semitic, and Aryan branches of speech; and though it is impossible to derive the Aryan system of grammar from the Semitic, or the Semitic from the Turanian, we can perfectly understand how, either through individual influences, or by the wear and tear of grammar in its own continuous working, the different systems of grammar of Asia and Europe may have been produced" (Max Müller, *Ibid.* pp. 479, 480). Once more, although it may not be possible simply to assign all Semitic tongues to the descendants of Shem, Aryan to the descendants of Japhet, and Turanian to the descendants of Ham; it is still observable that comparative philology seems to have reduced all languages to three distinct stocks, even the rapid degeneracy of barbarian dialects not wholly obscuring their relationship to one of these three families. This is the more to be noticed, when we learn that in savage tribes those who speak the same dialect will sometimes, by separation and estrangement, become in the course of a single generation unintelligible to each other.

Certain rules are to be observed for the clearing up of some difficulties in the genealogy of this chapter. 1. Though some notice may be taken of the progenitors of all nations, yet naturally those families, more or less connected with the Hebrews, are the longest dwelt upon. 2. Whereas all are said to have settled and dispersed themselves "after their families in their nations," it will appear that only the larger division by *nations* is traced in the case of more remote peoples, whereas those related to or bordering on the Hebrews are traced both according to the wider division of *nations*, and the narrower of *families*. 3. Although the first division of the earth is spoken of as made in the time of Peleg, and some families may be traced no farther than up to the time of such division, yet the developement of those more specially treated of is brought down to the time of Moses. 4. For none, however, must we seek a very remote settlement, as the original dispersion could not have extended so far. 5. In some cases the names of nations or tribes appear to be substituted for the names of individuals, such as the Jebusite, the Hivite, the Arkite &c., very probably also such as Kittim, Dodanim, Mizraim &c.; and even perhaps Aram, Canaan and the like. This may be accounted for in more than one way. The purpose of the sacred writer was to trace nations and families, rather than to give a history of individuals, and he therefore speaks of nations known by name to the Israelites as begotten by (*i.e.* descended from) certain patriarchs, in preference to tracing their descent through unknown individuals. Perhaps too individual patriarchs and progenitors had become known by tradition to posterity, not by their own original names, but by the name of the place they had settled in, or by the name of the tribe which they had founded and ruled. The origin of names is often very obscure, and it has been common in most rude societies for persons to be called after places or properties. It is quite possible that even the very earliest patriarchs, as, Shem, Ham and Japheth, Canaan and the like, may have been known in after ages by names which adhered to them through events in their history or places where they had fixed themselves. Thus Shem may have been the man of *name*, the most renowned of Noah's sons, Ham, the

3 And the sons of Gomer; Ash- kenaz, and Riphath, and Togarmah.

man who settled in the *warm regions* of Africa, Japheth the father of the *fair* people of Europe, or perhaps the man whose descendants *spread abroad* more widely than the rest. Canaan again may have been the dweller in *low* lands, while *Aram* may have derived a title from having chosen the *high* lands for his home. This theory, if true, would not interfere with the historical character of this Chapter; especially if we consider that Hebrew may not have been the primitive tongue, in which case all these names must either have been translations of the original names, or names by which the bearers had become known to posterity. We have many examples in Scripture of persons changing their names or adopting new names from events in their history, *e.g.* Abram changing into Abraham; Esau to Edom; Jacob to Israel; Saul to Paul, &c., &c. The whole number of families noticed in this chapter amounts to 70; but it is to be observed that in some cases the descent is traced only to the grandsons, in other cases to the great grandsons of Noah: in the family of Shem only, the ancestor of the Hebrews, the descent is traced through six generations.

2. *Japheth*] It is doubtful whether Japheth was the eldest or the second son of Noah, see in v. 21. He is generally mentioned last in order, Shem, Ham and Japheth, but from ix. 24, it is generally inferred that Ham was the youngest. In this genealogy he occurs first, the reason being probably this; Shem is reserved to the last that his descent may be traced to a greater length, and Ham last but one, because his descendants were those most closely connected with the descendants of Shem. The etymology of the name Japheth should seem from ix. 27 to be from the root *Pathah, to extend.* But the language in ix. 27, may be only an example of the paronomasia so common in Hebrew poetry; and Gesenius, Knobel and others prefer to derive from *Yaphah, to be fair*, from the fair complexion of Japheth and his descendants.

Gomer] Josephus ('Ant.' I. 7) says that Gomer was the ancestor of those whom the Greeks called Galatians, who were formerly called Gomarites. The descendants of Gomer have accordingly been generally identified with the Celtic race called in the time of Homer Cimmerii, who are first known as inhabiting the Chersonesus Taurica, which still retains the name *Crimea.* (See Herod. IV. 12, 45. Æsch. 'Prom.' V. 729.) The relation of Gomer to Magog and Madai corresponds with the original juxtaposition of the Cimmerians to the Scythians and Medes, the Cimmerians dwelling first on the confines of Asia and Europe. Being driven thence by the Scythians in the reign of Cyaxares, they made an irruption into Asia Minor, from which they were driven back again by Alyattes. Their name, which then nearly disappears in Asia, is recognized again in the Cimbri, who occupied the Cimbrian Chersonesus and other parts of the North of Europe, and in the great Celtic tribe of Cymry, the ancient inhabitants of Britain and the present inhabitants of Wales.

Magog] The statement of Josephus ('Ant.' I. 6), that the descendants of Magog were the Scythians is generally accepted as true. In Ezek. xxxviii. 2, 14; xxxix. 2. 6, we find Magog as the name of a people inhabiting "the sides of the North" closely connected with Meshech, the Moschi, and Tubal, the Tibarenes, with a prince named Gog, having horses and armed with bows, which corresponds with the local position and military habits of the Scythians. The Scythians, according to their own traditions, lived first in Asia near the river Araxes, afterwards they possessed the whole country to the ocean and the lake Mæotis, and the rest of the plain to the river Tanais (Diod. Sic. II. 3). Herodotus (I. 103—106) relates their descent upon Media, and Egypt, till they were surprised and cut off at a feast by Cyaxares. From their intermixture with the Medes, the Sarmatians appear to have arisen, and from them the Russians. See Knobel.

Madai] The Medes were called *Mada* by themselves, as appears from the arrow-headed inscriptions, changed in the Semitic to Madai, and by the Greeks to Medoi. They dwelt to the S. and S. W. of the Caspian, and coming over to Europe in small parties mingled with the Scythians, whence sprang the Sarmatians.

Javan] From Javan was "Ionia and the whole Hellenic people" (Jos. 'Ant.' i. 6). Cp. Is. lxvi. 19, Ezek. xxvii. 13, Daniel viii. 21, where Alexander is called king of Javan; Joel iii. 6, where "the sons of the Javanites" are put for the Grecians (υἷες Ἀχαίων), Zech. ix. 13. Greece is called *Ionia* in Egyptian hieroglyphics and Yuna in a Cuneiform inscription at Persepolis (Gesen. s.v.). The Ionians were the most Eastern of the Hellenic races, and so were the best known to the Asiatics. The course of migration had evidently been from Ionia to Attica and other parts of Greece.

Tubal, and Meshech] These names constantly occur together; see Ezek. xxvii. 13, xxxii. 26, xxxviii. 2, 3, xxxix. 1; where we find them joined with the invading army of Gog and Magog, and going with Javan to Tyre to purchase slaves and vessels of brass. Meshech is by Josephus said to be the father

4 And the sons of Javan; Elishah, and Tarshish, Kittim, and Dodanim.

of the Cappadocians, who had, he tells us, a city called Mazacha, and to Tubal he traces the Iberians who dwelt between the Euxine and the Caspian. Later writers have long identified Meshech with the Moschi, inhabitants of the Moschian mountains between Armenia, Iberia and Colchis. Bochart was the first to identify Tubal with the Tibareni, who dwelt on the Southern shore of the Euxine towards the East and near to the Moschi. Knobel considers the Tibareni to be connected with the Iberians: Tubal = Tibar = Iber.

Tiras] Josephus identifies the descendants of Tiras with the Thracians. So Jerome, the Targums, and most modern commentators. The Getæ and Daci, north of the Danube, belonged to the Thracian stock. According to Grimm and some other authorities, the Getæ were the ancestors of the Goths, which would immediately connect the Thracian and Teutonic races together. The chief reason, however, for considering Tiras the ancestor of the Thracians seems to be the similarity of the names. Accordingly other resemblances have been found. Tuch for instance is in favour of the Tyrseni or Tyrrheni.

3. *the sons of Gomer; Ashkenaz*] There is little to guide us to the identification of Ashkenaz, except the name and the mention of Ashkenaz Jer. li. 27 in company with Ararat and Minni, which makes it probable that the descendants of Ashkenaz dwelt near the Euxine and the Caspian. Bochart suggests Phrygia, where were the lake and river Ascanius. The Rabbi Saadias says the Slavi. Targ. of Jonathan gives Adiabene. Some have discovered a resemblance of sound in *Scandinavia*, and also to *Saxon*. The modern Jews called Germany Ashkenaz; and Knobel considers this to be the true interpretation of the name; though etymologically he finds in it the race of Asa or the Asiatics, Ash-genos. These Asa or Asiatics he thinks, dwelt in Asia Minor (comp. *Ascania*), and after the Trojan war migrated towards Pannonia and thence towards the Rhine. The Scandinavians traced their origin to Asia, and called the home of their gods Asgard. It has been conjectured by Bochart and others, that the Black sea was called the sea of Ashkenaz, which sounded to the Greeks like Axenos, their original name for it, and which by an euphemism they changed to Euxeinos.

Riphath] Josephus says Paphlagonia, in which he is followed by Bochart, Le Clerc, &c. Most modern commentators compare the Riphæan mountains, which the ancient geographers (Strab. VII. 3, § 1. Plin. 'H. N.' IV. 12. Mela, I. 19, &c.) place in the remote North. Mela (II. 2) places them East of the Tanais. Knobel conjectures that the Celts or Gauls were the descendants of Riphath, and that they first lived near the Carpathians, which he identifies with the Montes Riphæi.

Togarmah] Mentioned again Ez. xxvii. 14, xxxviii. 6. Josephus identifies with the Phrygians, Bochart with the Cappadocians. Michaelis, and after him most moderns, prefer the Armenians; so Rosenm., Gesen., Winer, Knobel, &c. The Armenians themselves traced their origin to Haic the son of Thogoreu or Thorgau (Mos. Choren. I. 4, § 9). Ezekiel (xxvii. 14) attributes to Togarmah great traffic in horses; and Strabo (XI. 13, § 9) speaks of the Armenians as famous for breeding horses. Modern philologists consider the Armenian as an Aryan or Indo-European language, which corresponds with the descent from Japheth.

4. *And the sons of Javan; Elishah*] Ezekiel (xxvii. 7) mentions the isles of Elishah as those whence the Tyrians obtained their purple and scarlet. Some of the Targums identify with Hellas, in which they are followed by Michaelis, Rosenm., and others. Josephus ('Ant.' I. 6) identifies with the Æolians, which is the view adopted by Knobel. Bochart preferred the Peloponnesus, which was famous for its purple dye, and of which the most important district was called *Elis*. Whichever view he adopted, there is little doubt that the descendants of Elishah in the time of Ezekiel were a maritime people of the Grecian stock.

Tarshish] By Josephus identified with Tarsus in Cilicia; by the LXX. (Is. xxiii. 1, &c.), Theodoret, and others, with Carthage; by Eusebius, who is followed by Bochart and most moderns, with Tartessus in Spain. Tarshish, from the various notices of it, appears to have been a seaport town towards the West (cp. Ps. lxxii.; Is. lx. 9); whither the Phœnicians were wont to traffic in large ships, "ships of Tarshish" (see 1 K. x. 22, xxii. 48; Ps. xlviii. 7; Is. ii. 16, xxiii. 1, 14, lx. 9) sailing from the port of Joppa (Jon. i. 3, iv. 2). It was a most wealthy and flourishing mart, whence came silver, iron, tin, and lead (Ps. lxxii. 10; Is. lxvi. 19; Jer. x. 9; Ezek. xxvii. 12, 25). The name Tartessus is identical with Tarshish, the *t* being constantly substituted by the Syriac for the Hebrew sibilant (cp. Bashan = Batanæa, Zor = Tyre, &c.). The Spanish were among the most famous of the Phœnician colonies, and were specially rich in metal (Diod. Sic. V. 35—38; Arrian. II. 16; Plin. 'H. N.' III. 3; Mela, II. 6, &c.); of which colonies Tartessus was the most illustrious. It appears to have been situated at the mouth of the Guadalquiver (Strabo, III. p. 148). Two passages in Chronicles (2 Chron. ix. 21, xx. 36) seem irre-

5 By these were the isles of the Gentiles divided in their lands; every one after his tongue, after their families, in their nations.

6 ¶ [b] And the sons of Ham; Cush, and Mizraim, and Phut, and Canaan.
7 And the sons of Cush; Seba, and Havilah, and Sabtah, and Raamah,

b 1 Chron. 1. 8.

concilable with this, and induced St Jerome ('in Jerem.' x. 9), and after him Bochart and others, to suppose that there must have been another Tarshish in the Indian Ocean, which could be approached by the Red Sea, an opinion now generally rejected. Knobel supposes that the original inhabitants of Tarshish were the Tusci, Tyrsenians, or Tyrrhenians, a Pelasgic, though not Hellenic race, inhabiting great part of Italy, Corsica, and Sardinia, and that very probably Tartessus in Spain was a colony or offshoot from these people.

Kittim (or *Chittim*)] Identified by Josephus with Cyprus, in which we meet with the town of Cittium; by Eusebius, and after him by Bochart, with the inhabitants of the part of Italy contiguous to Rome. In 1 Maccab. i. 1 Alexander is said to come from Chittim, and (1 Macc. viii. 5) Perseus is called King of the Kitiæans, which induced Michaelis and others to suppose the Chittim to be the Macedonians. Most modern interpreters seem to acquiesce in the opinion of Josephus, that Cyprus (see Is. xxiii 1, 12) may have been a chief seat of the Chittim, but add that probably their colonies extended to the isles of the Eastern Mediterranean (see Jer. ii. 10; Ezek. xxvii. 6). So Gesen., Knobel, Delitz., Kalisch.

Dodanim] has been compared with Dodona in Epirus. By Kalisch it is identified with the Daunians. Gesenius suspects Dodanim to be equivalent (perhaps by contraction) with Dardanim = Dardani or Trojans, an opinion which he confirms by the authority of the Bereschit Rabba on this verse. Knobel conjectures that we have traces of Dodanim both in Dodona (a name which he says prevailed through Illyricum and Northern Greece) and also in Dardania and the Dardans. There is another reading in 1 Chr. i. 7, and here also (Gen. x. 4) in the Gr. and Samaritan, viz. Rodanim, Rhodii, the people of Rhodes.

5. *isles of the Gentiles*] The word here rendered *Isle* very probably meaning originally "habitable region" (Is. xlii. 15), is generally used either of islands or of places on the sea coast. On the whole of this verse see Jos. Mede, Bk. 1. 'Disc.' XLIX. L. By the phrase "Isles of the Gentiles" were understood those countries of Europe and Asia Minor to which the inhabitants of Egypt and Palestine had access only by sea.

6. *Ham*] It is generally thought that the name means warm, which is to be compared with the Greek Aithiops (Ethiopian), which has a similar significance. The word *Kem*, the Egyptian name for Egypt, probably the same word as Ham, signifies *blackness*, with perhaps some notion of heat (see Plutarch, 'De Iside et Osiride,' § 33). The blackness is now generally admitted to refer to the soil, denoting its colour and fertility. (See Excursus.) In Ps. lxxviii. 51, cv. 23, cvi. 22, Egypt is called the land of Ham, which seems to confirm the belief that Kem (in Greek Chemia) is the same as Ham. The descendants of Ham appear to have colonized Babylonia, Southern Arabia, Egypt, Ethiopia, and other portions of Africa.

Much has been written of late about the Hamitic languages. The frequent mixture of the Hamites with the descendants of Shem makes it very difficult to discern clearly between their tongues. Bunsen considers Chamitism to be the most ancient form of Semitism, in fact Semitism, before the Hamites and Shemites thoroughly parted off from each other and from their primeval dwelling-place. The ancient Egyptian has a Semitic base with Turanian (negro) infusion, but the Hamitic races have so frequently been conquered, morally and physically, by the descendants of Shem and Japheth, that their original languages have been lost or corrupted by the prevalence of Semitism or Aryanism.

Cush] The name Cush is generally translated Ethiopia. The Ethiopians at the time of Josephus were called Chusæi, Cushites, and that is still the Syriac name for the Abyssinians. There is, however, good reason to believe, with Bochart, and others, that the first home of the Cushites was Chuzistan and the adjoining parts of Southern Asia, from whence they spread in different directions, a main body having crossed the sea and settled in Ethiopia.

Certainly some of those, who are here mentioned (*e.g.* Raamah, Sheba, Dedan, vv. 7, 8) as the descendants of Cush, established colonies in Asia. Some passages in the Old Testament seem to require that we should place Cush in Asia, as Gen. ii. 13; so also Exod. ii. 16, 21, compared with Num. xii. 1; in the latter of which Zipporah is called a Cushite, whilst in the former she is said to be a daughter of the priest of Midian. This connects Cush with Midian, which was in Arabia Felix, near the Red Sea. Again, in Hab. iii. 7 Cush and Midian appear to be connected. In Job xxviii. 19 we read of "the topaz of Cush." Now, there is no reason to suppose that Ethiopia produced topazes, but Pliny (XXXVII. 8) speaks of an island of Arabia in the Red Sea as famous for this

and Sabtechah: and the sons of Raamah; Sheba, and Dedan.

8 And Cush begat Nimrod: he began to be a mighty one in the earth.

---

gem, which is also noted by Diodorus (III. 39). All this connects Cush with Asia, and seems to prove that the first settlement of the Cushites was in Asia. Their subsequent emigration into Africa, so that one division was on the East and the other on the West of the Gulf of Arabia, may account for the language of Homer, who speaks of the Æthiopians as divided into two distinct tribes ('Od.' I. 23), a distinction observed by Strabo ('Geogr.' I. p. 21), by Pliny (lib. v. c. 8), and by Pomponius Mela (lib. I. cap. 2).

Mizraim] is undoubtedly Egypt. The origin and meaning of the word has been much debated, but with no certain conclusion. If the singular be the Hebrew Mazor, it should signify a *mound* or *fortified place*. Gesenius and others prefer the Arabic Meser, *a limit* or *boundary*. The dual form has been supposed to indicate Upper and Lower Egypt. It perhaps may be the rendering or transcription of Mes-ra-n "children of Ra," i.e. of the Sun. The Egyptians claimed to be sons of Ra. (See Excursus.) It certainly seems as if the name belonged rather to a race or nation than to a man; and, therefore, the son of Ham here named is probably designated as the founder or ancestor of the Egyptians or people of Mizraim.

Phut] The name *Phut* occurs several times in the Old Testament, and generally in connection with the Egyptians and Ethiopians, sometimes with Persia and Lud. See Jer. xlvi. 9; Ezek. xxvii. 10, xxx. 5, xxxviii. 5; Nah. iii. 9. The LXX. in Jeremiah and Ezekiel always render *Libyans*. So Josephus says ('Ant.' I. 6), that Phut colonized Libya, and that the people were from him called Phutites. The Coptic name of Libya is Phaiat ⲫⲁⲓⲁⲧ. St Jerome speaks of a river of Mauritania, and the region round it, as called Phut to his time. ('Tradit. Hebr.')

Canaan] The name is thought by some to be derived from the nature of the country in which the descendants of Canaan lived, viz. a flat, depressed region, from the Hebrew root *Cana* (hiph.) to depress. The fact, that the Canaanites appear to have spoken a Semitic tongue has been alleged as a reason why they should not have been of Hamitic descent. Knobel has well observed, however, that they are said by the ancients to have removed from the Red Sea to the Mediterranean, with which agrees the mythology which brought into relation the Phœnicians' ancestors Agenor and Phœnix sometimes with Belus and Babylonia, sometimes with Ægyptus and Danaus (the Æthiop), Cepheus and Libya. In the earliest days the Hamites and Shemites were near neighbours; there may have sprung from them a mixed race, which spread toward Tyre and Sidon and dispossessed, partly also intermingled with, a Semitic race originally inhabiting the region of Palestine and Phœnicia. As Abraham and his descendants appear to have changed their native Aramean for the Hebrew of Palestine, so very probably the Hamitic Canaanites, long mingled with Shemitic races, acquired the language of the children of Shem. The whole character of the Canaanitish civilization and worship was Hamite, not Semitic. Like the sons of Seth, the sons of Shem lived a nomadic, pastoral life; whilst, with a like resemblance to the descendants of Cain, the Hamites were builders of cities and fortresses, and rapidly grew into prosperous, mercantile races, with an advanced, but corrupt civilization. Compare Egypt, Babylon, Nineveh, Tyre, Sidon, and contrast with them the Israelites, Ishmaelites, Arabs, &c.

7. *the sons of Cush; Seba*] Seba appears to be the name of a commercial and wealthy region of Ethiopia; see Ps. lxxii. 10; Is. xliii. 3, xlv. 14. In the last passage the Sabeans (Sebaim) are called "men of stature;" and Herodotus says that the Macrobian Ethiopians "were reported to be the tallest and comeliest of men" (III. 20). According to Josephus ('Ant.' II. 10), Meroë was anciently called Seba, until Cambyses gave it the name of his sister Meroë. Meroë is described as a strong fortress situated in a most fertile country at the confluence of the rivers Astophus and Astaborus. The ruins of Meroë still remain to the north-east of the Nubian town of Shendy.

Havilah] Havilah, the son of Joktan, occurs, v. 29, among the descendants of Shem. Some identify the descendants of Havilah the son of Cush with the Avalitæ on the coast of Africa; whilst others place them in Chawlan of Arabia Felix. There is an inevitable confusion from the name of a grandson of Ham being the same as that of a descendant of Shem. Niebuhr and others have asserted that there were two Chawlans, and have ascribed one to the Shemite, the other to the Hamite. It seems very possible that the descendants of Havilah the son of Cush intermingled with the descendants of Havilah the Joktanide, and so ultimately formed but one people, whose dwelling-place was Chawlan, the well-known fertile region of Yemen.

Sabtah] By Gesenius and others, who confine the Cushites to Africa, the descendants of Sabtah are placed on the African shore of the Gulf of Arabia. More commonly, and more probably, their home is sought for in

9 He was a mighty hunter before the LORD: wherefore it is said, Even as Nimrod the mighty hunter before the LORD.

10 And the beginning of his kingdom was † Babel, and Erech, and Accad, and Calneh, in the land of Shinar.

† Gr. *Babylon.*

Hadramaut, a province of Southern Arabia, where Pliny (VI. 32) places the city of Sabbatha or Sabotha. It is said, that to this day in Yemen and Hadramaut there is a dark race of men distinguished from the fairer Arabs, and belonging evidently to a different original stock. (Knobel.)

Raamah] LXX. Rhegma. The connection of Raamah with Sheba and Dedan, of whom he is here said to be the father (cp. Ezek. xxvii. 22), leaves no doubt, even with those who confine the other Cushites to Ethiopia, that the settlement of Raamah must be sought for in Southern Arabia, in the neighbourhood of Sheba and Dedan. Ptolemy (VI. 7) places Rhĕgma, and Steph. Byzant. Rhĕgma on the shore of the Persian Gulf.

Sabtechah] is by some placed in Ethiopia. Bochart, who is followed by Knobel, places it in Caramania, on the Eastern shore of the Persian Gulf, where the ancients (Ptolem. VI. 8; Steph. Byz. 2) mention Samidace or Samydace.

Sheba, and Dedan] Sheba occurs again in v. 28 as a son of Joktan, and Sheba and Dedan together, Gen. xxv. 3, as children of Joktan, the son of Abraham and Keturah. This is evidently another example of the intermingling of the Cushites with the Joktanides, and generally of the early descendants of Shem and Ham. In Ezek. xxvii. 15—20 we find the Cushite Dedan supplying Tyre with merchandise brought from beyond the sea, while the Shemite Dedan supplies the produce of flocks. Sheba is known to us as an important and opulent region of Arabia Felix. (1 K. x. 1; Ps. lxxii. 10. 15; Job i. 15, vi. 19; Is. lx. 6; Jer. vi. 20; Ezek. xxvii. 22; Joel iii. 8.) The Sabeans are spoken of by Strabo (XVI. p. 777) as a most opulent and powerful people, famous for myrrh, frankincense, and cinnamon, their chief city being Mariaba, (in Arab. Marib). This was afterwards the famous kingdom of the Himyaritic Arabs, so called probably from the ruling family of Himyar. It is probable, that the Cushite Sheba, and his brother Dedan, were settled on the shore of the Persian Gulf (see Raamah above); but afterwards were combined with the great Joktanide kingdom of the Sabeans.

8. *Cush begat Nimrod*] Nimrod is here separated from the other sons of Cush, perhaps because of his great fame and mighty prowess; but it is quite possible, that the words "Cush begat Nimrod" may only mean that Nimrod was a descendant of Cush, not immediately his son, the custom of the Hebrews being to call any ancestor a father, and any descendant a son. The name Nimrod is commonly derived from the Hebrew *marad*, to *rebel*. The Eastern traditions make him a man of violent, lawless habits, a rebel against God, and an usurper of boundless authority over his fellow-men, at whose instigation men began the building of the tower of Babel. (Jos. 'Ant.' I. 4.) He has accordingly been identified with the Orion of the Greeks, and it has been thought that the constellation Orion, called by the Hebrew *Kesil* "the fool, the impious," and by the Arabs "the giant," was connected with Nimrod, who is said in the LXX. to have been a "giant on the earth." The Scripture narrative, however, says nothing of this violence and lawlessness, and the later tradition is very doubtful and vague. The LXX. spell the name Nebrod, so also Josephus, which some have referred to a Persian root signifying *war*, a warrior; but this etymology is altogether uncertain, and not to be relied on.

he began to be a mighty one in the earth] He was the first of the sons of Noah distinguished by his warlike prowess. The word "mighty one" (in the LXX. "giant") is constantly used for a great warrior, a hero, or man of renown. Cp. Gen. vi. 4; Judg. vi. 12; xi. 1; 1 S. ix. 1; 2 K. v. 1; Ps. xxxiii. 16, lxxviii. 65; Is. xiii. 3, &c.

9. *He was a mighty hunter*] LXX. "a giant hunter." Bochart says that by being a famous hunter, he gathered to himself all the enterprising young men of his generation, attached them to his person, and so became a kind of king among them, training his followers first in the chase, and then leading them to war. Compare Hercules, Theseus, Meleager, &c. among the Greeks. The Jerusalem Targum renders "He was mighty in hunting and in sin before the Lord, for he was a hunter of the sons of men in their languages." The Syriac also renders "a warrior." Following these, many have understood, that he was a hunter of men, rather than a hunter of beasts.

before the LORD] Is most likely added only to give emphasis, or the force of a superlative (cp. Gen. xiii. 10, xxx. 8, xxxv. 5; 1 S. xi. 7, xiv. 15, xxvi. 12; Ps. civ. 16; Jonah iii. 3; Acts vii. 20): though some understand "against the Lord," as 1 Chron. xiv. 8, where it is said "David went out against them," literally "before them."

10. *And the beginning of his kingdom was Babel*] The later Chaldæans and Babylonians

‖ Or, *he went out into Assyria.* ‖ Or, *the streets of the city.*

11 Out of that land ‖went forth Asshur, and builded Nineveh, and ‖the city Rehoboth, and Calah,

12 And Resen between Nineveh and Calah: the same *is* a great city.

---

spoke a Semitic language, but the most ancient Babylonian inscriptions shew that the earliest inhabitants spoke a Turanian or Cushite tongue, and were therefore of the same race as the Ethiopians and Southern Arabians. Moreover, the most ancient traditions bring the first colonists of Babylon from the South. Thus Belus, son of Poseidon and Libya, is said to have led a colony from Egypt into Babylonia, and there fixing his seat on the Euphrates, to have consecrated the priests called in Babylon Chaldæans (Diod. Sic. lib. I. c. ii.): and the fish-god Oannes, the great civilizer of Babylon, is said to have risen out of the Red Sea (Syncell. 'Chron.' p. 28). Nimrod is probably to be identified with Belus; but the word Belus itself (= Bel = Baal) is not so much a name as a title, meaning *lord* or *master*, and may have been given traditionally to the first founder of empire in the earth. The words "beginning of his kingdom" may signify that Babel was the *first*, or possibly that it was the chief city founded by Nimrod.

Erech] The Targums, Ephraim Syr. and Jerome, render *Edessa*. Bochart says Areca on the confines of Babylonia and Susiana: but it is now generally agreed to be Archoë, the ruins of which, called Warka, lie about thirty hours to the south east of Babylon. The numerous mounds and remains of bricks and coffins indicate that this was probably the burying place of the kings of Assyria. (See Rawlinson, 'Five Monarchies,' Vol. I. p. 23.)

Accad] Spelt Archad by the LXX. and Achar by the Syr., has been compared by Bochart with the river Argades in Sithacene, the whole region having perhaps been called Archada. Le Clerc, who is followed by Gesenius, suggests Sacada, a town lying not far below Nineveh, where the Lycus falls into the Tigris. Knobel proposes a tract north of Babylon called Accete. The only ancient authorities (the Targums of Jerusalem and Pseudo-Jonathan, Ephraim Syrus, Jerome, Barhebræus) render the word by *Nisibis*, a city on the river Khabour. Michaelis and many moderns adopt this as the probable site of Accad.

Calneh] (Calneh, Amos vi. 2. Calno, Is. x. 9, perhaps Canneh, Ezek. xxvii. 23, where one of De Rossi's MSS. reads Kalneh). Targg. Jer. and Pseudo-Jon., Euseb., Jerome, Ephr. Syr. give Ctesiphon on the east bank of the Tigris, opposite Seleucia, N.E. of Babylon. The name Calneh survived in Chalonitis, a region of Assyria, where Pliny places Ctesiphon. In this identification of Calneh with Ctesiphon most modern interpreters agree.

Shinar] Unquestionably the country round about Babylon, the great plain or alluvial country watered by the Tigris and Euphrates. The name seems to have been Jewish; though there was a town in Mesopotamia known to the ancients, called Singara (Arab. Sinjar); and Rawlinson found in the Assyrian and Babylonian inscriptions the name *Sinkareh* in cuneiform characters. The name too is found in Egyptian monuments of the 18th dynasty, from Thothmes I.

11. *Out of that land went forth Asshur*] So LXX., Syr., Vulg., Saad., Luth., Calv., J. D. Michael., Dathe, Ros., V. Bohlen. But the reading of the margin, "**From this land he went out into Assyria,**" is the rendering of all the Targums, of Nachmanides, and after them, of Drusius, Bochart, Le Clerc, De Wette, Baumg., Tuch, Gesenius, Knobel, Delitzsch, Kalisch, and most modern interpreters. The syntax fully admits of this interpretation; and the general sense of the passage requires it. Nimrod is the subject here treated of. Asshur, the son of Shem, v. 22, was at least a generation older than Nimrod, who may probably have first colonized the country called after him, Asshur (or Assyria); Nimrod, or one of his descendants, afterwards invading and governing that country. Asshur was a region through which the Tigris flowed, to the N.E. of Babylonia, including a portion of Mesopotomia.

and builded Nineveh] According to Herodotus, Ninus (the mythic founder of Nineveh) was the grandson of Belus, the mythic founder of Babylon (Herod. I. 7). This, the most ancient Greek tradition, well corresponds with the account of Scripture, for the words "he went out into Asshur," might be rendered "one went out into Asshur," not distinctly defining Nimrod as the individual who built Nineveh.

Nineveh, the ancient metropolis of Assyria, on the East branch of the Tigris, became in after ages the largest and most flourishing city of the old world. It is described in the book of Jonah as "an exceeding great city of three days' journey" (Jon. iii. 3), with 120,000 children "who knew not their right hand from their left" (Jon. iv. 11), which would make a population of about 2,000,000. According to Diodorus Siculus, it was no less than 55 miles in circumference (Diod. II. 3), built, no doubt, like the ancient cities of the East, with pastures and pleasure grounds interspersed among streets and houses. Even in Babylon, which was of less extent than Nineveh, Diodorus (II. 9) says, that there were gardens and orchards, and land sufficient

13 And Mizraim begat Ludim, and Anamim, and Lehabim, and Naphtuhim,

14 And Pathrusim, and Casluhim, (out of whom came Philistim,) and Caphtorim.

---

to provide corn for all the people in case of a siege. Nineveh is mentioned among the cities or fortresses captured by Thothmes III. (see Excursus, p. 1). It was attacked by Phraortes the Mede, who perished in the attempt to take it (Herod. I. 102). His successor, Cyaxares, having laid siege to it, B.C. 625, was obliged to raise the siege by an incursion of Scythians (Herod. I. 103); but finally succeeded in reducing it, B.C. 597 (Herod. I. 106). From that time it lay desolate, though Tacitus ('Ann.' XII. 13) and Ammianus (XVIII. 7) mention a fortress of the name. Its site has been identified by modern travellers with the ruins of Nebbi Yunus and Koyunjik, nearly opposite to Mosul on the East banks of the Tigris. (See esp. Layard, 'Ninev.' Vol. II. pp. 136 ff.) The language of the inscriptions discovered in these ruins appears to be an ancient Semitic dialect. This is not inconsistent with the foundation of the city by a descendant of Nimrod; for the indigenous race was no doubt derived from the colonization by Asshur, the son of Shem, and the adoption of the Semitic language has parallels in the cases of Babylon and Canaan (see above on v. 6). Moreover, it is thought that in Assyria, as well as in Babylonia, two distinct languages existed, the older being Turanian, the other Semitic; accordingly, at Koyunjik, vocabularies have been discovered with two languages arranged in parallel columns, and tablets apparently in a Turanian dialect have been found in the ruins.

11. *and the city Rehoboth*] Lit. "the streets of the city."

12. *the same is a great city*] It is extremely difficult to identify Rehoboth, Resen and Calah with any known sites. Perhaps the most probable conjecture is, that the four cities here named, viz. Nineveh, Rehoboth-Ir, Resen, and Calah, were all afterwards combined under the one name of Nineveh, and that the words, v. 12, "the same is a great city," applied to this united whole, not to the single state of Resen. This is adopted by Niebuhr, Grote, Knobel, Rawlinson, Delitzsch.

13. *Ludim*] There was also a son of Shem named Lud, v. 22; but these Ludim were an African tribe. They are probably the same as Retu, the Egyptian name for "man," especially the Egyptians. The name appears to have belonged to the old population of Central Egypt. In Jerem. xlvi. 9, Cush, Phut, and Ludim are mentioned together, the Ludim are said to "handle and bend the bow," and all are placed in the army of Pharaoh-Necho, king of Egypt. Again, in Ezek. xxx. 4, 5, Cush, Phut, and Lud are connected with Mizraim. In Isaiah, on the contrary, we find (lxvi. 19) Lud "that draw the bow" connected with Asiatic and European tribes, Tarshish, Pul, Tubal, and Javan. The existence of the two tribes both called Lud, the one Semite and the other Hamite, is inevitably a cause of confusion.

Anamim] Another Mizraite race, concerning whom no certain or very probable conjecture can be made. Knobel identifies them with an Egyptian name of the Delta.

Lehabim] Generally agreed to be the same as the Lubim, 2 Chr. xii. 3, xvi. 8, reckoned among the Ethiopian forces, and in Nah. iii. 9, Dan. xi. 43, named with the Egyptians; according to Josephus, the Libyans. The original home of this people appears to have been to the west of the Delta.

Naphtuhim] Mentioned only here and 1 Chr. i. 11. Bochart, followed by Michaelis, Jablonski, Gesenius and others, compares the name of the Egyptian goddess Nephthys, the wife of Typhon, to whom the parts of Egypt bordering on the Red Sea were consecrated. Plutarch ('De Is.' p. 355) says, "The Egyptians call the extremities of the land bordering on the sea by the name of Nephthys." If this be so, the Naphtuchim were probably a people dwelling on the Red Sea on the confines of Egypt. Knobel supposes them to have been the midland Egyptians, who in their great city Memphis worshipped Phthah, and were called in Coptic Phaphthah, "the (people) of Phthah."

14. *Pathrusim*] The people of Pathros, mentioned often in the prophets (as Is. xi. 11; Jer. xliv. 1; Ezek. xxix. 14, xxx. 14). The name Pathros occurs, sometimes as if it were separate from Egypt, sometimes as if it were part of Egypt; whence Bochart concluded that the Thebaid was intended, which at times is reckoned as in Upper Egypt, at times as distinct from it. Pliny mentions Phaturites as a præfecture of the Thebaid, ('Hist. Nat' l. v. c. 9, § 47). The words of Ezekiel (xxix. 14), where Pathros is called the land of the Egyptians' birth, is compared with Herod. (II. 15), who says Thebes was anciently called Egypt. Pa-t-res in Egyptian means "the land of the south."

Casluhim] Bochart conjectured the Colchians, who were an Egyptian colony (Herod. II. 104; Diod. Sic. I. 28; Strabo. I. 3). In this he is followed by Gesenius and others, though the similarity of name seems the chief reason for the identification. Forster ('Ep. ad Michael.' p. 16 sqq.) conjectured Casiotis,

15 ¶ And Canaan begat †Sidon his firstborn, and Heth,

† Heb. Zidon.

16 And the Jebusite, and the Amorite, and the Girgasite,

---

a region between Gaza and Pelusium, so called from Mount Casius. He is followed in this by Knobel, who says the name in Coptic signifies *burning*, hence applicable to a dry, arid, desert region. He combines Bochart's view with Forster's, supposing that the Colchians were a colony from Casiotis. This view is adopted and ably defended by Ebers ('Ægypten,' &c. p. 120).

Out of whom came Philistim] In Jer. xlvii. 4, Amos ix. 7, the Philistines are traced to the Caphtorim. Hence Michaelis and others think that there has been a transposition in this verse, and that it ought to run "and Caphtorim, out of whom came Philistim." The Samaritan text, however, and all Versions read as the Hebrew. Bochart therefore has conjectured, that the Casluchim and Caphtorim were tribes which intermingled, the Caphtorim having strengthened the Casluchian colony by immigration, and that hence the Philistines may have been said to have come from either. The name Philistine, which probably comes from an Æthiopic verb fălăsă, *to emigrate*, is often rendered by the LXX. (as Judg. xiv. 3, xiv. 1) by *allophyloi*, aliens, foreigners.

The following difficulties are urged against the Egyptian origin of the Philistines; first, that their language was probably, like that of the other inhabitants of Canaan, Semitic; secondly, that they were uncircumcised (1 S. xvii. 26), whilst Herodotus tells us that the Egyptians were circumcised. The linguistic difficulty may be explained by the very probable supposition, that the invading Philistines or Caphtorim adopted the language of the conquered Avim (Deut. ii. 23), or other tribe amongst whom they settled. The other disappears, if we consider, that everything in dress, customs, and religion of the Philistines indicates that they separated off from the other Mizraic tribes at a very early period, and that circumcision was probably adopted by the Egyptians at a much later date.

Caphtorim] It is plain from Jer. xlvii. 4, where the Philistines are called "the remnant of the isle (or maritime country) of Caphtor," that we must look for the site of the Caphtorim near the sea. The Targums and ancient Versions render Cappadocia, followed by most of the ancients, and by Bochart. Others (Swinton, Michaelis, Rosenmüller, &c.) have conjectured Cyprus, the original name of which has been thought to have been Cubdr or Cyptrus. Calmet and others prefer Crete, comparing the statement of Tacitus ('Hist.' v. 2) concerning the Cretan origin of the Jews, and supposing that he may have confounded the Jews with the Philistines. Gesenius mentions this with approval, and it is advocated by Knobel. Recent investigations in Egyptian identify Caphtor with Capht-ur, i. e. the Great Capht. This is compared with the Egyptian name Coptos. Again, the name Ægyptus is probably identical with Ai-Capht, i. e. the coast of Capht, (compare אִי כַּפְתּוֹר, *I-Caphtor*, "the isle or coast of Caphtor," Jer. xlvii. 4). This Capht, or Capht-ur, was probably the Northern Delta, from which the Phœnicians emigrated into Asia. Thus Capht became the Egyptian name for the oldest Phœnicians, whether in Asia or in Africa. (See Ebers, 'Ægypt.' &c. voc. *Caphtorim;* see also Excursus.)

15. *Sidon his first-born*] Sidon was, according to Justin (XVIII. 3), the oldest Phœnician state. Of all the Phœnicians Homer knew only Sidon. The city stood on the Eastern coast of the Mediterranean, about 20 miles North of Tyre, which latter is said by Justin to have been a colony of Sidon. So important was Sidon in most ancient times, that all the Phœnicians are comprised under the name of Sidonians (Josh. xiii. 6; Judg. xviii. 7): and this extension of the name was known to the Greeks and Romans (compare *Urbs Sidonia, i.e.* Carthage, which was a colony of Tyre, Virg. 'Æn.' I. 677; and *Sidonia Dido*, 'Æn.' I. 446, 613, &c.). The name Sidon is supposed to be derived from *fishing;* for the Phœnicians called fish Sidon (Gesen. 'Thesaur.' p. 1153).

Heth] The ancestors of the Hittites, who inhabited the hill country of Judea, especially in the neighbourhood of Hebron. These, however, were but one portion of the race, which according to Josh. i. 4 (cp. Ezek. xvi. 3) became more important. In the time of Solomon and Joram there were independent kings of the Hittites, 1 K. x. 29; 2 K. vii. 6. They are by most Egyptologers identified with the Kheta, a very powerful tribe, and masters of Syria.

16. *the Jebusite*] Inhabitants of Jebus, the ancient name of Jerusalem, mentioned Judg. xix. 10, 11; 1 Chr. xi. 4, 5. The Jebusites, a mountain tribe (Num. xiii. 29; Josh. xi. 3), seem never to have been conquered, or to have recovered possession of Jerusalem and to have retained it, till David took Jebus, 1 Chr. xi. 4, 5: and even after the conquest we find Araunah the Jebusite, who is called "Araunah the king" (2 S. xxiv. 23) living in peace and prosperity in the land.

the Amorite] Apparently the most powerful and widespread of all the Canaanitish tribes, dwelling chiefly in the hill-country of Judæa, subject to five kings (Josh. x. 5), but

17 And the Hivite, and the Arkite,
and the Sinite,
18 And the Arvadite, and the Zemarite,
and the Hamathite: and afterward
were the families of the Canaanites
spread abroad.
19 And the border of the Canaanites
was from Sidon, as thou comest
† Heb *Azzah.* to Gerar, unto † Gaza; as thou goest,
unto Sodom, and Gomorrah, and Admah,
and Zeboim, even unto Lasha.
20 These *are* the sons of Ham,
after their families, after their tongues,
in their countries, *and* in their nations.
21 ¶ Unto Shem also, the father
of all the children of Eber, the brother
of Japheth the elder, even to
him were *children* born.

---

also spreading to the other side of Jordan, to the North of the Arnon (Numb. xxi. 13), even to the river Jabbok (Num. xxi. 24). Simonis, followed by Gesenius, traces the name to an old word Amor or Emor, *elevation*, *mountain*, the Amorites being mountaineers or highlanders.

the Girgasite] Josephus ('Ant.' I. 6) says we have the name and nothing else of this people. Eusebius and others have identified them with the Gergesenes (Matt. viii. 28), who lived to the East of the Lake of Gennesaret. There is a difference of reading in St Matt.; some MSS. having Gerasenes, others Gadarenes; but Gesenius thinks, that Gerasa is but a corruption by the omission of *g* from Girgasa.

17. *the Hivite*] A people living in the neighbourhood of Hermon and Lebanon (Josh. xi. 3, Judg. vi. 3), near Sichem also (Gen. xxxiv. 2), and Gibeon (Josh. ix. 1, 7): Gesenius interprets the name to signify *pagani*, the inhabitants of villages.

the Arkite] Inhabitants, according to Josephus, of Arca a city of Phœnicia, near Libanus, 12 miles to the north of Tripoli. It was afterwards called Cesarea Libani, a name found on coins of the reign of Vespasian. Alexander Severus was born here. Shaw and Burckhardt describe the ruins of a fine city as still to be found there, called *Tell Arka*.

the Sinite] St Jerome ('Quæst. in Genes.' ad h. l.) says, that "near Arca was another city called Sini, which, though ruined, still retained its ancient name." Michaelis ('Spicil.' Pt. II. p. 29) quotes Breidenbach ('Itiner.' p. 47) as mentioning a city of the name of *Syn* in the same neighbourhood in the fifteenth century.

18. *the Arvadite*] Inhabitants probably of the city of Aradus, on an island of the same name, about three miles from the Phœnician coast. The LXX. render here and elsewhere the Aradite, and Josephus ('Ant.' I. 6) says "the Aradite inhabited the island of Aradus." Gesenius derives the name from a root, signifying "to wander," and quotes Strabo (XVI. 2, § 13) as saying that the city was built by fugitives from Sidon.

the Zemarite] There is little certainty as to the habitation of this race. The ancient interpreters, Targg., Rashi, Saad., and probably Jerome, give Emesa; Michaelis, led by Bochart's conjecture and followed by Rosenm., Gesen., Knobel, suggests Samyra, a city of Phœnicia on the sea coast, near the river Eleutherus, the ruins of which are still called Samra.

the Hamathite] Hamath was an important city, called by Amos (vi. 2) "Great Hamath," the chief city of Upper Syria on the Orontes at the foot of Libanus (Judg. iii. 3; Jer. xlix. 23; Zech. ix. 2), the metropolis of a region called the "land of Hamath" (2 K. xxiii. 33). It was called Epiphaneia by the Macedonians (Jos. 'Ant.' I. 6). It still however in the East retains the name of Hamah, and has been visited and described by Burckhardt and other modern travellers.

and afterward were the families of the Canaanites spread abroad] The first place of habitation of the Canaanites was probably on the Mediterranean, in Phœnicia, in the neighbourhood of Tyre and Sidon; but by degrees they spread abroad through the whole of Palestine, from Tyre and Sidon on the North to Gerar and Gaza and even to Lasha.

19. *Lasha*] The Targum of Jerusalem and Jerome ('Quæst. ad Genes.') identify Lasha with Callirrhoë, which Pliny ('N. H.' v. c. 6) and Josephus ('B. J.' I. 33) speak of as famous for its warm springs. It was situated on the East of the Red Sea.

21. *Shem also, the father of all the children of Eber*] As Ham is specially called the father of Canaan, so probably Shem is designated as the father of Eber. The Hebrews and the Canaanites were brought into constant conflict and exemplified respectively the characters of the Hamites and the Shemites, their characters and their destinies.

the brother of Japheth the elder] There is a great ambiguity in the original of these words. The LXX., Symm., Targ. of Onkelos render as in the English text; so Rashi, Abenezra, Luther, Cleric., J. D. Michael., Dathe, &c. But the Syriac, Arab., Vulg. render "the elder brother of Japheth," in which they are followed by Rosenm., Gesenius, Knobel, Delitzsch and most modern com-c 1 Chron. 1. 17. † Heb. Arpachshad.

22 The [c]children of Shem; Elam,
and Asshur, and †Arphaxad, and Lud,
and Aram.
23 And the children of Aram; Uz,
and Hul, and Gether, and Mash.

24 And Arphaxad begat †Salah;
and Salah begat Eber.
25 [d]And unto Eber were born two
sons: the name of one *was* Peleg;
for in his days was the earth divid-

† Heb. Shelah. d 1 Chron. 1. 19.

---

mentators, who say, that if "the brother of Japheth the Elder" had been meant, the Hebrew idiom would have required the addition of "*son*"—"the elder son of Noah." This appears to be true: moreover, Shem is generally mentioned first, and is perhaps put last here, because the writer proceeds almost without interruption from this point with the history of the descendants of Shem. In Gen. ix. 24, Ham appears to be called the youngest son of Noah; but see note on that verse. On the whole, the common order of enumeration is probably the order of age.

22. *The children of Shem*] The Shemites dwelt chiefly in Western Asia, South of the Asiatic Japhethites.

Elam] Elymais, a region adjoining Susiana and Media, called by the Arabs Chuzistan. Daniel (viii. 2) places Shushan (*i. e.* Susa) in Elam, which immediately connects Elam with Susiana.

Asshur] Without doubt the ancestor o' the Assyrians. At first, perhaps, the name Asshur or Assyria was restricted to the region round about Nineveh, known to the Greeks as Adiabene. Afterwards it spread, especially to the North-west, and embraced the Syrians. The foundation of its principal greatness is ascribed to the Babylonians in v. 11. This corresponds with the tradition in Herodotus (I. 7), which attributes the foundation of Nineveh to Ninus, the son of Belus, the founder of Babylon.

Arphaxad] Bochart conjectured that the name Arrapachites, a province in Northern Assyria, bordering on Armenia, was derived from Arphaxad; and as this was the country of the Chaldees, it has been thought that in the three last consonants of the name Arphaxad, viz. ch-s-d, are contained the elements of the name Chasdim (i. e. Chaldæans). Josephus certainly tells us that "Arphaxad gave the name Arphaxadæans to those afterwards called Chaldæans" ('Ant.' I. 6).

Lud] Josephus says the Lydians ('Ant.' I. 6). He is followed by Euseb., Jerome, and by Bochart, and most moderns. The resemblance of their manners and of their more ancient names to the Semitic confirms this tradition. It is probable, that their first home was not far from Armenia, whence they migrated into Asia Minor.

Aram] The country called Aram in Scripture was the highland region lying to the north-east of the Holy Land, extending from the Jordan and the Sea of Galilee to the Euphrates. The name Aram has been supposed to mean *high* (from *Aram* = *rūm*, to be high). In Genesis we read of Aram-Naharaim, *i.e.* Aram between the two rivers = Mesopotamia, which, or part of which, is also called Padan-Aram; and Laban who dwelt there is called the Aramean (Gen. xxv. 20, &c.). Homer ('Il.' II. 783); Hesiod ('Th.' 304); Pindar ('Fr.' v. 3), &c. speak of the Syrians as Arimi.

23. *Uz*] From him no doubt was named "the land of Uz," in which Job lived. (Job i. 1.) It is there rendered by the LXX. Ausitis. Ptolemy (v. 19) mentions the Æsitæ as inhabiting the northern part of Arabia Deserta, near to Babylon and the Euphrates, which Bochart, Gesenius, and others, identify with the inhabitants of Uz or Ausitis. The name Uz occurs also among the descendants of Abraham (Gen. xxii. 21), and again (Gen. xxxvi. 28) among the descendants of Seir the Hivite; and it has been conjectured, with more or less probability, that these different Semitic families may have coalesced.

Hul] Josephus places in Armenia, according to Bochart, that part called Cholobotene by the Greeks, as though it were Beth-Chul, the home of Hul. Michaelis, followed by Knobel, suggests that the name Cælesyria may have come from Hul or Chul. Rosenmüller has suggested the Ard el Hhuleh, a district near the sources of the Jordan.

Gether] No probable site has been fixed on for the descendants of Gether.

Mash] Josephus ('Ant.' I. 6) says, "Mash founded the Mesanæans," *i.e.* the inhabitants of Mesene, near Bassora, where the Tigris and Euphrates fall into the Persian Gulf. The opinion of Bochart is adopted by Gesenius, Winer, Knobel, and others, that the descendants of Mash were the inhabitants of Mons Masius, a range of hills to the North of Mesopotamia.

24. *Arphaxad begat Salah; and Salah begat Eber*] The name *Salah* appears to signify *sending forth*, *extension*, as *Eber*, the name of his son, signifies *passing over*. Many of the names in these genealogies are significant, and were probably given to their bearers late in life, or even historically, after their deaths. Salah and Eber seem to point to this fact, that the descendants of Arphaxad were now beginning to spread forth from the first cradle of the Semitic race, and to cross over the

ed; and his brother's name *was* Joktan.
26 And Joktan begat Almodad,
and Sheleph, and Hazarmaveth, and
Jerah,
27 And Hadoram, and Uzal, and
Diklah,
28 And Obal, and Abimael, and
Sheba,
29 And Ophir, and Havilah, and

---

great rivers on their way to Mesopotamia, and thence to Canaan.

25. *Peleg; for in his days was the earth divided*] It is generally supposed from this, that Peleg lived contemporaneously with the dispersion of Babel. It is, however, quite possible, that the reference is to a more partial division of regions and separation of races. The genealogy is now specially concerned with the descendants of Shem and the ancestry of the promised race, which is here traced down to Peleg to be continued farther in ch. xi. 18 sqq. The two races, which sprang from Eber, soon separated very widely from each other, the one, Eber and his family, spreading north-westward towards Mesopotamia and Syria, the other, the Joktanides, southward into Arabia. As the sacred narrative in vv. 31, 32, speaks expressly of the general spreading forth of the sons of Noah, and in ch. xi. 1—9 relates the confusion of their languages, it is very probable that in this verse the division of the land concerns only the separation of the Shemites.

Joktan] There is a general consent in favour of the colonization of Southern Arabia by the descendants of Joktan, with the names of whom correspond several of the districts and cities of that country. The Arabs identify Joktan with Kahtan, who was the traditional ancestor of the Beni Kahtan, inhabitants of Yemen or Arabia Felix. In Arabia the Joktanides, no doubt, found some peoples settled there already, viz. the Cushite descendants of Ham (ver. 7), and the Ludite descendants of Shem (ver. 22). The Arabic authors are silent concerning any Cushites, but derive the ancient Arabic races from the Kahtanides (*i.e.* the Joktanides).

26. *Almodad*] The names Modad and Morad (*r* being often a corruption of *d* by a clerical error) occur frequently in Arabic genealogies. The syllable *Al* is probably the definite article.

Sheleph] has been compared by Bochart with the Salopeni of Ptolemy (VI. 7), inhabiting the interior of Arabia, and is identified with a tribe of Sulaph or Seliph in Yemen. The Arabic writers speak of a large region called Salfie, south-west of Sanaa.

Hazarmaveth] The name agrees in every letter with Hadramaut, the name of a province on the southern coast of Arabia, famous for its fertility in myrrh and frankincense, and for the unhealthiness of its climate.

Jerah] The name in Hebrew signifies the *moon.* Bochart has suggested the identification of his descendants with the Alilæi (Agatharch. c. 49; Strabo, XVI. p. 277) = the Beni Hilal ("the sons of the new moon"), who dwelt south of Chawlan.

27. *Hadoram*] There has been no satisfactory identification of the descendants of Hadoram with any known race, though Bochart compared the Adramitæ of Ptolemy (VI. 7) and the Atramitæ of Pliny (VI. 28) in the south of Arabia.

Uzal] This name is identified with Awzal, the ancient name of Sanaa, the capital city of Yemen.

Diklah] in Syriac signifies *Palm;* whence Bochart and Gesenius identified the descendants of Diklah with the Minæi, a people of Yemen, who inhabited a palm-growing country. Michaelis conjectured a people contiguous to the Tigris, the name of which river in Syriac and Arabic was Diklat.

28. *Obal, and Abimael*] Only very uncertain conjectures have been made as to these names.

Sheba] We read much of Sheba, a country in Arabia Felix, abounding in gold, precious stones, frankincense, and famous for its merchandise (1 K. x. 10; Job vi. 19; Ps. lxxii. 10, 15; Is. lx. 6; Jer. vi. 20; Ezek. xxvii. 22; Joel iii. 8). The Arabic and Greek accounts of the Sabæans, a people, whose capital was Saba or Mariaba, three or four days' journey from Senaa, correspond thoroughly with all this. See on ver. 7 above.

29. *Ophir*] On no geographical question has a greater diversity of opinion existed than on the site of Ophir. The position of Ophir, as a son of Joktan, and the settlement of the other Joktanides in Arabia, form a strong argument in favour of placing Ophir in Arabia also. The historical notices, however, in the books of Kings and Chronicles (1 K. ix. 26—28, x. 11, xxii. 48; 2 Chr. viii. 18, ix. 10) have inclined many to place Ophir either in India or in Africa: whilst others have thought, that two Ophirs are mentioned in Scripture, one in Arabia, the other in India or Ceylon. The question is discussed at length by Gesenius, 'Thes.' p. 142. See also 'Dict. of Bible,' s. v. Ophir.

Havilah] It is generally thought that Chawlan, in Arabia Felix, was the home of the descendants of Havilah. (On the Cushite Havilah, see note on v. 7.) Whilst some have thought that there were two Chaw-

Jobab: all these *were* the sons of
Joktan.
30 And their dwelling was from
Mesha, as thou goest unto Sephar a
mount of the east.
31 These *are* the sons of Shem,
after their families, after their tongues,
in their lands, after their nations.
32 These *are* the families of the
sons of Noah, after their generations,
in their nations: and by these were
the nations divided in the earth after
the flood.

CHAPTER XI.

1 *One language in the world.* 3 *The building of Babel.* 5 *The confusion of tongues.* 10 *The generations of Shem.* 27 *The generations of Terah the father of Abram.* 31 *Terah goeth from Ur to Haran.*

AND [a]the whole earth was of one
†language, and of one †speech.
2 And it came to pass, as they
journeyed from the east, that they
found a plain in the land of Shinar;
and they dwelt there.
3 And †they said one to another,
Go to, let us make brick, and †burn
them throughly. And they had brick
for stone, and slime had they for
mortar.
4 And they said, Go to, let us

[a] Wisd. 10. 5.
† Heb. *lip.*
† Heb. *words.*
† Heb. *a man said to his neighbour.*
† Heb. *burn them to a burning.*

---

lans, one belonging to the descendants of the Joktanide and the other to the sons of the Cushite Havilah; others have thought that the two races were intermingled and confounded.

Jobab] Ptolemy (VI. 7) mentions the Jobaritæ near the Indian Sea, which Bochart conjectured to have been Jobabitæ, in which he is followed by Gesenius. Bochart and Gesenius think the name to be = the Arabic Jebab, *a desert.*

30. *And their dwelling was from Mesha, as thou goest unto Sephar a mount of the East*] Mesha has been identified by Bochart with the seaport of Musa or Muza, mentioned by Ptolemy VI. 8; Pliny VI. 23, &c. Michaelis, followed by Rosenmüller, Gesenius, &c. preferred Mesene, a place at the mouth of the Tigris and Euphrates, not far from Bassora.

Sephar] is pretty certainly Zafâr or Dhafari, a seaport on the coast of Hadramaut. It is pronounced in modern Arabic Isfor, and is not so much one town as a series of villages near the shore of the Indian Ocean. (Fresnel, quoted by Gesenius, p. 968.)

CHAP. XI. 1. *one language*] The general opinion of the Jews and ancient Christians was that this language was Hebrew. The names of the most ancient places and persons mentioned in Scripture being Hebrew seems to countenance this belief. But it is impossible to arrive at any certainty on the question, it being notorious that names have been translated from one language into another in many instances.

2. *it came to pass, as they journeyed from the east*] On the difficulty in these words, and on the first home of the descendants of Noah, see note on viii. 4. If Armenia was that first home, we must suppose either that they had journeyed in a south-easterly direction before they turned towards Shinar, and then they would journey from the east, or we must render "eastward," lit. "on the sides of the east."

a plain] The word more naturally means a deep valley, but it is often used of a wide vale or plain.

Shinar] Without doubt the region round about Babylon, to which, besides Babylon, pertained the cities of Erech, Kalneh and Accad (Gen. x. 10, where see note). The fertility of this country for the production of wheat is greatly praised by Herodotus (I. 193).

3. *let us make brick, and burn them throughly*] The regions of Assyria and Babylonia consisting of rich alluvial plains would provide no stone and were specially abundant in brick earth. Hence, when Nimrod built Babel and other towns in Shinar (ch. x. 10), he and those with him must have learned the art of brick-making. The building of villages in the earlier settlements of the Noachidæ had been probably of wood or stone.

they had brick for stone, and slime had they for mortar] All the versions give *asphalte* or bitumen for the word *chemer*, "slime". Herod. (I. 179) describes the building of the walls of Babylon much as the sacred history describes this building of the tower of Babel. He says a deep foss was dug all round the city, from which the mud was taken in large bricks and burnt in furnaces. Then for mud or mortar, they used hot bitumen, and so built the walls of the city. He mentions a town called Is, with a river of the same name near it, about eight days' journey from Babylon, where much bitumen was obtained and carried to Babylon for the building of the city. See also Strabo (Lib. XVI. p. 74), who speaks of the excellence of the Babylonian bitumen for building. Justin also (Lib. I. 2) speaks of Semiramis as having built Babylon with brick and liquid bitumen, which flowed in great abundance in the neighbourhood. Diodor. Sicul. (II. 12),

build us a city and a tower, whose
top *may reach* unto heaven; and let
us make us a name, lest we be scattered abroad upon the face of the
whole earth.

5 And the LORD came down to
see the city and the tower, which the
children of men builded.
6 And the LORD said, Behold, the
people *is* one, and they have all one

Pliny ('H. N.' XXXI. 5), Athenæus (Lib. II. 5), and other ancient writers, mention a lake close to Babylon abounding in bitumen, which floated on the waters. (See Reland, 'Palestin.' II. pp. 244, 245). The town of Is, mentioned by Herodotus (as above), is identified by modern travellers with Heets, where bitumen pits are still found on the western bank of the Euphrates. Some of the heaps of ruins, which have been identified with the ruins of Babylon, exhibit specimens of sun-dried bricks laid in bitumen, producing walls of great strength and solidity. Mr Layard tells us that at Birs Nimrod, "The cement, by which the bricks were united, is of so tenacious a quality, that it is almost impossible to detach one from the other," ('Nineveh and Babylon,' p. 499).

4. *a tower, whose top may reach unto heaven*] That is to say "a very high tower," just as the cities of the Canaanites were said to be "great and walled up to heaven" (Deut. i. 28, ix. 1), or as Homer ('Od.' V. 239), speaks of a pine tree "high as heaven." Many have identified this tower with the temple of Belus (Herod. I. 181), which is described as consisting of eight squares one upon the other, the dimensions of the lowest or base being a stadium in length and in breadth. The mound called Birs Nimroud is generally supposed to be the ruin of the temple of Belus.

let us make us a name, lest we be scattered abroad upon the face of the whole earth] Josephus gives as the motive for building the tower of Babel, that the builders feared another deluge, and hoped that the tower would be high enough to save them from its waters; Nimrod, the leader in the scheme, boasting that he could so defy the vengeance of God. Again some have thought, that Noah had deliberately marked out the settlements of his posterity (Usher, ad A. M. 1757), and that Nimrod and his followers were unwilling to submit to this. Then some Jewish writers have interpreted the word *name* (Shem) to mean God, "the name of God" being often put for God Himself; and so have imagined that the builders of the tower proposed to make an idol temple. Others have supposed that the descendants of Ham under Nimrod made here some reference to Shem, the favoured son of Noah, as though they would have said, "A blessing has been promised to Shem, but we will make a Shem for ourselves." Clericus suggested that the word Shem meant here a monument (cp. 2 S. viii. 13). The simplest sense of the passage seems the true. In ch. x. 10, we find that Nimrod founded a kingdom in Shinar. He and his followers were apparently actuated by an ambitious spirit, not satisfied with the simplicity of a patriarchal life, nor willing to be scattered abroad, as so many were, by the migratory instinct that seems to have led the descendants of Noah thus early to form extensive settlements, but desiring to found an empire, to build a city, with a strong citadel, and so to hold together in a powerful commonwealth, and to establish for themselves a name, fame, importance, renown, thereby, it may be, attracting others to join their community. Perhaps there was an allusion to this in the prophecy (Is. xiv. 22), "I will... cut off from Babylon *the name* and remnant and son and nephew" (*i. e.* grandson or posterity) "saith the LORD." The tradition which assigns the lead in the building of the tower of Babel to Nimrod was ancient and general. (See Joseph. 'Ant.' I. 4, Aug. 'De Civit. Dei,' XVI. 4, &c.) It may have arisen chiefly from what is said of him in ch. x. 9, 10, 11. It is worthy of remark, that, though the descendants of Shem and Japheth shared in the judgment which confounded the tongues, yet their dialects have to this day a nearer resemblance between themselves than those which may perhaps be attributed to the children of Ham. As the Shemites and Japhethites have had a higher civilization, so they have retained a purer language. The Semitic dialects all have a strong family likeness. The Aryan or Indo-European (*i.e.* probably the Japhetic) dialects, though more diverse than the Semitic, are yet all easily assignable to a common origin; whilst the Turanian and other languages branch off into endless varieties.

5. *the LORD came down to see*] An instance of the natural anthropomorphic language suited to the teaching of man in a state of simple and partial civilization.

the children of men builded] It has been thought, though perhaps on insufficient ground, that "children of men" as in ch. vi. 2, designates the impious portion of the human race, bad men, as opposed to "children of God;" and possibly the rebellious offspring of Ham.

6. *this they begin to do*] Perhaps rather "this is the beginning of their deeds." This is their first act of daring and impiety, and unless they be effectually checked, nothing will restrain them from going farther and farther.

language; and this they begin to do:
and now nothing will be restrained
from them, which they have imagined
to do.
7 Go to, let us go down, and there
confound their language, that they
may not understand one another's
speech.
8 So the LORD scattered them
abroad from thence upon the face of
all the earth: and they left off to
build the city.
9 Therefore is the name of it called
‖Babel; because the LORD did there
confound the language of all the
earth: and from thence did the LORD
scatter them abroad upon the face of
all the earth.
10 ¶ [b]These *are* the generations
of Shem: Shem *was* an hundred years
old, and begat Arphaxad two years
after the flood:
11 And Shem lived after he begat
Arphaxad five hundred years, and begat sons and daughters.
12 And Arphaxad lived five and
thirty years, and begat Salah:
13 And Arphaxad lived after he

‖ That is, Confusion.

[b] 1 Chron. 1. 17.

---

8. *they left off to build the city*] It seems, therefore, very doubtful how far the builders could have proceeded in building their tower, and hardly likely that the famous temple of Belus should have been to any considerable extent erected by them, though not improbably that great structure may have been raised on the foundation laid at this time. The tradition that God overturned it with a tempest (Jos. 'Ant.' I. 6; Euseb. 'Præp. Evang.' IX. 4), though probably unfounded, witnesses to its not having been completed.

9. *Babel*] From *Balal*, to *confound*, contracted from *Balbal*, *confusion*. The Greek tradition was, that the city was named after Belus, its mythic founder. So the Etymologicum Magnum says that "Babylon was named after Belus, who founded it." Hence Eichhorn suggested, that the name originally was Bāb Bel, "the gate or court of Bel," *i.e.* Baal or Belus. So Rosenmüller, Gesenius and others have thought it might be Bāb Il, the "Gate of God." These derivations are really much less likely than that given by Moses. There was no such person as Belus, except that Nimrod, whose scriptural name probably signifies *rebel*, may by his own people have been called Baal, Belus, Lord.

10. *These are the generations of Shem*] We have here the third genealogical table. The 1st was given in ch. v. from Adam to Noah; the 2nd in ch. x, the genealogy of the three sons of Noah, the descendants of Shem being traced down as far as Peleg. Now we have the line of Shem farther carried down to Abraham, the father of the faithful, the ancestor of the promised seed. In ch. x. no account is given of the length of the generations or of the duration of life; but here in ch. xi. as before in ch. v., both these are supplied. Concerning the chronological question and the ages of the patriarchs, see Introduction and on ch. v. note A. It may be observed here, that we mark at once the transition from the antediluvian to the postdiluvian duration of life. Noah lived 950 years, Shem only 600, Arphaxad, the first born of Shem after the deluge, only 438; when we come to Peleg, who seems to have been contemporary with the dispersion, life is still shorter, Peleg lived 239 years, Reu 239, Serug 230, Nahor 148.

The following table exhibits the different calculations according to the Hebrew, the Samaritan, and the Septuagint texts respectively.

	Hebrew Text.			Samaritan.			Septuagint.			Hebrew Text.	
	Years before birth of Son.	Rest of Life.	Whole Life.	Years before birth of Son.	Rest of Life.	Whole of Life.	Years before birth of Son.	Rest of Life.	Whole Life.	Year of birth A.M.	Year of death A.M.
Shem	100	500	600	100	500	600	100	500	600	1558	2158
Arphaxad	35	403	438	135	303	438	135	400	535	1658	2097
Kainan							130	330	460		
Salah	30	403	433	130	303	433	130	330	460	1693	2126
Eber	34	430	464	134	270	404	134	270	404	1723	2187
Peleg	30	209	239	130	109	239	130	209	339	1757	1996
Reu	32	207	239	132	107	239	132	207	339	1787	2026
Serug	30	200	230	130	100	230	130	200	330	1819	1997
Nahor	29	119	148	79	69	148	179	125	304	1849	1997
Terah	70	135	205	70	75	145	70	135	209	1878	2083
Abraham										1948	2123

begat Salah four hundred and three
years, and begat sons and daughters.
14 And Salah lived thirty years,
and begat Eber:
15 And Salah lived after he begat
Eber four hundred and three years,
and begat sons and daughters.
16 [c]And Eber lived four and thirty years, and begat [d]Peleg:
17 And Eber lived after he begat
Peleg four hundred and thirty years,
and begat sons and daughters.
18 And Peleg lived thirty years,
and begat Reu:
19 And Peleg lived after he begat
Reu two hundred and nine years, and
begat sons and daughters.
20 And Reu lived two and thirty
years, and begat [e]Serug:
21 And Reu lived after he begat
Serug two hundred and seven years,
and begat sons and daughters.

[c] 1 Chron. 1. 19.
[d] Called, Luke 3. 35 *Phalec.*
[e] Luke 3. 35, *Saruch.*

22 And Serug lived thirty years,
and begat Nahor:
23 And Serug lived after he begat
Nahor two hundred years, and begat
sons and daughters.
24 And Nahor lived nine and
twenty years, and begat [f]Terah:
25 And Nahor lived after he begat
Terah an hundred and nineteen years,
and begat sons and daughters.
26 And Terah lived seventy years,
and [g]begat Abram, Nahor, and Haran.
27 ¶ Now these *are* the generations of Terah: Terah begat Abram,
Nahor, and Haran; and Haran begat
Lot.
28 And Haran died before his father Terah in the land of his nativity,
in Ur of the Chaldees.
29 And Abram and Nahor took
them wives: the name of Abram's
wife *was* Sarai; and the name of
Nahor's wife, Milcah, the daughter

[f] Luke 3. 34, *Tha*[rah].
[g] Joshua 24. 2. 1 Chron. [1.] 26.

---

27. *Now these are the generations of Terah*] Not perhaps a distinct genealogy, but the winding up of the genealogy which had already been traced to the sons of Terah, and the expanding it into a fuller account of the families of these sons and especially of Abraham.

28. *Ur of the Chaldees*] Mentioned only here. There is great diversity of opinion as to the site of this city, except that it was in Chaldæa, i.e. the southern part of Babylonia. Bochart, followed by Michaelis, Rosenmüller and many others, identified it with *Ur*, which is mentioned by Ammianus Marcellinus (XXV. 8. col. 26), when describing the return of the Roman army under Jovian after the death of Julian, as lying between Nisibis and the Tigris. Ancient tradition and the opinion of many moderns connect it with the modern Orfa, the Edessa of the Greeks, well known in Christian times as the capital of Abgarus, its first Christian King, who is said to have written a letter to, and to have received a letter from our Saviour. "The traditions of Abraham still live in the mouths of the Arab inhabitants of Orfa. The city lies on the edge of one of the bare rugged spurs which descend from the mountains of Armenia, into the Assyrian plains in the cultivated land, which, as lying under the mountains, was called Padan-Aram. Two physical features must have secured it from the earliest times as a nucleus for the civilization of those regions. One is a high crested crag, the natural fortification of the present citadel, doubly defended by a trench of immense depth, cut out of the living rock behind it. The other is an abundant spring (the Callirrhoe of the Greek writers) issuing in a pool of transparent clearness and embosomed in a mass of luxuriant verdure, which, amidst the dull brown desert all around, makes, and must always have made, this spot an oasis, a Paradise in the Chaldæan wilderness." (Dean Stanley 'On the Jewish Church,' I. p. 7.) Eupolemus as quoted by Euseb. 'Præp. Evang.' IX. 17, says that Abraham was born in the city of Babylonia called Camarine, which some say is the city Uria, and by interpretation city of the Chaldees, which Gesenius explains by saying that *Ur* in Sanscrit signifies *city*, *country*, (cognate perhaps with the Hebrew *Ir*, עִיר), the original language of the Chaldees having been cognate with the Indian and Persian. This city is supposed to be now represented by the ruins Umgheir on the right bank of the Euphrates, which appears by its bricks to have been called Hur by the natives. (Professor Rawlinson in 'Dict. of Bible.')

29. *Iscah*] According to Josephus ('Ant.' I. 6), Targum Pseudo-Jonathan and Jerome ('Qu. in Genes.') the same as Sarai. This, however, hardly seems consistent with Gen. XX. 12, where Abram speaks of Sarai as daughter of his father but not of his mother; though it is very difficult to say with what exactness the terms father, daughter, brother, &c. are used. Ewald has conjectured that Iscah was Lot's wife and therefore mentioned here; but there is no evidence for this

of Haran, the father of Milcah, and
the father of Iscah.
30 But Sarai was barren; she *had*
no child.
31 And Terah took Abram his
son, and Lot the son of Haran his
son's son, and Sarai his daughter in
law, his son Abram's wife; and they
went forth with them from [h]Ur of
the Chaldees, to go into the land of
Canaan; and they came unto Haran,
and dwelt there.
32 And the days of Terah were
two hundred and five years: and Terah died in Haran.

[h] Neh. 9. 7. Judith 5. 7. Acts 7. 4.

CHAPTER XII.

1 *God calleth Abram, and blesseth him with a promise of Christ.* 4 *He departeth with Lot from Haran.* 6 *He journeyeth through Canaan,* 7 *which is promised him in a vision.* 10 *He is driven by a famine into Egypt.* 11 *Fear maketh him feign his wife to be his sister.* 14 *Pharaoh, having taken her from him, by plagues is compelled to restore her.*

NOW the [a]LORD had said unto
Abram, Get thee out of thy
country, and from thy kindred, and
from thy father's house, unto a land
that I will shew thee:
2 And I will make of thee a great
nation, and I will bless thee, and

[a] Acts 7. 3.

---

31. *and they went forth with them*] i.e. Terah and Abram went forth with Lot and Sarai. The Samaritan (followed by LXX. and Vulg.) by a slight transposition of the letters and different pointing reads "He brought them forth."

Haran] The Carrhæ of the Greeks and Romans, where Crassus fell, defeated by the Parthians (Plutarch, 'Vit. Cras.' 25. 27. 28. Plin. v. 24). It is called Charran in Acts vii. 4.

32. *two hundred and five years*] The Samaritan Pentateuch has here *one hundred and forty five*, which Bochart and others consider the right number. St Stephen (Acts vii. 4) says the migration of Abram into Canaan was after his father's death: but from v. 26 *supra* it seems as if Terah was only 70 when Abram was born, and by xii. 4 we find that Abram was 75 when he left Haran. This, according to the Samaritan, would appear to be the very year of his father's death. It is certain that the Samaritan text cannot have been tampered with by any Christian hand to bring it into conformity with St Stephen's statement, and it may very likely have preserved the true reading. It is possible, however, that Terah may have been really 130 years old when Abram was born: for though it is said in ver. 26 that Terah lived seventy years and begat Abram, Nahor and Haran, yet it does not follow that Abram was the eldest son, having been named first as being the heir of the promises and the subject of the future history. Indeed some of the rabbins consider Abram to have been the youngest son, in which case he may have been born when his father was 130 years old (see Wordsworth on Acts vii. 4).

CHAP. XII. 1. *Now the LORD had said*] **Now the LORD said.** The former chapter had carried the history down to the death of Terah. The present chapter returns to the date of the call of Abram. In Acts vii. 2 St Stephen tells us, what also appears most likely from the history in Gen., that God appeared to Abram "when he was in Mesopotamia, before he dwelt in Charran." This led our translators to render "*had said.*" The Hebrew lacks the pluperfect tense; but the continuous character of the narrative from this point marks the propriety of adopting a simple perfect, which is also the rendering of the ancient versions. The recounting briefly of events up to the death of Terah in the last chapter was by a prolepsis. We have here the beginning of a new Chapter in the history, of a new dispensation and a new covenant. Henceforth the narrative concerns only the chosen people of God and those who affect them and their fortunes.

Get thee out of thy country] Lit. *Go thee*, a pleonasm of the pronoun, common in many languages. The call was evidently from the birthplace of Abram, Ur of the Chaldees; and not only Abram, but his father and other of his family seem at first to have obeyed the call: for Terah took Abram and Lot and Sarai, and "they went forth from Ur of the Chaldees to go into the land of Canaan" (ch. xi. 31). The land is here called by the Almighty "the land that I will shew thee," but Moses, in ch. xi. 31, calls it the land of Canaan, the destination of Abram being known to Moses, though it was not at the time of his call known to Abram himself.

2. *I will make of thee a great nation*] Literally fulfilled in the glories of Israel, spiritually and more largely in the spiritual sons of Abraham, "Abraham's seed and heirs according to the promise," Gal. iii. 29.

and thou shalt be a blessing] Kimchi on Zech. viii. 12, followed by Clericus and Knobel, interprets "shalt be an example or type of blessing," so that men shall say "Blessed be thou, as Abraham was blessed." Others, as Rosenmüller, Gesenius, &c. consider the substantive to be put for the parti-

make thy name great; and thou shalt
be a blessing:
3 And I will bless them that bless
thee, and curse him that curseth thee:
[b] and in thee shall all families of the
earth be blessed.
4 So Abram departed, as the LORD
had spoken unto him; and Lot went
with him: and Abram *was* seventy
and five years old when he departed
out of Haran.
5 And Abram took Sarai his wife,
and Lot his brother's son, and all
their substance that they had gathered, and the souls that they had gotten
in Haran; and they went forth to go
into the land of Canaan; and into the
land of Canaan they came.
6 ¶ And Abram passed through
the land unto the place of Sichem,
unto the plain of Moreh. And the
Canaanite *was* then in the land.

[b] chap. 18. 18. & 22. 18. Acts 3. 25. Gal. 3. 8.

---

ciple, *a blessing* for *blessed*, comp. Zech. viii. 12. More probable, as well as more natural, is the interpretation adopted by Tuch, Delitzsch, Keil, and others, and commended by the last words of v. 3, "Thou shalt be a blessing or cause of blessing to others besides thyself."

3. *I will bless them that bless thee, and curse him that curseth thee*] God's blessing was to extend to Abram's friends and followers, and the enemies of Abram were to be subject to God's curse. Two different Hebrew words are here translated by the one English word *curse*. Some think that the one expresses more properly the reviling and malediction of man, the other the withering curse of God. Both, however, are used of God and of man, cp. Job iii. 8; Deut. xxi. 23. The first in the English Version, that used of God, is undoubtedly the stronger of the two.

in thee shall all families of the earth be blessed] Here again Rashi, Cleric., Knobel, and some others interpret the words to mean that Abram should be so blessed in his family that all families of the earth should wish for like blessings (comp. Gen. xlviii. 20, "In thee shall Israel bless, saying, God make thee as Ephraim and Manasseh"). The words, however, can with no shew of reason be rendered otherwise than as rendered in the Authorized Version, following the LXX. and Vulg. Nor can it be understood otherwise than that all families of men should in some manner derive blessing through Abram. The Targum of Onkelos has *for thy sake*, and so the Jerusalem Targum; but this is an unauthorized exposition.

It is not necessary to assert that the prediction here given was such as to enlighten Abram with any full clearness as to the way in which his seed should bless all nations. Indeed the promise is twofold, general and particular. Generally it is true, that Abram's seed was for centuries the sole depositary of God's objective revelations, and that that knowledge of God which was confided to them has by them been spread to all nations. "Out of Zion went forth the law, and the word of the LORD from Jerusalem" (Is. ii. 3). It has indeed been said with truth, that the Semitic nations, and especially the descendants of Abram, were from the time of Abram to Christ the only believers in the unity of the Godhead, and that ever since the Christian era they only have taught monotheism to mankind. But that which was the special blessing to Abram's race, has also, springing from that race, become the universal blessing to mankind. Of him "as concerning the flesh Christ came."

4. *seventy and five years old*] See on ch. xi. 32.

5. *the souls that they had gotten*] that is, the slaves or dependants whom they had attached to them. So in Ezek. xxvii. 13, slaves are spoken of as "souls of men." Onkelos renders, "The souls which they had converted to the law in Charran." So the Pseudo-Jonathan and Jerusalem Targums render, "the souls whom they had proselyted." And following this tradition, Rashi says that Abram made proselytes of the men and Sarai of the women.

into the land of Canaan they came] Leaving Haran they must have crossed the river Euphrates, from which crossing it is very commonly supposed the name Hebrew was derived (rendered by the LXX. in Gen. xiv. 13, ὁ περάτης, *the crosser over*). Thence their course must have been southward over the desert, probably near to Mount Lebanon, and thence to the neighbourhood of Damascus. Josephus ('Ant.' I. 7) quotes from Nicolaus of Damascus ('Hist.' bk. IV.), "Abraham reigned in Damascus, being come with an army from the country beyond Babylon called the land of the Chaldæans. But not long after, leaving this country with his people he migrated into the land of Canaan, which is now called Judæa." Josephus adds, that the name of Abraham was even in his days famous in the country of the Damascenes, and a village was pointed out there, which was called Abraham's habitation.

6. *the place of Sichem*] So named by anticipation. The word *place* may perhaps indicate that the town did not yet exist.

7 And the LORD appeared unto
c Chap. 13. 15. Abram, and said, [c] Unto thy seed will
I give this land: and there builded he
an [d] altar unto the LORD, who ap- d chap. 13. 4.
peared unto him.
8 And he removed from thence

It is generally supposed that Sychar (Joh. iv. 5) is the name by which it was known among the later Samaritans, though the identity of Sychar with Shechem is not quite certain (see Smith's 'Dict. of the Bible,' Art. 'Sychar'). The word Shechem signifies *a shoulder*, and, unless the town derived its name from Shechem the son of Hamor, it probably was situated on a *shoulder* or *ridge* of land connected with the hills of Ebal and Gerizim. Josephus ('Ant.' IV. 8) describes the city of Shechem or Sicima as lying between Gerizim on the right and Ebal on the left. The name Neapolis was given to it by Vespasian; and the ancients clearly identify the later Neapolis with the ancient Shechem; *e.g.* Epiphanius ('Hær.' III. 1055), "In Sichem, that is in the present Neapolis." The modern name is Nabulus. The situation of the town is described by modern travellers as one of exceeding beauty. Dr Robinson writes, "All at once the ground sinks down to a valley running toward the West, with a soil of rich black vegetable mould. Here a scene of luxuriant and almost unparalleled verdure burst upon our view. The whole valley was filled with gardens of vegetables and orchards of all kinds of fruits, watered by several fountains which burst forth in various parts and flow westward in refreshing streams. It came suddenly upon us like a scene of fairy enchantment, we saw nothing to compare to it in all Palestine" (Vol. II. p. 275. See also Stanley's 'Sinai and Palestine,' p. 234.) This spot, probably not yet so cultivated, but even then verdant and beautiful, was the first dwellingplace of the Patriarch in the land of promise.

the plain of Moreh] **The oak** (or terebinth) **of Moreh.** There is considerable variety of opinion as to the nature of the tree here mentioned, called *Elon* in Hebrew. Celsius ('Hierob.' I. p. 34) has argued that all the cognate words, *El*, *Elon*, *Elah*, &c. signify the terebinth tree, the word *allon* only being the oak. So Michaelis ('Supplem.' p. 72), Rosenm., Delitzsch, Keil, &c. The question is discussed at great length by Gesen. ('Thes.' p. 50), who doubts the distinction between *Allon* and *Elon* (a distinction merely of vowel points), and interprets both by *oak*, or perhaps generally a *large forest tree*. The LXX. and Vulg. render *oak*. The Targums (followed by the English Version) render *plain* (see also Stanley, 'Sinai and Palestine,' p. 141). It may be a question also whether the *oak of Moreh* was a single tree, or whether the word used may be a noun of multitude, signifying *the oak grove*. A single tree of large size and spreading foliage would, no doubt, be a natural resting place for a caravan or Arab encampment in the desert; but the great fertility of the valley of Shechem favours the belief that there may have been a grove rather than a single tree. Nothing is known as to the meaning of the word *Moreh:* it may have probably been the name of a man, a prince of the land, or owner of the property.

the Canaanite was then in the land] The original settlement of the sons of Canaan seems to have been in the South near the Red Sea; a Semitic race probably occupied the regions of Palestine and Phœnicia; a colony of the Canaanites afterwards spreading northwards, partly dispossessed and partly mingled with the ancient Shemite inhabitants, and adopted their language (see note on ch. x. 6, see also Epiphan. 'Hæres.' LXVI. n. 84). The historian therefore most appropriately relates that, at the time of the emigration of Abram and his followers, the Canaanite was already in possession of the land. The conjecture, therefore, that these words were written by a later hand than that of Moses, after the ancient Canaanite inhabitants had been expelled, is altogether beside the mark.

7. *And the* LORD *appeared unto Abram*] This is the first mention of a distinct appearance of the LORD to man. His voice is heard by Adam, and He is said to have spoken to Noah and to Abram: but here is a visible manifestation. The following questions naturally arise, 1. Was this a direct vision of JEHOVAH in Bodily shape? 2. Was it an impression produced on the mind of the seer, but not a true vision of God? 3. Was it an angel personating God? 4. Was it a manifestation of the Son of God, a Theophania, in some measure anticipating the Incarnation? (1) The first question seems answered by St John (Joh. i. 18), "No man hath seen God (the Father) at any time." (2) The second to a certain extent follows the first. Whether there was a manifestation of an objective reality, or merely an impression on the senses, we cannot possibly judge; but the vision, whether seen in sleep or waking, cannot have been a vision of God the Father. (3) The third question has been answered by many in the affirmative, it being concluded that "the Angel of the LORD," a created Angel, was always the means of communication between God and man in the Old Testament. The great supporter of this opinion in early times was St Augustine ('De Trin.' III. c. xi. Tom. VIII. pp. 805—810), the chief arguments in its favour being the statements of the New Testament that the

unto a mountain on the east of Beth-
el, and pitched his tent, *having* Bethel
on the west, and Hai on the east:
and there he builded an altar unto the
LORD, and called upon the name of
the LORD.
9 And Abram journeyed, †going on
still toward the south.
10 ¶ And there was a famine in
the land: and Abram went down
into Egypt to sojourn there; for the
famine *was* grievous in the land.
11 And it came to pass, when he
was come near to enter into Egypt,
that he said unto Sarai his wife, Behold now, I know that thou *art* a fair
woman to look upon:
12 Therefore it shall come to pass,

† Heb. *in going and journeying.*

---

law was given "by disposition of angels," "spoken by angels," &c. (Acts vii. 53; Gal. iii. 19; Heb. ii. 22). It is further argued by the supporters of this view, that "the angel of the LORD" is in some passages in the Old Testament, and always in the New Testament, clearly a created angel (*e.g.* Zech. i. 11, 12, &c.; Luke i. 11; Acts xii. 23); and that therefore it is not to be supposed that any of these manifestations of the Angel of God or Angel of the Lord, which seem so markedly Divine, should have been anything more than the appearance of a created Angel personating the Most High. (4) The affirmative of the fourth opinion was held by the great majority of the fathers from the very first (see, for instance, Justin. 'Dial.' pp. 280—284; Tertull. 'adv. Prax.' c. 16; Athanas. 'Cont. Arian.' IV. pp. 464, 465 (Ed. Col.); Basil, 'adv. Eunom.' II. 18; Theodoret, 'Qu. V. in Exod.' The teaching of the fathers on this head is investigated by Bp. Bull, 'F. N. D.' IV. iii. In like manner the ancient Jews had referred the manifestation of God in visible form to the *Shechinah*, the *Metatron*, or the *Memra de Jah*, apparently an emanation from God, having a semblance of diversity, yet really one with Him, coming forth to reveal Him, but not truly distinct from Him. The fact, that the name *Angel of the Lord* is sometimes used of a created Angel, is not proof enough that it may not be also used of Him who is called "the Angel of mighty counsel" (μεγάλης βουλῆς Ἄγγελος, Is. ix. 6, Sept. Trans.), and "the Angel of the covenant" (Mal. iii. 1): and the apparent identification of the Angel of God with God Himself in very many passages (*e.g.* Gen. xxxii. 24, comp. vv. 28, 30, Hos. xii. 3, 4; Gen. xvi. 10, 13, xlviii. 15, 16; Josh. v. 14, vi. 2; Judg. ii. 1, xiii. 22; Isa. vi. 1; cp. Joh. xii. 41; Is. lxiii. 9) leads markedly to the conclusion, that God spake to man by an Angel or Messenger, and yet that that Angel or Messenger was Himself God. No man saw God at any time, but the only begotten Son, who was in the Bosom of the Father, declared Him. He, who was the Word of God, the Voice of God to His creatures, was yet in the beginning with God, and He was God.

Unto thy seed will I give this land: and there builded he an altar] This is the first definite promise to Abram, that the land of Canaan should be the inheritance of his children. Accordingly, he built an altar there, as consecrating the soil and dedicating it to God. It is not mentioned that he offered sacrifice, but as the Hebrew word for *altar* means the *place of slaughter* or *of sacrifice*, there can be no doubt, that it was an altar of burnt offering, which he built, as was Noah's altar (ch. viii. 20), the only altar spoken of prior to this time.

8. *he removed*] lit. *he plucked up* his tent pegs. The journeying was by repeated encampments, after the manner of the Bedouins.

Beth-el,] *i.e.* the House of God. This is by anticipation. It was called *Luz* at this time (see ch. xxviii. 19; Judg. i. 23). The present name is Beitan.

Hai] was about five miles to the East of Beth-el, the ruins of which bear the name of Medinet Gai.

called upon the name of the LORD.] See ch. iv. 26.

9. *going on still toward the south*] The words express a gradual change of place, after the nomadic fashion. As food offered itself he pitched his tent and fed his cattle, and when food failed he went onwards to fresh pastures.

10. *a famine*] A country like Canaan, imperfectly cultivated, would be very subject to droughts and famine. The part of Egypt, which lay immediately South of Canaan, appears to have been especially fertile. It was at that time inhabited by a people skilled in agriculture, and flooded periodically by the Nile. Egypt is still the refuge for neighbouring nations when afflicted with drought. It is said that Abram went down to Egypt "to sojourn," not to live there; for he had received the promise of inheritance in Canaan, and, though this famine may have tried, it did not shake his faith.

11. *Behold...thou art a fair woman*] Sarai was now more than sixty years old: but her life extended to 127 years, so that she was only then in middle life; she had borne no children, and at the age of ninety, though not naturally young enough to have a son, was yet preserved in a condition of unusual and

when the Egyptians shall see thee,
that they shall say, This *is* his wife:
and they will kill me, but they will
save thee alive.
13 Say, I pray thee, thou *art* my
sister: that it may be well with me
for thy sake; and my soul shall live
because of thee.
14 ¶ And it came to pass, that,
when Abram was come into Egypt,
the Egyptians beheld the woman that
she *was* very fair.
15 The princes also of Pharaoh
saw her, and commended her before
Pharaoh: and the woman was taken
into Pharaoh's house.
16 And he entreated Abram well
for her sake: and he had sheep, and
oxen, and he asses, and menservants,
and maidservants, and she asses, and
camels.
17 And the LORD plagued Pharaoh
and his house with great plagues because of Sarai Abram's wife.
18 And Pharaoh called Abram,
and said, What *is* this *that* thou hast
done unto me? why didst thou not
tell me that she *was* thy wife?
19 Why saidst thou, She *is* my
sister? so I might have taken her to
me to wife: now therefore behold
thy wife, take *her*, and go thy way.

---

preternatural youth, so that she bore Isaac; her fair complexion would contrast favourably with the swarthy complexion of the Egyptians. The Arab life of Abram naturally made him wary of danger. He was about to sojourn in a country with a despotic government, and among a licentious people. We see in the conduct of Abram an instance of one under the influence of deep religious feeling and true faith in God, but yet with a conscience imperfectly enlightened as to many moral duties, and when leaning to his own understanding suffered to fall into great error and sin. The candour of the historian is shewn by his exhibiting in such strong relief the dissimulation of Abram as contrasted with the straightforward integrity of Pharaoh.

15. *Pharaoh*] The name or title, by which the kings of Egypt are called in the Old Testament. Josephus tells us that "Pharaoh among the Egyptians signifies *king*." It used to be thought that it was the Coptic word *Ouro* with the article *Pi* or *Ph*. (Jablonski, Diss. iv. section 3, 'De Terra Gosen.') Later the opinion of Rosellini, Lepsius, Rawlinson, Poole and others has been that it corresponded with the title of the Sun-God RA, with the article, PH—RA, a name which was given to some of the kings of Egypt. Gesenius objects to this from its lacking the final *oh* ('Thes.' p. 1129); and there is insufficient evidence that the title was really a common title of the kings. Very recently M. De Rougé has shewn that the hieroglyphic, which is the regular title of the Egyptian kings, and which signifies "the great house" or "the double house," must be read Peraa or Perao. This singularly corresponds with the statement of Horapollo (I. 61), that the king was called οἶκος μέγας, "the great house." The identity of this with the name Pharaoh is admitted by Brugsch, Ebers ('Ægypten, &c.' p. 26), and is argued at length in the "Excursus on Egyptian Words" (by the Rev. F. C. Cook) at the end of this volume. It may be compared with the title "Sublime Porte."

It is difficult to fix the particular Pharaoh or dynasty under which Abram came into Egypt. Generally the characteristics of the Court, as briefly described in Genesis, point to a native dynasty of very remote date. Some circumstances, the friendly reception of a Semitic nomade and the use of camels (v. 16) among the Egyptians, have suggested the belief that Abram's Pharaoh must have been a shepherd king (see Smith's Dict. of the Bible, Artt. *Pharaoh* and *Zoan*); and Sir Gardiner Wilkinson ('Ancient Egyptians,' Vol. I. chap. ii. p. 42) has identified him with Apophis or Apepi, the sixth monarch of Manetho's 15th dynasty. It is, however, impossible to admit so late a date. The Pharaoh of Joseph was almost certainly a king of the 12th dynasty. Abram's Pharaoh must therefore at latest have been one of the first kings of that same dynasty, if not belonging to a dynasty earlier still. The objections, derived from the camels, and other apparent indications of a shepherd reign, are fully considered in Excursus I. "On the Bearings of Egyptian History on the Pentateuch," at the end of this volume, by Rev. F. C. Cook: and the period of Abram's sojourn in Egypt is shewn to be most probably under one of the earlier sovereigns of the 12th dynasty.

the woman was taken into Pharaoh's house] Probably even at that early period Egypt had reached such a pitch of corrupt civilization that the sovereign had a hareem, and Sarai was chosen to be one of his wives.

18. *Pharaoh called Abram*] Josephus says, that the priests told Pharaoh for what cause that plague had fallen on him ('Ant.' I. 8). It is more likely that Sarai herself, being

20 And Pharaoh commanded *his*
men concerning him: and they sent
him away, and his wife, and all that
he had.

CHAPTER XIII.

1 *Abram and Lot return out of Egypt.* 7 *By disagreement they part asunder.* 10 *Lot goeth to wicked Sodom.* 14 *God reneweth the promise to Abram.* 18 *He removeth to Hebron, and there buildeth an altar.*

AND Abram went up out of E-
gypt, he, and his wife, and all
that he had, and Lot with him, into
the south.
2 And Abram *was* very rich in
cattle, in silver, and in gold.
3 And he went on his journeys
from the south even to Beth-el, unto
the place where his tent had been at
the beginning, between Beth-el and
Hai;
4 Unto the [a] place of the altar, [a] chap. 12. 7.
which he had made there at the first:
and there Abram called on the name
of the LORD.
5 ¶ And Lot also, which went
with Abram, had flocks, and herds,
and tents.
6 And the land was not able to
bear them, that they might dwell together: for their substance was great,
so that they could not dwell together.
7 And there was a strife between
the herdmen of Abram's cattle and
the herdmen of Lot's cattle: and the

---

interrogated about it, confessed the truth (Patrick).

19. *so I might have taken her*] Heb. **So I took her.** LXX. Syr. Onk. Though the Vulgate followed by the Arabic has, "so that I might have taken her." The meaning is, Deceived by Abram's words, Pharaoh took her with the intention of making her his wife, but was hindered from doing so by the afflictions with which God visited him (see Theodoret, 'Qu. LXXII. in Gen.' Op. XII. Augustin, 'De Civit. Dei,' XVI. 18). St Jerome ('Trad. Heb. in Genes.') refers to Esth. ii. 12, where we learn that the custom of Eastern monarchs was, that a maiden should undergo twelvemonths of purification before she was actually taken to wife. It was, he thinks, during some such period that Pharaoh was plagued and prohibited from marrying Sarai. It deserves to be noticed, that throughout the history of the chosen race, Egypt was to them the scene of spiritual danger, of covetousness and love of riches, of worldly security, of temptation to rest on an arm of flesh, on man's own understanding, and not on God only. All this appears from the very first, in Abraham's sojourn there, Sarai's danger, their departure full of wealth and prosperity.

CHAP. XIII. 1. *and Lot with him*] Lot is not mentioned in the descent into Egypt, because no part of the narrative there concerns him. On the return to Canaan he becomes a principal actor.

into the south] That southern part of Canaan, whence he had gone down into Egypt, The south, or *Negeb*, is almost a proper name.

2. *very rich*] He had grown rich in Egypt. He has now to experience some of the dangers and evils of prosperity.

3. *on his journeys*] By his stations, or according to his encampments, *i.e.* either station by station, as before, pitching his tent for a time at one station and then removing it to another; or perhaps, returning by his former stations, according to his original encampments when he was journeying southwards.

unto the place where his tent had been at the beginning] Shechem was the first place at which he rested and built an altar; but he probably remained there a comparatively short time. The Canaanites then in the land (ch. xii. 6) would doubtless have occupied all the most fertile country about Shechem. His second place of sojourn was the mountain near Bethel, where he is said to have built an altar and called on the name of the Lord, and where very probably he had continued until the famine began to prevail. (See ch. xii. vv. 7, 8, 9, 10.)

6. *the land was not able to bear them*] Lot was the sharer of Abram's prosperity. They came up out of Egypt with much larger possessions than before, more "flocks and herds and tents" for their now more numerous retainers. The land too had but just recovered from a state of drought and dearth: "and the Canaanite and the Perizzite dwelt then in the land" (v. 7), and probably by their occupation contributed to the scarcity of pasture.

7. *Perizzite*] But little is known of this people. They are not mentioned in the catalogue of nations in Gen. x. They are mostly coupled, as here, with the Canaanites. They appear from Josh. xi. 3, xvii. 15, to have dwelt in the woods and mountains. Bochart describes them ('Phaleg.' IV. 36) as a rustic, agrarian race, living without cities and in villages only, the name itself signifying ***pagani***, ***villagers***, ***rustics***.

Canaanite and the Perizzite dwelled
then in the land.
8 And Abram said unto Lot,
Let there be no strife, I pray thee,
between me and thee, and between
my herdmen and thy herdmen; for
we *be* † brethren. † Heb. *men brethren.*
9 *Is* not the whole land before
thee? separate thyself, I pray thee,
from me: if *thou wilt take* the left
hand, then I will go to the right; or
if *thou depart* to the right hand, then
I will go to the left.
10 And Lot lifted up his eyes, and
beheld all the plain of Jordan, that it
was well watered every where, before
the LORD destroyed Sodom and Gomorrah, *even* as the garden of the
LORD, like the land of Egypt, as thou
comest unto Zoar.

11 Then Lot chose him all the
plain of Jordan; and Lot journeyed
east: and they separated themselves
the one from the other.
12 Abram dwelled in the land of
Canaan, and Lot dwelled in the cities
of the plain, and pitched *his* tent toward Sodom.
13 But the men of Sodom *were*
wicked and sinners before the LORD
exceedingly.
14 ¶ And the LORD said unto A-
bram, after that Lot was separated
from him, Lift up now thine eyes,
and look from the place where thou
art northward, and southward, and
eastward, and westward:
15 For all the land which thou [b] chap. 12. 7. & 26. 4. Deut. 34. 4.
seest, [b] to thee will I give it, and to
thy seed for ever.

---

dwelled then in the land] See on xii. 6.

8. *Let there be no strife*] A noble example of disinterestedness and love of peace exhibited by the father of the faithful.

10. *Lot lifted up his eyes*] They were probably encamped on that mountain on the east of Bethel, having Bethel on the west and Hai on the east, where Abram had built the altar and called on the name of the Lord (ch. xii. 8). The very spot can be traced from the indications of the sacred text (Stanley's 'Jewish Church,' Vol. I. p. 32). From this spot Lot and Abram chose their respective possessions. Lot saw the plains of Jordan, watered by fertilizing rivers, not yet broken up by the overflowing or outbursting of the great salt lake, very probably irrigated like the land of Egypt which he had lately left, where the Nile refreshed the soil, and the plague of famine never came. Taking no warning by the dangers, bodily and spiritual, which had beset them in Egypt, he feared not the proximity of the wealthy and luxurious inhabitants of Sodom and Gomorrah, but thought their land pleasant even as the garden of the Lord. He chose the rich pastures of the plain, and left Abram the less promising, but, as it proved, the safer inheritance of the hill country of Judæa. It was a selfish choice, and it proved a sad one.

as thou comest unto Zoar] See on ch. xiv. 3.

12. *land of Canaan*] That is, Canaan strictly so called.

the plain] Lit. "the circuit or neighbourhood," the country round about Jordan. So the LXX. (Ges. 'Thes.' p. 717. Stanley, 'Sinai and Palestine,' p. 287.) The low tract or plain along the river—through which it flows, perhaps as comprehensive as the Ghor itself. (Robinson, 'Phys. Geog.' p. 73.)

13. *sinners before the LORD*] Sodom, Gomorrah, Admah and Zeboim are mentioned, Gen. x. 19, as among the first settlements of the Canaanites. The fertility of the soil in this Valley of the Jordan, with the luxurious and enervating character of the climate, rapidly developed the sensual vices of this early civilized but depraved race. Their wickedness is mentioned here perhaps in anticipation of the history in ch. xix., but partly also in order to exhibit more clearly the thoughtlessness and worldliness of Lot in choosing their neighbourhood for his residence, as distinguished from the humility and unselfish spirit of Abram.

14. *Lift up now thine eyes*, &c.] He was probably still on the hill east of Bethel. Here once again, on his return from Egypt to the land of his inheritance, God renews his promise to Abram. The world, with its dangers and its honours, may have tempted Abram, but it had not corrupted him. He came back from Egypt with larger knowledge, probably all the more armed against sin by having had some experience of its seductions. He is still the chosen of God; and he is comforted under separation from his kinsman, and the discovery of that kinsman's lower motives and less disinterestedness, by the assurance that God was still ever with him and pledged to preserve and provide for him.

15. *to thee*] The land even in present possession was his, so far as was needed by him as a nomade chief, though its permanent occupation was to him and his seed after him.

16 And I will make thy seed as the dust of the earth: so that if a man can number the dust of the earth, *then* shall thy seed also be numbered.

17 Arise, walk through the land in the length of it and in the breadth of it; for I will give it unto thee.

18 Then Abram removed *his* tent, and came and dwelt in the †plain of Mamre, which *is* in Hebron, and built there an altar unto the LORD.

† Heb. *plains.*

CHAPTER XIV.

1 *The battle of four kings against five.* 12 *Lot is taken prisoner.* 14 *Abram rescueth him.* 18 *Melchizedek blesseth Abram.* 20 *Abram giveth him tithe.* 22 *The rest of the spoil, his partners having had their portions, he restoreth to the king of Sodom.*

AND it came to pass in the days of Amraphel king of Shinar, Arioch king of Ellasar, Chedorlaomer king of Elam, and Tidal king of nations;

2 *That these* made war with Bera king of Sodom, and with Birsha king of Gomorrah, Shinab king of Admah, and Shemeber king of Zeboiim, and the king of Bela, which is Zoar.

---

for ever] *i.e.* in perpetuity. But, when we consider that the promises to Abram have their full completion in Christ, to whom are given "the uttermost parts of the earth for a possession," there need be no limit to the sense of the words "for ever."

18. *the plain of Mamre*] **The Oaks** (or terebinths) **of Mamre**, see on ch. xii. 6. Probably it means "the oak grove" or "wood of Mamre," called after Mamre the Amorite, the friend and ally of Abram (ch. xiv. 13, 24).

Hebron] Called *Arba* or *Kirjath-arba* (see ch. xxiii. 2, xxxv. 4. Judg. i. 10) till after the death of Moses, when Caleb took the city and changed its name to Hebron. It has been thought therefore that the words here "which is Hebron," must have been inserted by a later hand than that of Moses. It is more probable that Hebron was the original name, changed to Kirjath-arba during the sojourn of the descendants of Jacob in the land of Egypt, and restored by Caleb at the conquest of Palestine. So Karme (cited by Rosenmüller), Hengstenberg, Keil, &c.; see also on ch. xxiii. 2. This was the third resting place of Abram: 1. Shechem, 2. Bethel, 3. Hebron. Near it was the cave of Machpelah, where he and Sarah were buried. It is now called *El Khalil*, "the friend," *i. e.* the house of the friend of God. Near to it stands an ancient Terebinth, once a place of heathen worship (Delitzsch). The cave of Machpelah still is there, surrounded by a mosque, in which lie probably the dust of Abraham and Isaac, and perhaps the embalmed body, the mummy, of Jacob, brought up in solemn state from Egypt, ch. l. 13 (Stanley, 'Sinai and Palestine,' p. 102).

CHAP. XIV. 1. *And it came to pass*] We come now upon a new scene in the life of Abram. The choice of Lot was soon seen not to be a wise choice, even for earthly happiness. The rich plains of Sodom and Gomorrah were likely to be scenes of strife, as in early times was the case with all fertile countries (Thucyd. I. 2). The history of this war is a remarkable episode, and is thought by many to be a very ancient document incorporated by Moses in his great work. So Tuch, Ewald, Kurtz, &c. who all bear testimony to its internal proofs of historical accuracy. The occurrence of the name JEHOVAH in it is inconsistent with the theory, which assigns the use of that name only to the later portions of the book of Genesis.

in the days of Amraphel king of Shinar] The king of Shinar, (*Babel*, Onkel., *Bagdad*, Arab. Erpen., *Pontus*, Jonathan,) as being the representative of Nimrod, founder of the great Babylonian Empire, is mentioned first. The name Amraphel is probably Assyrian, its derivation unknown.

Arioch] If, as it is supposed, the root of this word be *ari*, a *lion*, the bearer of it would appear to have been Semitic.

Ellasar] Jonathan *Telassar* (see 2 K. xix. 12; Isa. xxxvii. 12), a place not far off. It is more probably identified with Larsa or Larancha, the Larissa of the Greeks, a town in Lower Babylonia, or Chaldæa, between Ur and Erech, on the left bank of the Euphrates (Rawlinson, Kalisch, &c.).

Chedorlaomer king of Elam] It seems from the narrative that at this time the king of Elam was the most powerful of the Asiatic princes (Le Clerc). The Elamites appear to have been originally a Semitic people (ch. x. 22). If then they had now gained a superiority over the Hamitic races, it is not improbable that the Canaanites of the plain of Jordan, having been originally subject to the kings of Shinar, or Babylon, bore unwillingly the transference of their fealty to the Shemite king of Elam, and took the first opportunity of throwing off their allegiance, whereupon the king of Elam, now the head of the four kingdoms named in this verse, gathered his subjects or tributary allies, and strove to reduce the Canaanites again to subjection. Re-

3 All these were joined together
in the vale of Siddim, which is the
salt sea.

4 Twelve years they served Chedorlaomer, and in the thirteenth year
they rebelled.

5 And in the fourteenth year came
Chedorlaomer, and the kings that
were with him, and smote the Rephaims in Ashteroth Karnaim, and
the Zuzims in Ham, and the Emims
in ‖ Shaveh Kiriathaim,

‖ Or, *the plain of Kiriathaim.*

---

cent discoveries shew that Susa (the capital of Elymais) must have been one of the most ancient cities of the East. Sir Henry Rawlinson thought he discovered a name coresponding with Chedorlaomer on Chaldæan bricks, viz. Kadur-Mapula, the second portion of the word being of course distinct. Another title by which Kadur-Mapula was known was "Ravager of the West," which corresponds with the account here given of Chedorlaomer. Rawlinson and others consider the dynasty of Chedorlaomer not to have been Semitic, but belonging to a race of Hamites, who had subdued the original Elymæans.

Tidal king of nations] Symmachus renders "King of the Scythians," which is approved by some commentators, because Scythia was inhabited by many different tribes (Fuller, 'Miscell. SS.' Lib. II. c. 4, quoted by Rosenm.). Le Clerc, followed by Rosenmüller, prefers Galilee, called "Galilee of the Gentiles" or "nations" (Is. ix. 1; Matt. iv. 15. See also Strabo, Lib. XVI. § 34, who says that these northern parts of Judæa were inhabited by various mixed tribes, Egyptians, Arabs, Phœnicians). But all this was probably later in history, and the name Galilee of the nations was given to Galilee, because it was still inhabited by other tribes, whilst Judæa was inhabited by none but Israelites (Gesenius, 'Thes.' p. 272). We may most probably conjecture that Tidal was owned as the chief of several nomade tribes, who, like Abram, had no stationary home. For Tidal, the LXX. has *Thargal*, which is preferred by some, as having the meaning of "Great chief" in the early Hamitic dialect of the lower Tigris and Euphrates country (Rawlinson, in Smith's 'Dict. of Bible').

3. *vale of Siddim*] The meaning of this name has been a great puzzle to interpreters. The LXX. render it "the salt valley." Onkelos evidently refers the derivation to *Sadeh*, a plain (as though שִׂדִּים was plural of שָׂדֶה). So Aquila and Rashi. They are followed by Stanley ('Sinai and Palestine,' p. 491). Aben Ezra derives it from *Sid* (שִׂיד), *lime*, because of the abundance of bitumen, which was used as lime (see ch. xi. 3). Gesenius suggests an Arabic root signifying an obstacle, and so concludes that the valley of Siddim was a plain full of rocky valleys and irregularities. In v. 10 it is said to be full of bitumen pits, which was perhaps the reason why the five kings chose it for the field of battle, as being more favourable to the weaker party.

which is the salt sea] The extreme depression of the Dead Sea, 1316 feet (Robinson, 'Phys. Geog.' p. 190), and other geological phenomena, are thought to favour the belief, that there must have been originally some lake at the extremity of the valley of the Jordan; but perhaps after the destruction of Sodom and Gomorrah the lake greatly extended itself, so as to cover much which before may have been low valley land. The vale of Siddim is generally thought to have been at the southern extremity of the Dead Sea, where are now to be seen the principal deposits of salt and bitumen, the site being occupied by the shallow southern portion of that sea (see Robinson, 'Physical Geography of the Holy Land,' pp. 73, 213).

4. *Twelve years*, &c.] See on v. 1.

5. *Rephaims*] The LXX. renders "Giants," so virtually do Onk. and Syr. It is, no doubt, the name of an ancient people; very probably a tribe resident in the Holy Land before the immigration of the Canaanites. They appear to have been a people of large stature. Og, the king of Bashan, at the time of the Exodus, is mentioned as the last remaining of their race (Deut. iii. 11). Their habitation was to the north-east of the valley of the Jordan, the country afterwards called Peræa. They must also have extended to the south-west; for the valley of Rephaim, named after them, appears to have been in the neighbourhood of the valley of Hinnom and Bethlehem, to the south of Jerusalem (see Josh. xv. 8, xviii. 16; 2 S. v. 18, 22, xxiii. 13). The name "Rephaim," in later times, is constantly used for "the dead," or rather for the "ghosts or manes of the dead" (Job xxvi. 5; Ps. lxxxviii. 11; Prov. ii. 18; Is. xiv. 9, xxvi. 14). Whether there is a connection between the name of this ancient and afterwards extinct people, and this word thus used for "the dead," is very doubtful (Gesen. 'Thes.' p. 1302).

Ashteroth Karnaim] "Ashteroth of the two horns." It is most probable that this was the same as the Ashtaroth, where Og the king of Bashan dwelt (Deut. i. 4; Josh. ix. 10), in the east of the inheritance of the tribe of Manasseh; and that it was named from the worship of Astarte (Ashtoreth), whose image

6 And the Horites in their mount
Seir, unto ‖ El-paran, which *is* by the
wilderness.
7 And they returned, and came to
En-mishpat, which *is* Kadesh, and
smote all the country of the Amalekites, and also the Amorites, that
dwelt in Hazezon-tamar.

‖ Or, *the plain of Paran.*

---

was such as to suggest the idea of a horned figure (see Gesen. 'Thes.' p. 1082). In like manner Athor (the Egyptian Venus, as Astarte was the Phœnician), was depicted with horns like a cow (see Rawlinson's 'Herod.' Vol. II. pp. 61, 62). Some, however, think the two horns to refer to two hills, between which the city lay, and the name "horned" was intended to distinguish this town from the city commonly called Ashtaroth only (see Rosenm. in loc. and Smith's 'Dict. of Bible,' s. v. *Ashtaroth*).

Zuzims] Little is known concerning the name or place of this people. The LXX. and Onk. render "the strong or mighty ones." Le Clerc thinks the name means "wanderer," from the root Zuz זוּז, "to move oneself." Michaelis understands "dwarfs." Both derivations are rejected by Gesen. ('Thes.' p. 410). They are very generally thought to be the same with the Zamzummims (Deut. ii. 20), who are spoken of as a race of great stature, and connected with the Horim, as are the Zuzims here.

in Ham] If the Zuzim be the same as the Zamzummim, they must have dwelt in the territory of the Ammonites, and Tuch, followed by Knobel, considers that Ham here is the same as Rabbath-Ammon. There is another reading in seven Samaritan MSS. followed by the LXX. and Vulg. viz. (בָּהֶם ἅμα αὐτοῖς, *cum illis*) "with them;" but the pointing of the Masorites seems more likely to be the true.

the Emims] The name is supposed to be the Hebrew for "terrible ones." The Rev. F. C. Cook identifies the name with Amu, the Egyptian word for nomad Semites. In Deut. ii. 10, 11, where they are mentioned in the same connection as here, they are spoken of as "a people great and many and tall." They dwelt in the country afterwards occupied by the Moabites.

Shaveh Kiriathaim] or "the plain of Kiriathaim," or "the plain of the two cities." Kiriathaim is mentioned, Num. xxxii. 37, Josh. xiii. 19, as in the possession of the sons of Reuben. Eusebius says it was well known in his day, a village inhabited by Christians, close to the Baris, about 10 miles west of Medeba ('Onom.' Κιριαθιείμ).

6. *the Horites in their mount Seir*] The name "Horites" means "inhabitants of caves." These people dwelt in the mountain region called Seir (lit. "the hirsute," probably from its thick forests and brushwood), extending from the Dead Sea southward to the Elamitic Gulf. Mount Seir is called in the Samaritan Pentateuch and the Jerusalem Targum "Gabla," and the northern part of the range is still called "Jebal," or "the mountain," by the Arabs. The wonderful excavations in the rocks near Petra may very possibly be due to these "Horim," or cave-dwellers. They were driven out by the Edomites (Deut. ii. 12), who also after the manner of their predecessors "made their nest high like the eagle."

El-paran] *i.e.* "the oak or terebinth wood of Paran." The great wilderness, extending to the south of Palestine, the south-west of Idumæa, and thence to the Sinaitic range, appears to have been called the wilderness of Paran. It probably lay to the west of the wilderness of Sin, but at times is to be taken in a wider sense, as comprehending the desert of Sin (see Gesen. 'Thes.' pp. 47, 1090). El-paran is here said to be by the wilderness, *i.e.* on the eastern side of the great desert, marking the farthest point to which the expedition of Chedorlaomer reached. The wilderness of Paran is identified with the modern desert of El-Tih, the wilderness of Zin or Sin being the Wady-el-Arabah (Stanley, 'Sinai and Palestine,' p. 92).

7. *to En-mishpat, which is Kadesh*] The LXX. renders "to the well of judgment," the Vulg. "to the well of Mishpat." Some suppose it to have derived its name from the *judgment* pronounced on Moses and Aaron (Num. xx. 12), and that the name is here given proleptically; but it is evidently here given as the ancient name to which the more modern *Kadesh* corresponded. Syr., Onk., Jerus. render Kadesh by Rekam. Josephus calls it Arekem, which he says now bears the name of Petra ('A. J.' IV. 4). This identity of Kadesh with Petra is ably defended by Dean Stanley ('S. and P.' pp. 94, 95). Another site for the ancient Kades, or Ain-Mishpat, is vindicated for Kudes or Kades, lying to the east of the highest part of Djebel-Halal, about 12 miles to the E.S.E. of Morlakhi (see Williams, 'Holy City,' Vol. I. p. 467; Kalisch, Delitzsch, Keil, in loc.) Strong objections to both these sites are urged in the art. *Kades* in Smith's 'Dict. of the Bible.'

Amalekites] See note on ch. xxxvi. 12.

Hazezon-tamar] *i.e.* "The pruning of the palm," the same place which was afterwards called Engedi, "the fountain of the wild-goat" (2 Chr. xx. 2). The palm-groves, which gave the original name, and for which Pliny says Engedi was famous ('Nat. Hist.' v. 17), have

8 And there went out the king of
Sodom, and the king of Gomorrah,
and the king of Admah, and the king
of Zeboiim, and the king of Bela
(the same *is* Zoar;) and they joined
battle with them in the vale of Siddim;
9 With Chedorlaomer the king of
Elam, and with Tidal king of nations,
and Amraphel king of Shinar, and
Arioch king of Ellasar; four kings
with five.
10 And the vale of Siddim *was full
of* slimepits; and the kings of Sodom
and Gomorrah fled, and fell there;
and they that remained fled to the
mountain.
11 And they took all the goods of
Sodom and Gomorrah, and all their
victuals, and went their way.
12 And they took Lot, Abram's
brother's son, who dwelt in Sodom,
and his goods, and departed.
13 ¶ And there came one that had
escaped, and told Abram the Hebrew;
for he dwelt in the plain of Mamre
the Amorite, brother of Eshcol, and
brother of Aner: and these *were* con-
federate with Abram.
14 And when Abram heard that
his brother was taken captive, he
‖armed his ‖trained *servants*, born in his ‖ Or, *led forth.*
own house, three hundred and eigh- ‖ Or, *instructed.*
teen, and pursued *them* unto Dan.
15 And he divided himself against
them, he and his servants, by night,

---

disappeared, but the ibex, or Syrian chamois, still inhabits the cliffs in the neighbourhood (Stanley, 'S. and P.' p. 295). The place was situated in the wilderness of Judæa, to the west of the Dead Sea, according to Josephus 300 stadia from Jerusalem ('Ant.' IX. c. 1). The ruins found at a place called Ain Jiddi, with a fountain in the midst of a mountain country, to the west of the Dead Sea and of about the latitude of Hebron, are supposed to mark the original site of Engedi or Hazezon-tamar.

10. *slimepits*] **Bitumen-pits:** of asphalt or bitumen, from which the Dead Sea was afterwards called Lacus Asphaltites, or Sea of Asphalt.

fell there] *i.e.* were overthrown there; for the king of Sodom seems to have been one of those who fled to the mountains and escaped, see v. 17.

13. *one that had escaped*] Rather **those that escaped** (Ew. 277; Ges. 'Thes.' p. 1105).

the Hebrew] *i.e.* either "the descendant of Eber," which seems most accordant with the words in ch. x. 21, where Eber seems to have given a general name to his descendants, or (as the LXX., Aq., Vulg., and most ancient interpreters), "the stranger from beyond the Euphrates," an appellative from the Hebrew noun or preposition *Eber*, עֵבֶר, signifying the "opposite side, beyond." The mention of Abram as the Hebrew is due to the fact, that the messenger, who came and told him what had happened, was an inhabitant of the land, and Abram was to him one of a strange country and strange race.

the plain] **The oaks or oak groves.**

14. *He armed his trained servants*] **He led out his trained servants.** The verb here used means "to draw out," as a sword from its sheath: and the word *trained* is applied to the teaching of children (Prov. xxii. 6), and to initiation or consecration, as of a house (Deut. xx. 5), or a temple (1 K. viii. 63).

born in his own house] Of his own patriarchal family, not bought, hired, or taken in war.

unto Dan] Some taking this Dan to be the same as Laish, which was not called Dan till after the country was conquered by the Danites (Josh. xix. 47; Judg. xviii. 29), have thought that this passage was not from the hand of Moses. So Ewald ('Gesch.' I. 53), who supposes *Dan* to have been substituted by a later hand for Laish in the original MS. Others have thought that another place was meant here (so Deyling, Hävernick, Kalisch, Keil). Keil contends that the Dan, formerly called Laish, which was on the central source of the Jordan (see Joseph. 'Ant.' I. 10; Stanley, 'S. and P.' p. 395), could not have been the Dan here mentioned, as it did not lie in either of the two roads leading from the vale of Siddim to Damascus. Both he and Kalisch think this Dan to be the same as Dan-jaan (2 S. xxiv. 6), apparently belonging to Gilead, and to be sought for in northern Peræa, to the south-west of Damascus. The chief objection to this is, that Josephus (as above, 'Ant.' I. 10) and Jerome ('Qu. Hebr. in Gen.' ad h.l.) distinctly speak of the Dan here mentioned, as situated at the source of the Jordan. The conjecture of Le Clerc (Cleric. *in loc.*) is not contemptible, viz. that the original name of the fountain was "Dan," *i.e.* "judge," (cp. Ain-mishpat, the fountain of justice), the neighbouring town being called Laish; but that the Danites gave the name of the well, which corresponded with that of their own tribe, to the city as well as the fountain.

15. *he divided himself against them, he*

and smote them, and pursued them
unto Hobah, which *is* on the left hand
of Damascus.
16 And he brought back all the
goods, and also brought again his
brother Lot, and his goods, and the
women also, and the people.

17 ¶ And the king of Sodom went
out to meet him after his return from
the slaughter of Chedorlaomer, and
of the kings that *were* with him, at
the valley of Shaveh, which *is* the
[a]king's dale.
18 And [b]Melchizedek king of Sa-

[a] 2 Sam. 18. 18.
[b] Heb. 7. 1.

---

and his servants, by night] From v. 24 it appears that besides Abram's own servants there went out with him Aner, Eshcol and Mamre, with their followers. These divided their forces, surprised the invaders at different points of attack during the darkness, and so routed them.

Hobah, which is on the left hand of Damascus] *i.e.* to the north of Damascus, the north being to the left of a man, who looks toward the sunrising. A place called Choba is mentioned, Judith xv. 6; Eusebius ('Onom.' v. Χωβά) says that in his day a village existed in the neighbourhood of Damascus called by this name, which was inhabited by Ebionites. About two miles from Damascus is now a village called Hobah, said to be the place to which Abram pursued the kings (Stanley, 'S. and P.' p. 414 k).

17. *the valley of Shaveh, which is the king's dale*] In 2 S. xviii. 18, we read that Absalom in his lifetime "took and reared up for himself a pillar, which is in the king's dale: for he said, I have no son to keep my name in remembrance: and he called the pillar after his own name, and it is called unto this day, Absalom's place." Josephus ('Ant.' VII. 10) says, that the monument was two stadia from Jerusalem. This would correspond well with the valley of the Upper Kidron, where are the tombs of the judges and other ancient sepulchres, a very likely place for Absalom to have erected what was evidently intended as a sepulchral monument. The tomb now known as Absalom's is probably not his, as it appears to be of later date, corresponding with the rock-tombs of Petra belonging to a period later than the Christian era (Robinson, 'Phys. Geog.' p. 92). It is not, however, possible to determine the situation of the valley of Shaveh, and its identity with the later King's Dale of 2 S. xviii. 18, without first fixing the site of Salem, of which Melchizedek was king. If Salem be Jerusalem, then Shaveh may well have been the valley of the Kidron, close to Jerusalem: but if Salem were some more northern city, we must leave the position of Shaveh undetermined. See on v. 18.

18. *Melchizedek*] Various have been the conjectures in all ages as to the person of Melchizedek. Some have supposed the name to be a title, like Augustus or Pharaoh, rather than a proper name, comparing Malek-ol-Adel and Adel-Chan, *i.e.* "the just king," a title common to some Mahommedan kings, as the princes of the Deccan and Golconda: but the Hebrew form of the word seems to point to a proper name rather than to a title. Cp. Abi-melech, Gen. xx. 2, Adoni-zedek, Josh. x. 3. The Targums of Jerusalem and Pseudo-Jonathan say, that Melchizedek was Shem, and St Jerome ('Qu. ad Genes.' in loc.) tells us that the Jews of his day said he was Shem the son of Noah, and calculating the days of his life, shewed that he must have lived to the time of Isaac. (See also Epist. LXXIII. 'ad Evang.' Opp. I. p. 438). This opinion has been adopted by many moderns, and is defended at length by Jackson 'On the Creed,' Bk. IX. It probably arose from considerations of the great dignity of the king and priest, who blessed Abraham and took tithes of him, and from the readiness of the Jews to ascribe such dignity only to an ancestor of their own. The Jews very anciently considered him at least to be a type of Messiah (Schœttgen. 'Hor. Hebr.' T. II. p. 645); but they generally seem to have believed that he was a prince of the country, as the Targum of Onkelos and Josephus, which both describe him simply as king of Jerusalem, in which they are followed by most commentators of modern times. It is a question of interest, but impossible to solve, Was he of the Canaanitish race or Semitic? On ch. x. 6, some explanation is given of the fact that the Canaanites spoke a Semitic tongue. The name and titles of Melchizedek are Semitic, but this proves nothing. He dwelt among Canaanites; but there had probably been Semitic inhabitants of the land before the immigration of the Canaanites (see on ch. xii. 6); and so Melchizedek, who was a worshipper of the true God, may have been one of the original Shemite stock. There were, however, worshippers of the true God, besides the Israelites, retaining patriarchal truth, as Job, and Balaam, and so it is not certain that Melchizedek was a descendant of Shem. He is, in fact, as the Apostle tells us, introduced "without father, without mother, without descent," with no mention of the beginning of his priesthood or the ending of it, and so specially suited to be a type of the Son of God. He is mentioned once besides in the Old Testament, viz. in Ps. cx. 4, where the priesthood of Messiah is said to be after the

lem brought forth bread and wine:
and he *was* the priest of the most
high God.

19 And he blessed him, and said,
Blessed *be* Abram of the most high
God, possessor of heaven and earth:

---

order of Melchizedek; and again in the New Testament, Heb. v. vi. vii., where the comparison between the royal priesthood of Melchizedek and that of Jesus is drawn out at length. The special points of resemblance of Melchizedek to Christ are: 1. that he was not of the Levitical order, local, national, but previous to the giving of the Law, catholic, universal; 2. that he was superior to Abraham, blessed and took tithes of him; 3. that (as often in old times, Virg. 'Æn.' III. 80; Arist. 'Pol.' III. 14, &c.), he was both king and priest; 4. that no beginning and no end are assigned either to his priesthood or his life; 5. his name too "king of righteousness and king of peace," are eminently suited to a type of the Son of God (Heb. vii. 2, 3). The bringing forth bread and wine is not referred to by the Apostle; but the ancient Church loved to dwell on this as typical of the institution by the Saviour of the θυσία ἀναίμακτος, the *incruentum sacrificium*, as they were wont to call the Holy Eucharist; and later ages may have made more of it than Scripture will warrant. (See Jackson, as above, Bk. IX. sect. ii. ch. x.)

king of Salem] Josephus ('Ant.' I. 10), Onkelos and all the Targg. understand Jerusalem, which is called Salem in Ps. lxxvi. 2, and this is pretty certainly the true interpretation. Jerome however ('Epist. LXXIII. ad Evang.' Tom. I. p. 446, edit. Vallars.), says it was not Jerusalem, but a city near Scythopolis, called Salem up to his time, where the ruins of Melchizedek's palace were shewn, and of which it is written (Gen. xxxiii. 18), "Jacob came to Shalem." Yet *Shalem*, in Gen. xxxiii. is rendered by Onkelos and a majority of modern commentators, not as a proper name, but rather "in peace" (see note on ch. xxxiii. 19). Moreover, Jerome elsewhere ('Qu. in Gen.') speaks of Melchizedek as "king of Salem, which was the former name of Jerusalem." Probably Salem was the oldest, Jebus the next, and Jerusalem the more modern name of the same city, though some think that the Salem here was the same as Salim near Ænon, where John baptized (Joh. iii. 23). If, as is most probable, Siddim, Sodom and Gomorrah, lay to the south of the Dead Sea, there is no reason why Salem should not have been Jerusalem, or that the valley of Shaveh, which is the "king's dale," should not have been the valley of the Kidron. If the view advocated by Mr Grove ('Dict. of Bible,' art. *Shaveh*, *Siddim*, *Sodom*, *Zoar*), and defended by Dean Stanley ('S. and P.' pp. 249, &c.), viz. that the valley of Siddim was north of the Dead Sea, be correct, then no doubt, Salem must have been a place far north of Jerusalem; but the more ancient opinion, viz. that the cities of the plain lay south of the Dead Sea is ably defended by Kuinoel ('Ep. ad Hebr.' VII. 1), Robinson ('B. R.' II. 188, 'Phys. Geog.' 213), Kurtz, Knobel, Delitzsch, Kalisch, Keil, &c., and is most probably the true. See also note on the Dead Sea at the end of ch. xix.

the priest] This is the first time that the word *priest*, *Cohen*, ἱερεὺς, *sacerdos*, occurs in the Bible, and it is in connection with the worship of an ancient people, perhaps not related by blood to the chosen race. The etymological meaning of the word is unknown. The word itself is applied afterwards both to the Levitical priesthood and to the priesthood of false religions. The patriarchs seem to have had no other priesthood than that of the head of the family (Gen. viii. 20, xii. 8, xxii., xxvi. 25, xxxiii. 20; Job i. 5); but here we find Melchizedek designated as a priest and as performing many priestly acts, solemnly blessing, taking tithes, &c. There is no distinct mention of sacrifice, which was afterwards the most special function of the priesthood. As, however, sacrifice was a rite of common use among the patriarchs, and, later at least, among all surrounding nations, there is no reasonable doubt but that Melchizedek was a sacrificing priest, and so more fitly a type of Christ, who offered Himself a sacrifice without spot to God (see Kuinoel on Heb. vii. 1). Philo indeed asserts that Melchizedek offered the first fruits of the spoil in sacrifice, ἐπινίκια ἔθυε ('De Abrah.' p. 381), a thing by no means improbable; and connected with such a sacrifice may have been the bread and wine, corresponding with the *mola* and libations of later days.

the most high God] This is the first time we meet with this title, *Elion*. It occurs frequently afterwards, as Num. xxiv. 16 (where it is used by Balaam, also an alien from the family of Abraham), Deut. xxxii. 18, Ps. vii. 18, ix. 2, xviii. 13, xlvii. 2, lxxviii. 35, &c., where sometimes we have *Elion* alone, sometimes joined with *El*, sometimes with JEHOVAH. It is observed that Sanchoniathon (ap. Euseb. 'Præp. Evang.' I. 10) mentions *Elion* as the name of the Phœnician Deity. So the words *alonim walonuth*, which occur in the well-known Punic passage in the Pœnulus of Plautus, are supposed to correspond with the Hebrew *Elionim velionoth*, "gods and goddesses." This may be true; the worship of the Phœnicians, as of other heathen nations, was, no doubt, a corruption of the ancient patriarchal faith: but it is plain, that Abram here acknowledges Melchizedek as a worshipper of the true God: and in v. 22,

20 And blessed be the most high
God, which hath delivered thine enemies into thy hand. And he gave
him [c]tithes of all. c Heb. 7.

21 And the king of Sodom said
unto Abram, Give me the †persons, † Heb.
and take the goods to thyself. [illegible]ls.

22 And Abram said to the king of
Sodom, I have lift up mine hand unto
the LORD, the most high God, the
possessor of heaven and earth,

23 That I will not *take* from a
thread even to a shoelatchet, and
that I will not take anything that *is*
thine, lest thou shouldest say, I have
made Abram rich:

24 Save only that which the young
men have eaten, and the portion of
the men which went with me, Aner,
Eshcol, and Mamre; let them take
their portion.

CHAPTER XV.

1 God encourageth Abram. 2 Abram complaineth for want of an heir. 4 God promiseth him a son, and a multiplying of his seed. 6 Abram is justified by faith. 7 Canaan is promised again, and confirmed by a sign, 12 and a vision.

AFTER these things the word of
the LORD came unto Abram in
a vision, saying, Fear not, Abram: I
am thy shield, *and* thy exceeding
[a]great reward. a Ps. 16. 5.

Abram uses the very titles of God, which had been used by Melchizedek before, coupling with them the most sacred name JEHOVAH, the name of the Covenant God, under which He was ever adored by the chosen seed as specially their God.

19. *possessor of heaven and earth*] The LXX. and Vulg. have "Maker of heaven and earth." This is probably the true meaning, but the word may have either significance (Ges. 'Th.' p. 1221. So Delitzsch and Keil).

20. *he gave him tithes of all*] The sentence, as it stands, is ambiguous, but the sense is obviously (as LXX., Joseph., Jonathan, and Heb. vii. 6) "Abram gave Melchizedek tithes of all," *i.e.* the *spolia opima*, the tenth part of the spoil which he had taken from the enemy (Joseph. 'Ant.' I. 10).

21. *Give me the persons, and take the goods to thyself.*] *i.e.* restore those of my people, whom you have rescued, but keep whatever other property of mine you may have lighted on.

22. *I have lift up mine hand unto the LORD*] A common form of solemn attestation in all nations. (See Dan. xii. 7, Virg. 'Æn.' XII. 195.) On the identification of the name El-elion with JEHOVAH, and on the use of the latter name, see notes on vv. 1, 18.

23. *That I will not take*] Lit. "If I will take." The particle *if* was constantly used in swearing, there being an ellipsis of some such expression as "God do so to me and more also if," (1 S. iii. 17). The particle is literally rendered in Heb. iii. 11. There is a marked difference between Abram's conduct to Melchizedek, and his conduct to the king of Sodom. From Melchizedek he receives refreshment and treats him with honour and respect. Towards the king of Sodom he is distant and reserved. Probably the vicious lives of the inhabitants of Sodom made him careful not to lay himself under any obligation to their king, lest he should become too much associated with him and them.

24. *the young men*] Abram's trained servants, whom he had led to the fight (Cp. 2 S. ii. 14, 1 K. xx. 14).

CHAP. XV. 1. *After these things the word of the LORD came unto Abram in a vision*] We have in this chapter a repetition of the promises to Abram, given when he was first called (ch. xii. 1), and when he first entered into the land of Canaan (ch. xii. 7), with the farther assurance that his own son should be his heir. This is the first time that the expression so frequent afterwards "the word of the LORD" occurs in the Bible. It has been questioned whether the "vision" was a dream or waking vision. The same word is used of Balaam, "which saw the *vision* of the Almighty, falling, but having his eyes open" (Num. xxiv. 4, 16). The way in which Abram was led out and saw the stars, and the subsequent reality of the sacrifice, look like a waking vision, and it is not till v. 12, that he falls into a deep sleep.

Fear not] Abram had now become a great man, with wealth and a comparatively settled home: but he was in a land of strangers, and many of them of godless life. He had been engaged in a war, and his very victory might bring reprisals. In his old age he had no children to support and defend him. Accordingly he now is assured of God's farther protection, and secured against those feelings of despondency natural to one who was lonely, childless, and in danger. It is observed that the words "fear not" have introduced many announcements of Messiah, as Joh. xii. 15; Luke i. 13, 30, ii. 10 (Wordsworth).

thy exceeding great reward] The word *great* is here an infinitive absolute used ad-

2 And Abram said, Lord God,
what wilt thou give me, seeing I go
childless, and the steward of my house
is this Eliezer of Damascus?
3 And Abram said, Behold, to me
thou hast given no seed: and, lo, one
born in my house is mine heir.
4 And, behold, the word of the
LORD *came* unto him, saying, This
shall not be thine heir; but he that
shall come forth out of thine own
bowels shall be thine heir.
5 And he brought him forth a-
broad, and said, Look now toward
heaven, and tell the stars, if thou be
able to number them: and he said
unto him, [b] So shall thy seed be. [b] Rom. 4. 18.
6 And he [c] believed in the LORD; [c] Rom. 4. 3. Gal. 3. 6. Jam. 2. 23.
and he counted it to him for right-
eousness.

---

verbially, so that the more exact rendering may be, "Thy reward exceeding abundantly." The LXX. render "Thy reward shall be exceeding great," which is approved by Rœdiger (in Ges. 'Thes.' p. 1257), Rosenm., Delitzsch.

2. *Lord God*] *Adonai* JEHOVAH. This is the first use of these two words together. When separate, both are rendered by versions, ancient and modern, by the same word LORD. Except in v. 8, the same combination occurs again in the Pentateuch, only in Deut. iii. 24, ix. 26. In all these passages it is in the vocative case, and JEHOVAH alone does not occur in Genesis as a vocative (Quarry, 'Genesis,' p. 234).

seeing I go childless] Abram, though blessed personally, feels that the promises of God seem to extend into the future, and does not understand that they can be fulfilled in him alone.

the steward of my house is this Eliezer of Damascus] The literal rendering is "The son of the business" (or perhaps "of the possession") "of my house, he is Damascus Eliezer." It is most probable that "Damascus" is put for "a man of Damascus," as the Authorized Version. The words rendered "steward of my house" are very obscure, so that some ancient versions leave them untranslated. The older critics generally render "son of the business," *i.e.* "steward;" the majority of modern commentators, after the Syriac, preferring "son of possession," *i.e.* "heir." The passage, therefore, must be read either "the steward," or "the heir of my house is Eliezer of Damascus." The tradition of Abram's connection with Damascus has already been referred to (see Nicol. Damasc. Ap. Joseph. 'Ant.' I. 7; Justin. XXXVI. 2). If Abram came into Palestine by the way of Damascus, it is not unlikely that he should have taken his principal retainer from that place.

3. *one born in my house*] Lit. "son of my house." The expression is like, but not necessarily equivalent to that in ch. xvii. 12, 27 (יְלִיד־בָּיִת), *he that is born in the house*, as opposed to those *bought with money of any stranger*. It is quite possible that the title "son of my house," was applied to inmates of the house, especially those in honourable office in the household, whether born in the family, or afterwards adopted into it. The relation of the head of a family to his retainers was, in the case of Abram at least, truly paternal. It evidently more resembled the connection between a feudal chief and his vassals than that between a master and his slaves. That some of them were "bought with money," appears indeed from the passages above referred to; but they were evidently not in the abject condition which attached to slavery in later days, and the principal among them was marked out in default of his own offspring as heir to his master, though Abram had near relations, and some of them at no greater distance from him than Lot and his family, then living in the plains of Jordan.

5. *tell the stars*] In the promise to Noah the rainbow had been the sign given from on high, a sacramental promise of mercy to mankind. Now to Abram the still brighter and more enduring token is the starry firmament. His seed should abide as "the faithful witness in heaven." There is the pledge of a brilliant future for his house, even as regards material prosperity; the pledge of still greater blessings to that spiritual family, which by baptism into Christ became "Abraham's seed, and heirs according to the promise" (Gal. iii. 27, 29).

6. *And he believed in the LORD; and he counted it to him for righteousness*] The root of the word rendered *believed* has the sense of supporting, sustaining, strengthening. Hence in the Hiphil conjugation (as here), it signifies to hold as firm, to rest upon as firm, hence to believe and rely upon as true and stable (Ges. 'Thes.' p. 114). The promise here made by the LORD to Abram was given to him before circumcision, whilst there was yet not even the germ of Levitical Law. It contained in it the promise of Christ. It elicited from Abram the great evangelical principle of faith. God promised that which was opposed to all appearance and likelihood. Abram relied on that promise. He surrendered his own wisdom

7 And he said unto him, I *am* the
LORD that brought thee out of Ur of
the Chaldees, to give thee this land
to inherit it.
8 And he said, Lord GOD, whereby shall I know that I shall inherit it?
9 And he said unto him, Take me
an heifer of three years old, and a she
goat of three years old, and a ram of
three years old, and a turtledove, and
a young pigeon.
10 And he took unto him all these,
and divided them in the midst, and
laid each piece one against another:
but the birds divided he not.
11 And when the fowls came down
upon the carcases, Abram drove them
away.

---

to the wisdom of God, and so gave up his own will to the will of God. So he became the heir of the promises; and the internal principle of faith became to him the true principle of righteousness. It was the only righteousness possible for the feeble and the sinful; for it was a reposing on the power and the love of the Almighty and the Holy One. It was therefore reckoned to him as what may be called a passive righteousness, and at the same time it was productive in him of an active righteousness: for the soul which relies on the truth, power, and goodness of another, in the strength of that truth, power, and goodness, can itself be active in them all: taking advantage of the power and goodness relied upon, it becomes itself powerful and good and true. The Apostles naturally dwell upon this first recorded instance of faith, faith in God, implied faith in Christ, and consequent accounting of righteousness, recorded before all legal enactments, as illustrative of the great evangelical grace of faith, its power as resting on One who is all powerful, and its sanctifying energy, as containing in itself the principle of holiness and the germ of every righteous act. (Rom. iv. v.; Gal. iii.; Heb. xi.; Jas. ii., &c. &c.)

7. *I am the LORD that brought thee out of Ur of the Chaldees*] In ch. xi. 31, Terah is represented as having left Ur of the Chaldees and settled in Haran with Abram, Sarai and Lot; whilst in ch. xii. 1, Abram is represented as having been called by the Lord to go *out* of Haran, cp. v. 4. These different statements are thought to be inconsistent with each other and referable to three different hands. Whether there was a distinct command to Abram to leave Ur does not appear. The LORD by His Providence may have led him and his father out of Ur to Haran, with the design of leading him further onward, and afterwards by special revelation have called him to leave Haran and to go to Canaan (see Quarry, p. 430).

8. *whereby shall I know*] Abram believed God; but there may have been some misgiving as to the reality of what he saw and heard; like St Peter, who "wist not that it was true which was done by the angel, but thought he saw a vision" (Acts xii. 9): and even where there is much faith, a man may distrust himself, may feel that though now the belief is strong, yet ere long the first impression and so the firm conviction may fade away. Thus Gideon (Jud. vi. 17), Hezekiah (2 K. xx. 8), the Blessed Virgin (Luk. i. 34) asked a sign in confirmation of their faith, and, as here to Abram, it was graciously given them.

9. *Take me an heifer of three years old*] The age chosen was probably because then the animals were in full age and vigour (Chrysost. 'in Gen. Hom. XXVI.'). The animals were those which specially formed the staple of Abram's wealth: they were also those, which in after times were specially ordained for sacrificial offerings. It has been said, that the transaction was not a real sacrifice, as there was no sprinkling of blood, nor offering on an altar: but the essence of the true Hebrew sacrifice was in the slaying of the victim, for the very word זֶבַח (*Zebach*, sacrifice) signifies *slaying:* and it was rather with the shedding of blood than with its sprinkling that atonement was made (Heb. ix. 22). The covenant was made according to the custom of ancient nations. The sacrificed victims were cut into two pieces, and the covenanting parties passed between them (see Jerem. xxxiv. 18, 19). The very word covenant in Hebrew, *Berith*, is supposed by Gesenius to be from a root signifying *to cut* ('Thes.' p. 238); and the common formula for "to make a covenant" is *carath berith*, "to cut a covenant" (so v. 18), comp. the Greek ὅρκια τέμνειν (Hom. 'Il.' v. 124) and the Lat. *fœdus ferire* (see Bochart, 'Hieroz.' I. 332). The division into two is supposed to represent the two parties to the covenant; and their passing between the divided pieces to signify their union into one. In this case Abram was there in person to pass between the pieces, and the manifested presence of God passed between them under the semblance of fire (v. 17).

10. *the birds divided he not*] So under the Law the doves offered as burnt offerings were not cleft in two (Lev. i. 17).

11. *the fowls*] **The birds of prey.** The

12 And when the sun was going
down, a deep sleep fell upon Abram;
and, lo, an horror of great darkness
fell upon him.
13 And he said unto Abram, Know
d Acts 7. 6. of a surety [d]that thy seed shall be a
stranger in a land *that is* not theirs,
and shall serve them; and they shall
afflict them four hundred years;
14 And also that nation, whom
they shall serve, will I judge: and
afterward shall they come out with
great substance.
15 And thou shalt go to thy fathers
in peace; thou shalt be buried in a
good old age.
16 But in the fourth generation
they shall come hither again: for the
iniquity of the Amorites *is* not yet
full.
17 And it came to pass, that, when
the sun went down, and it was dark,
behold a smoking furnace, and †a burn- † Heb.
ing lamp that passed between those *a lamp of fire.*
pieces.
18 In the same day the LORD e chap. 12. 7. & 13. 15. & 26. 4. Deut. 34. 4.
made a covenant with Abram, say-
ing, [e]Unto thy seed have I given this

word used (*ait*) means any rapacious animal, especially vultures or other birds of prey. It is probably of the same root as the Greek ἀετός, eagle.

Abram drove them away] It is generally thought, that the vultures seeking to devour the sacrifice before the covenant was ratified typified the enemies of Israel, especially the Egyptians; and in a spiritual sense they represent the spiritual enemies, which seek to destroy the soul, keeping it from union with God through the accepted sacrifice of His Son (see Knobel in loc.).

12. *when the sun was going down*] The evening came on before all the preparations were made, a solemn time for concluding the covenant between God and the seed of Abram; but it may have been said that it was evening, not night, in order to shew that the great darkness was preternatural (V. Gerlach).

a deep sleep] The same word as that used Gen. ii. 21, when Eve was taken from Adam's side. The constant translation, ἔκστασις (ecstasy), by the LXX. shews the belief that the sleep was sent by God for purposes of Divine revelation.

an horror of great darkness] Lit. **a horror, a great darkness**. The prophets were frequently appalled when admitted to the special presence of God: but here perhaps the horror was connected also with the announcement about to be made to Abram of the sufferings of his posterity.

13. *four hundred years*] In Ex. xii. 40 it is called 430. Possibly here the reckoning is in round numbers; also the Hebrews were not ill-treated during the whole 430 years.

15. *And thou shalt go to thy fathers in peace*] A similar expression occurs ch. xxv. 8, xxxv. 29, xlix. 33. It is interpreted to mean either going to the grave, in which his father or his people had been buried, or, (as by Knobel and others) going to that place, where the souls of his ancestors are in the state of separate spirits. That it cannot mean the former here seems to follow from the fact, that Abram was not to be buried in his father's burying-place, but in a grave which he himself purchased in the land of his adoption.

16. *in the fourth generation*] On the chronology from the Descent into Egypt to the Exodus, see note on Exod.

the iniquity of the Amorites is not yet full] The Amorites, the most powerful people in Canaan, are here put for the Canaanites in general. Their state of moral corruption is abundantly manifest in the early chapters of Genesis; and in the Divine foreknowledge it was seen that they would add sin to sin, and so at length be destroyed by the Divine vengeance. Still the long-suffering of God waited for them, giving time for repentance, if they would be converted and live.

17. *when the sun went down, and it was dark*] Or, "when the sun had gone down, that there was a thick darkness." So the Vulgate.

a smoking furnace, and a lamp of fire] This was the token of the presence of God, as when He appeared to Moses in the burning bush, and to the Israelites in a pillar of fire. The word *lamp* may very probably here signify a flame or tongue of fire. The Hebrew word which is cognate with *lamp*, and the other Aryan words of like sound (λάμπω, λαμπὰς, &c.) has probably its radical significance *a lambendo*, a lambent flame. Compare *labium*, *lip*, &c. (see Ges. 'Th.' p. 759).

18. *made a covenant*] Lit. "cut a covenant." See above on v. 9.

land, from the river of Egypt unto the
great river, the river Euphrates:
19 The Kenites, and the Kenizzites, and the Kadmonites,
20 And the Hittites, and the Perizzites, and the Rephaims,
21 And the Amorites, and the Canaanites, and the Girgashites, and the
Jebusites.

CHAPTER XVI.

1 *Sarai, being barren, giveth Hagar to Abram.* 4 *Hagar, being afflicted for despising her mistress, runneth away.* 7 *An angel sendeth her back to submit herself,* 11 *and telleth her of her child.* 15 *Ishmael is born.*

NOW Sarai Abram's wife bare
him no children: and she had
an handmaid, an Egyptian, whose
name *was* Hagar.
2 And Sarai said unto Abram, Behold now, the LORD hath restrained
me from bearing: I pray thee, go in
unto my maid; it may be that I
may †obtain children by her. And
Abram hearkened to the voice of
Sarai.

† Heb. *be builded by her.*

---

the river of Egypt] Many understand not the Nile but the *Wady-El-Arisch* which, however, is called "the brook or stream of Egypt" as in Is. xxvii. 12, not "the river of Egypt." The boundaries of the future possession are not described with minute accuracy, but they are marked as reaching from the valley of the Euphrates to the valley of the Nile. And in 2 Chron. ix. 26, it is distinctly stated that "all the Kings from the river (i.e. Euphrates) even unto the land of the Philistines and to the border of Egypt" were tributary to Solomon. Cp. 2 S. viii. 3.

19. *The Kenites*] An ancient people inhabiting rocky and mountainous regions to the south of Canaan, near the Amalekites (Num. xxiv. 21 seq.; 1 S. xv. 6, xxvii. 10, xxx. 29), a portion of which afterwards migrated to Canaan (Judg. i. 16, iv. 11, 17).

the Kenizzites] Mentioned only here. Bochart ('Phaleg,' IV. 36) conjectures that they had become extinct in the period between Abraham and Moses.

the Kadmonites] i. e. "the Eastern people." They are not elsewhere named. Bochart thought they might be the Hivites, elsewhere enumerated among the Canaanites, and spoken of as inhabiting the neighbourhood of Mount Hermon (Josh. xiii. 3; Judg. iii. 3), which was to the east of Canaan.

20. *the Hittites, and the Perizzites, and the Rephaims*] See on ch. x. 15, xiii. 7, xiv. 5.

21. *the Amorites, the Girgashites, and the Jebusites.*] See on ch. x. 15, 16.

the Canaanites] here distinguished from the kindred tribes, are described as inhabiting the low country "from Sodom to Gerar, unto Gaza; as thou goest, unto Sodom, and Gomorrha, and Admah, and Zeboim, even unto Lasha" (Gen. x. 19).

CHAP. XVI. 1. *Now Sarai,* &c.] The recapitulatory character of this verse is consistent with the general style of the book of Genesis, and the connection of the first four verses perfectly natural. The promise of offspring had been made to Abram, and he believed the promise. It had not, however, been distinctly assured to him that Sarai should be the mother of the promised seed. The expedient devised by Sarai was according to a custom still prevalent in the east. Laws concerning marriage had not been so expressly given to the patriarchs as they afterwards were. Yet the compliance of Abram with Sarai's suggestion may be considered as a proof of the imperfection of his faith; and it is justly observed, that this departure from the primeval principle of monogamy by Abraham has been an example followed by his descendents in the line of Ishmael, and has proved, morally and physically, a curse to their race.

an handmaid, an Egyptian, whose name was Hagar] Hagar, no doubt, followed Sarai from Egypt after the sojourn there recorded in ch. xii., when it is said that Abraham obtained great possessions, among other things, in "menservants and maidservants," v. 16. It is generally thought that the name Hagar signifies *flight*, a name which may have been given her after her flight from her mistress, recorded in this chapter, in which case the name is here given her proleptically, a thing not uncommon in Scripture history. Others suppose that she derived her name from having fled with her mistress out of Egypt. As she was an Egyptian, it is not likely that the Hebrew or Arabic name of Hagar should have been given her by her own parents.

2. *it may be that I may obtain children by her*] Lit. "I may be built up by her." The words "house" and "family" are in most languages used figuratively the one of the other. The house, considered as representing the family, is built up by the addition of children to it, and so the very word for son, in Hebrew, *Ben*, is most probably connected with the root *banah*, "to build" (see Ges. 'Th.' p. 215). Comp. ch. xxx. 3, where also it appears that the wife, when she gave her handmaid to her

3 And Sarai Abram's wife took
Hagar her maid the Egyptian, after
Abram had dwelt ten years in the
land of Canaan, and gave her to her
husband Abram to be his wife.
4 ¶ And he went in unto Hagar,
and she conceived: and when she saw
that she had conceived, her mistress
was despised in her eyes.
5 And Sarai said unto Abram, My
wrong *be* upon thee: I have given
my maid into thy bosom; and when
she saw that she had conceived, I was
despised in her eyes: the LORD judge
between me and thee.
6 But Abram said unto Sarai, Behold, thy maid *is* in thy hand; do to
her †as it pleaseth thee. And when
Sarai †dealt hardly with her, she fled
from her face.
7 ¶ And the angel of the LORD

† Heb. *that which is good in thine eyes.*
† Heb. *afflicted her.*

found her by a fountain of water in
the wilderness, by the fountain in the
way to Shur.
8 And he said, Hagar, Sarai's maid,
whence camest thou? and whither
wilt thou go? And she said, I flee
from the face of my mistress Sarai.
9 And the angel of the LORD said
unto her, Return to thy mistress, and
submit thyself under her hands.
10 And the angel of the LORD said
unto her, I will multiply thy seed
exceedingly, that it shall not be numbered for multitude.
11 And the angel of the LORD said
unto her, Behold, thou *art* with child,
and shalt bear a son, and shalt call
his name ‖Ishmael; because the LORD
hath heard thy affliction.
12 And he will be a wild man; his
hand *will be* against every man, and

‖ That is, *God shall hear.*

---

husband, esteemed the handmaid's children as her own.

3. *after Abram had dwelt ten years in the land of Canaan*] Abram was now 85 and Sarai 75 years old (cp. xii. 4, xvi. 16, xvii. 17). These words are doubtless intended to account for the impatience produced in them by the delay of the Divine promise.

4. *her mistress was despised in her eyes*] Among the Hebrews barrenness was esteemed a reproach (see ch. xix. 31, xxx. 1, 23; Lev. xx. 20, &c.): and fecundity a special honour and blessing of God (ch. xxi. 6, xxiv. 60; Ex. xxiii. 26; Deut. vii. 14): and such is still the feeling in the east. But, moreover, very probably Hagar may have thought that now Abram would love and honour her more than her mistress (cp. ch. xxix. 33).

5. *My wrong be upon thee*] *i.e.* "my wrong, the injury done to me is due to thee, must be imputed to thee, thou art to be blamed for it, inasmuch as thou sufferest it and dost not punish the aggressor." So in effect all the versions, LXX., Vulg., Targg., &c.

7. *the angel of the LORD*] In v. 13 distinctly called *the* LORD. See on ch. xii. 7.

Shur] according to Joseph. ('Ant.' VI. 7) is Pelusium, near the mouth of the Nile, which, however, seems more probably to be the equivalent for Sin (see Ges. 'Thes.' p. 947). Onkelos renders here "Hagra." The desert of Shur is generally thought to be the north eastern part of the wilderness of Paran, called at present *Al-jifar*. Hagar, no doubt, in her flight from Sarai, took the route most likely to lead her back to her native land of Egypt; and Gesenius supposes that Shur very probably corresponded with the modern Suez.

8. *Hagar, Sarai's maid*] The words of the angel recal to Hagar's mind that she was the servant of Sarai, and therefore owed her obedience.

11. *Ishmael; because the LORD hath heard*] *i.e.* "God heareth, because JEHOVAH hath heard." The name of God, by which all nations might acknowledge Him, is expressed in the name Ishmael, but the name JEHOVAH, the covenant God of Abraham, is specially mentioned, that she may understand the promise to come to her from Him, who had already assured Abraham of the blessing to be poured upon his race.

12. *a wild man*] Lit. "a wild ass of, or among men;" *i.e.* wild and fierce as a wild ass of the desert. A rendering has been suggested, "a wild ass, a man, whose hand is against every man." The suggestion is very ingenious; but for such a rendering we should have expected to find the word *Ish* (*vir*) not, as it is in the original, *Adam* (*homo*). The word *pere*, wild ass, is probably from the root *para*, signifying "to run swiftly." This animal is frequently mentioned in Scripture, and often as a type of lawless, restless, unbridled dispositions in human beings (see Job xi. 12, xxiv. 5; Ps. civ. 11; Is. xxxii. 14; Jer. ii. 24; Dan. v. 21; Hos. viii. 9). In Job xxxix. 5, another Hebrew word is used, but most commentators consider that the same animal is meant. The description of their

[a] chap. 25. 18. every man's hand against him; [a]and
he shall dwell in the presence of all
his brethren.
13 And she called the name of the
LORD that spake unto her, Thou
God seest me: for she said, Have
I also here looked after him that
seeth me?
14 Wherefore the well was called
[b] chap. 24. 62. [b]‖Beer-lahai-roi; behold, *it is* between
‖ That is, *the well of him that liveth* and *seeth me.* Kadesh and Bered.
15 ¶ And Hagar bare Abram a son:
and Abram called his son's name,
which Hagar bare, Ishmael.
16 And Abram *was* fourscore and
six years old, when Hagar bare Ishmael to Abram.

CHAPTER XVII.

1 *God reneweth the covenant.* 5 *Abram his name is changed in token of a greater blessing.* 10 *Circumcision is instituted.* 15 *Sarai her name is changed, and she blessed.* 17 *Isaac is promised.* 23 *Abraham and Ishmael are circumcised.*

AND when Abram was ninety
years old and nine, the LORD
appeared to Abram, and said unto [a] chap. 5. 22.
him, I *am* the Almighty God; [a]walk ‖ Or, *upright,* or, *sincere.*
before me, and be thou ‖perfect.

---

great speed in Xen. 'Anab.' Lib. I. is well known. Gesenius refers to a picture of the wild ass of Persia in Ker Porter's 'Travels in Georgia and Persia,' Vol. I. p. 459, and says, that a living specimen which he saw in the London Zoological Gardens in 1835 exactly corresponded with this picture ('Thes.' p. 1123).

his hand will be against every man, &c.] or "upon every man," a common phrase for violence and injury (cp. Gen. xxxvii. 27; Exod. ix. 3; Deut. ii. 16; Josh. ii. 19; 1 S. xviii. 17, 21, xxiv. 13, 14). The violent character and lawless life of the Bedouin descendants of Ishmael from the first till this day is exactly described in these words.

in the presence of all his brethren] Lit. "in front" or "before the face of all his brethren." This may point to that constant attitude of the Bedouin Arabs, living every where in close proximity to their kindred races, hovering round them, but never mingling with them: or, we may render "to the east of all his brethren," a translation adopted by Rosenm., Gesen., Tuch, Knobel, Delitzsch, &c. The Arabs are called in Job i. 3, "the children of the east," and in some passages of Scripture the phrase "in the presence of," is explained to mean "eastward of" (see Numb. xxi. 11; Josh. xv. 8; Zech. xiv. 4); the rationale of this being, that when a man looked toward the sunrise, the east was *before* him.

13. *Thou God seest me: for she said, Have I also here looked after him that seeth me?*] **Thou art a God of seeing, for have I also seen here after seeing?** The Authorized Version has nearly followed the rendering of the LXX. and Vulg., which is inadmissible. The meaning of the words is probably, "Thou art a God that seest all things," (or perhaps "that revealest Thyself in visions"); "and am I yet living and seeing, after seeing God?" (cp. Judg. xiii. 21). So apparently Onkelos; and this rendering is adopted by Rosenm., Gesen., Tuch, Kalisch, Delitzsch, and most moderns. The name of God throughout this chapter is JEHOVAH, except when Hagar the Egyptian speaks; yet the God of vision who reveals Himself to her is carefully identified with the JEHOVAH of Abraham.

14. *Beer-lahai-roi*] "The well of life of vision," *i.e.* where life remained after vision of God. (See Ges. 'Thes.' p. 175.) This seems to be the meaning of the name according to the etymology derived from the last verse, though others render it "the well of the living One (*i.e.* the living God) of vision."

between Kadesh and Bered] On the site of Kadesh and its uncertainty see on ch. xiv. 7. The uncertainty of the site of Bered is still greater, and therefore the difficulty of arriving at the exact position of Beer-lahai-roi is almost insuperable. Mr Rowlands (in Williams' 'Holy City,' I. 465) thinks that he has discovered its site at a place called Moilahhi, about 10 hours south of Ruheibeh, in the road from Beersheba to Shur, or Jebel-es-sur, a mountain range running north and south in the longitude of Suez.

CHAP. XVII. 1. *And when Abram was ninety years old and nine*] *i.e.* just thirteen years after the events related in the last chapter, compare v. 25, where Ishmael is said to be now thirteen years old.

the Almighty God] El-Shaddai. The word Shaddai, translated by most versions "mighty," or "Almighty," is generally thought (by Gesen., Rosenm., Lee, &c. &c.) to be a plural of excellence (in this respect like Elohim), derived from the root *Shadad*, the primary meaning of which appears to have been "to be strong," "to act strongly," though more commonly used in the sense of "to destroy, to devastate." The later Greek versions Aq., Sym., Theod., render ἱκανός, "sufficient," "all-sufficient." So Theodoret, Hesych., Saad. Accordingly, Rashi and some of the Jewish writers consider it to be compounded of two words, signifying "who is sufficient?" the improbability

2 And I will make my covenant
between me and thee, and will multiply thee exceedingly.
3 And Abram fell on his face: and
God talked with him, saying,
4 As for me, behold, my covenant
is with thee, and thou shalt be a
† Heb. *multitude of nations.* father of † many nations.
5 Neither shall thy name any more
be called Abram, but thy name shall
b Rom. 4. 17. be Abraham; b for a father of many
nations have I made thee.
6 And I will make thee exceeding
fruitful, and I will make nations of
thee, and kings shall come out of thee.
7 And I will establish my covenant between me and thee and thy
seed after thee in their generations
for an everlasting covenant, to be a
God unto thee, and to thy seed after
thee.
8 And I will give unto thee, and to
thy seed after thee, the land † wherein † Heb. *of thy sojournings.*
thou art a stranger, all the land of
Canaan, for an everlasting possession;
and I will be their God.
9 ¶ And God said unto Abraham,
Thou shalt keep my covenant therefore, thou, and thy seed after thee in
their generations.
10 This *is* my covenant, which ye
shall keep, between me and you and
thy seed after thee; c Every man child c Acts 7. 8
among you shall be circumcised.
11 And ye shall circumcise the flesh
of your foreskin; and it shall be a
d token of the covenant betwixt me d Acts 7. 8. Rom. 4. 11.
and you.
12 And he that is † eight days old † Heb. *a son of eight days.*
e shall be circumcised among you, every e Lev. 12. 3.
man child in your generations, he that Luke 2. 21. John 7. 22.
is born in the house, or bought with
money of any stranger, which *is* not
of thy seed.

---

of which derivation is very great. The title, or character, El-Shaddai, is said, Exod. vi. 2, 3, to have been that by which God was revealed to the patriarchs, not then, at least in its full meaning, by the name JEHOVAH; and it is noted as occurring in those passages which the German critics call Elohistic. In this very verse, however, we read it in immediate juxtaposition with the name JEHOVAH, and in Ruth i. 20, 21, we find the identification of JEHOVAH with Shaddai. Probably, like Elohim, and Adonai, we may consider El-Shaddai (a title known to Balaam, Num. xxiv. 4, 16, and constantly used in Job), to have been one of the more general world-wide titles of the Most High, whilst JEHOVAH was rather the name by which His own chosen people knew and acknowledged Him. The title, which especially points to power, seems most appropriate when a promise is made, which seems even to Abram and Sarai to be well-nigh impossible of fulfilment.

2. *I will make my covenant*] The word for "make" is different from that used in xv. 18. There God is said to have "cut" a covenant with Abram by sacrifice, which phrase has probably special reference to the sacrifice and also to the two parties who made the covenant by sacrifice (see on xv. 9). Here He says, "I will *give* my covenant between Me and thee." The freedom of the covenant of promise is expressed in this latter phrase. It was a gift from a superior, rather than a bargain between equals; and as it was accompanied by the rite of circumcision, it was typical of the freedom of that covenant made afterwards to Christians in Christ, and sealed to them in the sacred rite of baptism.

4. *of many nations*] **Of a multitude of nations**; as in margin.

5. *Abraham*] *i.e.* "father of a multitude." He was originally *Ab-ram*, "exalted father." Now he becomes *Ab-raham*, "father of a multitude;" *raham*, in Arabic, being a vast number, a great multitude. Abraham was literally the ancestor of the twelve tribes of Israel, of the Ishmaelites, of the descendants of Keturah and of the Edomites; but spiritually he is the father of all the faithful, who by faith in Christ are "Abraham's seed, and heirs according to the promise" (Gal. iii. 29). It has been very generally believed that the letter *H* here introduced into the names both of Abraham and Sarah is one of the two radical letters of the name JEHOVAH (as the other radical *J* was introduced into the name Joshua), whereby the owner of the name is doubly consecrated and bound in covenant to the LORD (see Delitzsch, in loc.). The custom of giving the name at the time of circumcision (Luke i. 59) probably originated from the change of Abraham's name having been made when that rite was first instituted.

10. *This is my covenant*] *i.e.* the sign, token and bond of the covenant.

12. *eight days old*] Seven days, a sacred number, were to pass over the child before he was so consecrated to God's service. There was a significance in the number 7, and there was a reason for the delay that the child might grow strong enough to bear the operation.

13 He that is born in thy house, and he that is bought with thy money, must needs be circumcised: and my covenant shall be in your flesh for an everlasting covenant.

14 And the uncircumcised man child whose flesh of his foreskin is not circumcised, that soul shall be cut off from his people; he hath broken my covenant.

15 ¶ And God said unto Abraham, As for Sarai thy wife, thou shalt not call her name Sarai, but Sarah *shall* her name *be*.

16 And I will bless her, and give thee a son also of her: yea, I will bless her, and †she shall be *a mother* of nations; kings of people shall be of her.

† Heb. *she shall become nations.*

17 Then Abraham fell upon his face, and laughed, and said in his heart, Shall *a child* be born unto him that is an hundred years old? and shall Sarah, that is ninety years old, bear?

18 And Abraham said unto God, O that Ishmael might live before thee!

---

13. *He that is born in thy house,* &c.] "Moses has nowhere given any command, nor even so much as an exhortation, inculcating the duty of circumcision upon any person not a descendant, or a slave of Abraham, or of his descendants, unless he wished to partake of the passover .... In none of the historical books of the Old Testament do we find the smallest trace of circumcision as necessary to the salvation of foreigners, who acknowledge the true God, or requisite even to the confession of their faith: no not so much as in the detailed story of Naaman (2 K. v.); in which indeed every circumstance indicates that the circumcision of that illustrious personage can never be supposed" (Michaelis, 'Laws of Moses,' Bk. IV. Art. 184). There is a marked distinction in this between circumcision and baptism. Judaism was intended to be the religion of a peculiar isolated people. Its rites therefore were for them alone. Christianity is for the whole human race; the Church is to be catholic; baptism to be administered to all that will believe.

14. *that soul shall be cut off from his people*] The rabbinical writers very generally understand that the excision should be by Divine judgment. Christian interpreters have mostly understood the infliction of death by the hand of the magistrate: some (Cleric. and Michael. in loc.) either exile or excommunication. The latter opinion was afterwards retracted by Michaelis, and it is pretty certain that death in some form is intended (see Gesen. 'Thes.' p. 718).

15. *thou shalt not call her name Sarai, but Sarah shall her name be*] There is but little doubt that Sarah signifies "Princess," in allusion probably to the princely race which was to spring from her, though Ikenius, followed by Rosenmüller, argues in favour of a meaning to be derived from the Arabic root *Saraa*, signifying, "to have a numerous progeny." As to the original name *Sarai*, the older interpreters generally understood it to signify "my princess:" the change to Sarah indicating that she was no longer the princess of a single race, but rather that all the families of the earth should have an interest in her (Jerome, 'Qu. Hebr.' p. 522); many think that Sarai means simply "noble, royal," whilst Sarah more definitely means "princess;" which, however, seems neither etymologically nor exegetically probable. Ewald explains Sarai as meaning "contentious," from the verb Sarah, שָׂרָה, which (Gen. xxxii. 29; Hos. xii. 4) occurs in the sense of "to fight, to contend." This meaning is approved by Gesenius ('Thes.' p. 1338), but the more usual derivation is probably the true.

16. *she shall be a mother of nations*] Heb. "she shall become nations."

17. *laughed*] Onkel. renders "rejoiced." Pseudo-Jon. "marvelled." The Jewish commentators, and many of the Christian fathers, understood this laughter to be the laughter of joy not of unbelief (Aug. 'De Civ.' XVI. 26). So also many moderns, *e.g.* Calvin, "partly exulting with gladness, partly carried beyond himself with wonder, he burst into laughter." It is thought also that our Blessed Lord may have alluded to this joy of Abraham (Joh. viii. 56), "Your father Abraham rejoiced to see My day, *and* he saw it and was glad;" for it was at the most distinct promise of a son, who was to be the direct ancestor of the Messiah, that the laughter is recorded (cp. also the words of the Blessed Virgin, Luke i. 47). On the other hand it must be admitted, that Abraham's words immediately following the laughter, seem at first sight as implying some unbelief, or at least weakness of faith, though they may be interpreted as the language of wonder rather than of incredulity.

18. *O that Ishmael might live before thee!*] These words may be interpreted in two ways, according as we understand the laughter of Abraham. They may mean, "I dare not hope for so great a boon as a son to be born hereafter to myself and Sarah in our old

f chap. 18. 10. & 21. 2. 19 And God said, [f]Sarah thy wife
shall bear thee a son indeed; and thou
shalt call his name Isaac: and I will
establish my covenant with him for
an everlasting covenant, *and* with his
seed after him.

20 And as for Ishmael, I have heard
thee: Behold, I have blessed him,
and will make him fruitful, and will
g chap. 25. 12. multiply him exceedingly; [g]twelve
princes shall he beget, and I will
make him a great nation.

21 But my covenant will I establish
with Isaac, which Sarah shall bear unto
thee at this set time in the next year.

22 And he left off talking with him,
and God went up from Abraham.

23 ¶ And Abraham took Ishmael
his son, and all that were born in his
house, and all that were bought with
his money, every male among the men
of Abraham's house; and circumcised
the flesh of their foreskin in the selfsame day, as God had said unto him.

24 And Abraham *was* ninety years
old and nine, when he was circumcised in the flesh of his foreskin.

25 And Ishmael his son *was* thirteen years old, when he was circumcised in the flesh of his foreskin.

26 In the selfsame day was Abraham circumcised, and Ishmael his son.

27 And all the men of his house,
born in the house, and bought with
money of the stranger, were circumcised with him.

---

age, but O that Ishmael may be the heir of Thy promises!" or they may imply only a fear, that now, when another heir is assured to Abraham, Ishmael should be excluded from all future inheritance.

19. *Isaac*] *i.e.* "he laughs," the third person singular of the present tense: similar forms are Jacob, Jair, Jabin, &c.

20. *as for Ishmael, I have heard thee*] There is an allusion to the significance of the name Ishmael, viz. "God heareth."

25. *Ishmael his son was thirteen years old*] The Arabs have in consequence always circumcised their sons at the age of 13. Josephus mentions this ('Ant.' I. 13), and it is well known that the custom still prevails among the Mahometan nations.

NOTE A on CHAP. XVII. V. 10. CIRCUMCISION.

(1) Reasons for the rite. (2) Origin of circumcision, whether pre-Abrahamic or not. (α) Egyptians said to have first used it. (β) Answer from lateness and uncertainty of the testimony. (γ) Balance of arguments.

THE reasons for this rite may have been various, 1st, to keep the descendants of Abraham distinct from the idolatrous nations round about them, the other inhabitants of Palestine not being circumcised. 2ndly, to indicate the rigour and severity of the Law of God, simply considered as Law, in contrast to which the ordinance that succeeded to it in the Christian dispensation indicated the mildness and mercy of the new covenant. 3rdly, to signify that the body should be devoted as a living sacrifice to God, "our hearts and all our members being mortified from all carnal and worldly lusts," and so to typify moral purity. (See Deut. x. 16; Jer. iv. 4; Acts vii. 51).

An important question arises as to the origin of circumcision. Was it first made known and commanded to Abraham, having nowhere been practised before? Or, was it a custom already in use, and now sanctified by God to a higher end and purport? A similar question arose concerning sacrifice. Was it prescribed by revelation or dictated by natural piety and then sanctioned from above? As the rainbow probably did not first appear after the flood, but was then made the token of the Noachic covenant; as the stars of heaven were made the sign of the earlier covenant with Abraham (ch. xv. 5); may it have been also, that circumcision already prevailed among some nations, and was now divinely authorized and made sacred and authoritative? There would be nothing necessarily startling in the latter alternative, when we remember that the corresponding rite of baptism in the Christian dispensation is but one adaptation by supreme authority of natural or legal washings to a Christian purpose and a most spiritual significance.

It is certain that the Egyptians used circumcision (Herod. II. 36, 37, 104; Diod. Sicul. I. 26, 55; Strabo, XVII. p. 524; Phil. Jud. 'De Circumcis.' II. p. 210; Joseph. 'Ant.' VIII. 10; 'Cont. Apion.' I. 22; II. 13). The earliest writer who mentions this is Herodotus. He says, indeed, that the Egyptians and Ethiopians had it from the most remote antiquity, so that he cannot tell which had it first; he mentions the Colchians as also using it (whence Diodorus inferred that they were an Egyptian colony), and says that the Phœnicians and Syrians in Palestine admit that they "learned this practice from the Egyptians" (Herod. II. 104). This is evidently a very loose statement. The Phœnicians probably did not use it, and the Jews, whom Herodotus here calls "the Syrians in Palestine," admitted that they had once dwelt in Egypt, but never admitted that they derived circumcision from thence. The statements of Diodorus and Strabo, which are more or less similar to those of Herodotus, were no doubt partly derived from him, and partly followed the general belief among the Greeks, that the "Jews were originally Egyptians" (Strabo, as above). It is stated by Origen ('in Epist. ad Rom.' ch. II. 13) that the Egyptian priests, soothsayers, prophets, and those learned in hieroglyphics were circumcised; and the same is said by Horapollo (I. 13, 14). If these ancient writers were unsupported by other authorities, there would be no great difficulty in concluding that Herodotus had found circumcision among the Egyptian *priests*, had believed the Jews to be a mere colony from Egypt, and had concluded that the custom originated in Egypt, and from them was learned by the Ishmaelites and other races. It is, however, asserted by some modern Egyptologists, that circumcision must have prevailed from the time of the fourth dynasty, *i.e.* from at least 2400 B.C., therefore much before the date generally assigned to Abraham, B.C. 1996, and that it was not confined to the priests, as is, they say, learned from the mummies and the sculptures, where circumcision is made a distinctive mark between the Egyptians and their enemies (see Sir Gardiner Wilkinson, in Rawlinson's 'Herodotus,' pp. 52, 146, 147, notes). If this be correct, we must conclude, that the Egyptians practised circumcision when Abraham first became acquainted with them, that probably some of Abraham's own Egyptian followers were circumcised, and that the Divine command was not intended to teach a new rite, but to consecrate an old one into a sacramental ordinance. Some even think that they see in the very style of this and the following verses indications that the rite was not altogether new and before unknown; for had it been new and unknown, more accurate directions would have been given of the way in which a painful and dangerous operation should be performed (Michaelis, 'Laws of Moses,' Bk. IV. Ch. iii. Art. 185). The Egyptians, Ethiopians, and perhaps some other African races, are supposed to have adopted it, partly from regard to cleanliness (Herod. II. 36), which the Egyptians, and above all the Egyptian priests, especially affected, partly to guard against disease incident in those hot climates (see Philo, as above, p. 211; Joseph. 'C. Apion.' II. 13), partly for other reasons, which may have been real or imaginary (see Michaelis, as above, Art. 186). This side of the question is ably defended by Michaelis, 'Laws of Moses,' as above, and Kalisch, in loc.

In answer it is truly said, that the Greek historians are too late and too loose in their statements to command our confidence; that the tribes cognate with the Egyptians, such as the Hamite inhabitants of Palestine, were notoriously uncircumcised, that the Egyptians, especially the Egyptian priests, are not unlikely to have adopted the rite at the time when Joseph was their governor and in such high estimation among them, and that the question concerning the relative dates of Abraham and the different Egyptian dynasties is involved in too much obscurity to be made a ground for such an argument as the above to be built upon it. (See Bp. Patrick, in loc.; Heidegger, 'Hist. Patr.' II. 240; Wesseling and Larcher, 'ad Herod.' II. 37, 104; Graves 'on the Pentateuch,' Pt. II. Lect. V.; Wordsworth, in loc.) Again, the argument derived from the ancient Egyptian language proves nothing, the words are lost or doubtful. The argument from the mummies proves nothing, as we have no mummies of the ancient empire. The figures in the hieroglyphics are later still. The only argument of weight is that derived from the old hieroglyphic, common in the pyramids, which is *thought* to represent circumcision. It may on the whole be said, that we cannot conclude from the loose statements of Greek writers 15 centuries later than Abraham, nor even from the evidence of monuments and sculptures as yet perhaps but imperfectly read and uncertain as to their *comparative* antiquity, that circumcision had been known before it was given to Abraham; yet that on the other hand, there would be nothing inconsistent with the testimony of the Mosaic history in the belief, that it had been in use among the Egyptians and other African tribes, before it was elevated by a Divine ordinance into a sacred rite for temporary purposes, to be served in the Mosaic dispensation. A very able summary of the arguments on both sides, not, of course, embracing those drawn from the more recent discoveries in Egypt, is given by Spencer, 'De Legg. Heb.' lib. I. c. 5. § 4. See Deut. x. 16 and Note.

CHAPTER XVIII.

1 Abraham entertaineth three angels. 9 Sarah is reproved for laughing at the strange promise. 17 The destruction of Sodom is revealed to Abraham. 23 Abraham maketh intercession for the men thereof.

AND the [a] LORD appeared unto [a] Heb. 13. 2.
him in the plains of Mamre:
and he sat in the tent door in the
heat of the day;
2 And he lift up his eyes and

looked, and, lo, three men stood by
him: and when he saw *them*, he ran
to meet them from the tent door, and
bowed himself toward the ground,
3 And said, My Lord, if now I have
found favour in thy sight, pass not
away, I pray thee, from thy servant:
4 Let a little water, I pray you, be
fetched, and wash your feet, and rest
yourselves under the tree:
5 And I will fetch a morsel of bread,
and †comfort ye your hearts; after † Heb. *stay.*
that ye shall pass on: for therefore
†are ye come to your servant. And † Heb. *you have passed.*
they said, So do, as thou hast said.
6 And Abraham hastened into the
tent unto Sarah, and said, †Make ready † Heb. *Hasten.*
quickly three measures of fine meal,
knead *it*, and make cakes upon the
hearth.
7 And Abraham ran unto the herd,
and fetcht a calf tender and good, and

CHAP. XVIII. 1. *plains of Mamre*] **Oaks or oak grove of Mamre**, see xiii. 18; xiv. 13.

in the heat of the day] Abraham was sitting in his tent under the shade of the trees, at the noon day when the sun was oppressive, and when the duty of hospitality specially suggested to him the receiving of travellers, who might be wearied with their hot journey. The time of the day may be also mentioned, that it might be the more certain that this was an open vision, not a dream of the night.

2. *three men*] In v. 1 it is said, "The LORD appeared unto him;" in v. 22 it is said, "The *men* turned their faces from thence, and went towards Sodom; but Abraham stood yet before the LORD;" in ch. xix. 1 it is said, "There came *two Angels* to Sodom at even." It appears from the comparison of these passages, and indeed from the whole narrative, that of the three men who appeared to Abraham, two were angels, and one was JEHOVAH Himself. On the belief of the ancient Church that these manifestations of God were manifestations of God the Son, anticipations of the Incarnation, see note on ch. xii. 7. See also on this passage, Euseb. 'Demonst. Evan.' Lib. v. c. 9. There was, however, a belief among many of the ancients that the three men here appearing to Abraham symbolized the three Persons of the Trinity; and the Church by appointing this chapter to be read on Trinity Sunday seems to indorse this belief. This need not conflict with the opinion, that the only Person in the Trinity really manifested to the eyes of Abraham was the Son of God, and that the other two were created angels. Indeed such a manifestation may have been reason enough for the choice of this lesson on Trinity Sunday. It has been observed that One of the three mentioned in this chapter is called repeatedly JEHOVAH, but neither of the two in ch. xix. is ever so called.

bowed himself toward the ground] This was merely the profound eastern salutation (cp. ch. xxiii. 7, 12, xxxiii. 6, 7). Abraham as yet was "entertaining angels *unawares*" (Heb. xiii. 2). He may have observed a special dignity in the strangers, but could not have known their heavenly mission.

3. *My Lord*] It is to be noticed that Abraham here addresses One of the three, who appears more noble than the rest. The title which he gives Him is *Adonai*, a plural of excellence, but the Targum of Onkelos has rendered JEHOVAH (יְיָ), as supposing that Abraham had recognized the divinity of the visitor.

4. *wash your feet*] In the hot plains of the east travellers shod only with sandals found the greatest comfort in bathing their feet, when resting from a journey. (See ch. xix. 2, xxiv. 32; Judg. xix. 21; 1 Tim. v. 10.)

5. *comfort ye your hearts*] Lit. "support your hearts." The heart, considered as the centre of vital functions, is put by the Hebrews for the life itself. To support the heart therefore is to refresh the whole vital powers and spirits. (See Ges. 'Thes.' p. 738, 6, לבב, 1. *a.*)

for therefore are ye come to your servant] The patriarch recognizes a providential call upon him to refresh strangers of noble bearing, come to him on a fatiguing journey.

6. *three measures of fine meal*] **Three seahs of the finest flour.** A *seah* was the third part of an ephah according to the Rabbins. Josephus ('Ant.' IX. 4) and Jerome ('Comm. on Matt.' xiii. 33), say that the seah was a modius and a half. The accuracy of this comparison between the Hebrew and Roman measures is doubted, as it does not correspond with the calculations of Rabbinical writers. (See Ges. 'Thes.' pp. 83, 932; Smith, 'Dict. of Bible,' Vol. III. pp. 1741, 1742.) The two words, *Kemach soleth*, rendered "fine meal," are nearly synonymous, both appearing to mean fine flour, the latter being the finer of the two. They might be rendered "flour of fine flour." According to the Rabbinical Commentary, 'Vajikra Rabba,' *soleth* is the *kemach* of *kemachs*, the fine flour of fine flour. (See Ges. 'Thes.' p. 959.)

cakes upon the hearth] Probably the simpler form of cake baked in the midst of hot cinders.

gave *it* unto a young man; and he
hasted to dress it.
8 And he took butter, and milk, and
the calf which he had dressed, and set
it before them; and he stood by them
under the tree, and they did eat.
9 ¶ And they said unto him, Where
is Sarah thy wife? And he said, Behold,
in the tent.
10 And he said, I will certainly
return unto thee according to the time
of life; and, lo, [b]Sarah thy wife shall
have a son. And Sarah heard *it* in
the tent door, which *was* behind
him.
11 Now Abraham and Sarah *were*
old *and* well stricken in age; *and* it
ceased to be with Sarah after the
manner of women.
12 Therefore Sarah laughed within
herself, saying, After I am waxed old
shall I have pleasure, my [c]lord being
old also?
13 And the LORD said unto Abraham,
Wherefore did Sarah laugh,
saying, Shall I of a surety bear a
child, which am old?
14 Is any thing too hard for the
LORD? At the time appointed I will
return unto thee, according to the
time of life, and Sarah shall have a son.
15 Then Sarah denied, saying, I
laughed not; for she was afraid. And
he said, Nay; but thou didst laugh.

[b] chap. 17. 19. & 21. 2.
[c] 1 Pet. 3. 6.

---

8. *butter*] *i.e.* thick milk or clotted cream. The modern Arabs have a simple mode of churning, and make very good butter. Robinson ('Res.' II. p. 180) describes the baking of cakes and making of butter among them in the present day. It is, however, most probable, that the word, rendered *butter* in the Old Testament, was rather thick milk, or more probably, thick cream, though in one place (Prov. XXX. 33), it may perhaps be rendered *cheese*. The ancient inhabitants of Palestine used olive oil where we use butter. (See Rosenm. and Ges. 'Thes.' p. 486.)

they did eat] That spiritual visitants, though in human form, should eat, has been a puzzle to many commentators. Josephus ('Ant.' I. 11) and Philo ('Opp.' II. 18), say it was in appearance only, which is implied by Pseudo-Jonathan, Rashi and Kimchi. If the angels had assumed human bodies, though but for a time, there would have been nothing strange in their eating. In any case, the food may have been consumed, miraculously or not; and the eating of it was a proof that the visit of the angels to Abraham was no mere vision, but a true manifestation of heavenly beings.

10. *he said*] In v. 9 we read "they said," *i.e.* one of the three heavenly guests spoke for the others. Now we have the singular number, and the speaker uses language suited only to the Ruler of nature and of all things.

according to the time of life] There is some difficulty in the rendering of these words. The phrase occurs again, 2 K. iv. 16. It is now generally thought that the sense is the same as in ch. xvii. 21, "at this set time in the next year" (cp. xviii. 14); and that the words should be translated, "when the season revives," *i.e.* when spring or summer comes round again. Compare

χαῖρε, γύναι, φιλότητι· περιπλομένου δ' ἐνιαυτοῦ
τέξεις ἀγλαὰ τέκνα.
Hom. 'Od.' Λ. 247.

(See Rosenm. in loc.; Ges. 'Thes.' p. 470.) Prof. Lee ('Lex.' p. 193) denies the soundness of this criticism, and virtually indorses the Authorized Version, "as (at) the season, period, of a vigorous woman." There is, however, very little doubt that the criticism is correct.

12. *laughed*] Whatever may have been the nature of Abraham's laughter (see xvii. 17), this of Sarah's seems to have resulted from incredulity. She may scarcely have recognized the Divinity of the speaker, and had not perhaps realized the truth of the promise before made to Abraham. St Augustine distinguishes between the laughter of Abraham and that of Sarah thus, "The father laughed, when a son was promised to him, from wonder and joy; the mother laughed, when the three men renewed the promise, from doubtfulness and joy. The angel reproved her, because though that laughter was from joy, yet it was not of full faith. Afterwards by the same angel she was confirmed in faith also." 'De C. D.' XVI. 31.

my lord] See 1 Pet. iii. 6.

13. *the LORD said*] Here the speaker is distinctly called JEHOVAH, and it seems much more reasonable to believe that there was a Theophania of the Son of God, than that a created angel was personating God and speaking in His name.

14. *Is any thing too hard for the LORD?*] Lit. "Is anything too wonderful for the Lord?" Cp. Luke i. 37.

At the time appointed I will return unto thee, according to the time of life] See on v. 10.

16 ¶ And the men rose up from
thence, and looked toward Sodom:
and Abraham went with them to
bring them on the way.
17 And the LORD said, Shall I
hide from Abraham that thing which
I do;
18 Seeing that Abraham shall surely
become a great and mighty nation,
and all the nations of the earth shall
be [d]blessed in him?
19 For I know him, that he will
command his children and his household after him, and they shall keep
the way of the LORD, to do justice
and judgment; that the LORD may
bring upon Abraham that which he
hath spoken of him.
20 And the LORD said, Because the
cry of Sodom and Gomorrah is great,
and because their sin is very grievous;
21 I will go down now, and see
whether they have done altogether
according to the cry of it, which is
come unto me; and if not, I will
know.
22 And the men turned their faces
from thence, and went toward Sodom:
but Abraham stood yet before the
LORD.
23 ¶ And Abraham drew near,
and said, Wilt thou also destroy the
righteous with the wicked?
24 Peradventure there be fifty righteous within the city: wilt thou also
destroy and not spare the place for
the fifty righteous that *are* therein?
25 That be far from thee to do after
this manner, to slay the righteous with
the wicked: and that the righteous
should be as the wicked, that be far
from thee: Shall not the Judge of all
the earth do right?
26 And the LORD said, If I find in
Sodom fifty righteous within the city,
then I will spare all the place for their
sakes.
27 And Abraham answered and
said, Behold now, I have taken upon
me to speak unto the Lord, which *am*
but dust and ashes:
28 Peradventure there shall lack
five of the fifty righteous: wilt thou
destroy all the city for *lack of* five?

[d] chap. 12. 3. & 22. 18. Acts 3. 25. Gal. 3. 8.

---

16. *Abraham went with them*] The three heavenly visitors all go towards Sodom. Abraham goes some way with them, how far is not said. There is a tradition that he went as far as Caphar-berucha, from which the Dead Sea is visible, through a ravine.

17. *Shall I hide from Abraham*] The LXX. adds here "my son," which is quoted by Philo (I. p. 401, Mangey) as "Abraham, my friend:" so that in all probability, copies of the LXX. in the time of Philo had this afterwards familiar name of Abraham expressed in this verse. Cp. 2 Chr. xx. 7; Isa. xli. 8; James ii. 23.

19. *For I know him, that*] This is the general reading of the ancient Versions, LXX., Vulg., Targg., &c. &c. It does not, however, seem to correspond with the Hebrew idiom. The literal rendering would be, "I have known him, to the end that, in order that, he should command his children, &c." The word (ידע, *to know*) is sometimes used of the eternal foreknowledge and election of God, as in Amos iii. 2, "You only have I known of all the families of the earth." Cp. Exod. xxxiii. 12; Job xxii. 13; Ps. lxxiii. 11, cxliv. 3; Is. lviii. 3; Nah. i. 7. And compare a similar use in the Greek Testament, Rom. viii. 29, xi. 2. The meaning would then be, "I have foreknown and chosen Abraham, that he should be the depositary of my truth, and should teach his children in the way of religion and godliness, that so the promises made to him should be fulfilled in his seed and lineage. So Ges. ('Thes.' p. 571), Rosenm., Tuch, Knobel, Delitzsch, Keil, &c.

20. *the cry*] Cp. ch. iv. 10; Ps. ix. 13.

21. *I will go down*] Ch. xi. 5, 7; Ex. iii. 8. The reason for God's thus revealing His purpose to Abraham seems to have been, that, as Abraham was to be the heir of the promises, he might be taught and might teach his children, who were afterwards to dwell in that very country, that God is not a God of mercy only, as shewn to Abraham and his descendants, but a God of judgment also, as witnessed by His destruction of the guilty cities of the plain.

22. *the men turned their faces from thence, &c.*] The two created angels went on to Sodom (see ch. xix. 1), "but Abraham stood yet before the LORD," stood yet in the presence of that third Being who was not a created angel, but the eternal Word of God, "the Angel of Mighty counsel" (Isai. ix. 6, LXX.); "the Messenger of the covenant" (Mal. iii. 1).

And he said, If I find there forty and
five, I will not destroy *it*.
29 And he spake unto him yet again,
and said, Peradventure there shall be
forty found there. And he said, I
will not do *it* for forty's sake.
30 And he said *unto him*, Oh let not
the Lord be angry, and I will speak:
Peradventure there shall thirty be
found there. And he said, I will not
do *it*, if I find thirty there.
31 And he said, Behold now, I have
taken upon me to speak unto the
Lord: Peradventure there shall be
twenty found there. And he said, I
will not destroy *it* for twenty's sake.
32 And he said, Oh let not the Lord
be angry, and I will speak yet but this
once: Peradventure ten shall be found
there. And he said, I will not destroy *it* for ten's sake.
33 And the LORD went his way, as
soon as he had left communing with
Abraham: and Abraham returned
unto his place.

CHAPTER XIX.

1 Lot entertaineth two angels. 4 The vicious Sodomites are stricken with blindness. 12 Lot is sent for safety into the mountains. 18 He obtaineth leave to go into Zoar. 24 Sodom and Gomorrah are destroyed. 26 Lot's wife is a pillar of salt. 30 Lot dwelleth in a cave. 31 The incestuous original of Moab and Ammon.

AND there came two angels to
Sodom at even; and Lot sat in
the gate of Sodom: and Lot seeing
them rose up to meet them; and he
bowed himself with his face toward
the ground;
2 And he said, Behold now, my
lords, turn in, I pray you, into your
servant's house, and tarry all night,
and [a] wash your feet, and ye shall rise [a] chap. 18.
up early, and go on your ways. And 4.
they said, Nay; but we will abide in
the street all night.
3 And he pressed upon them greatly;
and they turned in unto him, and
entered into his house; and he made
them a feast, and did bake unleavened
bread, and they did eat.

---

32. *I will not destroy it for ten's sake*] A noted example of the efficacy of prayer, of the blessedness of a good leaven in a city or nation, and of the longsuffering mercy of God.

CHAP. XIX. 1. *two angels*] Lit. **the two angels.** So LXX. The two men, who left Abraham still standing in the presence of the LORD (ch. xviii. 22) now came to Sodom at even.

Lot sat in the gate of Sodom] The gate of the city was, in the ancient towns of the east, the common place of public resort, both for social intercourse and public business. This gate of the city nearly corresponded with the forum or market-place of Greece and Rome. Not only was it the place of public sale, but judges and even kings held courts of justice there. The gate itself was probably an arch with deep recesses, in which were placed the seats of the judges, and benches on either side were arranged for public convenience. (Cp. ch. xxxiv. 20; Deut. xxi. 19, xxii. 15; Ruth iv. 1. See also Hom. 'Il.' Lib. III. 148.)

bowed himself] See on ch. xviii. 2.

2. *my lords*] The Masorites mark this word as "profane," *i. e.* as not taken in the divine, but in the human sense. Lot, like Abraham, only saw in the angels two men, travellers apparently wearied with the way, and he offers them all the rites of hospitality. In those days there were neither inns nor perhaps even caravanserais, so that private houses only could give lodging to strangers.

we will abide in the street all night] The "street," lit. "the broad, open space," probably included all the streets, squares, and inclosures, frequently extensive in an eastern city, and in these early days perhaps less built over than in modern towns. The warmth of the climate would make it easy to pass the night in such a place. The words of the angels may be compared with our Lord's manner as recorded Luke xxiv. 28, "He made as though He would have gone further." The visit of the angels was one of trial previous to judgment (see ch. xviii. 21), trial of Lot as well as of the people of Sodom. Lot's character, though he is called "a righteous" or upright "man" (2 Pet. ii. 7), was full of faults and infirmities, but here he comes out well under the trial. His conduct is altogether favourably contrasted with that of the inhabitants of the city, and so he is delivered, whilst they are destroyed.

3. *a feast*] Lit. "a drink, or banquet, symposium." It is the word used commonly for a sumptuous repast.

unleavened bread] As having no time to leaven it. Literally the words mean "bread of sweetness," *i.e.* bread which had not been made bitter by leaven.

4 ¶ But before they lay down, the
men of the city, *even* the men of
Sodom, compassed the house round,
both old and young, all the people
from every quarter:
5 And they called unto Lot, and
said unto him, Where *are* the men
which came in to thee this night?
bring them out unto us, that we may
know them.
6 And Lot went out at the door
unto them, and shut the door after
him,
7 And said, I pray you, brethren,
do not so wickedly.
8 Behold now, I have two daughters
which have not known man; let me,
I pray you, bring them out unto you,
and do ye to them as *is* good in your
eyes: only unto these men do nothing;
for therefore came they under the
shadow of my roof.

9 And they said, Stand back. And
they said *again*, This one *fellow* came
in to sojourn, and he will needs be a
judge: now will we deal worse with
thee, than with them. And they
pressed sore upon the man, *even* Lot,
and came near to break the door.
10 But the men put forth their
hand, and pulled Lot into the house
to them, and shut to the door.
11 And they smote the men [b]that [b] Wisd. 19. 16.
were at the door of the house with
blindness, both small and great: so
that they wearied themselves to find
the door.
12 ¶ And the men said unto Lot,
Hast thou here any besides? son in
law, and thy sons, and thy daughters,
and whatsoever thou hast in the city,
bring *them* out of this place:
13 For we will destroy this place,
because the [c]cry of them is waxen [c] chap. 18. 20.

---

4. *all the people from every quarter*] The utter shamelessness of the inhabitants of Sodom, as well as their unbridled licentiousness, is briefly but most emphatically expressed in this verse. The Canaanitish nations in general, and the cities of the plain especially, were addicted to those deadly sins so strictly forbidden to the Israelites. See Lev. xx. 22, 23.

6. *Lot went out at the door unto them, and shut the door after him*] Lit. "went out at the doorway, and shut the door after him."

8. *I have two daughters*] These words of Lot have been much canvassed in all times. St Chrysostom thought it virtuous in him not to spare his own daughters, rather than sacrifice the duties of hospitality, and expose his guests to the wickedness of the men of Sodom ('Hom. XXIII. in Gen.'). So St Ambrose ('De Abrah.' Lib. I. c. 6), speaking as if a smaller sin were to be preferred to a greater. But St Augustine justly observes, that we should open the way for sin to reign far and wide, if we allowed ourselves to commit smaller sins, lest others should commit greater ('Lib. contr. Mend.' c. 9. See also 'Qu. in Gen.' 42). We see in all this conduct of Lot the same mixed character. He intended to do rightly, but did it timidly and imperfectly. He felt strongly the duty of hospitality, perhaps by this time he had even some suspicion of the sacred character of his guests, but his standard of right, though high when compared with that of his neighbours, was not the highest. The sacred writer relates the history simply and without comment, not holding up Lot as an example for imitation, but telling his faults as well as his virtues, and leaving us to draw the inferences. He brought all his troubles on himself by the home he had chosen. He was bound to defend his guests at the risk of his own life, but not by the sacrifice of his daughters.

9. *Stand back*] Lit. "Come near, farther off."

will needs be a judge] or, "judging, he will judge," referring, probably, as Tuch observes, to Lot's frequent remonstrances with them for their licentiousness and violence, which is referred to in 2 Pet. ii. 7, 8.

11. *they smote the men that were at the door of the house with blindness*] Perhaps the word for blindness rather indicates confused vision, LXX. ἀορασία. In Wisd. xix. 17, the darkness in which these men were involved is compared with the plague of 'darkness which may be felt," which fell on the Egyptians (Ex. x. 22). If it had been actual blindness, they would hardly have wearied themselves to find the door, but would have sought some one to lead them by the hand (August. 'De Civit. Dei.' XXII. 19). The same word, the root of which is very doubtful (see Gesen. 'Thes.' p. 961), occurs only once again, in 2 K. vi. 18, where, apparently (see vv. 19, 20), not real blindness, but indistinctness of vision and misleading error are described. Aben Ezra interprets it as meaning "blindness of eye and mind."

great before the face of the Lord;
and the Lord hath sent us to destroy it.
14 And Lot went out, and spake
unto his sons in law, which married
his daughters, and said, Up, get you
out of this place; for the Lord will
destroy this city. But he seemed as
one that mocked unto his sons in
law.
15 ¶ And when the morning arose,
then the angels hastened Lot, saying,
Arise, take thy wife, and thy two
daughters, which †are here; lest thou
be consumed in the ‖iniquity of the
city.
16 And [d]while he lingered, the
men laid hold upon his hand, and
upon the hand of his wife, and upon
the hand of his two daughters; the
Lord being merciful unto him: and
they brought him forth, and set him
without the city.
17 ¶ And it came to pass, when
they had brought them forth abroad,
that he said, Escape for thy life; look
not behind thee, neither stay thou in
all the plain; escape to the mountain,
lest thou be consumed.
18 And Lot said unto them, Oh,
not so, my Lord:
19 Behold now, thy servant hath
found grace in thy sight, and thou
hast magnified thy mercy, which thou
hast shewed unto me in saving my
life; and I cannot escape to the mountain, lest some evil take me, and I
die:
20 Behold now, this city *is* near to
flee unto, and it *is* a little one: Oh,
let me escape thither, (*is* it not a little
one?) and my soul shall live.
21 And he said unto him, See, I
have accepted †thee concerning this
thing also, that I will not overthrow
this city, for the which thou hast
spoken.
22 Haste thee, escape thither; for

† Heb. *are found.*
‖ Or, *punishment.*
[d] Wisd. 10. 6.
† Heb. *thy face.*

---

13. *the Lord hath sent us to destroy it*] The angels speak here as messengers of judgment, not as He, who conversed with Abraham, ch. xviii. 17—33.

14. *which married his daughters*] Lit. "the takers of his daughters." LXX. "who had taken his daughters." Vulg. "who were about to marry his daughters." Some, Knobel, Delitzsch, &c., have held that besides those mentioned, vv. 8, 30, Lot had other daughters, who had married men of the city, and who perished in the conflagration with their husbands. It is more commonly thought that he had only two daughters, who were betrothed, but not yet married; betrothal being sufficient to give the title "son in law" or "bridegroom" to their affianced husbands.

15. *which are here*] Lit. "which are found." This seems to Knobel and others to indicate that there were other daughters, but that these two only were at home, the others being with their husbands in the city (see on v. 14); but it very probably points only to the fact, that Lot's wife and daughters were at home and ready to accompany him, whilst his sons in law scoffed and refused to go.

16. *the Lord being merciful unto him*] Lit. "in the mercy" (the sparing pity) "of the Lord to him."

17. *that he said*] *i.e.* one of the angels.

the plain] The *kikkar*, the circuit of the Jordan. Lot was to escape from the whole of the devoted region, which he had formerly coveted for his own, and where, when he parted from Abraham, he had made his habitation, and sought to enrich himself.

18. *my Lord*] The Masorites have the note *kadesh*, *i.e.* "holy," but it is probably no more than the salutation of reverence, see v. 2. For, though Lot had now found out the dignity of his guests, there is no evidence that he thought either of them to be the Most High. Indeed the word might be rendered in the plural "my lords," as the Syr. and Saad.

19. *I cannot escape to the mountain*] Lot and his family were, no doubt, exhausted by fear and anxiety, and he felt that, if he had to go to the mountains of Moab, he would be exposed to many dangers, which might prove his destruction; another instance of defective courage and faith, which yet is pardoned by a merciful God.

some evil] The evil, *i.e.* the destruction about to fall on Sodom; all Lot's conduct here denotes excessive weakness.

20. *is it not a little one?*] Though Zoar may have been involved in the guilt of the other cities of the plain, Lot pleads that it has but few inhabitants, and that the sins of such a small city can be but comparatively small. So Rashi.

21. *I have accepted thee*] Lit. "I have lifted up thy face." It was the custom in the

I cannot do anything till thou be
come thither. Therefore the name
of the city was called Zoar.
23 ¶ The sun was †risen upon the
earth when Lot entered into Zoar.
24 Then [e]the LORD rained upon
Sodom and upon Gomorrah brimstone and fire from the LORD out of
heaven;
25 And he overthrew those cities,
and all the plain, and all the inhabitants
of the cities, and that which grew upon
the ground.
26 ¶ But his wife looked back from
behind him, and she became a pillar of
salt.
27 ¶ And Abraham gat up early in
the morning to the place where he
stood before the LORD:
28 And he looked toward Sodom

† Heb. *gone forth.*

[e] Deut. 29. 23. Luke 17. 29. Isai. 13. 19. Jer. 50. 40. Amos 4. 11. Jude 7.

East to make supplication with the face to the ground; when the prayer was granted, the face was said to be raised.

22. *Zoar*] *i.e.* "little." It appears by several ancient testimonies to have been believed that Zoar or Bela, though spared from the first destruction of the cities of the plain, was afterwards swallowed up by an earthquake, probably when Lot had left it, v. 30. (See Jerom 'ad Jos.' XV. and 'Qu. in Gen.' c. XIV.; Theodoret 'in Gen.' XIX.). This tradition may account for the statement in Wisdom x. 6, that five cities were destroyed, and of Josephus ('B. J.' IV. 8. 4), that the "shadowy forms of five cities" could be seen; whereas Deut. xxix. 23 only mentions four, viz. Sodom, Gomorrah, Admah and Zeboim: yet, on the other hand, Eusebius (v. βαλὰ) witnesses that Bela, or Zoar, was inhabited in his day, and garrisoned by Roman soldiers.

24. *the LORD rained upon Sodom and upon Gomorrah brimstone and fire from the LORD out of heaven*] The LORD is said to have rained from the LORD, an expression much noted by commentators, Jewish and Christian. Several of the Rabbins, Manasseh Ben Israel, R. Simeon, and others, by the first JEHOVAH understand the angel Gabriel, the angel of the LORD: but there is certainly no other passage in Scripture, where this most sacred name is given to a created angel. Many of the fathers, Ignatius, Justin M., Tertullian, Cyprian, Athanasius, Hilary, The Council of Sirmium, &c. see in these words the mystery of the Holy Trinity, as though it were said, "GOD the Word rained down fire from GOD the Father;" an interpretation which may seem to be supported by the Jerusalem Targum, where "the Word of the LORD" is said to have "rained down fire and bitumen from the presence of the LORD." Other patristic commentators of the highest authority (as Chrysostom, Jerome and Augustine) do not press this argument. Aben Ezra, whom perhaps a majority of Christian commentators have followed in this, sees in these words a peculiar "elegance or grace of language;" "The LORD rained...from the LORD" being a grander and more impressive mode of saying, "The LORD rained from Himself." It is a common idiom in Hebrew to repeat the noun instead of using a pronoun.

brimstone and fire...out of heaven] Many explanations have been offered of this. Whether the fire from heaven was lightning, which kindled the bitumen and set the whole country in a blaze, whether it was a great volcanic eruption overwhelming all the cities of the plain, or whether there was simply a miraculous raining down of ignited sulphur, has been variously disputed and discussed. From comparing these words with Deut. xxix. 23, where it is said, "The whole land thereof is brimstone and salt and burning," it may be reasonably questioned, whether the "brimstone" in both passages may not mean *bitumen*, with which unquestionably, both before (see ch. xiv. 10), and after the overthrow, the whole country abounded (see also Jerusalem Targum quoted in the last note). The Almighty, in His most signal judgments and even in His most miraculous interventions, has been pleased often to use natural agencies; as, for instance, He brought the locusts on Egypt with an East wind and drove them back with a West wind (Ex. x. 13, 19). Possibly therefore the bitumen, which was the natural produce of the country, volcanic or otherwise, was made the instrument by which the offending cities were destroyed. The revelation to Abraham, the visit of the angels, the deliverance of Lot, mark the whole as miraculous and the result of direct intervention from above, whatever may have been the instrument which the Most High made use of to work His pleasure.

26. *a pillar of salt*] All testimony speaks of the exceeding saltness of the Dead Sea, and the great abundance of salt in its neighbourhood (*e.g.* Galen. 'De Simp. Medic. Facult.' IV. 19). In what manner Lot's wife actually perished has been questioned. Aben-Ezra supposed that she was first killed by the brimstone and fire and then incrusted over with salt, so as to become a statue or pillar of salt. There was a pillar of salt near the Dead Sea, which later tradition identified with Lot's wife (Joseph. 'Ant.' I. 11; Iren. IV. 51; Tertullian, 'Carmen de Sodoma;' Benjamin of

and Gomorrah, and toward all the
land of the plain, and beheld, and, lo,
the smoke of the country went up as
the smoke of a furnace.

29 ¶ And it came to pass, when
God destroyed the cities of the plain,
that God remembered Abraham, and
sent Lot out of the midst of the overthrow, when he overthrew the cities
in the which Lot dwelt.

30 ¶ And Lot went up out of
Zoar, and dwelt in the mountain, and
his two daughters with him; for he
feared to dwell in Zoar: and he dwelt
in a cave, he and his two daughters.

31 And the firstborn said unto the
younger, Our father *is* old, and *there*
is not a man in the earth to come in
unto us after the manner of all the
earth:

32 Come, let us make our father
drink wine, and we will lie with him,
that we may preserve seed of our
father.

33 And they made their father
drink wine that night: and the firstborn went in, and lay with her father;
and he perceived not when she lay
down, nor when she arose.

34 And it came to pass on the
morrow, that the firstborn said unto
the younger, Behold, I lay yesternight
with my father: let us make him drink
wine this night also; and go thou in,
and lie with him, that we may preserve seed of our father.

35 And they made their father
drink wine that night also: and the
younger arose, and lay with him; and
he perceived not when she lay down,
nor when she arose.

36 Thus were both the daughters
of Lot with child by their father.

37 And the firstborn bare a son,

Tudela, 'Itin.' p. 44. See Heidegger, II. p. 269). The American expedition, under Lynch, found to the East of Usdum a pillar of salt about forty feet high, which was perhaps that referred to by Josephus, &c.

29. *God remembered Abraham*] He remembered Abraham's intercession recorded in ch. xviii. and also the covenant which He had made with Abraham, and which was graciously extended so as to benefit his kinsman Lot.

30. *he feared to dwell in Zoar*] Jerome ('Qu.' ad h.l.) supposes that Lot had seen Zoar so often affected by earthquakes that he durst no longer abide there, see on v. 22. Rashi thought that the proximity to Sodom was the reason for his fear. The weakness of Lot's character is seen here again, in his not trusting God's promises.

dwelt in a cave] These mountainous regions abound in caves, and the early inhabitants formed them into dwellingplaces; see on ch. xiv. 6.

31. *there is not a man in the earth*] Iren. (IV. 51;) Chrysostom ('Hom. 34 in Genes.'), Ambros. ('De Abrahamo,' I. 6), Theodoret, ('Qu. in. Gen.' 69), excuse this incestuous conduct of the daughters of Lot on the ground, that they supposed the whole human race to have been destroyed, excepting their father and themselves. Even if it were so, the words of St Augustine would be true, that "they should have preferred to be childless rather than to treat their father so." (*Potius nunquam esse matres quam sic uti patre debuerunt*, 'C. Faustum,' XXII. 43.) It is too apparent that the licentiousness of Sodom had had a degrading influence upon their hearts and lives.

32. *let us make our father drink wine*] It has been suggested in excuse for Lot, that his daughters drugged the wine. Of this, however, there is no intimation in the text. But the whole history is of the simplest character. It tells plainly all the faults, not of Lot only, but of Abraham and Sarah also. Still though it simply relates and neither praises nor blames, yet in Lot's history we may trace the judgment as well as the mercy of God. His selfish choice of the plain of Jordan led him perhaps to present wealth and prosperity, but withal to temptation and danger. In the midst of the abandoned profligacy of Sodom he indeed was preserved in comparative purity, and so, when God overthrew the cities of the plain, he yet saved Lot from destruction. Still Lot's feebleness of faith first caused him to linger, v. 16, then to fear escape to the mountains, v. 19, and lastly to doubt the safety of the place which God had spared for him, v. 30. Now again he is led by his children into intoxication, which betrays him, unconsciously, into far more dreadful wickedness. And then we hear of him no more. He is left by the sacred narrative, saved indeed from the conflagration of Sodom, but an outcast, widowed, homeless, hopeless, without children or grandchildren, save the authors and the heirs of his shame.

and called his name Moab: the same
is the father of the Moabites unto
this day.
38 And the younger, she also bare
a son, and called his name Ben-
ammi: the same *is* the father of
the children of Ammon unto this
day.

---

37. *Moab*] According to the LXX.=*me-ab*, *i.e.* "from the father." So also the Targ. of Pseudo-Jonathan, Augustine, Jerome, &c. alluding to the incestuous origin of Moab. The Moabites dwelt originally to the East of the Dead Sea, from whence they expelled the Emims (Deut. ii. 11). Afterwards they were driven by the Amorites to the South of the river Arnon, which formed their Northern boundary.

38. *Ben-ammi*] *i.e.* "son of my people," in allusion to his being of unmixed race. The Ammonites are said to have destroyed the Zam-zummim, a tribe of the Rephaim, and to have succeeded them and dwelt in their stead. (Deut. ii. 22.) They appear for the most part to have been an unsettled marauding violent race, of Bedouin habits, worshippers of Molech, "the abomination of the Ammonites." 1 K. xi. 7.

De Wette and his followers, Rosenmüller, Tuch, Knobel, &c. speak of this narrative, as if it had arisen from the national hatred of the Israelites to the Moabites and Ammonites, but the Pentateuch by no means shews such national hatred (see Deut. ii. 9, 19): and the book of Ruth gives the history of a Moabitess who was ancestress of David himself. It was not till the Moabites had seduced the Israelites to idolatry and impurity, Num. xxv. 1, and had acted in an unfriendly manner towards them, hiring Balaam to curse them, that they were excluded from the congregation of the Lord for ever. Deut. xxiii. 3, 4.

NOTE A on CHAP. XIX. 25. THE DEAD SEA, SITE OF SODOM AND ZOAR.

(1) Characteristics of Dead Sea. Testimonies ancient and modern. (2) Geological formation. (3) Were Sodom, Zoar, &c. on the North or South of the Dead Sea?

THE Dead Sea, if no historical importance attached to it, would still be the most remarkable body of water in the known world. Many fabulous characteristics were assigned to it by ancient writers, as that birds could not fly over it, that oxen and camels floated in it, nothing being heavy enough to sink (Tacit. 'Hist.' v. 6; Plin. 'H. N.' v. 16; Seneca, 'Qu. Nat.' lib. II.). It has been conjectured by Reland, with some probability, that legends belonging to the lake of Asphalt said to have existed near Babylon (see on ch. xi. 3) were mixed up with the accounts of the Dead Sea, and both exaggerated (Reland, 'Palest.' II. pp. 244 seq.).

The Dead Sea called in Scripture the Salt Sea (Gen. xiv. 3; Numb. xxxiv. 3, 12), the Sea of the Plain (Deut. iii. 17, iv. 49; Josh. iii. 16), and in the later books, "the East Sea" (Ezek. xlvii. 18; Joel ii. 20; in Zech. xiv. 8, "the former sea" should be rendered "the East Sea"), is according to Lynch 40 geographical miles long by 9 to $9\frac{3}{4}$ broad. Its depression is 1316 feet below the level of the Mediterranean. Its depth in the northern portion is 1308 feet. Its extreme saltness was known to the ancients. Galen. ('De Simplic. Medicam. Facultat.' c. 19) says that "its taste was not only salt but bitter." Modern travellers describe the taste as most intensely and intolerably salt, its specific gravity and its buoyancy being consequently so great that people can swim or float in it, who could not swim in any other water. This excessive saltness is probably caused by the immense masses of fossil salt which lie in a mountain at its South-west border, and by the rapid evaporation of the fresh water, which flows into it (Stanley, 'S. and P.' p. 292; Robinson's 'Phys. Geog.' p. 195). Both ancient and modern writers assert that nothing animal or vegetable lives in this sea (Tacit. 'Hist.' v. 6; Galen. 'De Simpl. Med.' IV. 19; Hieron. ad Ezech. XLVII. 18; Robinson, 'Bib. Res.' II. p. 226). The few living creatures which the Jordan washes down into it are destroyed (Stanley, 'S. and P.' p. 293). No wonder, then, that the Salt Sea should have been called the Dead Sea, a name unknown to the sacred writers, but common in after times. Even its shores, incrusted with salt, present the appearance of utter desolation. The ancients speak much of the masses of asphalt, or bitumen, which the lake threw up. Diodorus Sic. affirms that the masses of bitumen were like islands, covering two or three plethra (Diod. Sic. II. 48); and Josephus says that they were of the form and magnitude of oxen ('B. J.' IV. 8. 4). Modern travellers testify to the existence of bitumen still on the shores and waters of the Dead Sea, but it is supposed by the Arabs, that it is only thrown up by earthquakes. Especially after the earthquakes of 1834 and 1837, large quantities are said to have been cast upon the Southern shore, probably detached by shocks from the bottom of the Southern bay (Robinson, 'B. R.' II. p. 229; 'Physical Geog.' p. 201. See also Thomson, 'Land and Book,' p. 223).

There is great difference between the Northern and Southern portions of the sea. The great depth of the Northern division does not extend to the South. The Southern bay is shallow, its shores low and marshy, almost like a quicksand, (Stanley, 'S. and P.' p. 293). It has been very generally supposed from Gen. xiv. 3, that the Dead Sea now occupies the site of what was originally the Plain of Jordan, the vale of Siddim, and to this has been added the belief that the cities of Sodom, Gomorrah, &c. were situated in the vale of Siddim, and that they too were covered by the Dead Sea. Recent observations have led many to believe that probably a lake must have existed here before historic times. Yet it is quite conceivable that the terrible catastrophe recorded in Genesis, traces of which are visible throughout the whole region, may have produced even the deep depression of the bed of the Dead Sea, and so have arrested the streams of the Jordan, which may before that time have flowed onwards through the Arabah, and emptied itself into the Gulph of Akabah. At all events, it is very probable that the Southern division of the lake may have been formed at a comparatively recent date. The character of this Southern part, abounding with salt, frequently throwing up bitumen, its shores producing sulphur and nitre (Robinson, 'Phys. Geog.' p. 204), corresponds accurately with all that is told us of the valley of Siddim, which was "full of slime pits" (Gen. xiv. 10), and with the history of the destruction of the cities by fire and brimstone and the turning of Lot's wife into a pillar of salt. Very probably therefore the vale of Siddim may correspond with what is now the Southern Bay of the Dead Sea. There is, however, no Scriptural authority for saying that Sodom and the other guilty cities were immersed in the sea. They are always spoken of as overthrown by fire from heaven (cf. Deut. xxix. 23; Jer. xlix. 18, l. 40; Zeph. ii. 9; 2 Pet. ii. 6). And Josephus ('B. J.' IV. 8. 4) speaks of "Sodomitis, once a prosperous country from its fertility and abundance of cities, but now entirely burnt up," as adjoining the lake Asphaltites. This was observed long ago by Reland (II. p. 256), and is now generally admitted by travellers and commentators. All ancient testimony is in favour of considering the cities of the plain as having lain at this Southern extremity of the sea. The general belief at present that that portion only of the sea can have been of recent formation, and hence that that only can have occupied the site of the vale of Siddim, the belief that Sodom was near the vale of Siddim, the bituminous, saline, volcanic aspect of the Southern coast, the traditional names of Usdum, &c., the traditional site of Zoar, called by Josephus (as above) Zoar of Arabia, the hill of salt, said to have been Lot's wife, and every other supposed vestige of the destroyed cities being to the South, all tend to the general conviction that the cities of the plain (of the Kikkar) lay either within or around the present South bay of the Dead Sea. On the other hand, Mr Grove (in Smith's 'Dict. of the Bible') has argued with great ability in favour of a Northern site for these cities, and he is supported by Tristram ('Land of Israel,' pp. 360—363). The chief grounds for his argument are 1st, that Abraham and Lot, at or near Bethel, could have seen the plain of Jordan to the North of the Dead Sea, but could not have seen the Southern valleys (see Gen. xiii. 10): 2ndly, that what they saw was "the Kikkar of the Jordan," whereas the Jordan flowed into the Dead Sea at its Northern extremity, but probably never flowed to the South of that sea: 3rdly, that later writers have been misled by apparent similarity of names, by the general belief that the sea had overflowed the sites of the cities and by uncertain traditions. It is, however, to be observed, that Mr Grove's arguments rest on two somewhat uncertain positions: first, that, in Gen. xiii. 10—13, Lot must have been able to see, from between Bethel and Ai, the cities of the plain; whereas it is possible that the language is not to be pressed too strictly, Lot seeing at the time the river Jordan North of the present Dead Sea, and knowing that the whole valley both North and South was fertile and well watered; secondly, that no part of the Dead Sea can be of recent formation, notwithstanding the terrible catastrophes all around it, to which not only Scripture but tradition and the present appearance of the whole country bear testimony. On the other hand, both tradition, local names and local evidences are strongly in favour of the Southern site of the cities destroyed.

CHAPTER XX.

1 *Abraham sojourneth at Gerar,* 2 *denieth his wife, and loseth her.* 3 *Abimelech is reproved for her in a dream.* 9 *He rebuketh Abraham,* 14 *restoreth Sarah,* 16 *and reproveth her.* 17 *He is healed by Abraham's prayer.*

AND Abraham journeyed from thence toward the south country, and dwelled between Kadesh and Shur, and sojourned in Gerar.

2 And Abraham said of Sarah his wife, She *is* my sister: and Abime-

---

CHAP. XX. 1. *From thence*] *i.e.* from Mamre, where he had received the heavenly visitors, and whence he had beheld the smoke from the conflagration of the cities of the plain.

lech king of Gerar sent, and took
Sarah.
3 But God came to Abimelech in
a dream by night, and said to him,
Behold, thou *art but* a dead man, for
the woman which thou hast taken;
for she *is* †a man's wife.
4 But Abimelech had not come
near her: and he said, Lord, wilt
thou slay also a righteous nation?
5 Said he not unto me, She *is* my
sister? and she, even she herself said,

† Heb. *married an husband.*

He *is* my brother: in the ‖integrity
of my heart and innocency of my
hands have I done this.
6 And God said unto him in a
dream, Yea, I know that thou didst
this in the integrity of thy heart; for
I also withheld thee from sinning
against me: therefore suffered I thee
not to touch her.
7 Now therefore restore the man
his wife; for he *is* a prophet, and he
shall pray for thee, and thou shalt

‖ Or, *simplicity*, or, *sincerity.*

It may have been painful to him to abide in a place where he would be hourly reminded of this terrible catastrophe, or he may merely have travelled onward in search of fresh pasturage.

dwelled between Kadesh and Shur, and sojourned in Gerar] He settled apparently in a fertile country lying between the two deserts of Kadesh and Shur, and finally took up his residence as a stranger or sojourner (so the word "sojourned" signifies) at Gerar, a place which, St Jerome says, was on the southern border of the Canaanites. Gerar was not far from Gaza (Gen. x. 19), and Beersheba (xxvi. 26). Its site has probably been identified by Rowlands (Williams' 'Holy City,' I. 465) with the traces of an ancient city now called *Khirbet-el-Gerar*, near a deep Wady called *Jurf-el-Gerar*, about three hours to the south-south-east of Gaza.

2. *She is my sister*] This was Abraham's plan of action, when sojourning among strangers, of whose character he was ignorant, see v. 13. He has been defended as having "said she was his sister, without denying that she was his wife, concealing the truth but not speaking what was false" (August. 'c. Faust.' XXII. 3). But, though concealment may not necessarily be deception, we can scarcely acquit Abraham either of some disingenuousness or of endangering his wife's honour and chastity, in order to save his own life.

Abimelech] *Father of the king*, or perhaps *father king*, the common title of the Philistine kings, as Pharaoh was of the Egyptians. The age at which Sarah must have been at this time, some twenty-three or twenty-four years older than when Pharaoh took her into his house (ch. xii. 15), creates a considerable difficulty here. We may remember that Sarah after this became a mother, that though too old for childbearing under normal conditions, she had had her youth renewed since the visit of the angels (Kurtz), when it was promised that she should have a son. The assertion of modern critics that this is merely another version of ch. xii. 10—20, the work of the Elohist, whilst that was by the Jehovist, is ably combated by Keil (p. 170, Eng. Trans. p. 242). He observes, that the name *Elohim* indicates the true relation of God to Abimelech; but that in v. 18, JEHOVAH, the covenant God of Abraham, interposes to save him. All the more minute details of this history are different from that in ch. xii. In Abimelech we see a totally different character from that of Pharaoh; the character, namely, of a heathen imbued with a moral consciousness of right and open to receive a divine revelation, of which there is no trace in the account of the king of Egypt. It is not to be wondered at that the same danger should twice have occurred to Sarah, if we remember that the customs of the heathen nations, among which he was sojourning, were such as to induce Abraham to use the artifice of calling his wife his sister.

4. *had not come near her*] Apparently a divinely sent illness had been upon him, vv. 6, 18.

a righteous nation] *i.e.* a nation guiltless as regards this act of their king; but it may be, that the people of Gerar were really exempt from the worst vices of Canaan, and living in a state of comparative piety and simplicity.

6. *suffered I thee not to touch her*] See on v. 4.

7. *he is a prophet*] *i.e.* one inspired by God, or the medium of God's communications and revelations to mankind. Thus Exod. vii. 1, Aaron is said to be Moses' prophet, because he was to convey the messages and commands of Moses to Pharaoh. An objection has been made to the antiquity of the Pentateuch from the statement in 1 S. ix. 9, that "he that is now called a Prophet was beforetime called a Seer." Hence it is argued that the Pentateuch, which always uses the word prophet, cannot be of the great antiquity assigned to it. The difficulty is only on the surface. "Prophet" was the genuine name applied to all who declared God's will, who foretold the future, or even to great religious teachers. "Seer" had a more restricted sense, and was appropriated to those only who were favoured with visions from heaven. The word *prophet* occurs constantly in the Pentateuch in the

live: and if thou restore *her* not,
know thou that thou shalt surely die,
thou, and all that *are* thine.
8 Therefore Abimelech rose early
in the morning, and called all his
servants, and told all these things in
their ears: and the men were sore
afraid.
9 Then Abimelech called Abraham, and said unto him, What hast
thou done unto us? and what have
I offended thee, that thou hast brought
on me and on my kingdom a great
sin? thou hast done deeds unto me
that ought not to be done.
10 And Abimelech said unto Abraham, What sawest thou, that thou
hast done this thing?
11 And Abraham said, Because I
thought, Surely the fear of God *is*
not in this place; and they will slay
me for my wife's sake.
12 And yet indeed *she is* my sister;
she *is* the daughter of my father, but
not the daughter of my mother; and
she became my wife.
13 And it came to pass, when God
caused me to wander from my father's
house, that I said unto her, This *is*
thy kindness which thou shalt shew
unto me; at every place whither we
shall come, [a]say of me, He *is* my
brother.
14 And Abimelech took sheep, and
oxen, and menservants, and womenservants, and gave *them* unto Abraham, and restored him Sarah his
wife.
15 And Abimelech said, Behold,
my land *is* before thee: dwell †where
it pleaseth thee.
16 And unto Sarah he said, Behold,
I have given thy brother a thousand
pieces of silver: behold, he *is* to thee

[a] chap. 12. 13.

† Heb. *as is good in thine eyes.*

general sense of one in communion with God, and made the medium of God's communications to man. The word "seer" would generally be out of place in such a passage as this, or such as Ex. vii. 1, xv. 20; Num. xi. 29, xii. 6, &c.; but in the time of Samuel, when "the word of the LORD was precious there was no open vision," (1 S. iii. 1;) the application of the title "seer" to Samuel, who had visions specially vouchsafed to him, was very appropriate; yet after his time, though the name was sometimes employed to designate the inspired teachers of mankind, the older and more comprehensive title of "prophet" again came into common use, not only for teachers of religion generally, but also for the most favoured of God's servants. (See 'Mosaic Origin of the Pentateuch,' by a Layman, p. 97.)

he shall pray for thee] As the prophets were the instruments of God's revelations, His messengers, to man; so men made the prophets instruments for sending their prayers up to God (Cleric.). Cp. Jer. vii. 16, xi. 14, xiv. 11.

10. *What sawest thou*] Many recent commentators, Knobel, Delitzsch, Keil, &c., render, "What hadst thou in view?" The more simple sense is, what didst thou see in the conduct and manners of me or my people, that thou shouldest have done so to us? Didst thou see us taking away the wives of strangers and murdering the husbands?

11. *Surely the fear of God is not in this place*] Abraham had seen the impiety and heathenism of the Canaanitish races, and had lately witnessed the overthrow of Sodom for the licentiousness of its people, and he naturally thought that the inhabitants of Gerar might be equally forgetful of God, and therefore prone to all wickedness.

12. *she is my sister; she is the daughter of my father, but not the daughter of my mother*] Sarah's name does not occur in the genealogies, and we do not know any thing of her birth but that which is here stated. Such marriages, though afterwards forbidden (Lev. xviii. 9, 11, xx. 17; Deut. xxvii. 22), may not have been esteemed unlawful in patriarchal times, and they were common among the heathen nations of antiquity (Ach. Tatius, Lib. I.; Diod. I. 27; Herod. III. 31; Nepos, 'Cimon,' c. 1.) Many Jewish and Christian interpreters, however, think that *daughter* here means *granddaughter*, and that Sarah was the same as Iscah, the sister of Lot (ch. xi. 29), who is called "the brother of Abraham" (ch. xiv. 16).

13. *God caused me to wander*] In general the name of GOD (Elohim), though of plural form, is joined with a singular verb. In this case, however, the verb is in the plural. Similar constructions occur ch. xxxv. 7; Exod. xxii. 8; 2 S. vii. 23; (cp. 1 Chr. xvii. 21); Ps. lviii. 12. In Josh. xxiv. 19, the adjective is in the plural. The Samaritan Pentateuch here and in ch. xxxv. 7 has the verb in the singular.

16. *a thousand pieces of silver*] Lit. "a thousand of silver." The versions insert "shekels" or "didrachmas;" nothing can be known of the weights and measures of this early time.

a covering of the eyes, unto all that *are* with thee, and with all *other:* thus she was reproved.

17 ¶ So Abraham prayed unto God: and God healed Abimelech, and his wife, and his maidservants; and they bare *children.*

18 For the LORD had fast closed up all the wombs of the house of Abimelech, because of Sarah Abraham's wife.

CHAPTER XXI.

1 Isaac is born. 4 He is circumcised. 6 Sarah's joy. 9 Hagar and Ishmael are cast forth. 15 Hagar in distress. 17 The angel comforteth her. 22 Abimelech's covenant with Abraham at Beer-sheba.

AND the LORD visited Sarah as he
had said, and the LORD did
unto Sarah [a] as he had spoken. [a] chap. 17.
2 For Sarah [b] conceived, and bare 19. & 18. 10.
Abraham a son in his old age, at the [b] Acts 7. 8. Gal. 4. 22.
set time of which God had spoken to Heb. 11.
him. 11.
3 And Abraham called the name
of his son that was born unto him,
whom Sarah bare to him, Isaac.
4 And Abraham circumcised his
son Isaac being eight days old, [c] as God [c] chap. 17.
had commanded him. 12.
5 And Abraham was an hundred
years old, when his son Isaac was
born unto him.
6 ¶ And Sarah said, God hath

Probably the thousand pieces of silver indicate the value of the sheep and oxen, which Abimelech gave to Abraham, though some think it was an additional present.

16. *he is to thee a covering of the eyes*] There is great variety of opinion as to the sense of these words. If we follow the rendering of the Authorized Version, the most probable interpretation is that of Heidegger, Schrœder, Rosenmüller, &c., viz. this, that in early times in the East unmarried women often went unveiled, but married women always veiled themselves. Cp. Gen. xxiv. 65. Hence Abimelech meant to say, that Abraham should be like a veil to Sarah, screening her from the eyes of all other men. See Rosenm. in loc. Heidegger, II. p. 163. The words might have been rendered, as by the LXX., Vulg., Targg., Syr., "it" or "they," *i.e.* the one thousand pieces of silver "are to thee a covering of the eyes," in which case the meaning would probably be "this gift is to thee for a covering to the eyes, so that thou shouldest overlook or condone the injury done to thee." So St Chrysostom, and among moderns, Gesenius, Tuch, Knobel, &c.

thus she was reproved] Here also there is great diversity of interpretation; but the Authorized Version is probably correct, and we must understand the words to be those of the historian, not of Abimelech. So apparently Onk., Arab., Saad., Kimchi, Gesen., Rosenm., &c.

18. *the LORD*] Keil has observed, that the various names of the Most High are used very significantly in these two last verses. The care of Abimelech and his wives belonged to the Deity (*Elohim*). Abraham directed his intercession not to *Elohim*, an indefinite and unknown god, but to *Ha-Elohim*, "the" true "God;" and it was JEHOVAH, the covenant God, who interposed for Abraham and preserved the mother of the promised seed.

CHAP. XXI. **1.** *the LORD did unto Sarah as he had spoken*] In ch. xvii. 16, GOD promised that He would give Abraham a son by Sarah his wife, on which promise Abraham fell on his face and laughed, whether from incredulity or for joy. What God (Elohim) then promised here the LORD (JEHOVAH) fulfils.

2. *at the set time of which God had spoken to him*] The "set time" was fixed, ch. xvii. 21, and xviii. 10, 14. (See note on ch. xviii. 10.) Modern critics see in ch. xvii. and in this ch. xxi. an Elohistic portion of the history of Abraham, and in ch. xviii. a Jehovistic portion. Yet this present chapter seems clearly to point back to both ch. xvii. and ch. xviii., and in its first verse it uses twice the name JEHOVAH, whilst in the second and subsequent verses it has constantly the name Elohim until we come to v. 33, when both names are conjoined, for Abraham is said to have called on the name of "The LORD, the everlasting God."

3. *Isaac*] The name which God had appointed for him, ch. xvii. 19. See also note on ch. xviii. 12.

6. *God hath made me to laugh*] Whatever was the nature of Sarah's laughter when the promise was made to her (see ch. xviii. 12), she now acknowledges that God had made her to laugh for joy; and she recognizes that He, whom she then took for a traveller and who made the promise, at which she laughed, was truly GOD.

will laugh with me] The Hebrew might mean "laugh at me" or "laugh with me." The Authorised Version rightly follows the LXX., Vulg., Targg., &c.

made me to laugh, *so that* all that
hear will laugh with me.
7 And she said, Who would have
said unto Abraham, that Sarah should
have given children suck? for I have
born *him* a son in his old age.
8 And the child grew, and was
weaned: and Abraham made a great
feast the *same* day that Isaac was
weaned.
9 ¶ And Sarah saw the son of
Hagar the Egyptian, which she had
born unto Abraham, mocking.
10 Wherefore she said unto Abra-
Gal. 4. ham, [d]Cast out this bondwoman and
30. her son: for the son of this bondwoman shall not be heir with my son,
even with Isaac.
11 And the thing was very grievous in Abraham's sight because of his
son.
12 ¶ And God said unto Abraham,
Let it not be grievous in thy sight
because of the lad, and because of thy
bondwoman; in all that Sarah hath
said unto thee, hearken unto her
voice; for in Isaac shall thy seed be
called.
13 And also of the son of the bondwoman will I make a nation, because
he *is* thy seed.
14 And Abraham rose up early in

---

7. *Who would have said*] The rendering of the Authorised Version is most likely correct. The obscurity of the passage probably arises from its poetical form. It has been long ago observed, that the words are apparently those of a short poem or hymn, like the hymn of Hannah, 1 S. ii. 1—7, or the Magnificat of the Blessed Virgin, Luke i. 46—55, the resemblance to which is the more noticeable, as Isaac was an eminent type of the Lord Jesus (see Wordsworth ad loc.). That these words were of the nature of a hymn or poem is seen in the use of a poetical word (*millel*) for "said," instead of the more common words (*dibber* or *amar*); and also in the appearance of regular parallelism of the members of the sentence.

8. *the child grew, and was weaned*] From 1 S. i. 23, 24; 2 Macc. vii. 27; Joseph. 'Ant.' II. 9. 6, it has been inferred that children were not weaned among the Hebrews till they were three years old. Ishmael was thirteen years old when he was circumcised, ch. xvii. 25, and one year after Isaac was born, ch. xvii. 21. If therefore Isaac was three years old at his weaning, Ishmael must have been then seventeen. If Isaac was but one year old, Ishmael would have been fifteen.

made a great feast] By comparing 1 S. i. 24, 25, it would seem that this was very probably a religious feast.

9. *mocking*] The word, which naturally means *to laugh*, is rendered by the LXX. and Vulg., "playing with Isaac." Tuch, Knobel, &c. say the word means merely, "playing like a child." Gesenius thinks it was "playing and dancing gracefully," and so attracting the favour of his father, which moved the envy of Sarah. The Targum of Onkelos appears to give the sense of "deriding" (see Buxtorf, 'Lex. Chald. and Talmud.' p. 719), as does the Syriac. The later Targums (Pseudo-Jon. and Jerusalem) understand some acts of idolatrous worship or perhaps impurity, (comp. Ex. xxxii. 6, where the same word is used for "play," and 1 Cor. x. 7). It is quite untrue that the word "laugh," here rendered "mocking," is never used but in a good sense. In ch. xix. 14, it is rightly rendered "mocked." See also Gen. xxvi. 8, xxxix. 14, 17; Ex. xxxii. 6. It probably means in this passage, as it has generally been understood, "mocking laughter." As Abraham had laughed for joy concerning Isaac, and Sarah had laughed incredulously, so now Ishmael laughed in derision, and probably in a persecuting and tyrannical spirit (see Gal. iv. 29).

10. *Cast out*] These words are quoted by St Paul (Gal. iv. 30), introduced by "But what saith the Scripture?" The words were those of Sarah, but they are confirmed by the Almighty, v. 12.

12. *in Isaac shall thy seed be called*] Here is the distinct limitation of the great promises of God to the descendants of Abraham in the line of Isaac (see Rom. ix. 7). God's promises gradually developed themselves in fulness, and yet were gradually restricted in extent: to Adam first; then to Noah; to Abraham; then to one race or seed of Abraham, viz. Isaac; to one of Isaac's children, viz. Jacob; to one of the twelve patriarchs, viz. Judah; then to his descendant David; and lastly to the great Son of David, the true promised Seed; but as all centred in Him, so too from Him they have spread out to all redeemed by Him, though more especially taking effect in those, who are "the children of God by faith in Christ Jesus" (Gal. iii. 26).

the morning, and took bread, and a
bottle of water, and gave *it* unto
Hagar, putting *it* on her shoulder, and
the child, and sent her away: and she
departed, and wandered in the wilderness of Beer-sheba.
15 And the water was spent in the
bottle, and she cast the child under
one of the shrubs.
16 And she went, and sat her down
over against *him* a good way off, as it
were a bowshot: for she said, Let me
not see the death of the child. And
she sat over against *him*, and lift up
her voice, and wept.
17 And God heard the voice of the
lad; and the angel of God called to
Hagar out of heaven, and said unto

---

14. *a bottle*] A skin or leathern bottle, probably made of the skin of a goat or a kid. (See the word *bottle* in Smith's 'Dict. of the Bible.')

putting it on her shoulder] Hagar was an Egyptian, and Herod. (II. 35) says that the women in Egypt carried burdens on their *shoulders*, but the men carried them on their heads. According to the testimony of the sculptures both men and women carried burdens on their shoulders. It is common now in the East to see women carrying skins of water in this way. (See Robinson, 'B. R.' I. p. 340, II. pp. 163, 276.)

and the child] The sacred writer has been charged with an anachronism here, both from his use of the word "child," when Ishmael must have been from fifteen to seventeen years old (see note on v. 8), and because it is said that the original indicates that he, as well as the bread and water, was placed on Hagar's shoulder. The word for "child" (*yeled*), however, is used for boys of adolescent age, as in Gen. xlii. 22, of Joseph, when he was seventeen. It is true, the Vatican MS. of the LXX. renders "he placed the boy on her shoulders," which Tuch adopts as the right rendering; but the Alexandrian MS. of the LXX. has simply "and the boy," whilst the Vulg., Targg., Syr., connect the words "putting it on her shoulder" only with the bread and the bottle of water, which is perfectly consistent with the Hebrew, whether the verb be rendered by the past tense, or, as probably with accuracy in the Authorised Version, by the participle. The promise, which Abraham had just received, that God would make a nation of Ishmael also, v. 13, may probably have led him to trust that the boy and his mother would be provided for, and so to leave them with only provision for their immediate wants.

in the wilderness of Beer-sheba] Abraham, who had been now for at least a year dwelling in the neighbourhood of Gerar (ch. xx. 1), may very probably have by this time taken up his residence at Beersheba (see vv. 33, 34). The name Beersheba is here given proleptically (see v. 31), unless the events in the latter part of this chapter took place before those in the former part, not having been related at first, lest there should be a break in the continuity of the history of Isaac and Ishmael.

15. *she cast the child under one of the shrubs*] From this expression again it is inferred that Ishmael must have been a child in arms. Such a conclusion, however, is not borne out by these words, nor by the whole narrative. The boy was young, but he was evidently old enough to give offence to Sarah by mocking (v. 9). At a time when human life was much longer than it is now (Ishmael himself died at 137), fifteen or sixteen would be little removed from childhood. The growing lad would easily be exhausted with the heat and wandering; whilst the hardy habits of the Egyptian handmaid would enable her to endure much greater fatigue. She had hitherto led the boy by the hand, now she left him fainting and prostrate under the shelter of a tree. (So Le Clerc followed by Rosenmüller.)

16. *a good way off, as it were a bowshot*] Lit. "as far off as the drawers of a bow," or "as they who draw a bow," *i.e.* as far as archers can shoot an arrow.

17. *the angel of God*] No where else in Genesis does this name occur. Elsewhere it is always "the Angel of the LORD." We meet with it again in Exod. xiv. 19, "And the Angel of God, which went before the camp of Israel, removed, and went behind them." The identification of the *Malach Elohim* with *Elohim* (cp. vv. 17, 19, 20,) here is exactly like the identification of the *Malach* JEHOVAH with JEHOVAH in other passages; a clear proof that there is not that difference between the Elohistic and Jehovistic passages in the Pentateuch, of which so much has been written. In ch. xvi. 7, whilst Hagar was still Abraham's secondary wife, we read that the Angel of the LORD, the covenant God of Abraham, appeared to her. She and her son, by Isaac's birth and their expulsion from Abraham's household, are now separated from the family and covenant of promise, yet still objects of care to Him who is "the God of the spirits of all flesh," and "of all the ends of the earth."

her, What aileth thee, Hagar? fear not; for God hath heard the voice of the lad where he *is*.

18 Arise, lift up the lad, and hold him in thine hand; for I will make him a great nation.

19 And God opened her eyes, and she saw a well of water; and she went, and filled the bottle with water, and gave the lad drink.

20 And God was with the lad; and he grew, and dwelt in the wilderness, and became an archer.

21 And he dwelt in the wilderness of Paran: and his mother took him a wife out of the land of Egypt.

22 ¶ And it came to pass at that time, that Abimelech and Phichol the chief captain of his host spake unto Abraham, saying, God *is* with thee in all that thou doest:

23 Now therefore swear unto me here by God †that thou wilt not deal falsely with me, nor with my son, nor with my son's son: *but* according to the kindness that I have done unto thee, thou shalt do unto me, and to the land wherein thou hast sojourned.

† Heb. *if thou shalt lie unto me.*

24 And Abraham said, I will swear.

25 And Abraham reproved Abimelech because of a well of water, which Abimelech's servants had violently taken away.

26 And Abimelech said, I wot not who hath done this thing: neither didst thou tell me, neither yet heard I *of it*, but to day.

27 And Abraham took sheep and oxen, and gave them unto Abimelech; and both of them made a covenant.

28 And Abraham set seven ewe lambs of the flock by themselves.

29 And Abimelech said unto Abraham, What *mean* these seven ewe lambs which thou hast set by themselves?

30 And he said, For *these* seven ewe lambs shalt thou take of my hand, that they may be a witness unto me, that I have digged this well.

31 Wherefore he called that place ‖Beer-sheba; because there they sware both of them.

‖ That is, *The well of the oath.*

32 Thus they made a covenant at Beer-sheba; then Abimelech rose up, and Phichol the chief captain of his

---

18. *Arise, lift up the lad, and hold him in thine hand*] So the Versions, according to the common use of the same verb with the same preposition. Cp. Deut. xxii. 25; Judg. xix. 25, 29; 2 S. xiii. 11, &c.; and see Gesen. 'Thes.' p. 463. "From this," says St Jerome, "it is plain that the boy whom she held in her hand had been her companion on the journey, not a burden on her shoulders," 'Qu. in Gen'.

19. *God opened her eyes, and she saw a well of water*] Very probably the mouth of the well had been purposely covered by the inhabitants of the desert, and was now by God's gracious intervention discovered to Hagar.

21. *in the wilderness of Paran*] (See on ch. xiv. 6). Probably the great desert, now called the desert El-Tih, *i.e.* "the wanderings," extending from the Wady-el-Arabah on the east, to the gulf of Suez on the west, and from the Sinaitic range on the south to the borders of Palestine on the north.

took him a wife out of the land of Egypt] According to the custom then prevalent in the East for parents to choose wives for their sons. (See ch. xxiv. 4, 55; Exod. xxi. 10.)

22. *Phichol*] The name occurs again in ch. xxvi. 26, and, as it signifies "the mouth of all," it has been supposed to have been the name of an officer, the grand vizier or prime minister of the king, through whom all complaints and petitions were to be made to him. Abimelech was also an official name. See on ch. xx. 2.

23. *that thou wilt not deal falsely with me*] Lit. "if thou shalt lie unto me;" the common form of an oath in Hebrew. See above, on xiv. 23.

31. *Beer-sheba*] *i.e.* "the well of the oath," or, it might be, "the well of the seven." There was a connection between the sacred number seven and an oath; oaths being ratified with the sacrifice of seven victims or by the gift of seven gifts (as seems to have been the case here), or confirmed by seven witnesses and pledges. (See Herod. III. 8; Hom. 'Il.' XIX. 243). Beer-sheba was in the Wady-es-Seba, a wide water-course or bed of a torrent, twelve hours south of Hebron, in which there are still relics of an ancient town or village, called Bir-es-Seba, with two deep wells of good water. See Robinson, 'B. R.' I. p. 204, seq. St Jerome speaks of the city as remaining in his day ('Qu. ad Gen.' XXI. 31).

host, and they returned into the land
of the Philistines.
‖ Or, tree. 33 ¶ And *Abraham* planted a ‖ grove
in Beer-sheba, and called there on the
name of the LORD, the everlasting
God.
34 And Abraham sojourned in the
Philistines' land many days.

CHAPTER XXII.

1 *Abraham is tempted to offer Isaac.* 3 *He giveth proof of his faith and obedience.* 11 *The angel stayeth him.* 13 *Isaac is exchanged with a ram.* 14 *The place is called Jehovah-jireh.* 15 *Abraham is blessed again.* 20 *The generation of Nahor unto Rebekah.*

AND it came to pass after these
things, that [a]God did tempt a Heb. 11. 17.

---

33. *Abraham planted a grove*] Rather **a tamarisk tree.** This is the rendering of Kimchi, which is adopted by Gesenius ('Th.' p. 159), Rosenm., and most of the German critics. (The ancient versions vary very much in their interpretation.) The hardiness of this evergreen shrub would fit it to be a perpetual memorial to Abraham and his followers that this well was theirs.

the LORD, the everlasting God] "JEHOVAH, the God of eternity." The word, rendered everlasting, means probably "the hidden time," that, whose beginning and ending are hidden in darkness, hence "eternity" (Ges. 'Th.' p. 1035). It signifies also "the world," "the universe," and hence, according to Maimonides, it means here the God of the universe, the Creator of the world. So the Samaritan, Syr., and Arab. versions. The more probable sense, however, is that given in the Authorised Version, which corresponds with the LXX., Vulg., Onk., and other Targg. The JEHOVAH whom Abraham worshipped is here identified with "El-Olam," the God of eternity, which was very probably a local name for the supreme Being. Compare "Elion" in ch. xiv. 22.

CHAP. XXII. 1. *And it came to pass after these things*] This is the only note of time that we have in this chapter, excepting the fact that Isaac was now grown old enough to bear the wood of the burnt offering, and to carry it up the mountain. The words "after these things," rather refer us to all that had been passing before. Abraham, after long wanderings and many trials, is presented to us in the last chapter, as eminently comforted and in a condition of peaceful prosperity. The promised, longed-for son has been given to him; his other son Ishmael, though no longer in his household, is growing up and prospering, Abraham is in treaty and at peace with his neighbours the Philistines, he sojourns for many days at Beer-sheba and its neighbourhood, with abundance of cattle, in a place well watered and fertile. Thus it appears to have been with him till now, when his son, his only son Isaac, whom he loved, is growing up to early manhood, his chief comfort and stay and hope in this world. But times of prosperity are often times when trial is needed for us, and so we find it here. There is great variety of tradition, but no evidence, as to the age of Isaac in this chapter. According to Josephus ('Ant.' I. 14), he was twenty-five. Aben-Ezra supposes that he was only thirteen, whilst some of the rabbins put him even at thirty-seven (see Heidegger, II. 282).

God did tempt Abraham] Lit. "The God did tempt," &c. possibly referring to the last two verses of the last chapter (where JEHOVAH is called El-olam), meaning "this same God." Much difficulty has been most needlessly found in these words. St James tells us (i. 13) that "God cannot be tempted with evil, neither tempteth He any man," language which it has been thought difficult to reconcile with this history in Genesis. So, some have endeavoured to explain away the words of this passage, as though Abraham had felt a strong temptation rising in his own heart, a temptation from Satan, or from self, a horrible thought raised perhaps by witnessing the human sacrifices of the Phœnicians, and had then referred the instigation to God, thinking he was tempted from above, whereas the real temptation was from beneath. The difficulty, however, has arisen from not observing the natural force of the word here rendered "did tempt," and the ordinary use of that word in the language of the Old Testament, especially of the Pentateuch. According to the highest authorities, the primary sense of the verb corresponds with that of a similar word in Arabic, viz. "to smell," and thence "to test by smelling" (see Ges. 'Thes.' p. 889, and the testimonies there cited). Hence it came to signify close, accurate, delicate testing or trying. It is translated by "prove," "assay," "adventure," "try," and that very much more frequently than it is translated by "tempt." For instance, David would not take the sword and armour of Saul, because he had not "proved them," 1 S. xvii. 39. Again, he prayed in the words "examine me, O LORD, and *prove* me" (Ps. xxvi. 2); and in very numerous and familiar passages in the Pentateuch, we read of God "proving" men, whether they would be obedient or disobedient, the same Hebrew verb being constantly made use of. (See Ex. xv. 25, xvi. 4, xx. 20; Deut. iv. 34, viii. 2, 16, xiii. 3, xxxiii. 8). Accordingly, whilst most of the versions adhere closely to the sense of

Abraham, and said unto him, Abraham: and he said, †Behold, *here* I am.

† Heb. *Behold me.*

2 And he said, Take now thy son, thine only *son* Isaac, whom thou lovest, and get thee into the land of Moriah;

"try," *tentare*, in this passage, the Arabic renders it very correctly, "God did prove Abraham." Words having the sense of "try" may generally be used either in a good or a bad sense. This particular word has generally a good sense, except where men are said to try or tempt God, *e.g.* Ex. xvii. 2; Num. xiv. 22; Deut. vi. 16; Ps. lxxviii. 18; cvi. 14, &c. The whole history of Abraham is a history of his moral and spiritual education by the teaching of God himself. He was to be the head of the chosen seed, the father of the faithful, himself the type of justifying faith. Here then, after long schooling and training, in which already there had been many trials (such as his first call, his danger in Egypt, his circumcision, his parting with Lot, &c. &c.), one great test of his now matured and strengthened faith is ordained by God. We have many instances of the trial of men's faith by the Most High. One remarkable example is that recorded in Matt. xix. 21. It cannot be that He who sees the heart needs such trials for His own information: but it is important for our instruction and correction, for example to future ages, and for the vindication of God's justice, that such trials should be permitted, and that so men's characters should be drawn out and exhibited to themselves and others. So St Augustine, "all temptation is not to be blamed, but that whereby probation is made is rather to be welcomed. For the most part a man's spirit cannot be known to himself, unless his strength be proved not by word but by actual trial." ('De Civit. Dei,' XVI. 32. See also Ambros. 'De Abr.' I. 8.)

2. *Take now thy son, thine only son*] In more ways than one Isaac might be called his "only son." He was the only son by his wife Sarah: he was the only son of promise, and to whom the promises were given and assured: by the expulsion of Hagar and Ishmael he was the only son left to his father's house. The rendering therefore of the LXX. "beloved" is not necessary. The words, emphatic as they are, "Thy son, thine only son, whom thou lovest," are all calculated to impress and enhance the sacrifice which Abraham is called on to make.

Moriah] The meaning of the name seems clearly to be *Mori-jah*, "the vision" or "the manifested of JEHOVAH." To this root it is evidently referred by Sym., Vulg. ("the land of vision"), Aq. ("the conspicuous land"), LXX. ("the lofty land"). In 2 Chr. iii. 1, Solomon is said to have built his temple on Mount Moriah; and the Jewish tradition (Joseph. 'Ant.' I. 13. 2; VII. 13. 4) has identified this Mount Moriah of the temple with the mountain in the land of Moriah, on which Abraham was to offer his son, whence probably here Onkelos and the Arab. render "the land of worship." No sufficient reason has been alleged against this identification except that in v. 4, it is said that "Abraham lifted up his eyes, and saw the place afar off," whereas Mount Zion is said not to be conspicuous from a great distance. Thence Bleek, De Wette, Tuch, Stanley ('S. and P.' p. 251, 'Jewish Church,' I. 49), and Grove ('Dict. of Bible,' s. v. *Moriah*), have referred to Moreh (Gen. xii. 6), and attempted to identify the site of the sacrifice with "the natural altar on the summit of Mount Gerizim," which the Samaritans assert to be the scene of the sacrifice. Really, however, the words in v. 4, mean nothing more than this, that Abraham saw the spot to which he had been directed at some little distance off, not farther than the character of the place readily admits. The evident meaning of the words "the mount of the vision of the LORD" (see v. 14); the fact that the mount of the temple bore the same name (2 Chr. iii. 1), the distance, two days' journey from Beer-sheba, which would just suffice to bring the company to Jerusalem, whereas Gerizim could not have been reached from Beer-sheba on the third day, are arguments too strong to be set aside by the single difficulty mentioned above, which is in fact no difficulty at all. This identity is ably defended by Hengstenberg ('Genuineness of the Pentateuch,' II. 162, translated by Ryland), Knobel (*in loc*), Kalisch (*in loc.*), Kurtz ('Hist. of Old Covenant,' Vol. I. 271), Thomson ('The Land and the Book', p. 475), Tristram ('Land of Israel,' p. 152).

offer him there for a burnt offering] It cannot justly be urged that the command was (1) in itself immoral, or (2) that it was a virtual sanction of human sacrifice. (1) As to the objection that it was immoral, it may be said, that the true basis of all morality is obedience to the will of God; but further than this, it is plain from the whole story, that the command was wholly of the nature of a trial. Abraham was the special type of trustful, obedient, loving faith. He believed that all which God commanded must be right, all that He promised must be true. Hence he knew that when the injunction was clear, the obedience must be undoubting. The wisdom, the justice, and the goodness of God, were such that, though he might not understand the reason of the dispensation, he must reverently and patiently submit to it. This too was not a mere blind credulity. He had lived a long life under the special guiding,

and offer him there for a burnt offering upon one of the mountains which
I will tell thee of.
3 ¶ And Abraham rose up early in
the morning, and saddled his ass, and
took two of his young men with him,
and Isaac his son, and clave the wood
for the burnt offering, and rose up,
and went unto the place of which God
had told him.
4 Then on the third day Abraham
lifted up his eyes, and saw the place
afar off.
5 And Abraham said unto his young
men, Abide ye here with the ass; and
I and the lad will go yonder and worship, and come again to you.
6 And Abraham took the wood of
the burnt offering, and laid *it* upon
Isaac his son; and he took the fire in
his hand, and a knife; and they went
both of them together.
7 And Isaac spake unto Abraham
his father, and said, My father: and
he said, †Here *am* I, my son. And † Heb. *Behold me.*
he said, Behold the fire and the wood:
but where *is* the ‖lamb for a burnt ‖ Or, *kid.*
offering?
8 And Abraham said, My son, God
will provide himself a lamb for a burnt
offering: so they went both of them
together.
9 And they came to the place which
God had told him of; and Abraham

---

training, and teaching of the Lord, and so he knew in whom he had believed. The command therefore, strange as it was, was but a final test of the firmness of his faith; and his obedience to that command testified that the faith was intelligent as well as unconditional and unwavering. (2) The objection that this was a virtual sanction to the heathen custom of offering human sacrifices is still less tenable. That such sacrifices were common in later times is unquestionable, and probably they may have been already adopted by the Canaanites, who certainly were afterwards much addicted to them. Although we must ascribe them not to Divine but to Satanic influence, their observance plainly shewed the devotion of the offerers to the religion of their demon gods. The God of Abraham would have His special servant, the father of the chosen race and of the promised Seed, manifest his faith and obedience to the true God to be not less than the faith and obedience of idolaters to their false gods. This could not be more signally done than by his readiness to overcome all scruples and all natural feelings at the command of Him whose voice he knew, and whose leading he had so long followed. But the conclusion of the history is as clear a condemnation of human sacrifice as the earlier part might have seemed, had it been left incomplete, to sanction it. The intervention of the angel, the substitution of the lamb, the prohibition of the human sacrifice, proved that in no case could such an offering be acceptable to God, even as the crowning evidence of faith, devotion, and self-sacrifice. The following is the well-known perverted account of the sacrifice of Isaac in the Phœnician traditions, as preserved from Sanchoniatho by Philo Byblius, "Cronus, whom the Phœnicians call Israel, being king over that country, who after his death was deified and consecrated into the planet bearing his name, having an only son by a nymph named Anobret, called therefore *Jehoud*" (= Heb. Jahid), "which is even now the name for *only-begotten* among the Phœnicians, when great perils from wars were impending over the land, having clothed his son in royal apparel offered him up upon an altar which he had built," (Euseb. 'Præp. Evang.' Lib. I. c. 10).

3. *rose up early in the morning*] The promptness and steadiness of Abraham's obedience are plainly marked in all the simple details of this verse.

5. *come again to you*] It may be questioned whether this had in it a prophetic significance, Abraham "accounting that God was able to raise his son up even from the dead" (Heb. xi. 17). In fact it was proved by the event to be a prophecy, though Abraham may have uttered it unconsciously (so Rashi): and that faith in God, which never forsook the patriarch, probably in the lowest depth of his anxiety brought a gleam of hope, that in some unforeseen way his son, even though slain, should yet be restored to him at last (see Origen, 'Homil. VIII. in Gen.' § 5).

6. *laid it upon Isaac his son*] Compare Joh. xix. 17, the great Antitype bearing the wood for the sacrifice of Himself (Origen, 'Hom. VIII. in Gen.' § 6; Aug. 'De C. D.' XVI. 32; 'De Trin.' III. 6).

8. *God will provide himself a lamb for a burnt offering*] **The lamb.** The fathers see in this again an unconscious prophecy by Abraham (see Origen as above, and Ambrose 'De Abr.' lib. I. 8). He probably meant to say that God had provided that Isaac should be the lamb or victim for the burnt-offering: but his words were more literally fulfilled in the

built an altar there, and laid the wood in order, and bound Isaac his son, and [b]laid him on the altar upon the wood.

b James 2. 21.

10 And Abraham stretched forth his hand, and took the knife to slay his son.

11 And the angel of the LORD called unto him out of heaven, and said, Abraham, Abraham: and he said, Here *am* I.

12 And he said, Lay not thine hand upon the lad, neither do thou any thing unto him: for now I know that thou fearest God, seeing thou hast not withheld thy son, thine only *son* from me.

13 And Abraham lifted up his eyes, and looked, and behold behind *him* a ram caught in a thicket by his horns: and Abraham went and took the ram,

---

unexpected event, the ram caught in a thicket, and in a deeper spiritual significance when God sent His Son to be "the Lamb of God that taketh away the sin of the world."

9. *Abraham built an altar there*] R. Eliezer in 'Pirke Avoth,' c. 31, has a tradition that this was the same place at which Adam sacrificed, at which Abel offered his burnt-offering, and where Noah built an altar and offered a sacrifice: so that it was apparently supposed that Abraham merely repaired the ruins of the ancient altar. Whatever the tradition is worth, it may illustrate the history. An altar of earth or of loose stones would be very quickly raised.

bound Isaac his son] It was common to bind victims, especially human victims (Ovid, 'Eleg. ex. Ponto.' III. 2; Virg. 'Æn. II. 134). The Jews agree that Isaac yielded submissively to his father's will and consented to be bound and sacrificed (Joseph. 'A. J.' I. 13; Eliezer, 'in Pirke,' c. 31; so also Chrysost. 'Homil. in Gen.' 46). Herein he was the truer type of Him, "who, when He was reviled, reviled not again; when He suffered, He threatened not; but committed Himself to Him that judgeth righteously" (1 Pet. ii. 23).

10. *stretched forth his hand*] The steady deliberate purpose of Abraham, and yet all the natural shrinking of his spirit, are admirably expressed in the details of the history.

11. *the Angel of the LORD*] Up to this verse we have only the name Elohim, God. Now that the Divine intervention to save Isaac and to accept a ransom for his life is related, we find the name, JEHOVAH, the great covenant name frequently made use of, though the name Elohim occurs again in the next verse. The Being here called "the Angel of JEHOVAH," who speaks as with Divine, supreme authority, is doubtless the Angel of the Covenant (Mal. iii. 1), the everlasting Son of the Father, who alone "hath declared Him" (John i. 18).

12. *now I know that thou fearest God*] "God tried Abraham," says Theodoret, "not that He might learn what He knew already, but that He might shew to others, with how great justice He loved the patriarch" ('Qu. in Gen.' LXXIII). Compare Origen ('Homil. VIII. 8), who refers to those words of the Apostle: "God spared not His own Son, but freely gave Him up for us all."

thou hast not withheld thy son] These words in the LXX. (οὐκ ἐφείσω τοῦ υἱοῦ σου) appear to be referred to in Rom. viii. 32 (τοῦ ἰδίου υἱοῦ οὐκ ἐφείσατο). Whence we may learn that St Paul held the sacrifice of Isaac to be prophetic of Christ.

13. *behold behind him a ram caught in a thicket by his horns*] There is a various reading (supported by many MSS., by the Samaritan Pentateuch, LXX., Vulg., Syr., Sam., and perhaps Onkelos), which might be rendered thus: "Behold a single ram caught," &c. a ram, that is, separated from the flock. There is a similar expression in Dan. viii. 3: "Behold, there stood before the river a ram," lit. "one ram," or a "single ram." The separation of the ram thus caught is significant, both historically, as shewing the Providential agency of God, and also as pointing to that Lamb of God, who was "separate from sinners" (Heb. vii. 26), bearing alone the burden of our iniquities. St Augustine thinks the horns caught in the thicket typical of the Lord Jesus crowned with thorns before His sacrifice ('De C. D.' XVI. 32).

offered him up for a burnt offering in the stead of his son] It has been argued that the lamb substituted for Isaac, not Isaac himself, was the true type of the Lord Jesus, who died that we might live. This, however, would be a very imperfect explication of the mystery. The antitype is always greater than the type, and hence in the prophetic system of the Old Testament, types are multiplied that they may express collectively that which can but partially be expressed by one of them. The fathers recognize the double type in this whole history. The father with full deliberate purpose offering up his dearly beloved, only-begotten son, the son willingly obedient unto death, the wood for the sacrifice carried by the victim up the hill, the sacrifice fulfilled in purpose though not in act, and then the father receiving his son in a figure from the dead (Heb. xi. 19) after three days of death in the father's purpose and belief; all

and offered him up for a burnt offering in the stead of his son.
14 And Abraham called the name
of that place ‖Jehovah-jireh: as it is
said *to* this day, In the mount of the
LORD it shall be seen.

‖ That is, *The LORD will see,* or, *provide.*

15 ¶ And the angel of the LORD
called unto Abraham out of heaven
the second time,
16 And said, [c]By myself have I
sworn, saith the LORD, for because
thou hast done this thing, and hast

[c] Ps. 105. 9. Ecclus. 44. 21. Luke 1. 73. Heb. 6. 13.

---

this is as much an actual prophecy of the sacrifice and resurrection of the Son of God as was possible without a true slaying of Isaac, for which was substituted the slaying of the ram. That which Isaac's sacrifice wanted to make it perfect as a type was actual death and the notion of substitution. These therefore were supplied by the death of the ram, and his substitution for a human life. Theodoret says ('Qu. in Gen.' LXXIII.) that "Isaac was the type of the Godhead, the ram of the manhood." This perhaps sounds fanciful at first; but the correspondence is in truth very exact. Isaac was of too noble a nature to be slain upon the altar; God would have abhorred such an offering. Hence the Most High prepares a victim to be as it were joined with Isaac and then to suffer, that thus the sacrifice should not be imperfect. So the ever blessed Son of God was by nature above the possibility of suffering; hence the Eternal Father prepares for Him a perfect humanity ("a Body hast Thou prepared me"), that He might die in that nature which was mortal, the immortal, impassible nature being yet inseparably united with it. Thus, Isaac and the ram together symbolized and typified in almost all particulars the sacrifice, the death and the resurrection of the Son of God, who also was the Son of man.

We may observe too, that not only was Isaac thus made the most memorable type of the Redeemer of the world (Isaac, who otherwise seems less noticeable than either Abraham or Jacob), but also that Abraham had the singular honour of representing the highest, holiest God and Father, who "spared not His own Son, but freely gave Him up for us all" (Rom. viii. 32. See Aug. 'De Civ. D.' XVI. 32).

14. *JEHOVAH-jireh*] *i.e.* "the Lord will see," or "the Lord will provide." The same words which Abraham had used in v. 8, but with a change in the sacred names. In v. 8, when Isaac had asked, "where is the Lamb?" Abraham answered, *Elohim jireh*, "God will see," or "provide a lamb for Himself." Now he perceives that he had uttered an unconscious prophecy, and that the God (Elohim) in whom he trusted had shewn Himself indeed JEHOVAH, the Eternal Truth and the covenated Saviour of his servants, and so he names the place JEHOVAH-jireh. The connection which there is between these words and the word Moriah (see on v. 2) has suggested the belief, that the name Moriah in v. 2 is used proleptically, and that it really originated in this saying of Abraham.

as it is said to this day, In the mount of the LORD it shall be seen] Or, "it shall be provided."

There is great variety of renderings in the ancient Versions. Indeed, if we disregard the vowel points, it would be equally possible to translate "In the mount of the Lord it shall be seen or provided," or "In the mount the Lord will see or provide," or "In the mount the Lord will be seen." The LXX. takes the last, the Vulgate, Syriac and Samaritan take the second. Onkelos departs from his habit of translating, and paraphrases, like the late Targums; "And Abraham worshipped and prayed there and said before the Lord, Here shall generations worship; whereupon it shall be said in that day, In this mountain Abraham worshipped before the Lord." St Jerome, taking the Latin, explained it thus: "This became a proverb among the Hebrews, that if any should be in trouble and should desire the help of the Lord, they should say, *In the mount the Lord will see*, that is, as He had mercy on Abraham, so will He have mercy on us" ('Qu. Hebraic. in Gen.' XXII).

On the whole, the pointing of the Masorites, a tradition never lightly to be rejected, which is followed by the Authorised Version, seems to give the most probable sense of the passage (So Ges. 'Thes.' p. 1246; Rosemn., Knobel). But, in any case, there seems not only a general assurance of God's providential care of His people, who in trouble may remember that "the Lord will provide," but also a special prophecy, 1st of the manifestation of the Lord in His temple at Jerusalem, where He was to be seen in the Shechinah or cloud of glory between the Cherubim, where He provided access to Himself and sacrifices for His service; 2ndly, of the coming of the Lord to His temple (Mal. iii. 1), thereby making "the glory of the latter house greater than of the former" (Hagg. ii. 9); and of His providing there a Lamb for a sacrifice, which should save not only from temporal but from eternal death, taking away the sin of the world.

16. *by myself have I sworn*] This is the final promise of the Lord to Abraham, confirming all the former promises by the solemnity of an oath, and "because He could swear by no greater, He sware by Himself"

not withheld thy son, thine only
son:
17 That in blessing I will bless
thee, and in multiplying I will multiply thy seed as the stars of the heaven,
and as the sand which *is* upon the sea
†shore; and thy seed shall possess the
gate of his enemies;
18 [d]And in thy seed shall all the
nations of the earth be blessed; because thou hast obeyed my voice.
19 So Abraham returned unto his
young men, and they rose up and went
together to Beer-sheba; and Abraham
dwelt at Beer-sheba.

† Heb. *lip.*

[d] chap. 12. 3. & 18. 18. Ecclus. 44. 22. Acts 3. 25. Gal. 3. 8.

20 ¶ And it came to pass after
these things, that it was told Abraham, saying, Behold, Milcah, she hath
also born children unto thy brother
Nahor;
21 Huz his first-born, and Buz his
brother, and Kemuel the father of
Aram,
22 And Chesed, and Hazo, and
Pildash, and Jidlaph, and Bethuel.
23 And Bethuel begat [e]Rebekah:
these eight Milcah did bear to Nahor,
Abraham's brother.
24 And his concubine, whose name
was Reumah, she bare also Tebah,

[e] Called, Rom. 9. 10, *Rebecca.*

(Heb. vi. 13). The vast importance of the revelation and of the promise here recorded is proved by this remarkable act of the Most High. "God, willing more abundantly to shew unto the heirs of promise the immutability of His counsel, interposed Himself by an oath" (or "made Himself the Mediator to be sworn by," ἐμεσίτευσεν ὅρκῳ); "that by two immutable things" (*i.e.* His word and His oath, Chrysost., Theod., Theophyl.), "in which it was impossible for God to lie, we might have a strong consolation, who have fled for refuge to lay hold upon the hope set before us" (Heb. vi. 17, 18). Abraham had by Divine grace achieved a victory of faith unheard of before in the world's history; and so to him personally a most blessed and most solemn promise is given of prosperity, honour and enlargement to him and to his seed after him. But this great victory of Abraham's was the type of a still greater victory to be won hereafter by God and God's only begotten Son; and so the promise to Abraham includes a promise still greater to all mankind, for in the seed of Abraham all the nations of the earth were to be blessed for ever. N. B. Onkelos renders here, "I have sworn by My Word," *Memra;* and the Arabic, "I have sworn by My own Name."

20. *it was told Abraham*] This is introduced for the sake of tracing the genealogy of Abraham's brother Nahor down to Rebekah the wife of Isaac, v. 23.

21. *Huz*] See on ch. x. 23, where we have seen Uz and Aram together before. It is only natural that names should have been repeated in the same race, the race of Shem. Uz and Aram also occur among the posterity of Esau (Gen. xxxvi. 28), whence Idumea is called "the land of Uz" (Lam. iv. 21). This recurrence of names in juxtaposition creates some obscurity as to the sites to be assigned to their descendants in the division of the nations. St Jerome ('Qu. in Gen.') thinks that Job was a descendant of Huz or Uz the son of Nahor. It is said that Job was of the land of Uz (Job i. 1), and his friend Elihu was "a Buzite of the kindred of Ram" (xxxii. 2). If Ram be the same as Aram, we have then the three names in this verse—Huz, Buz and Aram occurring in the history of Job. In Jerem. xxv. 23 Buz is placed with Dedan and Tema, apparently in Arabia Petræa.

22. *Chesed*] Jerome supposes the Chasdim (or Chaldæans) to have derived their name from him, to which conjecture the occurrence of the Chasdim also in the Book of Job, gives some colour (see on v. 21). If, indeed, "Ur of the Chaldees" was so called when Abraham dwelt there (Gen. xi. 31), this would be an anachronism, but very probably it may have been known as Ur of the Chaldees when Moses wrote, and so designated by him, though the Chaldees or Chasdim may not have been in existence in the days of Abraham.

23. *Bethuel begat Rebekah*] The relationship therefore of Rebekah to Isaac was that Rebekah was daughter of Isaac's first cousin. They were, as we should say, first cousins once removed. Nahor was the elder brother of Abraham, and his granddaughter may have been of a suitable age to be the wife of Abraham's son.

these eight] The sons of Nahor, like the sons of Ishmael and of Jacob, were twelve in number. But though it happens that among the descendants of Terah three persons had twelve sons, there is such a diversity in the other circumstances of the family, such a difference with regard to their mothers, and there are so many other patriarchs, Abraham, Isaac, &c., the numbering of whose children were quite unlike these, that the notion of a mystic number is utterly untenable (see Keil in loc.).

and Gaham, and Thahash, and Maa-
chah.

CHAPTER XXIII.

1 *The age and death of Sarah.* 3 *The purchase of Machpelah,* 19 *where Sarah was buried.*

AND Sarah was an hundred and
seven and twenty years old:
these were the years of the life of Sarah.
2 And Sarah died in Kirjath-arba;
the same *is* Hebron in the land
of Canaan: and Abraham came to
mourn for Sarah, and to weep for
her.
3 ¶ And Abraham stood up from
before his dead, and spake unto the
sons of Heth, saying,
4 I *am* a stranger and a sojourner
with you: give me a possession of a
buryingplace with you, that I may
bury my dead out of my sight.
5 And the children of Heth answered Abraham, saying unto him,
6 Hear us, my lord: thou art a
†mighty prince among us: in the choice
of our sepulchres bury thy dead; none
of us shall withhold from thee his
sepulchre, but that thou mayest bury
thy dead.
7 And Abraham stood up, and

† Heb. *a prince of God.*

CHAP. XXIII. 1. *And Sarah was an hundred and seven and twenty years old*] Sarah is the only woman whose age is mentioned in the Scriptures (Lightfoot, 'Har. of Old Testament,' Gen. xxiii.), because as the mother of the promised seed, she became the mother of all believers. (1 Pet. iii. 6) (Del., Keil.) She died 37 years after the birth of Isaac, as she was 90 when he was born.

2. *Kirjath-arba; the same is Hebron in the land of Canaan*] See on ch. xiii. 18. The supposition that the name Hebron was not given till the time of Joshua, and that the use of it in Genesis indicates a later hand, is contradicted by the natural force of these words. They appear plainly to have been written by some one not then living in the land of Canaan. Hebron was apparently the original name, which was changed to Kirjath-arba, and restored again by Caleb, Josh. xiv. 15.

Abraham came to mourn for Sarah] Aben-ezra and others infer from this that Abraham was not with Sarah when she died. It may mean no more than that Abraham went into Sarah's tent to mourn for her.

4. *I am a stranger and a sojourner*] (Cp. Heb. xi. 13). Abraham had only pastured his flocks, moving from place to place, as a nomad chief; but the various Canaanitish tribes had settled in the land, building cities and cultivating fields; and so as Lightfoot observes ('Harm.:' on Gen. xxiii.), "a burial place is the first land that Abraham has in Canaan." The heir of the promises was but a stranger and a pilgrim, never to rest but in the grave, but with a glorious future before him for his race and for himself; assured that his seed should possess the land, and himself "desiring a better country, that is a heavenly."

Give me a possession of a buryingplace with you] This is the first mention of burial. It was noted by the heathen historian as a characteristic of the Jews, that they preferred to bury their dead rather than to burn them; *corpora condere quam cremare* (Tac. 'Hist.' v. 5). It is observable that this is thus mentioned first, when the first death takes place in the family of him, who had received the promises. The care of the bodies of the departed is a custom apparently connected with the belief in their sanctity as vessels of the Grace of God, and with the hope that they may be raised again in the day of the restitution of all things. The elaborate embalming of the Egyptians had perhaps a very different significance, looking rather to retain the beloved body in its former shape, and perhaps to preserve the living principle in permanent existence with it, rather than hoping that the body, being "sown a natural should be raised a spiritual body."

5. *saying unto him*] The Sam. Pent. and LXX. read (by the variation of a single letter), "saying, Not so."

6. *thou art a mighty prince among us*] lit. "a prince of God." See on ch. x. 9, the name of God being apparently added to give a superlative force: cp. 1 Sam. xxvi. 12, where R. D. Kimchi writes, "When the Scripture would magnify anything, it joins it to the name of God."

in the choice of our sepulchres bury thy dead] The Hittites in the complimentary manner common in oriental bargains (see Thomson, 'Land and Book,' p. 578) offer Abraham to bury his dead in their sepulchres; but there was a separation between them of faith and life, which forbade Abraham to deposit the body of Sarah in the same grave with the people of the land. We know nothing of the funeral rites of the Canaanites at this early period, nor whether they buried the bodies of the departed or only their ashes. It is, however, very probable, that there were idolatrous rites connected with their sepulture, which it would have been unlawful for Abraham to countenance.

bowed himself to the people of the land, *even* to the children of Heth.
8 And he communed with them, saying, If it be your mind that I should bury my dead out of my sight; hear me, and intreat for me to Ephron the son of Zohar,
9 That he may give me the cave of Machpelah, which he hath, which *is* in the end of his field; for †as much money as it is worth he shall give it me for a possession of a buryingplace amongst you.
10 And Ephron dwelt among the children of Heth: and Ephron the Hittite answered Abraham in the †audience of the children of Heth, *even* of all that went in at the gate of his city, saying,
11 Nay, my lord, hear me: the field give I thee, and the cave that *is* therein, I give it thee; in the presence of the sons of my people give I it thee: bury thy dead.
12 And Abraham bowed down himself before the people of the land.
13 And he spake unto Ephron in the audience of the people of the land, saying, But if thou *wilt give it*, I pray thee, hear me: I will give thee money for the field; take *it* of me, and I will bury my dead there.
14 And Ephron answered Abraham, saying unto him,
15 My lord, hearken unto me: the land *is worth* four hundred shekels of silver; what *is* that betwixt me and thee? bury therefore thy dead.

† Heb. *full money.*

† Heb. *ears.*

---

7. *bowed himself*] The Vulgate has "adoravit coram populo." It was simply the deep reverence common in the East (cp. 1 Sam. xxv. 24; xxviii. 14; 1 Kings xviii. 7; 2 Kings ii. 15; Esth. viii. 3). It was a matter of courtesy and respect, also of entreaty or of gratitude.

9. *the cave of Machpelah*] The soil of Palestine being rocky naturally suggested sepulture in caves (see Winer, 'Realw.' s.v. *Grabes*, Smith, 'Dict. of Bible,' s.v. *Burial*). All the ancient Versions render the words "cave of Machpelah" by "the double cave," deriving Machpelah from the verb *Caphal* to divide, to double. Interpreters have explained this in various ways, as either that there were two entrances to the cave, or that it had a double structure such that two bodies (as e.g. that of Abraham and Sarah) might be laid there (see Heidegger, II. 131). Others, however, treat the word as a proper name, and Gesenius considers it more probably to signify "portion" than "duplication." The site of this ancient burialplace is well ascertained. Josephus tells us that "Abraham and his descendants built monuments over the sepulchres" here (A. J. I. 14), which were said to be still visible in the days of Jerome ('Onomast.'). Now a mosque is erected over the ground believed to cover the sepulchres. The Haram or sacred precinct of the mosque is surrounded by a wall, believed to be as ancient as anything now remaining in Palestine. The present condition and appearance of it are described by Robinson ('B. R.' II. p. 431 sq.), see also Thomson, 'Land and Book,' p. 580, and a full account of the sepulchre in the appendix to Stanley's 'Sermons in the East.'

for as much money as it is worth] lit. "for full money." The same words are rendered 1 Chron. xxi. 22, "for the full price."

10. *all that went in at the gate of his city*] The transaction took place publicly at the gate of the city, the forum or public place of the ancient cities of the East, see on ch. xix. 1.

11. *the field give I thee*] Compare 2 Sam. xxiv. 20, 24. Both conversations, that between Abraham and Ephron, and that between David and Araunah, are specimens of the extreme courtesy of the Eastern people in the transaction of business.

13. *But if thou wilt give it, I pray thee, hear me*] Rather perhaps, "But do thou, I pray thee, hear me." Two particles of wishing or intreating are used.

money for the field] Lit. "the money of the field," i.e. the value of the field.

15. *four hundred shekels of silver*] The word *shekel* means merely *weight*, cp. *pondus*, *pound*. See on ch. xx. 16, where no name fo a coin or weight occurs, but only the words "a thousand of silver." Here we first have the name of a weight, though probably not of a coin. There is no mention of coinage in Scripture before the Babylonish Captivity; but the Egyptians had rings of gold and silver of fixed weight long before Moses, which are represented on the monuments. The first actual Jewish money appears to have been coined by Simon Maccabæus (1 Macc. xv.). It is not easy to conjecture accurately what the value of a shekel may have been in the time of Abraham. In later times the LXX. and the New Testament (Matt. xvii. 24)

16 And Abraham hearkened unto Ephron; and Abraham weighed to Ephron the silver, which he had named in the audience of the sons of Heth, four hundred shekels of silver, current *money* with the merchant.

17 ¶ And the field of Ephron, which *was* in Machpelah, which *was* before Mamre, the field, and the cave which *was* therein, and all the trees that *were* in the field, that *were* in all the borders round about, were made sure

18 Unto Abraham for a possession in the presence of the children of Heth, before all that went in at the gate of his city.

19 And after this, Abraham buried Sarah his wife in the cave of the field of Machpelah before Mamre: the same *is* Hebron in the land of Canaan.

20 And the field, and the cave that *is* therein, were made sure unto Abraham for a possession of a buryingplace by the sons of Heth.

CHAPTER XXIV.

1 *Abraham sweareth his servant.* 10 *The servant's journey:* 12 *his prayer:* 14 *his sign.* 15 *Rebekah meeteth him,* 18 *fulfilleth his sign,* 22 *receiveth jewels,* 23 *sheweth her kindred,* 25 *and inviteth him home.* 26 *The servant blesseth God.* 29 *Laban entertaineth him.* 34 *The servant sheweth his message.* 50 *Laban and Bethuel approve it.* 58 *Rebekah consenteth to go.* 62 *Isaac meeteth her.*

AND Abraham was old, *and* †well stricken in age: and the LORD had blessed Abraham in all things. († Heb. *gone into days.*)

2 And Abraham said unto his eldest servant of his house, that ruled over all that he had, [a]Put, I pray thee, thy hand under my thigh: ([a] chap. 47. 29.)

3 And I will make thee swear by the LORD, the God of heaven, and the God of the earth, that thou shalt not take a wife unto my son of the daughters of the Canaanites, among whom I dwell:

---

identify the half shekel with the didrachma, which would make the shekel nearly half an ounce, 220 grains of our weight, or a little less in value than half-a-crown of our present money. The field therefore would have been purchased for about fifty guineas, 52*l.* 10*s.* (See Gesenius, 'Thes.' p. 1474; Winer, 'R. W. B.' s.v. *sekel;* Smith's 'Dict. of Bib.' s.vv. *money*, *shekel*, *weights and measures.*)

16. *current money with the merchant*] Lit. "silver passing with the merchant." The Canaanites were great merchants, so much so that the very word Canaanite became a synonym for merchant, see Job xl. 30 (in Authorised Version xli. 6); Prov. xxxi. 24. It is therefore very probable that they early learned the use of silver as a means of barter: and though it may not have been coined, yet the masses or bars of silver may have been early formed into conventional shapes, or marked with some rude sign to indicate their weight (see Ges. 'Thes.' p. 982).

17. *the field*, &c.] Not only the cave, as first proposed by Abraham, but the whole field with trees in it, which may have formed part of that grove of Mamre, where Abraham dwelt before the overthrow of Sodom and where he built an altar to the Lord.

were made sure unto Abraham] Lit. "stood firm to Abraham."

CHAP. XXIV. 1. *Abraham was old*] He was 137 at the death of Sarah. Isaac was then 37; and when he married Rebekah, he was 40 (see ch. xxv. 20). Abraham therefore must have been in his 140th year at this time, and he lived 35 years after it (ch. xxv. 7).

2. *unto his eldest servant of his house*] Lit. "to his servant, the elder of his house." The word *elder* in Hebrew as in most languages is used as a title of honour, cp. *Sheykh*, *Senatus*, *γέροντες*, *presbyter*, *Signor*, *Mayor*, &c. (Ges. 'Thes.' p. 427; Hammond, on Acts xi. 30). It is generally supposed that this was Eliezer of Damascus, see ch. xv. 2.

Put, I pray thee, thy hand under my thigh] A form of adjuration mentioned only here and of Jacob, ch. xlvii. 29. Various conjectures have been made by Jews (Joseph. 'Ant.' I. 16; Hieron. 'Qu. in Gen.;' Ambrose, 'De Abraham.' I. 6; Eliezer, in 'Pirke,' c. 39), and by the fathers (Ambros. 'De Abrahamo, I. 9; Hieron. ubi supra; August. 'De C. D.' XVI. 33); but nothing is known with certainty of the signification of the action. Aben-Ezra supposes that it was a form of oath prevalent in patriarchal times but only taken by inferiors, as here by Abraham's steward, and in Gen. xlvii. 29 by a son to his father; that accordingly it was a kind of homage, the servant or son thereby indicating subjection and the purpose of obedience. (See Heidegger, II. pp. 134, 135; Rosenm. in loc.)

3. *of the daughters of the Canaanites*]

4 But thou shalt go unto my country, and to my kindred, and take a
wife unto my son Isaac.
5 And the servant said unto him,
Peradventure the woman will not
be willing to follow me unto this
land: must I needs bring thy son
again unto the land from whence
thou camest?
6 And Abraham said unto him,
Beware thou that thou bring not my
son thither again.
7 ¶ The LORD God of heaven,
which took me from my father's house,
and from the land of my kindred, and
which spake unto me, and that sware
[b] chap. 12. 7. & 13. 15. & 15. 18. & 26. 4. unto me, saying, [b]Unto thy seed will
I give this land; he shall send his
angel before thee, and thou shalt take
a wife unto my son from thence.
8 And if the woman will not be
willing to follow thee, then thou shalt
be clear from this my oath: only bring
not my son thither again.
9 And the servant put his hand
under the thigh of Abraham his master,
and sware to him concerning that
matter.
10 ¶ And the servant took ten
camels of the camels of his master, and
departed; ‖for all the goods of his ‖ Or, *and.*
master *were* in his hand: and he arose,
and went to Mesopotamia, unto the
city of Nahor.
11 And he made his camels to kneel
down without the city by a well of

The licentiousness of the Canaanites had probably determined Abraham against marrying his son to one of their daughters. He had also, no doubt, reference to the Promised Seed, and desired that the race from which He was to come should be kept pure from admixture with the race of Ham.

6. *Beware thou that thou bring not my son thither again*] Abraham had been distinctly called of God to leave his own country, and to be a stranger and sojourner in the land which was to be his hereafter. It would therefore have been an act both of unbelief and of disobedience, to send his son back again. He trusted that He, who had so called him, would provide his son with a wife from his own kindred, not defiled, at least as the Canaanites were, with heathen worship and heathen morality; but in any case he would rather his son should wed among the aliens than return to the place whence he himself had been bidden to depart.

10. *ten camels*, &c.] The journey was long and could only be performed in safety by a considerable company or caravan. The words which follow, "for all the goods of his master were in his hand," very probably are no more than an explanation of his taking so many camels with him, his master sparing nothing to make the journey successful. The LXX. and Vulgate render "and he took part of all his master's goods in his hand," as though Abraham had sent a present with the servant to conciliate the favour of the bride's family.

to Mesopotamia] Lit. "Aram of the two rivers," or "Aram-Naharaim." The name *Naharina* constantly occurs in Egyptian inscriptions of the 18th and 19th dynasties. In other passages in Genesis (xxv. 20; xxviii. 2, 6, 7; xxxi. 18; xxxiii. 18; xxxv. 9, 26; xlvi. 15) we read of Padan Aram or simply Padan (Gen. xlviii. 7), "the Plain of Syria," "the flat land of Syria." *Aram-Naharaim* occurs again Deut. xxiii. 5; Judg. iii. 8; Ps. lx. 2 (Heb.). Both names describe the low flat country lying between the two rivers Tigris and Euphrates, though Padan Aram was more limited in extent than Aram-Naharaim. The whole highland country of Syria appears to have been called Aram, as many think to distinguish it from Canaan, the low country, Aram meaning "high" and Canaan "low" land. The country, however, which lies between the two rivers, is chiefly a vast plain, though intersected by the Sinjar range, and becoming more mountainous towards the North (see Stanley, 'S. and P.' p. 129; Smith's 'Dict. of Bible,' II. p. 338). Aram-Naharaim was the whole region afterwards called Mesopotamia, lying between the two rivers: Padan Aram being a limited portion of this country of flat character in the neighbourhood of Haran (see on xxv. 20, xxvii. 43).

the city of Nahor] i.e. Haran or Charran (compare ch. xxvii. 43, and see ch. xi. 31; Acts vii. 2).

11. *made his camels to kneel down*] That they might be unloaded, and rest there. (See on the whole of this scene, Thomson, 'Land and Book,' p. 592.)

the time that women go out to draw water] Le Clerc compares Hom. Od. VII. 20, where Minerva, in the form of a girl carrying a pitcher, meets Ulysses as he is about to enter the city of the Phœnicians in the evening. See also Robinson, 'B. R.' vol. II. p. 368, where a somewhat similar scene to this is described.

water at the time of the evening, *even*
the time † that women go out to draw
water.

† Heb. *that women which draw* water *go forth*.

12 And he said, O LORD God of
my master Abraham, I pray thee,
send me good speed this day, and shew
kindness unto my master Abraham.
13 Behold, [c] I stand *here* by the
well of water; and the daughters of
the men of the city come out to draw
water:

c Ver. 43.

14 And let it come to pass, that
the damsel to whom I shall say, Let
down thy pitcher, I pray thee, that I
may drink; and she shall say, Drink,
and I will give thy camels drink also:
let the same be she *that* thou hast
appointed for thy servant Isaac; and
thereby shall I know that thou hast
shewed kindness unto my master.
15 ¶ And it came to pass, before
he had done speaking, that, behold,
Rebekah came out, who was born to
Bethuel, son of Milcah, the wife of
Nahor, Abraham's brother, with her
pitcher upon her shoulder.
16 And the damsel *was* † very fair
to look upon, a virgin, neither had
any man known her: and she went
down to the well, and filled her pitcher,
and came up.

† Heb. *good of countenance*.

17 And the servant ran to meet
her, and said, Let me, I pray thee,
drink a little water of thy pitcher.
18 And she said, Drink, my lord:
and she hasted, and let down her
pitcher upon her hand, and gave him
drink.
19 And when she had done giving
him drink, she said, I will draw *water*
for thy camels also, until they have
done drinking.
20 And she hasted, and emptied
her pitcher into the trough, and ran
again unto the well to draw *water*,
and drew for all his camels.
21 And the man wondering at her
held his peace, to wit whether the
LORD had made his journey prosperous
or not.
22 And it came to pass, as the
camels had done drinking, that the
man took a golden ‖ earring of half a
shekel weight, and two bracelets for

‖ Or, *jewel for the forehead*.

---

12. *O LORD God of my master Abraham*] The Damascene recognizes JEHOVAH, the God of his master Abraham, the Supreme Disposer of all things. He had probably been born a heathen idolater; but Abraham, to whom God had been revealed as JEHOVAH, the eternal self-existing, had no doubt taught his household to acknowledge Him as the Covenant God of Abraham and his family. It is very observable, however, that when Abraham administers an oath to his servant, he makes him swear not only by JEHOVAH, but adds the God of heaven and the God of the earth, which might be a stronger sanction to one brought up in ignorance of the faith of his master.

give me good speed] Lit. "cause to meet me," i. e. the person of whom I am in quest.

14. *the damsel*] The word here used for *damsel* is of common gender, signifying a child or young person of either sex. This is a peculiarity of the Pentateuch. In all the later books the distinction of gender is observed, the feminine affix (ה) being used when a girl is intended. It is important to notice this here; first as shewing the antiquity of the Pentateuch generally; secondly, as shewing that this chapter, which is markedly Jehovistic, is also of marked antiquity. Those, who accuse the so-called Jehovistic chapters of being modern (of the date of Samuel for instance), ground their arguments on a minute criticism of the difference of the words used by the Elohist and the Jehovist writers respectively. It is, however, here very apparent that the word child, "nangar," had not, in the time of the writer of this most Jehovistic history, been distinguished in the singular number into masculine and feminine, *nangar* and *nangarah*, boy and girl.

thereby shall I know] Perhaps more correctly "by her shall I know;" though the Versions generally render the feminine pronoun here by a neuter, the Hebrew having no neuter gender.

15. *who was born to Bethuel*] See ch. xxii. 20 and note.

21. *wondering at her*] "Amazed and astonished" at finding his prayer so suddenly answered.

22. *earring*] So LXX., Vulg., but perhaps more probably "nose-ring." St Jerome in Ezek. xvi. 11, 12, mentions that to his day the women in the East wore golden rings hanging down from their foreheads, on their noses. Hence here the marginal reading gives "jewel for the forehead." To the present

her hands of ten *shekels* weight of gold;

23 And said, Whose daughter *art* thou? tell me, I pray thee: is there room *in* thy father's house for us to lodge in?

24 And she said unto him, I *am* the daughter of Bethuel the son of Milcah, which she bare unto Nahor.

25 She said moreover unto him, We have both straw and provender enough, and room to lodge in.

26 And the man bowed down his head, and worshipped the LORD.

27 And he said, Blessed *be* the LORD God of my master Abraham, who hath not left destitute my master of his mercy and his truth: I *being* in the way, the LORD led me to the house of my master's brethren.

28 And the damsel ran, and told *them of* her mother's house these things.

29 ¶ And Rebekah had a brother, and his name *was* Laban: and Laban ran out unto the man, unto the well.

30 And it came to pass, when he saw the earring and bracelets upon his sister's hands, and when he heard the words of Rebekah his sister, saying, Thus spake the man unto me; that he came unto the man; and, behold, he stood by the camels at the well.

31 And he said, Come in, thou blessed of the LORD; wherefore standest thou without? for I have prepared the house, and room for the camels.

32 ¶ And the man came into the house: and he ungirded his camels, and gave straw and provender for the camels, and water to wash his feet, and the men's feet that *were* with him.

33 And there was set *meat* before him to eat: but he said, I will not eat, until I have told mine errand. And he said, Speak on.

34 And he said, I *am* Abraham's servant.

35 And the LORD hath blessed my master greatly; and he is become great: and he hath given him flocks, and herds, and silver, and gold, and menservants, and maidservants, and camels, and asses.

36 And Sarah my master's wife bare a son to my master when she was old: and unto him hath he given all that he hath.

37 And my master made me swear, saying, Thou shalt not take a wife to my son of the daughters of the Canaanites, in whose land I dwell:

38 But thou shalt go unto my father's house, and to my kindred, and take a wife unto my son.

39 And I said unto my master, Peradventure the woman will not follow me.

40 And he said unto me, The LORD, before whom I walk, will send his angel with thee, and prosper thy way; and thou shalt take a wife for my son of my kindred, and of my father's house:

41 Then shalt thou be clear from *this* my oath, when thou comest to

---

day some Eastern nations wear nose-rings. Schrœder ('De Vest. Mul. Hebr.' c. xxii. § 2). Hartmann ('Hebr.' II. 166); Winer ('R. W.B.' II. 162); Gesen. ('Th.' p. 870); Rosenmüller (in loc.), argue for the rendering "nose-ring" in this passage. The word, however, simply signifies a ring.

half a shekel] Probably about 2 drachms or a quarter of an ounce. See on ch. xxxiii. 14.

28. *her mother's house*] Her father Bethuel was still living (see v. 50); but the mother is mentioned, perhaps because even thus early women may have lived in separate tents from the men (Rashi): which appears also from v. 67, where Sarah's tent is named, and Rebekah is installed in it at her marriage. The daughter naturally went to tell her mother rather than her father of what the servant of Abraham had done; the jewel, which he gave her, being perhaps intended to denote the nature of his embassage.

33. *I will not eat, until I have told mine errand*] Ancient hospitality taught men to set meat before their guests before asking them their names and their business; but here the servant of Abraham felt his message to be so momentous, that he would not eat till he had unburdened himself of it.

my kindred; and if they give not
thee *one*, thou shalt be clear from my
oath.
42 And I came this day unto the
well, and said, O LORD God of my
master Abraham, if now thou do prosper my way which I go:
Ver. 13. 43 [d]Behold, I stand by the well of
water; and it shall come to pass, that
when the virgin cometh forth to draw
water, and I say to her, Give me, I
pray thee, a little water of thy pitcher
to drink;
44 And she say to me, Both drink
thou, and I will also draw for thy
camels: *let* the same *be* the woman
whom the LORD hath appointed out
for my master's son.
45 And before I had done speaking
in mine heart, behold, Rebekah came
forth with her pitcher on her shoulder;
and she went down unto the well, and
drew *water*: and I said unto her, Let
me drink, I pray thee.
46 And she made haste, and let
down her pitcher from her *shoulder*,
and said, Drink, and I will give thy
camels drink also: so I drank, and
she made the camels drink also.
47 And I asked her, and said,
Whose daughter *art* thou? And she
said, The daughter of Bethuel, Nahor's
son, whom Milcah bare unto him: and
I put the earring upon her face, and
the bracelets upon her hands.
48 And I bowed down my head,
and worshipped the LORD, and blessed
the LORD God of my master Abraham, which had led me in the right
way to take my master's brother's
daughter unto his son.
49 And now if ye will deal kindly
and truly with my master, tell me:
and if not, tell me; that I may turn
to the right hand, or to the left.
50 Then Laban and Bethuel answered and said, The thing proceedeth
from the LORD: we cannot speak unto thee bad or good.
51 Behold, Rebekah *is* before thee,
take *her*, and go, and let her be thy
master's son's wife, as the LORD hath
spoken.
52 And it came to pass, that, when
Abraham's servant heard their words,
he worshipped the LORD, *bowing himself* to the earth.
53 And the servant brought forth
†jewels of silver, and jewels of gold, † Heb. *vessels*.
and raiment, and gave *them* to Re-
bekah: he gave also to her brother
and to her mother precious things.
54 And they did eat and drink, he
and the men that *were* with him, and
tarried all night; and they rose up in
the morning, and he said, [e]Send me [e] Ver. 56. & 59.
away unto my master.
55 And her brother and her mother
said, Let the damsel abide with us ‖*a* ‖ Or, *a full year*, or, *ten* months.
few days, at the least ten; after that
she shall go.
56 And he said unto them, Hinder
me not, seeing the LORD hath prospered my way; send me away that
I may go to my master.
57 And they said, We will call the
damsel, and inquire at her mouth.
58 And they called Rebekah,

---

50. *Laban and Bethuel*] The brother is here put before the father, and in v. 39 the brother only is mentioned. It appears that in those days the brother was much consulted concerning the marriage of his sisters (Cp. ch. xxxiv. 13; Judg. xxi. 22): but it has also been observed that Bethuel is altogether kept in the background in this history, as though he were a person of insignificant character, see ch. xxix. 6, where he is altogether passed over, Laban being called the son of Nahor, who was his grandfather. (See Blunt's 'Coincidences,' p. 35, and Wordsworth in loc.) Laban was evidently an active stirring man, as is manifested throughout the subsequent history of Jacob. The Hebrew tradition was that Bethuel died on the day that Eliezer, Abraham's servant, arrived (Targum of Pseudo-Jonathan, on v. 55). Josephus ('Ant.' I. 16) speaks of him as dead, which, however, is unlikely, see on ch. xxvii. 2.

53. *jewels of silver*, &c.] Lit. "vessels of silver," &c.

55. *days, at the least ten*] Lit. "days or ten." Certain days or at least ten; unless "days" be a phrase for the regular period of seven days, i.e. a week, when it would be "a week of days or ten days."

and said unto her, Wilt thou go with
this man? And she said, I will go.
59 And they sent away Rebekah
their sister, and her nurse, and Abraham's servant, and his men.
60 And they blessed Rebekah, and
said unto her, Thou *art* our sister, be
thou *the mother* of thousands of mil-
lions, and let thy seed possess the gate
of those which hate them.
61 ¶ And Rebekah arose, and her
damsels, and they rode upon the
camels, and followed the man: and
the servant took Rebekah, and went
his way.
62 And Isaac came from the way
f chap. 16. 14. & 25. 11. of the f well Lahai-roi; for he dwelt
in the south country.
‖ Or, *to pray.* 63 And Isaac went out ‖ to meditate in the field at the eventide: and
he lifted up his eyes, and saw, and,
behold, the camels *were* coming.
64 And Rebekah lifted up her eyes,
and when she saw Isaac, she lighted
off the camel.
65 For she *had* said unto the servant, What man *is* this that walketh
in the field to meet us? And the servant *had* said, It *is* my master: therefore she took a vail, and covered herself.
66 And the servant told Isaac all
things that he had done.
67 And Isaac brought her into his
mother Sarah's tent, and took Rebekah, and she became his wife; and he
loved her: and Isaac was comforted
after his mother's *death.*

CHAPTER XXV.

1 *The sons of Abraham by Keturah.* 5 *The division of his goods.* 7 *His age, and death.* 9 *His burial.* 12 *The generations of Ishmael.* 17 *His age, and death.* 19 *Isaac prayeth for Rebekah, being barren.* 22 *The children*

---

59. *their sister*] Only one brother is mentioned, viz. Laban: but her relatives generally are spoken of here, as saying of her, "Thou art our sister," sister being used in that wide sense for relation, in which brother is so often found in Scripture.

her nurse] Her name, Deborah, and her death are mentioned ch. xxxv. 8.

62. *And Isaac came from the way of the well of Lahai-roi*] Perhaps "Isaac had come from a journey to Lahai-roi," or "had returned from going to Lahai-roi."

for he dwelt in the south country] Probably at Beer-sheba. Abraham's later dwelling places had been Hebron and Beer-sheba. After the sacrifice of Isaac, we find him dwelling at Beer-sheba (xxii. 19), until we hear of the death of Sarah at Hebron. Very probably Abraham returned after this to Beer-sheba. And so Isaac, whether living with his father, or pitching his tent and feeding his flocks near him, is here represented as dwelling in the south country. In ch. xxv. 11 we find that, after Abraham's death, Isaac took up his residence at Lahai-roi, to which we find that he had been on a visit, when Rebekah arrived, where perhaps he had already been pasturing his flocks and herds (Knobel). All this is in the strictest harmony; though the German critics discover the hand of the Elohist in chapter xxiii., and in the earlier verses of xxv., and that of the Jehovist throughout xxiv.

63. *to meditate*] So LXX., Vulg., but the Targg., Sam., Arab., Saad., Rashi, render "to pray;" some (Syr., Aben-Ezra) "to walk." The word, however, appears most probably to signify religious meditation (see Ges. 'Thes.' p. 1322). Such occupation seems very characteristic of Isaac, whose whole life was so tranquil, and his temper and spirit so calm and submissive, as suiting one who was made an eminent type of Him, who "was oppressed and afflicted, yet He opened not His mouth: He was brought as a lamb to the slaughter; and as a sheep before her shearers is dumb, so He opened not His mouth" (Is. liii. 7). St Jerome ('Qu. in Gen.') sees in this quiet meditation and prayer a type of Him "who went out into a mountain apart to pray" (Matt. xiv. 23).

64. *lighted off the camel*] "It is customary for both men and women, when an Emir or great personage is approaching, to alight some time before he comes up with them. Women frequently refuse to ride in the presence of men; and when a company of them are to pass through a town, they often dismount and walk." (Thomson, 'Land and Book,' p. 593.)

65. *a vail*] The long cloak-like vail, with which the Eastern women covered their faces (see Jerome in loc. and in 'Comment. ad Jes.' III.; Tertullian, 'De velandis Virginibus' (Cap. XVI.). Even at this early period it seems to have been the custom for brides not to suffer the bridegroom to see their faces before marriage (cp. ch. xxix. 23, 25).

67. *Sarah's tent*] See on v. 28.

strive in her womb. 24 *The birth of Esau and Jacob.* 27 *Their difference.* 29 *Esau selleth his birthright.*

THEN again Abraham took a wife,
and her name *was* Keturah.
a 1 Chron. i. 32. 2 And [a]she bare him Zimran, and
Jokshan, and Medan, and Midian, and
Ishbak, and Shuah.
3 And Jokshan begat Sheba, and
Dedan. And the sons of Dedan
were Asshurim, and Letushim, and
Leummim.
4 And the sons of Midian; Ephah,
and Epher, and Hanoch, and Abidah,
and Eldaah. All these *were* the children of Keturah.
5 ¶ And Abraham gave all that he
had unto Isaac.
6 But unto the sons of the concubines, which Abraham had, Abraham
gave gifts, and sent them away from
Isaac his son, while he yet lived, eastward, unto the east country.
7 And these *are* the days of the years

CHAP. XXV. 1. *Then again Abraham took a wife, and her name was Keturah*] The later Targg. and some other Jewish commentators (Rashi and R. Eliezer, in 'Pirke,' c. 30; see also Jerome, 'Qu. in Gen.'), say that Keturah was the same as Hagar, whom Abraham took again, after Sarah's death. This seems inconsistent with v. 6, which speaks of "the concubines" in the plural, meaning, doubtless, Hagar and Keturah. The latter, though called wife here, is called concubine in 1 Chron. i. 32. Moreover, in 1 Chron. i. 28, 32, the sons of Keturah are named separately from Isaac and Ishmael. The concubine (Pilegesh) was a kind of secondary wife, sometimes called "the concubine wife," Judg. xix. 1; 2 S. xv. 16; xx. 3. It is generally supposed, that Abraham did not take Keturah to wife, till after Sarah's death. So the fathers generally. Abraham lived to the age of 175. If we consider this extreme old age as equivalent to eighty-five or ninety in the present day, his age at the time of Sarah's death would correspond to that of a man of from sixty-five to seventy now.

Some, however, think, that Abraham took Keturah to be a secondary wife, during Sarah's life, though no mention is made of this marriage till this time, as the chief purpose of mentioning it was that some account should be given of Keturah's children. So Keil, Poole (in 'Dict. of Bible'), &c. It is impossible to decide this question, as the text gives no note of time. The Authorised Version indeed renders, "Then again Abraham took a wife," but the Hebrew only conveys the notion that Abraham took another wife.

2. *she bare him Zimran*] Josephus ('A. J.' I. 15) tells us that the descendants of Keturah occupied the Troglodyte country and Arabia Felix, which statement is repeated by Jerome ('Qu. Heb. in Gen.'). Some of their names occur among the Arab tribes, but it is not easy to identify them all clearly

Zimran has been thought to be identified with the Zabram of Ptolemy (VI. 7, 5), the royal city of the Cinædocolpitæ to the West of Mecca, on the Red Sea; Jokshan with the Cassanitæ on the Red Sea (Ptol. VI. 7, 6); Ishbak with Shobek, in Idumæa (Knobel, Del., Keil).

Medan, and Midian] In ch. xxxvii. 28, 36, the Midianites and Medanites are identified. The Midianites dwelt partly in the peninsula of Sinai, partly beyond Jordan, in the neighbourhood of the Moabites. We meet with them first as the merchants to whom Joseph was sold by his brethren (as ch. xxxvii. 28 sqq.), trafficking between Egypt and Canaan. Next we find Moses flying to the land of Midian, and marrying the daughter of a priest of Midian, Exod. ii. 15, 16, 21, whose flocks pastured in the desert, in the neighbourhood of Mount Horeb (Ex. iii. 1). Later we find the people of Midian in immediate juxta-position with the Moabites (Num. xxii. 4, xxv. 6, 17, 18). We find them afterwards as formidable neighbours to the Israelites, invading and oppressing them, though afterwards expelled and conquered (Judg. vi. vii. viii.). It has been thought that traces of the name of Midian may be found in Modiana on the Eastern coast of the Elanitic Gulf mentioned by Ptolemy (VI. 7), (Knobel).

3. *Sheba, and Dedan*] Are named, ch. x. 7, among the descendants of Cush. It has been thought that in these, as in other instances, the Shemite and Hamite races intermarried, and that there consequently arose a certain confusion in their names, or that very probably they adopted names from those with whom they were thus connected (see on ch. x. 6, 7; also Ges. 'Thes.' p. 322).

4. *Ephah*] We meet with this Midianitish tribe in Is. lx. 6, as a people rich in camels and gold and incense. The attempts to identify the various descendants of Keturah, mentioned in this chapter, with the names of tribes or cities known to later geographers and historians, may be seen in Knobel, Del., Keil, &c. The uncertainty of such identification is very great.

6. *eastward, unto the east country*] That

of Abraham's life which he lived, an
hundred threescore and fifteen years.
8 Then Abraham gave up the
ghost, and died in a good old age, an
old man, and full *of years;* and was
gathered to his people.
9 And his sons Isaac and Ishmael
buried him in the cave of Machpelah,
in the field of Ephron the son of
Zohar the Hittite, which *is* before
Mamre;
[b chap. 23. 16.] 10 [b]The field which Abraham purchased of the sons of Heth: there was
Abraham buried, and Sarah his wife.
11 ¶ And it came to pass after the
death of Abraham, that God blessed
his son Isaac; and Isaac dwelt by the
[c chap. 16. 14. & 24. 62.] [c]well Lahai-roi.
12 ¶ Now these *are* the generations
of Ishmael, Abraham's son, whom
Hagar the Egyptian, Sarah's handmaid, bare unto Abraham:
[d 1 Chron. 1. 29.] 13 And [d]these *are* the names of
the sons of Ishmael, by their names,
according to their generations: the
firstborn of Ishmael, Nebajoth; and
Kedar, and Adbeel, and Mibsam,
14 And Mishma, and Dumah, and
Massa,
15 ‖Hadar, and Tema, Jetur, Na-
phish, and Kedemah:
16 These *are* the sons of Ishmael,
and these *are* their names, by their
towns, and by their castles; twelve
princes according to their nations.
17 And these *are* the years of the
life of Ishmael, an hundred and thirty
and seven years: and he gave up the
ghost and died; and was gathered
unto his people.
18 And they dwelt from Havilah
unto Shur, that *is* before Egypt, as
thou goest toward Assyria: *and* he
†died in the presence of all his bre- [† Heb. *fell.*]
thren.
19 ¶ And these *are* the generations of Isaac, Abraham's son: Abraham begat Isaac:
20 And Isaac was forty years old
when he took Rebekah to wife, the
daughter of Bethuel the Syrian of
Padan-aram, the sister to Laban the
Syrian.
21 And Isaac intreated the LORD

---

is into Arabia, the inhabitants of which were called Bene-Kedem, "children of the East" (Judg. vi. 3; 1 K. iv. 30; Job i. 3, Is. xi. 14). and afterwards "Saracens," i.e. "Easterns."

8. *Abraham gave up the ghost*] The history of Abraham is thus wound up before the history of Isaac's family is told. Abraham did not die till Jacob and Esau were born. Indeed they were fifteen years old at Abraham's death: for he died at 175, Isaac was then seventy-five years old, but Esau and Jacob were born when Isaac was sixty (see v. 26).

was gathered to his people] This cannot mean that he was buried where his fathers had been buried, for he had been a hundred years a pilgrim in the land of Israel, far from the home of his ancestors, and he was buried in the cave of Machpelah. The place therefore seems to indicate the belief of the patriarchal ages in a place of departed spirits, to which the souls of the dead were gathered. Thus Jacob expected to "go down into the grave (to Sheol) unto his son," though he did not believe his son to have been buried, but to have been devoured by wild beasts (ch. xxxvii. 35; compare also Deut. xxxii. 50). St Augustine ('Qu. in Gen.' 268) interprets the words "his people," of "the people of that city, the heavenly Jerusalem," spoken of in Heb. xii. 22, and which God is said to have prepared for the faithful patriarchs, Heb. xi. 16.

9. *his sons Isaac and Ishmael*] From this we see that Ishmael, though sent to dwell Eastward, had not lost sight of his father and Isaac; and very probably their father's death reconciled the two brothers to each other. Isaac is put first as the heir, and the heir of the promises.

16. *castles*] See on Num. xxxi. 10.

19. *And these are the generations of Isaac, Abraham's son*] This is the beginning of a new Section in the history of Genesis, which continues to the end of ch. xxxv. According to the uniform plan of the author, there is a brief recapitulation, in order to make the Section complete. In this case it is very brief, consisting of the latter part of v. 19, and v. 20.

20. *the Syrian of Padan-aram*] **The Aramean of Padan-aram.** Padan-aram is the "plain or flat land of Aram," translated or paraphrased in Hosea xii. 12 by Sĕdeh-Aram, "the field or plain of Aram." In the last chapter the country of Rebekah is called Aram-Naharaim, or Aram of the two rivers. See on ch. xxiv. 10. There is no reasonable foundation for the belief that Padan-aram

for his wife, because she *was* barren:
and the LORD was intreated of him,
and Rebekah his wife conceived.
22 And the children struggled together within her; and she said, If *it*
be so, why *am* I thus? And she went
to inquire of the LORD.
23 And the LORD said unto her,
Two nations *are* in thy womb, and
two manner of people shall be separated from thy bowels; and *the one*
people shall be stronger than *the other*
people; and [e] the elder shall serve the [e] Rom. 9. 12.
younger.
24 ¶ And when her days to be delivered were fulfilled, behold, *there*
were twins in her womb.
25 And the first came out red, all

---

was the old name used by the so-called Elohist, Aram-Naharaim being the name which had been adopted by the later Jehovist. It was natural that the historian, when relating the embassy of Eliezer of Damascus to Mesopotamia to seek a wife for Isaac, should have used the general name of the country into which Eliezer was sent, whereas in the present Section more particularity is to be expected, where Jacob is described as sojourning for years in Padan-aram, the land of Laban; just as in one case it might be natural to speak of going into Scotland, whilst in a more detailed account, we might prefer to speak of the Highlands of Scotland, or the Lowlands, or of some particular county or district.

21. *Isaac intreated the* LORD *for his wife, because she was barren*] This barrenness had lasted twenty years (v. 26). Another instance of the delay in the fulfilment of God's promises, and of the trial of the faith of those for whom the greatest blessings are reserved. The word here used for prayer is by many thought to mean frequent and repeated prayer; implying the anxious desire of Isaac to be blessed with offspring. Gesenius (p. 1085) thinks the word is connected with a root signifying "to offer incense," which certainly appears to belong to it in Ezek. viii. 11. If it be so, we must believe that the patriarchal worship, which from the earliest times was accompanied with sacrifice, had also, whether from Divine revelation or from an instinctive feeling, adopted the use of incense.

22. *If it be so, why am I thus?*] An obscure saying. The Vulg. and Targums render, "If it was to be thus with me, why did I conceive?" The Arabic has, "If I had known it would be thus, I would not have sought for offspring." Much to the same effect Rashi, "If such be the sufferings of pregnancy, why did I desire it?" The Syriac and most of the German Comm. understand it, "If it be so, wherefore do I live?"

And she went to inquire of the LORD] By prayer, or by sacrifice, perhaps at some special place of prayer; as to the domestic altar of Isaac (Theodor. 'Qu. in Gen.'), or more likely, by going to a prophet. The Jerusalem Targum, followed by several Jewish commentators says, she went to Shem; others say to Melchizedec. Abraham, who was still living, was the head of the family then dwelling in Palestine; he had been specially honoured by revelations from heaven; and was probably esteemed the patriarch-priest of the whole race. It is most likely, therefore, that if the inquiry was made through a man, it would have been made through him. Still we may conclude with St Augustine ('Qu.' 72), that nothing is certain except that Rebekah went to ask of the Lord, and that the Lord answered her.

23. *Two nations*, &c.] The response is in antistrophic parallelisms, a poetic form, in which no doubt it was more readily handed down from father to son:

Two nations are in thy womb:
and two peoples shall be separated from thy bowels;
and nation shall be stronger than nation,
and the elder shall serve the younger.

To this see the reference Mal. i. 2, 3, "Jacob have I loved, and Esau have I hated," and in Rom. ix. 10—13, where St Paul shews that election to the privilege of being the depositories of God's truth and the Church of God on earth is inscrutable, but not therefore necessarily unjust or unmerciful. Such election indeed plainly marks that God does not choose men as His instruments because of their merits, but it does not shew that He is therefore simply arbitrary. In all there is a hidden stream of mercy flowing. The chosen race shall be made the means of salvation to others as well as to themselves. Their privileges will be blessed to them, if they use those privileges faithfully. Otherwise whilst they are the channels of God's grace to their brethren, they themselves will be cast out, and others shall come into their inheritance.

25. *red, all over like an hairy garment*] He seemed as if covered with a kind of fur, a thick down, which is said to be found on some new born infants. It gave an animal appear-

over like an hairy garment; and they
called his name Esau.
26 And after that came his brother
out, and [f]his hand took hold on Esau's
heel; and his name was called Jacob:
and Isaac *was* threescore years old
when she bare them.
27 And the boys grew: and Esau
was a cunning hunter, a man of the
field; and Jacob *was* a plain man,
dwelling in tents.
28 And Isaac loved Esau, because
†he did eat of *his* venison: but Rebekah loved Jacob.
29 ¶ And Jacob sod pottage: and
Esau came from the field, and he *was*
faint:
30 And Esau said to Jacob, Feed
me, I pray thee, †with that same red
pottage; for I *am* faint: therefore was
his name called ‖Edom.
31 And Jacob said, Sell me this
day thy birthright.
32 And Esau said, Behold, I *am*

[f] Hos. 12. 3.

† Heb. *venison was in his mouth.*

† Heb. *with that red, with that red* pottage.

‖ That is *Red.*

---

ance to Esau, and probably indicated his more sensual nature. Owing to this he was called Esau, "hairy."

Jacob] Meaning, literally, "he holds the heel;" but, from the act of a person tripping up an adversary in wrestling or running by taking hold of the heel, it signifies also to "trip up," "to outwit," "to supplant." (See xxvii. 36).

27. *a cunning hunter*] **Skilled in hunting.** Instead of following the quiet pastoral life of his forefathers, Esau preferred the wilder life of a hunter, betokening his wild, restless, self-indulgent character, and leading him probably to society with the heathen Canaanites round about.

a man of the field] This is antithetic to what follows, "a dweller in tents." It probably indicates still more fully the wild life of Esau. Instead of spending his life in the society of his family, returning to his tent after the day's labour at night, he roved over the country, like the uncivilized hunters in half savage lands.

Jacob was a plain man] **An upright man,** a man of steady, domestic, moral habits.

dwelling in tents] *i.e.* staying at home, attending to the pasturing of the flocks and the business of the family, instead of wandering abroad in search of pleasure and amusement. (See Ges. 'Thes.' p. 634.)

28. *Isaac loved Esau, because he did eat of his venison*] Lit. "because venison was in his mouth." The bold daring of Esau was, perhaps by force of contrast, pleasant to the quiet spirit of Isaac. That quiet temper was not strong enough to rule such a restless youth; there was also a marked selfishness in Isaac's affection, which brought with it its own punishment. The mother, on the contrary, loved the well-conducted and helpful Jacob. Yet her love too was not guided by the highest principle, and so led her and her favourite son to sin against truth and justice, and brought heavy trials and sorrows on them both.

30. *Feed me, I pray thee, with that same red pottage*] **Let me, I pray thee, devour some of that red, that red.** The words express the vehemence of the appetite, and probably the very words uttered by Esau in his impatient hunger and weariness. The red lentil is still esteemed in the East, and has been found very palatable by modern travellers (Robinson, 'Bib. Res.' I. 246). Dr Kitto says he often partook of a red pottage made of lentils. "The mess had the redness, which gained for it the name of red" ('Pict. Bib.' Gen. xxv. 30, quoted in Smith's 'Dict. of Bib.' II. 92). It is also described by Thomson, 'Land and Book,' p. 587, as exhaling an odour very tempting to a hungry man.

therefore was his name called Edom] Names appear to have been frequently given from accidental causes, especially in the East; and sometimes the occurrence of more than one circumstance to the same person seems to have riveted a name. Thus we read above that Esau was born with red hair and colour. His frantic demand for *red* pottage and selling his birthright to gain it, may have conspired with his hair and complexion to stamp the name Edom (or Red) upon him. The conjecture of Tuch and others, that the name was connected with the Red Sea, near which the Edomites dwelt, is wholly groundless. The Red Sea was never so called in early times, or in Semitic tongues. The name Red was given in later days to this sea by the Greeks.

31. *Sell me this day thy birthright*] It is doubtful what privileges the birthright carried with it in patriarchal times. In after times a double portion of the patrimony was assigned to the firstborn by law (Deut. xxi. 15—17); but in the earliest days the respect paid to the eldest son is very apparent; and as the family spread out into a tribe, the patriarchal head became a chieftain or prince.

† Heb. *going to die.* †at the point to die: and what profit
shall this birthright do to me?
33 And Jacob said, Swear to me
this day; and he sware unto him:
g Heb. 12. 16. and [g]he sold his birthright unto
Jacob.
34 Then Jacob gave Esau bread
and pottage of lentiles; and he did
eat and drink, and rose up, and went
his way: thus Esau despised *his* birthright.

CHAPTER XXVI.

1 *Isaac because of famine went to Gerar.* 2 *God instructeth, and blesseth him.* 7 *He is reproved by Abimelech for denying his wife.* 12 *He groweth rich.* 18 *He diggeth Esek, Sitnah, and Rehoboth.* 26 *Abimelech maketh a covenant with him at Beer-sheba.* 34 *Esau's wives.*

AND there was a famine in the land, beside the first famine that was in the days of Abraham. And

---

It also looks as if the head of the family exercised a kind of priesthood. Then the father's chief blessing was given to his firstborn son. Above all, in the family of Abraham, there was a promise of peculiar spiritual privileges, which, if not fully understood, would have been much dwelt upon by believing minds. All this was to Esau of little account compared with the desire of present gratification of appetite. It has been thought, not improbably, that the famine impending (see xxvi. 1) was already, more or less, pressing on the family of Isaac (Lightfoot, 'Harm. of O. T.' in loc.). Esau had perhaps been seeking in vain for food in the chase, whilst Jacob had prepared a mess of pottage, sufficient to relieve the pains of hunger. If it were so, Esau, wearied and famished, may have been strongly tempted to give up much for food. But his worldly and "profane" character is exhibited in his contempt for that, which was, whether in a worldly or in a spiritual point of view, rather an object of faith or sentiment, than of sight and sense. Jacob, a man of widely different character, had probably looked with reverence on the spiritual promises, though with culpable ambition for the personal pre-eminence of the firstborn. He and Esau were twins, and it may have seemed hard to him to be shut out from the chief hope of his house by one not older than himself, and whose character was little worthy of his position. This may be some excuse for his conduct, but the sacred history, whilst exposing the carnal indifference of Esau, does not extenuate the selfishness of Jacob. Throughout their history, Esau is the bold, reckless, but generous and openhearted man of this world; Jacob, on the contrary, is a thoughtful, religious man, but with many infirmities, and especially with that absence of simplicity and uprightness, which often characterizes those who have made their choice of heaven and yet let their hearts linger too much on earth.

The events correspond with the characters of the men. Esau lives on his rough and reckless life; though towards the end of it we see his better feelings overcoming his vindictiveness. Whatever his own final state with God may have been, he has disinherited his children, left them wild men of the desert and the rocks, instead of leaving them heirs of the promises and ancestors of the Messiah. Jacob, with a less prosperous life, has yet gone through a long training and chastening from the God of his fathers, to whose care and guidance he had given himself; he suffers heavily, but he learns from that he suffered; at last he goes down to Egypt to die, comforted in having his children yet alive, confessing that few and evil had been the days of the years of his pilgrimage, but yet able to say in peaceful confidence upon his deathbed, "I have waited for thy salvation, O LORD." He has inherited the promises; but for trying by unworthy means to anticipate the promise of inheritance, he has to go through a life of trial, sorrow, and discipline, and to die at last, not in the land of promise, but in the house of bondage.

CHAP. XXVI. 1. *Abimelech*] It has been doubted whether this be the Abimelech with whom Abraham was concerned or not. The events related in this chapter took place about eighty years after those related in ch. xx. It is not therefore impossible, when men lived to 180, that the same king may still have been reigning over the Philistines; and it has been thought that the character described here is very similar to that in ch. xx. It seems more probable that the present Abimelech should have been the son or successor of the earlier king. Names were very frequently handed down to the grandson, recurring alternately, and this may very possibly have been the case here: but moreover, *Abimelech* (*father king*, or *father of the king*), may very likely have been, like Pharaoh, a title rather than a name, so also Phichol (*the mouth of all*, i.e. commanding all), sounds like the title of the commander in chief or the grand vizier. Cp. xxi. 22, xxvi. 26.

Gerar] The chief city of the Philistines, now Kirbet el Gerar.

Isaac went unto Abimelech king of
the Philistines unto Gerar.
2 And the LORD appeared unto
him, and said, Go not down into
Egypt; dwell in the land which I
shall tell thee of:
3 Sojourn in this land, and I will
be with thee, and will bless thee; for
unto thee, and unto thy seed, [a]I will
give all these countries, and I will
perform the oath which I sware unto
Abraham thy father;
4 And I will make thy seed to
multiply as the stars of heaven, and
will give unto thy seed all these countries; and in thy seed shall all the
nations of the earth be [b]blessed;
5 Because that Abraham obeyed
my voice, and kept my charge, my
commandments, my statutes, and my
laws.
6 ¶ And Isaac dwelt in Gerar:
7 And the men of the place asked
him of his wife; and he said, She *is*
my sister: for he feared to say, *She is*
my wife; lest, *said he*, the men of
the place should kill me for Rebekah;
because she *was* fair to look upon.
8 And it came to pass, when he
had been there a long time, that
Abimelech king of the Philistines looked out at a window, and saw, and,
behold, Isaac *was* sporting with Rebekah his wife.
9 And Abimelech called Isaac, and
said, Behold, of a surety she *is* thy
wife: and how saidst thou, She *is* my
sister? And Isaac said unto him, Because I said, Lest I die for her.
10 And Abimelech said, What *is*
this thou hast done unto us? one of
the people might lightly have lien with
thy wife, and thou shouldest have
brought guiltiness upon us.
11 And Abimelech charged all *his*
people, saying, He that toucheth this
man or his wife shall surely be put to
death.
12 Then Isaac sowed in that land,
and †received in the same year an

[a] chap. 13. 15 & 15. 18.

[b] chap. 12. 3. & 15. 18. & 22. 18.

† Heb. *found.*

2. *the LORD appeared unto him*] The last recorded vision was at the sacrifice of Isaac more than sixty years before, ch. xxii. These revelations were not so frequent as they seem to us, as we read one event rapidly after the other, but just sufficient to keep up the knowledge of God and the faith of the patriarchs in the line of the chosen people and of the promised seed.

Go not down into Egypt] "In the first famine, which was in the days of Abraham," Abraham had gone down to Egypt. Probably, after this example, and from the plenty with which Egypt was blessed, Isaac had purposed to go down there now.

3. *Sojourn in this land*] He was the heir, to whom the land had been promised. He is to dwell in it, as a stranger and sojourner, and not to be tempted by suffering to go down to that land of spiritual danger, from which his father so narrowly escaped.

4. *all these countries*] The lands of the different Canaanitish tribes named in ch. xv. 19—21. The pronoun here rendered "these" is one of those ancient forms peculiar to the Pentateuch (*ha-el;* in the later books it would be *ha-eleh*).

7. *She is my sister*] Isaac acted on this occasion just as Abraham had done in Egypt and in Philistia. Probably too, he called Rebekah his sister because she was his cousin, and the deep importance of strict truthfulness had not been fully unfolded to the patriarchs in their twilight state of faith. The difference in the details of this story and the events in the life of Abraham is too marked to allow it to be thought that this is only a repetition of the histories in ch. xii. and xx. In the history of Abraham Sarah was taken into the house of Pharaoh, and afterwards into that of Abimelech, and in both cases preserved by Divine intervention. In the history of Isaac, there is no apparent intention on the part of Abimelech to take Rebekah into his house, but he accidentally discovers that Isaac and Rebekah were not brother and sister but husband and wife, and then reproves Isaac for his concealment of the truth, on the ground that so some of his people might have ignorantly taken Rebekah to wife.

12. *sowed in that land*] The patriarchs were not so wholly nomadic and pastoral in their habits of life as to neglect agriculture entirely. Even the Bedouins practise agriculture at the present day as well as grazing (Robinson, 'B. R.' Vol. I. p. 77).

an hundredfold] **An hundred measures;** *i. e.* probably a hundred measures for each measure sown, a very unusual increase, though not quite unknown in a virgin soil, especially if the corn were barley. (The LXX. and Syr. render here "a hundred of barley,"

hundredfold: and the LORD blessed
him.
13 And the man waxed great, and
†went forward, and grew until he became very great:
† Heb. *went going.*
14 For he had possession of flocks,
and possession of herds, and great
store of ‖servants: and the Philistines
envied him.
‖ Or, *husbandry.*
15 For all the wells which his father's servants had digged in the days
of Abraham his father, the Philistines
had stopped them, and filled them
with earth.
16 And Abimelech said unto Isaac,
Go from us; for thou art much
mightier than we.
17 ¶ And Isaac departed thence,
and pitched his tent in the valley of
Gerar, and dwelt there.
18 And Isaac digged again the
wells of water, which they had digged
in the days of Abraham his father;
for the Philistines had stopped them
after the death of Abraham: and he
called their names after the names by
which his father had called them.
19 And Isaac's servants digged in
the valley, and found there a well of
†springing water.
† Heb. *living.*
20 And the herdmen of Gerar did
strive with Isaac's herdmen, saying,
The water *is* ours: and he called the
name of the well ‖Esek; because they
strove with him.
‖ That is, *Contention.*
21 And they digged another well,
and strove for that also: and he called
the name of it ‖Sitnah.
‖ That is, *Hatred.*
22 And he removed from thence,
and digged another well; and for that
they strove not: and he called the
name of it ‖Rehoboth; and he said,
For now the LORD hath made room
for us, and we shall be fruitful in the
land.
‖ That is, *Room.*
23 And he went up from thence
to Beer-sheba.
24 And the LORD appeared unto
him the same night, and said, I *am*
the God of Abraham thy father: fear
not, for I *am* with thee, and will bless
thee, and multiply thy seed for my
servant Abraham's sake.
25 And he builded an altar there,
and called upon the name of the LORD,
and pitched his tent there: and there
Isaac's servants digged a well.
26 ¶ Then Abimelech went to him
from Gerar, and Ahuzzath one of his
friends, and Phichol the chief captain
of his army.
27 And Isaac said unto them,
Wherefore come ye to me, seeing ye
hate me, and have sent me away from
you?
28 And they said, †We saw certainly that the LORD was with thee:
and we said, Let there be now an oath
betwixt us, *even* betwixt us and thee,
and let us make a covenant with thee;
† Heb. *Seeing we saw.*
29 †That thou wilt do us no hurt,
as we have not touched thee, and as
we have done unto thee nothing but
good, and have sent thee away in
peace: thou *art* now the blessed of
the LORD.
† Heb. *If thou shalt, &c.*

---

which Michaelis and others have adopted. The reading and rendering of the Authorised Version are more generally supported, and are probably correct.) The fertility of the soil in this neighbourhood is still very great.

17. *the valley of Gerar*] The word for *valley* signifies properly the bed or course of a stream or mountain torrent, a *wady*. It is not easy to say which of the valleys running to the sea, South of Beer-sheba, may be identified with this valley of Gerar (see Robinson, 'Physical Geography,' p. 112).

22. *Rehoboth*] Probably identified as to site with the Wady er-Ruhaibeh, where are the ruins of an extensive city, eight hours South of Beer-sheba. Here is an ancient well, now filled up, twelve feet in diameter, and regularly built with hewn stone (Robinson, 'Phys. Geog.' p. 243; see also 'B. R.' p. 289).

26. *Phichol*] See on v. 1. The name signifies "the mouth of all," which would be applicable to a grand vizier, through whom all might have access to the sovereign, or to a general whose voice gave command to all. The former sense would seem the more probable, if it had not been said that Phichol was "'the chief captain of the army."

29. *thou art now the blessed of the LORD*] We have here twice (see v. 28) the sacred name JEHOVAH, used by the heathen king of Gerar. This does not, however, indicate that the writer of this portion of the

30 And he made them a feast, and they did eat and drink.

31 And they rose up betimes in the morning, and sware one to another: and Isaac sent them away, and they departed from him in peace.

32 And it came to pass the same day, that Isaac's servants came, and told him concerning the well which they had digged, and said unto him, We have found water.

33 And he called it ‖ Shebah: therefore the name of the city *is* ‖ Beer-sheba unto this day.

‖ That is, *an oath.*
‖ That is, *the well of the oath.*

34 ¶ And Esau was forty years old when he took to wife Judith the daughter of Beeri the Hittite, and Bashemath the daughter of Elon the Hittite:

35 Which [c] were † a grief of mind unto Isaac and to Rebekah.

c chap. 27. 46.
† Heb. *bitterness of spirit.*

CHAPTER XXVII.

1 *Isaac sendeth Esau for venison.* 6 *Rebekah instructeth Jacob to obtain the blessing.* 15 *Jacob under the person of Esau obtaineth it.* 30 *Esau bringeth venison.* 33 *Isaac trembleth.* 34 *Esau complaineth, and by importunity obtaineth a blessing.* 41 *He threateneth Jacob.* 42 *Rebekah disappointeth it.*

AND it came to pass, that when Isaac was old, and his eyes were dim, so that he could not see, he called Esau his eldest son, and said

---

history had so-called Jehovistic tendencies, or that he simply identified the name JEHOVAH with the name Elohim. Abraham had dwelt for some time in Gerar, either under this very Abimelech, or under his immediate predecessor. Abraham was known as a worshipper of JEHOVAH, and was seen to be blessed and prospered by his God. Now again Abraham's son Isaac comes and sojourns for a long time in the same country. He too worships his father's God, and is seen, like his father, to prosper abundantly. The Philistines therefore recognize him, as his father, to be a worshipper of JEHOVAH, and perceive that he has succeeded to his father in the favour of their great Protector. Abimelech does not profess himself a worshipper of the LORD, but looks on the LORD as the God of Abraham, and sees that Abraham's son Isaac is "*now* the blessed of the LORD."

33. *he called it Shebah: therefore the name of the city is Beer-sheba unto this day*] "Shebah" means both *seven* and *oath;* the number seven being a sacred number among the Hebrews, and oaths being apparently ratified with presents or sacrifices seven in number (see ch. xxi. 28). There is no inconsistency in the history which tells us that Abraham gave the name of Beer-sheba to this well long before, and under similar circumstances. The well, dug by Abraham, and secured to him by oath, had been covered and lost. It is found by Isaac's servants just after the covenant made between him and Abimelech. The whole series of events recalls to Isaac's mind the original name, and that which gave rise to the name, and so he restores, not the well only, but the name also. "Upon the Northern side of the Wady es-Seba are the two deep and ancient wells, which gave occasion to this name" (Robinson, 'Phys. Geog.' p. 242; 'B. R.' I. p. 300). It is supposed by Robinson, that the one is that dug by Abraham, the other that dug by Isaac; the name having been afterwards given to both.

34. *Esau was forty years old,* &c.] Isaac was now a hundred years old. Esau marries two wives and both of them Canaanites. On account of his polygamy and his marrying without consent of his parents from among the idolatrous Hittites and Hivites (see ch. xxxvi. 2), he is called "a fornicator" by the Apostle (Heb. xii. 16). These two verses do not belong so much to this chapter as to the next. The account of Esau's marriage, and the consequent grief of Isaac and Rebekah, is intended to prepare the way for the succeeding history.

35. *a grief of mind*] **A bitterness of spirit.**

CHAP. XXVII. 1. *Isaac was old*] The Jewish intepreters say he was now one hundred and thirty-seven years old, the age at which Ishmael died fourteen years before, and it is not improbable that the thought of his brother's death at this age put Isaac in mind of his own end. The calculation on which it is inferred that Isaac was one hundred and thirty-seven, Esau and Jacob being seventy-seven at this time, is as follows; Joseph was thirty years old when he stood before Pharaoh (Gen. xli. 46), then came seven years of plenty (v. 47—53), which made Joseph thirty-seven; then two years of famine ere Jacob came into Egypt (ch. xlv. 6), which brings Joseph's age to thirty-nine; but at this time Jacob was one hundred and thirty; therefore Jacob must have been ninety-one when Joseph was born. Now Joseph was born in the last year of the second seven, or in the fourteenth year of Jacob's service with Laban, at the very end of that year

unto him, My son: and he said unto
him, Behold, *here am* I.
2 And he said, Behold now, I am
old, I know not the day of my
death:
3 Now therefore take, I pray thee,
thy weapons, thy quiver and thy bow,
and go out to the field, and †take me
some venison;
4 And make me savoury meat, such
as I love, and bring *it* to me, that I
may eat; that my soul may bless thee
before I die.
5 And Rebekah heard when Isaac
spake to Esau his son. And Esau
went to the field to hunt *for* venison,
and to bring *it*.
6 ¶ And Rebekah spake unto Jacob her son, saying, Behold, I heard
thy father speak unto Esau thy brother,
saying,
7 Bring me venison, and make me
savoury meat, that I may eat, and
bless thee before the LORD before my
death.
8 Now therefore, my son, obey my

† Heb. *hunt*.

(ch. xxx. 25, 26). Take fourteen years out of ninety-one, Jacob's age when Joseph was born, and we have seventy-seven for the age of Jacob, when he was sent away from the wrath of Esau to the house of Laban. (See Lightfoot's 'Harmony of Old Testament' in loc., works by Pitman, 1822, Vol. II. pp. 96, 97). If this calculation be true, Isaac had still forty-three years to live, his quiet life having been extended to an unusual length. There is however great risk of numerical calculations from various causes being inexact. The last chapter had brought us down only to the hundredth year of Isaac's life, Esau being then but forty; and in some respects an earlier date seems more accordant with the tenor of the subsequent history, it being hardly probable that Jacob should have been seventy-seven when he fled to Laban and served seven years for his wife, and then another seven years for his second wife; even at a period when human life was still extended so far beyond that of future generations. On the chronology of Jacob's life see note at the end of ch. xxxi.

3. *quiver*] So LXX., Vulg., Pseudo-Jon.: but Onkelos, Syr. have "sword." The Jewish commentators are divided between the two senses. The word occurs nowhere else, but is derived from a verb meaning to "hang," to "suspend," which would suit either the quiver which hung over the shoulder, or the sword, the "hanger," which was suspended by the side.

4. *that my soul may bless thee*] There appears a singular mixture of the carnal and the spiritual in this. Isaac recognizes his own character as that of the priestly and prophetic head of his house, privileged to bless as father and priest, and to foretell the fortunes of his family in succession to Abraham in his office of the prophet of God. Yet his carnal affection causes him to forget the response to the enquiry of Rebekah, "the elder shall serve the younger," and the fact that Esau had sold his birthright and alienated it from him for ever by a solemn oath. Moreover, in order that his heart may be the more warmed to him whom he desires to bless, he seeks to have some of that savoury meat brought to him which he loved.

6. *Rebekah spake unto Jacob*] She had no doubt treasured up the oracle which had assured her, even before their birth, that her younger son Jacob, whom she loved, should bear rule over Esau, whose wild and reckless life, and whose Canaanitish wives had been a "bitterness of soul" to her. She probably knew that Jacob had bought Esau's birthright. Now, believing rightly that the father's benediction would surely bring blessing with it, she fears that these promises and hopes would fail. She believed, but not with that faith, which can patiently abide till God works out His plans by His Providence. So she strove, as it were, to force forward the event by unlawful means; even, as some have thought that Judas betrayed Christ that he might force Him to declare Himself a king and to take the kingdom. Every character in this remarkable history comes in for some share of blame, and yet some share of praise. Isaac, with the dignity of the ancient patriarch and faith in the inspiring Spirit of God, prepares to bless his son, but he lets carnal and worldly motives weigh with him. Rebekah and Jacob, seeing the promises afar off and desiring the spiritual blessings, yet practise deceit and fraud to obtain them, instead of waiting till He who promised should shew Himself faithful. Esau, defrauded of what seems his right, exhibits a natural feeling of sorrow and indignation, which excites our pity and sympathy; but we have to remember how "for a morsel of meat he sold his birthright," and that so, when he would have inherited the promises he was rejected, being set forth as an example of the unavailing regret of such as wantonly despise spiritual privileges, and when they have lost them, seek too late for the blessings to which they lead.

voice according to that which I command thee.
9 Go now to the flock, and fetch
me from thence two good kids of the
goats; and I will make them savoury
meat for thy father, such as he loveth:
10 And thou shalt bring *it* to thy
father, that he may eat, and that he
may bless thee before his death.
11 And Jacob said to Rebekah his
mother, Behold, Esau my brother *is*
a hairy man, and I *am* a smooth man:
12 My father peradventure will feel
me, and I shall seem to him as a de-
ceiver; and I shall bring a curse upon
me, and not a blessing.
13 And his mother said unto him,
Upon me *be* thy curse, my son: only
obey my voice, and go fetch me *them*.
14 And he went, and fetched, and
brought *them* to his mother: and his
mother made savoury meat, such as
his father loved.
15 And Rebekah took †goodly raiment of her eldest son Esau, which
were with her in the house, and put
them upon Jacob her younger son:
16 And she put the skins of the
kids of the goats upon his hands, and
upon the smooth of his neck:

† Heb. *desirable.*

17 And she gave the savoury meat
and the bread, which she had prepared,
into the hand of her son Jacob.
18 ¶ And he came unto his father,
and said, My father: and he said,
Here *am* I; who *art* thou, my son?
19 And Jacob said unto his father,
I *am* Esau thy firstborn; I have done
according as thou badest me: arise, I
pray thee, sit and eat of my venison,
that thy soul may bless me.
20 And Isaac said unto his son,
How *is it* that thou hast found *it* so
quickly, my son? And he said, Because the LORD thy God brought *it*
†to me.
21 And Isaac said unto Jacob,
Come near, I pray thee, that I may
feel thee, my son, whether thou *be*
my very son Esau or not.
22 And Jacob went near unto Isaac
his father; and he felt him, and said,
The voice *is* Jacob's voice, but the
hands *are* the hands of Esau.
23 And he discerned him not, because his hands were hairy, as his
brother Esau's hands: so he blessed
him.
24 And he said, *Art* thou my very
son Esau? And he said, I *am*.

† Heb *before me*

---

15. *goodly raiment of her elder son Esau*] St Jerome ('Qu. Hebr.' in loc.) mentions it as a tradition of the rabbins, that the firstborn in the patriarchal times, holding the office of priesthood, had a sacerdotal vestment in which they offered sacrifice; and it was this sacerdotal vestment which was kept by Rebekah for Esau, and which was now put upon Jacob. See on ch. xxxvii. 3.

16. *the skins of the kids of the goats*] Martial (Lib. XII. Epig. 46) alludes to kid skins as used by the Romans for false hair to conceal baldness. The wool of the oriental goats is much longer and finer than of those of this country. (Cp. Cant. iv. 1. See Bochart, 'Hieroz.' p. 1, Lib. II. c. 51. See also Rosenm., Tuch, &c.)

18. *who art thou, my son?*] The anxiety and trepidation of Isaac appear in these words. He had perhaps some misgiving as to the blessing of Esau, and doubted whether God would prosper him in the chase and bring him home with venison to his father.

20. *Because the LORD thy God brought it to me*] The covering of his falsehood with this appeal to the Most High is the worst part of Jacob's conduct. In the use of the names of God, Jacob speaks of JEHOVAH as the God of his father. A little further on in the history, Jacob vows that, if he is prospered in his journey, then JEHOVAH shall be his God (ch. xxviii. 21). This is exactly accordant with the general use of these sacred names. Elohism would, so to speak, correspond with our word Theism. Though Jacob was a believer in JEHOVAH, yet revelation in those early days was but slight, and the knowledge of the patriarchs imperfect. There were gods of nations round about. JEHOVAH had revealed Himself to Abraham and was Abraham's God, and again to Isaac, and Isaac had served Him as his God. It is quite possible that Esau, with his heathen wives, may have been but a half worshipper of JEHOVAH; but Jacob recognizes Him as the God of his father Isaac (cp. ch. xxxi. 53), and afterwards solemnly chooses Him as the object of his own worship and service. See however note on ch. xxviii. 2.

25 And he said, Bring *it* near to me, and I will eat of my son's venison, that my soul may bless thee. And he brought *it* near to him, and he did eat: and he brought him wine, and he drank.

26 And his father Isaac said unto him, Come near now, and kiss me, my son.

27 And he came near, and kissed him: and he smelled the smell of his raiment, and blessed him, and said, See, the smell of my son *is* as the smell of a field which the LORD hath blessed:

Heb. 11.
28 Therefore [a]God give thee of the dew of heaven, and the fatness of the earth, and plenty of corn and wine:

29 Let people serve thee, and nations bow down to thee: be lord over thy brethren, and let thy mother's sons bow down to thee: cursed *be* every one that curseth thee, and blessed *be* he that blesseth thee.

30 ¶ And it came to pass, as soon as Isaac had made an end of blessing Jacob, and Jacob was yet scarce gone out from the presence of Isaac his father, that Esau his brother came in from his hunting.

31 And he also had made savoury meat, and brought it unto his father, and said unto his father, Let my father arise, and eat of his son's venison, that thy soul may bless me.

32 And Isaac his father said unto him, Who *art* thou? And he said, I *am* thy son, thy firstborn Esau.

33 And Isaac †trembled very exceedingly, and said, Who? where *is* he that hath †taken venison, and brought *it* me, and I have eaten of all before thou camest, and have blessed him? yea, *and* he shall be blessed.

† Heb. *trembled with a great trembling greatly.*
† Heb. *hunted.*

34 And when Esau heard the words of his father, he cried with a great and exceeding bitter cry, and said unto his father, Bless me, *even* me also, O my father.

35 And he said, Thy brother came with subtilty, and hath taken away thy blessing.

36 And he said, Is not he rightly named ‖Jacob? for he hath supplanted me these two times: he took away my birthright; and, behold, now he hath taken away my blessing. And he said, Hast thou not reserved a blessing for me?

‖ That is, *a supplanter.*

37 And Isaac answered and said unto Esau, Behold, I have made him

---

26. *kiss me*] Tuch has suggested that Isaac asked his son to kiss him, that he might distinguish the shepherd who would smell of the flock from the huntsman who would smell of the field. It may have been so (see next verse), or it may have only been paternal love.

28. *God*] Lit. *The God*, i.e. that God just named, the God of thy Father, viz. JEHOVAH. It does not indicate (as Keil) "the personal God," nor is it (as some would have it) a Jehovistic formula. The article is perfectly natural as referring to Jacob's words v. 20. The blessing is, as usual, thrown into the poetic form of an antistrophic parallelism.

29. *Let people serve thee, and nations bow down to thee*] This was fulfilled in the extensive dominions of the descendants of Jacob under David and Solomon, but, no doubt, has a fuller reference to the time when "the LORD should arise upon Israel, and His glory should be seen on her, when Gentiles should come to her light, and kings to the brightness of her rising"...when "the abundance of the sea should be converted unto her, the forces of the Gentiles should come unto her" (Isa. lx. 5, 6. Cp. Rom. xi. 25).

29. *cursed be every one*, &c.] This is the continued promise to the chosen race, first given (Gen. xii. 3) to Abraham. It is observed, however, that Isaac does not pronounce on Jacob that emphatic spiritual blessing, which God Himself had assured to Abraham twice (xii. 3; xxii. 18), and to Isaac once (xxvi. 4), "In thy seed shall all the nations of the earth be blessed." There was something carnal and sinful in the whole conduct of the persons concerned in the history of this chapter, Isaac, Rebekah, Jacob, Esau: and it may have been this which withheld for the time the brightest promise to the family of Abraham; or perhaps it may have been that that promise should come only from the mouth of God Himself, as it is given afterwards in ch. xxviii. 14.

36. *Is not he rightly named Jacob?*] Lit. "Is it that he is called Jacob, and he supplanteth or outwitteth me these two times?"

thy lord, and all his brethren have I
given to him for servants; and with
‖ Or, *supported.* corn and wine have I ‖sustained him:
and what shall I do now unto thee,
my son?
38 And Esau said unto his father,
Hast thou but one blessing, my father? bless me, *even* me also, O my
father. And Esau lifted up his voice,
b Heb. 12. 17. [b]and wept.
39 And Isaac his father answered
c ver. 28. and said unto him, Behold, [c]thy dwell-
‖ Or, *of the fatness.* ing shall be ‖the fatness of the earth,
and of the dew of heaven from above;
40 And by thy sword shalt thou
live, and shalt serve thy brother; and
it shall come to pass when thou shalt
have the dominion, that thou shalt
break his yoke from off thy neck.
41 ¶ And Esau hated Jacob because of the blessing wherewith his
father blessed him: and Esau said in
his heart, The days of mourning for
my father are at hand; [d]then will I d Obad. 10.
slay my brother Jacob.
42 And these words of Esau her
elder son were told to Rebekah: and
she sent and called Jacob her younger
son, and said unto him, Behold, thy
brother Esau, as touching thee, doth
comfort himself, *purposing* to kill thee.
43 Now therefore, my son, obey
my voice; and arise, flee thou to
Laban my brother to Haran;
44 And tarry with him a few days,
until thy brother's fury turn away;
45 Until thy brother's anger turn
away from thee, and he forget *that*
which thou hast done to him: then I
will send, and fetch thee from thence:
why should I be deprived also of you
both in one day?

A paronomasia on the name Jacob. See on ch. xxv. 26. The words seem to mean, Is there not a connection between the meaning of his name Jacob, and the fact that he thus supplants or outwits me?

39. *thy dwelling shall be the fatness of the earth, and of the dew of heaven from above*] Lit. "from the fatness of the earth and from the dew of heaven." Castalio, Le Clerc, Knobel, Del., Keil, render the preposition "from" by "far from." So apparently Gesenius ('Thes.' p. 805, *absque, sine*). But the Authorized Version corresponds with the ancient versions. The very same words with the very same preposition occur in v. 28, and it is difficult to make that preposition partitive in v. 28, and privative in v. 39.

40. *by thy sword thou shalt live, and shalt serve thy brother*, &c.] Josephus ('B. J.' IV. 4. 1) describes the Edomites as a tumultuous, disorderly race, and all their history seems to confirm the truth of this description. The prophecy thus delivered by Isaac was fulfilled in every particular. At first Esau, the elder, seemed to prosper more than his brother Jacob. There were dukes in Edom before there reigned any king over the children of Israel (Gen. xxxvi. 31); and whilst Israel was in bondage in Egypt, Edom was an independent people. But Saul defeated and David conquered the Edomites (1 S. xiv. 47; 2 S. viii. 14), and they were, notwithstanding some revolts, constantly subject to Judah (see 1 K. xi. 14; 2 K. xiv. 7, 22; 2 Chr. xxv. 11; xxvi. 2) till the reign of Ahaz, when they threw off the yoke (2 K. xvi. 6; 2 Chr. xxviii. 7). Judas Maccabæus defeated them frequently (1 Macc. v.; 2 Macc. x.). At last his nephew Hyrcanus completely conquered them, and compelled them to be circumcised, and incorporated them into the Jewish nation (Joseph. 'Ant.' XIII. 9. 1); though finally under Antipater and Herod they established an Idumæan dynasty, which continued till the destruction of the Jewish polity.

when thou shalt have dominion] More probably **when thou shalt toss** (the yoke). So the LXX., Vulg. (*excutias*); Gesen. 'Thes.' p. 1269; Hengst., Keil, &c. The allusion is to the restlessness of the fierce Edomite under the yoke of the Jewish dominion. The prophecy was fulfilled when they revolted under Joram and again under Ahaz; and finally when they gave a race of rulers to Judæa in the persons of Herod and his sons (see last note).

43. *Haran*] It appears that not only Abraham and the family of his brother Haran must have left Ur of the Chaldees (see ch. xi. 31); but that the family of Nahor must have followed them to Haran, which is therefore called "the city of Nahor" (ch. xxiv. 10). The name Harran still remains in the centre of the cultivated district at the foot of the hills lying between the Khabour and the Euphrates.

45. *why should I be deprived also of you both in one day?*] *i.e.* of Jacob by the hand of Esau, and of Esau by the hand of justice (ch. ix. 6). The sacred history has shewn us the sins and errors of the family of Isaac; it here briefly but emphatically exhibits the distress

[e] chap. 26. 35.
46 And Rebekah said to Isaac, [e]I
am weary of my life because of the
daughters of Heth: if Jacob take a
wife of the daughters of Heth, such
as these *which are* of the daughters of
the land, what good shall my life
do me?

CHAPTER XXVIII.

1 *Isaac blesseth Jacob, and sendeth him to Padan-aram.* 6 *Esau marrieth Mahalath the daughter of Ishmael.* 10 *The vision of Jacob's ladder.* 18 *The stone of Beth-el.* 20 *Jacob's vow.*

AND Isaac called Jacob, and blessed him, and charged him, and
said unto him, Thou shalt not take a
wife of the daughters of Canaan.
[a] Hos. 12. 12.
2 [a]Arise, go to Padan-aram, to
the house of Bethuel thy mother's
father; and take thee a wife from
thence of the daughters of Laban thy
mother's brother.
3 And God Almighty bless thee,
and make thee fruitful, and multiply
thee, that thou mayest be †a multitude of people;
† Heb. *an assembly of people.*
4 And give thee the blessing of
Abraham, to thee, and to thy seed
with thee; that thou mayest inherit
the land †wherein thou art a stranger,
† Heb. *of thy sojournings.*
which God gave unto Abraham.
5 And Isaac sent away Jacob:
and he went to Padan-aram unto
Laban, son of Bethuel the Syrian,
the brother of Rebekah, Jacob's and
Esau's mother.
6 ¶ When Esau saw that Isaac
had blessed Jacob, and sent him away
to Padan-aram, to take him a wife
from thence; and that as he blessed
him he gave him a charge, saying,
Thou shalt not take a wife of the
daughters of Canaan;
7 And that Jacob obeyed his father
and his mother, and was gone to
Padan-aram;
8 And Esau seeing that the daughters of Canaan †pleased not Isaac his
† Heb. *were evil in the eyes, &c.*
father;
9 Then went Esau unto Ishmael,
and took unto the wives which he
had Mahalath the daughter of Ishmael Abraham's son, the sister of
Nebajoth, to be his wife.
10 ¶ And Jacob went out from
Beer-sheba, and went toward [b]Haran.
[b] Called, Acts 7. 2, *Charran.*
11 And he lighted upon a certain
place, and tarried there all night,

---

and misery which at once followed; Isaac and Rebekah left in their old age by both their children; idols become scourges; Esau disappointed and disinherited; Jacob banished from his home, destined to a long servitude and a life of disquietude and suffering. Even those, whom God chooses and honours, cannot sin against Him without reaping, at least in this world, the fruit of evil doings (1 Cor. xi. 32).

CHAP. XXVIII. 1. *Isaac called Jacob, and blessed him*] Isaac has learned that God had decreed that Jacob should be the heir of the promises, the recipient of the blessings. Accordingly, in v. 4, he invokes on Jacob "the blessing of Abraham," that "he and his seed should inherit the land of his sojourning," and no doubt also the spiritual blessings pronounced on the descendants of Abraham.

2. *Padan-aram*] See on xxiv. 10, xxv. 20, xxvii. 43.

Bethuel] This looks as if Bethuel were still living, not as the Jewish tradition says, that he died before Isaac's marriage. It is more likely that he was either naturally of weak character, or enfeebled by age. (See on ch. xxiv. 50.)

3. *God Almighty*] "El-Shaddai." It was under this name that God appeared to Abraham, ch. xvii. 1, and gave him the blessing to which Isaac now refers.

4. *the land wherein thou art a stranger*] Lit. **the land of thy sojournings.**

8. *pleased not*] Lit. **were evil in the eyes of.**

11. *he lighted upon a certain place*] Lit. **he lighted on the place.** The definite article probably indicates either that it was the place appointed by God, or that it was the place afterwards so famous from God's revelation to Jacob. We may well picture to ourselves the feelings of Jacob on this night, a solitary wanderer from his father's house, going back from the land of promise, conscious of sin and in the midst of danger, with a dark and doubtful future before him, yet hitherto having always cherished the hope of being the chosen of God to bear the honours and privileges of his house, to have the inheritance promised to Abraham, and now too with

because the sun was set; and he
took of the stones of that place, and
put *them for* his pillows, and lay down
in that place to sleep.
12 And he dreamed, and behold a
ladder set up on the earth, and the
top of it reached to heaven: and behold the angels of God ascending and
descending on it.
13 [c] And, behold, the LORD stood
above it, and said, I *am* the LORD
God of Abraham thy father, and the
God of Isaac: the land whereon thou
liest, to thee will I give it, and to thy
seed;
14 And thy seed shall be as the
dust of the earth, and thou shalt
† spread abroad [d] to the west, and to
the east, and to the north, and to the
south: and in thee and [e] in thy seed
shall all the families of the earth be
blessed.

[c] chap. 35. 1. & 48. 3.
† Heb. *break forth.*
[d] Deut. 12. 20.
[e] chap. 12. 3. & 18. 18. & 22. 18. & 26. 4.

15 And, behold, I *am* with thee,
and will keep thee in all *places* whither thou goest, and will bring thee
again into this land; for I will not
leave thee, until I have done *that*
which I have spoken to thee of.
16 ¶ And Jacob awaked out of his
sleep, and he said, Surely the LORD is
in this place; and I knew *it* not.
17 And he was afraid, and said,
How dreadful *is* this place! this *is*
none other but the house of God,
and this *is* the gate of heaven.
18 And Jacob rose up early in the
morning, and took the stone that he
had put *for* his pillows, and set it up
for a pillar, and poured oil upon the
top of it.
19 And he called the name of that
place ‖ Beth-el: but the name of that
city *was called* Luz at the first.
20 And Jacob vowed a vow, say-

‖ That is, *the house of God.*

---

the words of Isaac's blessing just ringing in his ears. Whether would fear or faith prevail?

12. *a ladder*] God takes this opportunity to impress Jacob more deeply with the sense of His presence, to encourage him with promises of protection and to reveal to him His purpose of mercy and love.

The ladder might only indicate that there was a way from God to man, and that man might by God's help mount up by it to heaven, that angels went up from man to God, and came down from God to man, and that there was a continual providence watching over the servants of God. So the dream would teach and comfort the heart of the dreamer. But we cannot doubt, that there was a deeper meaning in the vision thus vouchsafed to the heir of the promises, in the hour of his greatest desolation, and when the sense of sin must have been most heavy on his soul. Our Lord Himself teaches (John i. 51), that the ladder signified the Son of Man, Him, who was now afresh promised as to be of the Seed of Jacob (v. 14); Him, by whom alone we go to God (John xiv. 6); who is the way to heaven, and who has now gone there to prepare a place for us.

13. *the LORD stood above it*] Onkelos renders "the glory of the LORD."

16. *Surely the LORD is in this place*] It is possible that Jacob may not have had quite so intelligent a conviction of God's omnipresence as Christians have; but it is apparent throughout the patriarchal history that special sanctity was attached to special places. This feeling is encouraged by the highest sanction in Ex. iii. 5.

18. *set it up for a pillar, and poured oil upon the top of it*] This was probably the most ancient and simplest form of temple or place for religious worship; excepting the altar of stones or earth for a burnt sacrifice. Whether this is the first example of such an erection we cannot judge. It was a very natural and obvious way of marking the sanctity of a spot; as in Christian times wayside crosses and the like have been set up so frequently. The pouring oil on it was a significant rite, though what may have been the full significance to Jacob's mind it is not easy to say. St Augustine ('De C. D.' XVI. 38) says that it was not that he might sacrifice to the stone or worship it, but that as *Christ* is named from *chrism*, or unction, so there was a great mystery (*sacramentum*) in this anointing of the stone with oil. The constant connection in religious thought between unction and sanctification seems a more probable solution of the question.

19. *Beth-el*] Abraham had built an altar in this neighbourhood (xii. 8, xiii. 4); and it is possible that the spot thus sanctified may have been the very place which Jacob lighted on (v. 11), and which he found to be the house of God and the gate of heaven.

The place consecrated perhaps first by Abraham's altar, and afterwards by Jacob's vision and pillar, was plainly distinct from the *city* which was "called Luz at the first," and which afterwards received the name of Bethel

ing, If God will be with me, and
will keep me in this way that I go,
and will give me bread to eat, and
raiment to put on,
21 So that I come again to my
father's house in peace; then shall the
LORD be my God:
22 And this stone, which I have
set *for* a pillar, shall be God's house:
and of all that thou shalt give me I
will surely give the tenth unto thee.

CHAPTER XXIX.

1 *Jacob cometh to the well of Haran.* 9 *He taketh acquaintance of Rachel.* 13 *Laban entertaineth him.* 18 *Jacob covenanteth for Rachel.* 23 *He is deceived with Leah.* 28 *He marrieth also Rachel, and serveth for her seven years more.* 32 *Leah beareth Reuben,* 33 *Simeon,* 34 *Levi,* 35 *and Judah.*

THEN Jacob † went on his journey, and came into the land of
the † people of the east.
2 And he looked, and behold a
well in the field, and, lo, there *were*
three flocks of sheep lying by it; for
out of that well they watered the
flocks: and a great stone *was* upon
the well's mouth.
3 And thither were all the flocks

† Heb. *lift up his feet.*

† Heb. *children.*

---

from its proximity to the sanctuary. So late as the time of Joshua (see Josh. xvi. 1, 2) the two places were distinct. When the tribe of Joseph took the city (Judg. i. 21—26), they appear to have given to the *city* the name of Bethel, formerly attaching only to the sanctuary, and thenceforward, the name Luz having been transferred to another town, the old town of Luz is always called Bethel. According to Eusebius and Jerome ('Onomast.' art. βαιθήλ) it lay about twelve miles from Jerusalem on the road to Sichem. Its ruins are still called by the name of *Beitin*. The rocky character of the hills around, and the stony nature of the soil, have been much noted by travellers (see Robinson, 'B. R.' II. pp. 127—130, and Stanley, 'Sinai and Palestine,' pp. 217—223). It has been thought by many that this act of Jacob, in setting up a stone to mark a sacred spot, was the origin of Cromlechs and all sacred stones. Certainly we find in later ages the custom of having stones, and those too anointed with oil, as objects of idolatrous worship. Clem. Alex. ('Stromat.' Lib. VII. p. 713) speaks of "worshipping every oily stone," and Arnobius, ('Adv. Gentes,' Lib. I. 39), in like manner, refers to the worshipping of "a stone smeared with oil, as though there were in it a present power." It has been conjectured farther that the name *Bætulia*, given to stones, called animated stones (λίθοι ἔμψυχοι), by the Phœnicians (Euseb. 'Præp. Evang.' I. 10) was derived from this name of Bethel. (See Spencer, 'De Legg.' I. 2; Bochart, 'Canaan,' II. 2.) These Bætulia, however, were meteoric stones, and derived their sanctity from the belief that they had fallen from heaven: and the name has probably but a fancied likeness to the name Bethel. Still the connection of the subsequent worship of stones with the primitive and pious use of them to mark places of worship is most probably a real connection. The erection of all such stones for worship was strictly forbidden in later times (see Lev. xxvi. 1; Deut. xvi. 22, &c.). What was good in its origin had become evil in its abuse.

21. *then shall the* LORD *be my God*] So the LXX., Vulg., Syr.; but the Arab. and several of the Hebrew commentators put these words in the protasis; "And if the LORD will be my God, then shall this stone be God's house," &c. The Hebrew is ambiguous, and so is the Targum of Onkelos: but the change of construction and of tense certainly appears to be at the beginning of v. 22, for all the verbs, beginning with "will keep me" in v. 20 to the end of v. 21, are in the same form (the perfect with vau conversive); and in verse 22 there is a change to the future. If this be so, the whole passage will then run, "If God will be with me and will keep me in the way that I go, and will give me bread to eat, and raiment to put on, and if I come again to my father's house in peace, and if the LORD will be my God, then shall this stone, which I have set for a pillar, be the house of God, and of all that Thou shalt give me, I will surely give a tenth unto Thee." The fulfilment of this vow is related in ch. xxxv. 15, where God again appears to Jacob on his return from Padan-aram, and Jacob restores the pillar which he had before set up, and again solemnly gives it the name of Beth-el, "the house of God" (see Quarry, 'on Genesis,' p. 486).

22. *give the tenth unto thee*] In ch. xiv. 20, we have an instance of Abraham giving tithes to Melchizedek. Here we have another proof that the duty of giving a tenth to God was recognized before the giving of the Law.

CHAP. XXIX. **1.** *Then Jacob,* &c.] Lit. "Then Jacob lifted up his feet and came into the land of the children of the East," *i.e.* into Mesopotamia, which lies East of Judæa.

2. *he looked, and behold a well*] Cp. ch. xxiv. 11—15. The similarity of the two stories results from the unvarying customs of

gathered: and they rolled the stone
from the well's mouth, and watered
the sheep, and put the stone again
upon the well's mouth in his place.
4 And Jacob said unto them, My
brethren, whence *be* ye? And they
said, Of Haran *are* we.
5 And he said unto them, Know
ye Laban the son of Nahor? And
they said, We know *him*.
6 And he said unto them, †*Is* he
well? And they said, *He is* well:
and, behold, Rachel his daughter cometh with the sheep.
7 And he said, Lo, †*it is* yet high
day, neither *is it* time that the cattle
should be gathered together: water ye
the sheep, and go *and* feed *them*.
8 And they said, We cannot, until
all the flocks be gathered together,
and *till* they roll the stone from the
well's mouth; then we water the
sheep.
9 ¶ And while he yet spake with
them, Rachel came with her father's
sheep: for she kept them.
10 And it came to pass, when Jacob saw Rachel the daughter of Laban his mother's brother, and the
sheep of Laban his mother's brother,
that Jacob went near, and rolled the
stone from the well's mouth, and watered the flock of Laban his mother's
brother.
11 And Jacob kissed Rachel, and
lifted up his voice, and wept.
12 And Jacob told Rachel that he
was her father's brother, and that he
was Rebekah's son: and she ran and
told her father.
13 And it came to pass, when Laban heard the †tidings of Jacob his
sister's son, that he ran to meet him,
and embraced him, and kissed him,
and brought him to his house. And
he told Laban all these things.
14 And Laban said to him, Surely
thou *art* my bone and my flesh. And
he abode with him †the space of a
month.
15 ¶ And Laban said unto Jacob,
Because thou *art* my brother, shouldest
thou therefore serve me for nought?
tell me, what *shall* thy wages *be*?
16 And Laban had two daughters:
the name of the elder *was* Leah, and
the name of the younger *was* Rachel.
17 Leah *was* tender eyed; but
Rachel was beautiful and well favoured.
18 And Jacob loved Rachel; and
said, I will serve thee seven years for
Rachel thy younger daughter.
19 And Laban said, *It is* better

† Heb. Is there *peace to him?*

† Heb. *yet the day is great.*

† Heb. *hearing.*

† Heb. *a month of days.*

---

the East, and from the natural halting place being a well outside a city.

5. *Laban the son of Nahor*] *i.e.* the descendant, the grandson of Nahor. Just as in v. 12, Jacob calls himself the brother of Laban, being in truth his nephew. The omission of Bethuel is here again observable.

6. *Is he well?*] Lit. "Is it peace to him?"

8. *We cannot*] Probably because there was an agreement not to roll away the stone till all were assembled, not because the stone was too heavy for three shepherds to move.

9. *Rachel came with her father's sheep*] So Ex. ii. 16, the daughters of Reuel, the priest of Midian, led their father's sheep to water. And even now among the Arabs it is not beneath the daughter of an Emir to water the sheep.

13. *he told Laban all these things*] *i.e.* probably the cause of his exile from home, his father's blessing and command to him to marry a wife of his mother's kindred, and the various events of his journey.

14. *the space of a month*] Lit. "a month of days;" the word "days" being frequently added to a note of time, as we might say "a month long," or as here in the Authorized Version, "the space of a month."

17. *tender eyed*] *i.e.* weak eyed, so LXX., Vulg., &c.

18. *I will serve thee seven years for Rachel*] In the case of Isaac and Rebekah, Abraham's servant gives handsome presents to Rebekah, ch. xxiv. 53, the Eastern custom at marriages. Jacob could give neither presents nor dowry, for he was a fugitive from his father's house, and describes himself as having passed over Jordan with only his staff (ch. xxxii. 10). He proposes therefore to serve Laban seven years, if he will give him his daughter to wife, a proposal, which Laban's grasping disposition prompts him to accept, even from one whom he calls brother and of his own bone and flesh (vv. 14, 15).

19. *It is better that I should give her to thee*, &c.] It has always been the custom

that I give her to thee, than that I should give her to another man: abide with me.

20 And Jacob served seven years for Rachel; and they seemed unto him *but* a few days, for the love he had to her.

21 ¶ And Jacob said unto Laban, Give *me* my wife, for my days are fulfilled, that I may go in unto her.

22 And Laban gathered together all the men of the place, and made a feast.

23 And it came to pass in the evening, that he took Leah his daughter, and brought her to him; and he went in unto her.

24 And Laban gave unto his daughter Leah Zilpah his maid *for* an handmaid.

25 And it came to pass, that in the morning, behold, it *was* Leah: and he said to Laban, What *is* this thou hast done unto me? did not I serve with thee for Rachel? wherefore then hast thou beguiled me?

26 And Laban said, It must not be so done in our †country, to give the younger before the firstborn.

† Heb. *place.*

27 Fulfil her week, and we will give thee this also for the service which thou shalt serve with me yet seven other years.

28 And Jacob did so, and fulfilled her week: and he gave him Rachel his daughter to wife also.

29 And Laban gave to Rachel his daughter Bilhah his handmaid to be her maid.

30 And he went in also unto Rachel, and he loved also Rachel more than Leah, and served with him yet seven other years.

31 ¶ And when the LORD saw that Leah *was* hated, he opened her womb: but Rachel *was* barren.

32 And Leah conceived, and bare a son, and she called his name ‖Reuben: for she said, Surely the LORD hath looked upon my affliction; now therefore my husband will love me.

‖ That is, *see a son.*

33 And she conceived again, and bare a son; and said, Because the LORD hath heard that I *was* hated, he hath therefore given me this *son* also: and she called his name ‖Simeon.

‖ That is, *hearing.*

---

with Eastern tribes to prefer marrying among their own kindred.

20. *but a few days, for the love he had to her*] He loved Rachel so much, that he valued the labour of seven years as though it were the labour of but few days in comparison with the great prize, which that labour was to bring him.

24. *Zilpah his maid for an handmaid*] So ch. xxiv. 61.

25. *it was Leah*] This deception was possible, because there appears to have been no religious or other solemn ceremony, in which the bride was presented to the bridegroom, and the veil in which brides were veiled was so long and close that it concealed, not only the face, but much of the figure also.

27. *Fulfil her week*] *i.e.* celebrate the marriage feast for a week with Leah (cp. Judg. xiv. 12); and after that we will give thee Rachel also. "It was not after another week of years that he should receive Rachel to wife; but after the seven days of the first wife's nuptials." (St Jerome, 'Qu. Hebr.' in loc.) It has been observed that the fraud practised by Laban on Jacob was a fit penalty for the fraud practised by Jacob on Isaac and Esau. The polygamy of Jacob must be explained on the same principle as that of Abraham. It had not yet been expressly forbidden by the revealed law of God. The marriage of two sisters also was afterwards condemned (Lev. xviii. 18), but as yet there had been no such prohibition.

31. *was hated*] *i.e.* less loved (cp. Mal. i. 3).

32. *Reuben*] *i.e.* "Behold a son." The words which follow are but one of those plays on a name so general in these early days; they do not give the etymology of the name; they have however led some to think that the meaning of "Reuben" is rather "the son of vision," or as Jerome interprets it, "the son of God's gracious regard," *filium respectus gratuiti.* The Syr. and Josephus give the name as Reubel, the latter explaining it as "the pity of God" ('Ant.' I. 19. 8), which is supported by Michaelis, though it is obviously a corrupt reading (see Rosenm. in loc. and Gesen. p. 1247).

33. *Simeon*] *i.e.* "hearing." The birth of her first son convinces her that God hath *seen* her, the second that God hath *heard* her.

34 And she conceived again, and
bare a son; and said, Now this time
will my husband be joined unto me,
because I have born him three sons:
therefore was his name called ‖Levi.
35 And she conceived again, and
bare a son: and she said, Now will I
praise the LORD: therefore she called
his name [a]‖Judah; and †left bearing.

‖ That is, *joined.* [a] Matt. 1. 2. ‖ That is, *praise.* † Heb. *stood from bearing.*

CHAPTER XXX.

1 *Rachel, in grief for her barrenness, giveth Bilhah her maid unto Jacob.* 5 *She beareth Dan and Naphtali.* 9 *Leah giveth Zilpah her maid, who beareth Gad and Asher.* 14 *Reuben findeth mandrakes, with which Leah buyeth her husband of Rachel.* 17 *Leah beareth Issachar, Zebulun, and Dinah.* 22 *Rachel beareth Joseph.* 25 *Jacob desireth to depart.* 27 *Laban stayeth him on a new covenant.* 37 *Jacob's policy, whereby he became rich.*

AND when Rachel saw that she
bare Jacob no children, Rachel
envied her sister; and said unto Jacob,
Give me children, or else I die.
2 And Jacob's anger was kindled
against Rachel: and he said, *Am* I in
God's stead, who hath withheld from
thee the fruit of the womb?
3 And she said, Behold my maid
Bilhah, go in unto her; and she shall
bear upon my knees, that I may also
†have children by her.

† Heb. *be built by her.*

4 And she gave him Bilhah her
handmaid to wife: and Jacob went
in unto her.
5 And Bilhah conceived, and bare
Jacob a son.
6 And Rachel said, God hath
judged me, and hath also heard my
voice, and hath given me a son: therefore
called she his name ‖Dan.
7 And Bilhah Rachel's maid conceived
again, and bare Jacob a second
son.
8 And Rachel said, With †great
wrestlings have I wrestled with my
sister, and I have prevailed: and she
called his name ‖[a]Naphtali.
9 When Leah saw that she had left
bearing, she took Zilpah her maid, and
gave her Jacob to wife.
10 And Zilpah Leah's maid bare
Jacob a son.
11 And Leah said, A troop cometh:
and she called his name ‖Gad.
12 And Zilpah Leah's maid bare
Jacob a second son.
13 And Leah said, †Happy am I, for
the daughters will call me blessed: and
she called his name ‖Asher.
14 ¶ And Reuben went in the days
of wheat harvest, and found mandrakes
in the field, and brought them

‖ That is, *judging.* † Heb. *wrestlings of God.* ‖ That is, *my wrestling.* [a] Called, Matt. 4. 13, *Nephthalim.* ‖ That is, *a troop,* or, *company.* † Heb. *In my happiness.* ‖ That is, *happy.*

---

34. *Levi*] "Association" or "associated."

35. *Judah*] *i.e.* "praised" (from the Hophal future of *Jadah*).

CHAP. XXX. 3. *that I may also have children by her*] Lit. "that I may be built up by her." (See on ch. xvi. 2.)

6. *Dan*] *i.e.* "judge."

8. *With great wrestlings*] Lit. "with wrestlings of God." The LXX. renders "God has helped me," and Onkelos, "God has received my prayer." So virtually the Syriac. Though the addition of the name of God often expresses a superlative, yet "wrestling" being a type of prayer, it is most probable that in this passage the allusion is to Rachel's earnest striving in prayer with God for the blessing of offspring. (So Hengst., Del., Keil.) Above, v. 1, Rachel had manifested impatience and neglect of prayer, seeking from Jacob what only could be given of God. Jacob's remonstrance with her, v. 2, may have directed her to wiser and better thoughts.

11. *A troop cometh*] Rather, **Good fortune cometh**, or, "in good fortune," *i.e.* happily, prosperously. The rendering of the Authorized Version is favoured by the Samaritan version, and has been supposed to be in accordance with ch. xlix. 19. The latter, however, may have no reference to the derivation, but be only the common Oriental play upon a word. The LXX., Vulg., Syr., Onk., Jerus., Pseudo-Jon., all interpret *Gad* to mean "success," "good fortune," "prosperity." So Gesen., Rosenm., Knobel, Del., Keil, &c.

13. *Happy am I,* &c.] Lit. **in my happiness** (*am I*), **for the daughters call me happy; and she called his name Asher,** *i.e.* happy.

14. *mandrakes*] So with great unanimity the ancient versions and most of the Jewish commentators. There is little doubt that the plant was really the *atropa mandragora*, a species closely allied to the deadly nightshade (*atropa belladonna*). It is not uncommon in Palestine (Tristram, pp. 103, 104). It is said to be a narcotic, and to have stupefying and even intoxicating properties. It has

unto his mother Leah. Then Rachel
said to Leah, Give me, I pray thee,
of thy son's mandrakes.
15 And she said unto her, *Is it* a
small matter that thou hast taken my
husband? and wouldest thou take
away my son's mandrakes also? And
Rachel said, Therefore he shall lie
with thee to night for thy son's mandrakes.
16 And Jacob came out of the
field in the evening, and Leah went
out to meet him, and said, Thou
must come in unto me; for surely
I have hired thee with my son's mandrakes. And he lay with her that
night.
17 And God hearkened unto Leah,
and she conceived, and bare Jacob the
fifth son.
18 And Leah said, God hath given
me my hire, because I have given my
maiden to my husband: and she called
his name ‖Issachar. ‖ That is, *an hire.*
19 And Leah conceived again, and
bare Jacob the sixth son.
20 And Leah said, God hath en-
dued me *with* a good dowry; now
will my husband dwell with me, because I have born him six sons: and
she called his name ‖ *b* Zebulun. ‖ That is, *dwelling.*
21 And afterwards she bare a daugh- *b* Called, Matt. 4. 13,
ter, and called her name ‖Dinah. *Zabulon.*
22 ¶ And God remembered Rachel, ‖ That is,
and God hearkened to her, and opened *judgment.*
her womb.
23 And she conceived, and bare a
son; and said, God hath taken away
my reproach:
24 And she called his name ‖Jo- ‖ That is, *adding.*
seph; and said, The LORD shall add
to me another son.
25 ¶ And it came to pass, when
Rachel had born Joseph, that Jacob

---

broad leaves and green apples, which become pale yellow when ripe, with a strong tuberous bifid root, in which Pythagoras discerned a likeness to the human form, whence many ancient fables concerning it. They are still found ripe about the time of wheat harvest on the lower ranges of Lebanon and Hermon. The apples are said to produce dizziness; the Arabs believe them to be exhilarating and stimulating even to insanity; hence the name *tuffah el jan*, "apples of the jan" (Thomson, 'Land and Book,' p. 577). The ancients believed them calculated to produce fruitfulness, and they were used as philtres to conciliate love, hence their name in Hebrew, *dudaim*, *i.e.* love-apples. Rachel evidently shared in this superstitious belief. (See Heid. Tom. II. Ex. xix.; Winer, 'R. W. B.' voc. *Abram;* Ges. 'Thes.' p. 324; Rosenm. in loc.; Smith's 'Dict.' voc. *mandrake*), &c.

18. *Issachar*] *i.e.* "there is a reward."

20. *Zebulun*] *i.e.* "dwelling," derived from *zabal*, to dwell, with a play on the word *Zabad*, "to give, to endow."

21. *Dinah*] *i.e.* "judgment." It is thought that Jacob had other daughters (see ch. xxxvii. 35; xlvi. 7). Daughters, as they did not constitute links in a genealogy, are not mentioned except when some important history attaches to them, as in this case the history in ch. xxxiv.

24. *Joseph*] *i.e.* "adding," from *jasaph*, "to add," with a play on *asaph*, "to take away."

25. *when Rachel had born Joseph*] It has been inferred from this, that Joseph was born at the end of the second seven years of Jacob's servitude; though it is by no means certain that Jacob demanded his dismissal at the first possible moment. The words of this verse seem to indicate that Jacob did not desire to leave Laban, at all events till after Joseph's birth. Many reasons may have induced him to remain in Padan-aram longer than the stipulated fourteen years; the youth of his children unfitting them for a long journey, the pregnancy of some of his wives, the unhappy temper of his beloved Rachel, whom he may have been unwilling to take from her parents, till she had a son of her own to comfort her; above all, the fear of Esau's anger, who had resolved to slay him. There is nothing necessarily inconsistent in the narrative. It is possible that Leah should have borne 6, Rachel 1, Bilhah 2, and Zilpah 2 sons in seven years. It is not certain that Dinah was born at this time at all. Her birth is only incidentally noticed. It would be possible even that Zebulun should have been borne by Leah later than Joseph by Rachel; it being by no means necessary that we should believe all the births to have followed in the order in which they are enumerated, which is in the order of mothers, not of births. The common explanation is, that the first four sons of Leah were born as rapidly as possible, one after the other, in the first four years of marriage. In the meantime, not necessarily after the birth of Leah's fourth son, Rachel gives her maid to Jacob, and so very probably Bilhah gave birth to Dan and Naphtali before the birth of Ju-

said unto Laban, Send me away, that
I may go unto mine own place, and
to my country.
26 Give *me* my wives and my
children, for whom I have served
thee, and let me go: for thou knowest my service which I have done
thee.
27 And Laban said unto him, I
pray thee, if I have found favour in
thine eyes, *tarry: for* I have learned
by experience that the LORD hath
blessed me for thy sake.
28 And he said, Appoint me thy
wages, and I will give *it*.
29 And he said unto him, Thou
knowest how I have served thee, and
how thy cattle was with me.
30 For *it was* little which thou
hadst before I *came*, and it is *now* † increased unto a multitude; and the
LORD hath blessed thee † since my
coming: and now when shall I provide for mine own house also?
31 And he said, What shall I give
thee? And Jacob said, Thou shalt
not give me any thing: if thou wilt
do this thing for me, I will again feed
and keep thy flock:
32 I will pass through all thy flock
to day, removing from thence all the
speckled and spotted cattle, and all
the brown cattle among the sheep,
and the spotted and speckled among
the goats: and *of such* shall be my
hire.
33 So shall my righteousness answer for me † in time to come, when
it shall come for my hire before thy
face: every one that *is* not speckled
and spotted among the goats, and
brown among the sheep, that shall be
counted stolen with me.
34 And Laban said, Behold, I
would it might be according to thy
word.
35 And he removed that day the
he goats that were ringstraked and
spotted, and all the she goats that were
speckled and spotted, *and* every one
that had *some* white in it, and all the
brown among the sheep, and gave
them into the hand of his sons.
36 And he set three days' journey

† Heb. *broken forth.*
† Heb. *at my foot.*
† Heb. *to morrow.*

---

dah. Leah, then finding that she was not likely to bear another son soon, may, in the state of jealousy between the two sisters, have given Zilpah to Jacob, of whom were born Asher and Naphtali, and then again in the very last year of the seven, at the beginning of it, Leah may have borne Issachar, and at the end of it Zebulun. Another difficulty has been found in Reuben's finding the mandrakes: but there is no reason why he should have been more than four years old, when he discovered them, and attracted by their flowers and fruits, brought them to his mother. (See Petav. 'De Doct. Temp.' x. 19; Heid. II. Exer. xv. xviii.; Kurtz 'on the Old Covenant,' in loc.; Keil in loc. &c., and note at end of ch. xxxi.)

27. *I have learned by experience*] **I have learned by divination**, literally either "I have hissed, muttered" (so Knobel on ch. xliv. 5), or more probably, "I have divined by omens deduced from serpents" (Boch. 'Hier.' I. 20; Gesen. 'Th.' p. 875). The heathenism of Laban's household appears by ch. xxxi. 19, 32; and though Laban acknowledged the LORD as Jacob's God, this did not prevent him from using idolatrous and heathenish practices. It is however quite possible that the word here used may have acquired a wider signification, originally meaning to "divine," but then having the general sense of "investigate," "discover," "learn by enquiry," &c.

30. *increased*] Lit. **broken forth**.

since my coming] Lit. "at my foot," *i.e.* God sent blessing to thee following on my footsteps, wherever I went. (See Ges. 'Th.' p. 1262.)

32. *removing from thence all the spotted and speckled cattle*] It is said, that in the East the sheep are generally white, very rarely black or spotted, and that the goats are black or brown, rarely speckled with white. Jacob therefore proposes to separate from the flock all the spotted and speckled sheep and goats, which would be comparatively few, and to tend only that part of the flock which was pure white or black. He is then to have for his hire only those lambs and kids, born of the unspeckled flock, which themselves should be marked with spots and speckles and ringstrakes. Laban naturally thinks that these will be very few; so he accepts the offer, and, to make matters the surer, he removes all the spotted and ringstraked goats, and all the sheep with any brown in them, three days' journey from the flock of white sheep and brown goats to be left under Jacob's care (see

betwixt himself and Jacob: and Jacob fed the rest of Laban's flocks.

37 ¶ And Jacob took him rods of green poplar, and of the hazel and chesnut tree; and pilled white strakes in them, and made the white appear which *was* in the rods.

38 And he set the rods which he had pilled before the flocks in the gutters in the watering troughs when the flocks came to drink, that they should conceive when they came to drink.

39 And the flocks conceived before the rods, and brought forth cattle ringstraked, speckled, and spotted.

40 And Jacob did separate the lambs, and set the faces of the flocks toward the ringstraked, and all the brown in the flock of Laban; and he put his own flocks by themselves, and put them not unto Laban's cattle.

41 And it came to pass, whensoever the stronger cattle did conceive, that Jacob laid the rods before the eyes of the cattle in the gutters, that they might conceive among the rods.

42 But when the cattle were feeble, he put *them* not in: so the feebler were Laban's, and the stronger Jacob's.

43 And the man increased exceedingly, and had much cattle, and maidservants, and menservants, and camels, and asses.

CHAPTER XXXI.

1 Jacob upon displeasure departeth secretly. 19
Rachel stealeth her father's images. 22 Laban
pursueth after him, 26 and complaineth of
the wrong. 34 Rachel's policy to hide the
images. 36 Jacob's complaint of Laban. 43
The covenant of Laban and Jacob at Galeed.

AND he heard the words of Laban's sons, saying, Jacob hath taken away all that *was* our father's; and of *that* which *was* our father's hath he gotten all this glory.

2 And Jacob beheld the countenance of Laban, and, behold, it *was* not toward him † as before. († Heb. *as yesterday and the day before.*)

3 And the LORD said unto Jacob, Return unto the land of thy fathers, and to thy kindred; and I will be with thee.

4 And Jacob sent and called Rachel and Leah to the field unto his flock,

5 And said unto them, I see your father's countenance, that it *is* not toward me as before; but the God of my father hath been with me.

6 And ye know that with all my power I have served your father.

7 And your father hath deceived me, and changed my wages ten times; but God suffered him not to hurt me.

8 If he said thus, The speckled shall be thy wages; then all the cattle bare speckled: and if he said thus,

---

vv. 35, 36), lest any of them might stray unto Jacob's flock and so be claimed by him, or any lambs or kids should be born like them in Jacob's flock.

37. *poplar*] So Celsius ('Hierobot.' I. 292), and many other authorities after the Vulg., but the LXX. and Arab. have the storax tree, which is adopted by Gesenius (p. 740) and many others.

hazel] **Almond**, Ges. (p. 747).

chesnut tree] **Plane-tree**, Ges. (p. 1071).

40. *And Jacob did separate the lambs*] The apparent inconsistency of this with the rest of the narrative, especially with v. 36, has induced some commentators to suspect a corruption in the text. The meaning, however, appears to be, that Jacob separated those lambs, which were born after the artifice mentioned above, keeping the spotted lambs and kids apart; but though he thus separated them, he contrived that the ewes and she goats should have the speckled lambs and kids in sight. "His own flocks" mentioned in the latter part of the verse were the young cattle that were born ringstraked and speckled; "Laban's cattle," on the contrary, were those of uniform colour in the flock tended by Jacob; not that flock which Laban had separated by three days' journey from Jacob.

CHAP. XXXI. 2. *as before*] Lit. "as yesterday and the day before."

5. *the God of my father hath been with me*] *i.e.* God has been present with me and has protected me. Jacob calls him the God of his father, so distinguishing the Most High from the gods of the nations and from the idols, which perhaps the family of Laban had worshipped. vv. 19, 30.

7. *ten times*] *i.e.* probably "very frequently." Cp. Num. xiv. 22; Job xix. 3.

The ringstraked shall be thy hire;
then bare all the cattle ringstraked.
9 Thus God hath taken away the
cattle of your father, and given *them*
to me.
10 And it came to pass at the time
that the cattle conceived, that I lifted
up mine eyes, and saw in a dream,
‖ Or, *he goats.* and, behold, the ‖rams which leaped
upon the cattle *were* ringstraked, speckled,
and grisled.
11 And the angel of God spake
unto me in a dream, *saying*, Jacob:
And I said, Here *am* I.
12 And he said, Lift up now thine
eyes, and see, all the rams which leap
upon the cattle *are* ringstraked, speckled,
and grisled: for I have seen all
that Laban doeth unto thee.
a chap. 28. 18. 13 I *am* the God of Beth-el, *a* where
thou anointedst the pillar, *and* where
thou vowedst a vow unto me: now
arise, get thee out from this land, and
return unto the land of thy kindred.
14 And Rachel and Leah answered
and said unto him, *Is there* yet any
portion or inheritance for us in our
father's house?
15 Are we not counted of him
strangers? for he hath sold us, and
hath quite devoured also our money.
16 For all the riches which God
hath taken from our father, that *is*
ours, and our children's: now then,
whatsoever God hath said unto thee,
do.
17 ¶ Then Jacob rose up, and set
his sons and his wives upon camels;
18 And he carried away all his
cattle, and all his goods which he had
gotten, the cattle of his getting, which
he had gotten in Padan-aram, for to
go to Isaac his father in the land of
Canaan.
19 And Laban went to shear his
sheep: and Rachel had stolen the † Heb. *teraphim*
† images that *were* her father's. † Heb. *the heart of Laban*
20 And Jacob stole away † una-

10. *the rams*] **The he goats.**

grisled] *i.e.* "sprinkled as with hail," the literal meaning of the word "grisled."

13. *I am the God of Beth-el*] (Heb. "El-Beth-el.") In v. 11 it is said, "the angel of God spake unto me." The Jewish commentators explain this by saying that God spoke through the mouth of the angel, and therefore though the angel actually spoke to Jacob, yet the words are the words of God. The Christian fathers generally believe all such visions to have been visions of the Son of God, who is both God and the angel of God: see on ch. xvi. 7.

There is no necessary contradiction between this dream and the account of Jacob's artifice given in the last chapter. If the dream occurred just before the flight of Jacob from Laban, it would be an indication to Jacob that all his artifices would have had no effect, had it not been God's pleasure that he should grow rich. The labours of the husbandman do not prosper but through the blessing of God. It seems, however, not improbable that Jacob is here relating to his wives two dreams, that concerning the sheep and goats having occurred at the beginning of his agreement with Laban, and that in which he was commanded to depart from Padan-aram just before his actual departure. This was suggested by Nachmanides and is approved by Rosenmüller. If so, we may infer, that Jacob believed the promise that the sheep which were to be his hire should multiply rapidly: but yet consistently with his mixed character, partly believing and partly impatient of the fulfilment, he adopted natural means for bringing about this event which he desired (so Kurtz and apparently Keil).

15. *he hath sold us*] Probably referring to Laban's giving his daughter to Jacob as wages for his service.

19. *And Laban went to shear his sheep*] The force of the tenses in the Hebrew will perhaps be better explained as follows: "Now Laban had gone to shear his sheep, and (or, whereupon) Rachel stole the Teraphim which were her father's, and Jacob stole away unawares to (lit. stole the heart of) Laban the Syrian." There may be a series of paronomasias in the Hebrew, "Rachel *stole* the Teraphim," "Jacob *stole* the heart of Laban;" and again, "the heart of Laban" is *Leb-Laban*, the first syllable of Laban corresponding with the word for "heart."

images] **Teraphim.** These were undoubtedly images in the human form, but whether whole length figures or only busts has been much doubted. In 1 S. xix. 13, Michal puts teraphim (the plural perhaps for a single image) in David's bed to deceive the messengers of Saul; which looks as if the image was of the size of life. In the present history as Rachel hides them under the camel's saddle, they were probably not so large. Laban calls them his gods v. 30, which corresponds with

wares to Laban the Syrian, in that he
told him not that he fled.
21 So he fled with all that he had;
and he rose up, and passed over the
river, and set his face *toward* the
mount Gilead.
22 And it was told Laban on the
third day that Jacob was fled.
23 And he took his brethren with
him, and pursued after him seven
days' journey; and they overtook him
in the mount Gilead.
24 And God came to Laban the
Syrian in a dream by night, and said
unto him, Take heed that thou speak
not to Jacob †either good or bad.
25 ¶ Then Laban overtook Jacob.
Now Jacob had pitched his tent in
the mount: and Laban with his brethren pitched in the mount of Gilead.
26 And Laban said to Jacob,
What hast thou done, that thou hast
stolen away unawares to me, and
carried away my daughters, as captives *taken* with the sword?
27 Wherefore didst thou flee away
secretly, and †steal away from me;
and didst not tell me, that I might
have sent thee away with mirth, and
with songs, with tabret, and with harp?

† Heb. *from good to bad.*

† Heb. *hast stolen me.*

28 And hast not suffered me to
kiss my sons and my daughters? thou
hast now done foolishly in *so* doing.
29 It is in the power of my hand
to do you hurt: but the God of your
father spake unto me yesternight, saying, Take thou heed that thou speak
not to Jacob either good or bad.
30 And now, *though* thou wouldest needs be gone, because thou sore
longedst after thy father's house, *yet*
wherefore hast thou stolen my gods?
31 And Jacob answered and said
to Laban, Because I was afraid: for
I said, Peradventure thou wouldest
take by force thy daughters from
me.
32 With whomsoever thou findest
thy gods, let him not live: before
our brethren discern thou what *is*
thine with me, and take *it* to thee.
For Jacob knew not that Rachel had
stolen them.
33 And Laban went into Jacob's
tent, and into Leah's tent, and into
the two maidservants' tents; but he
found *them* not. Then went he out
of Leah's tent, and entered into Rachel's tent.
34 Now Rachel had taken the im-

---

what we find afterwards concerning their worship (see Judg. xvii. 5; xviii. 14, 17, 18, 20). They are condemned with other idolatrous practices (1 S. xv. 23; 2 K. xxiii. 24), and in later times we find that they were consulted for purposes of divination (Ezek. xxi. 21; Zech. x. 2). They have been generally considered as similar to the Penates of the classical nations. Most probably they were of the nature of a fetish, used for purposes of magic and divination, rather than strictly objects of divine worship. In them we perhaps see the earliest form of patriarchal idolatry; a knowledge of the true God not wholly gone, but images, perhaps of ancestors, preserved, revered and consulted. There have been numerous conjectures as to the derivation of the name. The majority of recent Hebraists refer to the Arab. root *tarafa*, "to enjoy the good things of life," and think that teraphim were preserved and honoured, like the penates, or the household fairy, to secure domestic prosperity (see Ges. 'Thes.' p. 1520). Other but improbable derivations are that suggested by Castell from the Syriac *Teraph*, "to enquire," alluding to their use as oracles; and that by Prof. Lee, from the Æthiopic root, signifying "to remain, survive," so that the name may originally have meant "relics." The motive of Rachel's theft has been as much debated as the root of the word and the use of the images. It is at all events probable, that Rachel, though a worshipper of Jacob's God, may not have thrown off all the superstitious credulity of her own house, and that she stole the teraphim for some superstitious purpose.

20. *stole away unawares to Laban*] Lit. "stole the heart of Laban," i.e. deceived his mind and intelligence.

21. *the river*] The Euphrates.

mount Gilead] So called by anticipation. It received the name from what occurred below, vv. 46, 47.

26. *as captives taken with the sword*] As captives of the sword.

29. *It is in the power of my hand*] So probably, not as Hitzig, Knobel, Keil, &c., "my hand is for God," i.e. my hand serves me for God, is powerful.

ages, and put them in the camel's
furniture, and sat upon them. And
† Heb. *felt.* Laban †searched all the tent, but
found *them* not.
35 And she said to her father, Let
it not displease my lord that I cannot
rise up before thee; for the custom of
women *is* upon me. And he searched, but found not the images.
36 ¶ And Jacob was wroth, and
chode with Laban: and Jacob answered and said to Laban, What *is*
my trespass? what *is* my sin, that
thou hast so hotly pursued after me?
† Heb. *felt.* 37 Whereas thou hast †searched
all my stuff, what hast thou found of
all thy household stuff? set *it* here
before my brethren and thy brethren,
that they may judge betwixt us both.
38 This twenty years *have* I *been*
with thee; thy ewes and thy she
goats have not cast their young, and
the rams of thy flock have I not eaten.
39 That which was torn *of beasts*
I brought not unto thee; I bare the
b Ex. 22. 12. loss of it; of *b*my hand didst thou
require it, *whether* stolen by day, or
stolen by night.
40 *Thus* I was; in the day the
drought consumed me, and the frost
by night; and my sleep departed from
mine eyes.
41 Thus have I been twenty years
in thy house; I served thee fourteen
years for thy two daughters, and six
years for thy cattle: and thou hast
changed my wages ten times.
42 Except the God of my father,
the God of Abraham, and the fear of
Isaac, had been with me, surely thou
hadst sent me away now empty. God
hath seen mine affliction and the labour of my hands, and rebuked *thee*
yesternight.
43 ¶ And Laban answered and
said unto Jacob, *These* daughters *are*
my daughters, and *these* children *are*
my children, and *these* cattle *are* my
cattle, and all that thou seest *is* mine:
and what can I do this day unto
these my daughters, or unto their
children which they have born?
44 Now therefore come thou, let
us make a covenant, I and thou; and
let it be for a witness between me
and thee.
45 And Jacob took a stone, and
set it up *for* a pillar.
46 And Jacob said unto his brethren, Gather stones; and they took
stones, and made an heap: and they
did eat there upon the heap.
47 And Laban called it ‖ Jegar-sa- ‖ That is, *the heap of witness.*
hadutha: but Jacob called it Galeed.

34] *the camel's furniture*] The word for furniture (*Car*, perhaps cognate with *currus*, *car*, *carry*, *carriage*, &c.), seems to have signified a covered seat, litter, or palanquin, which was placed on the back of the camel for carrying women and children and supplied with curtains for concealing them, not only from sun and wind, but also from public view (see Ges. 'Thes.' p. 715 and the authorities there referred to). The Teraphim, being probably not of large size, would easily be concealed under such apparatus.

38. *This twenty years*] See above, v. 41. On the chronology, see Note A at the end of this chapter.

40. *in the day the drought consumed me, and the frost by night*] In the East it is common for extremely hot days to be succeeded by very cold nights.

42. *the fear of Isaac*] That is to say, the object of Isaac's reverential awe. The whole history of Isaac points him out to us as a man of subdued spirit, whilst his father Abraham appears as of livelier faith and as admitted to a more intimate communion with God. Hence Jacob not unnaturally calls his father's God "the fear of Isaac."

47. *Laban called it Jegar-sahadutha: but Jacob called it Galeed*] Jegar-sahadutha is the Aramaic (Chaldee or Syriac) equivalent for the Hebrew Galeed; both meaning the "heap of witness." It appears therefore that at this time Jacob spoke Hebrew whilst his uncle Laban spoke Syriac. We can only account for this by supposing either that the family of Nahor originally spoke Syriac and that Abraham and his descendants learned Hebrew in Canaan, where evidently the Hebrew language was indigenous when he first went there, having probably been acquired by the Hamitic Canaanites from an earlier Shemite race—or else, which is not otherwise supported, that the ancestors of Laban having left the early seat of the family had unlearned their original Hebrew and acquired the Syriac dialect of Padan-aram.

48 And Laban said, This heap *is*
a witness between me and thee this
day. Therefore was the name of it
called Galeed;
49 And ‖Mizpah; for he said, The
LORD watch between me and thee,
when we are absent one from another.
50 If thou shalt afflict my daughters, or if thou shalt take *other* wives
beside my daughters, no man *is* with
us; see, God *is* witness betwixt me
and thee.
51 And Laban said to Jacob, Behold this heap, and behold *this* pillar,
which I have cast betwixt me and
thee;
52 This heap *be* witness, and *this*
pillar *be* witness, that I will not pass
over this heap to thee, and that thou
shalt not pass over this heap and this
pillar unto me, for harm.
53 The God of Abraham, and the
God of Nahor, the God of their father, judge betwixt us. And Jacob
sware by the fear of his father Isaac.
54 Then Jacob ‖offered sacrifice
upon the mount, and called his brethren to eat bread: and they did eat
bread, and tarried all night in the
mount.
55 And early in the morning Laban rose up, and kissed his sons and
his daughters, and blessed them: and
Laban departed, and returned unto
his place.

‖ That is, *a beacon*, or, *watch-tower*.

‖ Or, *killed beasts*.

---

49. *Mizpah*] *i.e.* "watch-tower."

The LORD watch] Here Laban adopts both the language and the theology of Jacob. He calls the place Mizpah, which is a Hebrew name, and he acknowledges the watchfulness of JEHOVAH the God of Abraham.

53. *The God of Abraham, and the God of Nahor, the God of their father, judge between us*] The verb *judge* is in the plural. This looks as if Laban acknowledged JEHOVAH as Jacob's God and Abraham's God, but being himself descended from Nahor and Terah and doubting whether the God who called Abraham from his father's house was the same as the God whom Terah and Nahor had served before, he couples the God of Abraham with the God of Nahor and Terah, and calls on both to witness and judge. Polytheism had still hold on Laban, though he felt the power of the God of Jacob We learn from Josh. xxiv. 2, that the ancestors of Abraham worshipped strange gods. There is a very marked unity of purpose throughout this chapter in the use of the names of the Most High, utterly inconsistent with the modern notion of a diversity of authors, according to some not fewer than four, in the different portions of the same chapter. To Jacob He is JEHOVAH, v. 3, and the God of his father, v. 5, &c., whilst Laban acknowledges Him as the God of Jacob's father, v. 29. Once more Jacob refers to Him as the God of Abraham and the fear of Isaac (v. 42), by appeal to whom it was but likely that Laban would be moved; and lastly Laban, being so moved, himself appeals to the watchfulness of JEHOVAH, v. 49, but yet joins with Him, as possibly a distinct Being, the God of their common ancestor Nahor.

NOTE A on CHAP. XXXI. V. 41. ON THE CHRONOLOGY OF JACOB'S LIFE.

(1) Difficulty of the question. Common reckoning. (2) Suggestion of Dr Kennicott. (3) Dates on this hypothesis. (4) Greater facility for explaining the events thus obtained.

THE difficulties in the Chronology of the life of Jacob and his sons are very great, so great that Le Clerc has said, "There occur entanglements (*nodi*) in these things which no one has yet unravelled, nor do I believe will any one ever unravel them." It has been generally held by commentators, Jewish and Christian, that Isaac was 137 and Jacob 77 when Jacob received his father's blessing, and left his father's house to go to Padan-aram. (See note, ch. xxxvii. 1.) This calculation rests mainly on the following two points: the 1st is that Joseph was born just fourteen years after Jacob went to Haran, *i.e.* at the end of the second hebdomade which Jacob served for his wives; an inference, which would oblige us to conclude that all the sons of Jacob except Benjamin, eleven in number, were born in six years, a thing not quite impossible, but highly improbable (see on ch. xxx. 25). The second is, that Jacob, in vv. 38, 41, of this ch. xxxi, seems to say that his whole sojourn in Padan-aram was only twenty years. If these points be made out, we cannot deny the conclusion, that as Joseph was 39 when Jacob was 130, and so born when Jacob was 91, therefore Jacob must have been $91 - 14 = 77$, when he fled from Beer-sheba to Padan-aram.

As regards the first point, however, it has

already been seen (note on ch. xxx. 23), that it is not necessary to conclude that Jacob should have wished to leave Laban immediately on the conclusion of his 14 years' servitude. On the contrary, with his children too young to carry on so long a journey, with but little independent substance, and with the fear of Esau before his eyes, it is far more likely that he should have been willing to remain longer in the service of Laban. But, if this be so, we have then an indefinite time left us for this additional sojourn, limited only by the words "when Rachel had born Joseph" (ch. xxx. 25). Jacob may have lived and worked for twenty years longer with Laban, and not have asked for his dismissal, till Joseph was old enough to travel, or at all events till he was born.

As to the second point, almost all commentators take the statements in vv. 38 and 41 as identical, v. 41 being but a repetition, with greater detail, of the statement in v. 38, as appears in the translation of the Authorized Version. It has, however, been suggested by Dr Kennicott, that very probably the twenty years in v. 38 are not the same twenty years as those mentioned in v. 41, and that the sense of the Hebrew would be better expressed as follows, v. 38, "one twenty years I was with thee" (*i.e.* taking care of thy flocks for thee but not in thy house); and (v. 41), "another twenty years I was for myself in thy house, serving thee fourteen years for thy two daughters and six years for thy cattle." This, he contends, is a legitimate mode of rendering the repeated particle (*zeh*, *zeh*). Each mention of the twenty years is introduced with the word *zeh*, "this," which word, when repeated, is used in opposition or by way of distinction (see Ex. xiv. 20; Job xxi. 23, 25; Eccl. vi. 5). He understands Jacob therefore as saying, that he had served Laban fourteen years for his wives, after that he had for twenty years taken care of his cattle, not as a servant but as a neighbour and friend; and then, not satisfied to go on thus without profit, at last for six years more he served for wages, during which short period Laban had changed his hire 10 times.

If this reasoning be correct, and Bp Horsley has said that Dr Kennicott assigns unanswerable reasons for his opinion, then the following table will give the dates of the chief events in Jacob's life.

	Years of Jacob's life	
	0	Jacob and Esau born.
	40	Esau marries two Hittite wives, Gen. xxvi. 34.
14 years' service.	57	Jacob goes to Padan-aram, Isaac being 117.
	58	Esau goes to Ishmael and marries his daughter, Gen. xxviii. 9.
	63	Ishmael dies, aged 137, Gen. xxv. 17.
	64	Jacob marries Leah and Rachel, Gen. xxix. 20, 21, 27, 28.
		Reuben, Simeon, Levi, and Judah, born of Leah.
		Dan and Naphtali born of Bilhah.
	71	End of fourteen years' service.
20 years' assistance.	72	Beginning of 20 years mentioned in Gen. xxxi. 38.
		Gad and Asher born of Zilpah.
		Issachar and Zebulun born of Leah.
		Dinah born.
	91	Joseph born of Rachel.
6 years' service for cattle.	92	Agreement made, Gen. xxx. 25—34.
		Events in the family unknown.
	97	Flight from Padan-aram.
	98	Benjamin born, Rachel dies.
	108	Joseph at 17 is carried to Egypt, Gen. xxxvii. 2.
	120	Isaac dies at 180, Gen. xxxv. 28.
	121	Joseph, aged 30, Governor of Egypt.
	130	Jacob goes down to Egypt, Gen. xlvi. 1.
	147	Jacob dies, Gen. xlvii. 28.

It is not possible to date accurately the events in ch. xxxiv., xxxviii., but the above seems a far more probable chronology than that commonly acquiesced in. According to the common calculation, Judah and his sons Er and Onan must have been quite children when they married, whereas the assigning 40 instead of 20 years to the sojourn of Jacob in Padan-aram, will allow time for them to have grown up, though even so their marriages must have been for that time unusually early. The common calculation, which makes Jacob 84 at his marriage, whilst his son Judah could not have been more than 20, and his grandchildren Er and Onan not above 15 when they married (see Keil on ch. xxxviii.), must surely require some correction, even allowing for the length of patriarchal lives on the one side and for the early age of eastern marriages on the other.

CHAPTER XXXII.

1 *Jacob's vision at Mahanaim.* 3 *His message to Esau.* 6 *He is afraid of Esau's coming.* 9 *He prayeth for deliverance.* 13 *He sendeth a present to Esau.* 24 *He wrestleth with an angel at Peniel, where he is called Israel.* 31 *He halteth.*

AND Jacob went on his way, and
the angels of God met him.
2 And when Jacob saw them, he
said, This *is* God's host: and he
called the name of that place ‖ Mahanaim. ‖ That is, *two hosts, or, camps*
3 And Jacob sent messengers before him to Esau his brother unto the
land of Seir, the † country of Edom. † Heb. *field.*
4 And he commanded them, say-

ing, Thus shall ye speak unto my
lord Esau; Thy servant Jacob saith
thus, I have sojourned with Laban,
and stayed there until now:
5 And I have oxen, and asses,
flocks, and menservants, and womenservants: and I have sent to tell my
lord, that I may find grace in thy
sight.
6 ¶ And the messengers returned
to Jacob, saying, We came to thy
brother Esau, and also he cometh to
meet thee, and four hundred men
with him.
7 Then Jacob was greatly afraid
and distressed: and he divided the
people that *was* with him, and the
flocks, and herds, and the camels, into two bands;
8 And said, If Esau come to the
one company, and smite it, then the
other company which is left shall
escape.
9 ¶ And Jacob said, O God of
my father Abraham, and God of my
father Isaac, the LORD which saidst
unto me, [a] Return unto thy country,
and to thy kindred, and I will deal
well with thee:
10 † I am not worthy of the least

[a] chap. 31. 13.

† Heb. *I am less than all, &c.*

CHAP. XXXII. 1. *the angels of God met him*] The conjectures of various Jewish interpreters concerning this vision of angels may be seen in Heidegger, Tom. II. Ex. XV. § 37. The real purpose of it seems to have been this. When Jacob was flying from Esau's anger into Mesopotamia, he had a vision of angels ascending and descending on the ladder of God. He was thus assured of God's providential care over him, and mysteriously taught that there was a way from heaven to earth and from earth to heaven. Now he is again about to fall into the power of Esau; and so the angels encamped, perhaps on each side of him (*Mahanaim*, v. 2, signifying "two camps"), may have been sent to teach him, as a similar vision taught afterwards the servant of Elisha (2 K. vi. 16, 17), that, though he was encompassed with danger, there were more with him than could be against him, or, as the Psalmist wrote afterwards, that "the angel of the LORD encampeth round about them that fear him, and delivereth them" (Ps. xxxiv. 7). Thus Josephus ('A. J.' I. 20) says, "these visions were vouchsafed to Jacob returning into Canaan, to encourage him with happy hopes of what should befal him afterwards," and St Chrysost. ('Hom. 58 in Gen.'), "the fear of Laban having passed away, there succeeded to it the fear of Esau; therefore the merciful Lord, willing that the pious man should be encouraged and his fear dispelled, ordained that he should see this vision of angels."

2. *Mahanaim*] *i.e.* "two camps." Some have thought the dual here used for the plural; others that Jacob thought of his own camp and the camp of angels. (So Abenezra, and after him Clericus.) More likely the angels were encamped on the right-hand and on the left, so seeming to surround and protect Jacob (see on v. 1). The place called Mahanaim was in the tribe of Gad, and was assigned to the Levites, Josh. xxi. 38. The name *Mahneh* is still retained in the supposed site of the ancient town (Robinson).

3. *unto the land of Seir, the country of Edom*] It does not follow necessarily from this verse, that Seir had by this time become Esau's permanent place of residence. The historian calls Seir the country of Edom, because it had become so long before Moses wrote. Esau was a great hunter, and very probably a conqueror, who took possession of Seir, driving out or subjugating the Horites. It may have been for this very conquest, that he was now at the head of 400 armed men (v. 6). He had not yet removed his household from Canaan (ch. xxxvi. 6); and did not settle permanently in his newly conquered possession till after his father's death, when, yielding to the assignment made to Jacob by Isaac's blessing, he retires to Idumæa, and leaves Canaan to Jacob (ch. xxxvi. 1—8). (See Kurtz in loc.)

7. *Jacob was greatly afraid and distressed*] Though he had just seen a vision of angels, he was not unnaturally alarmed at the apparently hostile approach of Esau. He makes therefore all preparation for that approach, and then takes refuge in prayer. His faith was imperfect, but he was a religious man, and so he seeks in his terror help from God.

9. *O God of my father Abraham, and God of my father Isaac, the LORD*] This combination of names is natural and exact. He appeals to the Most High as the Covenant God, who had given promises to his fathers, of which promises he himself was the heir, and who had revealed Himself to the chosen family as the self-existent JEHOVAH, who would be their God. The whole prayer is one of singular beauty and piety.

10. *I am not worthy of the least of all the mercies*] Lit. "I am less than all the mercies."

of all the mercies, and of all the
truth, which thou hast shewed unto
thy servant; for with my staff I
passed over this Jordan; and now I
am become two bands.
11 Deliver me, I pray thee, from
the hand of my brother, from the
hand of Esau: for I fear him, lest
he will come and smite me, *and* the
† Heb. *upon.* mother † with the children.
12 And thou saidst, I will surely
do thee good, and make thy seed as
the sand of the sea, which cannot be
numbered for multitude.
13 ¶ And he lodged there that
same night; and took of that which
came to his hand a present for Esau
his brother;
14 Two hundred she goats, and
twenty he goats, two hundred ewes,
and twenty rams,
15 Thirty milch camels with their
colts, forty kine, and ten bulls, twenty
she asses, and ten foals.
16 And he delivered *them* into the
hand of his servants, every drove by
themselves; and said unto his servants, Pass over before me, and put
a space betwixt drove and drove.
17 And he commanded the foremost, saying, When Esau my brother meeteth thee, and asketh thee,
saying, Whose *art* thou? and whither goest thou? and whose *are* these
before thee?
18 Then thou shalt say, *They be*
thy servant Jacob's; it *is* a present
sent unto my lord Esau: and, behold,
also he *is* behind us.
19 And so commanded he the second, and the third, and all that followed the droves, saying, On this
manner shall ye speak unto Esau,
when ye find him.
20 And say ye moreover, Behold,
thy servant Jacob *is* behind us. For
he said, I will appease him with the
present that goeth before me, and
afterward I will see his face; peradventure he will accept † of me. † Heb. *my face.*
21 So went the present over before
him: and himself lodged that night in
the company.
22 And he rose up that night,
and took his two wives, and his
two womenservants, and his eleven
sons, and passed over the ford Jabbok.
23 And he took them, and † sent † Heb. *caused to pass.*
them over the brook, and sent over
that he had.
24 ¶ And Jacob was left alone;

---

11. *the mother with the children*] Lit. "upon the children." Whence some have thought that there was allusion to the mother protecting the child, as a bird covers its young (Tuch, Knobel, Keil), or to the slaying of the child before the parent's eyes, and then the parent upon him (Ros.); but the sense seems correctly expressed by "with," as in Ex. xxv. 22; Num. xx. 11; Deut. xvi. 3; Job xxxviii. 32, &c. (See Ges. 'Thes.' p. 1027.)

13. *of that which came to his hand*] or perhaps "that which had come to his hand," *i.e.* into his possession, what he possessed.

20. *I will appease him*, &c.] The sentence literally rendered would be, "I will cover his face with the present that goeth before me, and afterward I will see his face, peradventure he will accept my face." "To cover the eyes or the face" was an expression apparently signifying to induce the person to turn away from or connive at a fault. (Ges. pp. 700, 706.) "To accept or lift up the face" was equivalent to accepting a person favourably (*Ib.* p. 915).

22. *the ford Jabbok*] or "the ford of Jabbok." The name Jabbok is either derived from *bakak*, "to pour forth, to gush forth," or from *abak*, "to wrestle," from the wrestling of Jacob there. It flowed into the Jordan about half way between the Dead Sea and the sea of Galilee, at a point nearly opposite to Shechem. It is now called *Zerka*, *i.e.* "blue" (Ges. 'Thes.' p. 232).

23. *the brook*] The word signifies either a brook, a torrent, or the bed of a torrent, sometimes dry and sometimes flowing, like the Arabic *Wady*.

24. *Jacob was left alone*] He remained to the last that he might see all his family pass safely through the ford, that he might prevent anything being left behind through carelessness; and most probably that he might once more give himself to earnest prayer for God's protection in his expected meeting with his brother Esau.

and there wrestled a man with him
until the † breaking of the day.
25 And when he saw that he prevailed not against him, he touched
the hollow of his thigh; and the
hollow of Jacob's thigh was out of
joint, as he wrestled with him.
26 And he said, Let me go, for the
day breaketh. And he said, [b] I will
not let thee go, except thou bless me.

† Heb. *ascending of the morning.*

[b] Hos. 12. 4.

---

there wrestled a man with him] He is called "the angel," Hos. xii. 4, and Jacob says of him (v. 30), "I have seen God face to face." The Jews of course believed that he was a created angel, and said that he was the angel of Esau, *i.e.* either Esau's special guardian angel (cp. Acts xii. 15), or the angel that presided over Esau's country (cp. Dan. x. 13). So Abenezra and Abarbanel. Many Christian commentators also prefer to consider this a vision of a created angel, as thinking it inconsistent with the greatness of the Creator to have manifested Himself in this manner to Jacob. Most of the fathers, however, thought this to have been one of the manifestations of the Logos, of the eternal Son, anticipatory of His incarnation. Theodoret (Qu. 92 in Gen.) argues thus at length. (See also Justin M. 'Dial.' § 126; Tertull. 'Contra Marcion.' c. 3; Euseb. 'H. E.' I. 22; August. 'De C. D.' XVI. 39, &c. &c.). From vv. 29, 30, this seems the true opinion. The word for 'wrestle" (*abak*) is derived from *abak*, "dust," from the rolling of athletes in the dust when wrestling with each other.

until the breaking of the day] lit. "till the rising of the dawn."

25. *when he saw that he prevailed not against him*] There must have been some deep significance in this wrestling, in which an Angel, or more probably the God of angels, Himself "the Angel of the LORD," prevailed not against a man. The difficulty of believing that man could prevail against God led to some forced interpretations, such as that of Origen ('De Principiis,' Lib. III.), and Jerome ('in Epist. ad Ephes.' c. VI.), that Jacob wrestled against evil spirits, and that the "Man" is said to have wrestled *with* him in the sense of assisting him, wrestling on his side; an interpretation refuted by the words of the "Man" Himself in v. 28. The mystical meaning of the whole transaction seems probably to be of this kind. The time was an important epoch in Jacob's history. It was a turning-point in his life. There had been much most faulty in his character; which had led him to much trouble, and subjected him to a long penitential and reformatory discipline. He was now returning after an exile, of 20 or more probably 40 years, to the land of his birth, which had been promised to him for his inheritance. It was a great crisis. Should he fall under the power of Esau and so suffer to the utmost for his former sins? or should he obtain mercy and be received back to his father's house as the heir of the promises? This eventful night, this passage of the Jabbok, was to decide; and the mysterious conflict, in which by Divine mercy and strength he is permitted to prevail, is vouchsafed to him as an indication that his repentance, matured by long schooling and discipline and manifested in fervent and humble prayer, is accepted with God and blessed by the Son of God, whose ancestor in the flesh he is now once more formally constituted.

the hollow of the thigh] The socket of the hip-joint, the hollow place like the palm of a hand (Heb. *Caph*) into which the neck-bone of the thigh is inserted. The reason of this act of the Angel was very probably lest Jacob should be puffed up by the "abundance of the revelations;" he might think that by his own strength and not by grace he had prevailed with God; as St Paul had the thorn in the flesh sent to him lest he "should be exalted above measure," 2 Cor. xii. 7. (So Theodoret in loc.).

26. *Let me go, for the day breaketh*] Lit. "for the dawn ariseth." The contest had taken place during the later hours of the night. It was now right that it should be ended: for the time had arrived, the breaking of the day, when Jacob must prepare to meet Esau and to appease his anger. It was for Jacob's sake, not for His own convenience, that the Divine wrestler desired to go. (So Abarbanel, Heidegger, &c. &c.).

except thou bless me] Jacob had plainly discovered that his antagonist was a heavenly Visitor. Though he had been permitted to prevail in the contest, he still desired blessing for the future.

28. *Israel: for as a prince hast thou power*], The verb *Sarah* and its cognate *Sūr* signify "to contend with," and also "to be a prince or leader." See Judg. ix. 22; Hos. xii. 4 (Ges. pp. 1326, 1338, Ros. in loc.). It is quite possible that both senses are conveyed by the word, and it might be rendered either, "thou hast contended with God," or "thou hast been a prince with God." The Authorised Version combines both. The best Vss., LXX., Vulg., render, "Thou hast had power with God, and how much more wilt thou prevail with men," which has been followed by many moderns, as Heidegger, Rosenm., &c. The sense is thus rendered more perspicuous, as implying a promise of safety from

27 And he said unto him, What *is*
thy name? And he said, Jacob.
28 And he said, [c] Thy name shall
be called no more Jacob, but Israel:
for as a prince hast thou power with
God and with men, and hast prevailed.
29 And Jacob asked *him*, and said,
Tell *me*, I pray thee, thy name. And
he said, Wherefore *is* it *that* thou
dost ask after my name? And he
blessed him there.
30 And Jacob called the name of
the place ‖ Peniel: for I have seen
God face to face, and my life is preserved.
31 And as he passed over Penuel
the sun rose upon him, and he halted
upon his thigh.
32 Therefore the children of Israel
eat not *of* the sinew which shrank,
which *is* upon the hollow of the
thigh, unto this day: because he
touched the hollow of Jacob's thigh
in the sinew that shrank.

c chap. 35. 10.

‖ That is, *the face of God.*

CHAPTER XXXIII.

1 *The kindness of Jacob and Esau at their meeting.* 17 *Jacob cometh to Succoth.* 18 *At Shalem he buyeth a field, and buildeth an altar called El-elohe-Israel.*

AND Jacob lifted up his eyes, and
looked, and, behold, Esau came,
and with him four hundred men. And
he divided the children unto Leah,
and unto Rachel, and unto the two
handmaids.
2 And he put the handmaids and
their children foremost, and Leah and
her children after, and Rachel and
Joseph hindermost.
3 And he passed over before them,
and bowed himself to the ground
seven times, until he came near to
his brother.
4 And Esau ran to meet him, and
embraced him, and fell on his neck,
and kissed him: and they wept.
5 And he lifted up his eyes, and
saw the women and the children;
and said, Who *are* those † with thee?
And he said, The children which God
hath graciously given thy servant.
6 Then the handmaidens came
near, they and their children, and
they bowed themselves.
7 And Leah also with her children
came near, and bowed themselves:
and after came Joseph near and Rachel, and they bowed themselves.
8 And he said, † What *meanest* thou

† Heb. *to thee?*

† Heb. *What is all this band to thee?*

Esau. The difficulty, however, of thus explaining the particle *Vau* before "hast prevailed" is great.

29. *Wherefore is it that thou dost ask after my name?*] Comp. Judg. xiii. 18, "And the Angel of the Lord said unto him (*i. e.* Manoah), Why askest thou after my name seeing it is secret?" lit. "wonderful." In the present instance perhaps the words mean, "Why dost thou ask my name? as it may be plain to you who I am."

30. *Peniel*] *i. e.* "the face of God." Elsewhere it is always *Penuel*, and the Samaritan Pentateuch and the Vulg. have Penuel here. The LXX. does not give this name itself, but translates it both here and in v. 31. Josephus has Phanuel only. The words only differ by a single line in one letter, and have no difference of meaning. Strabo ('Geogr.' L. XVI. c. 2, §§ 15, 18) mentions a town among the Phœnician cities with a Greek name of the same meaning, viz. *Theou prosopon.*

32. *the sinew which shrank*] This is the rendering of LXX., Vulg., Onk. Many Jewish and Christian commentators have rendered it "the nerve of contraction" or "the nerve of oblivion." Whatever be the literal sense of the words, they doubtless mean the "sciatic nerve," the *nervus ischiadicus*, which is one of the largest in the body, and extends down the thigh and leg to the ankle. The Arabs still use this same word (*Nasheh* or *Naseh*) to designate the sciatic nerve (see Ros. in loc., Ges. 'Thes.' p. 924). The custom prevailing among the Jews to this day of abstaining religiously from eating this sinew seems a lasting monument of the historical truth of this wonderful event in the life of Jacob.

CHAP. XXXIII. 3. *bowed himself to the ground*] A deep oriental bow, not probably such profound prostration as is expressed in ch. xix. 1: "he bowed himself with his face to the ground."

5. *Who are those with thee?*] Lit. "to thee;" *i. e.* that thou hast.

8. *What meanest thou by all this drove*] Lit. "What to thee is all this camp?" The sheep with their shepherds assumed the appearance of a band or troop, hence called "camp."

by all this drove which I met? And
he said, *These are* to find grace in the
sight of my lord.
9 And Esau said, I have enough,
my brother; †keep that thou hast
unto thyself.
10 And Jacob said, Nay, I pray
thee, if now I have found grace in
thy sight, then receive my present at
my hand: for therefore I have seen
thy face, as though I had seen the
face of God, and thou wast pleased
with me.
11 Take, I pray thee, my blessing
that is brought to thee; because God
hath dealt graciously with me, and
because I have enough. And he
urged him, and he took *it*.
12 And he said, Let us take our
journey, and let us go, and I will go
before thee.
13 And he said unto him, My
lord knoweth that the children *are*
tender, and the flocks and herds with
young *are* with me: and if men should
overdrive them one day, all the flock
will die.
14 Let my lord, I pray thee, pass
over before his servant: and I will
lead on softly, †according as the cattle
that goeth before me and the children
be able to endure, until I come unto
my lord unto Seir.
15 And Esau said, Let me now
†leave with thee *some* of the folk that
are with me. And he said, †What
needeth it? let me find grace in the
sight of my lord.
16 ¶ So Esau returned that day on
his way unto Seir.
17 And Jacob journeyed to Succoth, and built him an house, and
made booths for his cattle: therefore
the name of the place is called ‖Suc-
coth.
18 ¶ And Jacob came to Shalem,

† [H]eb. *[L]et that be [th]at is thine.*

† Heb. *according to the foot of the work, &c. and according to the foot of the children.*

† Heb. *set, or, place.*

† Heb. *Wherefore is this?*

‖ That is, *booths*

---

10. *for therefore I have seen thy face,* &c.] Rather "for I have seen thy face, as though I had seen the face of God." The same particles are rendered "because," Gen. xxxviii. 26; "forasmuch as," Num. x. 31; "because," Num. xiv. 43 (see Ges. 'Thes.' p. 682). Jacob pleads as a reason why Esau should accept his present, that Esau's face had seemed as gracious and favourable to him as though it had been God's face. It is highly probable that Jacob here refers to his vision of God in the night past at Peniel. The words he uses are "for I have seen thy face, like a vision of *Peney El-ohim*," *i.e.* "the face of God." It might have seemed likely that Jacob on his meeting with Esau would use the special name of their father's God, JEHOVAH; but this, in addition to the reason given above, would have been like claiming to be the heir of the promises and under the peculiar care of JEHOVAH, which would have been very offensive to Esau.

11. *my blessing*] That is, "this gift which is meant to express good will and affection, offered with prayers for blessing on the recipient" (cp. Judg. i. 15; 1 S. xxv. 32, xxx. 26; 2 K. v. 15).

I have enough] Lit. "I have all."

13. *with young*] **In milk.**

if men should overdrive them one day] Esau's 400 horsemen would be likely to move too rapidly for the milch cattle.

14. *according as the cattle that goeth before me and the children be able to endure*] **According to the pace** (lit. "the foot") **of the cattle that is before me, and according to the pace of the children.** The word for cattle is literally "work;" thence anything acquired by labour, property, and hence cattle, the chief possession of a pastoral people.

until I come unto my lord unto Seir] It is probable that Jacob here intimated a hope that he might one day visit Esau at Seir. It does not necessarily mean that he was directly on his way thither; his course being evidently towards Shechem.

17. *booths*] Perhaps only wattled enclosures, or very possibly some simple contrivance of branches and leaves made for sheltering the milch cattle from the heat of the sun.

Succoth] "Booths," from *saccac*, to entwine, to shelter. Jacob could easily visit his father from this place. Jerome ('Qu. Heb.' ad h.l.) says that "Sochoth is to this day a city beyond Jordan in Scythopolis." According to Josh. xiii. 27, Judg. viii. 4, 5, Succoth was in the valley of the Jordan, "on the other side of the Jordan eastward," and was allotted to the tribe of Gad.

18. *to Shalem*] Or "in peace." The LXX., Vulg., Syr. render "Shalem." Robinson ('B. R.' III. 322) and Wilson ('Lands of the Bible,' II. 72) mention a place still called Salim to the east of Nablus. On the other hand the Sam. Pent. has *Shalom*, *i.e.* "safe."

a city of ‖Shechem, which *is* in the
land of Canaan, when he came from
Padan-aram; and pitched his tent
before the city.

‖ Called, Acts 7. 16, Sychem

19 And he bought a parcel of a
field, where he had spread his tent,
at the hand of the children of ‖Ha-
mor, Shechem's father, for an hundred
‖pieces of money.

‖ Called, Acts 7. 16, Emmor.

‖ Or, lambs.

20 And he erected there an altar,
and called it ‖El-elohe-Israel.

‖ That is, God the God of Israel.

CHAPTER XXXIV.

1 Dinah is ravished by Shechem. 4 He sueth to marry her. 13 The sons of Jacob offer the condition of circumcision to the Shechemites. 20 Hamor and Shechem persuade them to accept it. 25 The sons of Jacob upon that advantage slay them, 27 and spoil their city. 30 Jacob reproveth Simeon and Levi.

AND Dinah the daughter of Leah,
which she bare unto Jacob, went
out to see the daughters of the land.
2 And when Shechem the son of
Hamor the Hivite, prince of the
country, saw her, he took her, and
lay with her, and †defiled her.

† Heb. humbled her.

3 And his soul clave unto Dinah
the daughter of Jacob, and he loved
the damsel, and spake †kindly unto
the damsel.

† Heb. to her heart.

4 And Shechem spake unto his father Hamor, saying, Get me this damsel to wife.
5 And Jacob heard that he had defiled Dinah his daughter: now his
sons were with his cattle in the field:
and Jacob held his peace until they
were come.
6 ¶ And Hamor the father of Shechem went out unto Jacob to com-
mune with him.
7 And the sons of Jacob came out
of the field when they heard *it:* and
the men were grieved, and they were
very wroth, because he had wrought

Onkelos renders "in peace," and he is followed by Saadias, Rashi and most Jewish commentators, by Rosenm., Schum, Gesen., Tuch, Del., Knobel, Keil.

a city of Shechem] If instead of "to Shalem" we adopt the rendering "in peace," or "in safety;" then we must render here "to the city of Shechem." It was perhaps called after Shechem the son of Hamor (v. 19). In ch. xii. 6 (where see note), we read of "the place of Sichem," *i.e.* perhaps the site on which Sichem or Shechem was afterwards built. It was the first place in which God appeared to Abraham, and it is the place at which Jacob re-enters the promised land; for Succoth, whence he came to it, was on the other side of Jordan. Abraham only purchased a burial-place, Jacob purchases a dwelling-place. Perhaps the country had now become more fully inhabited, and therefore land must be secured before it could be safely lived upon.

19. *an hundred pieces of money*] "A hundred Kesita." All the ancient Versions (except Targg. Jerus. and Jonath.) render "a hundred lambs," whence it has been inferred that the *Kesita* was a piece of money bearing the impression of a lamb. It appears however to have been either an ingot or bar of silver of certain weight, or perhaps merely a certain weight of silver; a word of the same root in Arabic signifying "a balance," "a pair of scales." (See Ges. 'Thes.' p. 1241. Lee, 'Lex.' in voc.).

20. *El-elohe-Israel*] The name *Israel* contains in it the syllable *El*, one of the names of God. Jacob therefore calls *El* the God of Israel, and gives this title to the altar, which he built on the spot which had already been consecrated by Abraham (ch. xii. 7). Jacob had hitherto always spoken of JEHOVAH as the God of Abraham, and the God, or the Fear, of his father Isaac. Now on his gracious acceptance by Him, his change of name by His appointment, his return to Canaan as the heir of the land, he calls Him his own God, El, the God of Israel.

CHAP. XXXIV. **1.** *Dinah the daughter of Leah*] Her birth is mentioned (ch. xxx. 21) before the birth of Joseph (vv. 22, 23). If Jacob's sojourn in Padan-aram was 40 years long and not 20 only (see note at the end of ch. xxxi.), it is quite possible that Dinah may have been some years older than Joseph, who was 17 at the beginning of the history related in ch. xxxvii. (see v. 2), *i.e.* probably about a year or two after the events related in this present chapter. In any case therefore she was not less than 15 years old at this time, supposing her to have been no older than Joseph; so that the objection urged by Tuch and others that at this time she was but 6 or 7 years old cannot be maintained.

went out to see the daughters of the land] Josephus ('Ant.' I. 21) states that a feast among the Shechemites was the occasion of this visit.

3. *spake kindly unto the damsel*] Lit. "Spake to the heart of the damsel." So ch. l. 21; Judg. xix. 3; Isa. xl. 2; Hos. ii. 14, &c.

7. *he had wrought folly in Israel...which*

folly in Israel in lying with Jacob's
daughter; which thing ought not to
be done.
8 And Hamor communed with
them, saying, The soul of my son
Shechem longeth for your daughter:
I pray you give her him to wife.
9 And make ye marriages with us,
and give your daughters unto us, and
take our daughters unto you.
10 And ye shall dwell with us:
and the land shall be before you; dwell
and trade ye therein, and get you possessions therein.
11 And Shechem said unto her father and unto her brethren, Let me
find grace in your eyes, and what ye
shall say unto me I will give.
12 Ask me never so much dowry
and gift, and I will give according as
ye shall say unto me: but give me
the damsel to wife.
13 And the sons of Jacob answered
Shechem and Hamor his father deceitfully, and said, because he had
defiled Dinah their sister:
14 And they said unto them, We
cannot do this thing, to give our sister
to one that is uncircumcised; for that
were a reproach unto us:
15 But in this will we consent unto you: If ye will be as we *be*, that
every male of you be circumcised;
16 Then will we give our daughters unto you, and we will take your
daughters to us, and we will dwell
with you, and we will become one
people.
17 But if ye will not hearken unto us, to be circumcised; then will
we take our daughter, and we will be
gone.
18 And their words pleased Hamor,
and Shechem Hamor's son.
19 And the young man deferred
not to do the thing, because he had
delight in Jacob's daughter: and he
was more honourable than all the
house of his father.
20 ¶ And Hamor and Shechem his
son came unto the gate of their city,
and communed with the men of their
city, saying,
21 These men *are* peaceable with
us; therefore let them dwell in the
land, and trade therein; for the land,
behold, *it is* large enough for them;
let us take their daughters to us for
wives, and let us give them our
daughters.
22 Only herein will the men consent unto us for to dwell with us, to
be one people, if every male among
us be circumcised, as they *are* circumcised.
23 *Shall* not their cattle and their
substance and every beast of theirs *be*
ours? only let us consent unto them,
and they will dwell with us.
24 And unto Hamor and unto Shechem his son hearkened all that went
out of the gate of his city; and every
male was circumcised, all that went
out of the gate of his city.
25 ¶ And it came to pass on the
third day, when they were sore, that

---

thing ought not to be done] Lit. "and so it is not done." These are not the words of the sons of Jacob, but of the sacred historian. It is not likely that the family of Jacob should by this time have acquired the generic name of Israel; but Moses uses the designation which had become familiar in his own day. The words of this verse seem to have become proverbial, they are almost repeated in 2 S. xiii. 12. But this is no reason for supposing that the words of this present verse should be ascribed to a later hand than that of Moses.

13. *and said*] Schultens, Gesen. (p. 315), Knobel, Del., &c. translate here "and plotted" or "laid snares:" others repeat the word "deceitfully" from the former clause, rendering and "spoke deceitfully:" but the rendering of the Authorised Version seems preferable.

18. *their words pleased Hamor*, &c.] The readiness of the Shechemites to submit to circumcision may be accounted for, if circumcision had by this time become a rite known to others besides the descendants of Abraham (Herod. II. 104). At all events, it was now practised not only by the sons of Jacob and his household, but by the Ishmaelites, and the family and household of Esau, all growing into important tribes in the neighbourhood of the Shechemites.

25. *Simeon and Levi, Dinah's brethren, took each man his sword*] *i.e.* sons of the same

two of the sons of Jacob, Simeon and
Levi, Dinah's brethren, took each man
his sword, and came upon the city
[a chap. 49. 6.] boldly, and [a]slew all the males.
26 And they slew Hamor and She-
[† Heb. *mouth.*] chem his son with the †edge of the
sword, and took Dinah out of She-
chem's house, and went out.
27 The sons of Jacob came upon
the slain, and spoiled the city, because
they had defiled their sister.
28 They took their sheep, and their
oxen, and their asses, and that which
was in the city, and that which *was*
in the field,
29 And all their wealth, and all
their little ones, and their wives took
they captive, and spoiled even all that
was in the house.
30 And Jacob said to Simeon and
Levi, Ye have troubled me to make
me to stink among the inhabitants of
the land, among the Canaanites and
the Perizzites: and I *being* few in
number, they shall gather themselves
together against me, and slay me; and
I shall be destroyed, I and my house.
31 And they said, Should he deal
with our sister as with an harlot?

CHAPTER XXXV.

1 God sendeth Jacob to Beth-el. 2 He purgeth his house of idols. 6 He buildeth an altar at Beth-el. 8 Deborah dieth at Allon-bachuth. 9 God blesseth Jacob at Beth-el. 16 Rachel travaileth of Benjamin, and dieth in the way to Edar. 22 Reuben lieth with Bilhah. 23 The sons of Jacob. 27 Jacob cometh to Isaac at Hebron. 28 The age, death, and burial of Isaac.

AND God said unto Jacob, Arise,
go up to Beth-el, and dwell there:
and make there an altar unto God,
that appeared unto thee [a]when thou [a chap. 27. 43.]
fleddest from the face of Esau thy
brother.
2 Then Jacob said unto his household, and to all that *were* with him,
Put away the strange gods that *are*
among you, and be clean, and change
your garments:
3 And let us arise, and go up to

---

mother, Leah, as well as of the same father, Jacob. In ch. xxiv. 50, 55, &c. we saw Laban taking a principal part in giving his sister in marriage Michaelis (in loc.) mentions it as a prevalent opinion in the East that a man is more affected by the dishonour of his sister than even by the dishonour of his wife, as he may divorce his wife but can never cease to be his sister's brother. We are not to suppose that Simeon and Levi without help from others attacked and slew all the males: they had no doubt a retinue from their father's household with them, and perhaps were accompanied by some of their brothers, though they only are specially mentioned, as having taken the lead in the assault, and as most strongly actuated by the spirit of revenge.

27. *the sons of Jacob*] *i.e.* others beside Simeon and Levi, for all appear to have joined in the original stratagem (see v. 13), and probably all assisted in spoiling the city.

30. *I being few in number*] Lit. "I being men of number." That is, I and my family and followers (compare "I am become two bands," ch. xxxii. 10) are men so few that we can easily be numbered. A common idiom: see Deut. iv. 27; 1 Chr. xvi. 19; Ps. cv. 12; Isa. x. 19; Jer. xliv. 28.

It seems strange that Jacob should have reproached his sons as having brought him into danger, not as having been guilty of treachery and murder. This is only another instance of Jacob's weak character, and of the fidelity of the historian. Jacob's own fault was want of straightforward honesty. It is reproduced with grievous aggravations in his sons. The timidity of his disposition, a kindred defect with untruthfulness, shews itself now in his exclamation of fear rather than of moral horror. His more righteous indignation, the result of calmer thought, is expressed in his final judgment on the fierceness of their anger and the cruelty of their wrath (ch. xlix. 5, 6, 7).

CHAP. XXXV. 1. *Beth-el*] See on ch. xxviii. 19.

2. *strange gods*] Not only had Rachel stolen her father's teraphim, but probably others of Jacob's company had secreted instruments of idolatrous worship in the camp. As they had just spoiled a heathen city (ch. xxxiv. 27), it is not unlikely that they brought such instruments from that also.

be clean] "Purify yourselves." The same word is frequently used under the Law for purification from legal uncleanness before access to sacred ordinances (Lev. xiv. 4; Num. viii. 7; 2 Chr. xxx. 18; Ezra vi. 20; Neh. xii. 30; xiii. 22). Such purification was probably in the patriarchal times, as often even under the law, by washing merely, all such

Beth-el; and I will make there an
altar unto God, who answered me in
the day of my distress, and was with
me in the way which I went.

4 And they gave unto Jacob all the
strange gods which *were* in their hand,
and *all their* earrings which *were* in
their ears; and Jacob hid them under
the oak which *was* by Shechem.

5 And they journeyed: and the
terror of God was upon the cities that
were round about them, and they did
not pursue after the sons of Jacob.

6 ¶ So Jacob came to Luz, which
is in the land of Canaan, that *is*,
Beth-el, he and all the people that
were with him.

7 And he built there an altar, and
[b]called the place ‖El-beth-el: because [b] chap. 28. 19.
there God appeared unto him, when ‖ That is, *the God of Beth-el.*
he fled from the face of his brother.

8 But Deborah Rebekah's nurse
died, and she was buried beneath
Beth-el under an oak: and the name
of it was called ‖Allon-bachuth. ‖ That is, *the oak of weeping.*

9 ¶ And God appeared unto Jacob
again, when he came out of Padan-aram,
and blessed him.

10 And God said unto him, Thy
name *is* Jacob: thy name shall not be
called any more Jacob, [c]but Israel [c] chap. 32. 28.
shall be thy name: and he called his
name Israel.

11 And God said unto him, I *am*
God Almighty: be fruitful and multiply;
a nation and a company of na-

---

ceremonial washings being the prototypes of baptism, by which, false religions being rejected, men are brought into the Church of the living God.

4. *ear-rings*] perhaps talismans or idolatrous symbols worn in the ear. Augustine ('Qu.' ad h. l.) calls them "idolatrous phylacteries," *idolorum phylacteria*, and ('Epist.' CCXLV.) he mentions a superstitious use of ear-rings even in his own day among the African Christians "not to please men but to serve demons."

the oak which was by Shechem] See note on ch. xii. 6. It may have been under the very oak, or oak-grove, where Abraham pitched his tent, and which seems to have been sacred even in Joshua's time (Josh. xxiv. 26).

5. *the terror of God*] God inspired into the minds of the neighbouring tribes a sense of fear, so that they did not pursue Jacob in order to avenge the slaughter of the Shechemites.

6. *Luz*] See ch. xxviii. 19.

7. *El-beth-el*] *i.e.* "the God of Beth-el," or "the God of the House of God." At Bethel God first appeared to him. Then he devoted himself to God's service and received the promises of God's protection. He accordingly called the place Bethel, which name he now renews with addition of *El.*

God appeared unto him] The word for God, "Elohim," being here as generally in the plural, the verb is by a kind of attraction put in the plural also. Some have discovered in this a relic of polytheism, and Onkelos has rendered angels, a most unwarrantable translation. The Samaritan Pentateuch and the LXX. and Vulg. Versions have the verb in the singular, which may be the true reading; but see on ch. xx. 13.

8. *Allon-bachuth*] "The oak of weeping."

9. *God appeared unto Jacob again, when he came out of Padan-aram*] He was now at Bethel, the place from which he may be considered to have set out for Padan-aram, and where he made his vow that if God would be with him and be his God, he would make that place the house of God. He had now come back again to the same spot; he had fulfilled his vow by consecrating Bethel as the temple of God; this might then well be considered as the accomplishment of his return from Padan-aram. Accordingly God appears to him here once more, promises him again, and more emphatically, protection, blessing, inheritance, confirms the name of Israel to him, a name given by the angel at the ford of the brook Jabbok, but now fixed and ratified, and assures him that his posterity shall be numerous, powerful and blessed Accordingly Jacob, recognizing the fulfilment of all that had been promised him when he fled from Esau, and of all that his vows had pointed to, rears again a stone pillar as he had done forty years before, and again solemnly names the place Bethel. The whole of this history thoroughly fits in to all that has gone before, there being nothing whatever to support the notion that it is a mere legendary repetition of the previous vision.

11. *I am God Almighty*] *El-Shaddai.* It was by this name that God revealed Himself to Abram, when he changed his name to Abraham, and promised him the land of Canaan for an everlasting possession (see ch. xvii. 8). The use of the same name here is

tions shall be of thee, and kings shall
come out of thy loins;
12 And the land which I gave
Abraham and Isaac, to thee I will
give it, and to thy seed after thee will
I give the land.
13 And God went up from him in
the place where he talked with him.
14 And Jacob set up a pillar in the
place where he talked with him, *even*
a pillar of stone: and he poured a
drink offering thereon, and he poured
oil thereon.
15 And Jacob called the name of
the place where God spake with him,
Beth-el.
16 ¶ And they journeyed from
Beth-el; and there was but †a little
way to come to Ephrath: and Rachel
travailed, and she had hard labour.
17 And it came to pass, when she
was in hard labour, that the midwife
said unto her, Fear not; thou shalt
have this son also.
18 And it came to pass, as her soul
was in departing, (for she died) that
she called his name ‖Ben-oni: but
his father called him ‖Benjamin.
19 And Rachel died, and was buried in the way to Ephrath, which *is*
Beth-lehem.
20 And Jacob set a pillar upon her
grave: that *is* the pillar of Rachel's
grave unto this day.
21 ¶ And Israel journeyed, and
spread his tent beyond the tower of
Edar.
22 And it came to pass, when Israel dwelt in that land, that Reuben
went and [d]lay with Bilhah his father's concubine: and Israel heard *it*.
Now the sons of Jacob were twelve:
23 The sons of Leah; Reuben,
Jacob's firstborn, and Simeon, and
Levi, and Judah, and Issachar, and
Zebulun:
24 The sons of Rachel; Joseph,
and Benjamin:
25 And the sons of Bilhah, Rachel's
handmaid; Dan, and Naphtali:
26 And the sons of Zilpah, Leah's
handmaid; Gad, and Asher: these
are the sons of Jacob, which were
born to him in Padan-aram.
27 ¶ And Jacob came unto Isaac
his father unto Mamre, unto the city
of Arbah, which *is* Hebron, where
Abraham and Isaac sojourned.

† Heb. *a little piece of ground.*

‖ That is, *the son of my sorrow.*

‖ That is, *the son of the right hand.*

[d] chap. 49. 4.

---

therefore singularly appropriate, and Jacob refers to it with evident comfort and satisfaction at the close of his life (see ch. xlviii. 3).

16. *a little way*] These words probably in the original denote a definite space. The LXX. does not translate the principal word. The Vulg. improperly renders "in the Spring time." Onk. has "an acre of land;" the Syr. "a parasang;" Saad. and Arab. Erpen. "a mile." The Jews generally incline to understand "a mile," because of the traditions that Rachel's tomb was a mile from Bethlehem or Ephrath (v. 19).

18. *Ben-oni*] *i.e.* "son of my sorrow."

Benjamin] *i.e.* "son of the right hand," a name of good significance, the right hand being connected with prosperity, as the left hand was with calamity. Some ancient versions (favoured by the Samaritan Pentateuch) interpret Benjamin as "son of days," *i.e.* "son of old age." There is evidently, however, an antithesis between Benoni, "son of sorrow," and Benjamin, "son of prosperity." It might possibly be interpreted "son of strength," from the "strong right hand."

20. *unto this day*] *i.e.* till Moses wrote. It was worthy of notice that the pillar still stood after the land had been so long inhabited by unfriendly tribes. On the knowledge of the geography of Palestine by Moses, see Introduction to the Pentateuch, p. 17.

21. *tower of Edar*] *i.e.* "tower of the flock." It was apparently a watch-tower for the protection of flocks against robbers and wild beasts. (Cp. 2 K. xviii. 8; 2 Chr. xxvi. 10, xxvii. 4.)

22. *Reuben*] The incest of Reuben is punished by his being deprived of his right of primogeniture, ch. xlix. 3, 4; 1 Chr. v. 1.

and Israel heard it] The LXX. adds "and it was evil in his sight." The silence of the Hebrew expresses more eloquently the indignation of the offended patriarch.

26. *in Padan-aram*] *i.e.* except Benjamin, whose birth has just been recorded in Canaan (v. 18).

27. *Jacob came unto Isaac his father*] Whether this was just before Isaac's death, or whether Jacob spent some time at Mamre with his father, we do not read. If this were only just before his death it is very probable that Jacob had visited him from time to time before.

28 And the days of Isaac were an
hundred and fourscore years.
29 And Isaac gave up the ghost,
[e] chap. 25. 8. and died, and [e]was gathered unto his
people, *being* old and full of days: and
his sons Esau and Jacob buried him.

CHAPTER XXXVI.

1 *Esau's three wives.* 6 *His removing to mount Seir.* 9 *His sons.* 15 *The dukes which descended of his sons.* 20 *The sons and dukes of Seir.* 24 *Anah findeth mules.* 31 *The kings of Edom.* 40 *The dukes that descended of Esau.*

NOW these *are* the generations
of Esau, who *is* Edom.
2 Esau took his wives of the daughters of Canaan; Adah the daughter
of Elon the Hittite, and Aholibamah
the daughter of Anah the daughter
of Zibeon the Hivite;
3 And Bashemath Ishmael's daughter, sister of Nebajoth.
[a] 1 Chron. 1. 35. 4 And [a]Adah bare to Esau Eliphaz; and Bashemath bare Reuel;
5 And Aholibamah bare Jeush, and
Jaalam, and Korah: these *are* the
sons of Esau, which were born unto
him in the land of Canaan.
6 And Esau took his wives, and
his sons, and his daughters, and all
the †persons of his house, and his cat- † Heb. souls
tle, and all his beasts, and all his
substance, which he had got in the
land of Canaan; and went into the
country from the face of his brother
Jacob.
7 For their riches were more than
that they might dwell together; and
the land wherein they were strangers
could not bear them because of their
cattle.
8 Thus dwelt Esau in [b]mount Seir: [b] Josh. 24. 4.
Esau *is* Edom.
9 ¶ And these *are* the generations
of Esau the father of †the Edomites † Heb. Edom.
in mount Seir:
10 These *are* the names of Esau's
sons; [c]Eliphaz the son of Adah the [c] 1 Chron. 1. 35, &c.
wife of Esau, Reuel the son of Bashe-
math the wife of Esau.
11 And the sons of Eliphaz were
Teman, Omar, Zepho, and Gatam,
and Kenaz.
12 And Timna was concubine to
Eliphaz Esau's son; and she bare to
Eliphaz Amalek: these *were* the sons
of Adah Esau's wife.
13 And these *are* the sons of Reu-

CHAP. XXXVI. 2, 3. *Adah*, &c.] See note A at the end of the Chapter.

6. *went into the country*] Lit. "into a land." Onk. and Vulg. has "into another land." The Sam. Pentat. has "from the land of Canaan." The LXX. "from the land." The Syr. reads "into the land of Seir," which is adopted by Ewald, Knobel, Delitzsch, Keil, &c. In ch. xxxii. 3, Esau is mentioned as in the land of Seir, but then probably he was only there for a time, perhaps engaged in its conquest, now he finally takes up his abode there. See note on xxxii. 3.

7. *the land wherein they were strangers could not bear them because of their cattle*] They were not settled inhabitants, but only sojourners in the land: and though they were allowed to pasture their flocks in the land, yet it was not to be expected that the settled inhabitants would tolerate more than a reasonable number of cattle from one family to eat up the produce of their fields.

8. *mount Seir*] Mount Seir was the mountainous country between the Dead Sea and the Elamitic Gulf, the northern part of which is called *Jebal*, *i.e.* "the hill country," by the Arabs. So the Targums of Jerusalem and Pseudo-Jonathan put here *Gabala* for *Seir*. The southern part is called Sherah.

9. *the father of the Edomites*] Lit. "the father of Edom," *i.e.* either "the father of the Edomites," or "the founder of Idumæa."

11. *Teman*] We read elsewhere of a district in Idumæa called Teman, famous for its wisdom (Jer. xlix. 7, 20; Amos i. 12; Hab. iii. 3); and in Job we meet with Eliphaz the Temanite, probably descended from this Teman, the son of Eliphaz, the son of Esau. Pliny ('H. N.' VI. 32) speaks of the Thimanæi in connection with Petra.

Omar] is compared by Knobel with the Beni Ammer in Southern Palestine and Northern Idumæa, and with the Amarin Arabs and the Amir Arabs, all mentioned by Seetzen, Burckhardt, and Robinson.

Zepho] Compare Zaphia, a place to the south of the Dead Sea (Knobel).

Kenaz] Compare Aneizeh, the name of an Arab tribe, and of a fortress to the north-east of Petra (Knobel).

12. *Amalek*] The ancestor of the Amalekites, who probably at an early period separated themselves from the rest of the Edom-

el; Nahath, and Zerah, Shammah,
and Mizzah: these were the sons of
Bashemath Esau's wife.
14 ¶ And these were the sons of
Aholibamah, the daughter of Anah
the daughter of Zibeon, Esau's wife:
and she bare to Esau Jeush, and
Jaalam, and Korah.
15 ¶ These *were* dukes of the sons
of Esau: the sons of Eliphaz the firstborn *son* of Esau; duke Teman, duke
Omar, duke Zepho, duke Kenaz,
16 Duke Korah, duke Gatam, *and*
duke Amalek: these *are* the dukes
that came of Eliphaz in the land of
Edom; these *were* the sons of Adah.
17 ¶ And these *are* the sons of
Reuel Esau's son; duke Nahath, duke
Zerah, duke Shammah, duke Mizzah:
these *are* the dukes *that came* of Reuel
in the land of Edom; these *are* the
sons of Bashemath Esau's wife.
18 ¶ And these *are* the sons of
Aholibamah Esau's wife; duke Jeush,
duke Jaalam, duke Korah: these *were*
the dukes *that came* of Aholibamah
the daughter of Anah, Esau's wife.
19 These *are* the sons of Esau, who
is Edom, and these *are* their dukes.
20 ¶ [d]These *are* the sons of Seir [d] 1 Chron.
the Horite, who inhabited the land; i. 38.
Lotan, and Shobal, and Zibeon, and
Anah,
21 And Dishon, and Ezer, and Dishan: these *are* the dukes of the Horites, the children of Seir in the land
of Edom.
22 And the children of Lotan were
Hori and Hemam; and Lotan's sister
was Timna.
23 And the children of Shobal
were these; Alvan, and Manahath,
and Ebal, Shepho, and Onam.
24 And these *are* the children of

---

ites, and formed a distinct and powerful tribe. The Arabs have a legend concerning an aboriginal tribe of Amalek, with whom it has been thought that the Edomitish Amalekites were fused. Nöldeke has a monograph on the Amalekites, in which he shews that the Arabian legends concerning them are drawn directly or indirectly from the Old Testament, and are utterly valueless when they depart from that only historical source. There is no authority in the Old Testament for the existence of this aboriginal tribe, except the mention in ch. xiv. 7 of "the country of the Amalekites." This name, however, is probably given by anticipation, not because the country was so called in Abraham's time, but because it had become known by that title before the time of Moses and the Exodus. The Amalekites, having their chief seat to the south of the mountains of Judah, as far as Kadesh (Num. xiii. 29, xiv. 43, 45), spread over the whole of the northern part of Arabia Petræa, from Havilah to Shur on the border of Egypt (1 S. xv. 3, 7, xxvii. 8); whilst one branch penetrated into the heart of Canaan (Judg. xii. 15).

13. *Nahath*] "A descent." Cp. with the valley of Akaba of like significance (Knob.).

Shammah] Cp. the Sameni, a tribe of Nomad Arabs mentioned by Steph. Byzant. (Knob.)

14. *Aholibamah*] See note A on vv. 2, 3 below.

Korah] Perhaps perpetuated in the modern tribe of Kurayeh (Knobel).

15. *dukes*] *i.e. duces*, leaders of tribes, phylarchs. The Hebrew *alluph* is connected with *eleph*, which signifies either "a thousand" or "a family." Hence Bochart and others understand here *chiliarchs*, leaders of thousands; whilst others, with more probability, understand *phylarchs*, heads of tribes or families, (see Ges. 'Thes.' pp. 105, 106). Rosenmüller thinks that the word is used metonymically for a family, and would render "These are the families (or tribes) of the sons of Esau." This interpretation would apply well throughout the catalogue, but does not so well correspond with the etymology and formation of the word.

16. *Duke Korah*] These words are omitted in one MS. in the Sam. Pent. and Version. They are considered as having crept in through a clerical error from v. 18, by Kennicott, Tuch, Knobel, Delitzsch, Keil, &c.

20. *sons of Seir the Horite*] The inhabitants of the country previously to the Edomitish invasion. The Horites (*i.e.* Troglodytes or dwellers in caves), mentioned ch. xiv. 6 as an independent people, were partly exterminated and partly subdued by Esau and his descendants (Deut. ii. 12, 22).

Lotan] is compared with *Leyathan*, the name of a fierce tribe in the neighbourhood of Petra (Knobel).

22. *Hemam*] Cp. *Homaima*, a place to the south of Petra (Knobel).

23. *Alvan*] Cp. the *Alawin*, a tribe of Arabs of evil notoriety to the north of Akaba (Knobel)

Zibeon; both Ajah, and Anah: this
was that Anah that found the mules
in the wilderness, as he fed the asses
of Zibeon his father.
25 And the children of Anah *were*
these; Dishon, and Aholibamah the
daughter of Anah.
26 And these *are* the children of
Dishon; Hemdan, and Eshban, and
Ithran, and Cheran.
27 The children of Ezer *are*
these; Bilhan, and Zaavan, and A-
kan.
28 The children of Dishan *are*
these; Uz, and Aran.
29 These *are* the dukes *that came*
of the Horites; duke Lotan, duke
Shobal, duke Zibeon, duke Anah,
30 Duke Dishon, duke Ezer, duke
Dishan: these *are* the dukes *that came*
of Hori, among their dukes in the
land of Seir.
31 ¶ And these *are* the kings that
reigned in the land of Edom, before
there reigned any king over the children of Israel.
32 And Bela the son of Beor
reigned in Edom: and the name of
his city *was* Dinhabah.
33 And Bela died, and Jobab the

Manahath] Ptolemy, v. 17, 3, mentions *Manychiates* west of Petra (Knobel).

Shepho] Cp. the hill *Shafeh* north of Akaba (Robinson, 'B. R.' I. 256; Knobel).

24. *Anah that found the mules*] **Anah that found the hot springs.** (See note on vv. 2, 3 below.) The Greek Versions do not translate the word *yemim* (the LXX. has τὸν Ἰαμεὶν). The Samaritan text has "the Emim," a gigantic people, with which agrees the Targum of Onkelos, "the giants." This is followed by Bochart, Patrick, and others. The Targum of Pseudo-Jonathan renders "mules," being followed herein by Saad., Kimchi, and many Rabbins, by Luther, and the Authorised Version. The Vulgate renders "warm waters," *aquas calidas*, and the Syriac has "waters," a rendering adopted by Gesen. (see 'Thes.' p. 586), Rosenm., Schumann, and most modern interpreters. There were many warm springs in this region, the most famous being Callirrhoe, in the Wady Zerka Maein, which some suppose to have been the very springs discovered by Anah.

31. *And these are the kings that reigned in the land of Edom, before there reigned any king over the children of Israel*] These words have led many to suppose that this and the following verses were a late interpolation, as, it is thought, they must have been written after kings had reigned in Israel. Spinoza argued from them that it was clearer than midday that the whole Pentateuch was written centuries after the time of Moses; a most illogical conclusion, for the utmost that could be inferred would be that (as Kennicott supposed) these verses were taken from 1 Chron. i. 43—54, and having been inserted in the margin of a very ancient MS. of Genesis, had crept into the text.

There is however nothing inconsistent with the Mosaic origin of the whole passage. In the last chapter (ch. xxxv. 11) there had been an emphatic promise from God Almighty (El-Shaddai) to Jacob that "kings should come out of his loins." The Israelites, no doubt, cherished a constant hope of such a kingdom and such a kingly race. Moses himself (Deut. xxviii. 36) prophesied concerning the king that the Israelites should set over them; and hence it was not unnatural that, when recording the eight kings, who had reigned in the family of Esau up to his own time, he should have noted that as yet no king had risen from the family of his brother Jacob, to whom a kingly progeny had been promised. The words in the original are "before the reigning of a king to the sons of Israel;" and might be rendered, "whilst as yet the children of Israel have no king;" there being nothing in the words expressive of a past tense, or indicating that before the writing of the sentence a king had reigned in Israel.

The other difficulty in the passage is chronological, it being thought that so many dukes and kings could not have succeeded one another in the period which elapsed from Esau to Moses. But there is no reason to suppose that the dukes, mentioned from v. 15 to 19, reigned in succession, then the kings from v. 31 to 39, and then again the dukes mentioned from v. 40 to 43. On the contrary, a comparison of Num. xx. 14 with Exod. xv. 15 shews, that a single king was reigning in Edom contemporaneously with several dukes or phylarchs. The dukes (as their title indicates) were not sovereigns of the whole of Idumæa, but princes or rulers of tribes or provinces: moreover the kings do not appear to have succeeded by inheritance, the son never succeeding to his father. Hence they were probably elected by the dukes.

33. *Jobab*] The LXX. and some of the fathers consider this to have been the same person as Job; and the mention of Eliphaz in v. 11 in connection with Teman, and of **Eli-**

son of Zerah of Bozrah reigned in
his stead.
34 And Jobab died, and Husham
of the land of Temani reigned in his
stead.
35 And Husham died, and Hadad
the son of Bedad, who smote Midian
in the field of Moab, reigned in his
stead: and the name of his city *was*
Avith.
36 And Hadad died, and Samlah
of Masrekah reigned in his stead.
37 And Samlah died, and Saul of
Rehoboth *by* the river reigned in his
stead.
38 And Saul died, and Baal-hanan
the son of Achbor reigned in his
stead.
39 And Baal-hanan the son of
Achbor died, and Hadar reigned in
his stead: and the name of his city
was Pau; and his wife's name *was*
Mehetabel, the daughter of Matred,
the daughter of Mezahab.
40 And these *are* the names of the
dukes *that came* of Esau, according
to their families, after their places, by
their names; duke Timnah, duke
Alvah, duke Jetheth,
41 Duke Aholibamah, duke Elah,
duke Pinon,
42 Duke Kenaz, duke Teman, duke
Mibzar,
43 Duke Magdiel, duke Iram:
these *be* the dukes of Edom, according to their habitations in the land of
their possession: he *is* Esau the father of † the Edomites. † Heb. *Edom.*

---

phaz the Temanite in the book of Job favours this belief.

Bozrah] A famous city of Idumæa (see Isa. xxxiv. 6, lxiii. 1, &c.), remains of which are still traced in *El Buseireh*, a ruined village in *Jebal.* (Burckhardt, 'Syr.' 407; Robinson, II. 167.)

37. *Rehoboth by the river*] or *Rehoboth Hannahar*, so distinguished from *Rehoboth Ir*, ch. x. 11. The river here is probably the Euphrates.

39. *Hadar*] Called Hadad in 1 Chr. i. 50, and here also in the Samaritan text. He probably was living when Moses wrote, as no mention is made of his death, an argument for the Mosaic origin of this chapter; for Hadad could hardly have been living after the time of the kings of Israel, to which period those who from v. 31 consider it to be an interpolation would assign this genealogy, or perhaps the whole chapter.

40. *And these are the names of the dukes*, &c.] From comparing the words in this verse "after their places, by their names" with those in v. 43, "according to their habitations in the land of their possession," it is inferred with great probability, that this second catalogue of dukes is, not a catalogue of dukes who reigned subsequently to the kings of the preceding verses, nor a different version of the catalogue given in vv. 15 to 19, but rather a territorial catalogue, recounting, not the names, but the cities in which the various dukes or phylarchs before named had their seat of government. If so, we must render "the duke of Timnah, the duke of Alvah, the duke of Jetheth, &c." Two of the names in this list correspond with two in the former list, viz. Timnah and Kenaz, because, as it is supposed, the dukes Timnah and Kenaz called their cities after their own names. Aholibamah may have been a city called after the Horite princess (v. 25). (So Schumann, Knobel, Del., Keil, Kalisch, &c.).

43. *the father of the Edomites*] See on v. 9.

NOTE A on Chap. xxxvi. vv. 2, 3.

Adah the daughter of Elon the Hittite, and Aholibamah the daughter of Anah, the daughter of Zibeon the Hivite; and Bashemath, Ishmael's daughter, sister of Nebajoth] The difficulty of reconciling this with the names of the three wives of Esau, as given in ch. xxvi. 34, xxviii. 3, will be seen by comparing the two accounts as follows:

Ch. xxvi. 34, xxviii. 9.

1. Judith, daughter of Beeri the Hittite.
2. Bashemath, daughter of Elon the Hittite.
3. Mahalath, daughter of Ishmael, sister to Nebaioth.

Ch. xxxvi. 2.

1. Aholibamah, daughter of Anah daughter of Zibeon the Hivite.
2. Adah, daughter of Elon the Hittite.
3. Bashemath, daughter of Ishmael, sister to Nebaioth.

From this table it appears that every one of the three wives is designated by a different name in the earlier history from that in the later genealogy. Yet there can be little doubt that 2 Bashemath the daughter of Elon = Adah the daughter of Elon, nor that 3 Mahalath = Bashemath, both being described as daughter of Ishmael, and sister of Nebaioth. We may therefore conclude also that 1 Judith = Aholibamah. This excludes the explanation suggested by several commentators, that the wives of Esau, named in ch. xxvi. 34 had died without offspring, and that Esau had married others. It seems far more probable that the one set of names were those which they bore in their father's house, the other set having been given to them by Esau, or by the Edomites, after they had become mothers of tribes.

1. The identity of Judith and Aholibamah may appear thus. Judith is called the daughter of Beeri the Hittite, whilst Aholibamah is called "the daughter of Anah, the daughter of Zibeon the Hivite." Anah was probably not the mother, but the father of Aholibamah, the second "daughter" being referrible back to Aholibamah, and not attributable to Anah (unless the reading of the Samaritan, LXX., and Syriac, "the son of Zibeon," be the right reading); for in v. 24 we find that Anah was the son of Zibeon, and the grandson of Seir the Horite. The reason why the same person has been called Anah and Beeri has been derived by Hengstenberg and others from the fact that Anah is said, in v. 24, to have discovered the hot springs, from which very probably he acquired the name of Beeri, *i.e. fontanus*, "the well-finder." A greater difficulty is apparent in his being called a "Hittite" (xxvi. 34), a "Hivite" (xxxvi. 2), and a "Horite" (xxxvi. 20). It is observed that these three words "Hittite," "Hivite," and "Horite," differ in Hebrew by one letter only, and that they were easily interchanged in transcription. It is, however, clear (from xxvii. 46) that Rebekah calls Judith a daughter of Heth. And from xxxvi. 20, 24, 25, that Aholibamah, the daughter of Anah, was a Horite. The difficulty seems therefore rather to admit of solution by saying that Hittite (like Amorite) was a generic name for a large portion of the Canaanitish people, comprehending both Hivites and Horites. It is not improbable that Hivite in v. 2 may be an error of transcription for Horite (חוי for חרי), in which case we have only to conclude that the Horites of Mount Seir were reckoned by Isaac and Rebecca as among the Hittite inhabitants of Canaan. If, however, the reading Hivite be correct, it is not impossible that the Hivites, a southern people, may originally have come from Mount Seir, and have been dwellers in its rocky fastnesses, which is the meaning of the word Horite (troglodyte, dweller in caves). If this be correct, then we must conclude that Judith the daughter of Anah, called Beeri, from his finding the hot springs, and the granddaughter of Zibeon the Horite, one of the tribes reckoned in the great Hittite family, when she married Esau, assumed the name of Aholibamah ("the tent of the height").

2. Bashemath is described exactly as Adah is, *i.e.* as the daughter of Elon the Hittite. There is no difficulty here except in the change of name into Adah, "ornament," a change not improbable for Esau to have made.

3. In the same manner Mahalath is the daughter of Ishmael the sister of Nebaioth, and Bashemath is the daughter of Ishmael the sister of Nebaioth. There would be no difficulty in this, except that Bashemath, the second name of the daughter of Ishmael, is the same with the first name of the daughter of Elon the Hittite. If this seems to some irreconcileable with probability, it may be ascribed to an error of transcription, likely enough to occur in the writing out of genealogies, and the Samaritan text reads Mahalath in the genealogy as well as in the history.

CHAPTER XXXVII.

2 *Joseph is hated of his brethren.* 5 *His two dreams.* 13 *Jacob sendeth him to visit his brethren.* 18 *His brethren conspire his death.* 21 *Reuben saveth him.* 26 *They sell him to the Ishmeelites.* 31 *His father, deceived by the bloody coat, mourneth for him.* 36 *He is sold to Potiphar in Egypt.*

AND Jacob dwelt in the land
†wherein his father was a stranger, († Heb. *of his father's sojournings.*)
in the land of Canaan.
2 These *are* the generations of Jacob. Joseph, *being* seventeen years
old, was feeding the flock with his
brethren; and the lad *was* with the

CHAP. XXXVII. 1. *And Jacob dwelt in the land,* &c.] Ch. xxxv. concluded the history of Isaac. Ch. xxxvi. disposed of the history of Esau and his descendants down to the very time of the Exodus. (See on ch. xxxvi. 39.) This first verse of ch. xxxvii. now lands us in the time and place, from whence the succeeding history is to begin. **Jacob dwelt in the land of his father's sojournings, in the land of Canaan.** Esau had left Canaan to Jacob, who after their father's death became the sojourner in the land, which his posterity were to possess.

2. *These are the generations of Jacob.*] The *Toledoth*, or genealogical history of Isaac began (ch. xxv. 19) after the death of his father Abraham, a few verses having been allotted (vv. 12—18) to dispose of the history of his brother Ishmael. In the same manner, the *Toledoth* of Jacob are given in this chapter after the death of his father Isaac, ch. xxxvi. having intervened to account for Esau and his family. Many of the preceding chapters had been occupied with the history of Jacob and his sons, but Jacob's *Toledoth* begin at this point, because now he has become

sons of Bilhah, and with the sons of Zilpah, his father's wives: and Joseph
brought unto his father their evil report.
3 Now Israel loved Joseph more
than all his children, because he *was*
the son of his old age: and he made
him a coat of *many* ‖ colours.
4 And when his brethren saw that
their father loved him more than all
his brethren, they hated him, and
could not speak peaceably unto him.
5 ¶ And Joseph dreamed a dream,
and he told *it* his brethren: and they
hated him yet the more.
6 And he said unto them, Hear, I
pray you, this dream which I have
dreamed:
7 For, behold, we *were* binding
sheaves in the field, and, lo, my sheaf
arose, and also stood upright; and, behold, your sheaves stood round about,
and made obeisance to my sheaf.
8 And his brethren said to him,
Shalt thou indeed reign over us? or
shalt thou indeed have dominion over
us? And they hated him yet the
more for his dreams, and for his
words.
9 ¶ And he dreamed yet another
dream, and told it his brethren, and
said, Behold, I have dreamed a dream
more; and, behold, the sun and the
moon and the eleven stars made obeisance to me.
10 And he told *it* to his father,
and to his brethren: and his father

‖ Or, *pieces.*

---

the sole head and father of the chosen seed. The *Toledoth*, or family history, of Jacob continues now till his death ch. l.

2. *Joseph, being seventeen years old.*] This history goes back a few years; for Isaac must have been living when Joseph was seventeen. (See note at the end of ch. xxxi.) But the historian had fully wound up the history of Isaac, before commencing the *Toledoth* of Jacob; and he now gives unity to the history of the descent into Egypt by beginning with the adolescence of Joseph, his father's fondness for him, and his brothers' jealousy of him.

3. *the son of his old age*] It is not impossible that the greater part of this narrative may have been chronologically before the birth of Benjamin and the death of Rachel, related in ch. xxxv. 18.

coat of many colours] (1). The LXX. Vulg. and most modern versions render a garment made of different pieces, of patchwork, and so of many colours. In the well-known scene from the tomb of Chnoumhotep at Beni Hassan, a tomb of the XIIth dynasty, the Semitic visitors who are offering presents to the Governor are dressed in robes of rich colouring, apparently formed of separate small pieces or patches sewn together. There is an excellent engraving and explanation in Brugsch, 'Histoire d'Egypte,' p. 63.

(2). The versions of Aquila, Symm., Syr. render a tunic with sleeves or fringes extending to both hands and feet, *tunica manicata et talaris* (see Hieron. 'Qu.' ad h. l.), which is the interpretation adopted by most modern Hebraists (see Ges. 'Thes.' p. 1117). We find Thamar, the daughter of David, wearing this same dress (2 S. xiii. 18): and Josephus ('Ant.' vii. 8. 1) speaks of long garments reaching to the hands and ankles as worn by Jewish maidens. But the engraving at Beni Hassan just mentioned makes the former interpretation (1) the more probable.

It has been thought by some that Jacob, in his anger at the sins of his elder sons, especially of Reuben his firstborn, and in his partiality for Joseph, the firstborn of Rachel, designed to give him the right of primogeniture, that this robe was the token of birthright, and perhaps even designating the priestly office of the head of the family. (See Heidegger, Tom. II. p. 581. Braunius 'de Vestitu sacerdotali,' pp. 473 sqq., Kurtz, Vol. I. p. 378, Clark's translation, Blunt, 'Undesigned Coincidences,' p. 15.)

7. *we were binding sheaves in the field*] It appears from this, that Jacob was not a mere nomad, but, like his father Isaac (ch. xxvi. 12), had adopted agricultural as well as pastoral employments.

10. *his father rebuked him*] Joseph may have told the dream in the simplicity of his heart, or perhaps he may have been elated by his father's partiality and by "the abundance of the revelations" (2 Cor. xii. 7).

thy mother] It is possible that Rachel may have been living now, for neither the date of the dream nor of Rachel's death are clearly given. The dream may have been some time before the selling of Joseph, and is only related here as one of the reasons which caused his brethren to hate him. If, however, Rachel was dead, we must then understand Jacob to mean by "thy mother" either Leah, who would be his step-mother, or perhaps more likely Bilhah, who was Rachel's handmaid, and at once nurse and step-mother to Joseph; and it is not impossible that in either Leah or Bilhah the dream may have been fulfilled; for we do not know whether they were

rebuked him, and said unto him,
What *is* this dream that thou hast
dreamed? Shall I and thy mother
and thy brethren indeed come to bow
down ourselves to thee to the earth?
11 And his brethren envied him;
but his father observed the saying.
12 ¶ And his brethren went to feed
their father's flock in Shechem.
13 And Israel said unto Joseph,
Do not thy brethren feed *the flock*
in Shechem? come, and I will send
thee unto them. And he said to
him, Here *am I*.
14 And he said to him, Go, I pray
thee, † see whether it be well with thy
brethren, and well with the flocks;
and bring me word again. So he
sent him out of the vale of Hebron,
and he came to Shechem.
15 ¶ And a certain man found
him, and, behold, *he was* wandering
in the field: and the man asked him,
saying, What seekest thou?
16 And he said, I seek my brethren: tell me, I pray thee, where
they feed *their flocks*.
17 And the man said, They are
departed hence; for I heard them say,
Let us go to Dothan. And Joseph
went after his brethren, and found
them in Dothan.
18 And when they saw him afar
off, even before he came near unto
them, they conspired against him to
slay him.
19 And they said one to another,
Behold, this † dreamer cometh.
20 Come now therefore, and let
us slay him, and cast him into some
pit, and we will say, Some evil beast
hath devoured him: and we shall see
what will become of his dreams.
21 And [a] Reuben heard *it*, and he
delivered him out of their hands; and
said, Let us not kill him.
22 And Reuben said unto them,
Shed no blood, *but* cast him into this
pit that *is* in the wilderness, and lay
no hand upon him; that he might rid
him out of their hands, to deliver him
to his father again.
23 ¶ And it came to pass, when
Joseph was come unto his brethren,
that they stript Joseph out of his
coat, *his* coat of *many* ‖ colours that
was on him;
24 And they took him, and cast
him into a pit: and the pit *was* empty,
there was no water in it.

† Heb. *see the peace of thy brethren, &c.*

† Heb. *master of dreams.*

a chap. 42. 22.

‖ Or, *pieces.*

---

alive or not when Jacob went down into Egypt.

14. *out of the vale of Hebron, and he came to Shechem*] It appears from this that Jacob was now dwelling in the neighbourhood of Hebron where his father Isaac was still living (see on v. 3). After the slaughter of the Shechemites (see ch. xxxiv.) Jacob journeyed southward; but from the fact that his sons were sent to feed sheep in Shechem, it is not impossible that he may have left some of his cattle still in their old pastures, and his anxiety here about his sons, who were thus feeding in Shechem, may have arisen in part from the enmity excited against them in that neighbourhood by their violence. In ch. xxxv. we trace Jacob's southward journeyings from Shechem first to Bethel, v. 6; then to Bethlehem, vv. 16, 19; then to the tower of Edar, v. 21; and finally to Hebron, v. 27, where Isaac died, v. 29. But from this verse, ch. xxxvii. 14, we infer that Jacob must have arrived at Hebron several years before his father's death.

17. *Dothan*] or *Dothain*, the two wells or cisterns. They may have gone there because of the water in these wells. Dothan is said (Euseb. 'Onomasticon') to have been twelve Roman miles north of Sebaste (*i.e.* Shechem or Samaria) towards the plain of Jezreel. It still retains its ancient name (Robinson, 'B. R.' III. 122).

20. *some pit*] A cistern, or well, dug by the shepherds of the country, to catch and preserve the rain-water. Some of these cisterns were very deep, and a lad thrown into one of them would have been unable to escape.

24. *the pit was empty, there was no water in it*] Apparently referred to by Zech. ix. 11, in a prophecy of the Messiah. Joseph has been recognised by most Christian interpreters as a type of Christ; in his father's love for him, in his being sent to his brethren, rejected by them, sold to the Gentiles, delivered to death, in the sanctity of his life, in his humiliation, in his exaltation to be a Prince and a Saviour, in that his father and mother and brethren all came and bowed down to him. We may notice here, that the counsels of his brethren to prevent the fulfilment of his dreams, like the counsels of Herod and the Jews to prevent the fulfilment of the prophecies con-

25 And they sat down to eat
bread: and they lifted up their eyes
and looked, and, behold, a company
of Ishmeelites came from Gilead with
their camels bearing spicery and balm
and myrrh, going to carry *it* down to
Egypt.
26 And Judah said unto his brethren, What profit *is it* if we slay
our brother, and conceal his blood?
27 Come, and let us sell him to
the Ishmeelites, and let not our hand
be upon him; for he *is* our brother
† Heb. *hearkened.* *and* our flesh. And his brethren †were
content.
28 Then there passed by Midianites merchantmen; and they drew and
[b] Psal. 105. 17. Wisd. 10. 13. Acts 7. 9. lifted up Joseph out of the pit, [b]and
sold Joseph to the Ishmeelites for
twenty *pieces* of silver: and they
brought Joseph into Egypt.
29 ¶ And Reuben returned unto
the pit; and, behold, Joseph *was* not
in the pit; and he rent his clothes.
30 And he returned unto his brethren, and said, The child *is* not;
and I, whither shall I go?
31 And they took Joseph's coat,
and killed a kid of the goats, and
dipped the coat in the blood;
32 And they sent the coat of *many*
colours, and they brought *it* to their
father; and said, This have we found:
know now whether it *be* thy son's
coat or no.
33 And he knew it, and said, *It is*
my son's coat; an [c]evil beast hath de- [c] chap. 44. 28.
voured him; Joseph is without doubt
rent in pieces.
34 And Jacob rent his clothes, and
put sackcloth upon his loins, and
mourned for his son many days.
35 And all his sons and all his
daughters rose up to comfort him;
but he refused to be comforted; and
he said, For I will go down into the
grave unto my son mourning. Thus
his father wept for him.

---

cerning Jesus, only served to bring about God's counsels, which were wrought out by the very means taken to defeat them. If Joseph had not been sold to the Midianites, he would never have been exalted to be governor in Egypt. If Christ had not been persecuted and at last crucified, He would not have worked out redemption for us, have risen from the dead, and ascended up into His glory.

25. *they sat down to eat bread*] In this heartless meal Reuben can have taken no part. It appears from verse 29, that he must have left his brethren, perhaps with the very purpose of seeking means to rescue Joseph. The simplicity and truthfulness of the narrative are all the more apparent by the indifference of the writer to the question how and why it was that Reuben was absent at this point of the history. A forger would have been likely to tell all about it, and make it all plain. Yet strangely enough, this very artlessness has been made an argument against the historical truth of the narrative, as being clumsily arranged, and inconsistent in these details.

25. *a company of Ishmeelites*] "A travelling company" or "caravan." Ishmaelites afterwards called Midianites in v. 28, and Medanim in v. 36. See note on ch. xxv. 2. Medan and Midian were sons of Abraham by Keturah; Ishmael his son by Hagar. The Ishmaelites and Midianites were near neighbours, and very probably joined together in caravans and commercial enterprizes. Very probably too the Ishmaelites, being the more powerful tribe, may have by this time become a general name for several smaller and associated tribes.

spicery] probably "storax," the gum of the styrax-tree. So Aqu. followed by Bochart, 'Hieroz.' II. p. 532, Gesen. 'Thes.' p. 883, &c. The LXX. and Vulg. give only "perfumes."

balm] Probably the gum of the opobalsam or balsam-tree, which grew abundantly in Gilead, and was especially used for healing wounds. This is the interpretation commonly given by the Jews, and adopted by Bochart ('Hieroz.' I. 628); Celsius ('Hierob.' II. 180); Ges. 'Thes.' 1185, &c.). Lee (Lex. in loc.) contends for "mastich" as the right rendering.

myrrh] According to almost all modern interpreters Ladanum, an odoriferous gum found on the leaves of the *cistus creticus* or *cistus ladanifera*. (See Celsius, 'Hierob.' I. 280—288, Gesen. 'Thes.' p. 748, Smith, 'Dict. of Bible,' s.v. *Myrrh*.)

27. *were content*] **hearkened.**

35. *his daughters*] See on ch. xxx. 21.

into the grave] **To sheol.** He thought his son devoured by wild beasts, therefore the word *Sheol* translated "grave" must here mean the place of the departed. The word appears to signify a hollow subterraneous place (comp. *hell*, *hole*, &c.). (See Ges. 'Thes.' p. 1348.)

36 And the Midianites sold him
into Egypt unto Potiphar, an †officer
of Pharaoh's, *and* †‖captain of the
guard.

† Heb. *eunuch.* But the word doth signify not only *eunuchs*, but also *chamberlains, courtiers*, and *officers.*
† Heb. *chief of the slaughtermen*, or, *executioners.*
‖ Or, *chief marshal.*

CHAPTER XXXVIII.

1 *Judah begetteth Er, Onan, and Shelah.* 6 *Er marrieth Tamar.* 8 *The trespass of Onan.* 11 *Tamar stayeth for Shelah.* 13 *She deceiveth Judah.* 27 *She beareth twins, Pharez and Zarah.*

AND it came to pass at that time,
that Judah went down from his
brethren, and turned in to a certain
Adullamite, whose name *was* Hirah.
2 And Judah saw there a daughter
of a certain Canaanite, whose name
was [a] Shuah; and he took her, and
went in unto her.
3 And she conceived, and bare a
son; and he called his name Er.
4 [b] And she conceived again, and
bare a son; and she called his name
Onan.
5 And she yet again conceived,
and bare a son; and called his name
Shelah: and he was at Chezib, when
she bare him.
6 And Judah took a wife for Er

[a] 1 Chron. 2. 3.
[b] Numb. 26. 19.

---

36. *Potiphar*] Generally supposed to be the same as Potiphera, *i.e.* "devoted to Ra," the Sun-God. (See Ges. 'Thes.,' p. 1094.) It is far more probably "devoted to Par or Phar," *i.e.* to the Royal House or Palace. (See 'Excursus on Egyptian Words' at the end of this volume.)

an officer of Pharaoh's] Heb. "an eunuch;" but used also of chamberlains and other officers about the court. The immediate predecessor in Manetho of Sesostris, who was of the same dynasty with Joseph's Pharaoh, was slain by his eunuchs.

captain of the guard] **Chief of the executioners**, or "commander of the body guard," who executed the sentences of the king. (Cp. 2 K. xxv. 8; Jer. xxxix. 9, lii. 12.) Herod. (II. 168) tells us that "a thousand Calasirians and the same number of Hermotybians formed in alternate years the body-guard of the king" of Egypt.

CHAP. XXXVIII. 1. *it came to pass at that time*] This chapter may appear to be an useless digression inserted at an inconvenient time; but in reality it supplies a very important link, and this was probably the best place for its introduction. In the *Toledoth*, or family history, of Jacob, the two chief persons were Joseph and Judah; Joseph from his high character, his personal importance, his influence in the future destinies of the race, and his typical foreshadowing of the Messiah; Judah, from his obtaining the virtual right of primogeniture, and from his being the ancestor of David and of the Son of David. Hence, at a natural pause in the history of Joseph, viz. when he had been now sold into Egypt and settled in Potiphar's house, the historian recurs to the events in the family of Judah, which he carries down to the birth of Pharez, the next link in the ancestry of the Saviour. Thus he clears away all that was necessary to be told of the history of the twelve patriarchs, with the exception of that which was involved in the history of Joseph. There is also a remarkable contrast brought vividly out by this juxtaposition of the impure line of Judah and his children with the chastity and moral integrity of Joseph as seen in the succeeding chapter.

at that time] It is by no means certain that this note of time is to be immediately connected with the events in the last chapter. The strict chronological sequence in these *Toledoth* is not always followed. Episodes, like the genealogies of Ishmael and Esau above referred to, are introduced here and there, in order to avoid interrupting the general order of another narrative, and so this episode of the history of Judah is brought in to prevent an interruption in the history of Joseph. If the chronology in note at the end of ch. xxxi. be adopted, Judah would have been at least 26 at the time of Jacob's flight from Padan-aram, and from that time to the going down to Egypt there would be an interval of 33 years.

went down from his brethren] *i.e.* went southward (Abenezra, Rosenm. &c.).

Adullamite] Adullam, a place afterwards famous in the history of David, 1 S. xxii. 1 (see also Josh. xii. 15; 2 S. xxiii. 13; 1 Chr. xi. 15; 2 Chr. xi. 7; Micah i. 15), is mentioned by Jerome as existing in his day, then a small village to the east of Eleutheropolis. It must have lain in the southern part of the plain of Judah, but its site has not been discovered by modern travellers.

2. *a certain Canaanite, whose name was Shuah*] Shuah was the name of the father of Judah's wife, not of the wife herself, as appears from the Hebrew and from v. 12. This marriage of Judah with one of the daughters of the land was the fruitful source of sin and misery in his family.

5. *at Chezib*] Probably the same as Achzib mentioned with Adullam, Mic. i. 14, 15.

his firstborn, whose name *was* Tamar.

[c Numb. 26. 19.]

7 And [c] Er, Judah's firstborn, was
wicked in the sight of the LORD; and
the LORD slew him.

8 And Judah said unto Onan, Go
in unto thy brother's wife, and marry
her, and raise up seed to thy brother.

9 And Onan knew that the seed
should not be his; and it came to
pass, when he went in unto his brother's wife, that he spilled *it* on the
ground, lest that he should give seed
to his brother.

10 And the thing which he did
† displeased the LORD: wherefore he
slew him also.

[† Heb. *was evil in the eyes of the LORD.*]

11 Then said Judah to Tamar his
daughter in law, Remain a widow at
thy father's house, till Shelah my son
be grown: for he said, Lest peradventure he die also, as his brethren
did. And Tamar went and dwelt in
her father's house.

12 ¶ And † in process of time the
daughter of Shuah Judah's wife died;
and Judah was comforted, and went
up unto his sheepshearers to Timnath, he and his friend Hirah the
Adullamite.

[† Heb. *the days were multiplied.*]

13 And it was told Tamar, saying,
Behold thy father in law goeth up to
Timnath to shear his sheep.

14 And she put her widow's garments off from her, and covered her
with a vail, and wrapped herself, and
sat in † an open place, which *is* by the
way to Timnath; for she saw that
Shelah was grown, and she was not
given unto him to wife.

[† Heb. *the door of eyes,* or, *of Enajim.*]

15 When Judah saw her, he thought
her *to be* an harlot; because she had
covered her face.

16 And he turned unto her by the
way, and said, Go to, I pray thee,
let me come in unto thee; (for he
knew not that she *was* his daughter
in law.) And she said, What wilt
thou give me, that thou mayest come
in unto me?

17 And he said, I will send *thee*
† a kid from the flock. And she said,
Wilt thou give *me* a pledge, till thou
send *it?*

[† Heb. *a kid of the goats.*]

---

6. *Tamar*] *i.e.* "a palm-tree."

8. *raise up seed to thy brother*] As this was before the law of Moses, it would appear probable that this *lex leviratus*, law of marriage with a brother's widow, rested on some traditional custom, very probably among the Chaldees. The law of Moses did not abolish it, but gave rules concerning it (Deut. xxv. 5), as was the case as regards many other ancient practices. This law of levirate marriage prevailed among Indian, Persian, African, and some Italian races (Diod. Sic. XII. 18).

11. *Then said Judah to Tamar*] Judah perhaps superstitiously seems to have thought Tamar in some way the cause of his son's death (cp. Tobit iii. 7); or he may have thought Shelah too young to marry.

12. *Timnath*] Probably not the border town of Dan and Judah, between Ekron and Beth Shemesh (Josh. xv. 10), but Timnah in the mountains of Judah (Josh. xv. 57).

his friend] The LXX., and Vulg. have "his shepherd," but Onkelos, Syr., Arab. and most modern interpreters, render as the Authorised Version, which is probably right.

14. *in an open place*] **In the gate of Enaim.** So the LXX., Jerome (in 'Loc. Heb.'), Gesen., Winer and most modern interpreters. Enaim is probably the same as Enam, Josh. xv. 34. Enam is a place in the plain which lay on the road from Judah's dwelling-place to Timnath (Knobel). Other possible renderings are "at the opening of the eyes," *i.e.* in a public place, such as "the crossing of two roads," (so Vulg., Syr., and many Jewish interpreters); and "at the breaking forth of two fountains" (so Abenezra, Rosenm. and others): but the first is pretty certainly the true.

15. *an harlot; because she had covered her face*] Probably Judah thought her to be a woman having a vow. In v. 21, he calls her by a title translated "harlot," meaning literally "consecrated," *i.e.* to the impure worship of Astarte, as was the custom of Babylon in the worship of Mylitta (Herod. I. 199). This abominable worship was very early introduced into Canaan and Egypt. So *Kedeshah*, "a consecrated woman," appears to have come into use as a kind of euphemism. The veil probably led Judah to think her thus under a vow: for there is no reason to suppose that mere profligates so covered their faces (see Ges. 'Thes.' p. 1197). The worship of the *Dea Syra* at Byblos is recorded at a very early age. In the time of Rameses II. it was already very ancient.

18 And he said, What pledge shall
I give thee? And she said, Thy signet, and thy bracelets, and thy staff
that *is* in thine hand. And he gave
it her, and came in unto her, and she
conceived by him.
19 And she arose, and went away,
and laid by her vail from her, and
put on the garments of her widow-
hood.
20 And Judah sent the kid by the
hand of his friend the Adullamite, to
receive *his* pledge from the woman's
hand: but he found her not.
21 Then he asked the men of that
place, saying, Where *is* the harlot,
that *was* ‖ openly by the way side?
And they said, There was no harlot
in this *place*.
22 And he returned to Judah, and
said, I cannot find her; and also the
men of the place said, *that* there was
no harlot in this *place*.
23 And Judah said, Let her take
it to her, lest we † be shamed: behold, I sent this kid, and thou hast
not found her.
24 ¶ And it came to pass about
three months after, that it was told
Judah, saying, Tamar thy daughter
in law hath played the harlot; and
also, behold, she *is* with child by
whoredom. And Judah said, Bring
her forth, and let her be burnt.
25 When she *was* brought forth,
she sent to her father in law, saying,
By the man, whose these *are*, *am* I
with child: and she said, Discern, I
pray thee, whose *are* these, the signet,
and bracelets, and staff.
26 And Judah acknowledged *them*,
and said, She hath been more righteous
than I; because that I gave her not
to Shelah my son. And he knew her
again no more.
27 ¶ And it came to pass in the
time of her travail, that, behold, twins
were in her womb.
28 And it came to pass, when she
travailed, that *the one* put out *his* hand:
and the midwife took and bound upon
his hand a scarlet thread, saying, This
came out first.
29 And it came to pass, as he drew
back his hand, that, behold, his brother
came out: and she said, ‖ How hast
thou broken forth? *this* breach *be* upon thee: therefore his name was called
‖ *d* Pharez.
30 And afterward came out his
brother, that had the scarlet thread
upon his hand: and his name was
called Zarah.

‖ Or, *in Enajim.*

† Heb. *become a contempt.*

‖ Or, *Wherefore hast thou made this breach against thee?*

‖ That is, *a breach.*

d 1 Chron. 2. 4. Matt. 1. 3.

CHAPTER XXXIX.

1 *Joseph advanced in Potiphar's house.* 7 *He resisteth his mistress's temptation.* 13 *He is falsely accused.* 20 *He is cast in prison.* 21 *God is with him there.*

AND Joseph was brought down to
Egypt; and Potiphar, an officer
of Pharaoh, captain of the guard, an
Egyptian, bought him of the hands

---

18. *Thy signet*] A seal or signet-ring. The ancients wore it sometimes, not as a ring on the finger, but hanging round the neck by a cord or chain (Ges. 'Thes.' p. 534).

thy bracelets] **Thy cord**: the cord or string by which the seal was suspended (so Ges., Rosenm., Schum., Lee).

staff] It was probably of considerable value, as among the Babylonians, and on Egyptian monuments.

21. *openly*] **At Enaim**. See on v. 14.

26. *She has been more righteous than I*] Judah acknowledges that he had done wrong to Tamar in not giving her his son Shelah, according to the *lex leviratus*, that the brother should raise up seed to his brother. It appears further from Ruth ch. iii. iv. that, according to the patriarchal custom, the nearest of kin was to take the widow to wife, hence when Shelah does not take her, she considers Judah the right person with whom to form such an alliance.

29. *How hast thou broken forth? this breach be upon thee*] Or, "why hast thou made a rent for thyself?" or "hast rent a rent for thyself?"

Pharez] *i.e.* "breach" or "breaking forth."

30. *Zarah*] *i.e.* "rising."

CHAP. XXXIX. 1. *And Joseph was brought down to Egypt*, &c.] A recapitulation of the narrative in ch. xxxvii. 36, which had been interrupted by the history of Judah's family in ch. xxxviii.

Ishmeelites] See on ch. xxxvii. 25.

of the Ishmeelites, which had brought
him down thither.
2 And the LORD was with Joseph,
and he was a prosperous man; and he
was in the house of his master the
Egyptian.
3 And his master saw that the
LORD *was* with him, and that the
LORD made all that he did to prosper
in his hand.
4 And Joseph found grace in his
sight, and he served him: and he
made him overseer over his house,
and all *that* he had he put into his
hand.
5 And it came to pass from the
time *that* he had made him overseer
in his house, and over all that he had,
that the LORD blessed the Egyptian's
house for Joseph's sake; and the blessing of the LORD was upon all that he
had in the house, and in the field.
6 And he left all that he had in
Joseph's hand; and he knew not
ought he had, save the bread which
he did eat. And Joseph was *a* goodly
person, and well favoured.
7 ¶ And it came to pass after these
things, that his master's wife cast her
eyes upon Joseph; and she said, Lie
with me.
8 But he refused, and said unto
his master's wife, Behold, my master
wotteth not what *is* with me in the
house, and he hath committed all that
he hath to my hand;
9 *There is* none greater in this house
than I; neither hath he kept back any
thing from me but thee, because thou
art his wife: how then can I do this
great wickedness, and sin against God?
10 And it came to pass, as she
spake to Joseph day by day, that he
hearkened not unto her, to lie by her,
or to be with her.
11 And it came to pass about this
time, that *Joseph* went into the house
to do his business; and *there was* none
of the men of the house there within.
12 And she caught him by his garment, saying, Lie with me: and he
left his garment in her hand, and fled,
and got him out.
13 And it came to pass, when she

2. *the* LORD *was with Joseph*] The variety in the use of the Divine names in the history of Joseph is very observable. The name JEHOVAH occurs only where the narrator is speaking in his own person; until we come to ch. xlix. where Jacob uses it in the midst of his blessing on Dan, ch. xlix. 18. In all other speeches in the history we have Elohim, sometimes Ha-Elohim with the article, and sometimes El, or Ha-El. The reason of this is generally apparent. The whole history, though given by an inspired writer to whom the name JEHOVAH was familiar, concerns the history of Joseph and his kindred in contact with a heathen people. It is therefore on all accounts natural that the general name Elohim, and not the specially revealed name JEHOVAH, should be used in dialogue. Even the narrative, as in ch. xlvi., is most naturally carried on in a so-called Elohistic form, the name Elohim being of common use to both Hebrews and Egyptians. The adoption of the name *El* (or Ha-El) in xlvi. 3, is probably with marked reference to the blessing on Abraham pronounced in the name of *El-Shaddai* in ch. xvii. 1.

4. *overseer*] The Egyptian sculptures represent the property of rich men as superintended by scribes or stewards, who are exhibited as carefully registering all the operations of the household, the garden, the field, &c.

6. *Joseph was a goodly person, and well favoured*] Lit. "was fair of form and fair of aspect," or "appearance."

7. *his master's wife*] The licentiousness of the Egyptian women has always been complained of (see Herod. II. 111; Diod. I. 59). The same appears from the monuments, which prove also that women did not live so retired a life in Egypt as in other ancient and especially Eastern countries (Wilkinson, Vol. II. p. 389, Hengstenb. 'Egypt.' p. 26). There is a very remarkable resemblance between this passage in the history of Joseph and a very ancient Egyptian Romance in the Papyrus d'Orbiney in the British Museum, called "The Two Brothers," in which the wife of the elder brother acts in the same manner and uses almost the same words towards the younger brother as Potiphar's wife uses towards Joseph (see Ebers, 'Ægypten,' p. 311).

9. *sin against God*] The direct sin would have been against his master; but Joseph clearly recognized that the true guilt of all sin consists in its breach of the law, and disobedience to the will of God.

saw that he had left his garment in
her hand, and was fled forth,
14 That she called unto the men
of her house, and spake unto them,
saying, See, he hath brought in an
Hebrew unto us to mock us; he came
in unto me to lie with me, and I cried
with a †loud voice: † Heb. *great.*
15 And it came to pass, when he
heard that I lifted up my voice and
cried, that he left his garment with
me, and fled, and got him out.
16 And she laid up his garment
by her, until his lord came home.
17 And she spake unto him according to these words, saying, The Hebrew servant, which thou hast brought
unto us, came in unto me to mock me:
18 And it came to pass, as I lifted
up my voice and cried, that he left his
garment with me, and fled out.
19 And it came to pass, when his
master heard the words of his wife,
which she spake unto him, saying,
After this manner did thy servant to
me; that his wrath was kindled.
20 And Joseph's master took him,
and put him into the prison, a place
where the king's prisoners *were* bound:
and he was there in the prison.
21 ¶ But the LORD was with Jo-
seph, and †shewed him mercy, and † Heb. *extended kindness unto him.*
gave him favour in the sight of the
keeper of the prison.
22 And the keeper of the prison
committed to Joseph's hand all the
prisoners that *were* in the prison; and
whatsoever they did there, he was the
doer *of it.*
23 The keeper of the prison looked
not to anything *that was* under his
hand; because the LORD was with
him, and *that* which he did, the LORD
made *it* to prosper.

CHAPTER XL.

1 The butler and baker of Pharaoh in prison. 4 Joseph hath charge of them. 5 He interpreteth their dreams. 20 They come to pass according to his interpretation. 23 The ingratitude of the butler.

AND it came to pass after these
things, *that* the butler of the
king of Egypt and *his* baker had offended their lord the king of Egypt.
2 And Pharaoh was wroth against
two *of* his officers, against the chief
of the butlers, and against the chief
of the bakers.
3 And he put them in ward in the
house of the captain of the guard,
into the prison, the place where Joseph *was* bound.

---

20. *prison*] The word here used occurs only here and in ch. xl. It probably means a turret or rounded (perhaps arched) building or apartment, arched or rounded for strength, used as a prison or dungeon. It appears from ch. xl. 3, to have been a part of the house of the captain of the guard or chief of the executioners, in which the state prisoners were kept, and to have had a special jailer or keeper of the prison, an officer of the chief of the executioners, placed over it. In ch. xl. 15, Joseph speaks of it as "a dungeon" or pit, which would quite correspond with the character of an arched or vaulted room. In Ps. cv. 17, 18, the imprisonment of Joseph is represented as having been very severe, "whose feet they afflicted with the fetters, the iron entered into his soul." It is most probable that at first Joseph's treatment may have been of this character, the crime with which he was charged having been such that a slave would most likely have been instantly put to death for it. By degrees, however, he gained, under God's Providence, the confidence of the jailer (v. 22), when the rigour of his confinement was mitigated, and at length the chief of the executioners himself (either Potiphar, or, as some think, his successor) intrusts him with the care of important state prisoners. The fact that Joseph was not put to death, and by degrees treated kindly in prison, has given rise to the conjecture, that Potiphar did not wholly believe his wife's story, though he to a certain extent acted on it (Cleric in loc., Keil, &c.).

CHAP. XL. 2. *the chief of the butlers*] **The chief of the cupbearers.** The office of cupbearer to the sovereign was one of importance and high honour in the East. See Herod. III. 34.

chief of the bakers] or "confectioners." The Targum of Pseudo-Jonathan adds that "they had taken counsel to throw the poison of death into his food and into his drink, to kill their master, the king of Mizraim." This is probably only a conjecture from the fact that the two offending persons were immediately concerned with the food and the drink of the king.

4 And the captain of the guard
charged Joseph with them, and he
served them: and they continued a
season in ward.
5 ¶ And they dreamed a dream
both of them, each man his dream in
one night, each man according to the
interpretation of his dream, the butler
and the baker of the king of Egypt,
which *were* bound in the prison.
6 And Joseph came in unto them
in the morning, and looked upon them,
and, behold, they *were* sad.
7 And he asked Pharaoh's officers
that *were* with him in the ward of his
lord's house, saying, Wherefore † look
ye *so* sadly to day?

† Heb. *are your faces evil?*

8 And they said unto him, We
have dreamed a dream, and *there is*
no interpreter of it. And Joseph said
unto them, *Do* not interpretations *be-*
long to God? tell me *them*, I pray you.
9 And the chief butler told his
dream to Joseph, and said to him, In
my dream, behold, a vine *was* before
me;
10 And in the vine *were* three
branches: and it *was* as though it
budded, *and* her blossoms shot forth;
and the clusters thereof brought forth
ripe grapes:
11 And Pharaoh's cup *was* in my
hand: and I took the grapes, and
pressed them into Pharaoh's cup, and
I gave the cup into Pharaoh's hand.
12 And Joseph said unto him, This
is the interpretation of it: The three
branches *are* three days:
13 Yet within three days shall
Pharaoh ‖ lift up thine head, and restore thee unto thy place: and thou
shalt deliver Pharaoh's cup into his
hand, after the former manner when
thou wast his butler.

‖ Or, *reckon.*

14 But † think on me when it shall
be well with thee, and shew kindness,
I pray thee, unto me, and make mention of me unto Pharaoh, and bring
me out of this house:

† Heb. *remember me with thee.*

15 For indeed I was stolen away
out of the land of the Hebrews: and
here also have I done nothing that
they should put me into the dungeon.
16 When the chief baker saw that

---

4. *they continued a season*] Lit. "days," by which the Jews very generally understand a year.

9. *a vine*] Herodotus denies the existence of vines in ancient Egypt, and says that the Egyptian wine was made of barley (II. 77). Yet Herodotus himself (II. 42, 48, 144) and Diodorus (I. 11) identify Osiris with the Greek Bacchus, the discoverer of the vine, and Diodorus (I. 15) expressly ascribes to Osiris the first cultivation of the vine. But, moreover, it now appears from the monuments that both the cultivation of grapes and the art of making wine were well known in Egypt from the time of the Pyramids. Wine was universally used by the rich throughout Egypt, and beer supplied its place at the tables of the poor, not because "they had no vines in the country, but because it was cheaper." (Sir G. Wilkinson's note in Rawlinson's Herod. II. 77. See also Rosellini, Vol. II. pp. 365, 373, 377; Wilkinson, Vol. II. 143; Hengstenberg, 'Egypt,' &c. p. 16; Hävernick, 'Introd. to Pentateuch,' in h. l.; Ebers, 'Ægypten,' p. 323.)

11. *I took the grapes, and pressed them*] Some have thought that this indicates that the Egyptians did not at this time practise the fermentation of the grape, but merely drank the fresh juice, which would accord with the statement of Plutarch ('Is. et Osir.' § 6) that the Egyptians before the time of Psammetichus neither drank wine nor made libations thereof, as esteeming it to have sprung from the blood of those who made war with the gods; but the monuments represent the process of fermenting wine in very early times. See last note.

13. *shall Pharaoh lift up thine head*] Some think this expression merely means "will take count of thee," "will remember thee." Cp. Ex. xxx. 12; Num. i. 49; where the marginal reading is "reckon." More probably the meaning is, "will take thee out of prison" (see Ges. p. 914).

15. *the land of the Hebrews*] Though the patriarchs had been strangers and pilgrims, yet Abraham, Isaac and Jacob had effected something like permanent settlements in the neighbourhood of Mamre, Hebron, Shechem, &c. Probably too the visit of Abraham to Egypt and the intercourse of the Egyptians with the Hittites and other Canaanitish tribes, had made the name of Hebrew known to the Egyptians. Joseph does not say "the land of Canaan," lest he should be confounded with the Canaanites, who were odious to himself as being idolaters.

the interpretation was good, he said
unto Joseph, I also *was* in my dream,
and, behold, *I had* three ‖white baskets on my head:

‖ Or, *full of holes.*

17 And in the uppermost basket
there was of all manner of † bakemeats
for Pharaoh; and the birds did eat
them out of the basket upon my head.

† Heb. *meat of Pharaoh, the work of a baker,* or, *cook.*

18 And Joseph answered and said,
This *is* the interpretation thereof:
The three baskets *are* three days:
19 Yet within three days shall
Pharaoh ‖lift up thy head from off
thee, and shall hang thee on a tree;
and the birds shall eat thy flesh from
off thee.

‖ Or, *reckon thee,* and take thy office *from thee.*

20 ¶ And it came to pass the third
day, *which was* Pharaoh's birthday,
that he made a feast unto all his servants: and he ‖lifted up the head of
the chief butler and of the chief baker
among his servants.

‖ Or, *reckoned.*

21 And he restored the chief butler unto his butlership again; and he
gave the cup into Pharaoh's hand:
22 But he hanged the chief baker:
as Joseph had interpreted to them.
23 Yet did not the chief butler remember Joseph, but forgat him.

CHAPTER XLI.

1 *Pharaoh's two dreams.* 25 *Joseph interpreteth them.* 33 *He giveth Pharaoh counsel.* 38 *Joseph is advanced.* 50 *He begetteth Manasseh and Ephraim.* 54 *The famine beginneth.*

AND it came to pass at the end
of two full years, that Pharaoh
dreamed: and, behold, he stood by
the river.
2 And, behold, there came up out
of the river seven well favoured kine
and fatfleshed; and they fed in a
meadow.
3 And, behold, seven other kine
came up after them out of the river,
ill favoured and leanfleshed; and stood
by the *other* kine upon the brink of
the river.
4 And the ill favoured and leanfleshed kine did eat up the seven well
favoured and fat kine. So Pharaoh
awoke.
5 And he slept and dreamed the
second time: and, behold, seven ears
of corn came up upon one stalk,
† rank and good.
6 And, behold, seven thin ears and
blasted with the east wind sprung up
after them.

† Heb. *fat.*

---

16. *three white baskets*] Probably "baskets of white bread;" so LXX., Aq., Vulg., Syr., Onk. Some prefer "baskets full of holes," "perforated," or "wicker baskets."

on my head] See Herod. II. 35, of the men bearing burdens on their heads.

17. *bakemeats for Pharaoh*] Lit. "food for Pharaoh, the work of a baker." The Egyptians appear to have been very luxurious in the preparation of different kinds of bread and pastry. (See Rosellini, Vol. II. 264; Wilkinson, II. 384; Hengstenberg, p. 27.)

19. *shall Pharaoh lift up thy head from off thee*] The same words as those used in v. 13, with the addition of "from off thee," making the most vital difference. The mode of punishment was probably decapitation, the most common form of execution in Egypt (Ges. p. 915); though some have thought hanging or crucifixion, as Onkelos in loc. Possibly the words may only indicate *capital* punishment, like the *capite plecti* of the Latins.

CHAP. XLI. 1. *the river*] The "yeor," an Egyptian word signifying "great river," or "canal," used in Scripture for the Nile. The Nile had a sacred and a profane name. The sacred name was *Hapi*, i.e. Apis. The profane name was *Aur*, with the epithet *aa* great. The Coptic forms ⲓⲁⲣⲟ, ⲓⲁⲣⲱ, correspond exactly to the Hebrew *yeor*.

2. *kine*] The Egyptians esteemed the cow above all other animals. It was sacred to Isis (Herod. II. 41), or rather to Athor, the Venus Genetrix of Egypt, and was looked on as "a symbol of the Earth and its cultivation and food" (Clem. Alex. 'Strom.' v. p. 671). Hence it was very natural that in Pharaoh's dream the fruitful and unfruitful years should be typified by well-favoured and ill-favoured kine (see Hengstenb. 'Egypt,' p. 28).

in a meadow] **In the reed grass.** The word (Achu) is of Egyptian origin. It is not common, but occurs in a papyrus of early date (*akh-akh*, green, verdant). Jerome (on Isai. xix. 7) says that "when he enquired of the learned what the word meant, he was told by the Egyptians that in their tongue every thing green that grows in marshes is called by this name." It probably therefore means the sedge, reed, or rank grass by the river's side.

7 And the seven thin ears devoured the seven rank and full ears. And
Pharaoh awoke, and, behold, *it was* a
dream.
8 And it came to pass in the
morning that his spirit was troubled; and he sent and called for
all the magicians of Egypt, and all
the wise men thereof: and Pharaoh
told them his dream; but *there was*
none that could interpret them unto
Pharaoh.
9 ¶ Then spake the chief butler
unto Pharaoh, saying, I do remember my faults this day:
10 Pharaoh was wroth with his
servants, and put me in ward in the
captain of the guard's house, *both* me
and the chief baker:
11 And we dreamed a dream in
one night, I and he; we dreamed
each man according to the interpretation of his dream.
12 And *there was* there with us a
young man, an Hebrew, servant to
the captain of the guard; and we told
[a] chap. 40. 12, &c. him, and he [a] interpreted to us our
dreams; to each man according to
his dream he did interpret.
13 And it came to pass, as he interpreted to us, so it was; me he
restored unto mine office, and him
he hanged.
14 ¶ [b] Then Pharaoh sent and called Joseph, and they † brought him [b] Psal. 105 20.
hastily out of the dungeon: and he † Heb. *made him run.*
shaved *himself*, and changed his rai-
ment, and came in unto Pharaoh.
15 And Pharaoh said unto Joseph,
I have dreamed a dream, and *there*
is none that can interpret it: and
I have heard say of thee, *that* ‖ thou ‖ Or, *when thou hearest a dream, thou canst interpret it.*
canst understand a dream to inter-
pret it.
16 And Joseph answered Pharaoh,
saying, *It is* not in me: God shall
give Pharaoh an answer of peace.
17 And Pharaoh said unto Joseph,
In my dream, behold, I stood upon
the bank of the river:
18 And, behold, there came up
out of the river seven kine, fatfleshed
and well favoured; and they fed in a
meadow:

---

6. *east wind*] Probably put for the S. E. wind (Chamsin), which blows from the desert of Arabia. The East wind of Egypt is not the scorching wind, and indeed seldom blows; but the South-east wind is so parching as to destroy the grass entirely, if it blows very long (see Hengstenberg, p. 10).

7. *behold, it was a dream*] The impression on Pharaoh's mind was so strong and vivid, that he could hardly believe it was not real. The particulars of the dream are all singularly appropriate. The scene is by the Nile, on which depends all the plenty of Egypt. The kine and the corn respectively denote the animal and the vegetable products of the country. The cattle feeding in the reed grass shewed that the Nile was fertilizing the land and supporting the life of the beasts. The lean cattle and the scorched-up corn foreshadowed a time when the Nile, for some reason, ceased to irrigate the land. The swallowing up of the fat by the lean signified that the produce of the seven years of plenty would be all consumed in the seven years of scarcity.

8. *magicians*] Apparently "sacred scribes;" the name, if Hebrew, being composed of two words signifying respectively *a style* and *sacred*. Some have thought the word to be of Egyptian origin, or perhaps a Hebrew compound imitating an Egyptian name (see Ges. 'Thes.' p. 521). There has, however, no Egyptian name been found like it. The magicians appear to have been a regular order of persons among the Egyptians, learned priests, who devoted themselves to magic and astrology (see Hengstenberg, p. 28, and Poole in Smith's 'Dict. of the Bible,' art. *Magic*).

13. *me he restored*] Joseph prophesied that I should be restored, and, as he prophesied, so it came to pass.

14. *shaved himself*] The Hebrews cherished long beards, but the Egyptians cut both hair and beard close, except in mourning for relations, when they let both grow long (Herod. II. 36). On the monuments when it was "intended to convey the idea of a man of low condition or a slovenly person, the artists represented him with a beard" (Wilkinson, Vol. III. p. 357; Hengstenberg, p. 30). Joseph, therefore, when about to appear before Pharaoh, was careful to adapt himself to the manners of the Egyptians.

15. *that thou canst understand a dream to interpret it*] Lit. **that thou hearest a dream to interpret it.**

18. *in a meadow*] **In the reed grass.** See on v. 2.

19 And, behold, seven other kine
came up after them, poor and very
ill favoured and leanfleshed, such as
I never saw in all the land of Egypt
for badness:
20 And the lean and the ill favoured kine did eat up the first seven
fat kine:
21 And when they had † eaten — † Heb. *come to the inward parts of them.*
them up, it could not be known that
they had eaten them; but they *were*
still ill favoured, as at the beginning.
So I awoke.
22 And I saw in my dream, and,
behold, seven ears came up in one
stalk, full and good:
23 And, behold, seven ears, ‖ wi- — ‖ Or, *small.*
thered, thin, *and* blasted with the
east wind, sprung up after them:
24 And the thin ears devoured the
seven good ears: and I told *this* unto
the magicians; but *there was* none
that could declare *it* to me.
25 ¶ And Joseph said unto Pharaoh, The dream of Pharaoh *is* one:
God hath shewed Pharaoh what he *is*
about to do.
26 The seven good kine *are* seven
years; and the seven good ears *are*
seven years: the dream *is* one.
27 And the seven thin and ill
favoured kine that came up after
them *are* seven years; and the seven
empty ears blasted with the east wind
shall be seven years of famine.
28 This *is* the thing which I have
spoken unto Pharaoh: What God *is*
about to do he sheweth unto Pharaoh.
29 Behold, there come seven years
of great plenty throughout all the
land of Egypt:
30 And there shall arise after them
seven years of famine; and all the
plenty shall be forgotten in the land
of Egypt; and the famine shall consume the land;
31 And the plenty shall not be
known in the land by reason of that
famine following; for it *shall be* very
† grievous. — † Heb. *heavy.*
32 And for that the dream was
doubled unto Pharaoh twice; *it is*
because the thing *is* ‖ established by — ‖ Or, *prepared of God.*
God, and God will shortly bring it
to pass.
33 Now therefore let Pharaoh look
out a man discreet and wise, and set
him over the land of Egypt.
34 Let Pharaoh do *this*, and let
him appoint ‖ officers over the land, — ‖ Or, *overseers.*
and take up the fifth part of the
land of Egypt in the seven plenteous
years.
35 And let them gather all the
food of those good years that come,
and lay up corn under the hand of
Pharaoh, and let them keep food in
the cities.
36 And that food shall be for store
to the land against the seven years of
famine, which shall be in the land of
Egypt; that the land † perish not — † Heb. *be not cut off.*
through the famine.
37 ¶ And the thing was good in
the eyes of Pharaoh, and in the eyes
of all his servants.
38 And Pharaoh said unto his servants, Can we find *such a one* as
this *is*, a man in whom the Spirit of
God *is?*
39 And Pharaoh said unto Joseph,
Forasmuch as God hath shewed thee
all this, *there is* none so discreet and
wise as thou *art:* — c Psal. 105. 21. 1 Mac. 2. 53. Acts 7. 10.
40 c Thou shalt be over my house,
and according unto thy word shall all
my people be † ruled: only in the — † Heb. *armed,* or, *kiss.*
throne will I be greater than thou.

---

34. *take up the fifth part of the land*] *i.e.* Let him exact a fifth of the produce of the land. The Hebrew is literally "let him fifth the land." (Compare our phrase "to tithe the land.") It has been questioned whether the advice was to purchase a fifth of all the produce, or rather to impose a tax amounting to one fifth of the produce of the land. It has been not improbably conjectured that the Egyptian kings usually imposed a tribute of one tenth, and that in this season of unusual abundance Joseph advises Pharaoh to double the impost, with the benevolent intention of afterwards selling the corn so collected in the time of famine (Cleric. in loc.). On the large storehouses and granaries of Egypt, see Hengstenb., p. 36, Wilkinson, II. 135.

40. *according unto thy word shall all my*

41 And Pharaoh said unto Joseph,
See, I have set thee over all the land
of Egypt.

42 And Pharaoh took off his ring
from his hand, and put it upon Joseph's hand, and arrayed him in ves-
tures of ‖ fine linen, and put a gold
chain about his neck;

‖ Or, *silk.*

43 And he made him to ride in
the second chariot which he had; and
they cried before him, ‖ † Bow the
knee: and he made him *ruler* over
all the land of Egypt.

‖ Or, *Tender father.* † Heb. *Abrech.*

44 And Pharaoh said unto Joseph,
I *am* Pharaoh, and without thee shall
no man lift up his hand or foot in all
the land of Egypt.

45 And Pharaoh called Joseph's
name Zaphnath-paaneah; and he gave
him to wife Asenath the daughter

---

people be ruled] So, or nearly so, ("at thy word shall all my people arm themselves, or dispose themselves,") the Versions, Targg. and most commentators. But Kimchi, Gesenius, Knobel, &c., render "and all my people shall kiss thy mouth," as a token of reverence and obedience. The objections to the latter interpretation are that the kiss of reverence was on the hand or the foot, not on the mouth, which was the kiss of love, and that the construction here is with a preposition never used with the verb signifying "to kiss."

42. *ring*] The signet-ring was the special symbol of office and authority. The seal to this day in the East is the common mode of attestation, and therefore when Pharaoh gave Joseph his ring he delegated to him his whole authority.

fine linen] The byssus or fine linen of the Egyptians. The word used for it is *Shes*, a well-ascertained Egyptian word. It is mentioned in Ezek. xxvii. as imported into Tyre from Egypt. It was the peculiar dress of the Egyptian priests.

a gold chain] Probably "a simple gold chain in imitation of string, to which a stone scarabæus set in the same precious metal was appended." (Wilkinson, III. 376. See also Hengstenberg, p. 31.)

43. *Bow the knee*] **Abrech.** If the word be Hebrew, the rendering of the Authorised Version is probably correct. The Targums all give "father of the king" (cp. ch. xlv. 8), deriving from the Hebrew *Ab*, a father, and the Chaldee *Rech*, a king, which, however, is thought to be a corruption of the Latin *Rex*. It is generally thought to be an Egyptian word signifying "Bow the head," having some resemblance in form to the Hebrew (De Rossi, 'Etymol. Egypt.' p. 1. So Gesen. 'Thes.,' p. 19, and most of the Germans). A more probable interpretation is that which is given in the Excursus on Egyptian Words at the end of this volume, viz. "Rejoice" or "Rejoice thou!"

45. *Zaphnath-paaneah*] In the LXX. *Psonthomphanek*. The Vulg. renders *Salvator Mundi*, "Saviour of the World." Several learned in the language and antiquities of Egypt, Bernard (in Joseph, 'Ant.' II. 6); Jablonski ('Opusc.' I. 207); Rosellini ('Monuments,' I. p. 185), have so interpreted it. They are followed in the main by Gesenius (p. 1181, "the supporter or preserver of the age") and a majority of modern commentators. The true meaning appears to be "the food of life," or "of the living." (See Excursus on Egyptian Words at the end of this volume.) The Targg., Syr., Arab. and Hebrew interpp. render "a revealer of secrets," referring to a Hebrew original, which is on every account improbable. There can be no doubt that Pharaoh would have given his Grand Vizier an Egyptian name, not a Hebrew name, just as the name of Daniel was changed to Belteshazzar, and as Hananiah, Azariah and Mishael, were called by Nebuchadnezzar, Shadrach, Meshach, and Abednego.

Asenath] either "devoted to Neith," the Egyptian Minerva (Ges. 'Thes.' p. 130), or perhaps compounded of the two names Isis and Neith, such a form of combination of two names in one being not unknown in Egypt. (See Excursus on Egyptian Words at the end of this volume.)

Poti-pherah] *i.e.* "belonging" or "devoted to Ra," *i.e.* the Sun, a most appropriate designation for a priest of On or Heliopolis, the great seat of the Sun-worship. (See Excursus on Egyptian Words at the end of this volume.)

On] Heliopolis (LXX), called, Jer. xliii. 13, Beth-shemesh, the city of the Sun. Cyril (ad. Hos. v. 8), says, "On is with them the Sun." The city stood on the Eastern bank of the Nile a few miles north of Memphis, and was famous for the worship of Ra, the Sun, as also for the learning and wisdom of its priests (Herod. II. 3). There still remains an obelisk of red granite, part of the Temple of the Sun, with a dedication sculptured by Osirtasen or Sesortasen I. It is the oldest and one of the finest in Egypt; of the 12th dynasty. (Ges. p. 52, Wilkinson, Vol. I. p. 44; also Rawlinson's Herod. II. 8, Brugsch, 'H. E.' p. 254.)

The difficulty of supposing that the daughter of a priest of On should have been married to Joseph, a worshipper of JEHOVAH, has been unduly magnified. Neither the Egyptians nor the Hebrews were at this time as exclusive as

‖ Or, *prince.* of Poti-pherah ‖ priest of On. And
Joseph went out over *all* the land of
Egypt.
46 ¶ And Joseph *was* thirty years
old when he stood before Pharaoh
king of Egypt. And Joseph went
out from the presence of Pharaoh,
and went throughout all the land of
Egypt.
47 And in the seven plenteous
years the earth brought forth by
handfuls.
48 And he gathered up all the
food of the seven years, which were
in the land of Egypt, and laid up
the food in the cities: the food of
the field, which *was* round about
every city, laid he up in the same.
49 And Joseph gathered corn as
the sand of the sea, very much, until
he left numbering; for *it was* without number.
d chap. 46. 20. & 48. 5. 50 *d* And unto Joseph were born
two sons before the years of famine
came, which Asenath the daughter
‖ Or, *prince.* of Poti-pherah ‖ priest of On bare
unto him.
51 And Joseph called the name of
‖ That is, *Forgetting.* the firstborn ‖ Manasseh: For God,
said he, hath made me forget all my
toil, and all my father's house.
52 And the name of the second
‖ That is, *Fruitful.* called he ‖ Ephraim: For God hath
caused me to be fruitful in the land
of my affliction.
53 ¶ And the seven years of plen-
teousness, that was in the land of
Egypt, were ended.
54 *e* And the seven years of dearth *e* Psal. 105. 16.
began to come, according as Joseph
had said: and the dearth was in all
lands; but in all the land of Egypt
there was bread.
55 And when all the land of Egypt
was famished, the people cried to Pharaoh for bread: and Pharaoh said unto all the Egyptians, Go unto Joseph;
what he saith to you, do.
56 And the famine was over all
the face of the earth: And Joseph
opened † all the storehouses, and sold † Heb. *all wherein* was.
unto the Egyptians; and the famine
waxed sore in the land of Egypt.
57 And all countries came into
Egypt to Joseph for to buy *corn;*
because that the famine was *so* sore
in all lands.

CHAPTER XLII.

1 *Jacob sendeth his ten sons to buy corn in Egypt.* 16 *They are imprisoned by Joseph for spies.* 18 *They are set at liberty, on condition to bring Benjamin.* 21 *They have remorse for Joseph.* 24 *Simeon is kept for a pledge.* 25 *They return with corn, and their money.* 29 *Their relation to Jacob.* 36 *Jacob refuseth to send Benjamin.*

NOW when *a* Jacob saw that *a* Acts 7. 12.
there was corn in Egypt, Ja-
cob said unto his sons, Why do ye
look one upon another?
2 And he said, Behold, I have

---

they became afterwards. The Semitic races were treated with respect in Egypt. Joseph had become thoroughly naturalized (see v. 51 and ch. xliii. 32), with an Egyptian name and the rank of Viceroy or Grand Vizier. Abraham had before this taken Hagar, an Egyptian, to wife, which would make such an alliance less strange to Joseph. Whether Asenath adopted Joseph's faith we are not told, but, in the end at least, she probably did. (See also Excursus on Egyptian Words, on "Asenath wife of Joseph," at the end of this volume.)

46. *thirty years old*] He must therefore have been thirteen years in Egypt, either in Potiphar's house or in prison. (See ch. xxxvii. 2.)

51. *Manasseh*] *i.e.* "causing to forget." He was comforted by all his prosperity, so that he no longer mourned over his exile. It does not follow that he was ungratefully forgetful of his home.

52. *Ephraim*] *i.e.* "doubly fruitful," a dual form.

54. *the dearth*] Notwithstanding the fertility generally produced in Egypt by the overflowing of the Nile, yet the swelling of the Nile a few feet above or below what is necessary, has in many instances produced destructive and protracted famines, such that the people have been reduced to the horrible necessity of eating human flesh, and have been almost swept away by death. (See Hengstenberg, 'Egypt,' &c., pp. 37, 38; Hävernick, Int. to Pentateuch, p. 218; also Smith's 'Dict. of Bible,' art. *Famine.*)

in all lands] The drought which affected Egypt reached the neighbouring countries also. Ethiopia, Arabia, Palestine, and Syria, would be especially affected by it; and the Egyptians, and Hebrews also, would look on these lands as comprehending the whole known world.

heard that there is corn in Egypt:
get you down thither, and buy for
us from thence; that we may live,
and not die.
3 ¶ And Joseph's ten brethren
went down to buy corn in Egypt.
4 But Benjamin, Joseph's brother,
Jacob sent not with his brethren; for
he said, Lest peradventure mischief
befall him.
5 And the sons of Israel came to
buy *corn* among those that came: for
the famine was in the land of Canaan.
6 And Joseph *was* the governor
over the land, *and* he *it was* that
sold to all the people of the land: and
Joseph's brethren came, and bowed
down themselves before him *with*
their faces to the earth.
7 And Joseph saw his brethren,
and he knew them, but made himself strange unto them, and spake
† roughly unto them; and he said un- † Heb. *hard things with them.*
to them, Whence come ye? And
they said, From the land of Canaan
to buy food.
8 And Joseph knew his brethren,
but they knew not him.
9 And Joseph [b] remembered the [b] chap. 37. 5.
dreams which he dreamed of them,
and said unto them, Ye *are* spies; to
see the nakedness of the land ye are
come.
10 And they said unto him, Nay,
my lord, but to buy food are thy
servants come.
11 We *are* all one man's sons; we
are true *men*, thy servants are no spies.
12 And he said unto them, Nay,
but to see the nakedness of the land
ye are come.
13 And they said, Thy servants
are twelve brethren, the sons of one
man in the land of Canaan; and,
behold, the youngest *is* this day with
our father, and one *is* not.
14 And Joseph said unto them,
That *is it* that I spake unto you,
saying, Ye *are* spies:
15 Hereby ye shall be proved: By
the life of Pharaoh ye shall not go
forth hence, except your youngest
brother come hither.
16 Send one of you, and let him
fetch your brother, and ye shall be
† kept in prison, that your words may † Heb. *bound.*
be proved, whether *there be any* truth
in you: or else by the life of Pharaoh
surely ye *are* spies.
17 And he † put them all together † Heb. *gathered.*
into ward three days.
18 And Joseph said unto them the
third day, This do, and live; *for* I
fear God:
19 If ye *be* true *men*, let one of
your brethren be bound in the house
of your prison: go ye, carry corn for
the famine of your houses:

CHAP. XLII. 6. *he it was that sold to all the people of the land*] We are not to suppose that Joseph personally sold the corn to all buyers, but that he ordered the selling of it, and set the price upon it; and very probably, when a company of foreigners came to purchase in large quantities, they were introduced personally to Joseph, that he might enquire concerning them and give directions as to the sale of corn to them.

7. *spake roughly unto them*] Lit. "spake hard things with them," as the margin. This did not arise from a vindictive spirit. It was partly that he might not be recognized by them, and partly that he might prove them and see whether they were penitent for what they had done to him.

8. *they knew not him*] He was only 17 when they sold him; he was now at least 37, and had adopted all the habits and manners of the Egyptians; probably even his complexion had been much darkened by living so long in a southern climate.

9. *the nakedness of the land*] *i.e.* the defenceless and assailable points of the country; like the Latin phrases, *nuda urbs præsidio*, *nudata castra*, *nudi defensoribus muri* (Ros.; Cp. Hom. 'Il.' XII. 399, τεῖχος ἐγυμνώθη). The Egyptians were always most liable to be assailed from the East and North-east. (See Herod. III. 5.) The various Arab and Canaanitish tribes seem to have constantly made incursions into the more settled and civilized land of Egypt. Particularly the Hittites were at constant feud with the Egyptians. Moreover the famous Hycsos invasion and domination may have been very nearly impending at this period.

15. *By the life of Pharaoh*] Cp. similar phrases (1 S. i. 26; xvii. 55; 2 S. xiv. 19; 2 K. ii. 2, 4, 6). Not distinctly an oath, but a strong asseveration.

[c] chap. 43. 5.

20 But [c] bring your youngest brother unto me; so shall your words be verified, and ye shall not die. And they did so.

21 ¶ And they said one to another, We *are* verily guilty concerning our brother, in that we saw the anguish of his soul, when he besought us, and we would not hear; therefore is this distress come upon us.

[d] chap. 37. 21.

22 And Reuben answered them, saying, [d] Spake I not unto you, saying, Do not sin against the child; and ye would not hear? therefore, behold, also his blood is required.

† Heb. *an interpreter* was *between them.*

23 And they knew not that Joseph understood *them;* for † he spake unto them by an interpreter.

24 And he turned himself about from them, and wept; and returned to them again, and communed with them, and took from them Simeon, and bound him before their eyes.

25 ¶ Then Joseph commanded to fill their sacks with corn, and to restore every man's money into his sack, and to give them provision for the way: and thus did he unto them.

26 And they laded their asses with the corn, and departed thence.

27 And as one of them opened his sack to give his ass provender in the inn, he espied his money; for, behold, it *was* in his sack's mouth.

28 And he said unto his brethren, My money is restored; and, lo, *it is* even in my sack: and their heart † failed *them*, and they were afraid, saying one to another, What *is* this *that* God hath done unto us?

† Heb. *went forth.*

29 ¶ And they came unto Jacob their father unto the land of Canaan, and told him all that befell unto them; saying,

30 The man, *who is* the lord of the land, spake † roughly to us, and took us for spies of the country.

† Heb. *with us hard things.*

31 And we said unto him, We *are* true *men;* we are no spies:

32 We *be* twelve brethren, sons of our father; one *is* not, and the youngest *is* this day with our father in the land of Canaan.

33 And the man, the lord of the country, said unto us, Hereby shall I know that ye *are* true *men;* leave one of your brethren *here* with me, and take *food for* the famine of your households, and be gone:

34 And bring your youngest brother unto me: then shall I know that ye *are* no spies, but *that* ye *are* true *men: so* will I deliver you your brother, and ye shall traffick in the land.

35 ¶ And it came to pass as they emptied their sacks, that, behold, every man's bundle of money *was* in

---

20. *bring your youngest brother unto me*] There seems some needless severity here on the part of Joseph in causing so much anxiety to his father. We may account for it perhaps in the following ways. 1st, Joseph felt that it was necessary to test the repentance of his brethren and to subject them to that kind of discipline which makes repentance sound and lasting. 2ndly, He may have thought that the best mode of persuading his father to go down to him in Egypt was first of all to bring Benjamin thither. 3rdly, He was manifestly following a Divine impulse and guiding, that so his dreams should be fulfilled, and his race brought into their house of bondage and education.

24. *Simeon*] It has been thought that he took Simeon, either because he was the next in age to Reuben, whom he would not bind as having been the brother that sought to save him, or perhaps because Simeon had been one of the most unfeeling and cruel towards himself, according to the savage temper which he shewed in the case of the Shechemites. See ch. xxxiv, xlix. 5.

25. *their sacks*] Rather, **their vessels**; the word is different from that elsewhere used for sacks, and apparently indicates that they had some kind of vessel for corn which they carried within their sacks.

27. *in the inn*] The khan, or caravanserai, in the East was, and is still, a place, where men and cattle can find room to rest, but which provides neither food for man nor fodder for cattle. It is doubtful, however, whether anything of this kind existed so early as the time of Joseph. The word means only "a resting place for the night," and very probably was only a station, at which caravans were wont to rest, near to a well, to trees, and to pasture, where the tents were pitched and the cattle were tethered.

his sack: and when *both* they and their father saw the bundles of money, they were afraid.

36 And Jacob their father said unto them, Me have ye bereaved *of my children:* Joseph *is* not, and Simeon *is* not, and ye will take Benjamin *away:* all these things are against me.

37 And Reuben spake unto his father, saying, Slay my two sons, if I bring him not to thee: deliver him into my hand, and I will bring him to thee again.

38 And he said, My son shall not go down with you; for his brother is dead, and he is left alone: if mischief befall him by the way in the which ye go, then shall ye bring down my gray hairs with sorrow to the grave.

CHAPTER XLIII.

1 *Jacob is hardly persuaded to send Benjamin.* 15 *Joseph entertaineth his brethren.* 31 *He maketh them a feast.*

AND the famine *was* sore in the land.

2 And it came to pass, when they had eaten up the corn which they had brought out of Egypt, their father said unto them, Go again, buy us a little food.

3 And Judah spake unto him, saying, The man †did solemnly protest unto us, saying, Ye shall not see my face, except your [a] brother *be* with you.

† Heb. *protesting he protested.*
[a] chap. 42. 20.

4 If thou wilt send our brother with us, we will go down and buy thee food:

5 But if thou wilt not send *him*, we will not go down: for the man said unto us, Ye shall not see my face, except your brother *be* with you.

6 And Israel said, Wherefore dealt ye *so* ill with me, *as* to tell the man whether ye had yet a brother?

7 And they said, The man †asked us straitly of our state, and of our kindred, saying, *Is* your father yet alive? have ye *another* brother? and we told him according to the †tenor of these words: †could we certainly know that he would say, Bring your brother down?

† Heb. *asking he asked us.*
† Heb. *mouth.*
† Heb. *knowing could we know.*

8 And Judah said unto Israel his father, Send the lad with me, and we will arise and go; that we may live, and not die, both we, and thou, *and* also our little ones.

9 I will be surety for him; of my hand shalt thou require him: [b] if I bring him not unto thee, and set him before thee, then let me bear the blame for ever:

[b] chap. 44. 32.

10 For except we had lingered, surely now we had returned ‖ this second time.

‖ Or, *twice by this.*

11 And their father Israel said unto them, If *it must be* so now, do this; take of the best fruits in the land in your vessels, and carry down the man a present, a little balm, and a little honey, spices, and myrrh, nuts, and almonds:

---

36. *Me have ye bereaved*] Jacob suspects that they had been in some way the cause of Joseph's supposed death and of Simeon's captivity.

against me] Lit. "upon me," *i.e.* upon me as a burden too heavy for me to bear.

CHAP. XLIII. 11. *of the best fruits in the land*] Lit. "of the song of the land," *i.e.* the most praised produce, the fruits celebrated in song.

balm] See xxxvii. 25.

honey] So rendered in all the Versions, though some think that it was composed of the juice of grapes boiled down to a syrup of the consistency of honey, called in Arabic *Dibs;* which even in modern times has been imported into Egypt annually from the neighbourhood of Hebron (see Ros. and Ges. p. 319).

spices] Probably *Storax*. See on xxxvii. 25.

myrrh] **Ladanum.** See on xxxvii. 25.

nuts] **Pistachio nuts.** So Bochart ('Hieroz.' II. iv. 12); Cels. ('Hierobot.' Tom. I. p. 24); Ges. (p. 202). The LXX., followed by Onk., Syr., Arab., renders *terebinth*, probably because the pistachio nut tree was considered as a species of terebinth. All these fruits may have grown in the land of Canaan, though the corn-harvest may have utterly failed. Thus also may we account for the fact, that the small supply, which could be carried from Egypt by ten asses, sufficed for a time to sup-

12 And take double money in your hand; and the money that was brought again in the mouth of your sacks, carry *it* again in your hand; peradventure it *was* an oversight:

13 Take also your brother, and arise, go again unto the man:

14 And God Almighty give you mercy before the man, that he may send away your other brother, and Benjamin. ‖If I be bereaved *of my children*, I am bereaved.

)r, *And as I* *ve been,* *c.*

15 ¶ And the men took that present, and they took double money in their hand, and Benjamin; and rose up, and went down to Egypt, and stood before Joseph.

16 And when Joseph saw Benjamin with them, he said to the ruler of his house, Bring *these* men home, and †slay, and make ready; for *these* men shall †dine with me at noon.

Ieb. *ll a kill-* *g.* Ieb. *t.*

17 And the man did as Joseph bade; and the man brought the men into Joseph's house.

18 And the men were afraid, because they were brought into Joseph's house; and they said, Because of the money that was returned in our sacks at the first time are we brought in; that he may †seek occasion against us, and fall upon us, and take us for bondmen, and our asses.

Ieb. *ll him-* *f upon*

19 And they came near to the steward of Joseph's house, and they communed with him at the door of the house,

:hap. 42. Ieb. *ning* *wn we* *me* *wn.*

20 And said, O sir, c†we came indeed down at the first time to buy food:

21 And it came to pass, when we came to the inn, that we opened our sacks, and, behold, *every* man's money *was* in the mouth of his sack, our money in full weight: and we have brought it again in our hand.

22 And other money have we brought down in our hands to buy food: we cannot tell who put our money in our sacks.

23 And he said, Peace *be* to you, fear not: your God, and the God of your father, hath given you treasure in your sacks: †I had your money. And he brought Simeon out unto them.

† Heb. *your money came to me.*

24 And the man brought the men into Joseph's house, and dgave *them* water, and they washed their feet; and he gave their asses provender.

d chap. 18. 4. & 24. 32.

25 And they made ready the present against Joseph came at noon: for they heard that they should eat bread there.

26 ¶ And when Joseph came home, they brought him the present which *was* in their hand into the house, and bowed themselves to him to the earth.

27 And he asked them of *their* †welfare, and said, †*Is* your father well, the old man of whom ye spake? *Is* he yet alive?

† Heb. *peace.* † Heb. Is there *peace to your father.*

28 And they answered, Thy servant our father *is* in good health, he *is* yet alive. And they bowed down their heads, and made obeisance.

29 And he lifted up his eyes, and

---

ply Jacob's household. There was a grievous famine, but still all the fruits of the earth had not failed. Corn was needed; but life can be supported, especially in a warm climate, with but a moderate amount of the more solid kinds of food.

14. *God Almighty*] *El Shaddai.* Jacob here uses that name of the Most High, by which He made Himself known to Abraham, and afterwards renewed His covenant with Jacob himself (ch. xvii. 1, xxxv. 11; where see note). Hereby he calls to mind the promise of protection to himself and his house, as well as the power of Him who had promised.

If I be bereaved of my children, I am bereaved.] Cp. Esth. iv. 16; 2 K. vii. 4. The expression seems partly of sorrow and partly of submission and resignation.

18. *that he may seek occasion against us*] Lit. "that he may roll himself upon us," that is, probably, "that he may rush out upon us."

20. *O Sir*] "Pray, my lord," or "Hear, my lord," the word translated *O* is a particle of earnest entreaty.

26. *and bowed themselves*] Joseph's first dream is now fulfilled. The eleven sheaves make obeisance to Joseph's sheaf. It is observable, that Joseph's dream, like Pharaoh's, had reference to sheaves of corn, evidently pointing to the supply of food sought by the brethren.

saw his brother Benjamin, his mother's
son, and said, *Is* this your younger
brother, of whom ye spake unto me?
And he said, God be gracious unto
thee, my son.
30 And Joseph made haste; for
his bowels did yearn upon his brother:
and he sought *where* to weep; and he
entered into *his* chamber, and wept
there.
31 And he washed his face, and
went out, and refrained himself, and
said, Set on bread.
32 And they set on for him by
himself, and for them by themselves,
and for the Egyptians, which did eat
with him, by themselves: because the
Egyptians might not eat bread with
the Hebrews; for that *is* an abomination
unto the Egyptians.
33 And they sat before him, the
firstborn according to his birthright,
and the youngest according to his
youth: and the men marvelled one
at another.
34 And he took *and sent* messes
unto them from before him: but
Benjamin's mess was five times so
much as any of theirs. And they
drank, and †were merry with him. † Heb. *they drank largely.*

CHAPTER XLIV.

1 *Joseph's policy to stay his brethren.* 14 *Judah's humble supplication to Joseph.*

AND he commanded †the steward † Heb. him *that* was *over his house.*
of his house, saying, Fill the
men's sacks *with* food, as much as
they can carry, and put every man's
money in his sack's mouth.
2 And put my cup, the silver cup,
in the sack's mouth of the youngest,
and his corn money. And he did
according to the word that Joseph had
spoken.
3 As soon as the morning was light,
the men were sent away, they and
their asses.
4 *And* when they were gone out
of the city, *and* not *yet* far off, Joseph
said unto his steward, Up, follow after
the men; and when thou dost overtake
them, say unto them, Wherefore
have ye rewarded evil for good?
5 *Is* not this *it* in which my lord
drinketh, and whereby indeed he ‖divineth? ‖ Or *maketh trial?*
ye have done evil in so doing.

---

29. *my son*] Joseph addresses Benjamin his younger brother with this paternal salutation, not only from the difference in their ages, but as being a governor he speaks with the authority and dignity of his position.

32. *the Egyptians might not eat bread with the Hebrews*] The Egyptians feared to eat with foreigners, chiefly because they dreaded pollution from such as killed and ate cows, which animals were held in the highest veneration in Egypt. Hence Herodotus says, that an Egyptian would not kiss a Greek, nor use a knife or a spit belonging to a Greek, nor eat any meat that had been cut with a Greek knife (Her. II. 45). Joseph probably dined alone from his high rank, the distinctions of rank and caste being carefully observed; but, as he was naturalized in Egypt, and had, no doubt, conformed to their domestic customs, he would probably not have needed to separate himself at meals from the native Egyptians, as would his brethren from the land of the Hebrews.

33. *they sat before him*] The Egyptians sat at their meals, though most of the ancients, and, in later times at least, the Hebrews, reclined.

the men marvelled one at another] They marvelled that strangers should have seated them exactly according to their ages.

34. *sent messes unto them*] The custom is met with elsewhere, as a mark of respect to distinguished guests (see 1 S. ix. 23, 24).

five times so much] Herodotus mentions the custom of giving double portions as a mark of honour. The Spartan kings "are given the first seat at the banquet, they are served before the other guests, and have a double portion of everything" (VI. 57; cp. also Hom. 'Il.' VII. 321, VIII. 162).

were merry] **Drank freely.** The word is chiefly used of drinking to excess, but not always; see for instance Hagg. i. 6.

CHAP. XLIV. 2. *my cup*] or rather **bowl**. In Jer. xxxv. 5 the word is rendered "pots." In Ex. xxv. 31, xxxvii. 17, it is used of the "bowl" or calix of the sculptured flowers. It was evidently a larger vessel, flagon or bowl, from which the wine was poured into the smaller cups.

5. *divineth*] Divination by cups was frequent in ancient times. Jamblichus ('De Myst.' III. 14) mentions it, so Varro (ap. August. 'Civ. Dei,' VII. 35), Pliny ('H. N.' XXXVII. 73, &c.). The latter says that "in

6 ¶ And he overtook them, and he
spake unto them these same words.
7 And they said unto him, Wherefore saith my lord these words? God
forbid that thy servants should do
according to this thing:
8 Behold, the money, which we
found in our sacks' mouths, we brought
again unto thee out of the land of
Canaan: how then should we steal
out of thy lord's house silver or gold?
9 With whomsoever of thy servants
it be found, both let him die, and we
also will be my lord's bondmen.
10 And he said, Now also *let* it *be*
according unto your words: he with
whom it is found shall be my servant;
and ye shall be blameless.
11 Then they speedily took down
every man his sack to the ground, and
opened every man his sack.
12 And he searched, *and* began at
the eldest, and left at the youngest:
and the cup was found in Benjamin's
sack.
13 Then they rent their clothes,
and laded every man his ass, and returned to the city.
14 ¶ And Judah and his brethren
came to Joseph's house; for he *was*
yet there: and they fell before him
on the ground.
15 And Joseph said unto them,
What deed *is* this that ye have done?
wot ye not that such a man as I can
certainly ‖divine? ‖ Or,
16 And Judah said, What shall we *make trial?*
say unto my lord? what shall we
speak? or how shall we clear ourselves? God hath found out the iniquity of thy servants: behold, we *are*
my lord's servants, both we, and *he*
also with whom the cup is found.
17 And he said, God forbid that
I should do so: *but* the man in whose
hand the cup is found, he shall be my
servant; and as for you, get you up
in peace unto your father.
18 ¶ Then Judah came near unto
him, and said, Oh my lord, let thy

---

this hydromantia images of the gods were called up." It was practised either by dropping gold, silver, or jewels, into the water, and then examining their appearance; or simply by looking into the water as into a mirror, somewhat probably as the famous Egyptian magician did into the mirror of ink, as mentioned by the duke of Northumberland and others in the present day. (See Lane, 'Mod. Egypt.' II. 362.)

The sacred cup is a symbol of the Nile, into whose waters a golden and silver patera were annually thrown. The Nile itself, both the source and the river, was called "the cup of Egypt" (Plin. 'H. N.' VIII. 71). This cup of Joseph was of silver, while in ordinary cases the Egyptians drank from vessels of brass (Hecatæus in 'Athen.' XI. 6; Herod. II. 37; see Hävernick, 'Introd. to Pentateuch,' ad h. l.).

15. *wot ye not that such a man as I can certainly divine?*] Joseph here adapts himself and his language to his character as it would naturally appear in the eyes of his brethren. We are not to assume that he actually used magical arts. This would be quite inconsistent with what he said to Pharaoh, ch. xli. 16, disclaiming all knowledge of the future, save as revealed by God. It has been questioned how far Joseph was justified in the kind of dissimulation which he thus used to his brethren. That he was perfectly justified in not declaring himself to them until he had tested their repentance and had brought his schemes concerning his father to a point, there can be little doubt. He was never tempted to deny that he was Joseph, for no one suspected that he was. In fact he simply preserved his disguise. But in the present passage he seems to have used words which, though not affirming that he could divine, yet nearly implied as much. It is to be observed, however, that whatever may be thought on this head, Joseph is not held up to us as absolutely perfect. As it was in the case of Abraham, Isaac, and Jacob, the history is simply told of the events as they occurred. Joseph was a man of singular piety, purity, and integrity, in high favour with Heaven, and even at times inspired to declare the will of God. It does not follow that he was perfect. If inspired apostles were sometimes to be blamed (Gal. ii. 11, 13), the holiest patriarchs are not likely to have been incapable of error. If the act was wrong, we must not consider it as the result of Divine guidance, but as the error of a good but fallible man, whilst in the main carrying out the designs of Providence. Making the worst that can be made of it, it is difficult to say that any character in Scripture, save One, (of which at least we have any detailed account) comes out more purely and brightly in the whole course of its history than the character of Joseph.

servant, I pray thee, speak a word in
my lord's ears, and let not thine anger
burn against thy servant: for thou *art*
even as Pharaoh.
19 My lord asked his servants, saying, Have ye a father, or a brother?
20 And we said unto my lord, We
have a father, an old man, and a child
of his old age, a little one; and his
brother is dead, and he alone is left of
his mother, and his father loveth him.
21 And thou saidst unto thy servants, Bring him down unto me, that
I may set mine eyes upon him.
22 And we said unto my lord, The
lad cannot leave his father: for *if* he
should leave his father, *his father* would
die.
23 And thou saidst unto thy ser-
[a] chap. 43. 3. vants, [a]Except your youngest brother
come down with you, ye shall see my
face no more.
24 And it came to pass when we
came up unto thy servant my father,
we told him the words of my lord.
25 And our father said, Go again,
and buy us a little food.
26 And we said, We cannot go
down: if our youngest brother be
with us, then will we go down: for
we may not see the man's face, except
our youngest brother *be* with us.
27 And thy servant my father said
unto us, Ye know that my wife bare
me two *sons:*
28 And the one went out from me,
[b] chap. 37. 33. and I said, [b]Surely he is torn in pieces;
and I saw him not since:
29 And if ye take this also from
me, and mischief befall him, ye shall
bring down my gray hairs with sorrow
to the grave.
30 Now therefore when I come to
thy servant my father, and the lad *be*
not with us; seeing that his life is
bound up in the lad's life;
31 It shall come to pass, when he
seeth that the lad *is* not *with us*, that
he will die: and thy servants shall
bring down the gray hairs of thy
servant our father with sorrow to the
grave.
32 For thy servant became surety
for the lad unto my father, saying,
[c]If I bring him not unto thee, then I [c] chap. 43. 9.
shall bear the blame to my father for
ever.
33 Now therefore, I pray thee, let
thy servant abide instead of the lad a
bondman to my lord; and let the lad
go up with his brethren.
34 For how shall I go up to my
father, and the lad *be* not with me?
lest peradventure I see the evil that
shall † come on my father. † Heb. *find my father.*

CHAPTER XLV.

1 Joseph maketh himself known to his brethren. 5 He comforteth them in God's providence. 9 He sendeth for his father. 16 Pharaoh confirmeth it. 21 Joseph furnisheth them for their journey, and exhorteth them to concord. 25 Jacob is revived with the news.

THEN Joseph could not refrain
himself before all them that
stood by him; and he cried, Cause
every man to go out from me. And
there stood no man with him, while
Joseph made himself known unto his
brethren.
2 And he † wept aloud: and the † Heb. *gave forth his voice in weeping.*
Egyptians and the house of Pharaoh
heard.
3 And Joseph said unto his bre-
thren, [a]I *am* Joseph; doth my father [a] Acts 7. 13.
yet live? And his brethren could not
answer him; for they were ‖ troubled ‖ Or, *terrified.*
at his presence.
4 And Joseph said unto his bre-

---

28. *Surely he is torn in pieces*] From these words probably for the first time Joseph learns what had been Jacob's belief as to his son's fate.

34. *how should I go up to my father*] The character of Judah comes out most favourably in this speech. He had, in the first instance, saved Joseph from death, but yet he had proposed the alternative of selling him as a slave. He is evidently now much softened; has witnessed Jacob's affliction with deep sympathy and sorrow, and so has been brought to contrition and repentance. The sight of his repentance finally moves Joseph at once to make himself known to his brethren.

CHAP. XLV. 2. *wept aloud*] Lit., as the margin, "gave forth his voice in weeping."

thren, Come near to me, I pray you.
And they came near. And he said,
I *am* Joseph your brother, whom ye
sold into Egypt.
5 Now therefore be not grieved,
†nor angry with yourselves, that ye
sold me hither: [b]for God did send
me before you to preserve life.
6 For these two years *hath* the
famine *been* in the land: and yet *there*
are five years, in the which *there shall*
neither *be* earing nor harvest.
7 And God sent me before you †to
preserve you a posterity in the earth,
and to save your lives by a great deliverance.
8 So now *it was* not you *that* sent
me hither, but God: and he hath
made me a father to Pharaoh, and lord
of all his house, and a ruler throughout all the land of Egypt.
9 Haste ye, and go up to my father,
and say unto him, Thus saith thy son
Joseph, God hath made me lord of
all Egypt: come down unto me, tarry
not:
10 And thou shalt dwell in the
land of Goshen, and thou shalt be
near unto me, thou, and thy children,
and thy children's children, and thy
flocks, and thy herds, and all that thou
hast:
11 And there will I nourish thee;
for yet *there are* five years of famine;
lest thou, and thy household, and all
that thou hast, come to poverty.
12 And, behold, your eyes see, and
the eyes of my brother Benjamin, that
it is my mouth that speaketh unto
you.
13 And ye shall tell my father of
all my glory in Egypt, and of all that
ye have seen; and ye shall haste and
bring down my father hither.
14 And he fell upon his brother
Benjamin's neck, and wept; and
Benjamin wept upon his neck.
15 Moreover he kissed all his bre-

† Heb. *neither let there be anger in your eyes.*
[b] chap. 50. 20.
† Heb. *to put for you a remnant.*

---

6. *earing*] *i. e.* "ploughing." To "ear" is an old English word from the Anglo-Saxon root *erian*, "to plough," cognate with the Latin *arare*. (See Bosworth, 'Anglo-Saxon Dict.' 25 k.) It occurs in the Authorised Version; Ex. xxxiv. 21; Deut. xxi. 4; 1 S. viii. 12; Isa. xxx. 24.

7. *to preserve you a posterity in the earth, and to save your lives by a great deliverance*] **To make you a remnant in the earth** (that is, to secure you from utter destruction), **and to preserve your lives to a great deliverance** (*i.e.* to preserve life to you, so that your deliverance should be great and signal).

8. *but God*] Lit. "The God." That great Personal God, who had led and guarded Abraham, Isaac, and Jacob, and who still watched over the house of Israel.

a father to Pharaoh] *i.e.* a wise and confidential friend and counsellor. The Caliphs and the Sultan of Turkey appear to have given the same title to their Grand Viziers. (See Burder, 'Oriental Customs,' ad h. l.; Gesen. p. 7; Ros. in loc.).

10. *the land of Goshen*] The land of Goshen was evidently a region lying to the north-east of lower Egypt, bounded apparently by the Mediterranean on the north, by the desert on the east, by the Tanitic branch of the Nile on the west (hence called "the field of Zoan" or Tanis, Ps. lxxviii. 12, 43), and probably extending south as far as to the head of the Red Sea, and nearly to Memphis. It appears, in Gen. xlvii. 11, to be called the land of Rameses, and the Israelites, before the Exodus, are said to have built in it the cities of Raamses and Pithom (Exod. i. 11). It was probably, though under the dominion of the Pharaohs, only on the confines of Egypt. Hence the LXX. here renders "Gesen of Arabia." In ch. xlvi. 28, where Goshen occurs twice, the LXX. call it "the city of Heroopolis in the land of Ramasses." Joseph placed his brethren naturally on the confines of Egypt, nearest to Palestine, and yet near himself. It is probable, that either Memphis or Tanis was then the metropolis of Egypt, both of which are in the immediate neighbourhood of the region thus marked out. (See Ges. p. 307; Poole, in Smith, 'Dict. of Bible' Art. *Goshen;* Hengstenb. 'Egypt,' &c. p. 42 sq.).

11. *and thy household*] The household of Abraham and of Isaac consisted of many servants and dependents, besides their own families. So Jacob, when he came from Padan-aram, had become "two bands." It is probable that some hundreds of dependents accompanied Jacob in his descent into Egypt, and settled with him in Goshen. So again in v. 18, Joseph's brethren are bidden to take their "father and their *households*."

thren, and wept upon them: and after that his brethren talked with him.

16 ¶ And the fame thereof was heard in Pharaoh's house, saying, Joseph's brethren are come: and it †pleased Pharaoh well, and his servants.

† Heb. *was good in the eyes of Pharaoh.*

17 And Pharaoh said unto Joseph, Say unto thy brethren, This do ye; lade your beasts, and go, get you unto the land of Canaan;

18 And take your father and your households, and come unto me: and I will give you the good of the land of Egypt, and ye shall eat the fat of the land.

19 Now thou art commanded, this do ye; take you wagons out of the land of Egypt for your little ones, and for your wives, and bring your father, and come.

20 Also †regard not your stuff; for the good of all the land of Egypt *is* yours.

† Heb. *let not your eye spare, &c.*

21 And the children of Israel did so: and Joseph gave them wagons, according to the †commandment of Pharaoh, and gave them provision for the way.

22 To all of them he gave each man changes of raiment; but to Benjamin he gave three hundred *pieces* of silver, and five changes of raiment.

23 And to his father he sent after this *manner;* ten asses †laden with the good things of Egypt, and ten she asses laden with corn and bread and meat for his father by the way.

† Heb. *carrying.*

24 So he sent his brethren away, and they departed: and he said unto them, See that ye fall not out by the way.

25 ¶ And they went up out of Egypt, and came into the land of Canaan unto Jacob their father,

26 And told him, saying, Joseph *is* yet alive, and he *is* governor over all the land of Egypt. And †Jacob's heart fainted, for he believed them not.

† Heb. *his.*

27 And they told him all the words of Joseph, which he had said unto them: and when he saw the wagons which Joseph had sent to carry him, the spirit of Jacob their father revived:

28 And Israel said, *It is* enough; Joseph my son *is* yet alive: I will go and see him before I die.

CHAPTER XLVI.

1 Jacob is comforted by God at Beer-sheba: 5 Thence he with his company goeth into Egypt. 8 The number of his family that went into Egypt. 29 Joseph meeteth Jacob. 31 He instructeth his brethren how to answer to Pharaoh.

AND Israel took his journey with all that he had, and came to Beer-sheba, and offered sacrifices unto the God of his father Isaac.

2 And God spake unto Israel in the visions of the night, and said,

---

24. *See that ye fall not out by the way*] So all the Versions; but as the word rendered "fall out" expresses any violent emotion as of fear or anger, some prefer to render, "Be not afraid in the journey;" so Tuch, Baumg., Gesen., and many moderns. The ancient interpretation is more probable. They had already travelled on that journey several times without meeting with any evil accident; but there was some danger that they might quarrel among themselves, now that they were reconciled to Joseph, perhaps each one being ready to throw the blame of former misconduct on the others (Calvin).

27. *wagons*] Carts and wagons were known early in Egypt, which was a flat country and highly cultivated; but they were probably unknown at this time in Palestine and Syria. The Egyptian carts, as depicted on the monuments, are of two wheels only, when used for carrying agricultural produce. The four-wheeled car, mentioned by Herodotus, was used for carrying the shrine and image of a deity. (See Sir G. Wilkinson's note to Rawlinson's Herodotus, II. 63, and the engraving there.) When Jacob saw the wagons, he knew that they had come from Egypt, and so he believed his sons' report, and was comforted.

CHAP. XLVI. 1. *to Beer-sheba, and offered sacrifices*, &c.] Here Abraham and Isaac, built altars (ch. xxi. 33, xxvi. 25), and worshipped. Jacob naturally felt it to be a place hallowed by sacred memories, and being anxious as to the propriety of leaving the land of promise and going down into Egypt, he here sacrificed to the God of his fathers, and no doubt sought guidance from Him. Beer-sheba was South of Hebron on the road by which Jacob would naturally travel into Egypt.

Jacob, Jacob. And he said, Here
am I.
3 And he said, I *am* God, the God
of thy father: fear not to go down
into Egypt; for I will there make of
thee a great nation:
4 I will go down with thee into
Egypt; and I will also surely bring
thee up *again:* and Joseph shall put
his hand upon thine eyes.
5 And Jacob rose up from Beer-
sheba: and the sons of Israel carried
Jacob their father, and their little ones,
and their wives, in the wagons which
Pharaoh had sent to carry him.
6 And they took their cattle, and
their goods, which they had gotten in
osh. 24. the land of Canaan, and came into
al. 105. Egypt, [a]Jacob, and all his seed with
52. 4 him:

7 His sons, and his sons' sons with
him, his daughters, and his sons'
daughters, and all his seed brought
he with him into Egypt.
8 ¶ And [b]these *are* the names of [b] Exod. 1.
the children of Israel, which came into 1. & 6. 14.
Egypt, Jacob and his sons: [c]Reuben, [c] Numb. 26. 5.
Jacob's firstborn. 1 Chron. 5.
9 And the sons of Reuben; Ha- 1.
noch, and Phallu, and Hezron, and
Carmi.
10 ¶ [d]And the sons of Simeon; [d] Exod. 6. 15.
Jemuel, and Jamin, and Ohad, and 1 Chron. 4.
Jachin, and Zohar, and Shaul the 24.
son of a Canaanitish woman.
11 ¶ And the sons of [e]Levi; Ger- [e] 1 Chron. 6. 1.
shon, Kohath, and Merari.
12 ¶ And the sons of [f]Judah; Er, [f] 1 Chron.
and Onan, and Shelah, and Pharez, 2. 3. & 4. 21.
and Zarah: but Er and Onan died in chap. 38. 3.

---

3. *I am God, the God of thy father*] "I am *El*"—a reference again to the name "El-Shaddai," by which the Most High so specially made covenant with the patriarchs. See on ch. xliii. 14.

fear not to go down into Egypt] Abraham had gone down there and been in great danger. Isaac had been forbidden to go thither (ch. xxvi. 2). Abraham, Isaac, Jacob had all been placed and settled in Canaan with a promise that they should in future possess the land. Moreover, Egypt was, not only a heathen land, but one in which heathenism was specially developed and systematized. Jacob might therefore naturally fear to find in it dangers both worldly and spiritual. Hence the promise of God's presence and protection was signally needed.

4. *Joseph shall put his hand upon thine eyes*] The ancients, Gentiles as well as Jews, desired that their dearest relatives should close their eyes in death (Hom. 'Il.' XI. 453; 'Od.' XXIV. 296; Eurip. 'Hec.' 430; 'Phœn.' 1465; Virg. 'Æn.' IX. 487; Ov. 'Heroid.' I. 162).

5. *the sons of Israel carried Jacob their father*] The scene depicted on the tomb of Chnoumhotep at Beni Hassan cannot be the Egyptian version of the arrival of the Israelites in Egypt; but it is strikingly illustrative of the history of that event. The date of the inscription is that of the 12th dynasty, which was probably the dynasty under which Joseph lived; a number of strangers, with beards (which the Egyptians never wore, but which in the sculptures indicate uncivilized foreigners), and with dress and physical characteristics belonging to the Semitic nomads, appear before the governor offering him gifts. They carry their goods with them on asses, have women and children with them, and are armed with bows and clubs. They are described as Absha and his family, and the number 37 is written over in hieroglyphics. The signs, which accompany the picture, indicate that they were either captives or tributaries. Sir G. Wilkinson, however, has suggested that possibly this indication may result from the contemptuous way in which the Egyptians spoke of all foreigners, and the superiority which they claimed over them. Moreover, they are armed, one of them is playing on a lyre, and others bring presents; which things point rather to an immigration than to a captivity. (See Wilkinson, Vol. II. p. 296, and plate. Brugsch, 'H. E.' p. 63, where the scene is well engraved, and a good description annexed.)

7. *his daughters*] Only one daughter is named and one granddaughter. This verse implies that there were more. Married women would not be mentioned in a Hebrew genealogy; hence Jacob's sons' wives are not recounted among the seventy souls that came into Egypt. See v. 26. Dinah remained unmarried. Hence she only of Jacob's daughters is named.

10. *Jemuel*] Called Nemuel, Num. xxvi. 12; 1 Chron. iv. 24.

Ohad] Not named in Num. xxvi. 12; 1 Chr. iv. 24.

Jachin] "Jarib," 1 Chr. iv. 24.

Zohar] "Zerah," Num. xxvi. 13; 1 Chr. iv. 24.

11. *Gershon*] 'Gershom,' 1 Chr. vi. 16.

12. *And the sons of Pharez were Hezron and Hamul*] The difficulties in the chro-

the land of Canaan. And the sons of
Pharez were Hezron and Hamul.
g 1 Chron. 7. 1. 13 ¶ [g] And the sons of Issachar;
Tola, and Phuvah, and Job, and
Shimron.
14 ¶ And the sons of Zebulun;
Sered, and Elon, and Jahleel.
15 These *be* the sons of Leah,
which she bare unto Jacob in Padan-aram, with his daughter Dinah: all
the souls of his sons and his daughters
were thirty and three.
16 ¶ And the sons of Gad; Ziphion, and Haggi, Shuni, and Ezbon,
Eri, and Arodi, and Areli.
h 1 Chron. 7. 30. 17 ¶ [h] And the sons of Asher; Jimnah, and Ishuah, and Isui, and Beriah,
and Serah their sister: and the sons of
Beriah; Heber, and Malchiel.
18 These *are* the sons of Zilpah,
whom Laban gave to Leah his daughter, and these she bare unto Jacob,
even sixteen souls.
19 The sons of Rachel Jacob's
wife; Joseph, and Benjamin.
20 ¶ [i] And unto Joseph in the land i chap. 41. 50.
of Egypt were born Manasseh and
Ephraim, which Asenath the daughter
of Poti-pherah ‖ priest of On bare unto ‖ Or, *prince*.
him.
21 ¶ [k] And the sons of Benjamin k 1 Chron. 7. 6 & 8. 1.
were Belah, and Becher, and Ashbel,

---

nology of this catalogue have suggested the thought that it did not form a part of the original history of Genesis. The difficulties are really no greater than we might expect to find in a document so ancient, and where names and numbers are concerned, which of all things are most likely to puzzle us. In this verse it appears that Er and Onan having died in Canaan, two of Judah's grandchildren are substituted for them. It has been said that Hezron and Hamul could not have been born before the descent into Egypt, as the events related in ch. xxxviii. took place after the selling of Joseph, and that, therefore, Pharez could not have been old enough to have two sons at the time of that descent. Moreover, it is argued, that Judah himself could not have been more than 42 at this time, which is inconsistent with the apparent statement that his third son, Pharez, not born till after the marriage and death of his two elder brothers, Er and Onan, should himself have had two sons. To this it may be replied, (1), that we must not assume that the events in chap. xxxviii. necessarily took place after those in ch. xxxvii. It is most likely that ch. xxxviii. was introduced episodically at a convenient point in the history, to avoid breaking the continuity of the story. (See note on xxxviii. 1.) (2) Again, if the chronology of the life of Jacob proposed in the note at the end of ch. xxxi. be correct, Judah was, not 42, but 62, at the descent into Egypt, in which case the two sons of Pharez may easily have been born then. (3) Moreover, it is quite possible that the names in this catalogue may have comprised, not only those that were actually of the company, which went down into Egypt, but also all the grandchildren or great grandchildren of Jacob born before Jacob's death. This would not be inconsistent with the common usage of Scripture language, and it would allow 17 years more for the birth of those two grandsons of Judah and for the ten sons of Benjamin. Now Judah was probably 79 at Jacob's death, at which age his son Pharez may easily have had two sons. Indeed, the statement immediately coupled with the names of Hezron and Hamul, viz. that Er and Onan had died in Canaan, seems introduced on purpose to account for the reckoning of these grandchildren of Judah, born in Egypt, with others who had been born in Canaan.

13. *Job*] Called 'Jashub' Num. xxvi. 24; 1 Chr. vii. 1.

15. *thirty and three*] that is, including Jacob himself, but not Er, or Onan, who were dead, nor perhaps Leah.

16. *Ziphion*] 'Zephon' in Num. xxvi. 15.

Ezbon] 'Ozni,' Num. xxvi. 16.

Arodi] 'Arod,' Num. xxvi. 17.

17. *Ishuah*] Not mentioned in Numbers. Probably he had not left descendants and founded families.

20. *And unto Joseph*, &c.] At the end of this verse the LXX. insert the names of Machir the son of Manasseh, and Galaad the son of Machir, and Sutalaam and Taam the sons of Ephraim, and Edem the son of Sutalaam. (See Numb. xxvi. 28—37; 1 Chr. vii. 14.) Thus the whole number of persons becomes 75. The passage however is not in the Samaritan, with which the LXX. mostly agrees.

21. *the sons of Benjamin*] These are ten in number. According to Numb. xxvi. 40 two of them, Naaman and Ard, were grandsons of Benjamin. According to the common chronology Benjamin was only 23 at the coming into Egypt; an age at which he could hardly have had ten sons, or eight sons and two grandsons, even if he had two wives and some of the children had been twins. The considerations alluded to at v. 12, however, will allow us to calculate that Benjamin was 32 at

Gera, and Naaman, Ehi, and Rosh,
Muppim, and Huppim, and Ard.
22 These *are* the sons of Rachel,
which were born to Jacob: all the
souls *were* fourteen.
23 ¶ And the sons of Dan; Hu-
shim.
24 ¶ And the sons of Naphtali;
Jahzeel, and Guni, and Jezer, and
Shillem.
25 These *are* the sons of Bilhah,
which Laban gave unto Rachel his
daughter, and she bare these unto
Jacob: all the souls *were* seven.
26 [l] All the souls that came with
Jacob into Egypt, which came out
of his † loins, besides Jacob's sons'
wives, all the souls *were* threescore
and six;
27 And the sons of Joseph, which
were born him in Egypt, *were* two
souls: all the souls of the house of
Jacob, which came into Egypt, *were*
threescore and ten.
28 ¶ And he sent Judah before
him unto Joseph, to direct his face
unto Goshen; and they came into
the land of Goshen.
29 And Joseph made ready his
chariot, and went up to meet Israel
his father, to Goshen, and presented
himself unto him; and he fell on his
neck, and wept on his neck a good
while.
30 And Israel said unto Joseph,
Now let me die, since I have seen
thy face, because thou *art* yet alive.
31 And Joseph said unto his brethren, and unto his father's house,
I will go up, and shew Pharaoh, and
say unto him, My brethren, and my
father's house, which *were* in the
land of Canaan, are come unto me;
32 And the men *are* shepherds,
for † their trade hath been to feed
cattle; and they have brought their
flocks, and their herds, and all that
they have.
33 And it shall come to pass, when
Pharaoh shall call you, and shall say,
What *is* your occupation?
34 That ye shall say, Thy servants'
trade hath been about cattle from our
youth even until now, both we, *and*
also our fathers: that ye may dwell
in the land of Goshen; for every
shepherd *is* an abomination unto the
Egyptians.

[l] Deut. 10. 22.
† Heb. *thigh.*
† Heb. *they are men of cattle.*

---

the going down to Egypt (see note at the end of ch. xxxi.), and therefore forty-nine at the death of Jacob, by which age he might easily have been the father of ten sons.

Three of Benjamin's sons, Becher, Gera and Rosh, are wanting in the table given in Num. xxvi., probably because they had not left children enough to form independent families.

Ehi, Muppim, and Huppim] Called 'Shupham, Hupham, and Ahiram,' in Num. xxvi. 38, 39.

27. *all the souls of the house of Jacob, which came into Egypt, were threescore and ten*] The number is made up of the 66 mentioned in the last verse, Jacob himself, Joseph, and the two sons of Joseph. The LXX. reads here "The sons of Joseph, which were born to him in Egypt, were nine souls. All the souls of the house of Jacob, who came with Jacob into Egypt, were seventy-five." See above note on verse 20. St Stephen (Acts vii. 14) adopts the number 75, probably because he, or St Luke, quotes the LXX. version, as all Greek-speaking Jews would naturally have done; and it may be fairly said, that both numbers were equally correct, and that the variation depends on the different mode of reckoning. The genealogical tables of the Jews were drawn up on principles unlike those of modern calculation. And there would be no impropriety, on these principles, in reckoning the children of Joseph only, or in adding to them his grandchildren also, especially if the latter became founders of important families in Israel.

28. *he sent Judah before him unto Joseph, to direct his face unto Goshen*] *i.e.* He sent Judah before himself (Jacob) to Joseph, that Joseph might direct him to Goshen.

34. *every shepherd is an abomination unto the Egyptians*] Herodotus speaks of the aversion of the Egyptians for swineherds (II. 47). The monuments indicate their contempt for shepherds and goatherds by the mean appearance always given to them. Neither mutton nor the flesh of goats was ever eaten or offered. Even woollen garments, though sometimes worn over linen, were esteemed unclean. No priest would wear them. They were never worn in temples, nor were the dead buried in them. To this day, sheep-feeding is esteemed the office of women and slaves. The fact that the Egyptians themselves were great agriculturists, tillers of land, and

CHAPTER XLVII.

1 *Joseph presenteth five of his brethren,* 7 *and his father, before Pharaoh.* 11 *He giveth them habitation and maintenance.* 13 *He getteth all the Egyptians' money,* 16 *their cattle,* 18 *their lands to Pharaoh.* 22 *The priests' land was not bought.* 23 *He letteth the land to them for a fifth part.* 28 *Jacob's age.* 29 *He sweareth Joseph to bury him with his fathers.*

THEN Joseph came and told Pharaoh, and said, My father and my brethren, and their flocks, and their herds, and all that they have, are come out of the land of Canaan; and, behold, they *are* in the land of Goshen.

2 And he took some of his brethren, *even* five men, and presented them unto Pharaoh.

3 And Pharaoh said unto his brethren, What *is* your occupation? And they said unto Pharaoh, Thy servants *are* shepherds, both we, *and* also our fathers.

4 They said moreover unto Pharaoh, For to sojourn in the land are we come; for thy servants have no pasture for their flocks; for the famine *is* sore in the land of Canaan: now therefore, we pray thee, let thy servants dwell in the land of Goshen.

5 And Pharaoh spake unto Joseph, saying, Thy father and thy brethren are come unto thee:

6 The land of Egypt *is* before thee; in the best of the land make thy father and brethren to dwell; in the land of Goshen let them dwell: and if thou knowest *any* men of activity among them, then make them rulers over my cattle.

7 And Joseph brought in Jacob his father, and set him before Pharaoh: and Jacob blessed Pharaoh.

8 And Pharaoh said unto Jacob, † How old *art* thou?

9 And Jacob said unto Pharaoh, [a] The days of the years of my pilgrimage *are* an hundred and thirty years: few and evil have the days of the years of my life been, and have

† Heb. *How many are the days of the years of thy life?*
[a] Heb. 11. 9, 13.

---

that their neighbours the Arab tribes of the desert, with whom they were continually at feud, were nomads only, may have been sufficient to cause this feeling. The Egyptians looked on all the people of Egypt as of noble race (Diod. v. 58), and on all foreigners as low-born. Hence they would naturally esteem a nomadic people in close proximity to themselves, and with a much lower civilization than their own, as barbarous and despicable. Whatever be the historical foundation for the existence of three dynasties of Hycsos or Shepherd-kings extending over a period of from 500 to 1000 years, there can be little doubt that the Egyptians were frequently harassed by incursions from the nomadic tribes in their neighbourhood. Some of these tribes appear to have subdued portions of Lower Egypt and to have fixed their seat of government at Tanis (Zoan), or even at Memphis. The great Hycsos invasion was after the time of Joseph, who probably lived under a Pharaoh of the twelfth dynasty (see Excursus); but the hostility between the Egyptians and the nomad tribes of Asia had no doubt been of long duration.

CHAP. XLVII. 6. *in the best of the land*] The modern province of Es-Shurkiyeh, which appears nearly to correspond with the land of Goshen, is said to "bear the highest valuation and to yield the largest revenue" of any in Egypt. (Robinson, 'B. R.' I. p. 78, 79; Kurtz, Vol. II. p. 15.) M. Chabas has collected notices of great interest showing the riches and beauty of the district under the 19th dynasty ('Mél. Egypt.' II.)

7. *and Jacob blessed Pharaoh*] Some here render "Jacob saluted Pharaoh," a possible translation, as the Eastern salutation is often with words of blessing: but the natural sense of the word is "to bless;" and if Jacob had bowed himself to the ground before Pharaoh according to a familiar Eastern custom, it would probably have been so related in the history. More probably the aged patriarch, with the conscious dignity of a prophet and the heir of the promises, prayed for blessings upon Pharaoh.

8. *How old art thou?*] **How many are the days of the years of thy life?**

9. *my pilgrimage*] Lit. "my sojournings." Pharaoh asked of the days of the years of his life, he replies by speaking of the days of the years of his pilgrimage. Some have thought that he called his life a pilgrimage, because he was a nomad, a wanderer in lands not his own: but in reality the patriarchs spoke of life as a pilgrimage or sojourning, because they sought another country, that is a heavenly (Heb. xi. 9, 13). Earth was not their home, but their journey homewards.

few and evil] The Jews speak of Jacob's

not attained unto the days of the years of the life of my fathers in the days of their pilgrimage.

10 And Jacob blessed Pharaoh, and went out from before Pharaoh.

11 ¶ And Joseph placed his father and his brethren, and gave them a possession in the land of Egypt, in the best of the land, in the land of Rameses, as Pharaoh had commanded.

12 And Joseph nourished his father, and his brethren, and all his father's household, with bread, ‖ † according to *their* families.

‖ Or, *as a little child is nourished.* † Heb. *according to the little ones.*

13 ¶ And *there was* no bread in all the land; for the famine *was* very sore, so that the land of Egypt and *all* the land of Canaan fainted by reason of the famine.

14 And Joseph gathered up all the money that was found in the land of Egypt, and in the land of Canaan, for the corn which they bought: and Joseph brought the money into Pharaoh's house.

15 And when money failed in the land of Egypt, and in the land of Canaan, all the Egyptians came unto Joseph, and said, Give us bread: for why should we die in thy presence? for the money faileth.

16 And Joseph said, Give your cattle; and I will give you for your cattle, if money fail.

17 And they brought their cattle unto Joseph: and Joseph gave them bread *in exchange* for horses, and for the flocks, and for the cattle of the herds, and for the asses: and he † fed them with bread for all their cattle for that year.

† Heb. *led them.*

18 When that year was ended, they came unto him the second year, and said unto him, We will not hide *it* from my lord, how that our money is spent; my lord also hath our herds of cattle; there is not ought left in the sight of my lord, but our bodies, and our lands:

19 Wherefore shall we die before thine eyes, both we and our land? buy us and our land for bread, and we and our land will be servants unto Pharaoh: and give *us* seed, that we may live, and not die, that the land be not desolate.

20 And Joseph bought all the land of Egypt for Pharaoh; for the Egyptians sold every man his field, because the famine prevailed over them: so the land became Pharaoh's.

21 And as for the people, he re-

---

seven afflictions: (1) the persecution of Esau; (2) the injustice of Laban; (3) the result of his wrestling with the Angel; (4) the violation of Dinah; (5) the loss of Joseph; (6) the imprisonment of Simeon; (7) the departure of Benjamin for Egypt. They might well have added the death of Rachel and the incest of Reuben (Schumann).

11. *the land of Rameses*] In Ex. i. 11, the Israelites are said to have built treasure cities for Pharaoh, Pithom and Raamses. It is possible that Goshen is here called the land of Rameses by anticipation, as it may have become familiarly known to the Israelites by the name "land of Rameses" after they had built the city Rameses in it. Very probably, however, the Israelites in the captivity only fortified and strengthened the city of Rameses then already existing, and so fitted it to be a strong treasure-city. The name Rameses became famous in after times from the exploits of Rameses II., a king of the 19th dynasty: but he was of too late a date to have given name to a city, either in the time of Joseph, or even at the time of the Exodus. Rameses, according to the LXX. corresponded with the Heroopolis of after times. (See on this city Hengstenberg, 'Egypt,' p. 51, and Excursus at the end of the volume.)

12. *according to their families*] Lit. "to the mouth of their children;" meaning very probably, "even to the food for their children."

20. *Joseph bought all the land of Egypt for Pharaoh*] All the main points in the statements of this chapter are confirmed by Herodotus, Diodorus, Strabo, and the monuments. Herodotus (II. 109) says that Sesostris divided the soil among the inhabitants, assigning square plots of land of equal size to all, and obtained his revenue from a rent paid annually by the holders. Diodorus (I. 54) says that Sesoösis divided the whole country into 36 nomes and set nomarchs over each to take care of the royal revenue and administer their respective provinces. Strabo (XVII. p. 787) tells us that the occupiers of land held it subject to a rent. Again, Diodorus (I. 73, 74) represents the land as possessed only by the priests, the king, and the warriors, which

moved them to cities from *one* end of the borders of Egypt even to the *other* end thereof.

‖ Or, *princes.*

22 Only the land of the ‖ priests bought he not; for the priests had a portion *assigned them* of Pharaoh, and did eat their portion which Pharaoh gave them: wherefore they sold not their lands.

23 Then Joseph said unto the people, Behold, I have bought you this day and your land for Pharaoh: lo, *here is* seed for you, and ye shall sow the land.

24 And it shall come to pass in the increase, that ye shall give the fifth *part* unto Pharaoh, and four parts shall be your own, for seed of the field, and for your food, and for them of your households, and for food for your little ones.

25 And they said, Thou hast saved our lives: let us find grace in the sight of my lord, and we will be Pharaoh's servants.

26 And Joseph made it a law over the land of Egypt unto this day, *that* Pharaoh should have the fifth *part;*

---

testimony is confirmed by the sculptures (Wilkinson, I. p. 263). The discrepancy of this from the account in Genesis is apparent in the silence of the latter concerning the lands assigned to the warrior caste. The reservation of their lands to the priests is expressly mentioned in v. 22; but nothing is said of the warriors. There was, however, a marked difference in the tenure of land by the warriors from that by the priests. Herodotus (II. 168) says that each warrior had assigned to him twelve *aruræ* of land (each *arura* being a square of 100 Egyptian cubits); that is to say, there were no landed possessions vested in the caste, but certain fixed portions assigned to each person: and these, as given by the sovereign's will, so apparently were liable to be withheld or taken away by the same will; for we find that Sethos, the contemporary of Sennacherib and therefore of Hezekiah and Isaiah, actually deprived the warriors of these lands, which former kings had conceded to them (Herod. II. 141). It is therefore, as Knobel remarks, highly probable that the original reservation of their lands was only to the priests, and that the warrior caste did not come into possession of their twelve *aruræ* each, till after the time of Joseph. In the other important particulars the sacred and profane accounts entirely tally, viz. that, by royal appointment, the original proprietors of the land became crown tenants, holding their land by payment of a rent or tribute; whilst the priests only were left in full possession of their former lands and revenues. As to the particular king to whom this is attributed by Herodotus and Diodorus, Lepsius ('Chronol. Egypt.' I. p. 304) supposes that this was not the Sesostris of Manetho's 12th dynasty (Osirtasen of the Monuments), but a Sethos or Sethosis of the 19th dynasty, whom he considers to be the Pharaoh of Joseph. The 19th dynasty is, however, certainly much too late a date for Joseph. It may be a question whether the division of the land into 36 nomes and into square plots of equal size by Sesostris be the same transaction as the purchasing and restoring of the land by Joseph. The people were already in possession of their property when Joseph bought it, and they received it again on condition of paying a fifth of the produce as a rent. But whether or not this act of Sesostris be identified with that of Joseph (or the Pharaoh of Joseph), the profane historians and the monuments completely bear out the testimony of the author of Genesis as to the condition of land tenure and its origin in an exercise of the sovereign's authority.

21. *he removed them to cities*] He had collected all the corn, which he had stored up for the famine, into the various cities of Egypt, and so he removed the people into the cities and their neighbourhood, that he might the better provide them with food (Schum.).

22. *Only the land of the priests bought he not*] See on v. 20.

the priests had a portion assigned them of Pharaoh, and did eat their portion which Pharaoh gave them] This does not mean that the priests were Pharaoh's stipendiaries, which would be inconsistent with the immediately preceding words, as well as with the statement of profane authors as to the landed possessions of the priests. On the contrary, it means, that Pharaoh had such respect for the ministers of religion, that, instead of suffering Joseph to sell corn to them and so to buy up their land, he ordered a portion of corn to be regularly distributed to them during the famine, and so they were not reduced to the necessity of selling their lands. This regard for the priests is expressly assigned to Pharaoh, not to Joseph, and so there can be no need to apologize for Joseph's respect to an idolatrous priesthood.

26. *Joseph made it a law*] The final result of Joseph's policy was that the land was restored to the Egyptians, with an obligation to pay one fifth of it to Pharaoh for the

‖ Or, *princes.*

except the land of the ‖ priests only,
which became not Pharaoh's.
27 ¶ And Israel dwelt in the land
of Egypt, in the country of Goshen;
and they had possessions therein, and
grew, and multiplied exceedingly.
28 And Jacob lived in the land of
Egypt seventeen years: so † the whole
age of Jacob was an hundred forty
and seven years.
29 And the time drew nigh that
Israel must die: and he called his son
Joseph, and said unto him, If now
I have found grace in thy sight,
[b] put, I pray thee, thy hand under
my thigh, and deal kindly and truly
with me; bury me not, I pray thee,
in Egypt:
30 But I will lie with my fathers,
and thou shalt carry me out of Egypt,
and bury me in their buryingplace.
And he said, I will do as thou hast
said.
31 And he said, Swear unto me.
And he sware unto him. And [c] Israel bowed himself upon the bed's
head.

† Heb. *the days of the years of his life.*

b chap. 24. 2.

c Heb. 11. 21.

CHAPTER XLVIII.

1 *Joseph with his sons visiteth his sick father.*
2 *Jacob strengtheneth himself to bless them.* 3
He repeateth the promise. 5 *He taketh
Ephraim and Manasseh as his own.* 7 *He
telleth Joseph of his mother's grave.* 9 *He
blesseth Ephraim and Manasseh.* 17 *He
preferreth the younger before the elder.* 21
He prophesieth their return to Canaan.

AND it came to pass after these
things, that *one* told Joseph,
Behold, thy father *is* sick: and he

---

purpose of maintaining the revenues of the state. Much has been written in condemnation, and again in vindication of these proceedings. Was Joseph a mere creature of Pharaoh's, desirous only of his master's aggrandizement? or was he bent on establishing a tyrannical absolutism in violation of the rights and liberties of the subject? The brevity of the narrative and our imperfect acquaintance with the condition of the people and the state of agriculture in ancient Egypt make it impossible fully to judge of the wisdom and equity of Joseph's laws. This much, however, is quite evident. The land in favourable years was very productive. In the plenteous years it brought forth by handfuls (ch. xli. 47). Even the fifth part of the revenue of corn (v. 34) was so abundant that it is described as like "the sand of the sea," and "without number" (v. 49). Yet there was a liability to great depression, as shewn by the seven years of famine: the monuments too indicate the frequent occurrence of scarcity, and there was evidently no provision against this in the habits of the people or the management of the tillage. If Pharaoh had not been moved to store up corn against the famine years, the population would most probably have perished. The peculiar nature of the land, its dependence on the overflow of the Nile, and the unthrifty habits of the cultivators, made it desirable to establish a system of centralization, perhaps to introduce some general principle of irrigation, in modern phraseology, to promote the prosperity of the country by great government works, in preference to leaving all to the uncertainty of individual enterprize. If this was so, then the saying, "Thou hast saved our lives," was no language of Eastern adulation, but the verdict of a grateful people.

The "fifth part" which was paid to Pharaoh for the revenues of the state, and perhaps for public works of all kinds, agricultural and others, was not an exorbitant impost. The Egyptians appear to have made no difficulty in paying one-fifth of the produce of their land to Pharaoh during the years of plenty; and hence we may infer that it would not have been a burdensome rent when the system of agriculture was put on a better footing.

28. *the whole age of Jacob*] Lit. **the days of Jacob, even the years of his life.**

29. *bury me not...in Egypt*] Jacob had a firm faith that his descendants should inherit the land of Canaan, and therefore desired to be buried there. Moreover, he very probably wished to direct the minds of his children to that as their future home, that they might be kept from setting up their rest in Egypt.

31. *bowed himself upon the bed's head*] So the Masorites point it. So the Targg., Symm., Aquila, Vulg., but the LXX., Syr., and Epistle to the Hebrews (xi. 21), read "on the top of his staff." The Hebrew word without the vowel points means either "bed" or "staff." The only distinction is in the vowel points, which do not exist in the more ancient MSS. It is therefore impossible to decide with certainty which was the original sense of the word. It is quite possible that the meaning is, as the Apostle quotes the passage, that after Joseph had sworn to bury him in Canaan, Jacob bowed himself upon the staff which had gone with him through all his wanderings (Gen. xxxii. 10), and so worshipped God. And this seems the more likely from the fact that it is not till after these things that one told Joseph, "Behold, thy father is

took with him his two sons, Manasseh and Ephraim.
2 And *one* told Jacob, and said,
Behold, thy son Joseph cometh unto
thee: and Israel strengthened himself,
and sat upon the bed.
3 And Jacob said unto Joseph,
God Almighty appeared unto me at
[a] chap. 28. 13. & 35. 6. [a]Luz in the land of Canaan, and
blessed me,
4 And said unto me, Behold, I
will make thee fruitful, and multiply
thee, and I will make of thee a multitude of people; and will give this
land to thy seed after thee *for* an
everlasting possession.
[b] chap. 41. 50. Josh. 13. 7. 5 ¶ And now thy [b]two sons, Ephraim and Manasseh, which were born
unto thee in the land of Egypt before
I came unto thee into Egypt, *are*
mine; as Reuben and Simeon, they
shall be mine.
6 And thy issue, which thou be-
gettest after them, shall be thine, *and*
shall be called after the name of their
brethren in their inheritance.
7 And as for me, when I came
from Padan, [c]Rachel died by me in [c] chap. 35. 19.
the land of Canaan in the way, when
yet *there was* but a little way to come
unto Ephrath: and I buried her there
in the way of Ephrath; the same *is*
Beth-lehem.
8 And Israel beheld Joseph's sons,
and said, Who *are* these?
9 And Joseph said unto his father,
They *are* my sons, whom God hath
given me in this *place*. And he said,
Bring them, I pray thee, unto me,
and I will bless them.
10 Now the eyes of Israel were
†dim for age, *so that* he could not see. † Heb. *heavy*.
And he brought them near unto him;
and he kissed them, and embraced
them.
11 And Israel said unto Joseph, I
had not thought to see thy face: and,
lo, God hath shewed me also thy
seed.
12 And Joseph brought them out
from between his knees, and he bowed
himself with his face to the earth.

---

sick" (ch. xlviii. 1), so that Jacob probably had not as yet taken to his bed. At the same time we must not always press the quotations in the New Testament as proof of the true sense of the Hebrew original, for it is natural for the Apostles to quote the LXX. as being the Authorised Version, just as modern divines quote modern versions in the vernacular languages without suggesting a correction of their language, when such correction is unnecessary for their argument.

CHAP. XLVIII. 3. *God Almighty*] "El-Shaddai." See on ch. xliii. 14.

at Luz] *i. e.* Bethel. See ch. xxviii. 17, 19, xxxv. 6, 7.

5. *as Reuben and Simeon, they shall be mine*] Thy two sons shall be as much counted to be my sons, as Reuben and Simeon, my own two eldest sons, are counted to be mine; accordingly Ephraim and Manasseh became patriarchs, *eponymi*, heads of tribes. Some think that, as Reuben was deprived of his birthright, so here the birthright is given to Ephraim, the elder son of the firstborn of Rachel. But the birthright seems rather to have been transferred to Judah, his three elder brothers being disinherited, the first for incest, the other two for cruelty (see ch. xlix. 8-10) Accordingly, Judah became the royal tribe, from whom as concerning the flesh Christ came, who is over all God blessed for ever. There was, however, a kind of secondary birthright given to Ephraim (see xlix. 22 sq.), who became ancestor of the royal tribe among the ten tribes of Israel.

6. *shall be called after the name of their brethren*] Shall not give names to separate tribes, but shall be numbered with the tribes of Ephraim and Manasseh. We hear nothing of any younger sons of Joseph, and do not know for certain that any were born to him; but it has been thought that they may be mentioned in Num. xxvi. 28—37, 1 Chr. vii. 14—29.

7. *Rachel died by me*] When adopting the sons of Joseph, Jacob turns his thoughts back to his beloved Rachel, for whose sake especially he had so dearly loved Joseph. Rosenm., Gesenius and some others propose to translate here "Rachel died to my sorrow," lit. "upon me," and therefore as a heavy burden to me; but the received translation is supported by the Versions, and by the frequent use of the preposition in the sense of "near me," "by my side."

12. *Joseph brought them out from between his knees*] Joseph brought them out from between Jacob's knees, where they had gone that he might embrace them, and probably placed them in a reverent attitude to receive the patriarch's blessing

13 And Joseph took them both,
Ephraim in his right hand toward
Israel's left hand, and Manasseh in
his left hand toward Israel's right
hand, and brought *them* near unto him.
14 And Israel stretched out his
right hand, and laid *it* upon Ephraim's head, who *was* the younger,
and his left hand upon Manasseh's
head, guiding his hands wittingly; for
Manasseh *was* the firstborn.
d Heb. 11. 21. 15 ¶ And [d] he blessed Joseph, and
said, God, before whom my fathers
Abraham and Isaac did walk, the God
which fed me all my life long unto
this day,
16 The Angel which redeemed me
from all evil, bless the lads; and let
my name be named on them, and the
name of my fathers Abraham and
† Heb. *as fishes do increase.* Isaac; and let them † grow into a
multitude in the midst of the earth.
17 And when Joseph saw that his
father laid his right hand upon the
head of Ephraim, it displeased him:
and he held up his father's hand, to
remove it from Ephraim's head unto
Manasseh's head.
18 And Joseph said unto his father, Not so, my father: for this *is*
the firstborn; put thy right hand upon
his head.
19 And his father refused, and said,
I know *it*, my son, I know *it:* he
also shall become a people, and he
also shall be great: but truly his
younger brother shall be greater than
he, and his seed shall become a † mul- † Heb. *fulness.*
titude of nations.
20 And he blessed them that day,
saying, In thee shall Israel bless, saying, God make thee as Ephraim and
as Manasseh: and he set Ephraim
before Manasseh.
21 And Israel said unto Joseph,
Behold, I die: but God shall be with
you, and bring you again unto the
land of your fathers.
22 Moreover I have given to thee
one portion above thy brethren, which
I took out of the hand of the Amorite
with my sword and with my bow.

---

and he bowed himself with his face to the earth] *i.e.* Joseph bowed down respectfully and solemnly before his father. The LXX. has "They bowed themselves," which differs but by the repetition of one letter from the received reading.

14. *guiding his hands wittingly*] So Gesen., Rosenm., and most modern interpreters; but the LXX. Vulg. &c. "putting his hands crosswise." This has been defended by some, comparing an Arabic root, which has the sense "to bind, to twist," but it cannot be shewn ever to have had the sense "to cross."

16. *The Angel which redeemed me from all evil*] There is here a triple blessing:

"The God, before whom my fathers walked,
"The God, which fed me like a shepherd, all my life long,
"The Angel, which redeemed (or redeemeth me) from all evil."

It is impossible that the Angel thus identified with God can be a created Angel. Jacob, no doubt, alludes to the Angel who wrestled with him and whom he called God (ch. xxxii. 24—30), the same as the Angel of the Covenant, Mal. iii. 1. Luther observes that the verb "bless," which thus refers to the God of his fathers, to the God who had been his Shepherd, and to the Angel who redeemed him, is in the singular, not in the plural, showing that these three are but one God, and that the Angel is one with the fathers' God and with the God who fed Jacob like a sheep.

22. *Moreover I have given to thee one portion*] There is little doubt but that this rendering is correct. The past tense is used by prophetic anticipation, and the meaning is, "I have assigned to thee one portion of that land, which my descendants are destined to take out of the hands of the Amorites." The word rendered portion is *Shechem*, meaning literally "a shoulder," thence probably a ridge or neck of land, hence here rendered by most versions and commentators "portion." Shechem, the city of Samaria, was probably named from the fact of its standing thus on a ridge or shoulder of ground. (See on Gen. xii. 6.) Accordingly here the LXX., Targ. of Pseudo-Jonath., as also Calvin, Rosenm., and some moderns, have rendered not "portion," but "Shechem," a proper name. The history of Shechem is doubtless much mixed up with the history of the Patriarchs, and was intimately connected with all their blessings. It was Abraham's first settlement in Palestine, and there he first built an altar (ch. xii. 6). There too Jacob purchased a piece of ground from Hamor the father of Shechem, and built an altar (xxxiii. 18—20). This was, however, not "taken out of the hand of the Amorite with sword and bow," but obtained peaceably

CHAPTER XLIX.

1 *Jacob calleth his sons to bless them.* 3 *Their blessing in particular.* 29 *He chargeth them about his burial.* 33 *He dieth.*

AND Jacob called unto his sons,
and said, Gather yourselves together, that I may tell you *that* which
shall befall you in the last days.
2 Gather yourselves together, and
hear, ye sons of Jacob; and hearken
unto Israel your father.
3 ¶ Reuben, thou *art* my firstborn,
my might, and the beginning of my
strength, the excellency of dignity,
and the excellency of power:
4 Unstable as water, †thou shalt
not excel; because thou [a]wentest up
to thy father's bed; then defiledst
thou *it:* ‖he went up to my couch.
5 ¶ Simeon and Levi *are* brethren;
‖instruments of cruelty *are in* their
habitations.

† Heb. *do not thou excel.*
a chap. 35. 22. 1 Chron. 5. 1.
‖ Or, *my couch is gone.*
‖ Or, *their swords* are *weapons of violence.*

---

by purchase. Some have thought therefore that the allusion is to the victory over the Shechemites by Simeon and Levi related in ch. xxxiv., the Shechemites being here called Amorites, though there Hivites, because Amorite was a generic name, like Canaanite: but it is hardly likely that Jacob should boast of a conquest by his sons, as though it were his own, when he strongly reprobated their action in it, and even "cursed their anger, for it was fierce, and their wrath, for it was cruel" (ch. xlix. 7). Though, therefore, it is undoubtedly told us, that Jacob gave Shechem to Joseph, and that Joseph was therefore buried there (Josh. xxiv. 32; John iv. 5. See also Jerome, 'Qu. in Gen.' xlix.); and though there may be some allusion to this gift in the words here made use of, by a paronomasia so common in Hebrew, it is most likely that the rendering of the Authorised Version is correct. The addition of "one" to "portion" seems to decide for this interpretation. "I have given thee one Shechem," would be very hard to interpret.

CHAP. XLIX. 1. *in the last days*] The future generally, but with special reference to the times of Messiah. The Rabbi Nachmanides says, "According to the words of all, the last days denote the days of Messiah." The passages in which it occurs are mostly Messianic predictions (see Num. xxiv. 14; Isa. ii. 2; Jer. xxx. 24; Ezek. xxxviii. 16; Dan. x. 14; Hos. iii. 5; Mic. iv. 1). The exact words of the LXX. are used in Heb. i. 1, and virtually the same in Acts ii. 17; 2 Tim. iii. 1; 1 Pet. i. 20; 2 Pet. iii. 3, where the reference is to the times of Christ. (See Heidegger, Vol. II. XXIII. 6; Gesen. 'Thes.' p. 73.) The prophecy of Jacob does not refer exclusively to the days of Messiah, but rather sketches generally the fortunes of his family; but all is leading up to that which was to be the great consummation, when the promised Seed should come and extend the blessings of the Spiritual Israel throughout all the world. It is to be carefully noted, that the occupation of Canaan by the twelve tribes under Joshua was not the point to which his expectations pointed as an end, but rather that from which his predictions took their beginning. It was not the *terminus ad quem*, but the *terminus a quo.* The return to Canaan was a fact established in the decrees of Providence, the certainty of which rested on promises given and repeated to the Patriarchs. Jacob therefore does not repeat this, farther than by the injunction, in the last chapter, and again at the end of this, that he should be buried, not in Egypt, but at Machpelah, the buryingplace of his fathers.

3. *the beginning of my strength*] Some important Versions (Aquila, Symm., Vulg.) render "the beginning of my sorrow," a possible translation, but not suited to the parallelisms. For the expression, as applied to firstborn sons, comp. Deut. xxi. 17; Ps. lxxviii. 51, cv. 36.

4. *Unstable as water*] or "boiling over like water." The meaning of the word is uncertain. The same root in Syriac expresses "wantonness;" in Arabic, "pride," "swelling arrogance." In this passage it is clearly connected with water. The Vulgate translates, "Thou art poured out like water." Symmachus renders "Thou hast boiled over like water." The translation of the LXX. is peculiar, but it also seems to point to boiling as well as to the insolence of pride (ἐξύβρισας ὡς ὕδωρ, μὴ ἐκζέσης). Modern lexicographers (as Gesen., Lee, &c.) generally give "boiling over."

thou shalt not excel] Perhaps, though, through thy swelling wantonness, thou risest up like water when it boils, yet it shall not be so as to excel and surpass thy brethren. Not one great action, not one judge, prophet, or leader from the tribe of Reuben is ever mentioned in history.

then defiledst thou it] "Thou hast polluted" or "desecrated it."

5. *instruments of cruelty are in their habitations*] Probably, "Their swords are instruments of violence;" so the Vulg., several Rabbins, and the most eminent moderns. The word occurs only here, is very variously rendered by the Versions, and is of doubtful derivation.

6 O my soul, come not thou into
their secret; unto their assembly,
mine honour, be not thou united:
for in their anger they slew a man,
and in their selfwill they ‖ digged down
a wall.

‖ Or, *houghed oxen.*

7 Cursed *be* their anger, for *it was*
fierce; and their wrath, for it was
cruel: I will divide them in Jacob,
and scatter them in Israel.
8 ¶ Judah, thou *art he* whom thy
brethren shall praise: thy hand *shall*
be in the neck of thine enemies; thy
father's children shall bow down before thee.
9 Judah *is* a lion's whelp: from
the prey, my son, thou art gone up:
he stooped down, he couched as a
lion, and as an old lion; who shall
rouse him up?
10 The sceptre shall not depart
from Judah, nor a lawgiver from be-

---

6. *mine honour*] Probably a synonym for "my soul" in the first clause of the parallelism. The soul as being the noblest part of man is called his glory. See Ps. viii. 5 (6 Heb.), xvi. 9, xxx. 12 (13 Heb.), lvii. 8 (9 Heb.), cviii. 1 (2 Heb.); (Ges. 'Thes.' p. 655).

digged down a wall] **Hamstrung an ox.** So the margin "houghed oxen." The singular "an ox" must be used to retain the parallelism with "a man" in the former clause, both have a collective intention. This is the rendering of the LXX. and gives the commoner sense of the verb. It is therefore adopted by most recent commentators. The same Hebrew word, with a distinction only in the vowel point, means "ox" and "wall."

7. *I will divide them in Jacob, and scatter them in Israel*] This was most literally fulfilled, for when Canaan was conquered, on the second numbering under Moses, the tribe of Simeon had become the weakest of all the tribes (Numb. xxvi. 14); in Moses' blessing (Deut. xxxiii.) it is entirely passed over; and in the assignment of territory it was merely mingled or scattered among the tribe of Judah, having certain cities assigned it within the limits of Judah's possession (Josh. xix. 1—9); whilst the Levites had no separate inheritance, but merely a number of cities to dwell in, scattered throughout the possessions of their brethren (Josh. xxi. 1—40). With regard to the latter, though by being made dependent on the tithes and also on the liberality of their fellow countrymen, they were punished, yet in process of time the curse was turned into a blessing. (See Mede, 'Works,' Bk. I. Disc. xxxv.) Of this transformation of the curse into a blessing there is not the slightest intimation in Jacob's address: and in this we have a strong proof of its genuineness. After this honourable change in the time of Moses (due in great part to the faithfulness of Moses himself and of the Levites with him), it would never have occurred to the forger of a prophecy to cast such a reproach, and to foretell such a judgment on the forefather of the Levites. In fact, how different is the blessing pronounced by Moses himself upon the tribe of Levi in Deut. xxxiii. 8 sqq. (See Keil.)

8. *Judah, thou art he whom thy brethren shall praise*] **Judah, thou, thy brethren shall praise thee.** The word "thou" is emphatic, probably, like "Judah," in the vocative, not, as some would render it, "Thou art Judah," which is far tamer. The reference is to the meaning of the name. Leah said, "Now will I *praise* the Lord, therefore she called his name *Judah*" (ch. xxix. 35). Judah, notwithstanding the sad history of him and his house in ch. xxxviii., shewed on the whole more nobleness than any of the elder sons of Jacob. He and Reuben were the only two who desired to save the life of Joseph (ch. xxxvii. 22, 26); and his conduct before Joseph in Egypt is truly noble and touching (see ch. xliv. 18—34). Hence, when Reuben is deprived of his birthright for incest, Simeon and Levi for manslaughter, Judah, who is next in age, naturally and rightly succeeds to it.

thy hand shall be in the neck of thine enemies; thy father's children shall bow down before thee] He was to be victorious in war, and the leading tribe in Israel; the former promise being signally fulfilled in the victories of David and Solomon, the latter in the elevation of Judah to be the royal tribe; but both most fully in the victory and royalty of David's Son and David's Lord.

9. *Judah is a lion's whelp: from the prey, my son, thou art gone up*] Judah is compared to the most royal and the most powerful of beasts. The image is from the lion retiring to the mountains after having devoured his prey: not probably, as Gesenius and others, "thou hast grown up from feeding upon the prey."

as an old lion] **As a lioness** (Bochart, 'Hieroz.' I. p. 719; Ges. 'Thes.' p. 738). The standard of Judah was a lion, very probably derived from these words of Jacob.

10. *The sceptre shall not depart from Judah, &c.*] Render

A sceptre shall not depart from Judah
Nor a lawgiver from between his feet,
Until that Shiloh come,
And to him shall be the obedience of the peoples.

tween his feet, until Shiloh come; and unto him *shall* the gathering of the people *be*.

11 Binding his foal unto the vine, and his ass's colt unto the choice vine; he washed his garments in wine, and his clothes in the blood of grapes:

12 His eyes *shall be* red with wine, and his teeth white with milk.

13 ¶ Zebulun shall dwell at the

A remarkable prophecy of the Messiah, and so acknowledged by all Jewish, as well as Christian, antiquity. The meaning of the verse appears to be "The Sceptre (either of royal, or perhaps only of tribal, authority) shall not depart from Judah, nor a lawgiver (senator or scribe) from before him, until Shiloh (*i.e.* either 'the Prince of peace,' or 'he whose right it is') shall come, and to him shall the nations be obedient." There are some obscure expressions, but we may confidently hold that the above paraphrase conveys the true sense of the passage.

1. The word *sceptre*, originally denoting a staff of wood, a strong rod taken from a tree and peeled as a wand, is used (1) for "the rod of correction, (2) for "the staff of a shepherd," (3) for "the sceptre of royalty" (as Ps. xlv. 7; cp. Hom. 'Il.' II. 46, 101), (4) for "a tribe," which may be because the sceptre denoted tribal as well as regal authority, or because tribes were considered as twigs or branches from a central stem. (See Ges. p. 1353.) It is probable that the sceptre in Balaam's prophecy (Num. xxiv. 17) has a reference to these words of Jacob.

2. "A lawgiver," so, more or less, all the Ancient Versions. The LXX. and Vulg. render "a leader," the Targums paraphrasing by "scribe or interpreter of the law." The word certainly means "a lawgiver" in Deut. xxxiii. 21; Isa. xxxiii. 22; and all ancient interpretation was in favour of understanding it of a person. The R. Lipmann, however, proposed the sense of "a rod or staff" answering to "the sceptre" in the former clause, in which he has been followed by eminent critics, such as Gesenius, Tuch, Knobel, who think that this sense is more pertinent here, and in Num. xxi. 18; Ps. lx. 7 (see Heidegger, Vol. II. p. 738; Ges. p. 514); but it requires proof that the word, naturally signifying "lawgiver," sometimes undoubtedly meaning "lawgiver," and always so rendered in the Versions, can mean lawgiver's staff or sceptre.

3. "From between his feet" is rendered by the Versions, and generally by commentators "from among his posterity. (See Ges. p. 204.)

4. "Until Shiloh come." For fuller consideration of the name "Shiloh," see Note A at the end of the Chapter. The only two admissible interpretations are that the word is (1) a proper name, meaning "the Peace-maker," "the Prince of peace," or, (2) according to the almost unanimous consent of the Versions and Targums, "He, whose right it is." All the Targums add the name of Messiah, and all the more ancient Jews held it to be an undoubted prophecy of Messiah.

5. "Unto him shall the gathering of the people be." Rather, "Unto him shall be the obedience of the nations." The word for obedience occurs only once besides, in Prov. xxx. 17; but, if the reading be correct, there is little doubt of its significance. (See Ges. pp. 620, 1200; Heidegger, Tom. II. p. 748.)

As regards the fulfilment of this prophecy, it is undoubted that the tribal authority and the highest place in the nation continued with Judah until the destruction of Jerusalem. It is true that after the Babylonish Captivity the royalty was not in the house of Judah; but the prophecy is not express as to the possession of absolute royalty. Israel never ceased to be a nation, Judah never ceased to be a tribe with at least a tribal sceptre and lawgivers, or expositors of the law, Sanhedrim or Senators, and with a general pre-eminence in the land, nor was there a foreign ruler of the people, till at least the time of Herod the Great, just before the birth of the Saviour; and even the Herods, though of Idumæan extraction, were considered as exercising a native sovereignty in Judah, which did not quite pass away till a Roman procurator was sent thither after the reign of Archelaus, the son of Herod the Great: and at that very time the Shiloh came, the Prince of peace, to whom of right the kingdom belonged. (On the meaning of the name *Shiloh*, see Note A at the end of the Chapter.)

11. *Binding his foal unto the vine*, &c.] Many think that the patriarch, having spoken of the endurance of the reign of Judah till the coming of Christ, returns to speak of Judah's temporal prosperity during all that period; but the Targums of Jerusalem and Pseudo-Jonathan refer this verse to the Messiah. So also several Christian fathers (*e.g.* Chrysostom, in loc., Theodoret, 'Qu. in Gen.'); interpreting the vine of the Jewish people, and the wild ass of the gentile converts brought into the vineyard of the Church. The washing of the garments in wine they consider an allusion to Christ as the true vine (John xv. 1), to His treading "the winepress alone" (Isa. lxiii. 1—3), and empurpling His garments with His own Blood. (See Heidegger, II. pp. 752, sqq.)

12. *His eyes shall be red with wine*,] &c. Or perhaps (as the LXX., Vulg., Targg. Jerus., and Pseudo-Jon.), "His eyes shall be

haven of the sea; and he *shall be*
for an haven of ships; and his border
shall be unto Zidon.
14 ¶ Issachar *is* a strong ass couching down between two burdens:
15 And he saw that rest *was* good,
and the land that *it was* pleasant;
and bowed his shoulder to bear, and
became a servant unto tribute.

16 ¶ Dan shall judge his people,
as one of the tribes of Israel.
17 Dan shall be a serpent by the
way, †an adder in the path, that biteth
the horse heels, so that his rider shall
fall backward.
18 I have waited for thy salvation,
O LORD.
19 ¶ Gad, a troop shall overcome

† Heb. *an arrow-snake.*

---

redder than wine, and His teeth whiter than milk." This is generally supposed to refer to the land flowing with milk and honey, and abounding in vineyards; but the fathers applied it to the Messiah's kingdom in the same manner with the last verse, *e.g.* "That His eyes shine as with wine know all those members of His Body mystical, to whom it is given with a sort of sacred inebriation of mind, alienated from the fleeting things of time, to behold the eternal brightness of wisdom." (Augustin. 'C. Faust.' XII. 42, Tom. VIII. p. 24).

13. *Zebulun shall dwell at the haven of the sea*] "Zebulun shall dwell on the shore of the sea, and he shall be for a shore of ships," (*i.e.* suited for ships to land on), "and his border" (or farthest extremity) "shall be by Zidon." As far as we know of the limits of Zebulun, after the occupation of Canaan, it reached from the sea of Gennesareth to Mount Carmel, and so nearly to the Mediterranean. It did not reach to the city of Zidon, but its most western point reaching to Mount Carmel brought it into close proximity to Zidonia, or the territory of Tyre and Sidon. The language here used, though in all material points fulfilled in the subsequent history, is just what would not have been written by a forger in after times. Zebulun had not properly a maritime territory; yet its possessions reached very nearly to both seas. It was far from the city of Zidon; and yet, as approximating very closely to the land of the Syrians, might well be said to have its border by or towards Zidon. Tyre probably was not built at this time, and therefore is not named in the prophecy.

14. *Issachar is a strong ass couching down between two burdens*] Probably "Issachar is a strong-boned ass, couching down between the cattle pens," or "sheepfolds." The last word occurs only here and in Judg. v. 16, where it is rendered sheepfolds (see Rœdiger in Ges. 'Thes.' p. 1470). The prediction all points to the habits of an indolent agricultural people, and to what is likely to accompany such habits, an endurance of oppression in preference to a war of independence.

16. *Dan shall judge his people*, &c.] A paronomasia on *Dan* (*i.e.* a judge). The words may mean that, though he was only a son of Bilhah, he shall yet have tribal authority in his own people. The word translated "tribe" is the same as that translated "sceptre" in v. 10. Onkelos and others after him suppose the allusion to be to the judgeship of Samson, who was of the tribe of Dan (Judg. xv. 20).

17. *Dan shall be a serpent by the way, an adder in the path*] The word for adder, *Shephiphon*, is translated by the Vulg. *cerastes* the horned snake, the *coluber cerastes* of Linnæus, a small snake about 14 inches long and one inch thick, lurking in the sand and by the way side, very poisonous and dangerous. (Bochart, 'Hieroz.' Pt. ii. Lib. III. c. 12.) The people of Dan in Judges xviii. 27, shewed the kind of subtlety here ascribed to them. Perhaps the local position of the tribe is alluded to. It was placed originally on the outskirts of the royal tribe of Judah, and might in times of war have to watch stealthily for the enemy and fall on him by subtlety as he was approaching. The comparison of Dan to a serpent lying in wait and biting the heel seems to imply some condemnation. It is certainly observable that the first introduction of Idolatry in Israel is ascribed to the tribe of Dan (Judg. xviii.), and that in the numbering of the tribes in Rev. vii., the name of Dan is omitted. From these or other causes many of the fathers were led to believe that antichrist should spring from the tribe of Dan (Iren. V. 30, 32; Ambros. 'De Benedict. Patriarch.' c. 7; Augustin. 'In Josuam,' Quæst. 22; Theodoret, 'In Genes.' Quæst. 109; Prosper, 'De Promiss. et Prædict.' p. 4; Gregorius, 'Moral.' c. 18, &c.).

18. *I have waited for thy salvation, O LORD*] This ejaculation immediately following the blessing on Dan is very remarkable, but not easy to interpret. The Targg. Jerus. and Pseudo-Jonath. (and according to the Complutensian Polyglot Onkelos also, though the passage is probably spurious) paraphrase the words by saying that Jacob looked not for temporal redemption, such as that wrought by Gideon or Samson, but for the eternal redemption promised by Messiah. Is it not possible, that Jacob, having been moved

him: but he shall overcome at the
last.
20 ¶ Out of Asher his bread *shall*
be fat, and he shall yield royal dainties.
21 ¶ Naphtali *is* a hind let loose:
he giveth goodly words.
22 ¶ Joseph *is* a fruitful bough,
even a fruitful bough by a well; *whose*
† branches run over the wall:

† Heb. *daughters.*

23 The archers have sorely grieved
him, and shot *at him*, and hated
him:
24 But his bow abode in strength,
and the arms of his hands were made
strong by the hands of the mighty
God of Jacob; (from thence *is* the
shepherd, the stone of Israel:)
25 *Even* by the God of thy father,

---

by the Spirit of God to speak of the serpent biting the heel, may have had his thoughts called back to the primal promise made to Eve, the Protevangelium, where the sentence that the serpent should bruise the heel was succeeded by the promise that the serpent's head should be crushed by the coming Seed? This combination of thoughts may easily have elicited the exclamation of this verse.

19. *Gad, a troop shall overcome him: but he shall overcome at the last*] Perhaps "Gad, troops shall press on him, but he shall press upon their rear" (so Gesen. p. 271; Ros., Schum.); the allusion being to the Arab tribes in the neighbourhood of Gad, who would invade him, and then retire, Gad following them and harassing their retreat. Every word but two in the verse is some form of the same root, there being a play of words on the name *Gad* and *Gedud*, *i.e.* a troop; we might express it, "Gad, troops shall troop against him, but he shall troop on their retreat." (See on ch. xxx. 11.)

20. *Out of Asher his bread shall be fat, and he shall yield royal dainties*] The translation may be a little doubtful; but the sense is probably that expressed by the Authorised Version. The allusion is to the fertility of the territory of Asher extending from Mount Carmel along the coast of Sidonia nearly to Mount Lebanon. It was specially rich in corn, wine and oil (Heidegger), containing some of the most fertile land in Palestine (Stanley, 'S. and P.' p. 265).

21. *Naphtali is a hind let loose: he giveth goodly words*] The Targg. Pseudo-Jon. and Jerus. explain this that "Naphtali is a swift messenger, like a hind that runneth on the mountains, bringing good tidings." So virtually the Syr. and Sam. Versions. The allusion is obscure, as we know so little of the history of Naphtali. The Targums above cited say that Naphtali first declared to Jacob that Joseph was yet alive. As the tribe of Naphtali occupied part of that region which afterwards became Galilee, some have supposed that there was contained in these words a prophecy of the Apostles (in Hebrew *Sheluchim*, the same word with *Shelucha* here rendered "let loose"), who were Galileans and of whom it was said, "How beautiful upon the mountains are the feet of him that bringeth good tidings."

Bochart, after whom Michaelis, Schulz, Dathe, Ewald and others, follow the LXX. altering the vowel points, and render, "Naphtali is a spreading tree, which puts forth goodly branches."

22. *Joseph is a fruitful bough*] Perhaps "Joseph is the son," or branch, "of a fruitful tree, the son of a fruitful tree by a well, as for the branches" (lit. the daughters) "each one of them runneth over the wall" (see Ges. 218, 220). The construction is difficult and the difference of translations very considerable; but so, or nearly so, Gesen., Tuch, Knobel, Delitzsch, &c. The prophecy probably refers to the general prosperity of the house of Joseph. The fruitful tree is by some supposed to be Rachel. The luxuriance of the tendrils running over the wall may point to Joseph's growing into two tribes, whilst none of his brethren formed more than one: so Onkelos.

23. *The archers have sorely grieved him*] Though the Targums and others have referred this to Joseph's trials in Egypt, the prophetic character of the whole chapter shows that they point rather to the future wars of his tribes and the strength which he received from the hands of the mighty God of Jacob.

24. *from thence is the shepherd, the stone of Israel*] "From thence," referring to "the mighty one of Jacob" in the last clause. Some understand here that Joseph, having been defended from the malice of his enemies, was raised up by God to be a Shepherd or Guardian both to the Egyptians and to his own family, and a stone or rock of support to the house of Israel. Others see in this a prophecy of Joshua, the great captain of his people, who came of the tribe of Ephraim, and led the Israelites to the promised land. Others again have thought that, when Jacob was speaking of the sufferings and subsequent exaltation of his son Joseph, his visions were directed forward to that greater Son, of whom Joseph was a type, whom the archers vexed, but who was victorious over all enemies, and that of Him he says "From God cometh the Shepherd, the

who shall help thee; and by the Almighty, who shall bless thee with
blessings of heaven above, blessings
of the deep that lieth under, blessings
of the breasts, and of the womb:
26 The blessings of thy father have
prevailed above the blessings of my
progenitors unto the utmost bound
of the everlasting hills: they shall be
on the head of Joseph, and on the
crown of the head of him that was
separate from his brethren.
27 ¶ Benjamin shall ravin *as* a
wolf: in the morning he shall devour
the prey, and at night he shall divide
the spoil.
28 ¶ All these *are* the twelve tribes
of Israel: and this *is it* that their father
spake unto them, and blessed them;
every one according to his blessing he
blessed them.
29 And he charged them, and said
unto them, I am to be gathered unto
my people: [b] bury me with my fathers [b] chap. 47.
in the cave that *is* in the field of Eph- 30.
ron the Hittite,
30 In the cave that *is* in the field of
Machpelah, which *is* before Mamre,
in the land of Canaan, [c] which Abra- [c] chap. 23.
ham bought with the field of Eph- 16.
ron the Hittite for a possession of a
buryingplace.
31 There they buried Abraham
and Sarah his wife; there they buried
Isaac and Rebekah his wife; and there
I buried Leah.
32 The purchase of the field and
of the cave that *is* therein *was* from
the children of Heth.
33 And when Jacob had made an
end of commanding his sons, he gathered up his feet into the bed, and
yielded up the ghost, and was gathered unto his people.

Rock of Israel." As both Joseph and Joshua were eminent shadows and forerunners of the Saviour, it is quite possible that all these senses, more or less, belong to the words, though perhaps with special reference to the last. The translation advocated by many recent commentators, "From thence—from the Shepherd—the Rock of Israel" is against the original and the Versions.

25. *Even by the God of thy father, who shall help thee*, &c.] Rather "From the God of thy father and He shall help thee, and with (the aid of) the Almighty, even He shall bless thee."

26. *The blessings of thy father have prevailed above the blessings of my progenitors unto the utmost bound of the everlasting hills*] If this be the right rendering of a very obscure passage in the original, the meaning obviously is, that the blessings of Jacob on the head of Joseph and his offspring are greater than those which Abraham had pronounced on Isaac and Isaac on Jacob, and that they should last as long as the everlasting hills. This is more or less the interpretation of all the Jewish commentators following the Targums and the Vulg. The LXX (with which agrees the reading of the Samaritan Pentateuch) has a rendering which is adopted by Michaelis, Dathe, Vater, Tuch, Winer, Maurer, Schumann, Knobel, and Gesen. (see Ges. pp. 38, 391), "The blessings of thy father prevail over the blessings of the eternal mountains, even the glory of the everlasting hills." By this the parallelism of the two clauses is preserved, and the violence done to the two words translated in Authorised Version "progenitors" and "utmost bounds" is avoided.

separate from his brethren] So Onkelos. The Vulg. and Saad. have "the Nazarite among his brethren." Either of these translations would allude to the separation of Joseph from his family, first by his captivity and afterwards by his elevation. The word for "separate" means "one set apart," "consecrated," especially used of a Nazarite like Samson (Judg. xiii., xvi. 17), and of the Nazarite under the law (Num. vi. 2). It is possible that this consecration may apply also to princes who are separated to higher rank in dignity, just as the word *nezer*, "consecration," signifies a royal or high-priestly diadem. Accordingly, the LXX., Syr., Targg. Jerus., Pseudo-Jon. and many recent interpreters, render "a prince or leader of his brethren" (see Ges. p. 871).

27. *Benjamin shall ravin as a wolf*, &c.] The reference is, no doubt, to the warlike character of the tribe of Benjamin. Examples of this may be seen Judg. v. 14, xx. 16; 1 Chron. vii. 7, xii. 17; 2 Chron. xiv. 8, xvii. 17. Also Ehud the Judge (Judg. iii. 15) and Saul the king, with his son Jonathan, were Benjamites. The fathers (Tertul., Ambrose, August., Jerom.) think that there is a reference also to St Paul, who before his conversion devastated the Church and in later life brought home the spoils of the Gentiles.

NOTE A on Chap. xlix. v. 10. Shiloh.

i. Different renderings of word. 1. "He who shall be sent." 2. "His son." 3. "Until he come to Shiloh." 4. "The Peace-Maker." 5. "He, whose right it is." ii. Choice of renderings, either 4 or 5. iii. Messianic, by consent of Jewish and Christian antiquity. iv. Answer to objections.

Shiloh. A word of acknowledged difficulty.

1. The Vulgate renders "He, who shall be sent" (comp. *Shiloah*, Isai. viii. 6; John ix. 7—11). This would correspond with a title of the Messiah, "He that should come" (Matt. xi. 3). Such a translation is unsupported from other sources and rests on a different reading of the original, the letter ח (cheth) being substituted for ה (he) of the received text.

2. The Targum of Pseudo-Jonathan and some rabbins render "his son." So Kimchi, Pagninus, Calvin and others: but it requires proof that the word *shil*, "a son," has any existence in Hebrew.

3. The Rabbi Lipmann, in his book called "Nizzachon," suggests that it was the name of the city Shiloh, and that we should render "until he (Judah) shall come to Shiloh." A similar construction occurs 1 S. iv. 12 (he "came to Shiloh"), and it is said that Judah, in the march to the encampments in the wilderness, always took the first place (Num. ii. 3—9, x. 14), but that, when the Israelites came to Shiloh, they pitched the tabernacle there (Josh. xviii. 1—10), and, the other tribes departing from Judah, his principality closed.

It seems fatal to this theory, that every ancient Version, paraphrase and commentator make Shiloh, not the objective case after the verb, but the subject or nominative case before the verb. Moreover, whether it were a prophecy by Jacob, or, as many who adopt this theory will have it, a forgery of after date, nothing could be less pertinent than the sense to be elicited from the words, "till he come to Shiloh." Probably the town of Shiloh did not exist in Jacob's time, and Judah neither lost nor acquired the pre-eminence at Shiloh. He was not markedly the leader in the wilderness, for the people were led by Moses and Aaron; nor did he cease to have whatever pre-eminence he may have had when they came to Shiloh. This has induced some to vary the words, by translating, "*when* he comes to Shiloh," a translation utterly inadmissible; but it will give no help to the solution of the passage, for Judah did not acquire any fresh authority at Shiloh. It was the place of the rest of the tabernacle and therefore perhaps was named Shiloh, "Rest:" but it was no turning point in the history of Judah. Notwithstanding therefore the authority of Teller, Eichhorn, Bleek, Hitzig, Tuch, Ewald, Delitzsch, Kalisch, &c., we may pronounce with Hofmann, that the rendering is utterly impossible.

4. Far more probable is the rendering which makes Shiloh a proper name, and the subject of the verb, signifying "Peace," or rather, "the Peace-maker," the "Prince of peace." So, with slight variations, Luther, Vater, Gesenius, Rosenmüller, Hengstenberg, Knobel, Keil and others of the highest authority. The title is one most appropriate to Messiah (see Isai. ix. 6). The word is legitimately formed from the verb *Shalah*, to rest, to be at peace; and if the received reading be the true reading, there need be little doubt that this is its meaning. It has been thought by some that Solomon received his name *Shelomo*, the "peaceful," with an express reference to this prophecy of Shiloh, and it may be said that in Solomon was a partial fulfilment of the promise. Solomon was very markedly a type of the Messiah, himself the son of David, whose dominion was from sea to sea, who established a reign of peace in the land and who built the temple of the Lord; but Solomon was not the true Shiloh, any more than he was the true "Son of David."

5. The authority of the Ancient Versions is all but overwhelming in favour of the sense, "He, to whom it belongs," or "He, whose right it is." So, more or less, LXX., Aq., Symm., Syr., Saad., Onk., Targ. Jer., all, in fact, except Vulg. and Pseudo-Jonathan.

The objections to this are:

(1) That if the letter *yod* (expressed by the *i* in Sh*i*loh) be genuine, the translation is inadmissible: but it is replied that very many Hebrew MSS. and all Samaritan MSS. are without the *yod*, and that the evidence is much in favour of the belief that the *yod* did not appear till the 10th century (see Prof. Lee, 'Lex.' in voc.). It may be added that, as the reading without the *yod* is the harder and apparently the less probable, the copyists were more likely to have inserted it by mistake than to have omitted it by mistake.

(2) It is said, that by this reading so interpreted, a form is introduced unknown to the Pentateuch, Aramæan and of later date. To this it is replied, that the form occurs in the Song of Deborah (Judg. v. 7), which is very ancient; that Aramæan forms were either very ancient or decidedly modern, to be met with in Hebrew when the patriarchs were in contact with the Chaldæans (and Jacob had been forty years in Mesopotamia), or not again till the Jews were in captivity at Babylon. An Aramaism or Chaldaism therefore was na-

tural in the mouth of Jacob, though not in the mouth of David or Solomon.

This rendering of the Vss. is supported by the early Christian writers, as Justin M. ('Dial.' § 120) and many others. It is thought that Ezekiel (xxi. 27) actually quotes the words, "Until he come whose right it is," expanding them a little, and St Paul (in Gal. iii. 19) is supposed to refer to them.

On the whole, rejecting confidently the senses 1, 2, 3, we may safely adopt either 4 or 5; 4, if the reading be correct; 5, if the reading without the *yod* be accepted.

All Jewish antiquity referred the prophecy to Messiah. Thus the Targum of Onkelos has "until the Messiah come, whose is the kingdom;" the Jerusalem Targum, "until the time that the king Messiah shall come, whose is the kingdom." The Targum of Pseudo-Jonathan, "till the king the Messiah shall come, the youngest of his sons." So the Babylonian Talmud ('Sanhedrim,' cap. II. fol. 982), "What is Messiah's name? His name is Shiloh, for it is written, Until Shiloh come." So likewise the Bereshith Rabba, Kimchi, Aben-ezra, Rashi, and other ancient Rabbins. The more modern Jews, pressed by the argument, that the time appointed must have passed, refer to David, Saul, Nebuchadnezzar and others (see Schœttgen, 'Hor. Heb.' p. 1264). There can be no doubt that this prophecy was one important link in the long chain of predictions which produced that general expectation of a Messiah universally prevalent in Judæa at the period of the Christian era, and which Suetonius, in the well-known passage in his life of Vespasian, tells us had long and constantly pervaded the whole of the East. With the Jewish interpreters agreed the whole body of Christian fathers, *e.g.* Justin M. 'Apol.' I. §§ 32, 54; 'Dial.' §§ 52, 20; Iren. IV. 23; Origen, 'C. Cels.' I. p. 41, 'Hom.' in Gen. 17; Cyprian, 'C. Jud.' I. 20; Cyril. Hieros. 'Cat.' XII.; Euseb. 'H. E.' I. 6; Chrys. 'Hom. 67, in Gen.'; Augustine, 'De Civ. D.' XVI. 41; Theodoret, 'Quæst. in Gen.' 110; Hieron. 'Quæst. in Gen.', &c.

The only arguments of any weight against the Messianic character of the prophecy, except of course a denial that prophecy is possible at all, seem to be the following.

1. The patriarchal age had no anticipation of a personal Messiah, though there may have been some dim hope of a future deliverance. This is simply a gratuitous assertion. Admitting even that the promise to Adam may have been vaguely understood, we cannot tell how much the rite of sacrifice, the prophecies of men like Enoch and Noah, and the promises to Abraham and Isaac, had taught the faith of the fathers. There is the highest of all authority for saying that "Abraham rejoiced to see the day of Christ; he saw it, and was glad" (Joh. viii. 56). It was not indeed to be expected, that much beyond general intimations should be given in very early times, the light gradually increasing as the Sun-rise was drawing near: but there seems no more likely time for a special teaching on this vital point than the time of Jacob's death. He was the last of the three patriarchs to whom the promises were given. He was leaving his family in a foreign land, where they were to pass some generations surrounded by idolatry and error. He was foretelling their future fortunes on their promised return to Canaan. What more natural than that he should be moved to point their hopes yet farther forward to that, of which the deliverance from Egypt was to be an emblem and type?

2. The New Testament does not cite this as a prediction of Christ.

Bishop Patrick has well observed, that the fulfilment of the prophecy was not till the destruction of Jerusalem, when not only the Sceptre of Royalty, but even the tribal authority, and the Sanhedrim or council of elders ("the lawgiver") wholly passed from Judah. Then, and not till then, had the foretold fortunes of Judah's house been worked out. The sceptre and the lawgiver had departed, and "He, whose right it was," had taken the kingdom. The "Prince of peace" had come, and nations were coming into His obedience. But it would have been no argument to the Jew to cite this prophecy, whilst the Jewish nation was still standing and still struggling for its freedom, still possessing at least a shadow of royal authority and judicial power. There is therefore abundant reason why the New Testament should not refer to it.

CHAPTER L.

1 *The mourning for Jacob.* 4 *Joseph getteth leave of Pharaoh to go to bury him.* 7 *The funeral.* 15 *Joseph comforteth his brethren, who craved his pardon.* 22 *His age.* 23 *He seeth the third generation of his sons.* 24 *He prophesieth unto his brethren of their return.* 25 *He taketh an oath of them for his bones.* 26 *He dieth, and is chested.*

AND Joseph fell upon his father's face, and wept upon him, and kissed him.

2 And Joseph commanded his servants the physicians to embalm his

---

CHAP. L. 2. *his servants the physicians*] Herod. (II. 84) tells us, that in Egypt all places were crowded with physicians for every different kind of disease. The physi-

father: and the physicians embalmed
Israel.
3 And forty days were fulfilled for
him; for so are fulfilled the days of
those which are embalmed: and the
Egyptians †mourned for him three- († Heb. *wept.*)
score and ten days.
4 And when the days of his mourning were past, Joseph spake unto the
house of Pharaoh, saying, If now I
have found grace in your eyes, speak,
I pray you, in the ears of Pharaoh,
saying,
5 [a] My father made me swear, say- (a chap. 47. 29.)
ing, Lo, I die: in my grave which
I have digged for me in the land
of Canaan, there shalt thou bury me.
Now therefore let me go up, I pray
thee, and bury my father, and I will
come again.
6 And Pharaoh said, Go up, and
bury thy father, according as he made
thee swear.
7 ¶ And Joseph went up to bury
his father: and with him went up all
the servants of Pharaoh, the elders of
his house, and all the elders of the
land of Egypt,
8 And all the house of Joseph,
and his brethren, and his father's
house: only their little ones, and
their flocks, and their herds, they left
in the land of Goshen.
9 And there went up with him
both chariots and horsemen: and it
was a very great company.
10 And they came to the threshingfloor of Atad, which *is* beyond Jordan,
and there they mourned with a great
and very sore lamentation: and he made
a mourning for his father seven days.
11 And when the inhabitants of
the land, the Canaanites, saw the
mourning in the floor of Atad, they
said, This *is* a grievous mourning to
the Egyptians: wherefore the name

---

cians of Egypt were famous in other lands also (Herod. III. 1, 129). It is not wonderful therefore that Joseph, with all his state, should have had several physicians attached to his establishment. Physicians, however, were not ordinarily employed to embalm, which was the work of a special class of persons (Herod. II. 85; Diodor. I. 91); and the custom of embalming and the occupation of the embalmer were probably anterior to Moses and to Joseph. Very probably the physicians embalmed Jacob because he was not an Egyptian, and so could not be subjected to the ordinary treatment of the Egyptians, or embalmed by their embalmers.

3. *And forty days were fulfilled for him*] The account given by Diodorus (I. 91) is that the embalming lasted more than 30 days, and that when a king died they mourned for him 72 days. This very nearly corresponds with the number in this verse. The mourning of 70 days probably included the 40 days of embalming. Herodotus (II. 86), who describes at length three processes of embalming, seems to speak of a subsequent steeping in natron (*i.e.* subcarbonate of soda) for 70 days. He probably expresses himself with some inaccuracy, as both the account in Genesis, which is very much earlier, and the account in Diodorus which is later, give a much shorter time for the whole embalming, *i.e.* either 30 or 40 days, and seem to make the whole mourning last but 70 days. It is possible, however, to understand Herodotus as meaning the same as the Scriptural account and that of Diodorus. His words are, "Having done this they embalm in natron, covering it up for 70 days. Longer than this it is not lawful to embalm." (See Sir G. Wilkinson in Rawlinson, 'Herod.' II. 86; Hengstenb. 'Egypt,' &c. p. 68.)

4. *Joseph spake unto the house of Pharaoh*] He probably did not go himself to Pharaoh, because in mourning for his father he had let his hair and beard grow long, which was the custom in Egypt at the death of relations (Herod. II. 36): and it would have been disrespectful to go into the presence of Pharaoh without cutting the hair and shaving the beard. (See on ch. xli. 14, and Hengstenb. 'Egypt,' p. 71.)

7. *with him went up all the servants of Pharaoh*] Such large funeral processions are often seen on the Egyptian monuments (Rosellini, II. p. 395; Hengstenb. p. 71; Wilkinson, 'A. E.' Vol. V. ch. XVI. and plates there).

10. *threshingfloor of Atad*] Or "Goren-Atad," or "the threshingfloor of thorns."

beyond Jordan] *i.e.* to the West of Jordan. Moses wrote before the Israelites had taken possession of the land of Israel, and therefore whilst they were on the East of Jordan. This accords with what we hear of the site of Goren-Atad and Abel-Mizraim; for Jerome ('Onom.' s. v. *Area-Atad*) identi-

of it was called [∥]Abel-mizraim, which
is beyond Jordan.

∥ That is, *the mourning of the Egyptians.*

12 And his sons did unto him according as he commanded them:
13 For [b]his sons carried him into
the land of Canaan, and buried him
in the cave of the field of Machpelah, which Abraham [c]bought with
the field for a possession of a buryingplace of Ephron the Hittite, before Mamre.

b Acts 7. 16.

c chap. 23. 16.

14 ¶ And Joseph returned into
Egypt, he, and his brethren, and all
that went up with him to bury
his father, after he had buried his
father.
15 ¶ And when Joseph's brethren
saw that their father was dead, they
said, Joseph will peradventure hate
us, and will certainly requite us all
the evil which we did unto him.
16 And they [†]sent a messenger
unto Joseph, saying, Thy father did
command before he died, saying,

† Heb. *charged.*

17 So shall ye say unto Joseph,
Forgive, I pray thee now, the trespass of thy brethren, and their sin;
for they did unto thee evil: and now,
we pray thee, forgive the trespass of
the servants of the God of thy father.
And Joseph wept when they spake
unto him.
18 And his brethren also went
and fell down before his face; and
they said, Behold, we *be* thy servants.
19 And Joseph said unto them,
[d]Fear not: for *am* I in the place of
God?

d chap. 45. 5.

20 But as for you, ye thought evil
against me; *but* God meant it unto
good, to bring to pass, as *it is* this
day, to save much people alive.
21 Now therefore fear ye not: I
will nourish you, and your little ones.
And he comforted them, and spake
[†]kindly unto them.

† Heb. *to their hearts.*

22 ¶ And Joseph dwelt in Egypt,
he, and his father's house: and Joseph
lived an hundred and ten years.
23 And Joseph saw Ephraim's
children of the third *generation:* [e]the
children also of Machir the son of
Manasseh were [†]brought up upon Joseph's knees.

e Numb. 32. 39.

† Heb. *borne.*

24 And Joseph said unto his brethren, I die: and [f]God will surely
visit you, and bring you out of this
land unto the land which he sware
to Abraham, to Isaac, and to Jacob.

f Heb. 11. 22.

25 And [g]Joseph took an oath of
the children of Israel, saying, God
will surely visit you, and ye shall
carry up my bones from hence.

g Exod. 13. 19.

---

fies it with Beth-Hoglah, which lay between the Jordan and Jericho, the ruins of which are probably still to be seen (Rob. I. 544; see Smith's 'Dict. of Bible,' I. p. 200.)

11. *Abel-mizraim*] Means either "the field of Egypt," or "the mourning of Egypt," according to the vowel-points. The violence of the Egyptian lamentations is described by Herodotus (II. 85). See also Wilkinson, 'A. E.' ch. XVI.

19. *Am I in the place of God?*] *i.e.* it is God's place to avenge, not mine. See Rom. xii. 19.

23. *Were brought up upon Joseph's knees*] Lit. "were born on Joseph's knees." Comp. the phrase ch. XXX. 3. It seems as if they were adopted by Joseph as his own children from the time of their birth.

26. *They embalmed him, and he was put in a coffin*] The word for coffin is literally "ark" or "chest;" a word used always of a wooden chest, elsewhere almost exclusively of "the ark of the covenant." Herodotus, after describing the embalming, says, "The relatives inclose the body in a wooden image which they have made in the shape of a man. Then fastening the case, they place it in a sepulchral chamber, upright against the wall. This is the most costly way of embalming the dead" (II. 86). The description is of that which we commonly call a mummy-case. Such coffins, made of wood, chiefly of sycamore wood, were the commonest in Egypt; and though some very rich people were buried in basaltic coffins, yet, both from Herodotus' description above and from other sources, we know that wooden coffins were frequent, for great men, even for kings. The coffin of king Mycerinus, discovered A.D. 1837 in the third Pyramid of Memphis, is of sycamore wood. The command of Joseph and the promise of the Israelites, that his bones should be carried back into Canaan, were reason enough for preferring a wooden to a stone coffin. (See Hengstenb. 'Egypt,' pp. 71, 72. Various coffins of wood, stone, and

26 So Joseph died, *being* an hundred and ten years old: and they embalmed him, and he was put in a coffin in Egypt.

---

earthenware are described and engraved in Wilkinson's 'A. E.' Vol. v. p. 479.) The coffin was, no doubt, deposited in some sepulchral building (see Herod. above) and guarded by his own immediate descendants till the time of the Exodus, when it was carried up out of Egypt and finally deposited in Shechem (Josh. xxiv. 32). The faith of Joseph (Heb. xi. 22) must have been a constant remembrance to his children and his people, that Egypt was not to be their home. His coffin laid up by them, ready to be carried away according to his dying request whenever God should restore them to the promised land, would have taught them to keep apart from Egypt and its idolatries, looking for a better country, which God had promised to their fathers.

Section V.—The Twelve Minor Prophets.

Right Rev. CONNOP THIRLWALL, D.D., Lord Bishop of St. David's, author of *History of Greece, Translation of Niebuler's Rome, &c., &c.*

HOSEA and JONAH	Rev. E. HUXTABLE, M.A., author of *Sacred Record of Creation Vindicated, Ministry of St. John the Baptist, &c.*
AMOS & other PROPHETS..	Rev. R. GANDELL, M.A., Professor of Arabic, Oxford.
JOEL and OBADIAH........	Rev. F. MEYRICK, M.A., author of *Theology of the Church of Rome, Ecclesiæ Anglicanæ Religio, &c.*
ZECHARIAH & MALACHI.	Rev. W. DRAKE, M.A., Chaplain in Ordinary to the Queen, author of *Sermons on Jonah, Amos, and Hosea, &c.*

Section VI.—The Gospels and Acts.

ST. MATTHEW & ST. MARK	Most Rev. W. THOMSON, D.D., Lord Archbishop of York, author of *Limits of Philosophical Inquiry, Life in the Light of God's Word, &c.* Very Rev. H. L. MANSEL, B.D., Dean of St. Paul's, author of *Metaphysics, Philosophy of the Conditioned, Limits of Religious Thought, &c.*
ST. LUKE..................	Ven. WM. BASIL JONES, M.A., Archdeacon and Prebendary of York, author of *Peace of God* (Sermons), &c.
ST. JOHN.......	Rev. B. F. WESTCOTT, M.A., Canon of Peterborough, author of *History of the English Bible, Elements of the Gospel Harmony, Sermons on Gospel Miracles, &c.*
THE ACTS................	Right Rev. W. JACOBSON, D.D., Lord Bishop of Chester, author of *Patres Apostolici, Sermons, &c.*

Section VII.—The Epistles of St. Paul.

ROMANS.....................	Rev. E. H. GIFFORD, D.D., Honorary Canon of Worcester.
I. and II. CORINTHIANS...	Rev. T. EVANS, M.A., Professor of Greek in Durham University. Rev. J. WAITE, M.A., Master of University College, Durham.
GALATIANS........	Very Rev. J. S. HOWSON, D.D., Dean of Chester, author of *Life and Epistles of St. Paul, Metaphors of St. Paul.*
PHILIPPIANS............	J. A. JEREMIE, Very Rev. Dean of Lincoln, Regius Professor of Divinity, Cambridge, author of *History of the Scenes in the Life of St. Paul, &c.*
EPHESIANS, COLOSSIANS, THESSALONIANS, & PHILEMON.	Rev. J. B. LIGHTFOOT, D.D., Hulsean Professor of Divinity, Cambridge, Chaplain in Ordinary to the Queen, author of *Commentary on St. Paul's Epistles to the Galatians and Philippians.* Rev. B. F. WESTCOTT, B.D., author of *History of the English Bible, &c.* Rev. E. W. BENSON, D.D., Head Master of Wellington College.
PASTORAL EPISTLES.....	Right Rev. JOHN JACKSON, D.D., Lord Bishop of London, author of *God's Word and Man's Heart.*
HEBREWS...	Rev. W. KAY, D.D., author of *The Psalms translated from the Hebrew.*

Section VIII.—The Catholic Epistles and Revelations.

EPISTLE OF ST. JOHN....	Right Rev. W. ALEXANDER, D.D., Lord Bishop of Derry.
EPISTLE OF ST. JAMES...	Rev. R. SCOTT, D.D., Master of Balliol College, Oxford.
ST. PETER and ST. JUDE..	THE EDITOR.
REVELATION of ST. JOHN	Ven. W. LEE, D.D., Archdeacon of Dublin, author of *Inspiration of the Holy Scriptures, Lectures on Ecclesiastical History, &c.*

The volumes of the BIBLE COMMENTARY will be sent, post-paid, to any address, upon receipt of the price ($5.00 per volume), *by the publishers,*

SOLD BY

SCRIBNER, ARMSTRONG & CO.,

654 Broadway, New York.

Critical Notices

BY THE CLERGY AND THE PRESS

From Rt. Rev. HORATIO POTTER, *Bishop of New York.*

There can be no manner of doubt of its great value, or of its eminent success. We have long felt the want of just such a comprehensive and complete Commentary on the Holy Scriptures for our Students of Divinity, our Clergy, and for a large class of general readers. The Editor, the Rev. Canon Cook, has for many years been one of my most highly valued friends. He is an able man; and most of the distinguished contributors are well known to me personally or by reputation.

HORATIO POTTER.

From Rev. Prof. W. G. T. SHEDD, *D.D.*

I have examined the first volume of *The Bible Commentary*, and find it a superior work. While it would be premature to pronounce a judgment respecting the manner in which the exposition of passages relating to disputed doctrinal points will be made, there can be no doubt that the Commentary, as a whole, will be firmly evangelical, and that the whole influence of the work will be to strengthen the reader's confidence in Divine Revelation, and put him in a way to popularize it either in the Sabbath-school or the pulpit.

W. G. T. SHEDD.

From Rt. Rev. ARTHUR CLEVELAND COXE, *Bishop of Western New York.*

"The Speaker's Commentary" is a feature of the age in which we live. It cannot fail to mark an era in the Scientific Exposition of Scripture for popular ends.

A. CLEVELAND COXE.

From Right Rev. F. D. HUNTINGDON, *Bishop of Central New York.*

The chief merits of this first volume seem to me to be: 1. A reverential, believing spirit; 2. Thorough learning, not ostentatiously displayed, but always present and indicated in the results of scholarly investigation; 3. Remarkable condensation of matter, 4. Clearness and simplicity of style; 5. A judicious selection of the points of exposition made prominent; 6. Moderate and fair views of the alleged issues between Faith and Modern Science, with a wise handling of objections; 7. A felicitous use of comparative exegesis; 8. A good balance of the critical faculty with spiritual insight.

F. D HUNTINGTON.

From Rev. HOWARD CROSBY, *D.D., Pastor of the Fourth Avenue Presbyterian Church.*

The *Speaker's Commentary* fully realizes the expectation of its most hopeful friends. It is pithy and clear, and exhibits the condensed results of the best and latest scholarship. It will do much to put into possession of all, that which hitherto has been the exclusive property of a few erudite investigators. I devoutly thank God for this publication, and expect great things from it for the cause of truth.

HOWARD CROSBY.

From Rev. M. W. JACOBUS, *D.D., of the Allegheny Theological Seminary.*

The *notes* themselves are brief, often meagre, and commonly too cursory for the popular need, and seem to be put at a disadvantage by the fuller treatises. *But this work will fill a place not wholly occupied by any that has preceded it, and will add to the scholarly facilities placed within reach of Bible students in our day, for thorough understanding of the word of God.*

The treatment of the great subject of *sacrifices*, in the introduction to *Leviticus*, "*The Bearings of Egyptian History upon the Pentateuch*," and other elaborate articles, will amply repay the reading. And, judging from this volume, we cordially recommend this work, more than seven years ago projected by dignitaries and scholars of the English Church, as well representing the present status of Biblical science.

M. W. JACOBUS,
Professor Exegesis, &c.

From Rt. Rev. THOMAS M. CLARK, *Bishop of Rhode Island.*

I have examined "The Bible Commentary," which you are now republishing, with sufficient care to satisfy me that it will probably be the most valuable work of the kind for general use which has ever been produced in the English tongue. The common reader will derive a vast amount of information from its pages, and the most accomplished scholar can read it to advantage.

THOMAS M. CLARK.

From Prof. CHARLES A. AIKEN, *D.D., LL.D., of Princeton.*

As a compendium it will be prized by many who have access to more exhaustive Commentaries, and will furnish helps fresh, solid, and sound to many who have no access to, or leisure for using the more extensive storehouses of Biblical learning.

CHARLES A. AIKEN.

From Rev. Dr. GEO. L. PRENTISS.

It is evidently the work of thoughtful, devout, and earnest Christian scholars. Its tone and spirit are excellent; and if the whole Commentary is executed in the manner of this first volume, the result will be a most desirable and important addition to our exegetical literature of the Holy Scriptures.

GEO. L. PRENTISS.

From the Church Journal.

Certainly, this first volume is marked by soundness of interpretation, by sufficient fulness of exposition, by fairly grappling with heretical and wicked perversions of truth, and by confuting errors of all kinds rife at the present day.

From the Pacific Churchman (San Francisco).

We hope our clergy will all be able to buy it—or what will be better, let their parishioners buy it for them and make them a present of it; they will be amply repaid from the pulpit.

From the Christian Union.

Thank God for this glorious constellation of talent, learning, and piety, combined to elucidate the Word of God for the use of those great masses of the people who are not and cannot be scholars.

From the Association Monthly.

It is emphatically a Commentary for the times, treating of what is latest in Biblical criticism and research. The evident effort to compress the work into the smallest possible compass, consistent with the object proposed, will make the book attractive and popular.

From the New York Tribune.

The execution of the work appears to have been successfully accomplished in conformity with the original plan. It exhibits ample learning, remarkable power of illustration, and an earnest desire to support the prevalent conceptions of the Bible amid the sceptical suggestions of current science.

Numerous other equally important and valuable notices are omitted for want of space.

PROSPECTUS

OF A

Theological and Philosophical Library.

EDITED BY

HENRY B. SMITH, D.D. AND PHILIP SCHAFF, D.D.

PROFESSORS IN THE UNION THEOLOGICAL SEMINARY, NEW YORK.

The undersigned propose to publish a select and compact Library of Text-Books upon all the main departments of Theology and Philosophy, adapted to the wants especially of ministers and students in all denominations.

Some of the works will be translated from the German and other languages; others will be based upon treatises by various authors; some will be written for the Library by English or American scholars. The aim will be to furnish at least one condensed standard work on each of the scientific divisions of Theology and Philosophy, giving the results of the best critical investigations, excluding, however, such histories and commentaries as extend through many volumes.

BIBLICAL THEOLOGY.

Introductions to the Old and New Testaments; a Critical Edition of the Greek New Testament; the Canon; Biblical Theology; Biblical Psychology; and perhaps a Grammar and Dictionary of the New Testament Greek.

PRACTICAL THEOLOGY.

History of Church Government; Canon Law; Homiletics; Catechetics; Liturgies, including Hymnology: Pastorial Theology.

PHILOSOPHY.

History of Philosophy; Logic and Metaphysics; the Philosophy of Nature; Psychology; Ethics; Æsthetics; the Philosophy of Religion; the Philosophy of History.

SYSTEMATIC THEOLOGY.

Encyclopædia of Theology; Apologetis; a Collection of the Creeds and Symbols of the Church; a Collection of Theological Definitions of Doctrine, in the various schools of Theology, on the basis of HASE, LUTHARDT. HEPPE, and SCHWEIZER; Symbolics, or the Comparative Theology of Confessions of Faith; Polemics, with particular reference to the Roman Catholic Controversy; Doctrinal Theology; Christian Ethics; Collections of Essays on particular Doctrines.

HISTORICAL THEOLOGY.

Compends of Church History, and of the History of Doctrines; Patristics; Ecclesiastical Statistics; Jewish and Christian Archæology; Monographs on the History of Special Doctrines or of Signal Epochs.

This scheme is not presented as final, but as indicating the aim of the editors. If sufficient encouragement be given, no pains will be spared to make the project complete, and thus to meet a great and acknowledged desideratum in the apparatus for study. On all these topics every student needs, at least, one good work. To supply this will be the aim of our Library.

The various volumes will be published in the best style, on reasonable terms, and as rapidly as the nature of the work and the encouragement of the public will allow.

The editors will be assisted by eminenf scholars of various denominations, who will respectively assume the literary responsibility for the volumes prepared by themselves within the general plan and aim of the Library.

NOW READY, THE INITIAL VOLUME

IN

The Theological and Philosophical Library.

UEBERWEG'S HISTORY OF PHILOSOPHY.

Vol. I.—History of the Ancient and Mediæval Philosophy.

By Dr. FRIEDRICH UEBERWEG. Translated from the fourth German edition, by GEO. S. MORRIS, A.M., with additions by NOAH PORTER, D.D., LL.D., President of Yale College, and a general Introduction by the Editor of the Philosophical Library. One vol. 8vo, cloth. $3.50.

These works sent, post-paid, on receipt of the price by the Publisher.

SCRIBNER, ARMSTRONG & CO.,

654 Broadway, New York,

PUBLISHERS

LANGE'S COMMENTARY,

Critical, Doctrinal, and Homiletical.

TRANSLATED, ENLARGED, AND EDITED

—BY—

PHILIP SCHAFF, D. D.,

Professor in the Union Theological Seminary, New York.

654 BROADWAY, New York, January, 1873.

THIS great work is rapidly approaching completion. The New Testament Part is finished, with the exception of the volume on Revelation and an Index, which are now in the hands of the printer. The Old Testament Part is more than half done.

The German work, on which the English edition is based, is the product of about twenty distinguished Biblical scholars, of Germany, Holland, and Switzerland, and enjoys a high reputation and popularity wherever German theology is studied.

The American edition is not a mere translation (although embracing the whole of the German), but to a large extent, an *original* work; about one-third of the matter being added, and the whole adapted to the wants of the English and American student.

The press has been almost unanimous in its commendation of LANGE'S COMMENTARY. It is generally regarded as being, on the whole, the most useful Commentary, especially for ministers and theological students—in which they are more likely to find what they desire than in any other. It is a complete treasure of Biblical knowledge, brought down to the latest date. It gives the results of careful, scholarly research; yet in a form sufficiently popular for the use of intelligent laymen. The Homiletical department contains the best thoughts of the great divines and pulpit orators of all ages on the texts explained, and supplies rich suggestions for sermons and Bible lectures.

The following are some of the chief merits of this Commentary:

1. It is orthodox and sound, without being sectarian or denominational. It fairly represents the exegetical and doctrinal *consensus* of evangelical divines of the present age, and yet ignores none of the just claims of liberal scientific criticism.

2. It is comprehensive and complete—giving in beautiful order the authorized English version with emendations, a digest of the Critical Apparatus, Exegetical Explanations, Doctrinal and Ethical Inferences and Reflections, and Homiletical and Practical Hints and Applications.

3. It is the product of about forty American (and a few British) Biblical Scholars, from all the leading denominations and Theological and Literary institutions of the United States. Professors in the Theological Seminaries of New York, Princeton, Andover, New Haven, Hartford, Cambridge, Rochester, Philadelphia, Cincinnati, Alleghany, Chicago, Madison, and other places, representing the Presbyterian, Episcopal, Congregational, Baptist, Methodist, Lutheran, and Reformed Churches, have contributed or are engaged now in contributing to this Commentary. It may, therefore, claim a national character more than any other work of the kind ever published in this country.

For Names of Contributors, Volumes issued, etc., see next page.

LIST OF AMERICAN CONTRIBUTORS TO
LANGE'S COMMENTARY.

Prof. PHILIP SCHAFF, D. D., *GENERAL EDITOR,* **Union Theo'l Sem'y, N. Y.**

Prof. CHARLES A. AIKEN, D. D.,	Presbyterian,	Theo'l Seminary, Princeton, N. J.
Rev. S. R. ASBURY,	Episcopalian,	Moorestown, N. J.
Prof. GEORGE BLISS, D. D.,	Baptist,	Lewisburg University, Pa.
Rev. CHARLES A. BRIGGS,	Presbyterian,	Roselle, N. J.
Prof. JOHN A. BROADUS, D. D.,	Bapt.,	Greenville Theo'l Sem'y, South Carolina.
Rev. T. W. CHAMBERS, D. D.,	Reformed	New York.
Rev. THOS. C. CONANT, D. D.,	Baptist	Brooklyn, L. I.
Rev. E. R. CRAVEN, D. D.,	Presbyterian,	Newark, N. J.
Prof. GEORGE E. DAY, D. D.,	Congregational,	Yale College, New Haven, Ct.
Prof. CHAS. ELLIOTT, D. D.,	Presb.,	N. W. Theo'l Sem'y, Chicago, Ills.
Prof. L. J. EVANS, D. D.,	Presb.,	Lane Theo'l Seminary, Cincinnati, O.
Prof. PATRICK FAIRBAIRN, D. D.,	Presb.	Prin. Free College, Glasgow, Scotland
Prof. JOHN FORSYTH, D. D.,	Reformed,	Chapl'n Mil'y Acad., West Point, N. Y.
Prof. FRED. GARDINER, D. D.,	Epis.,	Berkeley Divinity School, Middletown, Ct.
Rev. A. GOSMAN, D. D.,	Presbyterian,	Lawrenceville, N. J.
Prof. W. H. GREEN, D. D.,	Presbyterian,	Theo'l Seminary, Princeton, N. J.
Prof. H. B. HACKETT, D. D.,	Baptist,	Rochester University, N. Y.
Rev. E. HARWOOD, D. D.,	Episcopal,	New Haven, Ct.
Prof. W. H. HORNBLOWER, D. D.,	Presbyterian,	Theo'l Sem'y, Alleghany, Pa.
Prof. J. F. HURST, D. D.,	Methodist,	Drew Theo'l Sem'y, Madison, N. J.
Prof. A. C. KENDRICK, D. D.,	Baptist,	Rochester University, N. Y.
Rev. JOHN LILLIE, D. D.,	Presbyterian,	(Deceased.)
Rev. J. FRED. McCURDY,	Presbyterian,	Princeton, N. J.
Prof. C. M. MEAD, D. D.,	Congregational,	Theo'l Sem'y Andover, Mass.
Rev. J. ISIDOR MOMBERT, D. D.,	Episcopal,	Dresden, Germany.
Miss EVELINE MOORE,	Presbyterian,	Newark, N. J.
Prof. MURPHY, D. D.,	Presbyterian,	Queen's College, Belfast, Ireland.
Prof. J. PACKARD, D. D.,	Episcopal,	Theo'l Sem'y, Alexandria, Va.
Prof. D. W. POOR, D. D.,	Presbyterian,	San Francisco, Cal.
Prof. M. B. RIDDLE, D. D.,	Reformed,	Theological Seminary, Hartford, Ct.
Prof. CH. F. SCHAEFFER, D. D.,	Luth.,	Lutheran Seminary, Philadelphia, Pa.
Prof. W. G. T. SHEDD, D. D.,	Presbyterian,	Union Theo'l Sem'y, New York.
Rev. C. C. STARBUCK,	Congregational,	Berea College, Ky.
Prof. P. H. STEENSTRA,	Episcopal,	Divinity School, Cambridge, Mass.
Prof. CALVIN E. STOWE, D. D.,	Congregational,	formerly of Andover, Mass.
Prof. JAS. STRONG, D. D.,	Methodist,	Drew Seminary, Madison, N. J.
Prof. W. G. SUMNER,	Episcopal,	Yale College, New Haven, Ct.
Prof. TAYLER LEWIS, LL.D.,	Reformed,	Union College, Schenectady, N. Y.
Prof. C. H. TOY, D. D.,	Baptist,	Greenville Sem'y, South Carolina.
Rev. E. A. WASHBURN, D. D.,	Episcopal,	Rector Calvary Church, New York.
Prof. WILLIAM WELLS,	Methodist,	Union College, Schenectady, N. Y.
Rev. C. P. WING, D. D.,	Presbyterian,	Carlisle, Pa.
Rev. E. D. YEOMANS, D. D.,	Presbyterian,	(Deceased.)

There are now issued of LANGE'S COMMENTARY *six volumes* of the OLD TESTAMENT and *nine* of the NEW TESTAMENT, as follows:

OLD TESTAMENT:

I. GENESIS.
II. JOSHUA, JUDGES, and RUTH.
III. FIRST and SECOND KINGS.
IV. PSALMS.
V. PROVERBS, SONG OF SOLOMON, ECCLESIASTES.
VI. JEREMIAH and LAMENTATIONS.

In preparation: MINOR PROPHETS (1 vol.), JOB (1 vol.), EXODUS, LEVITICUS, NUMBERS, DEUTERONOMY (1 vol.), ISAIAH (1 vol.), DANIEL and EZEKIEL (1 vol.)

NEW TESTAMENT:

I. MATTHEW.
II. MARK and LUKE.
III. JOHN.
IV. ACTS.
V. ROMANS.
VI. CORINTHIANS.
VII. GALATIANS, EPHESIANS, PHILIPPIANS, COLOSSIANS.
VIII. THESSALONIANS, TIMOTHY, TITUS, PHILEMON, and HEBREWS.
IX. JAMES, PETER, JOHN, and JUDE.

Completing this section of the Scriptures, excepting Revelation, which, together with an Index to N. T., will be published shortly.

Each one vol. 8vo. Price per vol. in half calf, $7.50; in sheep, $6.50; in cloth, $5.00.

Any or all the volumes of LANGE'S COMMENTARY sent, post or express charges paid, to any address on receipt of the price.

SCRIBNER, ARMSTRONG & CO., 654 Broadway, N. Y.

www.ingramcontent.com/pod-product-compliance
Lightning Source LLC
LaVergne TN
LVHW050526100826
845148LV00002B/449

* 9 7 8 1 4 2 5 5 2 0 0 1 4 *